THE
PSYCHOLOGY
OF
LEARNING

McGRAW-HILL SERIES IN PSYCHOLOGY
CONSULTING EDITORS
Norman Garmezy
Lyle V. Jones

THE PSYCHOLOGY OF LEARNING

FOURTH EDITION

Stewart H. Hulse

Professor of Psychology
The Johns Hopkins University

James Deese

Commonwealth Professor of Psychology
The University of Virginia

Howard Egeth

Professor of Psychology
The Johns Hopkins University

McGRAW-HILL BOOK COMPANY

New York   St. Louis   San Francisco   Auckland   Düsseldorf   Johannesburg
Kuala Lumpur   London   Mexico   Montreal   New Delhi   Panama   Paris
São Paulo   Singapore   Sydney   Tokyo   Toronto

THE PSYCHOLOGY OF LEARNING

34567890KPKP79876

This book was set in Palatino by Black Dot, Inc. The editors were John Hendry, Richard R. Wright, Jean Smith, and Susan Gamer; the designer was Jo Jones; the production supervisor was Dennis J. Conroy. The drawings were done by Vantage Art, Inc. Kingsport Press, Inc., was printer and binder.

Library of Congress Cataloging in Publication Data

Hulse, Stewart H
    The psychology of learning.

    In earlier editions Deese' names appeared first on the title page.
    1. Learning, Psychology of. I. Deese, James Earle, date joint author. II. Egeth, Howard, joint author. III. Title. (DNLM: 1. Psychology, Educational. LB1051 H917p]
LB1051.D36   1975   153.1'5   74-23207
ISBN 0-07-031150-1

ACKNOWLEDGMENTS

CHAPTER 1

Quotation, p. 37 Breland, K., & Breland, M. The misbehavior of organisms. *The American Psychologist,* 1961, **16,** 681–684. Passage, p. 682. Copyright 1961 by the American Psychological Association. Reprinted by permission.

Table 1.1 Grant, D. A. Classical and operant conditioning. In A. W. Melton (Ed.), *Categories of human learning.* New York: Academic Press, 1964. Table 1, p. 12. By permission of Academic Press, Inc.

Figure 1.1 Yerkes, R. M., & Morgulis, S. The method of Pavlov in animal psychology. *Psychological Bulletin,* 1909, **6,** 257–273. Figure 2, p. 264. Copyright 1909 by the American Psychological Association. Reprinted by permission. Reus, J., Lynch, J., & Gantt, W. H. Motor response device. *Conditional Reflex,* 1966, **1,** 135–136. Figure 1, p. 136. By permission of J. B. Lippincott Co.

Figure 1.3 Skinner, B. F. *The behavior of organisms.* New York: Appleton-Century-Crofts, 1938. Figure 3, p. 67. By permission of Prentice-Hall, Inc. Englewood Cliffs, New Jersey.

Figures 1.5, 1.6 Estes, W. K. All-or-none processes in learning and retention. *The American Psychologist,* 1964, **19,** 16–25. Figure 2, p. 19, and Figure 3, p. 19. Copyright 1964 by the American Psychological Association. Reprinted by Permission.

Figure 1.7 Miller, N. E., & DiCara, L. Instrumental learning of heart rate changes in curarized rats: Shaping, and specificity to discriminative stimulus. *Journal of Comparative and Physiological Psychology,* 1967, **63,** 12–19. Figure 1, p. 14. Copyright 1967 by the American Psychological Association. Reprinted by permission.

CHAPTER 2

Table 2.1 Kelleher, R. T., & Gollub, L. A review of positive conditioned reinforcement. *Journal of the Experimental Analysis of Behavior,* 1962, **5,** 543–597. Table 2, p. 561. Copyright 1962 by the Society for the Experimental Analysis of Behavior, Inc. Used by permission.

Table 2.2 Egger, M. D., & Miller, N. E. Secondary reinforcement in rats as a function of information value and reliability of the stimulus. *Journal of Experimental Psychology,* 1962, **64,** 97–104. Table 1, p. 100. Copyright 1962 by the American Psychological Association. Reprinted by permission.

Figure 2.1 Hovland, C. I. The generalization of conditioned responses. IV. The effects of varying amounts of reinforcement upon the degree of generalization of conditioned responses. *Journal of Experimental Psychology,* 1937, **21,** 261–276. Figure 1, p. 268. Copyright 1937 by the American Psychological Association. Reprinted by permission.

Figure 2.2 Logan, F. A. *Incentive.* New Haven: Yale University Press, 1960. Figure 11, p. 52. Copyright 1960 by Yale University Press. By permission of Yale University Press.

Figure 2.3 Hutt, P. J. Rate of bar pressing as a function of quality and quantity of food reward. *Journal of Comparative and Physiological Psychology,* 1954, **47,** 235–239. Figure 2, p. 237. Copyright 1954 by the American Psychological Association. Reprinted by permission.

Figure 2.4 Grice, G. R., & Hunter, J. J. Stimulus intensity effects depend upon the type of experimental design. *Psychological Review,* 1964, **71,** 247–256. Figure 1, p. 247. Copyright 1964 by The American Psychological Association. Reprinted by permission.

Figure 2.5 Bower, G. H. A contrast effect in differential conditioning. *Journal of Experimental Psychology,* 1961, **62,** 196–199. Figure 1, p. 197. Copyright 1961 by the American Psychological Association. Reprinted by permission.

Figure 2.6 Hulse, S. H. Reinforcement contrast effects in rats following experimental definition of a dimension of reinforcement magnitude. *Journal of Comparative and Physiological Psychology,* 1973, **85,** 160–170. Figure 5, p. 166. Copyright 1973 by the American Psychological Association. Reprinted by permission.

Figure 2.7 Miles, R. C. The relative effectiveness of secondary reinforcers throughout deprivation and habit-strength parameters. *Journal of Comparative and Physiological Psychology,* 1956, **49,** 126–130. Figure 1, p. 127. Copyright 1956 by the American Psychological Association. Reprinted by permission.

Figure 2.8 Grice, G. R. The relation of secondary reinforcement to delayed reward in visual discrimination learning. *Journal of Experimental Psychology,* 1948, **38,** 1–16. Figure 7, p. 13. Copyright 1948 by the American Psychological Association. Reprinted by permission.

CHAPTER 3

Figures 3.1, 3.2 Miller, N. E., & Kessen, M. L. Reward effects of food via stomach fistula compared with those of food via mouth. *Journal of Comparative and Physiological Psychology,* 1952, **45,** 555–564. Figure 3, p. 561 and Figure 2, p. 560. Copyright 1952 by the American Psychological Association. Reprinted by permission.

Figure 3.3 Sheffield, F. D., Wulff, J. J., & Backer, R. Reward value of copulation without sex drive reduction. *Journal of Comparative and Physiological Psychology,* 1951, **44,** 3–8. Figure 1, p. 5. Copyright 1951 by the American

Psychological Association. Reprinted by permission.

Figures 3.4, 3.5 Campbell, B. A. The reinforcement difference limen (RDL) function for shock reduction. *Journal of Experimental Psychology,* 1956, **52,** 258–262. Figure 1, p. 259, and Figure 2, p. 260. Copyright by the American Psychological Association. Reprinted by permission.

Figure 3.6 Menzel, E. W. Chimpanzee spatial memory organization. *Science,* 1973, **182,** 943–945. Figure 1, p. 944. Copyright 1973 by the American Association for the Advancement of Science. Reprinted by permission.

Figure 3.7 Bandura, A. Influence of models' reinforcement contingencies on the acquisition of imitative responses. *Journal of Personality and Social Psychology,* 1965, **1,** 589–595. Figure 1, p. 592. Copyright 1965 by the American Psychological Association. Reprinted by permission.

CHAPTER 4

Figure 4.1 Skinner, B. F. *The behavior of organisms.* New York: Appleton-Century-Crofts, 1938. Figure 17, p. 91. By permission of Prentice-Hall, Inc., Englewood Cliffs, New Jersey.

Figure 4.2 Perin, C. T. Behavior potentiality as a joint function of the amount of training and degree of hunger at the time of extinction. *Journal of Experimental Psychology,* 1942, **30,** 93–113. Figure 4, p. 101. Copyright 1942 by the American Psychological Association. Reprinted by permission.

Figure 4.3 Amsel, A., & Roussel, J. Motivational properties of frustration: I. Effect on a running response of the addition of frustration to the motivational complex. *Journal of Experimental Psychology,* 1952, **43,** 363–368. Figure 1, p. 367. Copyright 1952 by the American Psychological Association. Reprinted by permission.

Figure 4.4 MacKinnon, J. R. Interactive effects of the two rewards in a differential magnitude of reward discrimination. *Journal of Experimental Psychology,* 1967, **75,** 329–338. Figure 1, p. 332. Copyright 1967 by the American Psychological Association. Reprinted by permission.

Figure 4.5 MacKinnon, J. R. Competing responses in a differential magnitude of reward discrimination. *Psychonomic Science,* 1968, **12,** 333–334. Figure 1, p. 333. Copyright 1968 by the Psychonomic Society, Inc. Reprinted by permission.

Figure 4.6 Amsel, A. Behavioral habituation, counterconditioning, and a general theory of persistence. In A. H. Black & W. F. Prokasy (Eds.), *Classical conditioning II: Current theory and research.* New York: Appleton-Century-Crofts, 1972. Figure 6, p. 417. By permission of Prentice-Hall, Inc., Englewood Cliffs, New Jersey.

Figures 4.7, 4.8 Uhl, C. N. Eliminating behavior with omission and extinction after varying amounts of training. *Animal Learning and Behavior,* 1973, **1,** 237–240. Figure 1, p. 238, and Figure 3, p. 239. Copyright 1973 by the Psychonomic Society, Inc. Reprinted by permission.

CHAPTER 5

Figures 5.1, 5.2, 5.3, 5.4 Ferster, C. B., & Skinner, B. F. *Schedules of reinforcement.* New York: Appleton-Century-Crofts, 1957. Figures 152, p. 159; 396, p. 334; 24, p. 52; and 475, p. 396. By permission of Prentice-Hall, Inc. Englewood Cliffs, New Jersey.

Figure 5.5 Yamaguchi, H. The effect of continuous, partial and varied magnitude of reinforcement on acquisition and extinction. *Journal of Experimental Psychology,* 1961, **61,** 319–321. Figure 1, p. 320. Copyright 1961 by the American Psychological Association. Reprinted by permission.

Figure 5.6 Jenkins, W. O., McFann, H., & Clayton, F. L. A methodological study of extinction following aperiodic and continuous reinforcement. *Journal of Comparative and Physiological Psychology,* 1950, **43,** 155–167. Figure 1, p. 158. Copyright 1950 by the American Psychological Association. Reprinted by permission.

Figure 5.7 Boren, J. J. Resistance to extinction as a function of the fixed ratio. *Journal of Experimental Psychology,* 1961, **61,** 304–308. Figure 3, p. 306. Copyright 1961 by the American Psychological Association. Reprinted by permission.

Figure 5.8 Amount and percentage of reinforcement and duration of goal confinement in conditioning and extinction. *Journal of Experimental Psychology,* 1958, **56,** 48–57. Figure 1, p. 52. Copyright 1958 by the American Psychological Association. Reprinted by permission.

Figure 5.9 Hulse, S. H. Patterned reinforcement. In G. H. Bower (Ed.), *The psychology of learning and motivation.* Vol. 7. New York: Academic Press, 1973. Figure 9, p. 349. By permission of Academic Press, Inc.

CHAPTER 6

Quotation, p. 185, Bolles, R. C. The avoidance learning problem. In G. Bower (Ed.), *The psychology of learning and motivation.* Vol. 6. New York: Academic Press, 1972. By permission of Academic Press, Inc.

Figure 6.1 Stellar, E. Hunger in man: Comparative and physiological studies. *American Psychologist,* 1966, **21,** 105–117. Figure 19, p. 112. Copyright 1966 by the American Psychological Association. Reprinted by permission.

Figure 6.2 Jordan, H. A., Wieland, W. F., Zebley, S. P., Stellar, E., & Stunkard, A. J. Direct measurement of food intake in man: A method for the objective study of eating behavior. *Psychosomatic Medicine,* 1966, **28,** 836–842. Figure 6, p. 840. By permission of the American Psychosomatic Society.

Figures 6.3, 6.4 Miller, N. E. Studies of fear as an acquirable drive: I. Fear as motivation and fear-reduction as reinforcement in the learning of new responses. *Journal of Experimental Psychology,* 1948, **38,** 89–101. Figure 1, p. 90 , and Figure 2, p. 94. Copyright by the American Psychological Association. Reprinted by permission.

Figure 6.5 Maier, S. F., Seligman, M. E. P., & Solomon, R. L. Pavlovian fear conditioning and learned helplessness: Effects on escape and avoidance behavior of (a) the CS-US contingency and (b) the independence of the US and voluntary responding. In Campbell, B. A., & Church, R. M. (Eds.), *Punishment and aversive behavior.* New York: Appleton-Century-Crofts, 1969. Figure 10.5, p. 307. By permission of Prentice-Hall, Inc. Englewood Cliffs, New Jersey.

Figure 6.6 Solomon, R. L., & Wynne, L. C. Traumatic avoidance learning: Acquisition in normal dogs. *Psychological Monographs,* 1953, **67,** No. 354. Figure 5, p. 6. Copyright 1953 by the American Psychological Association. Reprinted by permission.

Figure 6.7 Bolles, R. C. The avoidance learning problem. In G. H. Bower (Ed.), *The psychology of learning and* *motivation*. Vol. 6. New York: Academic Press, 1972. Figure 2, p. 115. By permission of Academic Press, Inc.

Figure 6.8   Maier, S. F., Seligman, M. E. P., & Solomon, R. L. Pavlovian fear conditioning and learned helplessness: Effects on escape and avoidance behavior of (a) the CS-US contingency and (b) the independence of the US and voluntary responding. In Campbell, B. A., & Church, R. M. (Eds.), *Punishment and aversive behavior*. New York: Appleton-Century-Crofts, 1969. Figure 10.12, p. 321. By permission of Prentice-Hall Inc., Englewood Cliffs, New Jersey.

Figure 6.9   Hulse, S. H. Patterned reinforcement. In G. H. Bower (Ed.), *The psychology of learning and motivation*. Vol. 7. New York: Academic Press, 1973. Figure 8, p. 343. By permission of Academic Press, Inc.

Figure 6.10   Church, R. M. Response suppression. In Campbell, B. A., & Church, R. M. (Eds.), *Punishment and aversive behavior*. New York: Appleton-Century-Crofts, 1969. Figure 5-2, p. 120. By permission of Prentice-Hall, Inc., Englewood Cliffs, New Jersey.

Camp, D. S., Raymond, G. A., & Church, R. M. Temporal relationship between response and punishment. *Journal of Experimental Psychology*, 1967, **74**, 114–123. Figure 1, p. 117. Copyright 1967 by the American Psychological Association. Reprinted by permission.

Figure 6.11   Boe, E. E., & Church, R. M. Permanent effects of punishment during extinction. *Journal of Comparative and Physiological Psychology*, 1967, **63**, 486–492. Figure 1, p. 487. Copyright 1967 by the American Psychological Association. Reprinted by permission.

Figure 6.12   Brown, J. S., Martin, R. C., & Morrow, W. M. Self-punitive behavior in the rat: Facilitative effects of punishment on resistance to extinction. *Journal of Comparative and Physiological Psychology*, 1964, **57**, 127–133. Figure 4, p. 131. Copyright 1964 by the American Psychological Association. Reprinted by permission.

CHAPTER 7

Figure 7.1   Hovland, C. I. The generalization of conditioned responses: I. The sensory generalization of conditioned responses with varying frequencies of tone. *Journal of General Psychology*, 1937, **17**, 125–148. Figure 2, p. 136. By permission of The Journal Press.

Figure 7.2   Moore, J. W. Stimulus control: Studies of auditory generalization in rabbits. In A. H. Black and W. F. Prokasy (Eds.), *Classical conditioning II: Current theory and research*. New York: Appleton-Century-Crofts, 1972. Figure 6, p. 215. By permission of Prentice-Hall, Inc., Englewood Cliffs, New Jersey.

Figure 7.3   Guttman, N., & Kalish, H. I. Discriminability and stimulus generalization. *Journal of Experimental Psychology*, 1956, **51**, 79–88. Figure 1, p. 81. Copyright 1956 by the American Psychological Association. Reprinted by permission.

Figures 7.4, 7.5   Jenkins, H. M., & Harrison, R. H. Effect of discrimination training on auditory generalization. *Journal of Experimental Psychology*, 1960, **59**, 246–253. Figure 1, p. 247 and Figure 2, p. 248. Copyright 1960 by the American Psychological Association. Reprinted by permission.

Figure 7.6   Lashley, K. S. The mechanism of vision: I. A method for rapid analysis of pattern-vision in the rat. *Journal of Genetic Psychology*, 1930, **37**, 453–460. Figure 1, p. 454. By permission of The Journal Press.

Figure 7.7   Spence, K. W. The differential response in animals to stimuli varying within a single dimension. *Psychological Review*, 1937, **44**, 430–444. Figure 1, p. 433. Copyright 1937 by the American Psychological Association. Reprinted by permission.

Figure 7.8   Hanson, H. M. Effects of discrimination training on stimulus generalization. *Journal of Experimental Psychology*, 1959, **58**, 321–334. Figure 1, p. 324. Copyright 1959 by the American Psychological Association. Reprinted by permission.

CHAPTER 8

Table 8.1   Kendler, H. H., & Kendler, T. S. Mediation and conceptual behavior. In K. W. Spence & J. T. Spence (Eds.), *Psychology of learning and motivation*. Vol. 2. New York: Academic Press, 1968. Table, p. 226. By permission of Academic Press, Inc.

Figure 8.1   Harlow, H. F. The formation of learning sets. *Psychological Review*, 1949, **56**, 51–56, Figure 2, p. 53. Copyright 1949 by the American Psychological Association. Reprinted by permission.

Figure 8.3   Kendler, H. H., & Kendler, T. S. Vertical and horizontal processes in problem solving. *Psychological Review*, 1962, **69**, 1–16. Figure 2, p. 5. Copyright 1962 by the American Psychological Association. Reprinted by permission.

Figures 8.4, 8.5   Kendler, H. H., & Kendler, T. S. Mediation and conceptual behavior. In Spence, K. W., & Spence, J. T. (Eds.) *The Psychology of learning and motivation*. Vol. 2. New York: Academic Press, 1968. Figure 3, p. 209, and Figure 5, p. 214. By permission of Academic Press, Inc.

Figure 8.7   Honig, W. K. Attentional factors governing the shape of the generalization gradient. In Gilbert, R. M., & Sutherland, N. S. (Eds.), *Animal discrimination learning*. New York: Academic Press, 1969. Figure 4, p. 45. By permission of Academic Press, Inc.

Figure 8.8   Katz, P. A. Effects of labels on children's perception and discrimination learning. *Journal of Experimental Psychology*, 1963, **66**, 423–428. Figure 1, p. 425. Copyright 1963 by the American Psychological Association. Reprinted by permission.

CHAPTER 9

Table 9.2   Neisser, U., & Weene, P. Hierarchies in concept attainment. *Journal of Experimental Psychology*, 1962, **64**, 640–645. Table 2, p. 643. Copyright 1962 by the American Psychological Association. Reprinted by permission.

Figure 9.2   Bruner, J., Goodnow, J. J., & Austin, A. *A study of thinking*. New York: Wiley, 1956. Figure 1, p. 42. By permission of John Wiley & Sons, Inc.

Figure 9.3   Bourne, L. E., Jr. Learning and the utilization of conceptual rules. In Kleinmuntz, B. (Ed.), *Memory and the structure of concepts*. New York: Wiley, 1967. Figure 1.2, p. 17. By permission of John Wiley & Sons, Inc.

CHAPTER 10

Table 10.1   Miller, G. A. Free recall of redundant strings of letters. *Journal of Experimental Psychology*, 1958, **56**, 485–491. Table 1, p. 487. Copyright 1958 by the American Psychological Association. Reprinted by permission.

Table 10.2 Saporta, S., Blumenthal, A., & Reiff, D. G. Grammatical models and language learning. Reprinted from: *Georgetown University Round Table on Languages and Linguistics 1963.* Edited by Robert J. DiPietro. Washington, D. C., Georgetown University Press. Figure III, p. 138.

Table 10.3 Epstein, W. The influence of syntactical structure on learning. *American Journal of Psychology,* 1961, **74**, 80–85. Table 1, p. 82. By permission of the University of Illinois Press.

Figures 10.1, 10.2 Miller, G. A. Free recall of redundant strings of letters. *Journal of Experimental Psychology,* 1958, **56**, 485–491. Figure 1, p. 486; Figure 2, p. 487. Copyright 1958 by the American Psychological Association. Reprinted by permission.

CHAPTER 11

Table 11.1 Archer, E. J. Re-evaluation of the meaningfulness of all possible CVC trigrams. *Psychological Monographs,* 1960, **74**, No. 497. Data from Table 1 beginning on p. 4. Copyright 1960 by the American Psychological Association. Reprinted by permission.

Table 11.2 Noble, C. E. An analysis of meaning. *Psychological Review,* 1952, **59**, 421–430. Table 1, p. 46. Copyright 1952 by the American Psychological Association. Reprinted by permission.

Table 11.3 Underwood, B. J., & Schulz, R. W. *Meaningfulness and verbal learning.* Philadelphia, Lippincott, 1960. A list of about 25 selected trigrams together with their frequencies from Appendix D. By permission of J. B. Lippincott Co.

Figure 11.1 Underwood, B. J., & Schulz, R. W. *Meaningfulness and verbal learning.* Philadelphia: Lippincott, 1960. Figure 1, p. 29. By permission of J. B. Lippincott Co.

McGeoch, J. The influence of associative value upon the difficulty of nonsense-syllable lists. *Journal of Genetic Psychology,* 1930, **37**, 421–426. Data from Table 1, p. 422. By permission of The Journal Press.

Figure 11.4 Underwood, B. J., & Schulz, R. W. *Meaningfulness and verbal learning.* Philadelphia: Lippincott, 1960. Figure 17, p. 133. By permission of J. B. Lippincott Co.

Figure 11.5 Murdock, B. B., Jr. The serial position effect of free recall. *Journal of Experimental Psychology,* 1962, **64**, 482–488. Figure 2, p. 484. Copyright 1962 by the American Psychological Association. Reprinted by permission.

Figure 11.6 Deese, J. Serial organization in the recall of disconnected items. *Psychological Reports,* 1957, **3**, 577–582. Figure 1, p. 580. Reprinted with permission of the publisher.

CHAPTER 12

Figure 12.1 Jenkins, J. G., & Dallenbach, K. M. Obliviscence during sleep and waking. *American Journal of Psychology,* 1924, **35**, 605–612. Figure 1, p. 610. By permission of the University of Illinois Press.

Figure 12.2 Duncan, C. P. The retroactive effect of electroshock on learning. *Journal of Comparative and Physiological Psychology,* 1949, **42**, 32–44. Figure 1, p. 35. Copyright 1949 by the American Psychological Association. Reprinted by permission.

Figure 12.3 Ward, L. B. Reminiscence and rote learning. *Psychological Monographs,* 1937, **49**, No. 220. Figure 3, p. 13. Copyright 1937 by the American Psychological Association. Reprinted by permission.

Figure 12.4 Osgood, C. E. The similarity paradox in human learning: A resolution. *Psychological Review,* 1949, **56**, 132–143. Figure 5, p. 140. Copyright 1949 by the American Psychological Association. Reprinted by permission.

Figure 12.5 Melton, A. W., & Irwin, J. M. The influence of degree of interpolated learning on retroactive inhibition and the overt transfer of specific responses. *American Journal of Psychology,* 1940, **53**, 173–203. Figure 3, p. 198. By permission of the University of Illinois Press.

Figure 12.6 Barnes, J. B., & Underwood, B. J. "Fate" of first-list associations in transfer theory. *Journal of Experimental Psychology,* 1959, **58**, 97–105. Figure 1, p. 101. Copyright 1959 by the American Psychological Association. Reprinted by permission.

Figure 12.7 Koppenaal, R. J. Time changes in the strengths of A-B, A-C lists; spontaneous recovery? *Journal of Verbal Learning and Verbal Behavior,* 1963, **2**, 310–319. Figure 1, p. 313. By permission of Academic Press, Inc.

Figure 12.8 Underwood, B. J. Interference and forgetting. *Psychological Review,* 1957, **64**, 49–60. Figure 3, p. 53. Copyright 1957 by the American Psychological Association. Reprinted by permission.

Figure 12.9 Tulving, E. Cue-dependent forgetting. *American Scientist,* 1974, **62**, 74–82. Figure 2, p. 78. By permission of Sigma Xi, The Scientific Research Society of America.

CHAPTER 13

Table 13.1 Baddeley, A. D. The influence of acoustic and semantic similarity on long-term memory for word sequences. *Quarterly Journal of Experimental Psychology,* 1966, **18**, 302–309. By permission of Academic Press—London.

Figure 13.1 Sperling, G. The information variable in brief visual presentations. *Psychological Monographs,* 1960, **74**, No. 498. Figure 8, p. 11. Copyright 1960 by the American Psychological Association . Reprinted by permission.

Figure 13.2 Sperling, G. A model for visual memory tasks. *Human Factors,* 1963, **5**, 19–31. Figure 5, p. 25. By permission of the Human Factors Society, Inc.

Figure 13.3 Melton, A. W. Implications of short-term memory for a general theory of memory. *Journal of Verbal Learning and Verbal Behavior,* 1963, **2**, 1–21. Figure 1, p. 9. By permission of Academic Press, Inc.

Figure 13.4 Keppel, G., & Underwood, B. J. Proactive inhibition in short-term retention of single items. *Journal of Verbal Learning and Verbal Behavior,* 1962, **1**, 153–161. Figure 2, p. 156. By permission of Academic Press, Inc.

Figure 13.5 Waugh, N. C., & Norman, D. A. Primary memory. *Psychological Review,* 1965, **72**, 89–104. Figure 1, p. 91. Copyright 1965 by the American Psychological Association. Reprinted by permission.

Figure 13.6 Glanzer, M. & Cunitz, A. R. Two storage mechanisms in free recall. *Journal of Verbal Learning and Verbal Behavior,* 1966, **5**, 351–360. Figure 2, p. 358. By permission of Academic Press, Inc.

Figure 13.7 Kintsch, W., & Buschke, H. Homophones and synonyms in short-term memory. *Journal of Experimental Psychology,* 1969, **80**, 403–407. Figure 1, p. 404, and Figure 3, p. 406. Copyright 1969 by the American Psychological Association. Reprinted by permission.

Figure 13.8 Shallice, T., & Warrington, E. K. Independent functioning of verbal memory stores: a neuropsychological study. *Quarterly Journal of Experimental Psychology,* 1970, **22**, 261–273. Figure 3, p. 270. By permission of Academic Press—London.

Figure 13.9 Tulving, E. Intratrial and intertrial retention: Notes toward a theory of free recall verbal learning. *Psychological Review,* 1964, **71**, 219–237. Figure 2, p. 227. Copyright 1964 by the American Psychological Association. Reprinted by permission.

CHAPTER 14

Quotations, pp. 407, 408, 409 Bartlett, F. C. *Remembering: A study in experimental and social psychology.* Cambridge: Cambridge University Press, 1932. By permission of Cambridge University Press.

Quotation, p. 410–411 Bransford, J. D., & Johnson, M. K. Contextual prerequisites for understanding: Some investigations of comprehension and recall. *Journal of Verbal Learning and Verbal Behavior,* 1972, **11**, 717–726. Passage, p. 722. By permission of Academic Press, Inc.

Quotation, p. 412–413 Potts, G. R. Information processing strategies used in the encoding of linear orderings. *Journal of Verbal Learning and Verbal Behavior,* 1972, **11**, 727–740. Passage, p. 730. By permission of Academic Press, Inc.

Figure 14.1, 14.2 Collins, A. M., & Quillian, M. R. Retrieval time from semantic memory. *Journal of Verbal Learning and Verbal Behavior,* 1969, **8**, 240–247. Figure 1, p. 241; Figure 2, p. 244. By permission of Academic Press, Inc.

Figure 14.3 Norman, D. R. A process model for long term memory. In Tulving, E., & Donaldson, W. (Eds.), *Organization and memory.* New York: Academic Press, 1973. Figure 7, p. 209. By permission of Academic Press, Inc.

Figure 14.4 Freedman, J. L., & Loftus, E. Retrieval of words from long-term memory. *Journal of Verbal Learning and Verbal Behavior,* 1971, **10**, 107–115. Figure 1, p. 112. By permission of Academic Press, Inc.

Figure 14.5 Carmichael, L. C., Hogan, H. P., & Walter, A. A. An experimental study of the effect of language on the reproduction of visually perceived form. *Journal of Experimental Psychology,* 1932, **15**, 73–86. Figure 2, p. 80. Copyright 1932 by the American Psychological Association. Reprinted by permission.

Figure 14.6 Sachs, J. S. Recognition memory for syntactic and semantic aspects of connected discourse. *Perception and Psychophysics,* 1967, **2**, 437–442. Figure 2, p. 441. By permission of The Psychonomic Society, Inc.

Figure 14.7 Bransford, J. D., & Franks, J. J. The abstraction of linguistic ideas. *Cognitive Psychology,* 1971, **2**, 331–350. Figure 4, p. 346. By permission of Academic Press, Inc.

With affection,
we dedicate this book to our wives,
Nancy, Ellin, and Sylvia

CONTENTS

PREFACE

Earlier editions of this book were designed to bring together all the many things that psychologists have included under the heading of the psychology of learning. At first that was entirely possible, and the first edition was intended to be a survey of all topics in learning—general and specific, theoretical and applied. With the second edition, and especially with the third, growth of the field required some judicious pruning if material was to be kept within reasonable bounds. It has been necessary to continue the pruning process with this edition. We have therefore maintained our emphasis on the core topics underlying the psychology of learning, leaving extensive treatment of topics with either a more applied bent (such as the acquisition of specific skills) or topics which have become highly specialized (such as mathematical learning theory) to other places where they are better handled in the detail necessary to do them justice. We have also maintained our conviction that this text should provide a solid foundation for more detailed study of all facets of the psychology of learning, and the student should find an adequate background here for further work in any more specialized area in the field.

The early chapters of the book stress the basic processes of conditioning and learning. Chapter 1 introduces the fundamental procedures of Pavlovian and instrumental conditioning—emphasizing our new understanding of the interaction between the two, and our renewed appreciation of the role of biological and natural constraints on the learning process. This theme carries into three chapters on the processes of reinforcement, and an extensively revised chapter on the contribution of learning to emotion and motivation.

Chapter 7, and especially a new Chapter 8, provide a bridge between topics most closely concerned with animal psychology and those of particular concern to human learning. The bridge is built upon a discussion of how organisms acquire their ability to discriminate among the events in the world that are important for the proper and orderly unfolding of behavior. The construction of the bridge represents a conscious effort on our part to weld together fact and theory in animal and human learning. Too often these domains within the psychology of learning are treated as if they were entirely separate fields of inquiry—

perhaps because they can lend themselves pedagogically to separate courses in the curriculum. We feel that both fields have much in common, if for no other reason than the fact that one builds upon the other in so many ways. Consequently, while much of this book is devoted to separate analyses of animal and human learning, we have taken frequent opportunity to examine the points they span in common.

Chapter 9 focuses attention on concept identification and the learning of rules, and with this chapter we begin that portion of the book which has received essentially complete new treatment. It is within the fields of verbal learning and memory that so much recent progress has been made as psychologists have moved away from earlier stimulus-response conceptualizations of these topics and developed a new emphasis on the cognitive or information-processing point of view. Chapters 10 and 11 deal with the nature of language and the methods used in studying the acquisition of verbal behavior. The subsequent chapters present data and theory pertaining to short- and long-term memory not only for arbitrary material but also for meaningful material such as ordinary prose.

As in the earlier editions, we have approached our field empirically; method and technique receive special stress. Theory is introduced in the interests of solving particular problems, not as a presentation of the "system" of a particular individual or school. While we have adopted no consistent general theoretical point of view—for that is impossible in the field today—we have been quick to turn to specialized theory when that helps clarify things. By the same token, we have frequently viewed certain problems from the vantage point of their place in the history of psychology. We feel there is much to be gained for a current understanding of a problem, and for an appreciation of its possible appearance in the future, by an examination of its color and form in the past. Psychology as a discipline is especially marked by the reechoing return to prominence of questions that have interested mankind for centuries. The problem of how we remember things, for example, has been with us since at least the time of the ancient Greeks.

Like the earlier editions, this revision of the book is intended primarily for junior and senior students in psychology and for graduate students in psychology or educational psychology. However, the text is self-sufficient, and a student can study it with profit without any particular background in psychology.

Several persons have read all or part of the manuscript, and we are grateful to them for their carefully-cocked eyes. We would especially like to thank Russell Church of Brown University; Robert Crowder of Yale University; Henry Ellis of the University of New Mexico; and James Myer of Kent State University. We owe Nancy Allchin and Renee Laniado our appreciation for their diligent and careful typing of the manuscript. Finally, we thank our students and colleagues for their patience and encouragement as we went about our task.

Stewart H. Hulse
James Deese
Howard Egeth

ONE

SOME FUNDAMENTAL PRINCIPLES OF PAVLOVIAN AND INSTRUMENTAL CONDITIONING

We begin our study of the psychology of learning by examining some of the things that are known to enter into two basic forms of the process: Pavlovian and instrumental conditioning. Pavlovian and instrumental conditioning represent simpler forms of learning, a process which grows from conditioning to include more refined structures like concept learning and thinking. But simple conditioning provides many of the empirical and theoretical underpinnings of more complex forms of learning, and a study of conditioning will furnish many of the elements required to build the more complicated structures we shall develop as the book progresses. We begin, then, with an examination of the concepts of stimulus and response, then go on to look at the basic procedures for Pavlovian and instrumental conditioning. In later sections of the chapter, we shall introduce you to some fundamental things associated with the principle of reinforcement, and to some constraints that new knowledge has placed upon our conceptions of the way organisms learn by means of Pavlovian and instrumental conditioning.

THE CONCEPTS OF STIMULUS AND RESPONSE

Psychologists have assumed, probably since the time of Aristotle, that the process by which learning takes place will be some form of the process of *association*. That is, when we learn something we learn to put things together in some new way, to pair them up, to recall that one thing leads to or goes with another. We learn that black lines and spaces on a printed page are words, that words have meaning, and that words can be classified into categories like synonyms and antonyms on the basis of their meaning. We learn that certain smells make our mouths water, that red lights mean stop, and that green lights mean go. Animals learn to recognize certain song patterns or postural displays as signals for appropriate reactions or responses, and many species such as dogs or monkeys can easily associate simple verbal commands (the sound of human voices, at any rate) with behavior that leads to reward or avoids punishment. Interestingly enough, although other models or plans which might organize the principles, procedures, and outcomes of the learning process are available (Weimer, 1973), Western man seems to have settled for the principle of association as the fundamental rule for learning and to have developed his psychology—if not most of his general thought and philosophy—according to the tenets derived from that basic assumption.

Western science in general, and psychology in particular, has been less able to settle on a commonly accepted notion of *what goes into* the process of learning when association occurs. Psychologists have not been able, in other words, to come up with consistent agreement about the *stuff* of learning, the fundamental characteristics of the things, the elements, which are in fact submitted to the process of association as learning runs its course. Put simply, they are not sure what gets associated with what when learning occurs.

This book is not the place to expand upon that essentially philosophical question in any great detail, but we do need some working rules of thumb to guide us through the chapters ahead. Let us look, accordingly, at the concepts of *stimulus* and *response* as they are used in the psychology of learning. These concepts—in one of the many guises they can assume—have provided one of the basic schemes to organize what is presumed to get put together through the process of association.

THE CONCEPT OF A STIMULUS

There are many ways of using the term *stimulus*. We shall distinguish three. First, there is the notion of a *physical stimulus*, a stimulus as the more physiologically oriented scientist might use the term. To the physiologist, a stimulus is apt to be some form of relatively "raw" physical energy which is involved in a basic physiological process. Thus, light triggers receptor cells in the eye, sound waves affect the action of hair cells in the inner ear and so begin the process of getting nerve impulses underway in the auditory nerve, and so on. As Gibson (1960, 1966) points out, there can be a great amount of information inherent in the physical stimulus itself, but the physiologist's emphasis is upon the presumably simple physical energy which gets things underway in sensory or motor systems.

A broader class of meanings of the concept of stimulus arises when we ask how organisms *use* information that impinges upon sense receptors, and this leads us to the concept of a *functional stimulus*. What features of the physiologist's stimulus, in other words, are *behaviorally effective* in the sense that they control or set the occasion for behavior, or in the sense that they are actively processed, digested, and stored by the learning organism? Here, things can rapidly become very much richer, and it is usually within *this* domain that modern psychologists are really operating when they use the term stimulus. Thus, a stimulus may be some environmental event—perhaps a very complicated one—which becomes correlated in some consistent fashion with a particular class of behavior (Skinner, 1935). Or a stimulus may be, quite simply, something to which one as opposed to another response is attachable (Miller & Dollard, 1941). The stimulus the psychologist uses most often, in other words, is a *functional* one. To borrow Gibson's phrase, it is something— anything—the organism comes to respond *to*. From the wealth of potential stimuli for perception and action, says Gibson, only certain ones become effective for modulating behavior. Which ones acquire such control depends upon many things: the nature of the species, past history, capacity and training for attention, and so on. But these stimuli are clearly not necessarily a barren, sterile array of physical energies. They can be as rich and complicated as a courtship dance which triggers mating behavior in gulls, a mother's facial expression and contact gestures which help the development of a strong attachment between mother and infant during the early months of life, or a complicated visual display that psychologists might set up as they design a perceptual learning experiment. These are, in Lawrence's (1963) terms, *stimuli-as-coded*, stimuli that are processed and given meaning by an active, attentive, remembering organism.

3

SOME
FUNDAMENTAL
PRINCIPLES OF
PAVLOVIAN AND
INSTRUMENTAL
CONDITIONING

The third and final use of the concept of stimulus we wish to identify is a purely practical one which we mention because we shall be using it frequently throughout this book. Sometimes, psychologists use the term stimulus, or *stimulus situation*, to describe the set of things they do in the simple organization of an experiment. Thus, a rat is trained to run into a white goal box as opposed to a black one at the end of a maze, and psychologists will refer to "black and white goal box stimuli" in describing their experimental plan. While they could and may very well have something akin to a functional, behaviorally effective stimulus of the sort we have just discussed in mind, they may also—as a convenient shorthand—use the phrase to refer to the way in which they set up their experiment. Considered from this point of view, a stimulus is just a handy label for a set of experimental procedures, often the procedures that define the independent variable under study.

THE CONCEPT OF A RESPONSE

As with stimuli, the classification of behavior into categories to which the label *response* is given can become a complicated process. Once again, it is possible to identify the response the physiologist might study—a *physiological response*, if you will. This could include the action of nerve cells or the action of single muscle fibers, or it could include a catalog of the many muscle movements that go into some complicated bit of behavior like walking, closing the door, operating a crane, or saying the word *psychology*. Psychologists are sometimes interested in such responses, particularly when they pursue the things that go on in Pavlovian conditioning, for example, and they may well be interested in distinguishing one bit of behavior from another in some qualitative way which depends upon the specific movements that each involves.

More commonly, however, psychologists use the term *response* to label the *function* or *end result* that can be ascribed to behavior. Thus, we speak of the *functional responses* of "closing the door," "eating your supper," "remembering a list of words," "taking a course in psychology," and so on. What we have here are descriptors for the many courses of action that behavior can take, action that is defined in terms of its end results upon some feature of the environment of the behaving organism.

Finally, the concept of the response is used like the concept of the stimulus as a convenient, practical shorthand for the things that are set to happen through some experimental procedure. Thus, the rat gives the "response" of running to black and white goal box "stimuli," or the human learner makes the response of writing a list of words after studying some common nouns comprising a list of stimulus items. In this view, a response is little more than a label for the dependent variable that the experimenter may happen to measure, just as a stimulus may be but a simple label for the independent variables that make up the experimental situation that the learning subject encounters.

To summarize, then, just as there are *physical* and *functional* definitions of stimuli, there are also *physiological* and *functional* definitions of responses. To these we have added, in a third category, the notion that the terms stimulus and response can provide a convenient way of describing the experimental conditions psychologists may choose in their research upon the learning process.

By now it should be clear that the concepts of stimulus and response can be extraordinarily rich, full of as much meaning and complexity as anyone could require in constructing the most elaborate description of the most complicated forms of human and animal behavior. Unfortunately, although they imply no particular viewpoint or approach at all, the two terms have also been used to describe a so-called stimulus-response psychology. This is a psychology that is sometimes presumed to be mechanistic (as opposed to humanistic), sterile (because of rigid rules which blindly govern and severely restrict what is admissible into a study of behavior), and rather old-fashioned (because it is associated with the names of J. B. Watson and other early behaviorists). Perhaps this has all happened because some critics have failed to recognize something that should now be clear: a stimulus and a response to most modern-day psychologists are *not* the stimulus and response of the early reflex physiologists, those who contributed most directly to the times of which Watson was a part. Modern interpretations of these concepts are *least* likely to be cast into the mold of the early behaviorists. Obviously, we have only been able to touch upon the essence of this fascinating question in the history of psychology, but Gibson (1960) and Hinde (1970) have provided useful, thoughtful, and extensive discussions of the concepts of stimulus and response in both the past and present of the science of behavior, and their comments will lead you to still other sources if you wish to pursue the matter.

We turn now to our introduction of the principles associated with Pavlovian conditioning. Here, you will have a chance to observe stimuli and responses at work which are not far removed conceptually from those that a physiologist would use, although we shall see in due course that they can go far beyond that relatively simple level even in Pavlovian conditioning.

PAVLOVIAN CONDITIONING

5

SOME
FUNDAMENTAL
PRINCIPLES OF
PAVLOVIAN AND
INSTRUMENTAL
CONDITIONING

Ivan P. Pavlov, who won the Nobel prize for his earlier work on the physiology of the digestive system, is nevertheless perhaps most famous for his later experiments with ringing bells, meat powder, and salivating dogs. Not all of us realize just how familiar we are with the results of Pavlovian conditioning in our own experience, a fact which is easy to demonstrate in just a moment or two. Think of selecting a nice yellow lemon, slicing it with a sharp knife, then taking a long, slow lick from one of the halves, rinsing your mouth thoroughly with the sour juices. Chances are that the saliva began to flow before you finished reading the sentence—yet there was no lemon juice in your mouth at all. Clearly, therefore, the flow of saliva must depend in some respect on your previous experience with sour things; it is much as if the *thought* of the lemon juice has come to act as some kind of signal which stands in place of the lemon juice itself. At least the two produce the same behavioral result: a copious flow of saliva. This phenomenon was noticed at least two hundred years before Pavlov began his work (Fearing, 1930), but it was Pavlov who brought the phenomenon of salivary conditioning under close laboratory control and provided us with much of our early scientific understanding of it. Let us turn to a typical experiment of his to illustrate the fundamental procedures that are involved (Pavlov, 1927).

Conditioned salivation First, small openings were made in the cheek of a dog so that the duct of the parotid salivary gland could be directed outward; this allowed the saliva to be collected and measured as it was secreted. The dog was placed in a harness, such as that shown in Figure 1.1, which permitted some freedom but restricted much of the animal's ability to move about. The dog and the apparatus were placed in a soundproof room which had a small window that permitted the experimenters to watch the dog. A tuning fork was sounded in the room, and a few seconds later, small amounts of powdered meat were presented for the dog to eat. The tuning fork, of course, did not produce saliva, but the sight of the meat and its presence in the mouth did. After a few pairings of the tuning fork with the meat powder, the tuning fork was sounded *without* being followed by the meat powder, and the dog salivated. The sound of the tuning fork had acquired the ability to elicit the salivary response that was initially limited to the meat powder.

COMPONENTS OF PAVLOVIAN CONDITIONING

What are the essential elements of the experimental situation we have just described? What, in other words, constitute the fundamental components and procedures of Pavlovian conditioning?

The UCS Pavlov referred to the meat powder in his salivary conditioning experiment as an *unconditional stimulus*, often abbreviated UCS. The essential feature of a UCS is that it reliably elicits a response without prior training. Sometimes the ability of the UCS to elicit a response may be because of learning that took place before the animal came to the

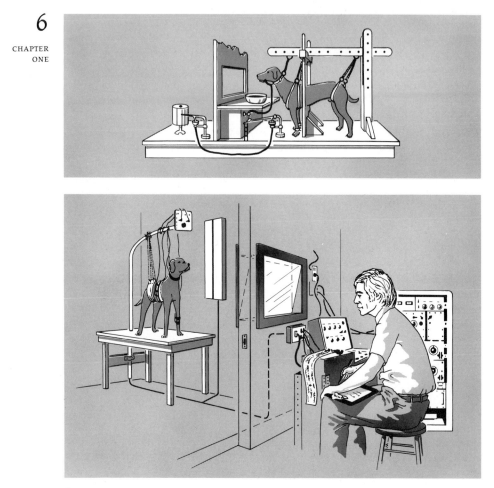

Figure 1.1
Top, an early experimental arrangement for Pavlovian conditioning of the salivary response. Drops of saliva were collected through the fistula in the dog's cheek, and their total number recorded by means of a system that moved a marker on a revolving smoked drum. *Bottom,* a modern laboratory for studying conditioned leg flexion to a mild electrical shock. The dog is in a soundproof room, while the experimenter is in an adjacent area controlling the delivery of CS and UCS and recording the dog's responses with automatic electronic equipment. (After Yerkes and Morgulis, 1909; Reus, Lynch, & Gantt, 1966.)

laboratory, although most experimenters do their best to eliminate or control such experience. Obviously, however, if one wishes to state that a particular UCS has an *innate,* unlearned eliciting tendency, he must carefully control the past history of the animal.

The UCR The *unconditioned response,* or UCR, is that response elicited by the UCS. Since the primary feature of the UCS-UCR relationship is that the UCS reliably elicits the UCR, the UCR is often a highly reflexive response, one which happens quickly and quite automatically when the

UCS occurs. Examples of UCRs include salivation, the eyeblink, and the knee jerk. In each case, appropriate UCSs would include food or weak acid (remember the lemon juice), a puff of air to the cornea of the eye or a mild electric shock to the margin of the eyelid, and a tap to the patellar tendon just below the kneecap.

7

SOME
FUNDAMENTAL
PRINCIPLES OF
PAVLOVIAN AND
INSTRUMENTAL
CONDITIONING

The CS   The *conditional stimulus*, or CS, is that stimulus which comes to elicit a response by being paired properly in time with the UCS. In a very real sense, the appearance of the newly emerging response comes to be *conditional* upon the presentation of the CS, hence its name. One obviously important feature of a CS is that it must be some stimulus which is within the sensory range of the organism; that is, it must be hearable, seeable, feelable, or tastable, and so on. A second important feature of the CS is that it must be neutral with respect to the reflex under study at the outset of the conditioning procedure. That is, it must not produce a response which looks like the to-be-conditioned response before any conditioning procedures take place. This is not to say that the CS does not produce any response, because in fact it often does. If a sound is used as a CS, for example, the dog may very well prick up its ears and look in the direction of the sound—particularly during early conditioning trials. This response to the CS is called an *orienting reflex* and has been taken, among other things, as an index of the attention-getting properties of the CS (Hinde, 1970). The important point once again, however, is that the orienting reflex to the CS does not have any direct topographical resemblance or relationship to the specific to-be-conditioned response produced by the UCS. The sound of the tuning fork does not produce salivation before conditioning occurs.

The CR   The *conditioned response*, or CR, is that learned reflex which arises when the CS is paired with the UCS. Quite simply, as a matter of fact, the operation of pairing CS with UCS provides the essential defining procedure for Pavlovian conditioning. Sometimes, incidentally, the CR is referred to as a *conditional* reflex for the reason we just noted—it becomes conditional upon the presentation of the CS.

It is important to recognize that the CR may *not* be exactly the same thing as the UCR. While both may share a great deal in common—a conditioned eyeblink is, after all, an eyeblink—there are often differences between them that are easy to distinguish. For example, a conditioned eyeblink may not have as great an *amplitude* as the unconditioned eyeblink; the eyelid may not close as completely to the CS as it does to the UCS of an air puff. By the same token, there may be differences in the *latency* of the conditioned as opposed to the unconditioned reflex; that is, the time which elapses between the onset of the CS and the occurrence of the CR may be longer (or shorter) than the time which elapses between the onset of the UCS and the occurrence of the UCR. Beyond these quantitative differences, it is also the case that the CR is sometimes best and most simply described as a *preparatory* response; in a real sense, the response prepares the organism for the arrival of the UCS. Thus, saliva prepares the mouth and the digestive system for the arrival of food, and so on. Consequently, it is well to remember that Pavlovian conditioning procedures do not literally *substitute* one response for another although, as we have seen, the CR and the UCR can share many features in common.

CS-UCS RELATIONS IN PAVLOVIAN CONDITIONING

It is one thing to say that the fundamental experimental operation for Pavlovian conditioning is the pairing in time of CS and UCS, and quite another to specify just how this should be done. In practice, psychologists have adopted the scheme outlined in Figure 1.2, a scheme which shows several ways in which CS and UCS can be arranged with respect to each other in time.

Look at the line labeled "CS" in Figure 1.2. It represents the tracing that a pen might make as it records the passage of time by moving across a piece of paper in the direction indicated by the arrow. The bump in the middle of the line labeled "CS" is intended to indicate that a CS was turned on and later turned off, the pen rising and then falling at these two points in time. Underneath the line labeled "CS" are several other lines labeled "UCS," each indicating, similarly, the onset and offset of a UCS. Comparison of the CS line with each of the UCS lines indicates various ways in which the CS and the UCS could be matched with each other in time. The line labeled "Simultaneous" indicates that both CS and UCS come on and go off together. The line labeled "Delayed" indicates that there was a delay in time between the onset of the CS and the onset of the UCS. The line labeled "Trace" indicates that the CS went on and off before the UCS went on at all. The line is labeled "Trace" because, with this procedure, any conditioning which occurs must depend on some trace of the CS left behind in the nervous system which persists until the UCS appears. This must be so because the actual CS, since it has been turned off, cannot be stimulating the organism directly. Finally, the line labeled "Backward" indicates that the UCS went on and off before the CS, itself, went on and off.

There are two further things to note about the scheme outlined in Figure 1.2. First of all, the figure does not exhaust all possible temporal relationships between CS and UCS. There are, for example, many other ways in which the UCS could be delayed with respect to the CS. Thus, the UCS could go off at the same time as the CS, it could go off before the CS goes off, or it could—as the example in the figure indicates—remain on for some time after the CS goes off. The only critical feature of the delayed procedure is that the onset of the UCS occurs after the onset of the CS. The second point of note about the scheme of Figure 1.2 is that the labels indicated in the figure for the various arrangements between CS and UCS are often used as a convenient shorthand to identify and distinguish the experimental operations incorporated into Pavlovian conditioning. Thus a psychologist may indicate that he used a trace procedure or a delayed procedure in his experiment. By this he means

9

SOME
FUNDAMENTAL
PRINCIPLES OF
PAVLOVIAN AND
INSTRUMENTAL
CONDITIONING

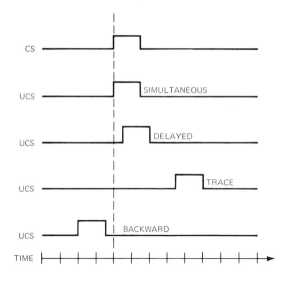

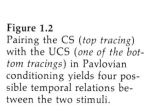

Figure 1.2
Pairing the CS (*top tracing*) with the UCS (*one of the bottom tracings*) in Pavlovian conditioning yields four possible temporal relations between the two stimuli.

basically that he set up certain fundamental time relations between the CS and the UCS in establishing his experimental design. Sometimes too, however, distinctions between the results of experiments incorporating trace, delayed, or backward conditioning can assume some theoretical as well as practical significance—as we shall see later.

THREE BASIC LAWS OF PAVLOVIAN CONDITIONING

During the course of his research with conditioning, Pavlov discovered many fundamental effects of putting conditional and unconditional stimuli together in one way or another. We shall be looking at some of these throughout much of the early part of this book, but it will prove useful to look at three of the most fundamental Pavlovian principles here. Our discussion owes much not only to Pavlov himself (Pavlov, 1927) but also to Rescorla and Solomon (1967).

The law of excitation   The law of excitation is really nothing more than a statement of the fact that Pavlovian conditioning occurs, but that is a pretty fundamental principle. Quite simply, the law of excitation says that if a previously neutral CS is paired with a UCS, the CS acquires excitatory properties; that is, it acquires the property of eliciting the CR. The significance of this law becomes even clearer if it is contrasted with the second law, a law which introduces a new idea not only to our discussion of Pavlovian conditioning but also to the development of the general psychology of learning.

The law of internal inhibition   One of the things that Pavlov did once he had established a conditioned salivary reflex in his dogs was to study what happened when he then sounded the tuning fork *without* delivering the food powder. The fundamental question, in other words, was what would happen to an established CR if the CS was turned on but was not followed by the UCS. As you might imagine, the dogs eventually stopped salivating. This procedure, known as *experimental extinction*, might take some time to produce complete results—perhaps several hundred trials if the conditional response were a well-established one— but eventually the dogs failed to salivate when the CS was turned on.

Pavlov gave the name *extinctive inhibition* to the process associated with the foregoing procedure, and he saw it as an example of a law encompassed by a more general process called *internal inhibition.* To understand this, it is necessary to ask what might have happened to the salivary CR as it underwent the extinction process. Perhaps it was simply forgotten—for example, the dog losing the association between CS and CR (or, perhaps, the UCS), so that late in extinction the animal could no longer remember what the CS signified when it appeared. This sounds a little farfetched, and there are a number of lines of evidence which indicate that animals do not, in fact, forget a conditioned response when they undergo extinction procedures (we shall look closely at some of that evidence when we get to the chapter on extinction). So it is safe to say that we are not dealing with a process of memory loss. Instead, the evidence points to the conclusion that the dog is coming to *actively inhibit* the CR when the CS is turned on. If, to go a step further, we have a dog with *two* responses conditioned according to Pavlovian procedures, and if we have extinguished one response, we can reduce the magnitude of the second CR by turning on the CS for the first one at the same time that we turn on the CS for the second. The extinction procedure, in other words, not only leads the animal to inhibit behavior associated directly with the CS, but also endows the CS with the power to actively inhibit or suppress other conditioned behavior.

A second line of evidence against a forgetting hypothesis comes from a consideration of our third law of Pavlovian conditioning, to which we shall turn in just a moment. Before we do, however, it is worthwhile noting that extinctive inhibition is just one example of internal inhibition. Pavlov was able to show internal inhibition at work in a number of different conditioning situations, and we shall have occasion to examine some of those in later portions of this book.

The law of external inhibition   If Pavlov had a dog with a well-established CR, and if he turned on some novel or distracting stimulus at the same time he presented the CS for the response, he often noted that a CR of reduced magnitude was the result. By the same token, if he had a well-extinguished CR and turned on a novel or distracting stimulus, he observed that the CR *reappeared,* often at considerable strength (which indicates incidentally, as we noted a moment ago, that extinction does not involve some loss in memory for events entering into the conditioning process). In each case, in other words, a novel *external* stimulus had the power to disrupt an ongoing process—either reducing the magnitude of an established CR or increasing the magnitude of (disinhibiting, if you will) an extinguished CR.

Pavlov's nomenclature may be a little confusing here—it is awkward, for example, to think things through to the necessary conclusion that an extinguished response reappears because internal inhibition is inhibited by an external inhibitor! The proper and fundamental sense of things is easy to keep in mind, however, if Pavlov's law of external inhibition is reduced to its essential feature: *Excitatory or inhibitory processes in conditioning can each be disrupted by novel, distracting stimuli.*

While we shall say more later about the basic procedures associated with Pavlovian conditioning, their fundamental characteristics are now before you. Pavlov's influence has been enormous in the psychology of learning, and the terms conditional and unconditional stimulus and conditioned and unconditioned response are a ready part of its vocabulary—if they are not actually a part of our everyday language. We turn, now, however, to a second major scheme for organizing and studying the learning process, a scheme which differs in a number of important respects from Pavlovian conditioning.

INSTRUMENTAL OR OPERANT CONDITIONING

One of the major operational features which characterizes Pavlovian conditioning—and there are others, as we shall see—is that the learning organism plays a purely passive role insofar as the delivery of the conditional and unconditional stimulus is concerned. In the case of experimental salivary conditioning, for example, the dog has absolutely no control over the delivery of the meat powder. Instead, the dog stands passively in its harness while the experimenter decides when conditional and unconditional stimuli are to be presented. A second operationally defined type of learning can be distinguished when we let the organism assume some active role in the learning situation. In particular, we can set things so that the organism cannot obtain reward or cannot escape from punishment of some kind until and unless it somehow makes the response we want it to make. This is a method which animal trainers sometimes utilize to help an animal learn to do tricks. In cases such as this, when reward is made deliberately *contingent* on the prior occurrence of the response we want the organism to learn, we speak of *instrumental* or *operant* conditioning. As the names imply, the organism quite literally plays an *instrumental* role in producing rewards for itself or in escaping from or avoiding some punishment (Hilgard & Marquis, 1940). The organism must literally *operate* upon its environment, in other words (Skinner, 1938).

BASIC PROCEDURES IN INSTRUMENTAL CONDITIONING

In general, psychologists have been satisfied to use a surprisingly small number of basic experimental arrangements in their study of the simple process of instrumental conditioning. At the risk of some oversimplification, but not too much, we can identify three basic features that characterize most instrumental conditioning experiments. First of all, the typical experimental plan will use procedures that involve *reward* or *punishment*. For example, we reward a hungry dog with a piece of food, or we punish an animal by subjecting it to some unpleasant stimulus like electric shock. The general term for the operations of reward or punishment is *reinforcement*, and particular kinds of reward or punishment are called *reinforcers* or *reinforcing stimuli*. Second, our experimental plan can lead an organism to either *produce* or *withhold* some specified response. An animal may have to do something actively, or the animal may have to withhold or inhibit a response before we give it a bit of food, for example. Third, a *discriminative cue* will be used in some experimental plans but not in others. A discriminative cue is a stimulus of some sort that tells the organism, in effect, when reinforcement can be obtained and when it cannot be obtained. Generally, the instrumental response will not be reinforced if it occurs when the discriminative cue is absent. In other words, a discriminative cue, if it is used in an experiment, "sets the appropriate occasion" for the behavior that leads to reinforcement.

A little reflection will show that eight experimental plans, or paradigms, can be specified by appropriate combinations of the types of reinforcement, response, and reinforcement cue that we have mentioned (Kimble, 1961; Grant, 1964). Table 1.1 summarizes the basic procedures that are involved in these paradigms.

We now have a convenient classification of some operationally defined types of instrumental conditioning. Let us look at some examples of experiments or experimental situations which fit these types of conditioning.

Reward training   A hungry white rat is placed in a 12-inch-square box that is relatively soundproof. At one end of the box is a small lever that projects from the wall. The lever is connected to an automatic recording

Table 1.1
Types of instrumental conditioning

TYPE	DISCRIMINATIVE CUE AVAILABLE?	RESPONSE COMES TO BE:	REINFORCEMENT BASED ON:
Reward training	No	Produced	Reward
Discrimination training	Yes	Produced	Reward
Escape training	No	Produced	Punishment
Avoidance training	Yes	Produced	Punishment
Omission training	No	Withheld	Reward
Punishment training	No	Withheld	Punishment
Discriminated omission training	Yes	Withheld	Reward
Discriminated punishment training	Yes	Withheld	Punishment

device and to an electrically operated magazine filled with pellets of rat food. When the lever is pressed, the magazine automatically delivers a pellet of food into a small cup near the lever. This device is often called a Skinner box after B. F. Skinner, who first described its use (but it is not called this by Skinner himself or many of his associates, who prefer to use the term "experimental space").

13

SOME
FUNDAMENTAL
PRINCIPLES OF
PAVLOVIAN AND
INSTRUMENTAL
CONDITIONING

When the rat is placed in the box, it will explore its new environment quite readily. It will sniff the air, paw the walls, and bite here and there. Eventually, it will stumble against the lever. Sooner or later it will depress the lever enough to release a pellet of food. The rat may not discover the food immediately, but when it does, it will certainly eat the food. There is a fair certainty also that the rat will press the lever a second time. This time, perhaps, it will discover the food immediately. At this point, the behavior of the rat may change dramatically. Instead of resuming its casual exploration of the box, it will now proceed to press the lever repeatedly. As a matter of fact, if the rat is hungry enough, it will press the lever at a rate which is limited only by the time it takes to put its nose down and eat the food from the cup.

The general procedures associated with simple reward training are hardly new. We owe their introduction into the psychology of learning to E. L. Thorndike, who, in a remarkable doctoral dissertation (Thorndike, 1898), described the techniques that cats learned to use to escape from "puzzle boxes" in order to get pieces of food. He found that the animals showed a great deal of exploratory behavior, stumbling, finally, onto the latch which operated the door and led to freedom and food. The process was a gradual one with his cats—the course of learning was marked by much trial and error and only a gradual reduction in the time it took the animals to solve the problem on any given trial.

Discrimination training   Let us use the same Skinner-box apparatus that we have just described, but let us add a discriminative cue—a small white light located in the wall of the box where the rat can easily see it. Let us turn the light on, place the rat in the box, and use reward training to a point where the rat is pressing the lever in a rapid and consistent fashion. Now we shall turn off the light and, at the same time, disconnect the food magazine from the lever so that lever presses no longer produce pellets of food. After a minute or two, we turn the light back on and reconnect the food magazine so that lever presses are once again reinforced when they occur. We continue to alternate periods of light-on with reinforcement and light-off with no reinforcement, choosing time intervals for these periods which are not consistently of the same length.

The first time that we omit the discriminative cue of the light, the rat will probably continue to press the lever for a considerable period of time, but since presses of the lever are not rewarded, the rat will eventually press the lever much less frequently than before. As a matter of fact, if we withheld reinforcement indefinitely, the rat would stop pressing the lever altogether (a process, remember, known as *experimental extinction*). Consequently, when the light is turned back on, we may have to wait awhile for the rat to return to the lever. When the rat does this and reward is forthcoming, however, the rat will return to pressing the lever just about as frequently as before. Eventually, after a number of periods in which the light is turned on and off—and reinforcement is delivered or withheld accordingly—the rat will reserve most of its lever presses for the period of time in which the light is on, and it will make very few lever presses when the light is off. The discriminative cue of the light has come to set the occasion for lever pressing. It tells the rat, in effect, when to behave in order to obtain reinforcement.

Escape training A dog is placed in one compartment of a two-compartment box. The two compartments are separated by a door, which can slide up and down. The door is arranged such that it can be dropped partway through a slot in the floor, creating a hurdle over which the dog can jump from the first compartment into the second. Both compartments are equipped with floors made of stainless-steel bars through which an electric current is passed. The bars are wired in such a way that when current is passed through them, a shock of moderate intensity is delivered to the dog through the dog's feet. The bars are also wired so that when current is on in one compartment it is off in the other. At some time determined by the experimenter, the door drops and, at the same instant, current is turned on in the first compartment. The shock continues until the dog jumps over the hurdle and reaches the "safe" compartment, in which the shock is not present. The door closes, and the dog then "rests" until the experimenter again drops the door and turns on the shock in the second compartment. The dog must then jump the hurdle once again, moving back to the original compartment, which is now safe. The process of shock in one compartment followed by escape to the other then continues for as many trials as the experiment may call for.

It is easy to imagine what the reaction of the dog will be the first time that it feels the punishing stimulus of the shock in such a "shuttle box." There will be a good deal of yelping, some urination and defecation, and a great deal of agitated activity. Eventually, however, the dog will stumble over the hurdle and reach the safe compartment. The second time the shock comes on, the dog will show much less agitation and will move over the hurdle much more rapidly than on the first trial. After a few trials, the dog will jump the hurdle and escape with a very short latency.

At this point we should stop and ask a pertinent question about the nature of reinforcement in escape training. We might guess that the actual process of reinforcement depends on the fact that shock stops when the dog moves from one compartment to the next. It might seem reasonable to think of escape training as a rather special case of reward training, on the assumption that escaping a noxious stimulus like shock is rewarding. There is, of course, much intuitive merit to this point of view. The important point at the moment, however, is that the procedure for escape training in instrumental conditioning depends upon a reinforcement operation which involves an aversive stimulus like electric shock, and an active response which gets the organism away from the punishing stimulus. Right now, we shall make no theoretical guesses about the precise nature of the process which underlies or which actually produces the improvement in the instrumental response in the situation. We shall have a good deal to say about that later on.

15

SOME
FUNDAMENTAL
PRINCIPLES OF
PAVLOVIAN AND
INSTRUMENTAL
CONDITIONING

Avoidance training We can describe the basic avoidance-training paradigm by using the same apparatus that we used for escape training. We shall modify the apparatus in one respect by adding an overhead light in each compartment that the dog can easily see when it is turned on. The dog is placed in one compartment of the shuttle box with the light turned off. At some appropriate moment, we provide the dog with a discriminative cue by turning on the light and dropping the door which separates the first compartment from the second. Ten seconds later, we apply current to the floor in the first compartment and shock the dog. However, the dog can avoid the punishing stimulus of the shock by leaping the hurdle into the safe compartment during the 10-second interval between the onset of the discriminative cue and the onset of the shock. Again, the discriminative cue sets the occasion for the dog's response. When the dog goes to the second compartment, we close the door, and the dog rests. The next trial begins when we again turn on the discriminative cue and, 10 seconds later, turn on the shock.

As with discrimination training, the discriminative cue will have essentially no effect on the behavior of the dog on the first trial. The first time we deliver the cue and follow it with shock, the dog will behave in essentially the same way that it would behave in an escape-training situation. As a matter of fact, early trials in avoidance training actually involve simple escape training so long as the dog fails to respond to the discriminative cue within the prescribed time interval, takes the shock, and then stumbles over the hurdle into the safe compartment. However, after a few trials during which the latency of the response to the shock may decrease considerably (but not enough to avoid it), the dog will begin to respond to the discriminative cue and leap to the second compartment before the shock comes on. Sometimes, if the situation is made sufficiently traumatic, the dog may never again take a shock once a trial occurs in which it successfully avoids shock.

The procedure we have just described also goes under the label "two-way active avoidance training," which indicates not only that the animal must actively produce a response to avoid punishment, but also that the avoidance response involves going back and forth across a hurdle between two compartments, each of which is "dangerous" at some time during a series of trials and "safe" at others. It is possible, of course, as an alternative, to arrange things so that the animal always starts each trial in one compartment, the dangerous compartment in which discriminative cue and shock are delivered, and leaps a hurdle to a safe compartment in which shock is never experienced. This procedure, which is called "one-way active avoidance training," obviously calls for moving the animal by hand from the safe compartment back into the dangerous compartment between each learning trial.

Punishment training   Another glance at Table 1.1 will show that, thus far, we have been discussing procedures for instrumental conditioning that involve the active *production* of a response by the organism in conjunction with reinforcement operations of reward or punishment. There are, by contrast, some procedures which call for the active *withholding* or *omission* of a response in order to obtain reward or avoid punishment. Probably the most common of these is simple *punishment training*, and it is easy to think of a situation in which this could be demonstrated. Quite simply, we could establish a lever-pressing response through simple reward training in a lever box, then suddenly change the outcome of responses from food pellets to brief electric shocks to the rat's feet. Under these conditions, the rat must learn to inhibit or withhold lever presses in order to avoid the punishing stimulus of the electric shock, a process which is in obvious conflict with the earlier habit of pressing for a reward. Nevertheless, assuming the punishment is strong enough, it behooves the animal to withhold the lever-pressing response, and this will be the outcome of the procedure. Note that the animal *avoids* the punishing stimulus by, in a sense, becoming passive in the situation—at least with respect to the lever-pressing response. For this reason, punishment training is sometimes called *passive avoidance learning*.

Omission training   Omission training is a direct analog to punishment training, except that reinforcement is based on a positive reward. Assume that we have used reward training to a point where a rat is pressing a lever for food pellets in a consistent, stable fashion. Now let us suddenly change things so that (1) lever presses are no longer reinforced but (2) *failure* to press the lever *is* reinforced. The latter could be done in some arbitrary way, perhaps by dropping a food pellet into the food cup at the end of each five-second period that the rat fails to press the lever. Under these conditions, obviously, the animal must learn to withhold or omit the response in order to assure a continued flow of food pellets.

Discriminated punishment and discriminated omission training   By now, you should be able to anticipate the procedures we would use to demonstrate these two remaining types of instrumental procedures. Basically, they simply require the addition of a discriminative cue that sets the occasion for reinforcement under the simple conditions of punishment training or omission training. Thus, if we choose a light as a discriminative cue, we could arrange things so that light onset sets the occasion for omitting lever presses in order to obtain rewards or to avoid punishments. In the absence of the discriminative cue—that is, when the light is off—we could reintroduce simple reward training, and lever presses could once again produce food pellets.

It is of some interest that while punishment training and discriminated punishment training have received considerable attention in the laboratory, there has been relatively little attention devoted to the behavior that is characteristic of omission training. Perhaps this is so because it is hard to think of many real situations in nature or in the world of human behavior in which responses are literally reinforced with a reward only when they fail to occur and when this is the single reinforcement arrangement involved. Nevertheless, a study of both simple and discriminated omission training may provide a very valuable tool to use in the investigation of processes which govern the inhibition of behavior.

17

SOME
FUNDAMENTAL
PRINCIPLES OF
PAVLOVIAN AND
INSTRUMENTAL
CONDITIONING

Learning which calls for the active withholding of behavior is by no means restricted to the world of Skinner boxes, food pellets, and electric shock. Parents learn, for example, that rewards given when children withhold some kind of unwanted behavior can sometimes (though not always!) prevent the recurrence of the unwanted behavior. Usually, they find that for this procedure to be effective it has to be combined with punishment for the unwanted behavior when it does occur. And parents sometimes use discriminative cues—often in the form of verbal commands—that set the occasion for the omission of the behavior in question. In the case of discriminated punishment training, for example, a parent may warn a child that unless some kind of unwanted behavior is omitted, punishment will ensue. Of course, the child may very well learn to omit the unwanted behavior in the presence of the discriminative cue represented by the parent, but go right ahead with things when the parent is absent. Such are the things that exasperate parents! Our general point, however, is that there are many occasions when responses must be withheld in order to satisfy some reinforcement contingency supplied by the environment.

Free versus controlled responding   Instrumental conditioning can involve either *free-responding* or *controlled-responding* procedures (sometimes called *free-operant* and *discrete-trial* procedures, respectively). The distinction is based on whether the *subject* or the *experimenter* controls the opportunity to make the instrumental behavior in question, and the distinction is an important one to keep in mind. First of all, the decision to use one as opposed to the other of the procedures may well determine the kind of measure of behavior that is used in the experiment. With a free-responding procedure such as that typically used in the Skinner box, for example, a frequently used measure of behavior is the *rate* at which a number of responses are produced, i.e., their frequency per unit time. Obviously, in a controlled-responding or discrete-trial situation, where the opportunity to respond is under the rigid control of the experimenter, it is not possible to use the rate at which a number of responses occur as an index of the effect of some variable upon behavior. Instead, the experimenter is more apt to record some feature of an *individual* response each time it occurs, such as the time that a rat takes to leave the start box of a maze or the time that a dog takes to get from one side of a shuttle box to the other.

A second important distinction between free- and controlled-responding procedures, however, is that they lend themselves in some cases to a study of different experimental variables. For example, as we shall see in much greater detail in Chapter 5, one interesting method for delivering rewards to subjects is based on the requirement that responses be spaced apart in time by a certain interval in order for them to be rewarded. Obviously, this procedure makes sense only in the case where the learning organism is free to distribute its responses as it wishes in time, and that can only happen with a free-responding arrangement.

THE DEFINITION OF REINFORCEMENT

We have just been using the terms *reinforcer* and *reinforcement* quite frequently, and now is the time to turn our attention to a somewhat more formal treatment of these concepts as they are used by the psychologist.

Recall, for a moment, the example of instrumental reward training given earlier in this chapter. In that example, a rat learned to press a lever, and this response was reinforced with a pellet of food.

If we had followed the lever-pressing response with the sound of a buzzer instead of a pellet of food, would the rat have learned to press the lever? Probably not, our common experience with rewards would tell us. [Sometimes our common experience can lead us to wrong conclusions. As Roberts, Marx, and Collier (1958) have shown, rats will learn to press a lever when the response is followed by the onset of a dim light! Here, however, our common experience would be right; in this situation food is a reinforcer and a buzzer is not.] Food is a reinforcer because it produces an increase in the frequency of the response that it follows. Obviously, because the buzzer cannot produce such an increase, it is not a reinforcer.

REINFORCERS AND REINFORCEMENT

With these thoughts in mind, we can now look at a formal definition of reinforcers and reinforcement. *A reinforcer is a stimulus event which, if it occurs in the proper temporal relation with a response, tends to maintain or to increase the strength of a response or of a stimulus-response connection.* In instrumental or operant conditioning, the reinforcer is contingent upon the occurrence of the response and thus follows the response in time. In Pavlovian conditioning, the reinforcer is the stimulus, the UCS, that elicits the unconditioned reflex, the UCR. Barring delays that are imposed by the speed with which impulses can be conducted in the nervous system and translated into effector activity, UCS and UCR occur simultaneously. The operations of using stimulus events in the ways described are known, collectively, as reinforcement (Meehl, 1950).

Positive and negative reinforcers In the case of instrumental or operant conditioning, it turns out to be convenient if we distinguish two subclasses of reinforcing stimuli: positive reinforcers and negative reinforcers (Skinner, 1938; Keller & Schoenfeld, 1950). The concept of positive reinforcement is clear enough from earlier discussion and from the general definition of reinforcement we have just given. In common terms, a positive reinforcer is a reward. It is a stimulus, like a piece of food, that we give to an organism after the organism has done something we want it to learn to do. But what of negative reinforcers? How, literally, can a response be negatively reinforced? The word *reinforce* connotes that a response is strengthened, while the word *negative* seems to add the implication that the response is somehow weakened at the same time. The use of the term *negative reinforcer* clearly raises some semantic problems, but these can be easily straightened out if we keep an operational definition in mind. Negative reinforcers are stimuli which strengthen a response when they are *removed* if the response occurs. Recall our example of simple escape training. In this instance, the dog's response of leaping from one side of the shuttle box to the other was reinforced by removing electric shock when the response occurred.

As you can easily infer, negative reinforcement involves the use of a stimulus event which has aversive properties, a stimulus event that an organism will ordinarily avoid if it can. And, as we saw earlier in this chapter, such stimulus events can also be used to punish a response. Thus, in the case of simple punishment training, a lever-pressing response that a rat had learned to make initially in order to obtain food pellets was punished by changing things so that lever presses began to produce electric shocks instead of morsels of food. And we noted that a procedure of this type would ordinarily tend to make the rat omit or withhold the lever-pressing response.

Since aversive, noxious stimuli like electric shocks can be used operationally to produce two very different effects, reinforcement and punishment, we had better be explicit about the experimental operations that will lead to one effect as compared with the other. Noxious stimulation can be used to reinforce a response when we supply noxious stimulation independent of anything the organism does, and when we set things so that the occurrence of the response we want the organism to learn *removes or turns off* the noxious stimulation. In everyday terms, if people are plunged into the middle of some traumatic situation owing to circumstances beyond their control, responses that get them away from trauma will be reinforced and learned. On the other hand, noxious stimulation can be used to punish a response when the occurrence of the response *supplies or turns on* noxious stimulation. In everyday terms once again, people tend to stop doing things that expose them to punishing, traumatic events.

The concepts of positive and negative reinforcement cannot be applied very meaningfully to Pavlovian conditioning. It is true that food, a substance that can function very efficiently as a positive reinforcer in instrumental conditioning, can be used as a UCS to elicit salivation, and thus to establish a Pavlovian conditioned salivary response. It is also true, however, that a weak acid solution injected into the mouth of a dog does the job as well (Pavlov, 1927), and it is doubtful that weak acid solutions would function very well as positive reinforcers for instru-

19

SOME
FUNDAMENTAL
PRINCIPLES OF
PAVLOVIAN AND
INSTRUMENTAL
CONDITIONING

mental conditioning. Offhand, we might guess that acid would be apt to have properties more closely akin to a negative rather than to a positive reinforcer.

Weak versus strong definitions of reinforcement   Our definitions of reinforcers and reinforcement are strictly operational. They are phrased in terms of the things that experimenters see, do, and measure. This definition is the "weak" or *empirical* definition of reinforcement; it simply describes the kinds of things that are done and the kinds of things that are supposed to happen if the concept of reinforcement is to be applied. Such a definition makes no assertions about the underlying mechanism by which a positive reinforcer like food for a hungry organism strengthens some response like lever pressing. One could, of course, ask why food works this way. Is it because the food reduces some drive or motive like hunger, or is it because the food has some special incentive value derived from its taste? Questions like these would lead us to the "strong" or *theoretical* definition of the concept of reinforcement. We would be asking *how* or *why* reinforcers in fact produce the changes in the strength of a response that we measure when we use them. We shall have more to say about theoretical approaches to reinforcement later on.

Trans-situational reinforcers   The definition of reinforcement we have given is open to the charge of being circular. One could say that reinforcers are things which change behavior, and then turn right around and assert that behavior is changed because it is reinforced. One path which leads partway out of this circularity comes from the notion that most, if not all, reinforcers for instrumental conditioning are *trans-situational* (Meehl, 1950). This means that a given reinforcer will strengthen *any* learnable response in a given species. In other words, if a particular stimulus is reinforcing for lever pressing for a rat, it ought to be reinforcing for other arbitrary responses such as running a maze.

The concept of the trans-situational nature of reinforcers does not apply in Pavlovian conditioning in the same way that it does in instrumental conditioning. A given unconditional stimulus can generally be used for only a few closely related reflexes, those that are directly elicitable by that stimulus. Pavlovian conditioning is trans-situational with respect to *conditional* stimuli in the sense that one can use almost any given CS for a given CR so long as it meets the usual requirements for conditional stimuli, such as being detectable by the organism.

THE CONCEPT OF RESPONSE STRENGTH

We have already used the phrase *response strength* on several occasions, and it is time to make explicit the meaning of that phrase—although its meaning has no doubt been reasonably clear from the various contexts in which it has been used. Response strength is an *intervening variable*, that is, a concept that must be inferred from some measurable aspect of overt behavior. If we were to say that reinforcement increases response strength, for example, this would imply that we have some index or measurement of behavior which will change in systematic fashion as we apply more and more reinforcement. If we have such an index, and if it behaves in orderly fashion as we increase, say, the number of reinforcements we use, then we apply the term response strength as a general label for that relationship.

21

SOME
FUNDAMENTAL
PRINCIPLES OF
PAVLOVIAN AND
INSTRUMENTAL
CONDITIONING

Indices of response strength fall into two broad classes. First, there are indices based on whether responses occur or fail to occur. Thus, response strength is great if there is high *probability* that a response will occur in a given unit of time or if a given stimulus appears. In free-operant situations, a high probability of a response in a given unit of time translates into a high *rate* of response, a frequently used index in the Skinner box. Thus, a strong tendency to press the lever might be indicated by a response rate of 2 presses per second, while a weak tendency to press the lever would be indicated by a response rate of 1 press per minute. If we are dealing with a learning problem that requires someone to make choices among several alternative courses of action, then we can use the probability of, say, a correct as opposed to an incorrect choice as an index of response strength.

The second class of indices of response strength is based on some measurable, quantitative feature of individual responses themselves. Included here are measures such as the latency of a response, the duration of a response, the amplitude of a response, and the force of a response. In any given experiment one or another of these indices might be well correlated with another—short response latencies might go with rapid responses, for example—although experience shows that sometimes this may not be the case.

TESTING THE EFFECTS OF REINFORCEMENT ON RESPONSE STRENGTH

In instrumental conditioning, the methods of assessing the effects of a procedure like reinforcement are quite simple. Usually the response before reinforcement is very low in strength; the probability of a response is small, or the amplitude is very low. The base-line strength of a response before conditioning begins is called its *operant level*—which must be at least finite, or else a response would never occur so that it could be reinforced and the process of learning begun. After a few reinforcements, however, the probability of occurrence per unit time of a typical operant response, that is, its *rate*, changes rapidly. Figure 1.3 shows this effect taking place. In the figure the cumulative frequency of responses is plotted against time. Thus early in the experiment the responses cumulate very slowly; the result is a nearly horizontal line with occasional bumps that show the occurrence of responses. As the response becomes conditioned, however, the response occurs much more frequently, so that the line goes up rapidly. The actual learning itself, in this example, is reflected by the change in the slope of the curve.

In Pavlovian conditioning, the situation is a bit more complicated. We have seen that the reinforcing stimulus in Pavlovian conditioning is the unconditional stimulus. Thus, the stimulus that elicits the response in the first place provides the reinforcement. The conditioned, or learned, response, however, occurs to the conditional stimulus, and because the conditional stimulus usually precedes the unconditional stimulus, the conditioned response often "anticipates" the occurrence of the unconditioned response. In cases like this, of which the conditioned eyeblink provides a good example, it is possible to obtain a record of, say, the amplitude of the conditioned response to the CS before the unconditioned response to the UCS begins to occur.

The conditioned response does not always anticipate the unconditioned response, however, either because of the nature of the response system itself that is being used or because of some feature of the way in which the CS is paired with the UCS. In cases like these, we must use special test trials in which we omit the UCS to find out whether any conditioning has taken place. Without these test trials we would have no way of knowing whether a particular response was the result of the conditional or unconditional stimuli. If we run a number of test trials during the course of an experiment, we can calculate the probability that a conditioned response will be obtained for a particular experimental variable by noting the frequency with which the conditioned response appears. If the CR appears on 9 out of 10 test trials for a given subject, for example, the probability of obtaining a CR for that subject is 0.90. Care must be used when a test-trial procedure is used to check for conditioning, however. If we omit the UCS on too many trials, we may find that the response begins to lose strength according to the process of extinctive inhibition.

Figure 1.3
A cumulative record of instrumental conditioning. All responses were reinforced. There is no evidence of learning following the first three responses, but the fourth is followed by a rapid change in the rate of responding—the responses cumulating quickly in time. (Skinner, 1938.)

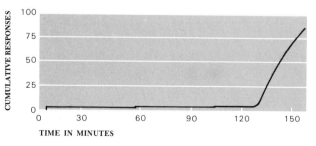

THE INFERENCE OF LEARNING FROM
CHANGES IN RESPONSE STRENGTH

23

SOME
FUNDAMENTAL
PRINCIPLES OF
PAVLOVIAN AND
INSTRUMENTAL
CONDITIONING

How do we decide when an organism has "learned" something, and how can we describe the course of such learning? The first thing that must be done is to recognize that learning itself cannot be observed. Learning itself must be considered an intervening variable which must be inferred from some observable aspect of behavior. Generally speaking, psychologists infer the concept of learning on the basis of two things. First, they postulate that the necessary independent variable which must be manipulated to produce learning is something that is akin to practice of, experience with, or repetition of a response. In order to learn, organisms must practice or have experience with things. For simple learning, a commonly accepted index of such practice is *number of reinforced trials*. Second, a dependent variable must be specified which will reflect the results of practice or experience. Psychologists are not always in agreement about the best one to use, and the appropriate measure may indeed vary from experiment to experiment or from learning situation to learning situation. But they do agree that the dependent variable must be some measure of the overt performance of the response that is practiced by the organism. The kinds of measures that we have identified under the heading of *response strength* are quite commonly used. Generally speaking, then, learning will be inferred if there is some change in the strength of a response with the practice of that response.

But how to describe that change in strength? A commonly accepted way to do this is to draw a *learning curve*, a curve which shows just how response strength increases with practice. You can see examples of learning curves in Figures 1.4 and 1.5, and there will be frequent occasion to call on them in the future. The concept of learning as a change in response strength with practice, and the technique of showing it graphically by means of a learning curve, are both simple ideas which lead to some further questions that rapidly become more complicated. One issue has to do with whether learning occurs gradually and incrementally over a relatively large number of practice trials or whether it tends to happen suddenly and all at once on just a single trial or two. Psychologists have not yet been able to settle that issue because the answer depends ultimately on the extent to which all the relevant variables can be identified in any given learning situation, variables which range from those having to do with the species of learning organism to the type of task that is there to be learned. But let us look at an example of an approach which emphasizes an incremental model for the learning curve, and then another example which emphasizes the jumpwise or all-at-once approach. There are some interesting things to be learned along the way.

AN INCREMENTAL MODEL FOR THE LEARNING CURVE

An incremental model for the learning curve generally postulates three things assumed to be fundamental to the learning process:

1. Strength of response increases as the number of reinforced practice trials increases. In instrumental conditioning, at least, we have to assume that the strength of a response is never actually zero, or else the response would never occur so that we could reinforce it and raise the probability that it be repeated. But for all practical purposes, we can think of response strength at the beginning of learning as essentially nil.

2. There is some upper limit beyond which response strength cannot increase. This upper limit, the asymptote of response strength, will be determined by many things, such as the nature of the species, the nature of the response that is to be learned, and the particular conditions of reinforcement, motivation, and the like that we impose. As these things change, so will the upper limit of response strength, but if they are held constant, the upper limit of response strength will be a constant.

3. Experience with a wide variety of responses in a wide variety of learning situations shows that the biggest additions to response strength occur early in learning; as the number of practice trials increases, smaller and smaller increments of response strength are added to the total strength of the response. This means, of course, that response strength ultimately approaches a limit, an asymptote.

There are many ways in which these assumptions can be put together in mathematical form, but one way to do it is given by the equation $\Delta R_n = k(M - R)$. This equation says that the response strength ΔR_n which is added to learning on any given trial is a function of the difference between the ultimate asymptote of response strength M and the amount of response strength already acquired on previous trials R. The symbol k stands for a constant which determines the rate at which response strength is added by successive trials.

Figure 1.4 shows four learning curves that were derived by the above reasoning. Two curves were derived on the assumption that the limit of response strength was 100 arbitrary units, but for one, $k = 0.10$ and for the other, $k = 0.50$. Two other curves were derived with the same values for k, but with M set at 300 arbitrary units of response strength. It is easy to see from the figure that all curves start with large increments to

Figure 1.4
Some hypothetical learning curves derived by reasoning discussed in the text. The solid curves are heading toward an asymptote of 300 units of response strength, while the dashed curves are heading toward an asymptote of 100 units of response strength. Note that the curves approach these limits faster when $k = 0.5$ than when $k = 0.1$.

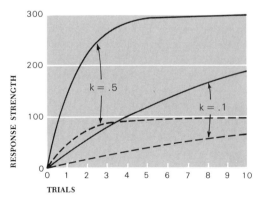

response strength during early practice trials, but the increments become smaller as trials increase. Also, when $k = 0.50$, response strength approaches its limit much more quickly than when $k = 0.10$.

25

SOME
FUNDAMENTAL
PRINCIPLES OF
PAVLOVIAN AND
INSTRUMENTAL
CONDITIONING

AN ALL-OR-NONE MODEL FOR THE LEARNING CURVE

Evidence also exists that the strength of certain learned relations can go from some low, perhaps chance, level to its maximum after just *one* trial (Estes, 1964; Estes, Hopkins, & Crothers, 1960; Bower, 1961a). The same data show that if this does not happen—that is, if a subject does not demonstrate complete learning in a single trial—the probability that he will make a correct response on the next trials remains at the initial chance level. Thus, learning is an all-or-none affair in the sense that a subject either learns completely on a trial or he does not learn at all.

Let us look at some further reasoning (Estes, 1964) based on data from human subjects to see in better detail how the process is presumed to work. Suppose we choose a task that involves the learning of paired associates. With a task of this sort, people are first presented with a pair of items—two English words like BALL-HOUSE, for example. The subjects are asked to associate the two so that on a subsequent test they will be able to give the response word HOUSE when the stimulus word BALL is shown to them by itself. A typical experiment will use a list of paired items so that the subject has a number of stimulus items and a number of response items which he must learn to associate in proper fashion. Let us suppose that, in addition to the response word HOUSE in our example, the subject has three other response words from which he might select when he is given the stimulus word BALL. In this case the probability by chance alone of making the correct response, HOUSE, will be 0.25. Assume further, however, that there is some fixed probability, say 0.50, that the subject will learn the correct association on a given trial; if he does, the probability that he will give the correct response shifts from the initial chance level of 0.25 to a probability of 1.0. For several subjects, the process is like that diagrammed in Figure 1.5.

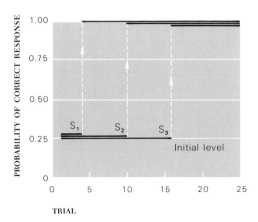

Figure 1.5
Learning "curves" for individual subjects according to a one-element learning model. For each subject (S_1, S_2, or S_3) the probability of a correct response goes from a chance level to 1.0 in just one trial, but this happens on different trials for different subjects. (Estes, 1964a.)

You can see from the example shown in the figure that different subjects learn the correct response on different trials; this happens because the probability is only 0.5 that any given subject will learn on any given trial. Note also that if a subject learns on a given trial, the probability of a correct response on all subsequent trials remains at 1.0. However, if a subject does not learn on a given trial, it is assumed that the probability of his giving a correct response on the next trial remains at the chance level; i.e., it remains at 0.25. Thus, with respect to individual subjects, learning is truly an all-or-none and not an incremental affair; a subject either learns completely or not at all on a given trial. But what happens if the data from a group of subjects are pooled so that the probability of a correct response on a given trial is averaged across a number of subjects? The result is shown in Figure 1.6.

The horizontal dashed line labeled $P(C_{n+1}|N_n)$ is to be read "the probability that subjects will be correct on trial $n + 1$, given that they were not correct on trial n." This value, 0.25, corresponds to the value we would expect for subjects who had not learned but who were simply correct now and then by chance guessing. As trials progress, however, more and more subjects will learn; that is, their probabilities of being correct will jump on a given trial from 0.25 to 1.0 and stay there. As we have seen, the probability that this will happen on a given trial for a given subject is 0.50. The net effect is that the proportion of subjects who have learned, as compared with those who have not, will increase steadily as the number of trials increases. This fact is reflected in the solid curve in Figure 1.6, which gives the mean proportion of correct responses per trial. It is quite apparent that this curve has the same characteristics as the one we developed based on the assumption that learning went by

Figure 1.6
A learning function based on data *pooled* across a number of subjects according to a one-element learning model. As trials progress, the proportion of subjects who have learned as compared with those who have not changes so that the overall probability of a correct response increases. For those subjects who have not learned, the probability of a correct response remains at the chance level. (Adapted from Estes, 1964a.)

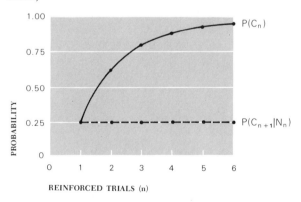

REINFORCED TRIALS (n)

incremental instead of all-or-none steps. It is important to remember, however, that it was generated by pooling data from a *group* of subjects, a group composed of some subjects who had learned completely and some who had not learned at all—a process which is quite different from the one we postulated for the curves of Figure 1.4.

27

SOME
FUNDAMENTAL
PRINCIPLES OF
PAVLOVIAN AND
INSTRUMENTAL
CONDITIONING

The latter point is one well worth emphasizing. If data from many subjects are grouped together for display—or even for statistical analysis—the average or mean performance of the group may not correspond at all to the behavior of any of the individuals composing the group. The question of whether or not group data are representative of individual data is one which experimental psychologists always keep in mind as they do their research, since that question shapes the interpretation that they place on their observations. They may very well be interested in the behavior of a group of subjects considered as a whole—on the assumption that they are willing to restrict their conclusions to the behavior of groups taken as a whole. But if they want to say something about the behavior of individual subjects, they take care to make sure that group data, to the extent they use them, are indeed representative of individual data.

As we end this section, you are probably wondering how psychologists reconcile the differences between the incremental and the all-or-none approaches to a description of the course of learning. You may ask which one is "correct." The best possible answer to that question is that "it depends." It depends, in fact, upon a great many things: the nature of the material to be learned, whether or not a learner is familiar with that material and simply has to learn to put it together in new ways, the species of the learning organism, and so on. Theoretically, the answer to the question is that the all-or-none approach provides the ultimate description of the learning curve, but it does so in a very special sense. In order to see why this is so, let us look at a bit of data.

If a monkey is given a simple discrimination task to perform, say picking a red object from a group made up of the red object and two other blue ones in order to earn a bit of food, the monkey may well take a fairly large number of trials before the task is mastered to some criterion like 9 out of 10 correct. But if the monkey is given a second task, say picking a round object from a group made up of the round object and two other square ones, learning may take fewer trials to criterion. On a third, fourth, and fifth task, and so on—each based on the principle that the odd object in a group of three is correct—the monkey will require fewer and fewer trials to master the discrimination. Eventually, the animal will require only *one* trial; that is, the correct response will be selected from the outset.

Harlow (1949, 1959) gave the name *learning set* to the foregoing phenomenon; the monkey becomes "set," in effect, to learn oddity problems with great diligence and efficiency, no doubt using some generalizable concept in the process. So efficient is the process, as a matter of fact, that it has been said that if the all-or-none approach to learning calls for "one-trial" learning, then Harlow's monkeys were demonstrating "no-trial" learning.

But the point we wish to make about learning sets is this: they call attention to the fact that a specific instance of learning can be rapid and very sudden, but that this can, in fact, be based on a painfully and slowly acquired skill derived from a lot of past experience. In other words, the shape of the learning curve for any given task depends fundamentally on our knowledge of the experience and past history that the learning organism brings with it to the new learning situation. The question becomes one of asking how quickly and efficiently the learning organism can apply what it knows or the skills it possesses to the new task—how quickly and efficiently, in other words, the learning organism can *transfer* past skills, both innate and acquired, to the acquisition of new knowledge and behavior. If the learner has little to go on, either genetically or in terms of experience, learning may proceed slowly, in small increments, if indeed it occurs at all. If, on the other hand, the learner has a wealth of experience to draw upon, learning may well be very rapid, and an all-or-none model may best describe the course of the learning process for a specific task of the moment.

PROCEDURAL DISTINCTIONS BETWEEN PAVLOVIAN AND INSTRUMENTAL CONDITIONING

We have now looked at the fundamentals of Pavlovian and instrumental conditioning, together with some of the considerations involved in the concepts of reinforcement, response strength, and the learning curve. We turn now to some further things that arise when we place Pavlovian and instrumental conditioning side by side and examine some similarities, differences, and interactions between them. First of all, are there any general features of these two procedures which distinguish them? The answer, of course, is yes. The distinctions fall into two classes: (1) those that arise from simple differences in the way that stimuli, responses, and reinforcement and the relations between them are arranged in an experiment and (2) those based on some theoretical and empirical ideas about how learning occurs when we use one as opposed to the other technique. We shall look at the distinctions which arise primarily from matters of procedure now, saving the rest of the matter until the next sections.

When we first introduced the concept of instrumental conditioning, we noted that the organism is required to do something—to produce or to withhold a response—before the experimenter provides reinforcement. This was contrasted with the procedure in Pavlovian conditioning, where the organism has no control over the delivery of the UCS. In the former case, the experimenter must pay close attention to what the organism is doing so as to be sure to provide reinforcement and so on at the proper time. In the case of Pavlovian conditioning, however, the necessary operations are performed entirely independently of what the organism happens to be doing. Given the onset of the CS, the onset of the UCS, say, is determined not at all by the organism's behavior, but instead by the fact that a clock has run a certain period of time. Put another way, we can say that in instrumental conditioning, the critical experimental contingency is between a *response*, supplied by the organism, and its *outcome* or *consequences*, supplied by the experimenter or the environment. In Pavlovian conditioning, on the other hand, the critical contingency is between one *stimulus*, the CS, and another *stimulus*, the UCS—both under the direct and exclusive control of the experimenter.

29

SOME
FUNDAMENTAL
PRINCIPLES OF
PAVLOVIAN AND
INSTRUMENTAL
CONDITIONING

The next distinction appears when we try to use Pavlov's terms for simple Pavlovian conditioning to describe the things we did in our example of simple reward training. Our first problem arises when we try to identify something analogous to a UCS in reward training. In a loose sense, pressing the lever during the course of initial exploration in the Skinner box may be thought of as a kind of UCR, but what was the stimulus that elicited this response? We can guess, but we can never know with any certainty what the stimulus actually was. It might have been the sight of the lever or the tactual stimulation obtained by sniffing along the walls of the box, but we cannot be sure. In other words, in a Pavlovian conditioning experiment, there is always a readily identifiable stimulus, the UCS, which elicits the response we wish to condition, while in an instrumental conditioning experiment, a comparable stimulus cannot be identified. In instrumental conditioning, instead, we must wait for the response we want to condition to occur spontaneously; we must wait for the organism to emit the response.

Similarly, what is the CS to which lever pressing is conditioned in our example of instrumental reward training? In other words, what leads the rat to press the lever after it has "discovered the connection" between the lever and food? Again we are reduced to a guess. Though the response may be occurring with considerable regularity after the rat has obtained several reinforcing stimuli, there is still no identifiable stimulus in instrumental conditioning which we can say with absolute certainty elicits the instrumental response. In this connection, do not confuse a discriminative cue, such as the one we described for discrimination training or for avoidance training, with a CS. As we have seen, the function of the discriminative cue is to set the occasion for some rather complex instrumental behavior, not to elicit a response reflexively. As Skinner (1935) has pointed out, the discriminative cue in discrimination training acquires its unique control over behavior when we reinforce a response when the cue is present, but withhold reinforcement when the cue is absent. In Pavlovian conditioning, on the other hand, the CS is always present, and it is always followed by the UCS.

Probably the most important operational distinction between Pavlovian and instrumental conditioning concerns the role of reinforcement in the two situations. Pavlov used the terms reinforcement and unconditional stimulus interchangeably. The UCS is a reinforcer in Pavlovian conditioning because without it no conditioning would occur; it literally reinforces or "strengthens" conditioning. In instrumental conditioning, the reinforcement operation is to provide a stimulus, like food, after the response takes place. We do not know what stimulus actually causes the response to be produced in the first place, but when the response is finally emitted by the organism, then we can reinforce it and thus strengthen it. Therefore, another difference between Pavlovian and instrumental conditioning is that in Pavlovian conditioning the UCS simultaneously elicits and reinforces the response, while in instrumental conditioning reinforcement occurs only when and if the response occurs.

THEORETICAL DISTINCTIONS BETWEEN PAVLOVIAN AND INSTRUMENTAL CONDITIONING

Psychologists do not always agree about how many *theoretical* processes or types of learning—as opposed to experimental operations that are used to study learning—should be identified. Should we assume, for example, that each set of procedures outlined in Table 1.1 involves a truly different learning *process*? Intuition tells us that there might be almost as many processes which could be used in acquiring a new response as there are responses to be acquired. We hope intuition is wrong in this instance! Yet until relatively recently, most psychologists were satisfied to account for essentially all simple learning phenomena with theoretical systems that distinguished exactly *two* basic learning processes. This was done by attaching some theoretical significance to the distinction between Pavlovian and instrumental conditioning and postulating that fundamentally different things happened when one as opposed to the other procedure was used. One of the important developments in the psychology of conditioning and learning over the past few years has been the breakdown in this distinction and its reemergence in an entirely new form, a form which blurs the distinction considerably. As this process has gone on, some fascinating discoveries have been made, discoveries with enormous practical as well as theoretical implications. Let us set the stage for an examination of these changes by taking a look at the state of affairs as it existed until about 1965. We shall borrow our historical account from thinking owed to psychologists such as Schlosberg (1937), Skinner (1938), Hilgard and Marquis (1940), Mowrer (1947, 1960), Kimble (1961), and Rescorla and Solomon (1967). Then we shall turn to the more recent literature to see what has become of the matter as a result of new experimentation.

OPERANT VERSUS RESPONDENT BEHAVIOR

A succinct version of the notion that Pavlovian and instrumental conditioning imply more than just convenient labels for two laboratory procedures comes from Skinner (1938). Skinner's theoretical distinction rests upon the basic idea that *different kinds of responses* are conditionable with the techniques of Pavlovian and instrumental conditioning. *Respondents*, the kinds of behavior supposed to be most typically conditionable with Pavlovian procedures, are classes of responses that are directly elicited by stimuli. They obey the classical physiological laws of reflexes, and, indeed, the terms respondent and reflex are identical for all practical purposes. Examples of respondents are salivation, the knee jerk, the eyeblink, the heartbeat, and the galvanic skin response. In contrast to respondents with their easily identified eliciting stimuli, *operants*—the kinds of behavior supposed to be most typically conditionable with instrumental procedures—have no identifiable external stimulus which produces them. Instead, they are *emitted* by the organism. In common terms, operants are voluntary responses, and they include the familiar examples of behavior that we have already discussed in some detail—dogs moving back and forth in shuttle boxes, rats pressing levers, children searching for candy, and so forth.

31

SOME
FUNDAMENTAL
PRINCIPLES OF
PAVLOVIAN AND
INSTRUMENTAL
CONDITIONING

What other features were thought to distinguish the learning processes associated with Pavlovian and instrumental conditioning? In discussing this question, Rescorla and Solomon (1967) cite several, some of which we can mention here. It has been proposed that Pavlovian versus instrumental procedures are especially adaptable to visceral or glandular responses under control of the autonomic nervous system as opposed to skeletal responses under control of the somatic nervous system (Mowrer, 1947); to diffuse emotional responses as opposed to highly precise, adaptive responses (Schlosberg, 1937); or to highly reflexive responses involving small amounts of body mass, like a toe twitch, as opposed to quite unreflexive responses involving large amounts of body mass, like the movement of an entire arm or leg (Turner & Solomon, 1962). It is also possible to make a distinction in terms of the reinforcers that are potentially most effective with one procedure as opposed to the other. It is hard to think of an instrumental response for which weak acid would function as a reinforcer, for example, yet this works very well as a reinforcer for the development of a Pavlovian salivary reflex (remember that lemon once again!).

Strictly speaking, of course—if the distinction between the processes associated with Pavlovian and instrumental conditioning is indeed a real one—it ought to be impossible to condition operant behavior with Pavlovian procedures and respondent behavior with instrumental procedures, and prior to 1965 this was presumed to be true. Hindsight shows, however, that this was largely a matter of blind faith because with a few isolated exceptions (e.g., Kimble, Mann, & Dufort, 1955; Fowler & Kimmel, 1962) which showed that there was some promise in pursuing the matter further, *no one had made a serious attempt to condition respondent behavior with instrumental techniques.* Somehow, a simple assumption had crept into a science and assumed the full colors of an accepted fact.

INSTRUMENTAL CONDITIONING OF VISCERAL RESPONSES

Neal Miller and his students and colleagues, together with Kimmel and his associates (e.g., Kimmel, 1974), were among the first to remedy this situation by undertaking a serious and extensive investigation of the possibility that visceral, autonomically controlled behavior could be changed with instrumental conditioning procedures. Miller and DiCara (1967) provide one of the first relevant experiments, an experiment in which they showed that it was possible to condition changes in the rate of rats' heartbeats using the basic techniques of simple discriminative reward learning. The exact experimental procedures that they used were fairly complicated, and they introduced some new terms and procedures as well as some new thinking; so let us look at them in some detail.

The first step was to do some surgical preparation of the rats. First, while the animal was under anesthesia, electrodes were properly located and sewn under its skin in such a way that they could be attached to an electrocardiograph—a machine that records and monitors the animal's heart rate. Second, electrodes were implanted in a portion of the rat's brain known as the medial forebrain bundle. It was well known from earlier research (some of which we will examine in Chapter 3) that minute electrical impulses delivered to this portion of the brain functioned just like positive rewards of food or water for a hungry or thirsty animal—in the very precise sense that animals would learn to press a lever or perform some other instrumental response for the sole payoff of brain stimulation. The next step was to paralyze the rat's musculature with a drug known as d-tubocurarine chloride (a pure form of curare). This substance blocks the transmission of nerve impulses from nerve to skeletal muscle; it does require that the animal be artificially respirated during the course of an experiment, but it leaves the animal awake with its sensory system entirely intact and functional.

Once the rats were prepared in this fashion, instrumental conditioning of the heart rate began. This was done by turning on a discriminative cue of a combination of light and a tone, monitoring the rat's heart rate, and waiting for a spontaneous increase (or decrease, for some rats) of an arbitrary amount—usually a 2 percent change. When the change occurred, the rat was rewarded for making it by turning on a brief electrical stimulus to the brain. Following this, the light-tone cue was turned off for 20 seconds, then turned on for the beginning of the next trial when, once again, the heart rate was monitored, and the rat was reinforced with brain stimulation just as soon as the heart rate increased (or decreased) by a preset, arbitrary amount. As the rat got better and better at the task, the criterion for reward was made progressively more stringent, and so the animal had to increase (or decrease) the rate by larger and larger amounts in order to obtain reward. Trials continued in this fashion for a period of 90 minutes. The results of the experiment are shown in Figure 1.7.

The results could not be clearer. Quite apparently, the rats rewarded for an increase in heart rate were able to do so, and the ones rewarded for a decrease in heart rate were able to do so, too. Moreover, the magnitude of the effects was large, on the order of 75 beats per minute.

Since the time that the initial experiments showed that instrumental conditioning of visceral responses was possible, the same general

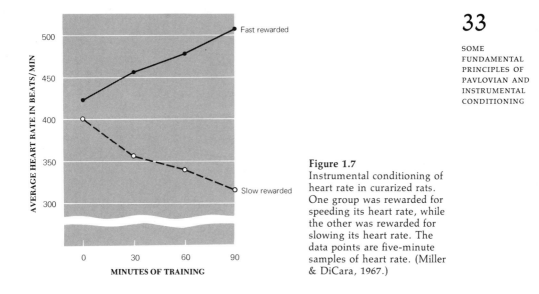

33

SOME
FUNDAMENTAL
PRINCIPLES OF
PAVLOVIAN AND
INSTRUMENTAL
CONDITIONING

Figure 1.7
Instrumental conditioning of
heart rate in curarized rats.
One group was rewarded for
speeding its heart rate, while
the other was rewarded for
slowing its heart rate. The
data points are five-minute
samples of heart rate. (Miller
& DiCara, 1967.)

procedure has been applied to a host of internal responses in the rat
under the primary control of the autonomic nervous system (Katkin &
Murray, 1968; Miller, 1969). The list includes changes in kidney function, intestinal contraction and relaxation, blood pressure, and, remarkably enough, dilation of blood vessels in one ear but not in the other.

Mediating responses and instrumental conditioning of visceral responses
There is an important concept which we must mention now because it is
of central importance for a convincing demonstration of the conditioning
of autonomic responses. It is also of central importance for a very great
deal of the psychology of learning, and we shall have frequent occasion
to refer to it (in many guises) in later portions of this book. It is
important at the moment because it provides the rationale for using
curare to paralyze the animals in the research we have just examined, a
procedure which may on the face of it seem a bit puzzling.

The concept to which we refer in general is that of *mediation*, and the
particular instance of it that we have at hand is that of a *mediating
response*. The basic idea here is that one item or process can be linked to
a second by some third thing that stands, literally, in the middle. Figure
1.8 may help to make the matter clear. At the top of the figure, we show a
direct *non*mediated connection between two things symbolized by *A* and
B. The letters *A* and *B* could stand for any number of things: stimulus
and response, one idea and another, a sensory process and a motor
response, a CS and a UCS, and so on. The connection between the
things symbolized by *A* and *B* can be an innate or already formed one,
such as that between a UCS and a UCR, or it can be one that is learned or
acquired through experience, such as that between a CS and a CR. At the
bottom of the figure, we show an indirect, *mediated* connection between
A and *B*. The letter *X* symbolizes something that stands between *A* and *B*

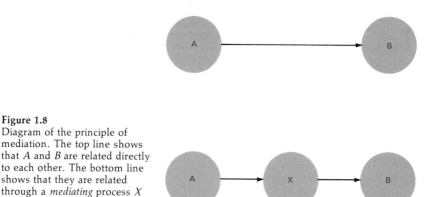

Figure 1.8
Diagram of the principle of
mediation. The top line shows
that *A* and *B* are related directly
to each other. The bottom line
shows that they are related
through a *mediating* process *X*
which intervenes between them.

and functions to build a bridge between them. In this case, *A* and *B* are
not connected directly; instead they are connected indirectly through
process or item *X*. Once again, the connections between *A*, *B*, and *X* can
be built-in, unlearned, and innate, or they can be learned or acquired
through experience. Sometimes, there may be a mixture of learned and
unlearned connections so that, say, an organism must learn that *A* leads
to *X*, but once *X* occurs, *B* follows automatically.

To return to the specific point at hand, suppose that the distinction
between the conditionability of autonomic and skeletal responses was
indeed highly valid, and that it was truly impossible to condition visceral
responses with instrumental techniques. Suppose too, however, that the
instrumental conditioning procedures that Miller used in his experiments
would simply lead his rats to search around for something, anything at
all, that they could do to produce the positive reward of brain stimulation.
Suppose, for example, that in their random activity they happened to
take a deep breath or tense the muscles of the diaphragm at the bottom of
the rib cage. Now it turns out that breathing patterns and tensing of the
muscles of the diaphragm have an interesting side effect: they produce
direct, reflexive changes in heart rate. So Miller ran the potential risk
that any changes he might observe in heart rate might not be due to his
instrumental conditioning of heart rate directly, but might be due instead
to his instrumental conditioning of some extraneous *skeletal* response
which would act, indirectly, as a mediator to produce changes in heart
rate. Perhaps, in other words, instrumental conditioning would cause the
rats to learn an association between the light-sound discriminative cue
(*A*) and the production of some response like taking a deep breath (*X*),
the deep breath leading automatically and reflexively to a change in heart
rate (*B*) and the delivery of the reward.

By now, you have probably guessed that the use of curare was
designed to eliminate the possibility that skeletal mediating responses
could produce changes in heart rate. Since curare produces a flaccid
paralysis of the entire skeletal musculature, it was literally impossible for
any skeletal response to function as a mediator, and this provided an

important experimental control for the conclusions that Miller wished to draw. This is not to say that there might not be some other mediating process going on, a mediating process taking place perhaps at some high point in the central nervous system. This is true, because if you stop to think about it, you can never *prove* that something *doesn't* exist (although you may feel you have rendered the possibility quite unlikely). But at least the use of curare eliminated the possibility that some peripheral mediator based on the actual occurrence of overt skeletal responses could be at work, a possibility that would have reduced Miller's observations to interesting but inconsequential ones for the theoretical point his work was designed to make.

While we have developed the notion of the learning of visceral responses pretty much as a theoretical issue marking one distinction between Pavlovian and instrumental conditioning, it is obvious that the procedures involved have enormous practical and applied potential quite apart from any role they may play in a theoretical controversy. If it were possible for people to learn to control their own heart rates or other visceral functions, for example, this would have tremendous medical and clinical significance. Furthermore, the accomplished fact of a voluntary change in heart rate would be important even if people found it necessary to bring mediating behavior into play in order to accomplish the change—as a *practical* matter, mediating behavior might prove helpful in spite of the fact that it raises some important problems when theoretical matters are under test, as we have seen.

Evidence is accumulating that higher animals and people can acquire some form of voluntary control over at least some of their internal "involuntary" behavior. The full story is by no means complete, and psychologists show proper caution (together with some inevitable disagreement) at this stage of things; but the available research is certainly promising at least. Harris, Gilliam, Findley, and Brady (1973) have been able to develop large-magnitude, long-lasting changes in blood pressure in baboons who had to increase their blood pressure in order to minimize or avoid electric shock. Shapiro, Schwartz, and Tursky (1972) were able to teach human subjects to control their own diastolic blood pressure, and there is now a fairly extensive literature concerning apparently successful attempts to condition a number of cardiac functions in humans with instrumental procedures. Blanchard and Young (1973) have taken a critical look at that literature, reaching the conclusion that it is premature to assert that cardiac conditioning in humans has been demonstrated beyond any doubt (but see Engel, 1974, for a rejoinder). The safest position to adopt at this point would be to view the question of instrumental conditioning of visceral responses in humans as one to which no unequivocal answers can yet be given. Things look promising right now, a great deal of research is underway, and it is to be hoped that the future looks bright in the practical application of the simple fundamentals of conditioning and learning to this most important problem.

This has been a fairly long section, but we have covered a good bit of territory. Remember not only the factual material we have discussed concerning the learning of visceral responses but also the notions of *mediation* and *mediating responses*—we will be returning to these concepts in many guises later on. We will also return in Chapter 6 to some further interactions between Pavlovian and instrumental conditioning procedures as they appear in learning situations that involve acquired motivation, so be prepared to meet the topic again.

CONSTRAINTS ON LEARNING

It would be natural to conclude as we end this chapter that, like Caesar's world, all the world of the psychology of conditioning and learning is divided into two parts, Pavlovian and instrumental learning—with perhaps a dash of concern about stimulus, response, reinforcement, and learning curves thrown in—and that psychologists have now settled down to the relatively simple task of working out the laws associated with the behavior generated by these two sets of procedures and the interactions between them. Indeed, this view was not far from the truth as it was perceived some few years ago. During the past few years, however, there has been a rapid resurgence of the general notion that not all species of organism learn all given responses to all possible stimuli at just the same stage of development and with precisely the same principles guiding the learning process. Of course, there were those—particularly European students of behavior such as Tinbergen (1951, 1953), Bowlby (1952), and Hinde (1970)—who had been saying much this sort of thing all along. But their work, and the work of many other ethologists like them such as Lorenz and Von Frisch, did not have much direct and effective influence on the development of the science of behavior as it was then establishing itself in America.

This is not to say that there wasn't anyone in America who wasn't concerned with a more naturalistic approach to the study of learning. Beach (1950) had decried the fact that most of the early behavioristic approach to learning was based on information obtained from a very few species of animal, with the rat leading the pack, so to speak. Breland and Breland (1961) were perhaps the first, however, to suggest that maybe all was not well within the well-ordered world of operant behavior in the Skinner box. The Brelands had, in a sense, staked their livelihood on that world because they had gone into the business of engineering and selling animal-behavior displays at fairs, conventions, amusement centers, and so on, training a great variety of species with operant, instrumental techniques to perform interesting tricks for commercial purposes. While they generally met with great success in their enterprise, the Brelands soon discovered that their work more often than not forced upon them some interesting variations on the things to be expected from standard operant procedures. Their description of an attempt to train a raccoon provides a good example.

The raccoon's task was simple. It was supposed to learn to use its forepaws (which are shaped much like human hands) to pick up a couple of coins, insert them into a slot in a 5-inch metal box, and so obtain food reinforcement. Training began by reinforcing the raccoon with food for picking up the coin. That was easy. Next the raccoon was required to insert one coin into a slot in the box—and here the troubles began. While training was eventually successful, the animal demonstrated great reluctance to let go of the coin, putting it in the slot, pulling it back out and clutching it, relinquishing it only after some seconds of this kind of behavior. Things really fell apart, however, when the animal was required to perform the complete task of putting *both* coins in the box in order to obtain food. In the Brelands' words (Breland & Breland, 1961):

37

SOME
FUNDAMENTAL
PRINCIPLES OF
PAVLOVIAN AND
INSTRUMENTAL
CONDITIONING

> Now the raccoon really had problems (and so did we). Not only could he not let go the coins, but he spent seconds, even minutes rubbing them together (in a most miserly fashion), and dipping them into the container. He carried on this behavior to such an extent that the practical application we had in mind—a display featuring a raccoon putting money into a piggy bank—simply was not feasible. The rubbing behavior became worse and worse as time went on, in spite of nonreinforcement [p. 682].

Breland and Breland go on to describe a number of instances of animals who gradually drift toward injecting instinctive behaviors into otherwise well-learned and straightforward operant responses. Usually, the extraneous behavior involved components of the standard responses the animals used to eat food. Thus pigs started rooting and nosing with large wooden "coins" they were supposed to simply pick up and place in a "bank" in order to get food, while chickens would start scratching while standing on a platform, even though the only contingency involved to obtain food was standing on the platform for 15 seconds (the Brelands capitalized on that one by incorporating the scratching behavior into the scheme of things and using the whole as a display of the "dancing chickens"). The point is that these were clear, and frustrating, departures from what was to be expected on the basis of generalizations from the animal laboratory.

Some of the more important new discoveries in the psychology of conditioning and learning have appeared since work such as that of the Brelands has appeared, although it has taken time for the implications of their work to be absorbed into the general course of things. Let us turn to some of that work now—maintaining our usual selective eye.

SPECIES-SPECIFIC DEFENSE REACTIONS AND THE CONCEPT OF PREPAREDNESS

From our initial description of escape and avoidance learning, it would be easy to reach the conclusion that we might choose literally *any* arbitrary response within the repertoire of possible responses for a given species of animal and require that it be used instrumentally in order to escape or avoid some punishing stimulus. Thus, lever pressing turns out to be a convenient response to use in simple reward training for rats, and hundreds and hundreds of experiments have been done which require that pigeons learn to peck a lighted key or disk in order to obtain food from a food hopper; why, then, shouldn't these same responses function just as well as escape or avoidance responses? The simple fact of the matter, however, is that they don't. It is extremely difficult to get rats or pigeons to use them to escape or avoid punishment, success often requiring either extensive training, in which the animal is "shaped" by gradual approximation toward the successful response over many trials, or some other special experimental techniques (D'Amato & Schiff, 1964; D'Amato, Fazzaro, & Etkin, 1968; Bolles, 1970).

This is not to say, of course, that animals lack responses that get them away from danger. The fundamental point is that in their natural habitat animals rarely have an opportunity to *learn* any response to avoid or to escape from some real or potentially dangerous thing. Nature is not apt to provide very many practice trials for a mouse, say, to become skillful at avoiding owls. Instead, mice, like other animals, are equipped with *innate*, *unlearned* responses which are always ready to be triggered instantly by novel stimuli which may or may not, in fact, represent danger. In developing this point, Bolles coins the term *species-specific defense reactions* to describe those response systems which animals of different species possess to enable them to cope with threatening events in their environments. Rats, for example, will freeze or run away at the sudden appearance of any novel stimulus. Birds will take flight. Monkeys may flee or adopt threatening postures and expressions. In no case does the animal linger to find out if the new thing in its environment is dangerous without taking some kind of *automatic* action to defend itself. Bolles then goes on to postulate the notion that a given response will be successfully acquired as an avoidance response—if that instrumental contingency should be imposed—only to the extent that it is an effective species-specific defense reaction in the situation in which it must be learned.

The notion of *preparedness* (Seligman, 1970) extends, in a sense, the basic premise of species-specific defense reactions not only to all classes of response, but also to all classes of the learning process itself. It says, in effect, that some response systems are innately better prepared than others to be modified by some experiential process—be it Pavlovian conditioning, instrumental learning, or what not—in the sense that fewer trials are required for learning. We have just seen that some forms of behavior in rats are extremely difficult, if not impossible, to use as arbitrary avoidance responses, while with other forms learning to avoid pain or danger becomes a trivial affair. By the same token, some response systems seem especially well adapted to be associated with particular sensory systems but not with others. Rats learn to associate being sick to the stomach with novel tastes or odors but not with novel sights or sounds (Garcia, Ervin, & Koelling, 1966), a phenomenon we shall develop at some length in another context.

Do different *laws* of learning apply to one end of the preparedness dimension as opposed to the other? Are the characteristics of learning associated with highly prepared species-specific defense reactions going to be different from those associated with unprepared or even contraprepared response systems? We do not have the answers to these questions yet, but there are now enough exceptions to the notion that there is some general law of learning that applies to all behavior to make the questions important and sensible to ask.

39

SOME
FUNDAMENTAL
PRINCIPLES OF
PAVLOVIAN AND
INSTRUMENTAL
CONDITIONING

SUPERSTITIOUS BEHAVIOR AND THE PHENOMENON OF AUTOSHAPING

We close this section and this chapter with two final examples of constraints on learning. Both involve the pecking response in pigeons, and both together show that while pecking can be acquired by the rules of instrumental conditioning, the development of this behavior is sometimes better described by completely different rules.

Suppose that we were to take a hungry pigeon and place it in a box which contained a translucent key or disk in one wall and a food hopper that would provide the bird with access to grain upon the experimenter's command; and suppose that we were to arrange things so that the food magazine would operate automatically once every 12 seconds—entirely independently of anything the bird might be doing. Skinner (1948) noted that pigeons came to produce highly stereotyped, regular responses under these conditions, responses such as wing flapping, circling in the box, and so on. He termed these responses "superstitious," noting that even though the experimental arrangement called for no particular response at all to assure the delivery of food, the birds came to volunteer their own idiosyncratic responses anyway. Skinner proposed that the response the birds hit upon was one which on occasion, and quite by accident, happened to be occurring just at the moment the food hopper was activated and food became available. The response was, in other words, conditioned by a kind of accidental application of the usual procedures for instrumental conditioning.

When Staddon and Simmelhag (1971) repeated Skinner's basic experiment, but ran their pigeons for many sessions, however, they observed that the birds eventually developed a variety of stereotyped "superstitious" responses which occurred just after food was delivered (named "interim" activities), but that as the time for the next food delivery approached, it became increasingly probable that the birds would begin pecking at the wall of the food hopper (a "terminal" activity). Pecking appeared in the situation, in other words, *even though there was absolutely no contingency which required it at all*.

Consider now a second experiment (Brown & Jenkins, 1968). Take another hungry pigeon and place it in the same box, but this time, turn on a light so that it shines through the translucent key from behind for 8 seconds. At the end of the 8-second period, quickly make food available at the food hopper but, as in the superstition experiment, do so independently of anything the pigeon happens to do. Notice that we *have* set up a contingency in the situation—the delivery of food is contingent upon the fact that the light has been on for 8 seconds—but the contingency is quite independent of anything having to do with the behavior of the bird. Under these conditions, pigeons rapidly acquired a pecking response, a pecking response directed at the lighted key.

Brown and Jenkins termed this phenomenon "autoshaping" after the fact that the procedure seemed to save the sometimes laborious process of getting animals to perform instrumental responses by reinforcing successive approximations to some final arbitrary response. The autoshaped pecking response is *not* just like the usual operantly conditioned key peck, however, because, for one thing, birds cannot learn to inhibit it through omission training—they continue pecking even though this ensures that reinforcement will be withheld (Williams & Williams, 1969). Furthermore, among other things, if a hungry pigeon is autoshaped to peck with food as a reinforcer, the pecks to the key look like those the bird makes when eating food, but if a thirst motive is used with water as a reinforcer, then the pecks to the key resemble those responses involved in drinking. Finally, the contingency between the lighted key and the reinforcer is critical; autoshaped keypecking does not appear if food is delivered to the bird during periods of time which are not properly correlated with the light (Jenkins, 1973).

In discussing the phenomenon of autoshaping, both Moore (1973) and Jenkins (1973) reach the conclusion that it is probably best described as the result of some kind of reflexive, Pavlovian process. While this bare conclusion may be premature, the procedures involved and the nature of the behavior which results certainly seem to suggest Pavlovian principles at work. No doubt you have already noticed that the pairing of light with grain is a straightforward Pavlovian procedure, and we need only add that Staddon and Simmelhag's experiment (together with a great many others Moore mentions) suggests that for pigeons, pecking is a highly prepared, highly probable response in situations which contain something nutritious to peck from time to time. Pecking, in other words, may be a highly reflexive UCR to food in pigeons and other birds, readily attachable to conditional stimuli which reliably predict that food is about to arrive. As a matter of fact, Moore lists half a dozen techniques for getting birds to peck at keys in Skinner boxes, only *one* of which involves withholding reinforcement until the bird actually emits a peck—and that procedure is by far the most laborious. All the others incorporate some procedure for getting the bird to respond initially to the key by eliciting the first few pecks with food—food placed directly on the key itself, for example.[1]

IN CONCLUSION

It is well to remember, then, that the fundamental point at hand is that the behavior of animals and people is modified according to rules of

---

[1]There is no small measure of irony in all this. Much of the Skinnerian approach to the experimental analysis of behavior has been based on the pecking response in pigeons as the prototype of instrumental, operant behavior under the "voluntary" control of the organism.

learning which are in part arbitrary, applying to arbitrary forms of
behavior, and in part genetic and instinctive, applying to more naturally
occurring forms of behavior. This theme, which is hardly new because it
is based fundamentally on the age-old (and probably unresolvable)
controversy over the relative contribution of nature and experience to the
behavior of organisms, is nevertheless of central importance. If you wish
to study it further, Hinde and Stevenson-Hinde (1973), from whom we
have borrowed the title of this section, provide an excellent recent
starting place, and Seligman and Hager (1972) should be of interest too.

41

SOME
FUNDAMENTAL
PRINCIPLES OF
PAVLOVIAN AND
INSTRUMENTAL
CONDITIONING

TWO

REINFORCEMENT AND LEARNING: BASIC PRINCIPLES

Since the time of Thorndike (1898, 1911), the notion that behavior can be strengthened or weakened by its own consequences, by reward or punishment, has occupied a central position in the psychology of learning. In this chapter we examine, first, some things that happen as a function of changes in the fundamental parameters of reinforcers, such as their number or amount, and second, some theoretical issues that have arisen both historically and more currently with regard to the reinforcement process. An enormous amount of experimental information has been compiled about the intricate effects of rewarding or punishing a response, and psychologists can now state with considerable confidence some general principles involving these effects. Sometimes, however, an empirical issue which seems well settled, such as how the strength of behavior changes as one introduces a delay between the occurrence of some response and the delivery of reinforcement, can be reopened forcefully by brilliant new discoveries which compel drastic empirical and theoretical changes in the way we perceive reinforcers to work. We shall have a chance to examine some of these new discoveries.

We begin, then, with a discussion of some fundamental parameters of the reinforcement process. Most of our discussion, though by no means all, will be based on things that have been learned using positive reinforcement. The whole question of negative reinforcement, punishment, and the like, is best reserved for detailed treatment in a later chapter.

BASIC REINFORCEMENT VARIABLES

NUMBER OF REINFORCEMENTS

One of the simplest and most straightforward ways to vary a reinforcement condition in an experiment is to vary the number of times that a response is reinforced and to measure the concomitant changes in response strength which occur. We have already looked at this process at work in our discussion of learning curves in the last chapter, and you should be reminded of the cautions we mentioned then about incremental versus all-or-none processes in the acquisition of a response. In other words, the effect of adding increasing numbers of reinforced trials to some response may well depend upon the nature of the specific response itself, its past history, and so on.

In a classic experiment, Hovland (1937) generated a learning curve based on increases in the number of reinforcers which followed an incremental course patterned quite accurately after the curves of Figure 1.4 of the last chapter. Hovland chose to condition the galvanic skin response (GSR) in man using Pavlovian procedures. The GSR is a change in electrical resistance of the skin due to some effectors in the skin, probably the sweat glands. It is a reflex under control of the autonomic nervous system. Hovland paired a vibrator to the skin (CS) with a mild electric shock (UCS) and watched the development of the GSR as more and more reinforced trials accrued. The results of the experiment are shown in Figure 2.1.

Notice from Figure 2.1 that, as in all long-term incremental learning curves, the greatest increment of response strength occurs with the first few reinforcements, additional reinforcements add less and less to response strength, and the curve gradually approaches a limit. Similar functions can, of course, be obtained with instrumental conditioning.

AMOUNT OF REINFORCEMENT

Variation in the amount of magnitude of the reinforcing agent provides a second variable which modifies response strength. With positive reinforcers, and with relatively simple learning tasks like training rats to run alleys or to press levers, this can be accomplished by varying the weight, volume, or intensity of a reward—in short, by varying the *quantity* or *quality* of a reward. With negative reinforcers, a commonly used method of varying amount of reinforcement is to vary the intensity-reduction of some noxious stimulus, like electric shock, that is given when the response under study occurs.

Quantity of reinforcement and response strength A large number of experiments have varied the weight of a food reinforcer, or the number of

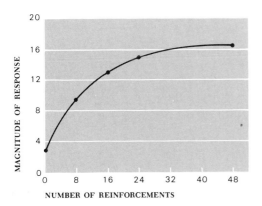

Figure 2.1
Amplitude of the galvanic skin response (GSR) as a function of number of reinforcements. (Hovland, 1937c.)

food pellets that animals find in a goal box, and shown that response strength increases as quantity of reinforcement increases. Zeaman (1949), for example, measured the latency with which rats ran from a start box at the beginning of a runway and provided different groups of rats with one of five amounts of reinforcement. Zeaman's reinforcers were, appropriately, pieces of cheese that varied in weight from 0.05 to 2.40 grams. Again, response strength increased as amount of reinforcement increased; the larger the piece of cheese, the shorter the latency of the running response at the end of training. Logan (1960, 1969) has summarized data such as these, together with data from a large number of experiments of his own, by means of the relationship between quantity of reinforcement (number of food pellets) and response strength shown in Figure 2.2.

The figure indicates that amount of reinforcement, like some forms of the relationship between number of reinforcements and response strength, is related to response strength according to an increasing, negatively accelerated function. That is, if we deal with very small quantities of reinforcement, it does not take much of an increase in amount to produce a rather large increase in response strength. As a response is reinforced with larger and larger quantities of reinforcement, however, the net addition to response strength becomes smaller and smaller.

Quality of reinforcement and response strength Certain substances like sucrose (common table sugar) seem to have an innate taste appeal for some animals as well as people, and these substances can be used effectively as reinforcing stimuli. Thus, the *qualitative* characteristics of a stimulus furnish another dimension which can be used to manipulate response strength in a way that seems to fit best under the heading of amount of reinforcement. An experiment by Hutt (1954), which used a technique first introduced by Guttman (1953), shows the relation between several qualities of reinforcement and response strength. This experiment is particularly interesting in that it also incorporated different quantities of reinforcement. Hutt was thus able to determine if quantity and quality would work together in their effect upon response strength;

Figure 2.2
Hypothetical curve showing the relationship between response speed and amount of reinforcement (number of food pellets in this case). The curve is typical of data from a number of experiments. (Logan, 1960.)

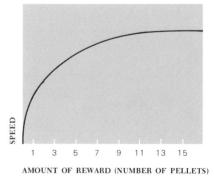

perhaps, for example, quantity of reward would have bigger effects upon response strength if used with a sweet as compared with a neutral reinforcer. That is, the two variables might *interact*. For his reinforcing substance, Hutt chose a liquid food which, if used as a complete diet, would provide proper nutrition for rats. This food was used in pure form (the *basic* reinforcer), or else it was adulterated with citric acid or with saccharin to give it a sour or sweet taste (the *citric* and *saccharin* reinforcers). The quantity of these substances that was used for each reward was 3, 12, or 50 milligrams. In all, nine groups of rats were required in the experiment in order to test response strength for each combination of quality and quantity of reinforcement.

Hutt used a Skinner box for his experiment. Rats were required to press a lever to obtain a reinforcer, and the reinforcers were automatically delivered to the rat by a dipper mechanism which measured·out the appropriate quantity of the reinforcing substance. To prevent satiation of the rats as they pressed the lever during a long experimental session, and to assure that one rat could not obtain a larger number of reinforcers than another, Hutt used a *fixed-interval schedule* of reinforcement. With this schedule, a lever press produced a reinforcer only if a certain amount of time had elapsed since the rat last obtained a reinforcer—one minute, in this case. The rat was free to respond during the one-minute interval, but these responses were not reinforced. Figure 2.3 shows the rates at which rats responded on the last day of training, after they had received 150 reinforcements (but had made a great many more responses because of the schedule of reinforcement).

In general, the figure shows that rate of responding, and hence response strength, was the highest for the saccharin reinforcer and lowest for the citric reinforcer, with the basic reinforcer coming somewhere between these extremes. Also, response strength increased as the quantity of reinforcer increased. The quantity and quality dimensions did not interact with each other in their effect upon response strength, however; the effect of the quality variable was just about the same regardless of the particular quantity of reinforcement which was used.

The definition of amount of reinforcement: some problems   In the experiments we have just examined, amount of reinforcement was defined in terms of some simple physical scale like weight, number, concentration, and so on. And organisms can clearly differentiate *something* about different points along these scales, since differences in a physical dimension such as weight of food or volume of sucrose solution can, in fact, produce appropriate differences in response strength. But what is it about a big, heavy piece of food, for example, that makes an animal respond to it as a larger amount of reinforcement than a small, light piece of food? Big pieces of food take longer to eat, require more bites, look bigger, and are very likely eaten in bigger chunks than small pieces of food (Kling, 1956; Pubols, 1960; Snyder & Hulse, 1961; Flaherty, Riley, & Spear, 1973). Which one of these variables, or which combination of several of them, is actually correlated with amount of reinforcement—from the learning subject's point of view?

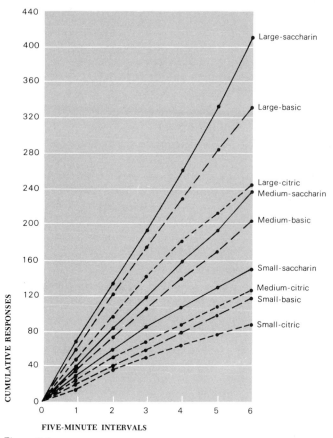

CUMULATIVE RESPONSES

FIVE-MINUTE INTERVALS

Figure 2.3
Cumulative response records for three volumes and three qualities of
reinforcement. The curves were computed from responses cumulated
over six successive five-minute intervals of responding. (Hutt, 1954.)

The research on this problem has been developing for some time, and
while some of the answers are available, much remains to be learned.
Part of the answer may lie in the fact that the *psychological* magnitude, so
to speak, of a given reward may be only a partial function of its physical
magnitude. In other words, rewards (and punishers, for that matter)
may assume quantitative control over response strength as a function of
some property they possess other than their weight, number, and so
forth. For example, evidence exists that the *functional* magnitude of a
reinforcer, that is, the extent to which different amounts of it actually
produce differences in response strength, may depend rather substantially on the *context* in which it is introduced in an experiment (Schrier,
1958; Bevan, 1968; Hulse, 1962a, 1973a). Thus, Schrier (1958) trained
monkeys on a series of very simple discrimination problems. On each
problem, the monkeys had to learn to choose one of two objects in order
to receive a reward. For four groups of monkeys, the amount of reward
was constant during a pretraining period, which was used to familiarize

the monkeys with the apparatus, and throughout the series of discrimination problems that followed. For one group, the reward was always one pellet, while for the other three groups, it was always two, four, or eight pellets. For a fifth group (the "shift" group), the amount of reward was shifted during the pretraining period and as the monkeys went from one discrimination problem to the next. On the first discrimination problem, for example, the monkeys might receive one pellet of food, but on the next, they would receive eight pellets, and so on. The shift group thus had extensive experience with all four of the amount-of-reinforcement conditions by the time the experiment had ended. The results were very clear-cut: For subjects that experienced only one amount of reinforcement during the course of the experiment (it did not matter which one), just about the same percentage of correct responses were made on the discrimination problems. A monkey that got one pellet did just about as well as a monkey that got eight. For the shift group that experienced all four amounts of reward, however, the percentage of correct responses on a problem increased as the amount of reward which was used with the problem increased. The monkeys made more correct responses on problems that involved an eight-pellet reward than they did on problems that involved a one-pellet reward, for example.

For human subjects, Bevan (1966) reported that the effectiveness of a punishing stimulus used to mark incorrect responses in learning a simple tabletop maze was a function of the context in which the punisher, an electric shock, had previously appeared. Some people were exposed to it in a context in which it was the strongest of a series of shocks, while others were exposed to it in a context in which it was the weakest of a series of shocks. Bevan found that if it had appeared in the past as the weakest of the series, it was less effective as a punisher for the learning task than if it had appeared as the strongest of the series. In other words, the context in which it had appeared in the past was an important determiner of its "apparent magnitude" and, consequently, its effectiveness as a reinforcing stimulus.

The important point, then, is that a reinforcing stimulus never exists in a vacuum; the manner in which an organism responds to different amounts of reinforcement can depend profoundly upon the conditions under which the organism is exposed to them and upon what the organism has to do to get them.

EFFECTS OF STIMULUS INTENSITY IN PAVLOVIAN CONDITIONING

There are, of course, two stimuli in Pavlovian conditioning, the CS and the UCS, which can produce changes in response strength if we vary their intensity. Changing the intensity of the UCS is directly analogous to changing magnitude of reinforcement in instrumental conditioning, since the UCS is that stimulus which constitutes the reinforcer in Pavlovian conditioning. It is easy to state what happens when one group of subjects is exposed to a strong UCS and another to a weak UCS in

Pavlovian conditioning: the stronger UCS produces a stronger conditioned response (Passey, 1948; Prokasy, Grant, & Meyers, 1958).

Things are not quite so straightforward when it comes to the role that the intensity of the CS plays in Pavlovian conditioning. Offhand, one might expect that a strong, intense CS would generate a strong conditioned response, and in a general way that is quite true. But it turns out that the method used to expose subjects to conditional stimuli of different intensities has profound effects upon the differences in response strength which emerge. Grice and Hunter (1964) did a Pavlovian eyelid conditioning experiment using human subjects which involved two sound intensities of a 1,000-hertz tone as a CS. One group of subjects was exposed to the more intense stimulus by itself, a second group was exposed to the weak stimulus by itself, while a third was exposed from trial to trial to *both* the intense and the weak stimulus. For the third group, in other words, some trials incorporated a weak CS, while others incorporated a strong CS, the two intermixed in random and unpredictable fashion. The results of the experiment appear in Figure 2.4.

As you can see, the effect of letting subjects experience *both* intensities of the tone CS produced a large difference in the strength of the CR elicited by one as opposed to the other. On the other hand, the difference between the strength of the CR elicited by the strong and weak CSs presented to separate groups of subjects—while in the expected direction—was much smaller. Grice has gone on to develop an elegant theoretical account for this and a number of other related phenomena (Grice, 1968, 1972), but the important point is that, once again, the *context* in which stimuli are presented to subjects can have an important bearing upon even so simple a function as the effect of their intensity upon the strength of some response. Subjects exposed to both CS intensities were, in some important sense, able to *compare* the two intensities, while those in the other two groups were unable to do so; and this seems to have had some important effects upon the ability of the two stimuli to produce effective Pavlovian conditioning.

Do comparable effects exist for the intensity of the unconditional

Figure 2.4
Percent conditioned eyeblinks as a function of the method of presenting two CS intensities to human subjects. Both the 50- and the 100-decibel intensities were presented to the same subjects under the "two-stimuli" condition, while the 50- and the 100-decibel intensities were presented to separate groups of subjects under the "one-stimulus" condition. (Grice & Hunter, 1964.)

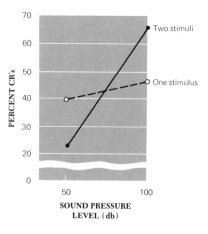

stimulus? The data are meager, but they suggest that the context in which that stimulus appears can modulate its effectiveness when it varies in intensity too—although the effects are apparently different from those for CS intensity. Passey and Wood (1963) found, for example, that subjects exposed to a multiple array of UCS intensities tended to "average" them insofar as their effect upon the magnitude of a Pavlovian eyelid CR was concerned. That is, they gave a response to each of the stimuli in the array which was of about the same magnitude as that generated in some other subjects who were exposed to a single UCS intensity near the middle of the array.

CONTRAST EFFECTS

What happens when a learning organism gets a chance to *compare* one set of reinforcement conditions with some other set as learning runs its course? Is behavior that is reinforced under one set of conditions influenced by the effects generated by the other when the two are contrasted with each other in some fashion? Put another way, can the effectiveness of a given reward or punishment be modified by an organism's past experience wth reward or punishment? Offhand, it would seem that historical familiarity of one kind or another with reinforcers for learning could have a profound effect upon their ef- ficiency; intuitively it would seem that a 10-dollar bill might well reinforce the behavior of an impoverished person while having relatively little influence on the behavior of someone from a more affluent background. Psychologists are, of course, hesitant to indulge in this kind of broad speculation, but it is nevertheless a well-established fact that placing conditions of reinforcement in contrast with one another can have important effects upon their behavioral consequences. We turn, accordingly, to some of the things that have been learned about contrast effects.

DIFFERENTIAL CONDITIONING AND INDUCTION

Pavlov provides us with an example of contrast at work in Pavlovian conditioning. He placed a dog in the standard harness and arranged to reinforce salivation with food. One conditional stimulus, CS+, was turned on, and when it appeared, it was always followed by food. A second conditional stimulus, CS−, was also turned on on some trials, but when this stimulus appeared, it was never followed by food. Under these conditions, the salivary CR rapidly became *differentiated*; that is, the dog learned to salivate profusely when CS+ appeared, but to reduce and actively *inhibit* salivation when CS− appeared.[1]

---

[1]Pavlov could show that the process was one of active inhibition because if the CS− was turned on *at the same time* as some other CS+ was turned on, the magnitude of the CR to the CS+ was reduced. That is, CS− interacted with CS+ in a direct subtractive fashion. This process, incidentally, is another example of internal inhibition (cf. Chapter 1).

Coupled with the phenomenon of differentiation, however, is a second one, that of *induction*, and it is induction which provides us with our first example of a reinforcement contrast effect. If a dog with a well-differentiated CR to CS+ and CS− is presented, say, CS− for several trials, and then CS+ is reintroduced on the next trial, an *exaggerated* conditioned reflex to CS+ will be observed on that trial. That is, the dog will produce an especially copious flow of saliva, returning to a more typical amplitude of the CR on the next trial if the CS+ is presented then. Similarly, an exaggerated inhibition to CS− may appear following a few trials on which CS+ has regularly appeared (assuming that inhibition to CS− is not altogether complete through the process of differentiation). Such exaggerated CRs to CS+ and CS− demonstrate *positive* and *negative* induction, respectively.

CONTRAST IN INSTRUMENTAL LEARNING

Psychologists have thus far chosen two primary dimensions along which to contrast conditions of reinforcement in instrumental learning. On the one hand, an organism can be asked to compare two *quantities* of reinforcement in some fashion and, on the other, to compare two *frequencies* or *densities* of reinforcement. The term *reinforcement contrast* has been applied to the first approach, while the term *behavioral contrast* has been applied to the second. Let us look at each of these, then turn to the gist of theory which has been put forward to help account for the phenomena which emerge.

Reinforcement contrast Bower (1961b) did an experiment on reinforcement contrast which is especially useful because it is directly analogous to an experiment designed to produce induction in Pavlovian conditioning. Bower ran rats in two 5-foot runways located side by side; one was painted white and the other black. Rats in the contrast group were run two trials per day to a reward of eight food pellets in one runway (S+), say the black one, and two trials per day to a reward of one pellet in the other (S−). A second group was run two trials per day in one runway (the subjects in the group were counterbalanced across the two runways), but the reward was a constant eight pellets. Similarly, a third group received a constant reward of one pellet on its two daily trials. Bower recorded the speeds with which the rats ran, and the results appear in Figure 2.5.

As you can see, the rats that ran to a constant eight-pellet reward ran just a trifle faster than the rats in the contrast group on the trials in which they ran to eight pellets in the S+ runway. The difference is not a reliable one in the statistical sense, however, so for all intents and purposes, performance to the eight-pellet reward can be considered identical under the two conditions. The contrast animals on their one-pellet trials in the S− runway ran much more slowly (and reliably so) than the animals which were run to a constant one-pellet reward. These animals, in other words, showed a reliable negative reinforcement contrast effect directly analogous to negative induction in Pavlovian conditioning.

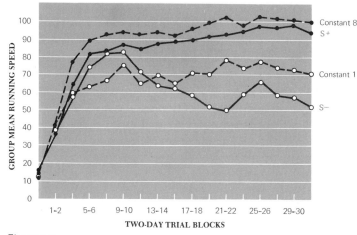

Figure 2.5
Running speeds to a constant eight-pellet reward, to a constant one-
pellet reward, or to an eight-pellet reward in a positive runway (S+) and
a one-pellet reward in a negative runway (S−). Slower speeds under the
S− as compared with the Constant 1 condition show negative reinforcement contrast. By statistical test, the Constant 8 and S+ curves are not
reliably different from each other. (Bower, 1961b.)

A great deal of experimentation has been done using the general
method that Bower used (Dunham, 1968; Black, 1968; Amsel, 1971). The
basic scheme, of course, is one in which subjects get to compare
conditions of reinforcement in a more or less *simultaneous* fashion,
either on the same trial or on closely neighboring trials. That is, the
critical experimental group gets experience with *both* or with *all* conditions of reinforcement in the experiment at pretty much the same time as
the experiment runs its course. The upshot of most of this work is that
negative reinforcement contrast effects are obtained fairly routinely, but
for some reason positive reinforcement contrast is an elusive phenomenon (Dunham, 1968). One possible reason for this comes from the fact
that subjects—both animal and human—can do just so well no matter
how much reinforcement may be available. A contrast group may not be
able to increase its performance sufficiently to surpass that of an
appropriate control group run with the same large reward, and so *ceiling
effects* may enter the picture, in other words. This may be part of the
story under some conditions, but we shall see in a moment that the
elimination of ceiling effects still does not generate a salient positive
reinforcement contrast effect based on the use of different magnitudes of
reward. If positive contrast exists as a phenomenon, the conditions
which will produce it reliably remain to be discovered.

A second general set of procedures for the study of reinforcement
contrast effects comes from an arrangement in which subjects are first
exposed to a set of reinforcement conditions for an extensive period of
time, then suddenly shifted to a new set for the very first time and their
behavior studied there. This constitutes *successive* exposure to two or
more conditions of reinforcement.

The basic successive procedure is simple and can be developed briefly using Zeaman's (1949) experiment, to which we referred earlier under the heading of amount of reinforcement. In part of Zeaman's experiment, animals trained to run the alley with a large reward for the initial course of the experiment, and those trained to run with a very small reward, were shifted suddenly so that rats which had been getting the large reward now got the small one and vice versa. As compared with some control measurements, the animals shifted to the large reward ran faster than the performance to be expected if the large reward were used alone, while those shifted to the small reward ran slower than they should have.[2]. Crespi (1942), whose experiment showing much the same thing preceded Zeaman's, attached the labels "elation" and "depression" to positive and negative reinforcement contrast effects such as these, labels which certainly seem to capture whatever emotional experience a learning subject might undergo if subjected to sudden switches in amount of reinforcement.

Typically, however, more recent work with successive procedures seems to substantiate the results obtained with simultaneous contrast procedures. In particular, if switches in magnitude of reinforcement are the reinforcement conditions under study, it is relatively easy to demonstrate negative reinforcement contrast, but quite difficult to demonstrate positive reinforcement contrast. An experiment of Hulse (1973a) provides a good example and also introduces another useful form of the successive contrast procedure, a form first used by Collier and Marx (1959). Hulse first trained some hungry rats in a lever box for 14 days to eat food pellets that were delivered automatically into a food dish; i.e., the food pellets were "free" in the sense that the animals did not have to do anything to get them. The food pellets were delivered during this "magazine training" phase of the experiment under one of three conditions: (1) some rats always got just 1 food pellet each time the magazine operated, (2) some other rats always got 10 food pellets, while (3) a third group of rats got 1 pellet sometimes and 10 pellets other times. The impending arrival of the food pellets was signaled by a tone that came on five seconds before the food magazine operated.

Following this initial phase of the experiment, the *learning* phase began. During each day of learning, the same five-second tone signaled the arrival of a lever into the box on each of 15 discrete trials. On each trial, the lever stayed in the box until it was pressed or until 80 seconds elapsed. Then it withdrew automatically until the next trial began. During the learning phase of the experiment, the groups that had been exposed during magazine training to 10 pellets or to 1 pellet were reinforced for each lever press with 10 pellets or 1 pellet, respectively. The group exposed initially to *both* 10 pellets and 1 pellet was split, half the

---

[2]Zeaman did not, unfortunately, run separate control groups of rats which ran to large and small rewards, respectively, throughout the experiment. Instead, contrast was judged based on a simple extrapolation of the animals' performance prior to the shift in reward magnitude; i.e., Zeaman assumed the rats would have continued to run at the same speed if rewards had not been changed.

animals working for 10 pellets per lever press, half working for 1 pellet.

The significant results of the experiment are shown in Figure 2.6, which
displays the trial-by-trial (lever-press-by-lever-press) performance of the
animals who learned to press the lever for a 1-pellet reward.

As you can see from the figure, the response latencies of the animals
with a variable (V) background of both 10-pellet and 1-pellet quantities
tapered off much more slowly than the latencies of the group trained
with a constant (C) background of nothing but single pellets. Both
conditions led to equivalent performance by the end of the nine-day
learning phase, but initially, in other words, the V condition led to slower
learning than the C condition and, therefore, to a negative contrast
effect. It was much as if the V rats remembered their earlier experience
with both quantities of food and were "chagrined" to conclude as they
learned to press for the single-pellet reward that the larger quantity had,
so to speak, gone forever. In accord with earlier experiments, other data
from the experiment (not shown in Figure 2.6) revealed no trace of a
positive contrast effect; the V animals rewarded with a 10-pellet reward
for lever pressing showed no better (nor worse) performance than the C
animals exposed to a 10-pellet quantity throughout both phases of the
experiment.

Behavioral contrast   Behavioral contrast is a phenomenon which appears
with methodology that is similar to that used to demonstrate induction in
Pavlovian conditioning. The basic idea is to teach an organism, say a
pigeon, to peck at a key which is sometimes transilluminated with red
light (S+) and sometimes with green light (S−). The bird is reinforced
according to a variable-interval schedule (remember the Hutt experiment
described a few pages ago), so that not all pecks to the key are reinforced.
After behavior has stabilized under these conditions, *reinforcement*

Figure 2.6
Learning a discrete-trial lever-pressing task following exposure to a constant 1-pellet stimulus during pretraining
(C-1) or to both 1-pellet and 10-pellet stimuli (V-1). All
animals learned to lever-press for a 1-pellet reward. (Hulse,
1973a.)

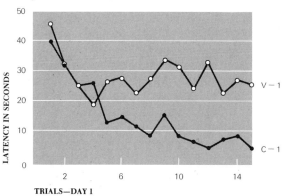

frequency in the presence of the S− stimulus is reduced in some fashion, perhaps to zero, by increasing the average length of time between the availability of successive rewards. Then, the response rates in the presence of S+ as opposed to S− are compared. If this is done, an increased frequency of responding to S+ is generally the result; that is, the bird "overshoots" and responds faster to S+ than formerly (Reynolds, 1961a). The parallel to Pavlovian positive induction is clear (Amsel, 1971). The parallel to reinforcement contrast effects using repeated sequential shifts in *amount* of reinforcement should also be clear.

THEORETICAL ACCOUNTS OF CONTRAST EFFECTS

In broad perspective, how shall we account for contrast effects in terms of some theoretical notions about what might be going on to produce them? We choose to emphasize two primary approaches to this point, though others could no doubt be mentioned as well. Dunham (1968) has provided a thoughtful discussion of the matter, and that is a good starting place for further study.

Emotion   One approach to the problem stresses the intuition that shifts in conditions of reinforcement may well generate *emotional* consequences in learning organisms which can, in turn, modify the overall level of motivation that prevails in the learning situation. As many have pointed out, one immediate problem here has to do with how one goes about defining emotion under the conditions which produce contrast, but the general sense of the idea is that shifts in conditions of reinforcement generate excitatory or inhibitory "states" which are perhaps quite transient but which can, nevertheless, work to modulate the vigor with which some response is produced by an organism. Proponents of this general view, in one or another of the many forms it can take, range from Crespi (1942), who gave us the terms *elation* and *depression*, to Amsel (1967, 1971), who stresses the emotional consequences of frustration arising from nonreinforcement or from reduced reinforcement (about which we shall have a great deal to say in the part of this book dealing with extinction).

Stimulus control   Another approach to the problem—which may complement more than stand in opposition to the emotional approach—stresses the fact that organisms must have, at a minimum, some appreciation that more than one condition of reinforcement exists in a contrast situation before contrast effects will emerge (Hulse, 1962a, 1962b, 1973b; Bevan, 1968). Put more technically, this position stresses the fact that the behavior of the organism which is going to show a contrast effect must be under differential control of the stimuli associated with one as opposed to another of the contrasting conditions of reinforcement. This, of course, is part and parcel of any contrast procedure which incorporates a direct and repeated comparison between contrasting conditions, such as the procedures used in differential conditioning, simultaneous reinforcement contrast, or behavioral contrast. There, the very procedures themselves assure that the learning organism will, at a minimum, get to compare—and presumably learn to discriminate among—the several conditions of reinforcement. Other procedures, however, such as that incorporating a single shift from one set of reinforcement conditions to another, do not provide for automatic development of such discriminative control, and sometimes these procedures fail to reveal contrast effects, as we have seen. Thus, if contrast effects are to emerge, the situation must provide some opportunity for the behaving organism to become familiar with—and to learn to tell the difference between—the relevant conditions of reinforcement. This seems like an obvious principle, but it is nevertheless a consideration which has sometimes failed to get the attention it deserves.

We undoubtedly oversimplify when we say that contrast effects reflect some combination of excitatory and inhibitory "emotional" factors on the one hand, and discriminative, attentional factors on the other, but a fundamental explanation of contrast effects will probably incorporate either or both these factors in one guise or another.

CONDITIONED REINFORCEMENT

Food pellets and sucrose solutions are examples of *primary* or *first-order* reinforcing stimuli. That is, they will operate as simple reinforcers even though the organism has little, if any, previous experience with them. Generally speaking, primary reinforcers in simple conditioning and learning are tied pretty closely to some basic physiological system: taste, hunger, thirst, and so on. It is obvious that to the extent human behavior is learned on the basis of straightforward reinforcement principles, reinforcement must be quite different from simple primary reinforcement. Money is an example of something that is a reinforcing stimulus for most people, but a stimulus which is certainly not tied in any direct fashion to a basic physiological system. Consequently, psychologists have found it necessary to add a concept to the basic principles of conditioning and learning which can help to account for the fact that organisms can learn in the absence of anything that could be called primary reinforcement. The concept is that of *secondary* or *conditioned* reinforcement. Again, we shall confine our discussion here primarily to conditioned reinforcement based on positive primary reinforcement. Similar considerations that involve negative reinforcement will be dealt with later.

At the end of this section of the chapter, we shall also have a few comments to make about the notion of *second-order conditioning* in Pavlovian conditioning. This phenomenon, conceptually at least, is a close cousin to that of conditioned reinforcement.

*A conditioned reinforcer is a neutral stimulus that acquires the functional
properties of a primary reinforcer by being paired with a primary reinforcer
or with another conditioned reinforcer.* In other words, conditioned
reinforcers are stimuli that acquire the power to reinforce by being paired
with other stimuli that already possess the power to reinforce. In this
sense, conditioned reinforcers are stimuli that acquire their reinforcing
properties through *learning*.

According to a straightforward interpretation of our definition of
conditioned reinforcement, we could establish a conditioned reinforcer
quite simply. In practice, psychologists have used three general techniques to do this. Let us look briefly at these techniques and examine some
experiments that furnish examples of each technique—and the principle
of conditioned reinforcement—at work.

The first technique involves pairing a stimulus with primary reinforcement in one situation and with one response, and then testing to see if
the stimulus has become a conditioned reinforcer by using it—and it
alone—to reinforce a *new* response in a *new* situation. If the stimulus
which we think is a conditioned reinforcer can, in fact, produce new
learning, then we have demonstrated that it is a conditioned reinforcer.

The second technique is to use *resistance to extinction* as a measure of
the establishment of a conditioned reinforcer. While we will develop the
concept of resistance to extinction in some detail in a later chapter,
suffice it to say here that the concept is an index of the extent to which an
organism is willing to *persist* in the performance of some response when
we stop reinforcing the response. For example, when one rat makes
more responses on a lever than another rat after the experimenter stops
giving food pellets for lever presses, we say that the first rat is more
resistant to extinction than the second rat. With respect to conditioned
reinforcers, we would expect a stimulus that had acquired some value as a
conditioned reinforcer to increase resistance to extinction if we followed
lever presses during extinction with the stimulus. Even though we have
withdrawn primary reinforcement, we would still be giving *some*, albeit
learned, reinforcement for lever-pressing behavior.

The third technique is to study conditioned reinforcement as it
operates in a *chain* of behavior. A chain of behavior is a *sequence* of
different responses, each response paired with a different stimulus, that
eventually leads to some primary reinforcement like food. The concept of
a chain of behavior, and the role that conditioned reinforcement plays in
such a chain, are best explained by means of an example from the
experimental literature, and so we shall return to this point in a moment.
First, let us look at experiments that are representative of our first two
techniques.

Saltzman (1949) trained rats to run down a straight runway to a goal
box that contained food. The goal box was either black or white. In one

condition, the goal box always contained food when it was black, but did not when it was white. After this training, the rats were taught a simple maze in which they had to choose between two pathways, one leading to a black goal box and the other to a white one. The rats learned to go to the black goal box, *even though it was never baited with food.* Thus it is clear that the black goal box itself was a stimulus complex that was reinforcing because it had been paired with primary reinforcement, food, in another situation. The black goal box was thus a conditioned reinforcer.

Miles (1956) did an experiment in which resistance to extinction was used to measure the strength of a conditioned reinforcer. His experiment incorporated two variables: the number of times that a conditioned reinforcer was paired with a food-reinforced lever press and the strength of hunger drive at the time extinction began. In the part of the experiment in which number of pairings of conditioned reinforcer with primary reinforcement was the independent variable, different groups of rats had the delivery of a food pellet paired with both a flash of light and an audible click (the conditioned reinforcer) following 0, 10, 20, 40, 80, or 160 lever presses. Then the food-delivery apparatus was turned off, and the rats pressed the lever without primary reinforcement. For half the rats, lever presses during extinction produced the conditioned reinforcer; for the other half, the conditioned reinforcer was omitted. Figure 2.7 shows part of the results. As you can see, resistance to extinction increased as number of reinforcements increased, but the group which was extinguished with the conditioned (secondary) reinforcer made more lever presses than the group which was extinguished without the conditioned reinforcer.

Miles's experiment also showed that the effect of the conditioned reinforcer on resistance to extinction also depended upon the strength of the hunger drive under which the rats entered extinction. Generally speaking, the conditioned reinforcer ·added more extra responses the longer the rats were deprived of food.

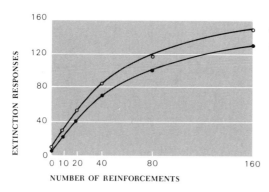

Group
○ Secondary reinforcement
● No secondary reinforcement

Figure 2.7
Effect of a conditioned reinforcer on resistance to extinction as a function of number of reinforcements. (Adapted from Miles, 1956.)

Let us now return to our third technique and examine the concept of conditioned reinforcement as it can be shown to operate in a chain of behavior. To do this, let us look at an experiment by Napalkov cited in Kelleher and Gollub (1962). Napalkov first trained pigeons to peck a lever (response 1) in order to obtain a primary reinforcer, food. Then he reinforced pecks only if they occurred when a white light (stimulus 1) was turned on. You will recognize that this procedure made a discriminative cue out of the light. After the pigeon had learned to confine most of its pecks to the time that the light was on, the pigeon was required to jump onto a platform (response 2) in order to turn on the light. But the light could only be turned on if the jumping response was made in the presence of another discriminative cue, a rotating black air vane (stimulus 2). This procedure was carried on until the pigeon had learned a sequence of responses, a chain of behavior, that involved component responses, each response correlated with a different discriminative cue. The whole experiment is outlined in Table 2.1. Note that the chain was established in reverse order; the response closest to primary reinforcement was established first, then earlier components were added, response by response.

Now it is clear that the first component of the chain, pecking the lever, was reinforced with a primary reinforcer, food. But what was the reinforcing stimulus for the second component response, jumping on the platform? Clearly, it must have been the discriminative cue of the white light. In other words, the jumping response was reinforced by a previously neutral stimulus that acquired its reinforcing power by being paired—as a discriminative cue—directly with primary reinforcement. Similarly, the third response, jumping onto the floor of the apparatus, was reinforced by the discriminative cue of the rotating black air vane. Thus, the black air vane was also a conditioned reinforcer, but it acquired its reinforcing power by being paired, not with primary reinforcement, but with another *conditioned* reinforcer. So this experiment demonstrates that conditioned reinforcers can be developed by pairing stimuli, as discriminative cues, not only with primary reinforcers but also with other conditioned reinforcers.

Some things that affect the strength of conditioned reinforcers Since conditioned reinforcers are developed through a learning process, we would expect that their strength might be correlated with variables which have been shown to affect the strength of a learned association. This turns out to be the case. Miles's (1956) experiment, if you will recall, showed that the strength of a conditioned reinforcer was a function of both the number of times a cue had been paired with primary reinforcement and the strength of hunger motivation during test trials. Other experiments have shown that the strength of a conditioned reinforcer increases with amount of reinforcement (D'Amato, 1955; Butter & Thomas, 1958), while still others show that, under some conditions at least, intermittent as opposed to regular reinforcement of the conditioned reinforcer with primary reinforcement can strengthen it. Wike

(1966) has provided an excellent review of these points, together with a great many others which are worth exploring.

THE NECESSARY CONDITIONS FOR ESTABLISHING A CONDITIONED REINFORCER

What experimental operations should we choose to *guarantee* that a particular stimulus will become a conditioned reinforcer? While psychologists have some good hunches about the answer to this question, they still must deal with it much as they have had to deal with the problem of selecting a variable that will properly describe different amounts of reinforcement. The choice of a technique remains pretty much a pragmatic affair. One of the best, in the sense that it does work most consistently, is to make a discriminative cue out of the neutral stimulus which is to acquire reinforcing value. This technique, first described by Skinner (1938), is characteristic of the Napalkov experiment as well as of a great many others (Keller & Schoenfeld, 1950; Kelleher & Gollub, 1962; Wike, 1966).

Conditioned reinforcers as information-carrying stimuli Another interesting approach to the question of the necessary and sufficient conditions for establishing a conditioned reinforcer comes from some work of Egger and Miller (1962, 1963). We mention it here because it is one forerunner

Table 2.1
Summary of Napalkov's experiment
(From Kelleher & Gollub, 1962)

RESPONSE	DISCRIMINATIVE CUE	REINFORCING STIMULUS	NO. OF TRIALS FOR RESPONSE TO OCCUR TO DISCRIMINATIVE CUE
1. Peck lever	White light (S_1)	Food	14–18
2. Jump onto a platform	Black air vane rotating (S_2)	White light	12–20
3. Jump onto floor of apparatus	Whistle (S_3)	Black air vane	20–30
4. Jump down onto a platform	Blue light (S_4)	Whistle	18–36
5. Jump onto rod	Horn (siren) (S_5)	Blue light	31–45
6. Jump into right section of apparatus	Bell (S_6)	Horn	40–55
7. Jump into left section of chamber and up onto a shelf	Large white air vane (S_7)	Bell	42–61

of a more general approach to an understanding of how stimuli come to be associated with other stimuli in conditioning experiments (Rescorla, 1967, 1972; Wagner, 1969; Rescorla & Wagner, 1972). Egger and Miller postulated that a neutral stimulus might become an effective conditioned reinforcer to the extent that it carried reliable *information* about the occurrence or nonoccurrence of primary reinforcement.

Suppose that two neutral stimuli, S_1 and S_2, are arranged with respect to primary reinforcement such that S_1 comes on, then S_2 comes on, then both go off together as primary reinforcement arrives. In this case, *both* stimuli reliably predict that primary reinforcement will be forthcoming—in the sense that primary reinforcement is arranged to appear following the onset of both stimuli—but S_2 is *redundant* with respect to S_1 in predicting the arrival of primary reinforcement. That is, given the onset of S_1, the subsequent appearance of S_2 adds no information about whether primary reinforcement will appear or not; the essential information has already been conveyed by S_1. Suppose, on the other hand, that things are arranged so that S_1 followed by S_2 always leads to primary reinforcement, but sometimes S_1 appears by itself and primary reinforcement fails to occur. Now, S_1 is no longer a reliable predictor of primary reinforcement; it carries no dependable information concerning the impending arrival of that stimulus. However, S_2 *does* carry reliable information under these conditions; primary reinforcement always occurs if S_2 is included in the preceding stimulus complex.

Egger and Miller set out to test the notion that informative cues would be efficient conditioned reinforcers by first training rats to press levers for food pellet reinforcers in lever boxes. Then, the levers were removed from the boxes, and things were arranged so that S_1 (say, a tone) and S_2 (say, a flashing light) and food pellets were paired together according to the arrangements described in the preceding paragraph. That is, for some rats S_2 was a redundant predictor of the arrival of a food pellet, while for others, it was an informative predictor of the arrival of the food pellet. Following a number of sessions in which the several stimuli were paired in this fashion, the lever was reintroduced into the box, and the effectiveness of S_1 and S_2 under the two conditions of presentation were tested by having lever presses produce the stimuli (but no food). Notice that this procedure tests during extinction for the establishment of conditioned reinforcement; i.e., a stimulus is a conditioned reinforcer to the extent that it prolongs persistence in the face of no reinforcement. The results of the experiment are shown in Table 2.2.

Table 2.2
Mean number of lever presses during test for conditioned-reinforcement value of S_1 and S_2

GROUP	S_1	S_2
S_2 redundant	115.1	65.8
S_2 informative	76.1	82.6

As you can see, S_1 and S_2 both prolonged extinction in general, but this happened to the extent that they had been established as reliable carriers of information about impending primary reinforcement. If S_2 were redundant to S_1 in predicting food pellets, only 65.8 responses were produced, but if it had to be depended on by the rats to predict food, it generated 82.6 presses on the average. Note that when S_1 had reliably predicted food (top row of the table), it generated 115.1 lever presses, substantially overshadowing S_2 as a conditioned reinforcer in the process.

The hypothesis that conditioned reinforcers are information carriers does *not* do any serious violence to the notion that a discriminative cue will be a good conditioned reinforcer or, for that matter, that a simple pairing of a stimulus with a primary reinforcer will generate an effective conditioned reinforcer. In both instances, the cue in question reliably predicts the arrival of primary reinforcement, and that is all that the Egger and Miller hypothesis calls for. Their hypothesis does have some things to say when *two* stimuli are arranged such that they can both become conditioned reinforcers potentially and when one must make predictions about which one will become the more effective. As a matter of fact, the information notion has implications which go far beyond the problem of conditioned reinforcement, and we shall be meeting it again later on.

TOKEN REWARDS AND THE PRACTICAL APPLICATION OF CONDITIONED REINFORCEMENT

So that concepts like that of conditioned reinforcement may shed some of the fur and dander of the animal laboratory, let us look at some accomplishments that have been achieved when the fundamental princi-ples we have just examined are put to use in a practical situation. Before we leave the animal laboratory for good in this regard, however, we must develop the concept of a *token reward*, and that comes from some experimental work with chimpanzees (Wolfe, 1936). Wolfe trained chimps to insert poker chips into a vending device in order to obtain food from it. After he had trained them to do this, Wolfe found that the poker chips as "tokens for food" had acquired the properties of a conditioned reinforcer in the sense that chimps would work at a weight-pulling task, which required considerable expenditure of effort, in order to obtain poker chips that could be exchanged for the primary reinforcement of food only after a considerable delay interval. As a matter of fact, Wolfe found that the delay interval could be extended to as much as an hour before the chimps would refuse to work for the poker chips, and in later work Kelleher (1957) was able to extend the interval to as much as two hours. Interestingly enough, both investigators noticed that during the delay interval, the chimps frequently put the poker chips in their mouths, manipulating them as if they were food—which should remind you of some experiences of the Brelands (1961) which we discussed in the last chapter. But the important point is that the poker chips had all the requisite characteristics of conditioned reinforcers.

Staats, Finley, Minke, Wolfe, and Brooks (1964) made one of the first attempts to apply the principle of token reinforcement to a practical situation involving human subjects. They were interested in teaching four-year-old children some of the rudiments of reading, and set up an experimental situation in which youngsters were reinforced with marbles dispensed from a magazine for performing correctly on various components of the reading task. The marbles had no (or very little) intrinsic reinforcing properties themselves, but they were "backed up" with a variety of "primary" reinforcers for which they could be exchanged. The backup objects included toys of one kind or another that the youngsters had picked out for themselves ahead of time or trinkets such as small plastic toys or bits of candy that were dispensed from another device. The various backup objects varied in their dollar value; some of the toys therefore required as much as 150 marble tokens for their "purchase," while others required less. Under all cases, however, the subjects were given the option of exchanging their tokens for whatever backup reinforcement they wished. Staats et al. report that the children found this general experimental arrangement to their liking and that they quickly went to work at the task, sticking with it successfully for long periods of time.

Since initial research by investigators such as Staats et al. has been accomplished, a very large number of programs have gotten under way in which token reinforcers have been used not only in laboratory situations but also directly in school classrooms. O'Leary and Drabman (1971) report that there is a large measure of success with these programs, many of which have been introduced in settings involving mentally disturbed or retarded children. Such programs are, of course, potentially beset with the problems that beset any new method of education, including variables which arise from teacher attitudes, parent attitudes, student attitudes, and so on, but the gist of the matter as things stand now is that token-reinforcement systems provide a powerful technique to use in the classroom. They have, incidentally, also been used with marked success in a variety of clinical settings, such as those involving psychiatric patients (Ayllon & Azrin, 1968).

HIGHER-ORDER CONDITIONING

Pavlov (1927) describes a phenomenon he called *secondary* conditioning, but which is now called *higher-order* or *second-order conditioning*, which is sufficiently similar to conditioned reinforcement—at least in the logic of the procedures used to establish it—that it is conveniently discussed here.

Higher-order conditioning is demonstrated as follows. Suppose that a hungry dog has been placed in the conventional Pavlovian harness and a salivary reflex is conditioned using food as a UCS and a tone as CS. Let us arrange things so that the dog is conditioned for a number of trials using a trace procedure in which the CS precedes the UCS by a second or two with a gap of a few seconds between the offset of the CS and the onset of the UCS. After we have established the CR in this fashion, let us switch the experimental procedure in the following way. Let us substitute the tone CS for the food UCS and introduce a *new* CS, say a flashing light, in place of the tone. Now we have an arrangement in which the CS of the flashing light is followed a few seconds later by the former CS of the tone, a CS which has acquired the ability to elicit salivation through its earlier pairing with food. Food, however, has been discarded from the situation, and if conditioned salivation is to be maintained, this must happen through whatever properties the tone CS has *acquired through learning* to produce salivation. As you can see, this makes the arrangement at least analogous to conditioned reinforcement in instrumental learning.

Pavlov found that higher-order conditioning was an obtainable phenomenon, particularly so if an aversive UCS was used with a conditioned reflex like leg flexion. He also reports that it was possible to get third-order conditioning in addition to second-order conditioning; that is, the chain of higher-order reflexes could be extended beyond the second order by adding yet another CS to the situation, using the second-order CS as the new UCS. Third-order conditioning is difficult to obtain, however, and even second-order conditioning wanes with repeated elicitation of the reflex due to increasing extinctive inhibition—remember that food is removed from the situation, just as primary reinforcement is removed as part of some procedures for testing for conditioned reinforcement in instrumental conditioning. Perhaps because of the fact that higher-order conditioning has not been a particularly robust phenomenon experimentally, it has failed to receive the empirical development it deserves. Recently, however, Rescorla (1973) has been able to demonstrate substantial and reliable second-order conditioning in the laboratory, and he has begun the outline of a theoretical account based on this which places important emphasis on higher-order conditioning as a process in basic associative learning. As a *model* for the formation of associations, higher-order conditioning is quite interesting, since it is one simple and straightforward way for describing how successive chains of associations might grow (or be inhibited and blocked, for that matter). Our present state of knowledge does not warrant further treatment here, but it should prove interesting to watch future developments in this area.

TIME RELATIONS IN CONDITIONING AND LEARNING

So far in our examination of basic reinforcement variables, we have postponed discussion of a very important set of relationships in the conditioning and learning of simple responses. This has to do with the way in which stimuli, responses, and reinforcers are related in time. Such matters are important because they are directed explicitly at a very general problem that has interested psychologists—and philosophers—

for a great many years. The basic question is this: How should two or more events be arranged in time so that an organism will associate them with each other?

In practice, psychologists have sought answers to these questions in two domains. First, Pavlovian conditioning techniques have been used to study the strength of a conditioned response when the interval varies between the CS and the UCS. Second, instrumental conditioning techniques have been used to study the strength of a response when the interval varies between the occurrence of the response and the delivery of the reinforcing stimulus.

THE CS-UCS INTERVAL IN PAVLOVIAN CONDITIONING

There are now many experiments which demonstrate the strength of a Pavlovian conditioned response as a function of the relation between the CS and UCS in time. It is hardly surprising that Pavlov was the first to devote some attention to this problem, and we shall now have a brief look at some of the things he did.

Pavlov's studies of time relations in conditioning Pavlov was especially interested in two techniques in his study of the temporal relation between CS and UCS, those to which we have given the labels *delayed* conditioning and *trace* conditioning (Chapter 1). When the UCS was delayed, Pavlov found that animals could learn to delay the onset of the CR for long periods of time. They would delay giving the CR until just before the UCS was about to appear, appropriately holding off salivation, say, until food was about to appear. He also found that animals could delay the CR with the trace procedure. The delays in each case were attributed to *inhibition of delay*, which Pavlov classified as another example of internal inhibition. He found, moreover, that it was more difficult to establish the trace CR than the delayed CR. More recent research shows that this observation may vary depending upon such things as the species or the specific CR involved. Schneiderman (1966) found that when he conditioned closure of the nictitating membrane in rabbits (one of the rabbit's three eyelids) to a tone CS and a puff of nitrogen to the cornea of the eye as UCS, delayed procedures produced much better conditioning than trace procedures, just as Pavlov found. Ross and Ross (1971), however, found no differences in human subjects in the extent to which eyelid conditioning could be obtained with trace versus delayed procedures.

Response strength and the CS-UCS interval At present there must be 50 or more experiments which were designed to show in one way or another how response strength changes when the CS-UCS interval varies. Three representative studies with human subjects (Spooner & Kellogg, 1947; Moeller, 1954; Kimble, Mann, & Dufort, 1955) used conditioned responses that were, variously, a hand movement, a galvanic skin response, and an eyeblink. These experiments, and most like them, are consistent in showing that conditioning is most rapid and terminal response strength is greatest when the CS *precedes* the UCS by approximately half a second.

Backward conditioning One curious case of the time relation between the CS and the UCS is that of backward conditioning: the UCS precedes the CS. Pavlov thought conditioning could not take place in this case, and in many cases where it seems to appear, it is probably not true conditioning, but more likely a sensitization of the whole response system. The UCS, often an electric shock or some other noxious stimulus in cases where backward conditioning appears to be successful, *sensitizes* the subject so that he will give a response to almost any stimulus. This implies, of course, that the stimulus need not be paired with the UCS in any fashion whatsoever.

More recently, evidence has been accumulating that the backward-conditioning paradigm can actually generate an *inhibitory* state to the CS; that is, the CS can become a conditioned inhibitor of Pavlovian reflexes (Rescorla, 1969; Siegel & Domjan, 1971). According to this line of reasoning, the CS is *negatively* correlated with the delivery of the UCS in the backward-conditioning paradigm; that is, the appearance of the CS predicts the *absence* of the UCS with perfect reliability. Under these conditions, says Rescorla, inhibition should result and conditioning levels should drop.

DELAY OF REINFORCEMENT IN INSTRUMENTAL CONDITIONING

Suppose we somehow coaxed a dog to make a response and then rather fiendishly failed to give the dog some appropriate reward until an hour or so had passed. Would the dog learn the response? Psychologists can say with considerable confidence that under most conditions, and with dogs the animal in question, the response will be learned with difficulty if it is learned at all. Suppose on the other hand that we fed a rat some novel food that it had never tasted before, then an hour or two later made the animal sick to its stomach by dosing it with some suitable chemical such as an injection of a substance called *apomorphine*. Under these conditions, rats will form a *permanent aversion* to the novel food, an aversion which somehow develops in spite of the long period of time between initial ingestion of the food and the onset of the illness. Clearly, some interesting things are going on here, and we shall look at them and some of their implications in this final section of the chapter.

A classical view First, let us look at the empirical and theoretical analysis of the problem of delay of reinforcement as it was understood until quite recently. There is still good reason to believe that this approach, or something like it, can account for a substantial portion of the more recent data coming from delay-of-reinforcement studies, although the classical view is relatively useless in accounting for certain varieties of experimental results now emerging from the laboratory. If nothing else, the classical view is of historical interest as a neat and elegant analysis of an important problem in the psychology of learning, and there is often much to be learned from a study of such analyses.

In an early experiment, Perin (1943) trained rats in a Skinner box that was modified so that movement of a rod to either the right or the left would produce a food pellet. Immediately after the rod was moved, it was withdrawn from the box until the next trial. After the rats had learned to move the rod in both directions and had displayed their preference for one direction, the apparatus was changed so that a movement of the rod in the preferred direction would produce no food. A movement of the rod in the other direction, however, would cause the food pellet to be delivered. Also, at this point, the apparatus was changed so that correct movement of the rod produced the food pellets for different rats after 0, 2, 5, 10, 20, or 30 seconds. Perin ran the rats under these conditions for 120 trials and measured the frequency with which the rats made the correct response, i.e., moved the rod in the new direction. He then calculated the *slope* of the learning curve associated with each of the delay periods at the point where the rats were making 50 percent correct responses—that is, at the point where the problem was "half learned." Perin's rationale was that if delay of reinforcement affected the facility with which the correct response would be acquired, rats who were learning the problem faster would show a greater *rate* of improvement (a steeper slope on the learning curve) than rats who were having more difficulty with the problem. A plot of the slopes as a function of delay of reinforcement, a *gradient of reinforcement*, is shown by the upper function in Figure 2.8.

It is very clear in this figure that the shorter the delay of reinforcement, the steeper the slope of the learning curve. Rats with short delays learned the problem at a much faster rate than rats with long delays. Looking at the curve, it would be predicted that no learning at all would

Figure 2.8
Delay-of-reinforcement gradients obtained by Perin (1943) and Grice (1948). Note that Grice's procedure, which presumably reduced conditioned reinforcement, produced little learning beyond a delay of five seconds. (Grice, 1948.)

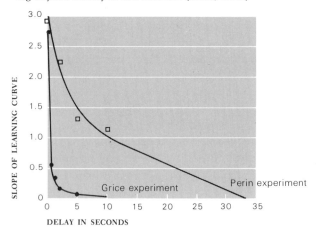

occur (that is, the slope of the learning curve would be 0) if reinforcement were delayed for about 35 to 40 seconds. As a matter of fact, about half the rats in the 30-second group extinguished during the course of the 120 learning trials; the delay was so long that they stopped moving the rod altogether.

In a paper analyzing the problem of delay of reinforcement, Spence (1947) argued that experiments which had shown a long gradient of reinforcement had used procedures which assured the presence of *conditioned* reinforcers during the delay period. Spence argued further that if it were possible to remove all conditioned reinforcers during the delay period, the gradient of reinforcement ought to almost vanish!

An experiment by Grice (1948) provided strong support for Spence's point of view. Grice set out to remove from the delay period as many cues with potential value as conditioned reinforcers as he could and predicted that if any gradient of reinforcement were obtained at all, it would be a very short one. He conditioned rats in a black-white "discrimination" apparatus in which they were trained to leave a start box and to choose between one of two straight alleys. The initial portion, the discrimination section, of one alley was painted white, while the initial portion of the other was painted black. After choosing a discrimination section (the white one was always correct), the rat ran into a gray delay section and then into a gray goal box, where food was available after a correct response. With this procedure, the white and black cues provided by the discrimination sections—the brightness cues the rats had to use to solve the problem—were never paired directly in time with primary reinforcement and should therefore have acquired little value as conditioned reinforcers. Further, the black and white cues were shifted randomly from side to side on different trials, and so the rats could not solve the problem by simply learning to go to the right or left. This assured that no particular pattern of proprioceptive cues could acquire differential value as a conditioned reinforcer by being paired consistently with primary reinforcement. Different delays of reinforcement for correct responses were introduced for different rats by reinforcing them directly in the discrimination section (0 delay), by varying the length of the delay section through which they ran, and for long delays, by confining rats in the delay section before permitting them to run into the goal box. With these techniques, delays of 0, 0.5, 1.2, 2.0, 5.0, and 10.0 seconds were used. The rats were considered to have learned the problem when they made 18 correct choices during 20 consecutive trials. Grice calculated the slopes of the learning curves for his rats in a manner which was essentially the same that Perin used, and obtained the bottom function shown in Figure 2.8. Clearly, Grice's results demonstrate that rats would not have been able to learn the problem if reinforcement were delayed much longer than 5 seconds; three out of five rats in the 10-second group did not learn at all. This is a striking confirmation of Spence's assertion.

Though the Spence-Grice approach appears to handle the problem very well, other data suggest that things might not be quite so simple even within this classical account of the phenomenon of delay of reinforcement. Lawrence and Hommel (1961) asked what would happen in a discrimination problem if control for conditioned reinforcement were maintained during the delay period, but the goal boxes into which the rats ran after a correct or incorrect choice were highly discriminable from each other. To answer this question, three groups of rats were trained in an apparatus which was basically the same that Grice used.

For all groups, a response to the white discrimination section was correct, and following both correct and incorrect choices, all animals were confined for 10 seconds in a gray delay section. Then they were permitted to run into a goal box. For group C, both goal boxes were identical in structure and were painted gray—the conditions Grice used. For group DG, both goal boxes were also gray, but they differed in shape and in floor texture. For group BW, one goal box was white and the other was black; however, the black goal box was used with the white discrimination section. Note that, since choice of the white discrimination section was correct, food was presented in the black goal box. Thus "black" as a cue presumably acquired the properties of a conditioned reinforcer. But note also that if "black" were a conditioned reinforcer, responses to the *black* discrimination section would be the ones that would receive immediate conditioned reinforcement, and *these were incorrect responses not followed by food.* And so if conditioned reinforcement were at work in the situation, it would operate *against* mediation of the delay and solution of the discrimination problem.

The results of the experiment show that for group C, only 2 of 10 rats reached the learning criterion of 18 correct choices in 20 successive trials during 300 learning trials. These results are quite comparable with those of Grice. For group DG, however, 7 of 9 rats reached the criterion in a median of 169 trials, and for group BW, all of 10 rats reached the criterion in a median of 119.5 trials. Further, when delays for the BW group were subsequently increased from 10 to as much as 60 seconds, the rats maintained the discrimination. Taken as a whole, the results indicate clearly that rats can solve a discrimination problem involving delay of reinforcement on some basis other than that of conditioned reinforcement alone. Lawrence and Hommel feel that when food appears in one place and not in another, and when the rat can distinguish between the two places, the rat will search for and attend selectively to other cues—notably those in the discrimination sections—that lead to primary reinforcement. In a sense, the rat is provided with some information which enables it to recognize that it does, in fact, have a discrimination problem to solve: it has to find its way to that unique place where food is consistently available and to avoid that unique place where food is never found. In Grice's experiment, on the other hand, both correct and incorrect responses (from the experimenter's point of view) lead to the *same* place, a gray goal box (from the rat's point of view). Though the experimenter has a discrimination problem in mind, the problem for the rat may never become a discrimination problem at all.

If Lawrence and Hommel's experiment raises some questions about the validity of the Spence-Grice scheme as a truly general principle applying to all forms of learning, more recent discoveries show that the approach must be truly limited in terms of the learning situations to which it can be applied. We turn to those newer facts now. As we do, however, it is well to remember that the Spence-Grice approach can still handle a great deal of data, and the principle which it incorporates of mediation of a delay through conditioned reinforcement and its behavioral correlates is an important and useful one.

Long-delay learning During the 1950s and early 1960s, a great deal of research was done in which the effects of radiation (X-rays, for example) upon the behavior of animals were studied (Revusky & Garcia, 1970). In a typical experimental arrangement (Garcia, Kimeldorf, & Koelling, 1955) rats were first permitted to choose freely between plain and saccharin-flavored water; of their total intake, about 85 percent was from the sweet saccharin solution which is a highly preferred substance in rats. Then the animals were allowed to drink saccharin-flavored water for six hours while they were simultaneously exposed to X-radiation. It is, of course, well known that prolonged or intense radiation will produce radiation sickness (general malaise, sickness to the stomach, diarrhea), but in this case, the strength of the radiation was kept at a level that did not produce overt symptoms. Presumably, the animals experienced these symptoms to some degree, however. Following the pairing of saccharin consumption with radiation, the animals were returned to their home cages in which supplies of both plain and saccharin-flavored water were continuously available, and the relative consumption of each solution was recorded for a period of 63 days. The results show that, initially, consumption of the saccharin solution fell almost to zero. Consumption recovered gradually during the test period, but never reached the preexperimental level even after *two months* of testing. And this effect, remember, resulted from a *single* pairing of the sweet taste with the sickness-producing radiation. Furthermore, and of particular importance from our present point of view, the delivery of the radiation took time. Possibly, therefore, the remarkable effects of the radiation upon behavior appeared in spite of considerable *delay* between the consumption of the saccharin and effects due to the radiation. This would certainly be true if the relevant property of the radiation was the sickness it produced, since symptoms of illness take some time to appear after radiation is initiated.

All these conjectures were confirmed in later work. Garcia, Ervin, and Koelling (1966), for example, did an experiment in which animals drank saccharin-flavored water and then were made sick to their stomachs by later injection of a substance, *apomorphine*, which we mentioned at the outset of this section. The interval of time between ingestion of the saccharin and injection of the apomorphine was varied for different animals from 30 minutes to 3 hours, and the animals were exposed to five pairings of saccharin and apomorphine each separated by 3 days. The amount of saccharin solution the animals then drank during a test period increased as a direct function of the amount of time that had elapsed during conditioning between saccharin consumption and apomorphine injection. The rats drank very little at the short delays, indicating they had formed an association between the saccharin and getting sick to their stomachs—they had a well-developed *learned aversion* to the formerly palatable substance. As the delay interval increased, the learned aversion became less severe—the animals drank more saccharin—but there was still some evidence that the association had been formed even at the most extreme intervals that were used. Now recall very carefully the range of delays that were employed in the experiment. The animals were learning an association when *reinforcement (punishment* in this case) *was delayed by as much as 3 hours.*

Clearly, this result—which has been obtained in many experiments (Revusky & Garcia, 1970; Rozin & Kalat, 1971)—is completely counter to any of the work we examined under the classical approach to the problem of delay of reinforcement. There, delays of a few minutes were quite long, but learned aversions have been reported with delays of as much as 12 *hours* or so. Analysis of the problem has contributed to our under-standing of this discrepancy and, incidentally, elaborated some other important constraints on learning of the sort we discussed in the last chapter.

First of all, long-delay learning appears to be pretty specific to certain sensory systems in the rat, the taste-smell system in particular. This was demonstrated in an experiment of Garcia and Koelling (1966). They hypothesized that aversions would develop only if the signaling and reinforcing stimuli *belonged* to each other. That is, aversions should appear when an internal stimulus, like taste, was associated with another internal stimulus, like stomach sickness, or when an external stimulus, like light and noise, was associated with another exteroceptive stimulus, like shock to the feet—but not when the two modalities were mixed. And the results of the experiment bear out their conjecture. Rats were quick to learn to avoid fluid if it was tasty and if they were made sick to their stomachs, or if it was bright and noisy and they were shocked to the feet—but not if it was tasty and they were shocked to their feet, or if it was bright and noisy and they were made sick to their stomachs.

The concept of *salience* or *novelty* provides a second dimension of importance for learned aversions over long delays (Kalat & Rozin, 1970). In particular, aversions are most easily formed if the substance entering into the aversion is novel to the animal, that is, the animal has no or relatively little prior experience tasting the substance. Kalat and Rozin were able to show, as a matter of fact, that the salience factor was more important (within limits, anyway) in the formation of the aversion than the amount of time that was introduced as a delay between ingestion of the substance and the subsequent induction of illness. Perhaps you have already guessed that factors such as novelty and belongingness may go a long way in accounting for the familiar "bait shyness" which rats demonstrate. They are extraordinarily wary of novel foods in their environment—as anyone who has to keep them under control in their natural habitat can readily testify.

What accounts for long-delay learning? How can rats (and other ani-mals) bridge such long intervals between two events and learn to associate them? We have seen that factors such as belongingness and salience can be important variables in this regard, but what process might be of fundamental theoretical significance in connection with the phenomenon? Several have been identified, and while the issue is by no means settled finally, it appears that a notion based on *learned safety* of novel substances may do the best job of accounting for the currently available data (Rozin & Kalat, 1971; Kalat & Rozin, 1973; but see Revusky & Garcia, 1971, for a very potent possible alternative). Before developing the concept of learned safety, however, let us look at one obvious preliminary explanation of the phenomenon.

Quite simply, long-delay learning might be a simple artifact. Suppose, for example, that after ingesting saccharin-flavored water and then becoming sick, rats simply regurgitate whatever is in their stomachs, retasting it in the process. This would mean that instead of a delay between the tasting of a substance and the experience of illness, there would be direct temporal contiguity between the taste of the (regurgitated) saccharin and becoming ill. This cannot account for things, however, because of a very simple physiological fact: rats do not have the necessary reflex mechanisms to throw up. They are simply stuck with whatever they permit to enter their stomachs.[3] Other evidence works against an *aftertaste theory* too. In summarizing this evidence, Rozin and Kalat (1971) note among other things that rats can develop an aversion to a fluid in which temperature is the relevant cue for the development of the aversion (an aftertaste for temperature is a little difficult to imagine), and they can develop delayed learning to the taste of substances, like hydrochloric acid, for which it is possible to demonstrate that the stimulus is gone from the tongue's surface within a minute or so after the animal stops drinking.

Learned safety The *learned safety* approach asserts that during long-delay learning an animal is undergoing an active process of *learning* that something that it has just ingested is *safe* (Rozin & Kalat, 1971). The longer the interval of time between the ingestion of a novel substance and the *absence* of any ill effects, the surer the animal is that the new substance is, in fact, a safe one. According to this reasoning, in other words, the gradient of delay in taste-aversion learning is a simple measure of how confident the animal has become about a new food at any given point in time since its ingestion.

Kalat and Rozin (1973) have provided a very interesting experimental analysis of the predictions this theory has to make about long-delay learning. In one set of experiments, they varied the amount and span of experience animals had with a novel substance prior to the time it was

---

[3]There is a cautionary tale here for those who are quick to see natural selection working in "obvious" ways in the behavior of both animals and men. It is hard to imagine that an animal like the rat, whose diet can range from reinforced concrete and electrical insulation to the rather more nutritious and palatable substances provided by mankind's larder, would evolve without developing a mechanism for rapidly expelling an occasional gastronomic mistake. Perhaps the rat, a truly remarkable creature, is wiser than we think: it seems to have developed an exquisite mechanism for avoiding bad foods in the first place.

paired with illness-inducing apomorphine. Thus, some rats had seven daily exposures to the novel substance, others had one exposure, while still others had none. Two other sets of rats all had just one exposure to the novel substance prior to the time it was paired with poison, but one group had the initial exposure one day prior to poisoning, while the other had it three weeks prior to poisoning. The results of this set of experiments showed that it did not take much familiarity with a novel substance to render it resistant to a learned aversion over a 30-minute delay. Compared with the animals for which the substance was novel at the time poisoning occurred, animals with one prior exposure to it were not much different from animals with seven, and all failed to develop much of an aversion. Furthermore, if three weeks were permitted to elapse between a single initial exposure to the substance and its subsequent pairing with poison, the animals were just as unlikely to develop the aversion as if just one day had elapsed.

In a second set of experiments, Kalat and Rozin were able to provide further evidence that rats do, in fact, undergo an active process of learning that a novel substance is safe the longer it has been since they have ingested it without any ill effects. They showed that if a rat was exposed to a novel solution once $3^1/_2$ hours before being poisoned and again $^1/_2$ hour before the same poisoning, it developed a weaker aversion than if it had been exposed to the solution once $^1/_2$ hour before poisoning. It was, as a matter of fact, little different from an animal exposed to the solution 4 hours before poisoning. These results suggest that the animals were not responding to how *recently* they had drunk the substance but instead to when they had *first* drunk it, a fact which implies in turn that long-delay gradients occur not because animals have forgotten some novel substance, but because the animals have, in effect, decided that the novel substance is safe and therefore do not associate it with illness induced at lengthy intervals.

We have covered a broad expanse of territory in the last section of this chapter. Yet the problems we have encountered are perhaps among the most fundamental to the psychology of learning. This is true because they deal with a question as old as Aristotle: If learning is by association, what temporal bounds must be placed on associations if they are to be formed successfully? This is fundamental to Pavlovian conditioning, to instrumental conditioning, and to a number of other learning processes that we will encounter later on. Clearly the answers to this question tap many things. One direction that seems to be emerging from current work is that temporal relations in learning may be another class of constraints on learning that is, in part at least, species typical. Not all species appear to show long-delay learned aversions, for example, although a full investigation of this point remains to be done before we can be sure about the matter. Clearly, much important and useful work lies ahead, and some new and exciting things will no doubt emerge from the endeavor.

THREE

CONDITIONING, LEARNING, AND REINFORCEMENT: SELECTED THEORETICAL ISSUES

Now that the basic principles of reinforcement and learning have been discussed, we can move on in this chapter to an examination of some of the theoretical issues that are raised by a consideration of those principles. While the concept of reinforcement will be our primary concern in this regard, we shall also discuss some other theoretical issues that have become important that are less directly related to the principle of reinforcement. In at least one instance—that having to do with some of the theories about how reinforcing events work—we shall adopt a historical approach and show how some present-day thinking in the psychology of learning depends upon older knowledge and how, in other cases, unfruitful thinking has been modified or discarded. In the same vein, we shall also take a rapid look at some of the older, broader systematic approaches to the study of behavior—such as those of Hull and Tolman—so that you can become briefly acquainted with them and discover that although they are no longer of direct importance in shaping current day-to-day empirical and theoretical development of the science of psychology, the general problems, principles, and issues that they raised and examined are still important and very much alive in many cases.

It would be quite appropriate at this point to go into some detail with regard to theoretical matters, but we shall avoid that temptation because it would quickly take us into many more pages of this book than we can devote to all the topics that would have to be covered. If you are interested, there are many excellent sources dealing with theories of learning in great detail, and you will be rewarded if you seek them out. Among them we can mention books by Hilgard and Bower (1974) and Hill (1971).

WHAT IS LEARNED?

At the outset of things, there are some fundamental questions that underlie all theoretical approaches to the learning process, and we shall take a look at them first. The first can be stated thus: *What does an organism actually acquire as a function of experience or practice in some learning situation?* Does the organism learn an association between a stimulus and response, for example, and should we adopt a *stimulus-response*, or S-R, theory of learning (Spence, 1951)? If we do, we have the related problem of defining exactly what we mean by the concepts of stimulus and response, a problem which we discussed in some detail in Chapter 1 if you will recall. On the other hand, perhaps learning is to be conceived of as a new association between one or more stimuli (a *stimulus-stimulus*, or S-S, theory of learning), where the basic function of practice or experience is to provide a kind of "restructuring" of the way in which an organism perceives the world in which it lives. Note, too, that Pavlovian conditioning can be viewed as a theoretical model in which two stimuli, the CS and the UCS, are viewed as the elements which become related to each other through association. Perhaps, to continue, learning involves *both* S-R and S-S processes (a so-called *two-factor theory*) with one process applicable at one time or in one situation and the other process applicable at another time or in another situation. More generally, should we even conceptualize the learning process in terms like stimulus and response, which carry a great deal of connotative meaning from reflex physiology? Perhaps we should talk about learning in terms which are more cognitively tinged, as Tolman (1932) and Irwin (1971) have done, or perhaps we should use a model which is based on computer programming and design, which Miller, Galanter, and Pribram (1960) did when they introduced the concepts of images, plans, and feedback loops. More generally still, does learning involve the principle of *association* at all? At least one recent theoretical development (Weimer, 1973) stresses the notion that learning by association may not be a truly basic and fundamental process at all. Instead, Weimer insists, much human behavior may arise fairly automatically by virtue of being "programmed in" through generations and generations of behavioral adaptation and natural selection. If learning by association exists, it may be there just to put the final embellishments—the final adaptive polish—on the things people and animals do.[1]

We are left then with two points about the question of what is learned. The first concerns itself with the problem of what *materials*—stimuli, responses, or what have you—go into the learning process. Just what is the stuff of learning, anyway? The second concerns itself with the *model* that makes the best sense out of how these materials get put together as the learning process runs its course. Psychologists are by no means in agreement about either of these points, as we have just seen, but the progress of the psychology of learning will no doubt be measured in major part by the progress that we make in seeking answers to them.

---

[1] Weimer refers specifically to the acquisition of language, but his thinking may mark a return on the part of the psychology of learning to a point of view which stresses in general the natural endowment of organisms as opposed to the things they learn from experience. Psychology is known for its swings from one pole to the other of this "nature-nurture" controversy, a controversy which is probably largely unresolvable because there is much of value to be said on both sides of the question.

A problem of central importance in this chapter has to do with the role that reinforcement is assumed to play when new learning occurs. Some theorists, Hull (1943) for example, have said that whatever the funda- mental nature of the learning process, experience or practice in a new situation has no effect—learning will not occur—unless practice is reinforced. For a *reinforcement theory* of this sort, there exists the problem of specifying the precise mechanism by which a reinforcer does, in fact, reinforce. Does food, for example, reinforce because it stimulates certain taste receptors on the tongue as it is eaten, or because its ingestion reduces the intensity of some motive or drive like hunger? In other words, when a theorist makes a reinforcement operation a necessary, integral part of the conditions under which learning occurs, he often goes on to adopt some "strong" definition of the concept of reinforcement.

Other theorists, Guthrie (1935, 1959) for example, postulate that reinforcement is not necessary for learning to occur. Generally, the only requirement is that the elements which are to constitute the new learning (whether they are stimuli, responses, or whatever) be contiguous—be closely paired or related to each other in time. Psychologists who maintain a *nonreinforcement* position of this sort must face the demon- strable fact that operations of reward and punishment are powerful tools to use in the control of behavior. Thus if the theorist maintains that reinforcement is not actually necessary for learning to occur, and if he satisfies himself with an operational, "weak" definition of reinforce- ment, we can ask what position he then assigns the concept of reinforcement in his theory. We shall examine some of these positions as we turn now to a brief discussion of some of the more fundamental theoretical approaches to the analysis of conditioning and learning.

SOME BASIC APPROACHES TO LEARNING THEORY

LEARNING BY CONTIGUITY

We owe to Aristotle the notion that two events will be associated when they occur closely together. To make this statement intelligible, as we have seen, we have to state what kinds of things become associated and under what conditions association will occur. In learning theory, one of the most common ideas is that stimuli and responses are the associated factors, and that simple contiguity in time is all that is required for an association to occur.

According to a *contiguity* view of learning, then, stimuli come to elicit responses that they had not previously elicited because, perhaps quite by accident, these stimuli occur simultaneously with certain responses. The model for this process is Pavlovian conditioning. Here we elicit an unconditioned response by using an appropriate unconditional stimulus at the same time that we present a conditional stimulus. Because the CS is simultaneous with the response (or nearly so, depending upon the time relations between CS and UCS), it comes—through association—to elicit the response.

We have just described a stimulus-response, or S-R, view based on learning by contiguity. While Pavlovian conditioning can provide an accurate model for such an S-R view, we should point out that an alternative view of Pavlovian conditioning stresses the fact that it involves the pairing of two *stimuli*, the CS and the UCS, and that it is this, a stimulus-stimulus, or S-S, association which is formed when the two stimuli are put together (e.g., Rescorla & Solomon, 1967). To keep this apparent discrepancy straight, remember that it is possible to build models for learning which view different things to be the critical factors that are put together through the learning process. The important point about the contiguity view is not so much the question of whether it is stimuli that are put together with stimuli, or stimuli with responses, but rather that the formation of the association between the elements depends upon their contiguous association and nothing else.

One of the early advocates of an S-R contiguity theory of learning was E. R. Guthrie (1935, 1952), who had this to say about the learning process: "A combination of stimuli which has accompanied a movement will on its recurrence tend to be followed by that movement." Later, Guthrie (1959) modified that position to require that an organism be paying attention to a particular combination of stimuli before learning occurs by contiguity, but the essence of his approach remained essentially the same. For Guthrie, Pavlovian conditioning of S and R provided the model for all learning processes.

In most cases of instrumental conditioning, however, we cannot observe conditional stimuli (remember, for example, our discussion of the rat pressing the lever in the Skinner box); and so in Guthrie's theory they take on the character of hypothetical constructs. That is to say, we invent some conditional stimuli for a particular set of learned responses. In the case of lever pressing, some of the conditional stimuli are presumed to be kinesthetic, according to Guthrie. In other words, the rat makes a series of movements, these stimulate the sense organs of the muscles, and this combination of muscular sensations serves as one primary source of conditional stimuli. Another important source of conditional stimuli, again chiefly internal, comes from sensations associated with a particular condition of motivation such as hunger or thirst; these are called *maintaining stimuli*. Maintaining stimuli have the important characteristic that they remain relatively constant throughout the learning of a long sequence of responses such as that required to traverse a maze or to run off a long chain of behavior. This, as we shall see, turns out to be a useful construct to have at hand when the role of reinforcement in S-R contiguity theory must be specified.

As you may have guessed, Guthrie's definition of a stimulus makes it pretty physiological and peripheral in character. Certainly his stimulus is not a very cognitive one of the type we discussed at the beginning of Chapter 1. By the same token, his definition of response is also quite physiological in tone; a response is quite literally something very close to a simple muscle movement.

With respect to the definition of response, as a matter of fact, Guthrie is dissatisfied with the typical experiment on instrumental behavior because, he claims, it examines the *results* of behavior, not the behavior itself. Take the lever-pressing case, for example. In the Skinner box we find out how many times per minute the rat presses the lever; we are not necessarily interested in the *way* in which the lever is pressed by the animal. Guthrie objected to this approach because he believed that it is the association of particular *movements* of the animal with stimuli that is really important and that the result of the movement is only secondary. Skinner—whose fundamental theoretical approach (to the extent that he admits of one at all) is probably closer to that of Guthrie than anyone else—takes the contrary view. He believes that the best way to define a response is, in fact, in terms of the end results of behavior upon the environment. The important thing is that the lever gets pressed and that the rate of lever pressing becomes a steady, consistent correlate of a set of experimental conditions. It is immaterial how the organism manages to accomplish this feat. Sometimes the animal does use its feet—or its mouth. We have seen at least one rat quite spontaneously courting the lever with a wiggle—its south pole preceding its north—to produce an emphatic lever press with a carefully placed squat, for hundreds of trials. A phenomenon such as this bears testimony to the ability of simple reward training to strengthen many types of behavior—even behavior that is patently not the most efficient to get the job done (though most organisms will usually "short-circuit" bizarre methods of responding and eventually adopt more efficient and direct methods of producing reinforcement). The phenomenon also bears testimony to Guthrie's point that much can be learned about the qualitative properties of behavior in particular from studying the precise movements that an organism makes (Guthrie & Horton, 1946).

Modern development of the theory of learning by contiguity has taken place in the hands of many, but perhaps W. K. Estes has been most consistently associated with it. We have already had a chance to see (Chapter 1) how he accounted for an example of sudden and rapid learning using a one-element model for the contiguous association of a stimulus and response, and that is but an example of a long history of theoretical contributions (e.g., Estes, 1950, 1959, 1964b, 1969, 1970, 1973). Estes' studies have ranged from an attempt to describe conditioning and learning in terms of statistical mathematical models for the manner in which a stimulus comes to be associated with 'a response, to theoretical treatments of human memory processes. While we shall have occasion to meet some of his work—and other examples of a basic contiguity approach, too—later on, his contributions have been prodigious and numerous to the point of being far beyond things to which we can do justice here. You will be rewarded, however, if you seek them out yourself.

The role of reinforcement in learning by contiguity By now it may be obvious that in an S-R contiguity theory, reinforcement does not have to occur in order for particular stimulus and response events to become associated; mere contiguity can bring that about. In Guthrie's parent theory, for example, reinforcement operations are assigned two rather simple mechanical functions. First and foremost, a reinforcing stimulus provides an end to the particular sequence of stimuli and responses that the experimenter wants the organism to learn. Reward serves to prevent the organism from unlearning what it has already learned by keeping it from reacting in other ways to the stimuli that lead to the desired response pattern. Food at the end of a maze for a hungry rat, for example, keeps the rat there instead of allowing it to wander through the maze unlearning proper turns and learning new turns into blind alleys. Thus, the rat eventually does learn the maze.

Estes' (1969, 1971) thoughts concerning reinforcement are in some respects consistent with those of Guthrie by and large, but they are considerably more developed and placed within a much more general theory of learning and performance. Estes' theory is rather complicated for outline in complete detail here, but the first of its primary notions is consistent with basic contiguity theory: learning is a process of formation of associations by contiguity. Estes locates learning not so much in the formation of associations between peripheral stimuli and responses as in the formation of associations between central, higher-order stimuli as well as between stimuli and responses. Furthermore, the concepts of stimulus and response, particularly when applied to complicated forms of behavior like human language and cognition, assume complex structures. Estes (1971) states that such behavior may be "better understood in terms of the operation of rules, principles, strategies, and the like than in terms of successions of responses to particular stimuli [p. 23]." Finally in this regard, newly formed associations are stored in *memory* where they are represented according to certain rules, and from which they can be retrieved when circumstances warrant, i.e., when appropriate environmental cues trigger recall.

Now the function of reinforcement in Estes' theory is not to strengthen directly the formation of new associations; simple contiguity suffices for that. In this regard he is in close harmony with Guthrie. Instead, reinforcing events have their effects upon *performance* which, in Estes' terms, means the tendency for a given sequence of learned responses to run to some final conclusion. The function of reinforcement is to provide *feedback* based on the anticipation (learned or otherwise) of impending reward or punishment which *summates* with current stimuli (or stimuli recalled from memory) in the learning situation and so *guides* behavior preferentially along one path as opposed to another. In essence, in other words, Estes' theory emphasizes a cybernetic model for the influence of reinforcement upon performance: behavior is guided toward goals and away from aversive situations through positive or negative feedback from the reinforcing event.

COGNITIVE OR SIGN LEARNING

Let us now look at a second general theory of learning, an approach closely associated with the name of E. C. Tolman. Tolman (1932, 1951, 1959) developed and expanded what he called a "purposive" theory of learning. His theory deemphasizes Pavlovian conditioning as the prime model for the learning process and replaces that model with what he calls "sign learning." This means that animals usually learn (when running a maze, for example) the succession of stimuli or "signs" that lead to or "signify" the goal. In contrast to Guthrie's approach, Tolman's theory stresses the notion that organisms learn relations among *stimuli* rather than relations among stimuli and responses per se. In a characteristically epigrammatical phrase, Tolman (1948) says that rats develop "cognitive maps" of the maze.

One of the chief characteristics of Tolman's theory is that it was subject to frequent change. Throughout a metamorphosis that lasted twenty years or so, however, Tolman consistently emphasized the importance of *purpose* in the learning of new behavior. Learned behavior is always directed and oriented toward some end, some *goal*.

In his last statement (Tolman, 1959), the chief learning construct for Tolman was the *means-end-readiness*. One form of a means-end-readiness can be diagramed $S_1R_1 \rightarrow S_2$. This says that if an organism is exposed to a stimulus pattern S_1 it acquires a "belief" that the performance of some behavior R_1 will lead to a second stimulus pattern S_2. A second form of means-end-readiness can be diagramed $S_1 \rightarrow S_2$. This signifies that an organism learns that the presence of one stimulus pattern S_1 will be accompanied or followed shortly by the occurrence of a second stimulus pattern S_2. This type of means-end-readiness is reserved for events associated with Pavlovian conditioning and conditioned reinforcement, for example, where learning is presumed to be an essentially pure association between stimuli.

A second important construct in Tolman's theory is that of *expectancy*. While a means-end-readiness is a general sort of "belief" acquired over a relatively long past history of an organism, an expectancy is a state aroused when a means-end-readiness is evoked on a particular single occasion. For example, when a rat is placed in the start box of a runway on, say, the twenty-fourth learning trial, the stimuli of the start box arouse an expectancy that a particular goal object such as food can be obtained in the goal box if the rat runs the runway. The expectancy elicited on trial 24 is due, however, to the fact that the rat has been placed in the start box on 23 preceding trials. From this previous experience, the rat has developed a means-end-readiness that start-box stimuli, followed by running the runway, will lead to food.

Two other things which distinguish Tolman's approach are his notions concerning the concepts of stimulus and response. Both are quite different from, say, Guthrie's. For Tolman, a stimulus is a *perception*; it is an environmental event that is *processed* by the organism and thus colored by the organism's past history. For example, the way in which an animal perceives the sights and sounds of the start box of a maze depends upon what has happened in the start box before, what has happened previously in the goal box, and so on. If the stimulus of Guthrie or Estes is a physiological, peripheral one, then Tolman's is at the other end of that dimension: it is a central, cognitive one. Similarly, Tolman does not think of a response as a collection of muscle twitches or glandular secretions, the general approach associated with Guthrie. Rather, learned behavior is composed of *performances*. Performances are *acts*. They are classes of behavior that are defined in terms of some end result or goal; they are "patterns of organism-environment rearrangements." Tolman notes, for example, that rats in a Skinner box adopt all sorts of methods of pressing the lever, sometimes using their noses, sometimes their paws, and—at least on one occasion that we have already noted— their rear ends. For him, as for Skinner (1935), these are all the same performances because they all accomplish the same end result. For Guthrie, however, they represent different responses because they involve different patterns of motor movements, each associated with its own unique set of conditional stimuli.

Sign learning and reinforcement　For Tolman, as we have seen, learning lies in the development of means-end-readinesses. Tolman's approach, strictly speaking, does not require that practice be reinforced for the means-end-readiness to develop; nor does Tolman advocate some particular strong definition of the concept of reinforcement. Yet he does attempt to account for the fact that positive and negative reinforcing stimuli (in their operational sense) have powerful effects upon behavior. This he does through the concepts of *value* and *valence*.

If a motive such as hunger is induced by depriving an animal of food, then food as a goal object has positive *value* for the animal in the sense that it is needed to repair internal deficits produced by starvation. Whether food, in fact, does have positive value for a particular animal could be determined objectively by finding out if the animal will eat food when given the opportunity, or, more generally, by finding out if the animal will repeat behavior that leads to food. In addition to their value, however, goal objects also have a *valence*. Valence, in Tolman's terms, reflects the "goodness" or "badness" of the particular goal object that the animal expects to find at the end of a maze on some particular occasion. If a hungry animal has been rewarded on a number of past occasions with positively valued food, for example, the animal expects something of the particular goodness associated with food to be in the goal box when it begins to run the maze on a new occasion. This expectancy constitutes the valence of the goal object of food on that particular trial.

Impact of Tolman's theory　It is almost impossible to give the true flavor of Tolman's approach in a few paragraphs. In some respects, his injection of surplus meaning—and his predilection for stringing together with hyphens the words which label the constructs (viz., sign-gestalt-expectation, means-end-readiness)—casts, for some, a bothersome aura about his point of view. Besides, Tolman consistently wrote with a chuckle lurking somewhere in the background, always called his theory programmatic, and was ready to shift a point of view at a moment's notice. Yet Tolman knew what he was up to, and the cognitive, purposive aspects of his theory are the parts of it that have survived to influence the theoretical side of the psychology of learning as we know it today. Whereas concepts like "attention" or "cognition" were taboo in theoretical camps apart from Tolman's at the time Tolman was developing his theory, they label areas of psychology which, 15 years later, are at the very center of both theory and research—as a good part of this book testifies.

EFFECT OR REINFORCEMENT THEORY

We have just had a broad look at two general approaches to learning which say that, fundamentally, reinforcement is unnecessary for learning to occur. An alternative theory, broadly conceived, is closely associated with the names of Thorndike (1898), Hull (1943, 1952), and Miller (1959, 1963). While these psychologists have developed theories of learning which have differed in important detail, they have all assumed somewhere that learning cannot occur unless behavior is *reinforced* during the learning process. Simple contiguity between stimulus and response is not enough. In general, there must also be some consequence or *effect* of the new behavior before new learning will occur, a reinforcement operation in particular.

The origins of effect theory   The origins of modern effect theory and of many of our notions about the things characteristic of stimuli that reinforce probably come from Darwin and the theory of natural selection. Darwin and his successors tried to explain the process of species evolution in terms of natural selective breeding. The adaptive characteristics of organisms survive, said Darwin, and the unadaptive ones die out. Naturalists have pointed out many examples of anatomical and physiological characteristics that are adaptive and that seem to be perpetuated through selective breeding. Thus, in evolution, biological changes in organisms have "good" and "bad" effects, and according to the theory of natural selection, only the changes with good effects survive.

It was apparent to many early workers in evolution that behavioral patterns also provide good examples of the survival of adaptive mechanisms. Furthermore, in the lifetime of an individual of a species there appears to be a process of selective adaptation. Organisms seem to learn those things which are useful—they learn the location of food supplies, water, hiding places, and so forth.

Thus, the argument goes, adaptive behavior (that which preserves the animal from harm and keeps it fed and sheltered) survives and becomes learned, but unadaptive behavior does not. This concept was combined with the hedonistic ideas of utilitarianism. Pleasure, it was held, is associated with adaptive behavior and pain with nonadaptive behavior. Thus pleasure and pain were brought into an adaptive theory. These notions—a behavioral hedonism combined with the survival of adaptive traits—have had an enormous influence on psychology in general and upon the psychology of learning in particular. One very important area in this regard is that of *behavior genetics*, an area which receives an enormous amount of current research attention (e.g., Bovet, Bovet-Nitti, & Oliverio, 1969; Hirsch, 1967), and there has been a growing reemphasis on Darwinian principles in some more specific regions of the psychology of learning as well (e.g., Staddon & Simmelhag, 1971; Hinde & Stevenson-Hinde, 1973).

Thorndike and Hull   E. L. Thorndike (1898, 1911) was one of the first experimental psychologists to explore the relation between reinforcement and adaptive mechanisms, and it is to him that we owe the term *principle of effect*. Thorndike had worked with animals and their ways of learning for many years and was struck by the extent to which a particular bit of behavior was shaped and fixated by its effects or consequences. His principle of effect states, in general, that behavior is *stamped in*, or increased in strength, when it is followed by a "satisfying state of affairs" (reward). Correspondingly, though Thorndike later modified his position in this regard, for reasons we shall discuss in Chapter 6, behavior is weakened when it is followed by an "annoying state of affairs" (punishment). As Hilgard and Bower (1974) note, Thorndike defines "satisfiers" and "annoyers" in terms that we would consider today to be quite operational. Thus, a satisfying state of affairs was "one which the animal does nothing to avoid, often doing things which maintain or renew it," while an annoying state of affairs was "one which the animal does nothing to preserve, often doing things which put an end to it."

Thorndike's work was of tremendous significance in providing a bridge between Darwin's theories of natural selection and adaptive behavior and the young experimental psychology of learning. He was also the first to identify many concepts—not only reinforcement but many others—which appear as major components of present-day psychologies of learning. It remained for Clark L. Hull (1943, 1952), however, to take a Darwinian-Thorndikian approach and turn it into a truly systematic and elegant theory of learning.

Hull's approach to science in general, and to the science of psychology in particular, was Newtonian. The learning process was to be described by means of postulates and corollaries, and the business of the experimental psychology of learning was to arrive at testable hypotheses about behavior by a process of logical *deduction* from the postulates and corollaries. If hypotheses turned out to be in error when put to experimental test, the elements of the theory were to be changed accordingly. A second general characteristic of Hull's approach was that the relationships among the elements which composed the system were expressed in quantitative mathematical terms using models borrowed from traditional physics. To see examples of this characteristic, one needs only to turn to any of Hull's books (e.g., Hull, 1943), but Hull's mathematical schemes have little impact per se on the psychology of learning today. Instead, his impact is currently expressed in terms of the problems he helped to identify, many of which are still important and worthy of additional development.

CONDITIONS FOR SIMPLE REINFORCEMENT

In this section, we shall look at some attempts that have been made to specify the necessary and sufficient conditions that one must establish to generate a reinforcing state of affairs. While we will be examining a good deal of experimental evidence, it is important to remember that much of the material we shall be covering was stimulated by theoretical mat- ters—some of which we have just discussed in the last section. It is also important to recognize that some of the material under discussion is important primarily in the historical sense. While it was once the case that argument raged over whether drive reduction was necessary for reinforcement, or whether some approach based on the concept of incentives was a better theoretical alternative, for example, such is no longer the case. Instead, psychologists have been forced into the more defensible position that there are likely to be many mechanisms through which reinforcement may work, some better described in physiological terms, some appropriate for one species at one particular time and place, and others appropriate for other species under still different circum- stances. It is no longer sensible, as Hull would once have had it, to regard reinforcement as a single unitary principle to be encompassed by just one theoretical postulate. Nevertheless, it is important to remember that much of what we study today is important because of both theoretical and empirical developments of the not-too-distant past, and much can be learned by seeking the historical roots of modern-day problems.

DRIVE REDUCTION AND REINFORCEMENT

The drive-reduction theory of reinforcement states, in its most general form, that reinforcers are always related to specific motives in animals and men. Events which reinforce, in Hull's initial formulation (Hull, 1943), are always those which reduce *organic needs*, an assumption which obviously derives from a Darwinian approach to things. According to a simple need-reduction point of view, responses which eventually lead to food and to eating will be reinforced and thus learned, because the ingestion of food reduces or eliminates the need state. By the same token, responses which lead an organism away from painful stimulation will be reinforced by a reduction in the intensity of the pain.

Hull modified his bare need-reduction definition of reinforcement to account for the fact that in many situations it *takes time* for physiological needs to be repaired. Given the effects of delay of reinforcement on at least some forms of learned behavior (cf. Chapter 2), you can see that this would place serious strain on a theory that postulated the reduction of actual physiological *needs* as the essential reinforcement mechanism. To avoid this problem, Hull introduced the concepts of *drive*, D, and *drive stimulus*, S_D. Drives are intervening variables that are correlated with operations that produce physiological needs, though strictly speaking they are defined in terms such as the time that an organism has been deprived of food, the strength of a punishing shock, and so forth. Drive stimuli are patterns of stimuli associated uniquely with individual drives. Thus, thirst would have a set of drive stimuli associated with it (like the feel of a dry mouth, for example), while hunger would have its unique set, too (like stimulation arising from stomach contractions). Furthermore, the strength of a drive stimulus would increase with the strength of the drive with which it was associated; longer periods of food deprivation should produce more intense drive stimuli. Given these concepts, Hull could assume that the intensity of a drive stimulus could be reduced very rapidly compared with the amount of time it would take to repair the need associated with the drive, and by this means, he solved the problem introduced by facts associated with delay of reinforcement. His final theory was then one which postulates drive-stimulus reduction as the necessary and sufficient condition for reinforcement.

Hull never embarked on very much of an experimental program to test his theory of reinforcement. It remained for Neal Miller to do that (Miller & Dollard, 1941; Miller, 1951, 1959). For Miller, a drive could be produced by any stimulus if it were made strong enough to "impel action." Thus, food deprivation produces hunger drive because it arouses "strong internal stimuli" and, presumably, initiates food-seeking behavior. Strong electric shocks and loud sounds could also function as drive stimuli. According to Miller, then, a reinforcing state of affairs is simply that which produces a rapid reduction in the intensity of a drive stimulus.

Mouth versus stomach effects and reinforcement by drive reduction
Although Miller and his students did many experiments testing the drive-reduction theory of reinforcement, let us look at just one issue that he studied experimentally. Take hunger as an example of a basic drive that provides strong internal stimuli and food as an example of a substance that reduces hunger-drive stimuli and so, according to drive-reduction theory, functions to reinforce the learning of new behavior. Food has two properties that are of special interest to us at the moment. First of all, once eaten, it enters the stomach, where the processes of digestion begin to occur. Correlated with this will be a number of things: changes in stomach distension, changes in the frequency of stomach contractions, and changes in a host of other internal physiological conditions. Some of these changes occur rather quickly; others take longer; but all fall into the general class of events that are presumed to constitute a reduction in hunger drive.

Food has a second property, however, which—in an intact organism—always goes along with the process of ingestion: food has taste, and in the process of eating, food is tasted. Furthermore, as we saw in Chapter 2, sugar (which is a sweet-tasting food) can function very well as a reinforcer for learning. Given these two properties of food, a problem is raised that is critical for drive-reduction theory: Does food function as a reinforcer because it reduces the intensity of hunger-drive stimuli, or because it has certain stimulus properties that trigger the sense of taste or smell in some special way, perhaps in a way that is innately "pleasant"? According to the latter view (about which we will have a great deal to say later), food as a reinforcing stimulus might function as a highly valued *incentive* and, if anything, *produce* drive in the learning situation rather than reduce it. Thus, it becomes crucial from a pure drive-reduction point of view to separate "mouth factors," like taste, from "stomach factors," like stomach distension, and to show that the latter—alone—can mediate the process of reinforcement.

The experiments that were done on this problem adopted the general strategy of feeding food to rats under one of two conditions: Food was eaten by mouth in the normal way, or the mouth was bypassed and food was injected directly into the stomach through a surgically placed gastric tube. Then a comparison was made between the relative efficiency of these two procedures in reducing hunger drive, on the one hand, and reinforcing the learning of a new response, on the other. If drive-reduction theory were correct, we would have expected that direct injection of food into the stomach would be sufficient to produce both these effects.

Miller and Kessen (1952) fitted rats with stomach fistulas—surgically implanted tubes leading from the skin surface on the back of the rat directly to the stomach—deprived the rats of food, and trained them to go to a goal box at the end of one arm of a T maze. Five rats in one group (the mouth–no delay group) found a dish which contained 13 cubic centimeters of milk that they could drink by mouth in the correct end box, and 13 cubic centimeters of an isotonic saline solution that they could drink the same way in the incorrect end box. Six rats in a second group (the stomach-injection group) received a direct stomach injection of 13 cubic centimeters of milk for a correct choice and an injection of 13 cubic centimeters of saline solution for an incorrect choice. Six rats in a third group (the mouth–delay group) also received 13 cubic centimeters of milk or saline solution by mouth for correct and incorrect choices, but the rewards were not presented to the rats until after they had been in the goal boxes for 7 minutes and 35 seconds—the time that was required to make stomach injections for the stomach-injection group. This delay group was run as a control to counter the possible argument that, in Miller and Kessen's (1952) terms, "The effect of reward begins with the first sip when milk is taken by mouth, but only after a considerable volume of milk has been injected directly into the stomach."

The results of the experiment are shown in Figures 3.1 and 3.2. All reinforcement conditions eventually led the rats to choose the correct arm of the T on 100 percent of the free-choice trials. The rats that received milk by mouth learned fastest, but after 35 to 40 free-choice

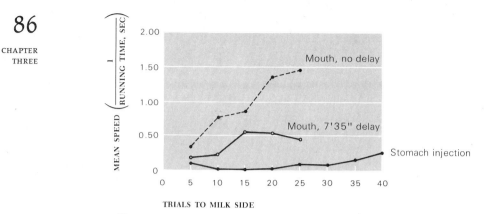

Figure 3.1
Mean speed of running as a function of method of giving a milk reinforcer.
Milk taken by mouth produces a progressive increase in speed across trials,
but milk injected directly into the stomach does not. (Miller & Kessen,
1952.)

trials, the rats rewarded with stomach injections of milk had also learned.
Figure 3.1 shows, however, that rats receiving milk by direct stomach
injection did not increase their running speed to the correct arm, while
rats receiving milk by mouth did. This result suggests that drinking milk
by mouth may produce an increase in a nonlearning, motivational factor
(due, perhaps, to some kind of mouth factor associated with taste) which
does not appear when milk is injected directly into the stomach.
However, the important result of the experiment is that rats could learn
which was the correct arm of the T on the basis of stomach injections
alone, though they may not have become as highly motivated to get
there as rats receiving milk by mouth.

Figure 3.2
Percent correct responses as a function of method of giving a milk reinforcer. In each case, learning occurs, but it takes somewhat longer for this
to happen if milk is injected directly into the stomach than if it is given by
mouth. (Miller & Kessen, 1952.)

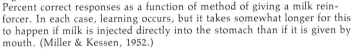
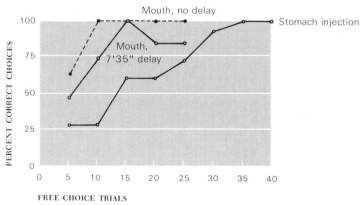

Taken as a whole, this experiment and a great many others like it (see Deese & Hulse, 1967, for a complete review), demonstrate in convincing fashion that food injected directly into the stomach can produce effects which have all the hallmarks of primary reinforcement and so support the drive-reduction theory of reinforcement. It should not be forgotten, however, that these same experiments show that food taken by mouth functions generally as a much more effective reinforcer than food injected directly into the stomach, and so it would be dangerous to conclude that stomach factors alone are responsible for reinforcement based on a substance like food. Another important point to remember about this work is that it stresses a very physiological approach to the problem of reinforcement. This is a good general emphasis to adopt in looking for the factors—both in the central nervous sytem and else-where—that modulate primary reinforcement processes; but alternative emphases are available, and we shall look at some of them shortly. Obviously, however, an understanding of what is going on beneath the skin will be of ultimate fundamental importance.

INCENTIVES AND REINFORCEMENT

Though drive-reduction theory can hold its own in accounting for many examples of simple reinforcement, there is an alternative approach that we mention at this time because it adopts a point of emphasis which is a polar opposite from that of drive reduction. The germ of the theory was contained in a portion of a talk given by F. D. Sheffield at Brown University in 1954 (Sheffield, 1966). Sheffield had this to say: "If one dangles a carrot in front of a rabbit, it does not relax the rabbit; on the contrary, it arouses him to action. [If] the carrot is on the wrong side of a wire screen, the action may involve considerable struggling." Sheffield then went on to develop the proposition that reinforcing stimuli operate as they do because they tend to act as *incentives*; that is, they are events that *increase* or *induce* drives. A proposition that emphasizes the drive-*producing* properties of reinforcing events is, of course, in complete contrast to the drive-reduction approach, which emphasizes the notion that reinforcing events are those which tend to reduce or eliminate the tensions associated with basic drives like hunger or thirst. An example from the experimental literature readily illustrates what Sheffield was talking about and demonstrates the contrast between an incentive and a drive-reduction approach to the problem of reinforcement.

Sheffield, Wulff, and Backer (1951) asked this question about the reinforcing effects of sexual behavior in rats: Would male rats learn an instrumental response when, as a reinforcing event, they were permitted to copulate with another rat, but not to ejaculate? This question distinguishes between the incentive properties of sexual stimulation (and the consummatory activity of intromission and copulatory movement that such stimulation elicits) and the drive reduction that would occur through ejaculation. First, 24 male rats were pretested, in a circular box 30 inches in diameter, to see if they would copulate with a female in heat.

Of the 24, 8 copulated with the female, but the investigators removed the female before actual ejaculation occurred. Of the remaining males, 6 showed "sustained pursuit" of the female, but never actually copulated. The 10 male rats who neither copulated nor showed interest were not used in the rest of the experiment.

All rats were trained to run a 32-inch runway which opened into the circular goal box in which they had been pretested. Half the rats who had copulated during the pretest (the experimental group) found a female in heat in the goal box and were permitted to copulate. However, the female was removed before ejaculation occurred. The other half of the copulators (the control group) found a male "companion" rat in the goal box; the male companion was removed after two minutes or after two attempts had been made to copulate (male rats will, on occasion, show copulatory activity with other male rats). Of the remaining 6 rats who had not copulated, but who had shown "interest" during the pretest (the noncopulator group), half were run to a male and half to a female in heat. A total of 28 trials, 2 per day, were run in the alley, and measures of running speed were taken over these trials. The results of the experiment are shown in Figure 3.3.

The figure indicates that the speed of running increased for all groups but that the rats in the experimental group eventually ran fastest. Note also that the rats in the control group ran faster than the rats in the noncopulator group. The investigators attribute this result to the fact that

Figure 3.3
Reinforcing effects of different types of sexual experience. Experimental animals found a female in the goal box, control animals found a male, while noncopulators found a male or female, but never attempted to copulate. While copulation was permitted for all animals, no animal was ever allowed to ejaculate (Sheffield, Wulff, & Backer, 1951.)

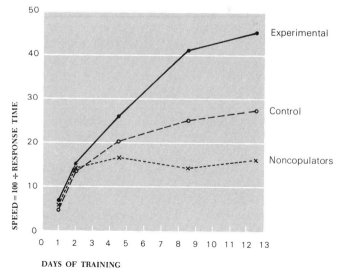

DAYS OF TRAINING

the control rats had copulated during the pretest and attempted to copulate during the learning task even though they found a male rat in the goal box. That is, they exhibited some of the consummatory behavior normally aroused by sexual stimulation, even though this behavior was aimed in rather misdirected fashion at male rats. The rats in the noncopulator group, on the other hand, never exhibited any of the behavior normally elicited by sexual stimulation. This was true even though some of them were run to a female in heat in the goal box. Taken as a whole, the results of the experiment show clearly that female rats are excellent reinforcing stimuli for male rats and that they function as such in the absence of anything that could reasonably be called a reduction in primary sex drive on the part of the male.

Consummatory responses and reinforcement In accounting for these data, Sheffield stressed the notion that incentives were effective because they evoked vigorous *consummatory activity*, activity which *completed* and thus *consummated* some goal-oriented activity. In the Sheffield, Wulff, and Backer experiment, the rats in the control group that ran to male lures ran faster than rats in the noncopulator group, even though some of the latter actually ran to females in heat. In other words, rats in the control group exhibited at least *some* of the consummatory behavior aroused normally by sexual stimulation, while rats in the noncopulator group never did. Thus, the aspect of the goal animal that was most consistently correlated with its incentive value was not its sex at all. Instead, the most consistent indicator of incentive value was the degree to which the goal animal, whether it was male or female, elicited the consummatory responses normally triggered by sexual stimulation. In other work in this regard, Sheffield, Roby, and Campbell (1954) showed that rats would run faster in a straight runway the greater the vigor of the consummatory response elicited by a liquid reward in the goal box. They varied the vigor of consummation by varying the sweetness of the fluid, using water, saccharin, dextrose, or dextrose plus saccharin as test solutions for different animals. The data show a remarkable correlation between the vigor of the consummatory response and the speed with which the rats ran the alley. Fast running was consistently associated with vigorous drinking, slow running with lackadaisical drinking.

As Sheffield and his associates pointed out, their experiment tends to rule out a drive-reduction theory as adequate to account for their data because saccharin was effective as a reinforcer even though it has no caloric value (but see Valenstein & Weber, 1965). However, as they also note, the sweetness of the various solutions may have been the critical feature determining their effectiveness as reinforcers. This is true because as the sweetness of the solutions that were used increased, so did the vigor of the consummatory response, and we cannot be sure which of these two variables was, in fact, producing the observed differences of running speed in the alley. Snyder and Hulse (1961) obtained data which also rule against a pure consummatory response explanation of reinforcement, and Miller (1963) brings together a great deal of evidence which shows that it cannot be a *peripheral* consummatory response, at least, which is the critical variable. That is, it cannot be literally the muscular movements of copulation or of drinking which account for the reinforcing effects of sexual activity or of fluids ingested by mouth (and that is a literal interpretation of Sheffield's position).

Perhaps the most recent outgrowth of a theoretical approach to reinforcement which stresses, at least in part, the importance of consummatory activity is the "biological" theory of reinforcement of Glickman and Schiff (1967). These theorists developed an approach which emphasizes the importance of species-typical behaviors of approach and withdrawal to appropriate stimuli in the organization of behavior and which goes on to postulate the view that "reinforcement basically involves selective facilitation of motor patterns organized within the brain stem." They postulate, in turn, that factors such as the sight of an appropriate goal object or the taste of a rewarding fluid work to get reinforcement underway by *activating* some appropriate underlying *neural circuit* that is intimately involved in the *motor* sequences of the appropriate consummatory activity. They point to a host of experiments, many based on a direct study of central nervous system structures, which indicate that regions of the brain involved, say, in the control of feeding and drinking or sexual behavior also mediate reinforcing effects associated with food, liquids, or sexual objects. In a very real sense, however, their theory appears to be but a removal of a consummatory response theory—together with some proper emphasis upon the importance of response-specific stimulation—from the periphery of the organism to the organism's central nervous system. And that is almost certainly the proper direction in which to go.

The fractional goal response Before we leave the general topics of reinforcement and incentives, we must introduce a concept that is of theoretical importance in connection not only with incentives but also with a good many other processes of learning that we shall be discussing later in the book. The concept, which has a long and venerable history and is interesting if for no other reason than that alone, is that of the *fractional goal response* r_g (Hull, 1930, 1931; Spence, 1956, 1960; Amsel, 1967). It is a particularly useful tool whenever the theoretician must account for the way events of one kind or another are *mediated* or *bridged* in time or space by an organism. It is, as a matter of fact, one of the earliest historical examples of a well-developed mediating mechanism in the psychology of learning.

Suppose, to take a very simple example, a hungry rat enters a goal box after running through a maze and finds a goal stimulus, an S_G, of a piece of food. Since the rat is hungry, it is quite likely that the goal stimulus will elicit, perhaps reflexively, a characteristic overt goal response R_G. The overt goal response would include behavior we have talked about under the general heading of consummatory responses; in the case of food, for example, it might consist of seizing, chewing, and swallowing the food.

Now R_G occurs directly as a function of the appearance of S_G, but there are other stimuli that could, through Pavlovian conditioning, become associated with R_G. One such class of stimuli would be those of the goal box itself, since these are present as the rat finds and eats the food. To the extent that stimuli in other parts of the maze are similar to those of the goal box, they too could become associated with the goal response. The same thing would be true of drive stimuli arising from the rat's particular state of deprivation (Guthrie called these maintaining stimuli, if you will remember). Drive stimuli are particularly important because they are present not only when the rat sees, seizes, and eats the food in the goal box but also as the rat responds throughout *every* part of the maze. In other words, since the drive stimulus is conditioned to the overt goal response, and since the drive stimulus is always present, it ought to come to elicit the goal response throughout the entire sequence of responses that the rat must make to get through the maze.

Of course, until the rat gets to the goal box, it cannot seize and eat a piece of food it does not have. But it could make anticipatory responses that are *fractional* components of the full-blown goal response. These fractional goal responses r_g might be chewing movements, salivation, or any other similar sort of response that would not interfere with the rat's main task of getting from one end of the maze to the other. Further, since they are conceived to have the properties of responses, the r_g's would produce their own proprioceptive stimuli. Such proprioceptive stimuli, in turn, would provide the rat as it runs through the maze with a kind of symbolic representation of the goal object, a *fractional goal stimulus*, or s_g, arising from the fractional goal response. And finally, because r_g's produce s_g's throughout the entire maze, the s_g's themselves should eventually become part of the general stimulus complex to which responses occurring at different points throughout the maze are conditioned. In effect, the r_g-s_g mechanism provides a means by which the rat, through conditioning, can come to "think ahead" and to anticipate whatever waits at future choice points and at the goal.

It is important to recognize that as Hull, Spence, or Amsel has used the term, the r_g-s_g mechanism is nothing more than a conceptual model, tied to independent and dependent variables, that has been assigned some properties which make it useful as a theoretical tool in accounting for certain learning phenomena. It is easy to lose sight of this fact, since terms like fractional goal response could lead one to think that the validity of the concept might depend upon actual measurement of "real" fractional goal responses in the laboratory. In fact, it *is* possible to measure fractional responses which occur in anticipation of some goal event, such as miniature licking responses that can be generated through Pavlovian conditioning in anticipation of the actual arrival of fluid (Deaux & Patten, 1964; Patten & Deaux, 1966). But if it were impossible to find a fractional goal response and to track it down in the laboratory, this would in no way invalidate the concept, nor would it destroy its utility as a theoretical tool. As a matter of fact, the only reason the r_g-s_g mechanism is so labeled is because Hull, who first developed it, wanted to emphasize an approach to learning where everything was to be explained in terms like stimulus and response. Today, of course, we may view such an approach as a rather tortured way of restricting oneself in the name of theoretical consistency—surely the phenomena associated with thinking and other cognitive processes are more conveniently explained in terms other than those of peripheral stimulus and response. But the r_g-s_g concept has had a long and venerable history, and we have, no doubt, yet to see the end of its usefulness. Remember it for what it is—a model for a process of mediation—and you should be able to live with it quite comfortably.

STIMULATION AND REINFORCEMENT

Still another way to view the fundamental reinforcement process lies in an emphasis upon the stimulus properties of reinforcers and the things that reinforcers share with stimuli in general. In a sense, of course, the incentive approach to reinforcement could fit very well under this heading because it is certainly the case that the concept of an incentive carries with it many meanings that imply stimuli at work. Incentives are lures, things "out there," stimuli that draw action of one kind or another toward them, and they have been studied as such by many investigators. Troland (1928), for example, discusses the concepts of *beneceptors* and *nociceptors*—hypothetical receivers of stimulation that is "good" or "attractive" on the one hand and "bad" or "aversive" on the other. Similarly, P. T. Young (e.g., 1936, 1961, 1973) has spent a career studying the "hedonic" aspects of stimuli—the features that make them attractive to organisms in the pleasurable sense—and both he and Pfaffmann (1960, 1969) have done much empirical work studying, for example, the manner in which organisms react to the taste of stimulus substances like sugar, salt, and quinine and how these substances function to reinforce new behavior. As a matter of fact, Hutt's (1954) experiment that we looked at in Chapter 2 is a very good example of an experiment in which the taste of a stimulus turned out to be a good correlate of its effectiveness as a reinforcer. Incentives, then, are classes of events which can be profitably viewed from the point of view of their stimulus properties. There are some other things characteristic of reinforcement at work which emphasize the role of stimuli and stimulation in the reinforcement process, however, and we turn to some of them now.

Psychophysics and reinforcement   If drives can be thought of as strong stimuli which impel action, and if reduction in the intensity of such stimuli can reinforce behavior, how much must a drive be reduced in intensity before a measurable reinforcement effect can be obtained? Further, is it true that we would have to have a greater reduction in the intensity of a very strong drive as compared with a weak one in order to produce equivalent reinforcing effects? Or again, suppose we reduce the intensity of *one* drive at the same time that we expose an organism to a second one. Would their effects summate (as Hull said they would in 1943), or would the presence of the second drive reduce the effectiveness of reductions in the first?

These questions, of course, are borrowed from psychophysics. For example, the psychophysicist asks how intense a light must be before the light can just barely be seen; this physical intensity is called an *absolute threshold*. Similarly, the psychophysicist asks how much two lights must differ in physical intensity before the *difference* between the lights is barely detectable; a difference of this sort is called a *just noticeable difference*, or *difference threshold*. The psychophysicist also asks how the size of a difference threshold changes when it is determined at different points along a dimension of stimulus intensity. In general, the magnitude of the difference threshold becomes larger as the physical intensities of stimuli increase. According to Weber's law, however, if difference thresholds are determined for a number of standard intensities, then the *ratios* of the difference thresholds to their respective standard intensities will all be the same. Thus, Weber's law says that $\Delta I/I$ is a constant, where I stands for the intensity of any standard stimulus and ΔI stands for the difference threshold determined for that particular standard stimulus. Weber's law holds pretty well for the middle ranges of intensity for a wide variety of stimuli, although it tends to break down at extreme intensities—those that are very high or very low.

Campbell (1955, 1956, 1958) reasoned that if a drive-reduction approach to reinforcement has merit, it ought to be possible to ask some psychophysical questions about reductions in the intensity of drive stimuli and their corresponding ability to reinforce a response. Since, as we have seen, the experimenter has many problems in controlling precisely the things that produce and, in particular, reduce drive stimuli like those associated with hunger, Campbell chose to use another type of drive-producing stimulus. In one experiment (Campbell, 1955), he exposed rats to intense noise, and in another (Campbell, 1956), he used electric shock. The chief advantage of using externally applied stimuli such as these is that the experimenter has very precise control over their onset, offset, and intensity. Consequently, he can easily vary drive strength and the amount by which drive is reduced.

Let us look at Campbell's shock experiment in some detail. The apparatus was a simple cage with a floor made of metal rods through which electric current could be passed. The floor was pivoted in the middle so that it would tilt slightly as the rats Campbell used for subjects went from one side to the other. When a rat was on one side of the floor, it received a "standard" shock of one intensity. When, and if, it moved to the other side of the floor, it received a "comparison" shock of a lower intensity. A clock measured the amount of time that the rat spent on the lower-shock side of the cage. The standard intensities that were used were 55, 72, 95, 165, 287, and 500 volts passed through a resistor that limited the current flow through the rat. For each standard intensity, several (at least three) comparison intensities were chosen; each comparison intensity was progressively less intense than its standard.

Separate groups of six rats each were run for each combination of standard and comparison intensity. This was done so that the behavior measured under one set of conditions would not be affected by earlier experience with another set of conditions. The procedure was simple. A rat was placed in the tilt cage and a standard and comparison shock were turned on for eight minutes. Then, for the last four minutes of the eight-minute session, the percentage of time that the rat spent on the side of the cage with the lower-intensity comparison shock was determined. Median percentages for the groups of rats run under each condition are shown in Figure 3.4, which also includes points at 50 percent for the hypothetical state of affairs that would occur, presumably, when the standard and comparison shocks were of the same intensity.

From the data shown in Figure 3.4, Campbell then calculated, for each standard intensity, the reduction in intensity that would lead the rat to spend 75 percent of its time on the side of the grid floor with the less intense shock. Campbell assumed that if a rat did this, it was demonstrating a reliable preference for this side as compared with the other. Then Campbell assumed that the difference in intensity between the standard and comparison shock at the point of 75 percent preference constituted a reduction in shock intensity which was "just noticeably reinforcing" for the response of going to and staying on the side of the cage with the weaker shock. The reductions in shock intensity that were required to produce a just noticeably reinforcing effect for each standard intensity are shown in Figure 3.5.

Figure 3.4
The curves show, for each of several standard intensities (filled circles), the percent preference for the side of the tilt cage with the lower shock as a function of the intensity of the lower shock (open circles). Campbell assumed that had each standard intensity been compared with itself, the rats would have spent equal amounts of time on each side of the cage, and so "preference" for each standard was set arbitrarily at 50 percent. (Campbell, 1956.)

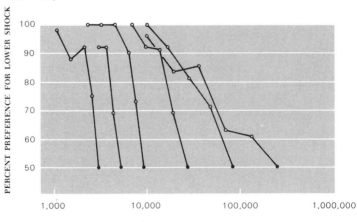

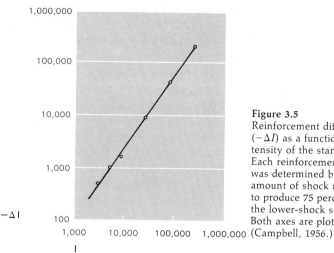

Figure 3.5
Reinforcement difference limens
$(-\Delta I)$ as a function of the log intensity of the standard shock I.
Each reinforcement difference limen was determined by calculating the amount of shock reduction required to produce 75 percent preference for the lower-shock side of the cage. Both axes are plotted in E^2 units. (Campbell, 1956.)

Figure 3.5 indicates that as the intensity I of the standard shock increased, there had to be a much larger decrease in intensity $(-\Delta I)$ before the decrease was sufficient to produce just noticeable reinforcement. For example, when I was about 100,000 units, there had to be a decrease in intensity of about 70,000 units for just noticeable reinforcement to occur. When I was about 10,000 units, however, a decrease of only 1,100 or 1,200 units was required.

Given this basic work, Campbell has gone on (e.g., Campbell, 1968; Messing & Campbell, 1971) to pursue the application of a psychophysical, stimulus-emphasizing approach to reinforcement. He has shown, for example, that if *two* aversive drives, electric shock and very intense noise, are combined so that movements from one side to another of a cage produce reductions in the intensity of the noise but not in the intensity of the shock, then noise reduction is much less effective as a reinforcing operation. In other words, it took a greater amount of noise reduction to produce a given reinforcing effect if an irrelevant aversive shock were present in the animals' environment, and the magnitude of the necessary decrease was greater the stronger the intensity of the shock. This phenomenon is very much like a phenomenon known as *masking* in the psychophysics of hearing: the ear is much less sensitive to changes in the loudness of a sound if an extraneous noise is also present in the environment. Campbell also showed, however, that if *both* noise and shock were reduced following a response, the reinforcing effects of the two summated; that is, the combination worked better than the two used separately.

By this time, you may have noticed that Campbell's work supports a drive-reduction model for reinforcement very well. While this is true, it is also the case that his work can be incorporated into any theory which stresses the stimulus properties of reinforcing events, and that is a broader class of theories than the fundamental drive-reduction account of things. For another example, we can note that Bevan and his associates (e.g., Bevan, 1966, 1968) have developed a model for reinforcement which is based on the principle of an *adaptation level* for a set of stimuli of differing intensities (Helson, 1964). It is beyond the scope of this book to go into this approach in detail, but suffice it to say that it views reinforcement as a function of the intensity of a reinforcing stimulus like an electric shock compared with some *average* intensity, some psychological norm that the organism develops for itself through experience with an entire array of reinforcement intensities. Basically, in other words, an important feature of reinforcing stimuli is the fact that they exist in a *context* of reinforcing stimuli, and the reinforcing effectiveness of any given stimulus depends upon how it stacks up against the context viewed as a whole. Hulse (1973b) has stressed and developed a similar approach.

Brain stimulation and reinforcement   Another important class of phenomena that can be placed under the general heading of reinforcement by stimulation is that in which direct stimulation of the brain can reinforce behavior. This phenomenon, first reported by Olds and Milner (1954), was demonstrated in the following way. Fine wire electrodes were implanted in portions of the limbic system of the rat's brain; the limbic system involves some of the basal, lower structures of the brain, including portions of the thalamus and hypothalamus. Then the rats were placed in a Skinner box, and lever presses were reinforced with a brief, half-second pulse of 30- to 90-microampere current delivered through the electrodes. The behavior that resulted was dramatic: after rats pressed the lever once, they began to press at a very high rate and continued to do so in some cases until physical exhaustion set in (Olds, 1958).

Since the original discovery of the phenomenon, further work has demonstrated a great many reinforcementlike effects of brain stimulation. As the voltage of the stimulating current increases, for example, so does the rate at which the rat will press the lever which turns on the current (Reynolds, 1958). This effect is certainly reminiscent of some of the things that happen when a conventional reinforcer, like food, varies in magnitude. It is also possible to obtain negative as well as positive reinforcing effects through brain stimulation. Delgado, Roberts, and Miller (1954) showed that for certain electrode placements, cats would perform a wheel-turning response in order to *avoid* electrical stimulation of the brain, and Bower and Miller (1958), using a T maze to test for learning, found loci in the medial forebrain bundle where the onset of the stimulus was reinforcing; but if stimulation then continued, the stimulation became functionally aversive and its *offset* was reinforcing. And finally, among other things that could be mentioned, it is possible to obtain positive and negative reinforcement *contrast effects* with sudden changes in the intensity of reinforcing brain stimulation (Trowill, Panksepp, & Gandelman, 1969).

While there is considerable evidence to show that brain stimulation is, in many respects, much like other standard forms of reinforcement, there are some anomalies which, at the very least, call for some special accounting. The first comes from the Bower and Miller (1958) experiment just cited in which brain stimulation was first a positive reinforcer—in the sense that a rat would work to turn it on—but then became a negative reinforcer—in the sense that the animal would now work to turn it off if it were prolonged. One argument would hold that such stimulation is "pleasant" at first but that it produces effects which become steadily aversive as stimulation continues. Another argument would hold that the positive effects of the stimulation simply decay or adapt with time, and so the animal must turn off the stimulus and wait awhile for central cells and pathways to "recover" before a further lever press can be rewarded by a renewed positive reinforcement effect. While there may be some merit to the proposition that stimulation may become aversive—particularly at certain sites in the central nervous system—there is considerable evidence to argue that the major explanation of the Bower and Miller phenomenon lies with the second possibility—the positive effects of central stimulation simply adapt with prolonged, continued stimulation (Keesey, 1964; Deutsch, 1973). A second anomalous fact about brain stimulation is that—compared with standard primary rewards like food, at any rate—it is relatively difficult to get a response to persist for very long if reinforcement is turned off altogether and the response is extinguished (Olds, 1958; Deutsch, 1963; Deutsch & Howarth, 1963). As we shall see in the next chapter, a food-reinforced response will often persist for many hundreds of trials when reinforcement is removed, but with brain stimulation, the response may persist for just two or three responses. Several factors may be important in accounting for this apparent discrepancy. First, as Trowill, Panksepp, and Gandelman (1969) point out, experiments which have found fast extinction have often not done a closely controlled job of regulating need states like hunger or thirst, or other environmental and procedural factors, at the time tests for rewarding effects of brain stimulation are made. Under proper conditions, prolonged extinction can often be obtained. Second, an animal apparently does a better job of bridging periods of nonreinforcement if an *external cue* is used to signal ahead of time that a given response is to be reinforced with brain stimulation (Cantor, 1971); perhaps central brain stimulation somehow bypasses an important source of information that organisms require to span intervals of time between successive reinforced responses. Finally, it is much as if the removal of brain stimulation turns off a motivational system that is basically independent of the reinforcing effects which brain stimulation also produces. As a matter of fact, one important theory of the operation of rewarding brain stimulation (Deutsch & Howarth, 1963; Gallistel, 1973) suggests that it contains two components: a rewarding or reinforcing function and a motivational or drive effect, the latter dependent upon some cumulative amount of brain stimulation that an organism has received in a situation—stimulation that need not be contingent upon responses at all.

There remains a final approach to reinforcement to be discussed, an approach we owe to Premack (1959, 1965, 1971). Premack's theory is interesting because it rests solely on some simple assumptions about how external responses of one class or another are related to each other in probabilistic terms. Quite simply, says Premack first of all, responses can be ranked along a single scale of their *value* to the behaving organism. Value is defined by the simple *probability* that one response as opposed to another will occur. This can be assessed by giving an organism a chance to choose between one or more responses, or by using some measure of the relative likelihood that one as opposed to another response will occur during a given span of time. Given the concepts of relative value and relative probability, Premack's statement of the necessary and sufficient conditions for positive reinforcement is quite simple: given two responses, one of which is more probable than the other, an opportunity to perform the more probable response will provide positive reinforcement for production of the less probable response. In other words, if response A is more probable than response B, then an opportunity to engage in A can be used to reinforce acquisition of response B.

This is a very simple set of assumptions, and because of that, it is potentially a very powerful description of a reinforcing state of affairs. It says, for example, that if drinking water for a thirsty rat (response A) is more probable than running in an alley or a running wheel (response B), drinking ought to reinforce running. This seems trivial, and would be predicted by essentially any theory of reinforcement. Premack's approach also says, however, that if conditions could be arranged such that running was a more probable response than drinking, then rats ought to learn to drink in order to get an opportunity to run! This sounds highly unlikely, but it turns out that the prediction holds very well: if drinking is made a highly unlikely response relative to running in an activity wheel (by satiating rats, for example), rats will learn to produce a few licks in order to gain access to an activity wheel in which they can run for a while. To top things off, Premack has also shown (Terhune & Premack, 1970; Premack, 1971) that a relationship between two responses which is the reverse of the one we have just examined describes a *punishing* state of affairs. That is, if response A is less probable than response B, and if response A is then made contingent upon response B, the result will be that response B will be inhibited; its likelihood of occurrence will decrease exactly as if it were being subjected to punishment.

The simple elegance of Premack's approach is not to be denied, and that is perhaps its greatest appeal. It has not, however, stimulated a great deal of research designed to provide strict and rigorous tests of its ability to make predictions that would not also be easily made by other theories. The best way to do this, it would seem, would be to pick response systems interrelated in such a way that an incentive or drive-reduction approach to reinforcement would have very little, if anything, to predict about which event would reinforce some other event. To mention a rather farfetched example, one could pick two highly unrelated response systems—like driving a car and kissing—assess their relative independent probability of occurrence, then make the more probable activity contingent upon engaging in the less probable activity. Premack's theory makes a straightforward prediction here: you should learn to engage in driving your car if that leads to lovemaking, or you should learn to engage in lovemaking if that leads to an opportunity to drive your car. Which way the relationship would go would depend solely upon which of the two "responses" was the more probable one when assessed independently. No doubt you can think of other examples which are as good as, or better than, this one; the key point is that Premack's theory makes statements about the necessary and sufficient conditions for reinforcement which are logically independent of any further statements about incentives, stimulation, motivation, drive reduction, or anything else we have looked at so far. It is truly an empirical theory in the sense that its only postulates are based on some simple statements about empirical relations among response systems. It will be interesting to watch the development of this potentially powerful approach to the problem of reinforcement.

IMITATIVE LEARNING AND VICARIOUS REINFORCEMENT

Thus far, our treatment of the reinforcement process has been based on situations in which reinforcement has been stripped to its bare essentials and studied in a context in which relatively uncomplicated response processes are used. After all, however, there is not really very much to *learn* in a Skinner box or in a runway, although reinforcement variables can have profound effects upon the *performance* of even very simple responses. Somehow, however, the world of rats and pigeons does not seem to do full justice to the complex richness of so much of the human behavior we see going on around us. And it is difficult to see, sometimes, how some of the fundamental reinforcement principles we have been examining in this chapter can have much to do with such behavior.

One path into the more complex world of primate behavior in this regard comes from some principles which have been studied under the general rubric of *vicarious reinforcement*. This, in turn, has been a subject of interest within the more general domain of *learning by imitation*. A thorough treatment of that subject is far, far beyond the scope of this book. The topic begins with Aristotle, and in modern times many people have had a hand in its development. Among them, we may list Miller and Dollard (1941), who provide an extensive history of the subject. A survey of the topic is provided by McLaughlin (1971). For our purposes, it will suffice to skim a fundamental principle or two from the surface of things and then take a brief look at how reinforcing events can function under circumstances of imitative learning.

Learning by observation It is the hallmark of primate behavior that much learning goes on without the actual overt performance of responses. We learn by watching others and learning, perhaps, to imitate them, and sometimes we learn a great deal about potentially reinforcing events by storing information about them that we gather quite passively. A case in point which is closely related to the general problem of reinforcement is provided by some research of Menzel (1973). Menzel worked with chimpanzees and set out to see how well the chimps could learn something about the location of food in a large field with which they were quite familiar (they had lived there for about a year). Six chimps were used in the study. One was carried passively by an experimenter around the field while a second experimenter placed pieces of fruit in 18 randomly selected locations in the field. The test chimp was able to watch the baiting of the locations (indeed it seemed to the experimenters that the animal was busy trying to mentally mark the location with respect to natural objects like trees, rocks, and so forth), but the animal was unable to do any active exploring and received no food during this phase of the experiment. After the food had been placed, the test chimp, together with the five other chimps who did not have the benefit of watching the food being stashed here and there, were released into the field, and the experimenters recorded how many pieces of fruit were retrieved by the animals, together with the order in which they went about things. The animals that were naive with respect to the location of the food provided a base-line control for locating food by accident and by means of olfactory cues.

The results are remarkable. Over a series of trials, four test chimps found an average of 12.5 (out of 18) pieces of fruit per trial, while the control animals found an average of about two-tenths of a piece of fruit per trial. Furthermore, Menzel describes behavior of the test animals as direct and unerring: the animals went in direct lines to this place or that where food had been placed. This fact, together with another interesting facet of the behavior of the animals, appears in Figure 3.6. Note from the figure, which shows data for the four test animals used in the experiment, not only that the chimps got most of the fruit on this, their best, trial but that they tended to minimize the effort involved. That is, they did not in any sense at all retrace the original path which had been followed when the baiting was done initially but instead collected most of the goodies in a single general area of the field before moving on to another general area. In other words, they optimized things, expending the least amount of effort possible in obtaining most of the fruit.

This experiment shows that chimps have a remarkable sense of the location of things in an area with which they are familiar, and, as Menzel suggests, if primary reward and motor movement are necessary in order to do well in a task such as that used in the experiment, this must be true in a developmental sense only. That is, such experience may have been necessary to learn to get around at some time in the past but certainly

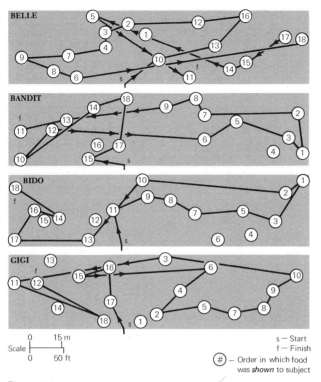

101

CONDITIONING,
LEARNING,
AND
REINFORCE-
MENT

Figure 3.6
Paths in a field taken by four chimpanzees as they retrieved
pieces of fruit they had watched being hidden earlier. The
numbers in the circles show the order in which the chimps
watched the original placement of the fruit, while the arrows
indicate the paths the chimps followed as they retrieved it. Note
that the animals optimized: they tended to collect all the fruit in
one area of the field before moving on to another area—
regardless of the order in which the fruit had been originally
cached. (Menzel, 1973.)

wasn't necessary to solve the immediate problem at hand. And, as
Menzel (1973) puts it in connection with his chimps,

> Their achievements are a good first approximation of those at which an
> applied scientist would arrive from his real maps, algorithms, and a priori
> criteria of efficiency. Mentalistic terms such as "cognitive mapping" do not
> necessarily explain the above facts, but they predict them accurately and
> describe them succinctly [p. 945].

The behavior of Menzel's chimps does not, of course, constitute an
isolated example of learning rather complex tasks by observation.
Another example of similar complex behavior which we now want to
examine is that of *imitative learning*. This phenomenon raises, in turn,
the notion of *vicarious reinforcement*, reinforcement experienced in-

directly through the observation of the reinforcement of another organism.

It will be convenient to introduce some of the important points to consider by describing an experiment of Bandura (1965) on imitative learning in children. Bandura had groups of four- to six-year-old children watch a five-minute televised movie which showed someone, the *model* for imitative learning, expressing four types of aggressive behavior toward an adult-sized, inflated plastic Bobo clown. Aggression ranged from laying the Bobo clown on its side and punching it to hitting it with a wooden mallet and kicking it. Each response was coupled with some form of distinctive, verbally aggressive remark, such as "Pow, right in the nose." In the closing scene of the film, a second adult entered the picture and for different groups of children in the experiment either *rewarded* the model for displaying aggressive behavior ("You are a strong champion"), *punished* the model for displaying aggression ("Hey there, you big bully, if I catch you doing that again, I'll give you a hard spanking"), or *remained neutral*, that is, neither rewarded nor punished the model. Following this initial experience, the children were ushered into a playroom in which there was a Bobo clown, objects such as the mallet that had been used aggressively in the film, and some other novel objects such as plastic farm animals. Then for 10 minutes, the children were observed to see if they would spontaneously generate, as they played, the specific aggressive responses and the verbal remarks that they had seen in the movie. The fundamental questions here were (1) would the children demonstrate that they had *learned* the aggressive behavior from watching the model do it and (2) would the extent to which the behavior was displayed be correlated with whether or not the model had been rewarded or punished?

Following the initial period of observation, the children were all exposed to a "game" in which they were asked specifically to recall and state what the model had done in the television movie. Each time they could come up with an accurate matching response, they were rewarded with some appetizing fruit juice and a pretty sticker picture which they used to add to a scene on the wall that they had been challenged to decorate by the experimenter. Here, Bandura was interested in finding out if the children had in fact all learned the aggressive responses involved in the movie, but had been biased in their tendency to *perform* what they knew by the reward and punishment administered to the model. He guessed that *direct reward* of the recall of the aggressive behavior might induce the children to reveal that they had learned the responses after all, but had simply been biased either for or against revealing what they knew by the reinforcement contingencies expressed in the movie. Bandura was interested, in other words, in whether the effects of reward and punishment in imitative learning were upon the actual learning of imitative responses or simply upon the subjects' willingness to perform what they knew, a problem which we have already looked at in other contexts (see Chapter 1).

As you can see from Figure 3.7, several things emerged from the

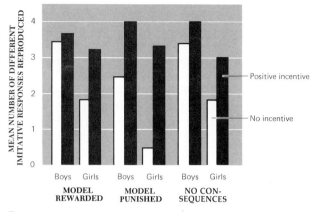

103

CONDITIONING,
LEARNING,
AND
REINFORCE-
MENT

Figure 3.7
Imitative responses produced by children after they had
watched a model be rewarded, punished, or treated neutrally
for displaying aggressive behavior. Imitative responses increased when the children were directly rewarded for making
them (solid bars). Earlier, imitative responses were less frequent when they were not directly rewarded (open bars).
(Bandura, 1965.)

experiment. First of all, during the "no incentive" phase of the experiment when the children were simply observed for imitative responses
that they might choose to display, the frequency of imitative responses
either increased or decreased if aggressive behavior had been, respectively, rewarded or punished in the television movie. When a positive
incentive was then introduced for specifically recalling and acting out the
aggressive acts shown in the movie, however, the children all responded
the same way (and demonstrated a great deal of learning) regardless of
whether the model had been rewarded or punished in the movie. In
other words, Bandura's data argue, the children all learned about the
aggressive behavior in the movie, but their willingness to *reveal* what
they knew was the thing that was modified by reward or punishment
applied to the model. You will also note in the figure that there was a
general factor correlated with sex of the children; girls were, in general,
more reluctant (or less able) to reveal that they had learned about the
aggressive behavior in the movie, a fact which matches well with a great
deal of other research on aggressive behavior.

While the foregoing shows unequivocally that human beings can learn
about things by watching the experiences of someone else, and while it
shows that the effects of such imitative learning can be modified by
reinforcement, the research does not tell us anything about the precise
mechanism that is involved when reinforcement works in the situation.
Bandura (1971) has offered a rather extensive discussion of this problem—which is of course the central one for this portion of the chapter
you are reading—and he identifies several factors which could have
contributing effects. For example, some vicarious *emotional conditioning*

could be at work (Church, 1959). While an observer does not experience the direct effects of reward and punishment upon a model, the observer can see cues correlated with the affective state of the model—such as facial expressions, vocalizations, body postures, and so on—and watch the overt behavior that then ensues, some of it aimed directly at the observer himself. Through a process of straightforward Pavlovian conditioning, the cues to emotion provided by the model then gradually come themselves to act as conditional stimuli and arouse affective feeling in the observer.

Another of the most important facts about reward and punishment in imitative or observational learning is that they provide *information* about the outcomes of specific modes of behaving. The observer has a chance to see what happens to the model in an imitative learning situation, for example, and can relate this information to potential outcomes of his own behavior. Recall, in this connection, that Estes said (p. 78) that learning was basically a process of forming associations by contiguity and storing them in memory. Reinforcement, on the other hand, has its effects essentially on the performance of behavior, acting through information and positive and negative feedback to facilitate or inhibit behavior both recalled from memory and triggered by current environmental cues. It would seem that Bandura's analysis of some of the things that go on in learning by imitation is well correlated with an approach such as that of Estes.

SUMMARY AND PERSPECTIVE

In this chapter we have examined in broad outline several of the basic theoretical approaches not only to the problem of reinforcement but also to the whole of the psychology of learning. We have used a historical perspective in part and found that most of the theoretical underpinnings of the psychology of learning can be encompassed by points of view which stress learning through a process of pure contiguity, on the one hand, and contiguity plus effect, on the other. If a dash of cognitive spice is added to this mix, we have a fairly representative view of the fundamentals of the wide landscape of this particular field of psychology as it exists today. There is little argument among psychologists regarding the merits of any of the approaches we have outlined. While there was a time—in the 1930s, 1940s, and 1950s during the era of the great systems of behavior associated with names like Hull and Tolman—when argument raged about the relative value of one or another approach to things, psychologists no longer find it productive or meaningful to pit one theory against another in the form of some "crucial" experiment or the like.

Today, the psychology of learning seems to have passed from an era of the grand, broad theory into an era of the microtheory. Behavior is much too complicated, and far too little is yet known and understood about it, to make the development of general theories of learning a fruitful undertaking at this time. Instead, the modern theorist attacks a rather specific bit of behavior, collects a lot of data about it, teases it apart, and then attempts to put it back together in the form of some necessarily limited, theoretical structure.

Nowhere is the microtheory better illustrated than in the case of some of the analytical approaches to reinforcement that we have scrutinized in this chapter. Reinforcement can be handled from the point of view of relative value and probability of response, as suggested by Premack. It can be handled from the aspect of brain stimulation and from the vantage point of incentive-motivation. How can one make sense out of this welter of seeming confusion (if not contradiction)? Unfortunately, there is no simple answer to that question. Each approach has its usefulness, each can handle some of the data better than another, each has its limitations. In this chapter we have attempted to sample some of that diversity, and you should not be dismayed if you are left with the feeling that a great deal needs to be done before valid general statements can be made about the reinforcement process. But don't forget that while we are not yet in a position to make valid statements in general, we are quite well equipped in particular to make important and useful comments about the application of the principles of reinforcement to many circumscribed features of behavior, both basic and applied. And, of course, it is the task of psychology to make that circle of its knowledge grow.

FOUR

EXTINCTION

What happens to behavior that is no longer needed or useful? Thus far it may seem that we have been discussing how living organisms acquire or learn new things on some tacit assumption that the primary task of the psychology of learning is a description of how creatures go about adding to their storehouse of available behavior. But it is clearly the case that for one reason or another, we stop doing things we once used to do, and we are all familiar with the phenomenon of forgetting—a phenomenon which, alas, becomes more of a problem as we grow older.

While other factors certainly contribute, too, there are three important processes which assure each in their own way that behavior will be dropped—either temporarily or permanently—from the response repertoire of an organism: (1) forgetting, (2) punishment and the application of aversive stimulation, and (3) extinction. While all would agree that forgetting is an independent process, some would argue that punishment and extinction have some things in common, and we shall have a chance to see why in this chapter. Nevertheless, the bulk of our discussion here will be devoted to the phenomenon of extinction, and both forgetting and punishment will receive complete treatment later on.

THE DEFINITION OF EXTINCTION

When learned acts are no longer reinforced, they usually diminish in strength. Children who have learned the location of the cookie jar will generally drop their foraging expeditions if experience shows that the supply of cookies has been cut off. Animals, too, will abandon locations where food has been found if something should happen to the food supply there. It is easy to think of other common examples of this sort, and in most cases, common sense does a reasonably good job of predicting the consequences of the withdrawal of some reinforcing substance—by and large, unreinforced responses are dropped from the organism's repertoire of behavior.

We turn, then, to a discussion of the phenomenon of *extinction*, a process defined operationally as the *removal of reinforcement following the occurrence of some response that has been reinforced in the past.*

Extinction is an important process. Imagine what the world would be like if learned responses were *not* dropped more or less promptly when they no longer were reinforced. Presumably, under these circumstances, given components of an organism's response store would disappear only through some other process like forgetting, a process which works by very different rules and which takes far longer under most circumstances to run its course (as we shall see later in this book). Extinction, then, helps assure that behavior does not persist which is no longer useful in producing rewards or avoiding punishment. And that is important if behavior is not to become a disorganized, maladaptive mess. As we pursue our examination of extinction, we shall look briefly at some of the variables that are known to modulate the process, and then examine some attempts that have been made to account for it in theoretical terms.

In the simplest examples we use to define the learning process, a response is reinforced every time it occurs (though nature might not be so cooperative in more naturalistic settings). Thus, in simple reward learning, the rat receives a pellet of food each time that it presses the lever in the Skinner box. After the rat learns the correlation between food and lever pressing, it will continue to press at a reasonably steady rate so long as it remains hungry. If reinforcement is now discontinued, the rat will continue to respond for a while, but it does so at a gradually diminishing rate and with decreasing regularity. Figure 4.1 shows the process of extinction taking place. From the figure it is clear that the rate of responding is high at the beginning of extinction, right after reinforcement has stopped: responses cumulate rapidly as time passes, and the slope of the cumulative record is steep. Soon, however, the rate of responding begins to decrease, and behavior becomes erratic, so that after the first hour or so of extinction, the rat is going for long periods of time without responding at all.

Figure 4.1
An extinction curve for lever pressing in a Skinner box. Cumulative number of responses appears on the ordinate. The rate of responding is high at the beginning, but then declines and becomes more irregular. Long periods of time pass without responding, until finally responding stops almost completely. (Skinner, 1938; data from F. S. Keller & Kerr.)

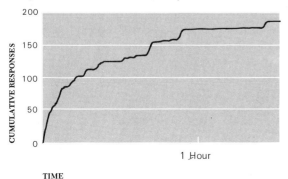

In the same way, a response that has been conditioned with Pavlovian procedures diminishes in strength if reinforcement, the unconditional stimulus in this case, is removed. Thus, in Pavlov's classic salivary conditioning experiment, the amount of salivation elicited by the tone CS will gradually diminish over trials if we withhold the food-powder UCS. As a matter of fact, if you will recall, we said in Chapter 1 that this was a standard procedure for developing one form of internal inhibition, *extinctive inhibition*.

Resistance to extinction   When reinforcement is withheld and extinction begins, it is apparent that behavior does not come to a stop very rapidly under standard conditions. The operation of learning with reinforcement, in other words, creates a response which *resists* the negative or inhibitory influence of the withdrawal of reinforcement. Consequently, we speak of the *resistance to extinction* of a response. Responses vary in resistance to extinction to the extent that an organism will continue to produce them after primary reinforcement has been withdrawn. As a matter of fact, Amsel (1967) stresses the notion of *persistence* of behavior in his theory of extinction, which we shall examine in this chapter.

In practice there are a number of ways in which resistance to extinction is measured, and we shall be looking at experiments which will furnish good examples of each method. Generally, the indices that are used to measure behavior during extinction are the same that are used to measure behavior during acquisition: indices which reflect the strength of the response. If you will recall, these include measures such as the probability that a response will occur, the latency and amplitude of the response, the speed or duration of the response, and so on. In addition to watching changes in these measures as extinction proceeds, the psychologist may also adopt some form of *extinction criterion*. When this criterion is met, he will conclude quite arbitrarily that extinction is complete. For example, it could be decided arbitrarily ahead of time that extinction is complete when an animal in a Skinner box fails to make a response for the duration of some preset period of time. Another way to establish an extinction criterion is to determine ahead of time that some arbitrary number of *trials* will be run during extinction, and to observe some index like response latency or response speed over the course of that block of trials. This criterion is often used in discrete-trial learning situations where the organism is not free in time to go from one response to the next and the opportunity to respond is controlled by the experimenter. You can probably think of still other criteria for extinction that might be used, too.

SOME BASIC VARIABLES

NUMBER OF REINFORCEMENTS AND EXTINCTION

Resistance to extinction depends, to some extent, upon the number of reinforcements given an organism before extinction begins. Figure 4.2 shows some classic data that were obtained from rats in the Skinner box

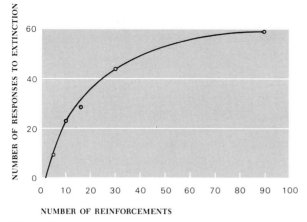

Figure 4.2
Number of lever presses during extinction as a function of
the number of reinforcements administered during training.
(Redrawn from Perin, 1942; data from Perin, 1942, and
Williams, 1938.)

by Perin (1942) and Williams (1938). The figure demonstrates that if a
small number of reinforcements is given, a few lever-pressing responses
are emitted in extinction before animals cease responding altogether. As
the number of reinforced responses increases, the number of responses
in extinction also increases, although resistance to extinction appears to
approach a limit rather quickly. Maximal resistance to extinction is
obtained with relatively few reinforcements, and after a certain point,
one can go on giving reinforcements without adding appreciably to the
number of responses an organism will give when reinforcement stops.

Evidence now exists, however, which shows that the function relating
number of reinforcements to resistance to extinction may not be so
simple. Under some conditions, as a matter of fact, it may be *nonmonotonic*. In general, a nonmonotonic function is one in which the relationship between a dependent and an independent variable *changes* from
positive to negative or from negative to positive. For the case at hand,
this means that resistance to extinction first increases (as in Figure 4.2),
but if more and more reinforcement is given, resistance to extinction
begins to decrease (that is, the curve in Figure 4.2 would eventually begin
to drop to some greater or lesser degree). The evidence for this effect is
by no means consistent, however. While some experimenters report the
nonmonotonic relation (e.g., North & Stimmel, 1960; Ison, 1962; Siegel
& Wagner, 1963), others do not (e.g., Bacon, 1962). In any event, it is
certainly the case that providing more and more reinforcement for a
response does not build up its strength indefinitely, as if some reservoir
of behavior were being endlessly filled to be tapped and drawn upon
when reinforcement is withheld (the concept of the *reflex reserve*,
Skinner, 1938). While responses must be reinforced for their persistence
to develop, and while persistence certainly increases for some period of
time as the number of reinforcements increases, a stage is apparently

reached under many circumstances in which other factors take over and tend to decrease the persistence of the response.

AMOUNT OF REINFORCEMENT

The empirical picture which holds for this variable and its effect upon resistance to extinction is quite similar to that for number of reinforcements. If every response is reinforced during acquisition, and if amount of reinforcement is defined by the weight or number of the reinforcing substance (e.g., food pellets for hungry rats), most of the available evidence shows that resistance to extinction *decreases* as the amount of reinforcement used during training increases.[1] Hulse (1958) and Wagner (1961) were the first to demonstrate this fact, and while some exceptions exist (e.g., Bacon, 1962), it has now been substantiated in a number of different experimental settings (Sutherland & Mackintosh, 1971).

At first glance, less persistence following large rewards seems counterintuitive, just as it is counterintuitive from one point of view to discover that resistance to extinction can decrease as the number of reinforcements increases. This would be true, at least, from the vantage point of any theory which views persistence to be a function of variables with dimensions of magnitude, amount, intensity, or quantity that add directly to some kind of generalized pool of response strength. As we shall see, however, there are other psychological features of large amounts of reinforcement or large numbers of reinforced practice trials which suggest that the available data are correct in spite of their lack of intuitive appeal. As a hint of things to come, the sudden disappearance of a large reward could lead to relatively dramatic emotional consequences, with upset and breakup of well-learned behavior following rapidly. All these things could lead in turn to fast disruption of behavior and to a rapid loss of measured response strength. It is well to remember, then, that an intuitive approach to the action of many variables in psychology can lead one astray, and such can certainly be the case for some variables entering into the extinction process unless one is careful.

DISTRIBUTION OF RESPONSES IN TIME

What happens to behavior when successive responses are spaced by different intervals of time? The effect of varying the intertrial interval in an experiment turns out to be of some theoretical interest for the phenomenon of extinction, and so let us look now at some of the data that have been obtained on this matter.

Interest in the effects on behavior of different intervals of time between responses begins, like many other things, with Pavlov. Pavlov (1927) reported that a Pavlovian conditioned response extinguishes more rapidly when trials occur close together than when they are spaced apart.

---

[1]An inverse relationship between amount of reinforcement and resistance to extinction holds only when *every* response is reinforced during training. We shall see in the next chapter that a very different state of affairs exists when irregular reinforcement is used.

More recently, experiments have been performed to see if this is also true

of instrumental conditioning.

First of all, if we look at the data that are available concerning the effect of different intertrial intervals upon instrumental behavior during *reinforcement*, we find a highly ambiguous state of affairs. While Hovland (1936) found that massing trials together in time impaired performance appreciably, the great weight of the evidence shows that learning proceeds at just about the same rate regardless of the interval of time that elapses between successive responses (e.g., Wilson, Weiss, & Amsel, 1955; Lewis & Cotton, 1959). Second, if we look at the effect of intertrial interval upon resistance to *extinction*, we find an almost equally ambiguous state of affairs. When significant effects are found (e.g., Lewis & Cotton, 1959), they generally indicate that resistance to extinction is greater if trials are spaced close together in time than if they are spaced farther apart. Exceptions to this rule are not hard to find, however; Gagne (1941) and Hill and Spear (1962) report that spaced trials during extinction produce greater resistance to extinction than massed trials.

Teichner (1952) and Cole and Abraham (1962), among others, point out one factor that may help to unravel things a bit—at least as far as the extinction data are concerned. Teichner, for example, suggests that extinction is faster under massed conditions (his data showed this to be true), but that this is a relatively small effect easily obscured by other conditions. Of much greater importance, Teichner feels, is the relation between the intertrial interval used during training and that used during extinction. The greatest resistance to extinction is found when the training and extinction intervals are the same; if they are different, resistance to extinction will be reduced. As we shall see in Chapter 7, response strength tends to decrease when an organism is conditioned to respond to one set of stimulus conditions and is then shifted to another set (a phenomenon known as stimulus generalization), and so there is good reason to believe that something akin to stimulus generalization could be at work when intertrial intervals change as part of the switch from conditioning to extinction.

In this connection, Cole and Abraham's experiment is of some interest, since they attempted to minimize the effects of a change in intertrial interval by exposing each of their subjects, during training in a Y maze, to a sample of the intertrial intervals that were to be used during extinction. Thus, while rats were learning to find food in a goal box at the end of one arm of the Y, trials were separated by either 20 seconds or 24 hours, with the two intervals used in random fashion so that there were from one to five trials per day. *All* rats in the experiment learned according to this procedure. Then, during extinction, subgroups of rats were run with a 20-second, 5-minute, or 24-hour intertrial interval. The results show that, in general, the group which was extinguished with the 24-hour intertrial interval persisted longer in making correct responses and ran faster for more trials than the groups which were extinguished with the two shorter intertrial intervals.

A well-known experiment by Mowrer and Jones (1943) provides evidence suggesting that the effort which must be expended in making a response during extinction affects the resistance to extinction of that response. These investigators trained rats to press a lever for food in a Skinner box. During training, the lever was counterweighted by different amounts so that the rats learned to press the bar when it required 5 grams to produce reinforcement, when it required 42.5 grams, and when it required 80 grams. At the end of training, the rats were divided into three groups, and each group was extinguished with a different counterweight attached to the lever. The results show that resistance to extinction decreased as more and more force was required to press the lever during extinction. Similar results were obtained by Capehart, Viney, and Hulicka (1958) in an experiment in which *all* rats received equal amounts of training on *all* the lever weights that were to be used during extinction (5, 40, and 70 grams). Under these conditions, a group extinguished with a 5-gram lever emitted a mean of 146 presses during the course of two extinction sessions, while groups extinguished with 40- and 70-gram levers gave means of 98 and 45 responses, respectively.

Offhand, it would seem on the basis of these data that resistance to extinction is a neat, straightforward, decreasing function of the amount of effort that an animal has to expend to produce responses during extinction. But, as you may well have anticipated, things are not quite that simple. For one thing, if reinforcement is made contingent upon pressing heavy levers during conditioning, the rat may learn not only the response of "pressing the lever" but also, in a sense, the response of "pressing the lever *hard*." And this might well be a *different* response from that which a rat learns when it must press a lighter lever to obtain reinforcement (Logan, 1956, 1960). If such were the case, we might expect that a rat trained on a 50-gram lever and then extinguished on a 100-gram lever would make just as many *attempted* depressions of the lever as a rat both trained and extinguished on a 100-gram lever. However—and this is the crux of the matter—these presses would not have sufficient force in all cases to be recorded as complete responses, and it might appear in the recorded data that the rat was extinguished when, in fact, it was still worrying the lever at a great rate. What is needed is an experiment in which both complete and incomplete presses are recorded during extinction. Neither Mowrer and Jones (1943) nor Capehart et al. (1958) obtained these data. Stanley and Aamodt (1954) did.

In their experiment, Stanley and Aamodt conditioned two groups of rats in a Skinner box to press a lever that required 50 grams of effort for one group, and 100 grams of effort for another. Then the two groups were split, and half the rats in each were extinguished with a 50-gram lever, half with a 100-gram lever. The results of the experiment show, first of all, that the groups extinguished with the 100-gram lever were far less resistant to extinction than the groups extinguished with the 50-gram lever. We would expect this observation on the basis of other experiments. This conclusion must be hedged extensively, however, because the rats which were trained on the 50-gram lever and extinguished on the 100-gram lever, for example, made a very large number of responses that did not meet the force criterion for extinction, but would have been sufficient to produce reinforcement during conditioning. While the data still showed that heavy levers produced faster extinction than lighter levers, in other words, this effect was attenuated sharply by lots of partial responses which simply did not meet the force criterion imposed during extinction. As part of the conditioning process, animals learn to press levers (or to work other manipulanda) with a certain force characteristic of the force required to produce reinforcement (Notterman & Mintz, 1965), and the effects of this procedure carry over to extinction to modify performance there.

Spontaneous recovery The phenomenon of spontaneous recovery appears when time is allowed to elapse, not between successive individual responses, but instead, between successive *sessions* or *periods* of extinction in each of which we fail to reinforce responses—perhaps to some extinction criterion. The phenomenon refers to the fact that there will be some *recovery* of response strength if time passes between the end of one session of extinction and the beginning of the next. Furthermore, the amount of recovery depends upon the duration of the time interval: the longer the time interval, the greater the recovery. Spontaneous recovery is an interesting phenomenon not only in its own right but also because it bears on certain theoretical matters to which we will turn in due course.

An experiment from Pavlov's laboratory provides, as usual, a good example of spontaneous recovery at work (Pavlov, 1927). Pavlov produced a conditioned salivary response by allowing a dog first to *see* some meat powder and then to eat it. After the dog had learned to salivate at the sight of the meat powder, Pavlov extinguished the response by no longer putting the meat powder into the animal's mouth. It took only a few trials of this sort to extinguish the conditioned response. The animal was then removed from the experimental room for approximately two hours. When the dog was brought back and allowed to look at the meat powder again, the conditioned response returned. True, the amount of saliva flow was not so great this time as it had been before the extinction process began, but there was no doubt that the conditioned response had recovered to a considerable extent—actually about one-sixth of the original amount under the conditions that Pavlov used.

Spontaneous recovery is a genuine and stable part of the extinction process. We may, for example, try to stop the family dog from begging at the dining-room table by ignoring it when it does so, and we may find that by the end of the meal the dog has retired to the living room. Nevertheless, the next evening it will probably beg as before. Since spontaneous recovery is incomplete, however, the dog will not be so persistent this time and will stop sooner. If we repeat the extinction process for a few days, and if we are *consistent* about doing so (which is not easy), the response will eventually stop occurring.

A pattern of reinforcement exists whenever the reinforcing event follow-ing a response *changes* in some fashion from one response to the next (Hulse, 1973b). In most examples of simple learning, certainly the vast majority of those we have examined so far, the reinforcing event is a constant thing; we are sure to reinforce each and every response with exactly the same, carefully calibrated reinforcing stimulus. This does not have to be true, however. Most simply, we could reinforce some responses and not others. Beyond that, it is possible to arrange ex-traordinarily complex patterns of reinforcing events and to study their effects upon various facets of behavior, including extinction. It is upon resistance to extinction, as a matter of fact, that patterns of reinforce-ment have one of their most profound effects: resistance to extinction tends to increase as reinforcement conditions during initial learning become more and more irregular and complex. The principles lying behind this fact, both empirical and theoretical, turn out to be both extremely broad and very important and interesting—so much so, as a matter of fact, that we will devote the entire next chapter to them. At this point, therefore, we mention patterns of reinforcement as a basic variable entering into the extinction process primarily for the sake of completing the list of variables which have been shown to modify behavior during extinction. Be prepared for a complete and thorough discussion of the concept of patterns of reinforcement when we turn to it later on.

THEORIES OF EXTINCTION

Organisms drop learned responses that are no longer reinforced. So simple a fact would hardly seem to demand very subtle theoretical explanation, yet extinction has been one of the aspects of learned behavior which has received a great deal of rather elaborate theoretical treatment. Actually, of course, a theory of extinction is fundamental to any theory of behavior because, as we have noted, the fact that organisms stop performing unreinforced acts is just as important as the fact that they learn reinforced acts in the first place. Think once again of the unimaginable chaos that would exist in the world if learned responses did not extinguish when the environment failed to provide reinforcement for them.

In the following sections, we shall look at two major theories of extinction. In each case, we shall see what a particular theory has to say about the extinction process, then see whether the theory thrives or wilts under the harsh light of laboratory test.

RESPONSE-PRODUCED INHIBITION THEORY

The response-produced inhibition theory is, in a certain historical sense, the major classical theory of extinction. Like "classical" theories in many other fields, however, it has been pretty thoroughly demolished in regard to detail by a number of critics—among them that ultimate critic, experimental data. Some of the rubble has been used to build new theories, and some of the empirical bits and pieces still hold and deserve their place in psychology today. But by and large, the last few years have seen little new empirical and theoretical development of the traditional inhibition theory of extinction.

This is not to say that the phenomenon of *inhibition* has been left to lie fallow. Quite the contrary. We saw in Chapter 1 how inhibitory processes are at the heart of Pavlovian conditioning, for example; and Pavlov's theory of extinction is basically one in which inhibition is postulated to develop when the UCS is removed and to counteract the excitatory effects of the application of the UCS. Inhibitory processes are currently under active study not only in their own right (Rescorla, 1969; Boakes & Halliday, 1972) but also as they enter into other phenomena in the psychology of learning—the phenomenon of discriminative learning providing a good case in point, as we shall see in Chapters 7 and 8. But it is the case that the response-produced inhibition theory of extinction is of current interest largely because of its historical importance, and our treatment of it will reflect that fact.

Reactive inhibition The most complete statement of the response-produced inhibition theory of extinction comes from Hull (1943). Hull started with the assumption that whenever an organism makes a response, it also generates some inhibition with respect to that response. This means that, all other things being equal, once a response takes place, it is somewhat less likely to occur in the immediate future. Such inhibition may be thought of as analogous to fatigue in that it makes the next response more difficult to produce. And like fatigue, reactive inhibition disappears after a period of rest. If there is not enough rest between responses, however, the inhibition accumulates from response to response.

Hull (1943) advanced the hypothesis that the amount of inhibition which results from a series of responses is a positively accelerated function of the amount of physical work the response requires. In other words, as the response requires more effort, the inhibition accumulates at an increasing rate. Later, Hull (1951) revised the substance of this assumption to the effect that for responses involving large amounts of work (relative to the ability of the organism involved), the inhibition generated is not much greater than that for smaller amounts of work. In other words, he said that the function which relates responding to work is S-shaped. In both cases, he specified that rest reduces the inhibition generated by each response in a way that is best described by a simple negative exponential function. Eventually, with enough rest, the response will completely recover its strength. It is important to recognize, too, that in Hull's theory, reactive inhibition will accumulate whether the response is reinforced or not.

The most important aspect of the response-produced inhibition theory concerns its statement about what goes on during extinction. When responses are no longer reinforced, reactive inhibition is thought to increase without the counteracting effects of positive reinforcement. The result is that the organism eventually ceases to respond. Since reactive inhibition decreases with time, however, we should predict spontaneous recovery after a period of rest. Remember, too, that Pavlov showed spontaneous recovery to be only about one-sixth the original response strength, and at best, we might expect only 50 percent recovery. Since spontaneous recovery is incomplete, Hull postulated a second factor, *conditioned inhibition*, to account for the permanent effects of extinction.

Conditioned inhibition   Hull regarded reactive inhibition as a negative motivational state. Presumably, animals are motivated to avoid reactive inhibition much as they are motivated to avoid an electric shock. If we accept the drive-reduction theory of reinforcement, it is easy to see how escape from, or avoidance of, reactive inhibition would constitute reinforcement. Thus, when an organism ceases to respond, its fatigue state, or reactive inhibition, is reduced. But this, in keeping with the drive-reduction point of view, is precisely the operation that is required for reinforcement to occur. Reduction of reactive inhibition supposedly reinforces the organism for doing nothing, and the state of affairs which results and produces failure to respond is a learned *habit* called *conditioned inhibition*.

How reactive and conditioned inhibition work in extinction   The theory of extinction based on reactive and conditioned inhibition seems complicated, but its essentials are simple. Extinction is the result of an active inhibition of a learned response. This inhibition is composed of two parts—reactive inhibition, which is temporary and disappears with rest, and conditioned inhibition, which is permanent and does not. Thus, spontaneous recovery—which the theory does an elegant job of accounting for—is predicted from the assumption that reactive inhibition disappears with rest. In the process, however, conditioned inhibition is produced, and so complete recovery of the extinguished response does not occur.

Hull's two-factor theory, as it has been called, has been applied to a variety of problems in behavior—in addition to its account of the extinction process. For example, it has a great deal to say about the relative utility of massed as compared with spaced practice trials in the acquisition of complex motor skills like learning to type or learning to track moving targets with a pointer. As you can imagine, massed trials ought to lead to a relatively rapid buildup of reactive inhibition, and to relatively slow learning of such tasks, and that prediction turns out to match with data quite well (Kimble & Shattel, 1952; Woodworth & Schlosberg, 1954; Kling & Riggs, 1971). But the theory does not, in the final analysis, do a very adequate job of handling some of the phenomena associated with extinction per se. Let us take a brief look at some of the empirical facts which embarrass it and see why this is so.

Time and effort in relation to response-produced inhibition The response-produced inhibition theory of extinction says that in the process
of extinguishing a response, resistance to extinction will be less if massed
trials as compared with spaced trials are used and if more effort as
compared with less effort is required. This follows directly from the fact
that resistance to extinction is supposed to decrease as a function of the
buildup of reactive inhibition on the one hand and the correlated buildup
of conditioned inhibition on the other. Massed trials and effortful
responses are precisely those things which should produce the greatest
rate of increase in reactive and conditioned inhibition, and so resistance
to extinction should be least under these conditions. Yet as we have seen,
the data from animal experiments involving fairly simple responses are
essentially, if not completely, at odds with this deduction. Since time and
effort are two of the simplest variables that we can introduce into
extinction to test the theory, and since the theory does not do a very
good job of predicting the data that appear when we do so, the
response-produced inhibition account of extinction is already in serious
trouble.

Latent extinction and extinction without responding Some of the most
telling data concerning the response-produced inhibition theory come
from experiments in which an animal, following training, is exposed
directly to a stimulus situation (such as a goal box) in which reward was
formerly available but from which it has now been removed. In the
process, things are set so that the animal *does not perform the complete
learned response at all.* Instead of running the runway to get to the goal
box, the animal is placed directly into the empty goal box by the
experimenter. Then, after a number of direct placements of this sort,
conventional extinction trials begin, and the animal runs once more. The
effect of the direct-placement procedure upon resistance to extinction of
running is checked by comparing the performance of animals subjected
to this procedure with the performance of other animals placed the same
number of times in some "neutral" location (such as a carrying cage or a
box not associated with reinforcement). The response-produced inhibition theory of extinction has to predict that direct placements in an empty
goal box will have essentially no effect upon the subsequent resistance to
extinction of running. This would be true because reactive inhibition of
running cannot build up unless an animal actually runs. Yet there is now
an overwhelming abundance of evidence which shows that direct,
nonreinforced exposure to a place formerly associated with reinforcement produces latent effects that carry over to reduce the resistance to
extinction of a conditioned response. The phenomenon is termed *latent
extinction* (Seward & Levy, 1949; Deese, 1951; Moltz, 1955; Clifford,
1964).

The theory behind the phenomenon of latent extinction Before we turn to
a general evaluation of the response-produced inhibition theory of
extinction, let us take a look at one way in which the phenomenon of

latent extinction, a very interesting effect in its own right, can be handled in theoretical terms. First of all, there is little question that whatever goes on to produce latent extinction must occur *during* the time that animals spend in the stimulus situation associated with reinforcement when they are placed directly there. One way of looking at this is to assume that changes take place in the strength of the Pavlovian conditioned r_g-s_g mechanism described in the last chapter (Moltz, 1957; Spence, 1960; Clifford, 1964). If you will recall, the strength of the fractional goal response is presumed to depend upon such things as the number of reinforcements, the size of each reinforcement, and so on. Furthermore, the elicitation of fractional goal responses by cues in the learning situation is supposed to add to the general level of *motivation* that is conditioned in the learning situation—specifically, in Spence's terms, to incentive motivation K.

Now when a rat is placed directly in a goal box that formerly contained reinforcement, the cues of the goal box elicit the fractional goal response. But since reinforcement is not there, the strength of the fractional goal response should decrease according to the general rules that hold for the extinction of any response. This, in turn, should reduce the strength of incentive motivation. The extent of the reduction will depend upon a number of things, such as the number of times the animal is exposed to the empty goal box and the length of the period the animal is confined there on each occasion—in general, that is, upon any experimental operation which will reduce, through extinction, the tendency for goal-box cues to elicit fractional goal responses. Of course, for control animals placed in some neutral location in which reward has never occurred, there are no cues associated with reinforcement, and so there is nothing to elicit the fractional goal response and produce its extinction. According to this reasoning, then, the latent-extinction procedure produces relatively fast extinction of running because it reduces that part of the motivational base for running which is conditioned to cues specific to the place where original learning occurs.

The fate of the response-produced inhibition theory Putting all the evidence together, we must conclude that the theory does not do a very successful job of withstanding the rigors of experimental test. In the light of phenomena like latent extinction, for example, there appears to be little question that the theory faces a formidable task if it is to extricate itself from the serious trouble in which the data place it. For the present, the task does not seem worth attempting, and it is perhaps for this reason that little attention has been devoted to the theory in recent years. Perhaps new evidence will be uncovered which will lead to a revival of the theory—certainly much behavior bears the stamp of inhibition and inhibitory processes of one kind and another—but that will remain for time to tell. We turn now to another theoretical approach to extinction which continues to capture a great deal of interest and which does a better overall job of accounting for the various phenomena associated with the extinction process.

A second theory of extinction is that put forward by Guthrie (1935, 1952) and by Estes (1950, 1959). In its most general form it is called a *competition* or *interference* theory. In a word, the theory attributes extinction of a particular response to the acquisition of competing response tendencies. Thus, when an animal stops responding in a particular situation, it may be because it has formed an association between "not responding" and the stimuli present in the situation. In some cases the animal will learn responses that are alternative to those conditioned during original learning, while in other cases it will learn to do nothing. In both instances, the important thing is that the animal learns behavior that competes or interferes with the behavior acquired during initial training.

Guthrie, following the above reasoning, says that there are three ways in which responses may be eliminated. The first method is to introduce the conditional stimulus subliminally, so that it is too weak to be detected by the organism and to produce a response, and then to increase its strength gradually. This is what we do when we train a horse to saddle by first putting on only a light blanket and then gradually working up to full gear. The blanket, by itself, is not a sufficient stimulus to set off bucking, and the horse is not disturbed by the gradual addition of heavier loads. A second method is to repeat the conditional stimulus until the original response is exhausted and the organism is too fatigued to give the original response (though it may, perhaps, be able to give other responses). This is the broncobusting technique. The third method is to present the conditional stimulus when it is mechanically impossible for the organism to respond in the way that it was formerly conditioned to respond.

The chief feature of these methods is that they tend to create a situation where, at the time the conditional stimulus is presented, there is a very low probability that the old response will occur and, therefore, a correspondingly high probability that other new responses will occur. This sets the stage for the association, by simple contiguity, of the new responses with the old conditional stimulus. As always, resistance to extinction will be a function of many things, but it will vary chiefly with the extent to which the conditions of the environment assure that new behavior can attach itself to and be triggered by the old conditional stimulus. The basic idea, then, is that a response extinguishes as it is displaced by other incompatible or alternative responses.

Guthrie left his analysis of the extinction process pretty much at this level. Estes, however, has gone quite a bit farther, and, among other things, his approach has the merit of considerable logical elegance. For one thing, conditioning and extinction become simply different aspects of the same thing—they are both learning by a process of contiguous association of elements of particular responses with elements of stimulus complexes. Furthermore, as Estes (1955, 1959) points out, spontaneous recovery under this theory is not a special phenomenon of inhibition.

Rather, it is a function of the fact that the elements of a stimulus compound which are conditioned (or extinguished) on one trial may not be present on the next. These elements, which may be both internal or external to the organism, *fluctuate* from trial to trial, and so the tendency to respond "spontaneously" can change between trials (see also Homme, 1956).

It is perhaps not surprising that competition theory—in its bare form—has difficulties which are similar in magnitude, if not in kind, to those we have seen to trouble the response-produced inhibition theory. For one thing, competition theory could not handle the phenomena associated with latent extinction, and extinction without responding, without being weighted with a large number of extra assumptions. Furthermore, there are few simple one-to-one relationships between the properties of conditioning and extinction—for example, a very high rate of responding can often be obtained in a Skinner box following a very few reinforcements, while extinction after just a few reinforced responses can require an extensively protracted period of time before responding returns to the unconditioned, or operant, level. And in Pavlovian conditioning, extinction is usually more rapid than the original conditioning.

Perhaps the greatest objection to the simple competition theory of extinction, however, is that there is good reason to believe that extinction reflects many factors other than the simple loss of the measured response per se. Extinction does not, for example, remove the effects of learning, because it takes far less time to recondition the animal after a period of extinction (Skinner, 1938). Furthermore, anyone who has handled animals like rats who have just undergone the extinction process is struck by their "emotionality": their jumpiness, their exaggerated startle responses to novel stimuli (disinhibition at work), their general excitability, and—sometimes—their aggression. Indeed, the experienced investigator knows that extinction is the time when he will most likely have a confrontation with his experimental subjects (requiring some antiseptic and a bandage) if such is ever to be the case. Extinction, in other words, appears to contain a measure of frustration-produced emotion which may have some very strong motivational properties. If we take the general logic of competition theory and add dashes of frustration-produced emotion and counterconditioning, we have a very potent tool to use in handling a number of the phenomena of extinction—as we shall now see.

FRUSTRATION AND REINFORCEMENT

There are obviously many ways in which we can frustrate an organism and so, perhaps, arrive at a definition of a frustrating state of affairs. We could, for example, train a rat to run a simple runway with food as a reward, and then introduce frustration by placing a barricade in the runway so that the rat could not get into the goal box (Lambert & Solomon, 1952). In this case, there would be two essential ingredients involved in the production of frustration: *initial training* with a food reward so that the rat, in effect, has a chance to learn that the response of running the alley leads to a fine-tasting morsel in the goal box, and subsequent *blocking* of the response so that the rat can no longer get into the goal box and obtain the reward. This is not the only way in which frustration can be produced, of course, and a technique that is of particular interest to us at the moment is the following: Let the rat continue to run into the goal box after initial training trials which were rewarded with food, but now remove the food. In this case, running trials continue, but frustration is produced by blocking the behavior most critically involved in obtaining reinforcement—the eating response itself. The eating response is blocked, obviously, in the sense that it cannot occur when there is no food to eat. What we now have is frustration produced by the *nonreinforcement* of a previously reinforced response, and as you can see, we also have the experimental operations that we use for extinction.

Many experimenters have observed that when an instrumental response is extinguished, animals tend to become emotionally excited, as if they were frustrated by the withdrawal of reinforcement. Skinner (1938), for example, has noted this in rats undergoing extinction and has proposed that it contributes to the comparative irregularity of extinction curves. Other investigators have assumed that extinction gives rise to a frustration drive and that this accounts for some of the effects we find in a study of extinction. Theoretical and experimental descriptions of the things that happen when frustration due to nonreinforcement occurs have been developed by Spence (1956, 1960), but the most extensive attention to this problem has been given by Amsel (1958, 1962, 1967, 1972). Much of what is known comes from experiments in which frustration has been introduced during the *conditioning* of a response, but this information has been used to generate ideas and experiments aimed directly at the extinction process per se.

In one of the very first experiments on the problem, Amsel and Roussel (1952) ran a single group of rats down a straight runway that consisted of a start box, an alley (alley 1), a goal box (goal box 1), a second alley (alley 2), and a second goal box (goal box 2). After some preliminary training, the rats were run for 84 trials, 3 trials per day, with food available in both goal boxes. At the end of these trials, running times had reached a low asymptote in both runways. Then the rats were run for 36 more trials with food available in goal box 1 on a random half of the trials, and no food available in goal box 1 on the other half of the trials. Food was always available in goal box 2. The experimenters report their results by comparing the running times in runway 2 for those trials where the rats had just eaten food in goal box 1 and those trials where they had not. The data appear in Figure 4.3. As you can see, the rats ran down runway 2 at just about the same speed they always had on those trials in which they had just been rewarded in goal box 1. However, on those trials in which they found no food in goal box 1, they ran significantly *faster* down runway 2.

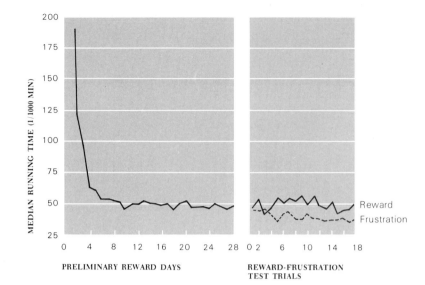

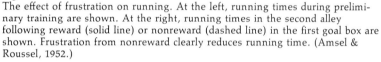

Figure 4.3
The effect of frustration on running. At the left, running times during preliminary training are shown. At the right, running times in the second alley
following reward (solid line) or nonreward (dashed line) in the first goal box are
shown. Frustration from nonreward clearly reduces running time. (Amsel &
Roussel, 1952.)

Amsel and Roussel interpret their data by assuming first of all that
during the initial 84 training trials, the rats were building a strong
tendency to approach and eat food in both goal boxes. They then
assumed that once this tendency was strongly established, *frustration*
was introduced by removing food in goal box 1 on some trials, and that
the effects of frustration showed up on those trials as an increase in
running speed in runway 2. In other words, they assumed that frustration induced by nonreinforcement of a previously reinforced response
has drive or *motivational* properties that channel into running down
runway 2.

Research over the years since Amsel's original work has demonstrated that the effects which can be generated in the double runway are
sometimes complex indeed, and not all data argue in favor of an analysis
based on a simple, uncomplicated application of the concept of frustration per se. For example, one deduction from the frustration approach
would be that some frustration could be generated in goal box 1 if the
reduction of amount of reinforcement on some trials in goal box 1 was
not to a zero amount but was, instead, to some small but finite amount.
In general, amount of frustration should be *graded* depending upon the
difference between the amount usually found in goal box 1 and the
smaller amount available there on trials testing for frustration. Bower
(1962), among others, obtained results which directly support this
prediction: running speed in runway 2 was greater the smaller the
amount of food given on test trials for frustration. A complication over

the interpretation of these data arises, however, when you stop to think that animals are getting fed in goal box 1 on test trials, and getting fed is going to make them less hungry. Furthermore, the extent to which hunger is ameliorated is going to be a direct function of the amount of food given in goal box 1. Thus, an animal getting nothing in goal box 1 on a frustration test trial is going to be maximally hungry as it enters alley 2 and scurries rapidly to the food waiting in goal box 2. An animal getting some larger amount in goal box 1 on frustration test trials will be proportionately less hungry and run, accordingly, proportionately slower. In general, in other words, the frustration effect might appear not because of frustration due to a thwarted expectancy of food, but, instead, because the animal is simply hungrier as it enters runway 2 on trials in which it finds nothing or some relatively small amount of food in goal box 1. While a *demotivation hypothesis* like this one has intuitive appeal—and may account for the data in some experiments—the bulk of the available research suggests that the frustration effect is real and does not occur because animals are simply more or less hungry as they run the second of the double alleys. Instead, it does appear that frustration can be graded depending upon the amount of reinforcement the animal receives on frustration test trials in goal box 1 (see Scull, 1973, for a review).

A second possible complication for a simple frustration analysis of the basic Amsel effect comes from a theoretical observation of Daly (1968) and McHose (1970). These researchers noted that the standard method for demonstrating the frustration effect in the double runway provides an excellent example of *differential conditioning* to cues associated with alley 1 as compared with alley 2. Perhaps, in other words, the frustration effect appears as a form of *contrast effect* between the cues of alley 1 and the partial reward in goal box 1 and the cues of alley 2 and the consistent reward in goal box 2, a contrast effect akin to Pavlovian induction (cf. Chapter 2). This may, in part at least, be true. Amsel (1971), as a matter of fact, has argued directly that the frustration effect looks a great deal like positive Pavlovian induction, and goes on to the contention that other phenomena like behavioral contrast may contain frustrative components.

A factor which strongly validates the frustration approach as expressed by Amsel is that it is possible to obtain differences in activity level after reinforced as compared with nonreinforced trials in a runway. Gallup and Altomari (1969), for example, placed rats in an open enclosure following runs in a runway, which were either reinforced or not, and measured the frequency with which several signs of general activity appeared, such as rearing and climbing. The results showed clearly that following a nonrewarded trial in the runway, when frustration should be high, activity was considerably greater in the open field than it was following rewarded trials in the runway. Other similar experiments support this observation, too (Wagner, 1963; Daly, 1969; Scull, 1973). Since activity in animals like the rat is often taken as an index of the level of generalized emotion or motivation of the animal, these data argue strongly for frustration as an important motivational factor when reinforcement is withheld following the occurrence of a response that is usually reinforced. Taken as a whole, in spite of some of the possible complicating factors which can also enter into situations in which the basic frustration effect is obtained, it appears that Amsel's fundamental assumptions are well supported: the thwarting of an expectancy for a positive reinforcer leads to frustration, and frustration provides motivation.

THE COMPETITION-FRUSTRATION THEORY OF EXTINCTION

Now that we have some basic demonstrations of the effects of frustration before us, let us see how the concept of frustration—together with the principles of competition theory—can fit together to account theoretically for the phenomenon of extinction. In order to do this, we need to develop the concept of the r_f-s_f *mechanism*; this is easy to do, because the *model* for the concept is the same as that for the r_g-s_g mechanism, a mechanism with which you should by now be very familiar. The approach we want to discuss specifically is due primarily to Amsel (1958) and to Spence (1960).

If an animal is first reinforced for a number of trials in some simple learning situation like a straight runway, and if we then remove the reinforcer on some subsequent trial, we have, as we have seen, performed the necessary operations to produce a *primary frustration response* R_f. If we wanted to see some aspect of R_f in action, we would look for overt signs of emotional activity which, in the rat, might consist of such things as urination, defecation, biting parts of the apparatus, and so on. Now it is assumed that, like the primary goal response R_g and its fractional component r_g, there can be a fractional component of the full-blown frustration response. Let us call this fractional component r_f. As primary frustration occurs over a series of nonreinforced trials, r_f, like r_g, is assumed to occur earlier and earlier in the chain of responses leading to the place where primary frustration takes place. That is, r_f can become *anticipatory*, and so the rat, in a manner of speaking, begins to "act frustrated" before it actually arrives at the place where reinforcement has been removed and primary frustration occurs. Just as the elicitation of r_g is presumed to add to general drive level (in the form of incentive motivation in Spence's system), the elicitation of r_f is also presumed to add to general drive level.

Now, to reach the crux of things, the r_f response is presumed to yield its own response-produced stimuli s_f. And the s_f stimuli, in turn, elicit overt responses in the learning situation. Some of these responses to s_f may be quite compatible with the original conditioned response of running to the goal box. But others will appear for the first time, and many of these will be *incompatible* with running. What the r_f-s_f mechanism yields in the end, then, is a source of incompatible responses that are both *triggered* and *motivated* uniquely by the frustration that nonreinforcement produces.

By now you may be able to anticipate the next and final step. Given
that frustration produces incompatible responses, all we have to do is add
the now-familiar propositions associated with learning by contiguity. As
incompatible responses which are stimulated and motivated by frustration occur, they become attached through simple contiguity to the stimuli
that have been eliciting the original learned response. In so doing, they
interfere or compete with that response and produce its extinction. The
process begins in the goal box, of course, but as nonreinforced trials
continue, interfering responses produced by frustration should occur
earlier and earlier in the chain of behavior leading from start box to goal
box. Thus, the sequence of behavior that was conditioned originally will
eventually disappear.

Most recently, Amsel (1972) has broadened his theory into a general
theory of *persistence*, emphasizing conditions under which extinction is
prolonged because of various experimental treatments that are introduced
during the learning of a response. The basic addition to the bare
competition-frustration theory that the broader scheme calls for is the
specification of conditions during initial training which assure that the
competing response to frustrationlike situations will become *habituated*
or *counterconditioned* to the stimuli which are evoking frustration. In
other words, the theory specifies how animals learn to maintain consistent responding in the face of cues which, initially, signal frustration and
trigger responses which are incompatible with the basic learned response. Most of the necessary conditions call for *intermittent reinforcement* of responding. That is a topic we will treat at great length in the
next chapter, so be prepared to meet some further extensive development
of Amsel's approach to persistence there. Right now, let us look briefly at
some experimental data which may help to underline the simple, basic
competition-frustration theory of extinction.

The competition-frustration theory at work   Adelman and Maatsch
(1955) studied the effect upon resistance to extinction of the type of
response elicited by frustration during extinction. They trained rats in a
short, straight runway and then extinguished different groups under one
of three conditions. One group was given regular extinction in that it was
simply confined in the empty goal box for a set period of time following a
run down the alley. A second group was encouraged to make a response
compatible with running as a function of the elicitation of frustration in
the empty goal box: the goal-box lid was raised, and the rat was coaxed
into jumping from the goal box onto a small ledge at the edge of the goal
box (it is not hard to get a rat to do this). A third group was encouraged to
make a response quite incompatible with running down the alley and
into the goal box: the goal-box door that was normally closed to prevent
retracing once the rat reached the goal box was opened on extinction
trials, and the rat was permitted to "recoil" from the empty goal box and
to make the incompatible response of running all the way back to the
start box.

The results of the experiment are quite striking. The rats in the group that could respond to frustration by running into the goal box and jumping directly out of the frustrating situation did not slow their running speeds at all during extinction. The rats in the group that was permitted to retrace extinguished quite rapidly, while the rats in the group that was simply confined in the empty goal box extinguished at an intermediate rate. In short, the experiment clearly demonstrates that the *nature* of the response elicited by frustration can have a marked effect upon the rate at which the response conditioned originally will extinguish. The greater the incompatibility of the response to frustration with the response that the rat has learned initially, the faster extinction proceeds. And this, of course, is an observation that would be predicted directly by the competition-frustration theory.[2]

Another experiment (MacKinnon, 1967, 1968) is especially interesting because it looked directly at the occurrence of competing responses to cues associated with frustrating nonreinforcement in a differential conditioning experiment based on two magnitudes of reward. MacKinnon ran rats in an apparatus in which a run down one distinctive alley (S_1) was always reinforced with a constant 500-milligram food reward, while intervening runs down a second alley (S_2) were reinforced, for different rats, with amounts of food ranging from 500 milligrams (the same as S_1) to 0 milligrams—that is, nothing at all. MacKinnon was interested in the relative speeds that would appear to S_1 and S_2, but he was also interested in the extent to which animals would retrace in the S_2 alley, that is, produce responses incompatible with running when faced with cues signaling a reduced magnitude of reward relative to that prevailing in the S_1 alley. The relevant data appear in Figures 4.4 and 4.5.

The lower curves marked by open circles in Figure 4.4 show that speed of running in S_2 decreased regularly as the amount of food available at the end of that alley decreased. This was true, with a few exceptions, regardless of whether running speeds were measured as the animals started to run, while they were running the main part of the alley, or as they entered the goal area. Speeds also decreased a small, but reliable, amount in S_1 as the amount of reinforcement in S_2 decreased— suggesting that the effects of nonreinforcement spread, or generalized, from alley 2 to alley 1. But the central thrust of the data indicate that as the amount of reward in S_2 decreased relative to that in S_1, the S_2 alley became an increasingly unpleasant place to be—generating slow running characteristic of an aversive state of affairs.

Figure 4.5 shows the retrace data from the experiment, and these data are of special interest insofar as the competition-frustration theory is concerned. Notice that the animals' tendency to retrace was greatest

---

[2]This experiment was actually designed to test some of the implications of an *elicitation* theory of learning in general, and of extinction in particular (Denny, 1971). Denny's approach is similar to the competition-frustration approach, except that it emphasizes the notion that incompatible responses are, in effect, innate, *unconditioned* responses to the sudden removal of primary reinforcement which get conditioned to learning cues by contiguity. Denny does not emphasize the motivational properties of frustrating situations except to note that motivational conditions in general help to assure that certain particular responses will be elicited and thus conditioned.

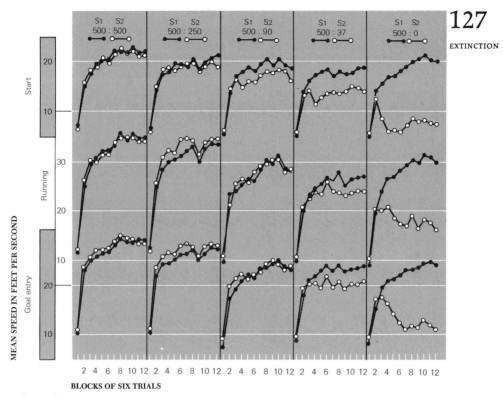

EXTINCTION

Figure 4.4
Running speeds at the beginning (start), middle (running), and end (goal entry) of runways S_1 and S_2. Running speeds decreased markedly in S_2 as the amount of reward decreased there. Speeds also decreased in S_1 although to a lesser degree. (MacKinnon, 1967.)

Figure 4.5
Tendency to retrace in the S_2 alley in MacKinnon's experiment. Notice that retracing tended to appear early in training. Notice, too, that retracing was greater the smaller the magnitude of reward in S_2, that is, the greater the frustration in S_2. (MacKinnon, 1968.)

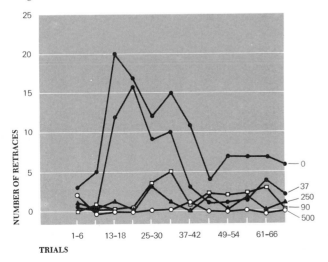

early in learning, but notice particularly that the tendency was greatest the less the amount of reward in S_2. In other words, the more aversive and frustrating the S_2 alley became relative to the S_1 alley, the greater the tendency for competing responses to occur in the S_2 alley.

Figure 4.6 shows some extinction data from MacKinnon's experiment, as discussed by Amsel (1972). The figure shows, first of all, the mean trials to an extinction criterion and, secondly, the mean number of alley retraces during extinction as a function of the magnitude of reward used in S_2 during acquisition. Notice that *extinction was carried out in the S_1 alley* which had always contained a constant, 500-milligram reward. The data show, first of all, that resistance to extinction decreased as the magnitude of reward that was used in S_2 had increased. This is a common finding (e.g., Hulse, 1958), but this experiment shows that it can be obtained when the effect must spread or generalize from one set (S_2) to a second set (S_1) of related cues, perhaps through a mediational process (see Amsel's discussion for a fuller development of this point). Most importantly, however, the data show that a tendency to make *competing responses*—alley retraces—appeared and tended to produce relatively rapid extinction as a function of the amount of reward that had been used in alley S_2 during acquisition. Again, the data argue strongly for the importance of frustration-produced competing responses as a substantial source of the effects associated with the extinction process.

All in all, the competition-frustration theory fares pretty well when put to a variety of experimental tests. Actually, as we have already indicated, the area in which it has received perhaps the greatest amount of experimental attention has to do with the effects of *patterns* of reinforcement upon behavior, a topic which we will treat at considerable length in the next chapter. So be prepared to meet the theory again.

Figure 4.6
Trials to extinction in S_1 (lighter bars) and retraces in alley S_1 (darker bars) as a function of magnitude of reward in S_2 during acquisition. (Amsel, 1972; data from MacKinnon, 1967.)

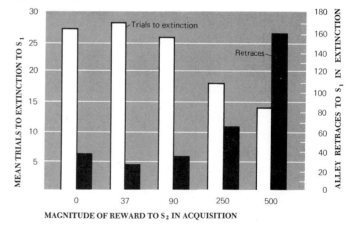

MAGNITUDE OF REWARD TO S_2 IN ACQUISITION

Following our general practice, we have taken a selective look at a small number of theories of extinction. We have done so, of course, at the expense of some other theories that psychologists have also developed to account for the things that go on during extinction. While we have occasionally mentioned other theories in passing (e.g., Denny, 1971), we have not been able to do them justice, and you are encouraged to pursue them in further detail to learn more about how the phenomena associated with the extinction process are handled in theoretical terms.

In this chapter, we have seen both the strengths and weaknesses of an account of the basic phenomena of extinction in terms of response inhibition, and in terms of the concept of competition among responses and of frustration. It is important to recognize that no single one of these approaches can handle all the things we know about the basic extinction process. For example, Pavlov (1927) did a very successful job of accounting for extinction following *Pavlovian* conditioning in terms of inhibition, yet we have seen that at least one form of an inhibition theory runs into serious trouble when it is applied to extinction following *instrumental* conditioning. By the same token, the competition-frustration theory can do a commendable job of handling extinction phenomena following instrumental conditioning, but the theory must be stretched to its breaking point when applied to Pavlovian conditioning. If we have conditioned an eyeblink with Pavlovian procedures, for example, does extinction really produce another response which *competes* and *interferes* with the eyeblink, and if so, what could the nature of that response possibly be? And how, if such is the case, could frustration possibly enter the picture? There may well be answers to these questions (though it seems highly illegitimate to speak of frustration when we extinguish an eyeblink by removing the UCS of a noxious air puff), but we do not have them all yet. Perhaps it will turn out that no unitary theory will be able to handle all the facts of extinction. While theoretical parsimony is always a commendable thing, nature may not provide it as frequently as we might wish.

There is another important question about the matter of extinguishing an "old" response by learning a "new," incompatible activity. It is not clearly established that learning the new response results in any sense at all in the "unlearning" of the old one. What does happen to the old behavior? The theories of Guthrie and Estes, even when supplemented by the notion of frustration, do not provide answers to this question. As we go about measuring behavior during extinction, we record a decrease in the strength of the old response, but this occurs presumably because there are so many other new responses occurring and interfering with the old response. And so we are left with this basic question: Does extinction actually *eliminate* the old response, does it simply supplant the old response with other new ones, or does it do both? We simply do not have a final answer to this question.

OMISSION TRAINING, EXTINCTION, AND THE PERSISTENCE OF BEHAVIOR

Before we leave this chapter and move on to other things, we shall take a brief look now at the effects that instrumental conditioning with the technique of *omission training* (Chapter 1) has upon the persistence of a response. Properly speaking, this topic is not directly associated with that of extinction, but this is a convenient place to raise it because our knowledge of it—what little there is—has been developed largely in the context of experiments which compare the effects of omission training with those of extinction.

Omission training, if you will recall, is a procedure in which a response which has been well learned on the basis of reward training is now placed on a contingency in which *failure* to produce the response for a certain period of time results in reward. In the everyday world it is possible to argue that behavior tends to be eliminated at least as much by omission training as it does by extinction (or even punishment, for that matter). As Uhl (Uhl & Garcia, 1969) points out, people are at least as apt to deliver rewards for the withholding of unwanted behavior ("Johnny, you get dessert if you don't spill your milk") as they are to withhold rewards when the unwanted behavior occurs ("Johnny, you spilled your milk, so you don't get dessert").

When the principles behind omission training are taken into the laboratory, contingencies are generally set up in which omission of the response for a certain period of time, the reinforcement-to-reinforcement (S^r-S^r) interval, results in the delivery of reward. If the experimenter selects an S^r-S^r interval of 20 seconds, for example, rewards will be delivered automatically into the learner's environment every 20 seconds *unless* a response occurs during the interval. In practice, this procedure is sometimes modified so that if a response *does* occur during the S^r-S^r interval, the clock that times that interval resets, perhaps (though not necessarily) adding an additional forced waiting period, an *extra* penalty for responding too soon. With omission training, it behooves the organism to learn to withhold responses, and that, by and large, is exactly what happens.

But how does omission training compare with ordinary extinction as an eliminator of unwanted behavior? Offhand, since omission of behavior is the process upon which reward is directly contingent, it might seem that it ought to be at least as effective as extinction in reducing response strength. Perhaps it might even do a better job. The question has been put to experimental test by a number of investigators (Uhl & Garcia, 1969; Uhl & Sherman, 1971; Uhl, 1973; Zeiler, 1971), although surprisingly little work has been done on the problem given the obvious potential that the technique seems to hold. In any event, let us look at one of Uhl's experiments (Uhl, 1973) to see a comparison between the effectiveness of extinction and omission training.

Uhl trained rats to press a lever for a sucrose reward in a Skinner box. He trained them on a schedule of reinforcement in which responses were rewarded with a drop of sucrose if they were spaced, on the average, by 30 seconds. Different amounts of this training were given, with some rats permitted to lever-press for one 30-minute session in the box, while others were given 3, 9, or 27 daily 30-minute sessions. Then, the groups were divided, half undergoing conventional extinction, while the other half underwent omission training. During omission training, reward was delivered if a response failed to occur for 20 seconds. A penalty of 40 seconds was imposed if the rat pressed the lever during the 20-second interval; if the rat continued to press the lever, additional 40-second periods were imposed until the rat finally stopped for at least 40 seconds. Each rat was run until it met a nonresponse criterion of 10 minutes (remember that the omission-training animals were getting rewards every 20 seconds during that 10 minutes, while the extinction animals got nothing).

The results showed, first of all, that the persistence of lever pressing under either the omission-training or extinction contingency increased with increasing amounts of initial reward training, a phenomenon we have already noted in an earlier section of this chapter. Furthermore, the increase was just about the same regardless of which of the two techniques was used. If we disregard the common effect of different amounts of training and look at a comparison of the persistence of responding as a function of the method of response elimination, we get the data shown in Figure 4.7.

Figure 4.7 shows quite clearly that the extinction procedure was more effective in eliminating behavior than the omission-training proce-dure—at first. As days of elimination training continued, however, the omission-training procedure eventually produced just as much reduction of response strength as the extinction procedure; by day 7 the two curves are not reliably different from each other.

Figure 4.7
Response rates in extinction relative to those at the end of training as a function of the omission and extinction tech-niques of eliminating the lever-pressing response. Extinction is more effective at first, but both techniques produce com-parable results by the seventh day. (Uhl, 1973.)

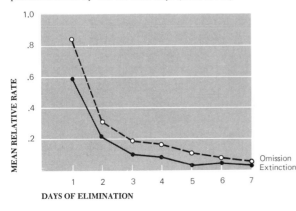

Uhl asked another interesting question in this experiment. He wondered how *durable* the effects of extinction as compared with omission training would be. To this end, the rats were retrained to press the lever using a new contingency in which rewards were programmed to be delivered *automatically* on the same 30-second schedule that had been used during the initial reward training in the experiment. It is important to recognize that this contingency is entirely independent of any rat's production of lever presses—rewards occur no matter what the rat does—and so this procedure is not one in which rats are returned directly to simple reward training (which Uhl had found in earlier work to lead to a rapid resumption of responding following either extinction or omission training). The procedure is one, as a matter of fact, which reintroduces conditions not dissimilar to those which prevailed during omission training for the rats subjected to that procedure, and so it is perhaps not altogether surprising that Figure 4.8 shows that the animals which had experienced *omission training* continue to withhold lever pressing during the durability test. So do rats which had had just one day of initial reward prior to the *extinction* procedure. But as you can see from the figure, other animals which had been extinguished returned rapidly to lever pressing, the more so the greater the amount of initial reward training they had had. Even though reward was not directly contingent on lever pressing at all, the extinction animals were unable to contain themselves, returning to a rapid production of the response which had produced reward at some time in the past.

Uhl analyzes this phenomenon on the basis that the arrival and consumption of a given reward during initial training is a cue for returning to the lever and pressing it again. The omission-training rats have an opportunity to learn that the reward cue no longer signals further rewards if the lever is pressed, while the extinction rats do not. So when rewards reappear—albeit automatically—for the extinction animals during the test for durability, they do what they have learned to do when pellets appear: they go press the lever.

Figure 4.8
Response rates during the test for durability of response elimination relative to those at the end of the elimination procedure. Omission training produces more durable elimination of the lever-pressing response. (Uhl, 1973.)

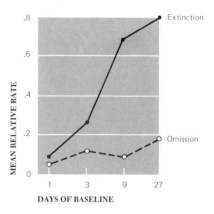

Uhl's test for the durability of response elimination may seem a bit unfair because the omission-training rats had been, in a sense, specifically trained to "resist the temptation" of resuming their old behavior upon the reappearance of a desirable reward, while the extinguished rats had not. But if the fundamental aim of a procedure is to get some bit of behavior to be dropped from an organism's repertoire on some relatively permanent basis, Uhl has described one method for assuring that this takes place. And that is an accomplishment well worth noting.

Two other points with respect to omission training must be made before we turn to the next chapter and our discussion of patterns of reinforcement. First of all, organisms subjected to omission training do not just curl up in the corner of their environments and go to sleep—rousing themselves every now and then to collect the good things that are accumulating automatically in a corner somewhere. Instead, they are quite apt to develop all kinds of other behavior, some of it looking very much like "superstitious" behavior that we have discussed in Chapter 1. As a matter of fact, another label for omission training (Zeiler, 1971) is a *DRO contingency*—differential reinforcement of other (responses). This leads one to the conjecture that omission training—like extinction—leads organisms to produce responses which *compete* directly with the response which is being "eliminated." The crucial difference is that whatever those responses may be, they are reinforced in omission training and they are not reinforced in extinction. Second, the phenomena associated with omission training deserve vigorous investigation, far more investigation than they have received to date. That is a comment which can be easily made about a great may things in the psychology of learning, but since it is very important—as we have seen—that organisms possess mechanisms by which unwanted or useless behavior is dropped from their behavioral repertoires, it is important that we know as much as possible about any mechanism which can help accomplish that end. Omission training deserves far more attention than it has received. Perhaps you will be challenged by our discussion to help provide some of that information.

FIVE

PATTERNS OF REINFORCEMENT

From all the things we have discussed in this book, it should be amply clear that behavior is maintained at high strength by reinforcement and that behavior declines in strength if it is not reinforced. Perhaps you have also remarked to yourself that we have done some substantial oversimplification with respect to conditions of reinforcement and nonreinforcement. But as we have noted before, there are good reasons for this, and we have simplified deliberately. It is much easier to develop some of the basic ideas about learning if we choose situations in which a response is always reinforced or situations in which reinforcement fails consistently. But simplicity has its price. It is quite doubtful if there are many instances in the real world where a given bit of behavior is *always* reinforced under *precisely* the same conditions, or, for that matter, where removal of reinforcement is utterly final and complete. The environment in which animals and people live is just not that consistent.

In this chapter we are going to complicate things somewhat and look at what happens when conditions of reinforcement *change* from response to response—that is, when conditions of reinforcement vary according to some *pattern* (Hulse, 1973b). There are, in fact, many ways in which patterning can occur. One way of establishing a pattern of reinforcement is to reinforce some, but not all, of the responses an organism makes. We simply omit reward or punishment on some trials in instrumental learning, or we omit the UCS now and then in Pavlovian conditioning. As you can see, this is a type of pattern that is, in a sense, intermediate between continuous reinforcement of all responses and continuous nonreinforcement of all responses (which is, of course, extinction). Psychologists have attached the general label of *partial reinforcement* to a pattern in which reinforcement occurs intermittently, but they also speak—particularly within the Skinnerian tradition—of *schedules* of reinforcement to describe specific methods for intermixing reinforcement and nonreinforcement. We shall examine some of these schedules in the next section.

A second procedure for establishing a pattern of reinforcement is to vary the *amount of reinforcement* that is given from response to response. In Pavlovian conditioning, the analogous procedure would be to vary the intensity of the UCS from response to response. Thus, we could reinforce some responses with a large amount of reinforcement (or an intense UCS) and some with a small amount, and we could intermix these according to any particular pattern we might want to use. Still a third method of developing a pattern of reinforcement is to change the *delay of reinforcement* from response to response. Again, in Pavlovian conditioning the analogous procedure would be to vary the CS-UCS interval from one occasion to the next. Some responses could be reinforced with no delay, with long delays, and so forth, or CS-UCS intervals could change from short to very long ones, and so on. It is not hard to think of ways in which some of the basic reinforcement variables can be used in a pattern of reinforcement, and perhaps you can add to this list yourself. The important point is that in the real world, the consequences of behavior vary. We are rewarded—and punished, for that matter—according to an intricate set of rules that are sometimes under our control and sometimes not. And these rules often involve not just one pattern of events, but many, many different patterns that are twined and intertwined in an enormously complex fashion.

Let us begin our discussion of specific patterns of reinforcement by looking at two of them: patterns based on *intermittency* of reinforcement and patterns based on variable *magnitudes* of reinforcement.

PARTIAL REINFORCEMENT

In Chapter 1, we made a precise distinction between a study of behavior in a free-responding situation as compared with a controlled-responding or discrete-trial situation. Nowhere is this distinction more important to keep in mind than it is in connection with a study of intermittent or *partial* reinforcement. In a discrete-trial situation, if you will recall, the experimenter administers isolated trials one by one, and generally measures something about an organism's behavior *within* a particular trial (such as response latency or amplitude) to assess the effects of an experimental procedure. In the case of partial reinforcement, these facts commit the experimenter to define a particular pattern of reinforcement and nonreinforcement in terms of the relative *number* of such trials that shall occur. Typically, this is done by establishing the *percentage* of trials that will be reinforced out of some total number of trials that will be run. Thus, if 75 percent reinforcement is to be used, and 100 trials are to be run, 75 trials will be reinforced and 25 will not. The common procedure is to distribute reinforced among nonreinforced trials in some random fashion, although other sorts of pattern can be used (like reinforcing 50 percent of the trials by systematically rewarding every other response).

In a free-responding situation, such as that of a Skinner box, the organism is free to respond and to distribute its responses in time as it chooses. Here, as in a discrete-trial situation, we can count responses and reinforce some particular percentage or ratio of the responses the organism makes, but we can also use *time itself* as an independent variable to establish a pattern of reinforcement. Let us turn now to free-responding techniques and to the topic of schedules of reinforcement to see how these things are done.

SCHEDULES OF REINFORCEMENT

There are two basic ways in which we can correlate a pattern of reinforcement and nonreinforcement with behavior in a free-responding situation. In the first case, we can set things so that a certain *period of time* must elapse after one reinforcement has been obtained before the next one can be obtained. In the Skinner box, for example, we could arbitrarily decide that at least five minutes must elapse after a lever press has produced one reinforcement before another lever press will produce a second reinforcement. The organism is free to respond as often as it chooses in the interim, but only those responses that follow prior reinforcement by at least five minutes produce the next reinforcement.

The other basic way in which we can develop a pattern based on reinforcement and nonreinforcement is to vary the *number of responses* that an organism must make to produce successive reinforcers. In this case, we might decide to reinforce every tenth response, withholding reinforcement on the intervening 9 responses. Here, it is up to the organism to determine how quickly the required number of responses is made—it does not matter whether it takes five minutes or one. When we use either of these two methods, we can alter the schedule of reinforcement so that it is either haphazard or highly systematic. We might set things, for example, so that successive reinforcements are obtained for 5 responses, then 10 responses, then 2 responses, and so on. Or we can reinforce systematically—as in our initial example above—by rewarding every tenth response. Since these different methods of scheduling reinforcement and nonreinforcement produce rather different effects upon behavior, let us look at them in greater detail.

Fixed-interval reinforcement Fixed-interval (FI) reinforcement occurs on a *fixed* time schedule. Only those responses which occur at intervals greater than some fixed interval of time are reinforced. This kind of schedule has a particular and systematic effect on previously learned behavior. When an animal becomes accustomed to a fixed-interval schedule of reinforcement for, say, pressing a lever, its behavior becomes stable. In general, the animal will emit a reasonably constant number of responses per reinforcement. If, for example, the animal gives an average of 20 responses for each reinforcement and it is being reinforced for responses spaced at least one minute apart, its overall average rate of responding will be 20 responses per minute. If, however, the animal is reinforced once every two minutes, the same 20 responses will be spread out over this period, so that the animal's average rate of responding will be only 10 per minute. The general rule—though there are exceptions—is that the rate of responding is inversely proportional to the interval between reinforcements (Skinner, 1938, 1950).

Basically, of course, an FI schedule of reinforcement presents an
organism with a *timing* problem. The optimum way to behave on this
type of schedule—if effort is to be minimized at least—is to make one
response just after the preset interval elapses, but organisms cannot time
the length of an interval that accurately (unless they can use external aids
like clocks). What can be learned fairly readily, however, is that
responses early in the interval are never reinforced immediately; and
from what you know about delay of reinforcement you would predict
correctly that such responses would come to occur very rarely. As the
interval of time runs its course, however, delays of reinforcement
become much shorter, and it becomes correspondingly more probable
that the fixed interval has elapsed and that any given response will be the
one that produces reinforcement. Consequently, the organism tends to
"pile up" its responses toward the end of the interval, and is usually
responding at a high rate as the end of the interval is reached. Figure 5.1
shows this phenomenon quite clearly for pigeons pecking at a key. There
is essentially no responding following the delivery of a reinforcement
(marked by the downward blip in the cumulative record), but as the fixed

Figure 5.1
A cumulative record of a pigeon pecking a key on a fixed-interval schedule of reinforcement (FI 4 minutes). Each time the pen on the recorder reached the top point of the
figure, it reset quickly to the bottom. To save space in displaying the data, the record
has been cut, and the individual segments have been squeezed to the left. Reinforcements are marked by occasional downward blips of the pen. Note the long pauses after
most reinforcements, and the steady acceleration of rate prior to reinforcement—giving
the record a scalloped appearance. (Ferster & Skinner, 1957.)

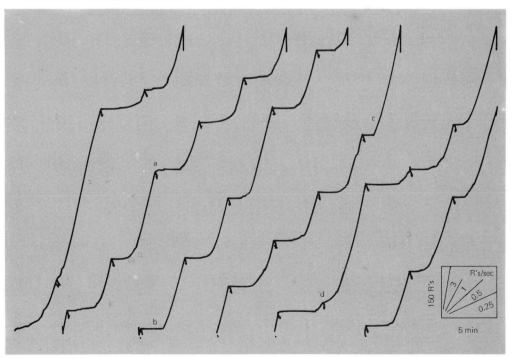

interval—four minutes in this case—runs its course, behavior gradually picks up and the pigeon is going at a steady maximal rate at the time the next reinforcement becomes available and is obtained. The consequence of all these factors is that the cumulative record assumes a *scalloped* appearance as the animal works from one reinforcement to the next.

Fixed-interval schedules are of great interest in the laboratory because they provide an opportunity to study, among other things, how organisms learn to manage their behavior when some internal system monitoring the passage of time is the only cue that is available to mark the availability of reinforcement. It is difficult, however, to think of examples of fixed-interval schedules of reinforcement at work in the everyday world outside the laboratory. This is true because while many things in our daily lives appear at fixed intervals of one kind or another—the arrival of the daily commuting train, the arrival of the dinner hour, final exams at the end of the term, and so on—the events marked by the interval are *not* also *contingent* upon the occurrence of some *response*. The train will come regardless of any behavior on the part of the commuter, and, as students are all too acutely aware, exams appear inexorably at the end of the term. A fixed-interval schedule requires *two* things, in other words: a certain interval of time must have elapsed since the last reinforcement was obtained, *and* some response must occur which directly *produces* the reinforcing event. Perhaps one everyday example satisfying both these conditions would be the behavior of going to the pay window to pick up one's weekly paycheck. Under these conditions, reward (the paycheck) is made available on a weekly fixed interval, but the reward is also contingent upon whatever responses must be made to get to that place where the reward can, in fact, be picked up. And it is those responses that are on the FI schedule.

Variable-interval reinforcement Instead of making reinforcers available at fixed intervals, we can change things so that reinforcement becomes available at *variable* intervals (VI) of time. Thus, after an organism has learned a particular response, we might make reinforcement available after 1 minute, after 30 seconds, after 3 minutes, and so on.[1] Under these conditions, it is not possible for the organism to learn to time the interval at all accurately; reinforcement is, in a sense, likely to be available at any time longer than the shortest interval used in the schedule. Consequently, an organism tends to respond at an extremely stable rate on a VI schedule. Figure 5.2 shows this effect quite clearly; although there are numerous local irregularities in the cumulative record generated on the VI 3-minute schedule, the overall slope of the record is remarkably constant.

---

[1]There are, of course, many ways in which variability among intervals can be set in a VI schedule. One way to do this is to select a number of different intervals of time, say 1, 3, 5, 7, and 9 minutes, and to pick randomly from this list to determine the interval of time between the availability of any two successive reinforcements. The variable-interval schedule is then labeled in terms of the *average* interval of time between reinforcements—5 minutes in this case.

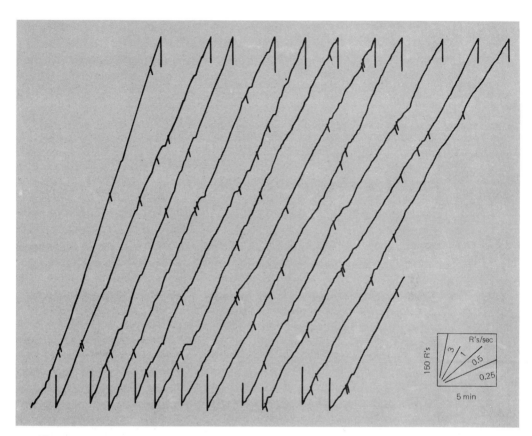

Figure 5.2
A cumulative record like that in Figure 5.1 showing pecking on a variable-interval schedule (VI 3 minutes). Pauses following reinforcement are not evident in the data, and behavior is characterized by a steady rate of responding. (Ferster & Skinner, 1957.)

Fixed-ratio reinforcement In fixed-ratio (FR) reinforcement, the reinforcement is contingent upon the occurrence of a *fixed number* of responses. Here, as you might expect, the effects on performance are dramatically different from those of FI schedules. First of all, reinforcement on a ratio schedule places a premium on rapid responding; the higher the rate of responding, the higher the rate of reinforcement. A peculiarity of performance on FR schedules, however, is that the organism tends to pause for a while (sometimes for several minutes or more) just after it has obtained a reinforcement; then it begins more or less at once to respond at a rapid, fairly constant rate until the next reinforcement is obtained. This so-called *postreinforcement pause* is quite evident in Figure 5.3. If we exclude the period of the postreinforcement pause, however, rate in the schedule is quite constant. Other experiments show that rate tends to increase, however, as the size of the fixed ratio becomes larger.

Everyday examples of ratio reinforcement are much easier to come by than examples of interval reinforcement schedules. An FR schedule is, basically, an example of *piecework* in which the amount of money that

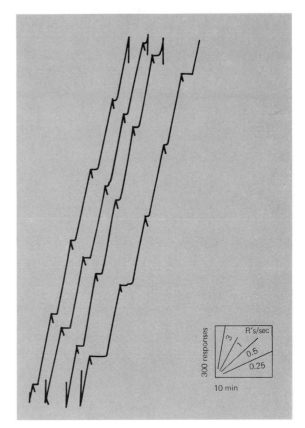

Figure 5.3
A cumulative record like that in Figure 5.1 showing pecking on a fixed-ratio schedule (FR 200). Note the marked
pauses after each reinforcement followed by an almost
immediate return to the high rate of responding characteristic of the schedule. (Ferster & Skinner, 1957.)

one makes depends upon how many of a given item, be it baskets of
tomatoes or bundles of widgets, get picked or produced. No doubt you
can think of a great many other examples of the reinforcement of
behavior which is describable in terms of fixed-ratio schedules.

Variable-ratio reinforcement Within the domain of ratio schedules,
variable-ratio (VR) schedules are perhaps the most interesting because
they are probably most characteristic of the conditions under which
natural behavior occurs—at least those conditions where patterns of
reinforcement involve nothing but reinforcement and nonreinforcement.
Variable-ratio reinforcement is analogous to VI reinforcement, but with a
VR schedule, of course, different numbers of responses are required to
produce successive reinforcers. If we reinforce a well-learned habit on a
VR schedule, postreinforcement pauses do not become a dominant part
of performance, and extraordinarily high rates of performance can be
generated, as Figure 5.4 shows.

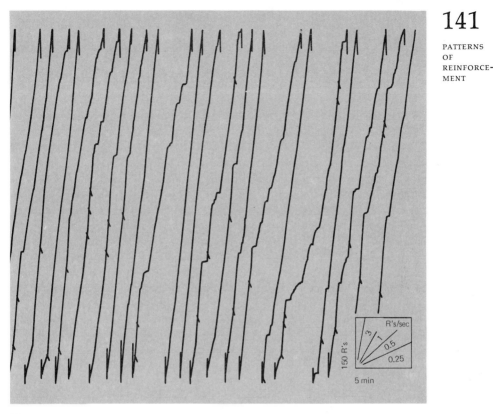

Figure 5.4
A cumulative record like that in Figure 5.1 showing pecking on a variable-ratio schedule (VR 360). Postreinforcement pauses are not evident, and the bird responds at a high, steady rate for the most part. (Ferster & Skinner, 1957.)

Other schedules of reinforcement   We have described only a few of the many possible schedules of reinforcement that can be generated, though we have carefully examined those that are most basic. It is possible, for example, to use combinations of different schedules, perhaps arranging them in sequence so that the animal responds on one schedule for a while, then must respond on another. We can, if we wish, pair stimuli with the schedules so that one kind of stimulus is present when one schedule is in effect (a so-called *multiple schedule*). Or we can reinforce only when responses occur at a rate faster or slower than some arbitrary rate we decide upon in advance (differential reinforcement, respectively, of high and low rates of responding). Of course, each schedule generates its own unique pattern of behavior. In general, the variety of schedules of reinforcement that can be studied is limited only by the complexity of experimenters' programming equipment and their ingenuity in making use of it. If you want to look at a good catalog of many kinds of schedules of reinforcement—and the behavior that each generates—consult Ferster and Skinner (1957).

A second class of patterns of reinforcement can be developed if we reinforce successive responses of some kind with different amounts of reinforcement. As a rat runs a runway, for example, we might reinforce the first run with 5 food pellets, the second with 15 food pellets, the third with 10 food pellets, and so on. In this case, the rat is *always* reinforced in the sense that it always gets something to eat when it arrives at the goal box. However, the amount of food that is used as a reward changes from trial to trial.

It is quite likely that a pattern of reinforcement based on variable amounts of reinforcement describes the things that go on in the environment of most organisms more realistically than a pattern of reinforcement based on a combination of simple reinforcement and nonreinforcement. If you stop and think for a moment, it is hard to imagine many examples where the environment pays off with something of exactly the same magnitude or with nothing at all each time that a response occurs. Instead, a bit of behavior is more apt to be reinforced from one occasion to the next with one of a *number* of different amounts or kinds of reinforcement. Thus, an employer rewards an employee from time to time with a raise in salary, a smile and a hearty handshake, a simple pat on the back, or perhaps just a quick nod. Similarly, an animal on the hunt for food is rewarded sometimes with a large kill that may supply food for several days, sometimes with a mere morsel, and sometimes with nothing at all—though the latter must not happen too often if the animal is to survive.

Mean amount of reinforcement   As you can imagine, the general concept of a pattern based on variable amounts of reinforcement can lead potentially to a very large and complex list of specific methods for reinforcing responses with different amounts of reinforcement. For simplicity's sake, let us look at just one example, an example which has some interesting properties and is based on the principle of *mean* or *average* amount of reinforcement.

Suppose we pick a certain mean amount of reinforcement that an organism is to receive over a large number of responses. We might decide, for example, that we are going to run a rat down an alley for 100 trials and that we want to reinforce each trial with 10 pellets of food, *on the average*. Having set our mean amount of reinforcement, there are many ways in which we could actually reward the rat from trial to trial, developing a pattern of reinforcement but still keeping within the restriction that the mean amount must equal 10 pellets per trial by the time we have given 100 trials.

To keep things simple, let us give the rat one of just two possible amounts of reinforcement on each trial. We can satisfy our mean-amount requirement by giving the rat 5 pellets on half the trials and 15 pellets on the other half, perhaps intermixing the two amounts in some random fashion. We could also do the same thing by giving 9 pellets on half the trials and 11 pellets on the other half, by giving 18 and 2 pellets, and so on. In each case, by the time we have completed all our training trials, the rat will have gotten a mean amount of 10 pellets per trial. In each case, too, the size of the *difference* between the two numbers of pellets changes. Thus, the rat is exposed to much greater changes in magnitude from trial to trial in the case of 18 pellets versus 2 pellets than it is in the case of 11 pellets versus 9 pellets. In a sense, the pattern of reinforcement from trial to trial wobbles over a much greater range of amounts in the former case than in the latter.

If you have this clearly in mind, let us carry things a stealthy step farther. Suppose we give the rat 10 pellets on half of the trials and 10 pellets, the same amount, on the other half of the trials. This, obviously, is consistent *continuous* reinforcement with exactly the same amount from trial to trial—the kind of "pattern" with which we have dealt throughout most of this book. But now suppose that we give the rat 20 pellets on a random half of the trials and 0 pellets (that is, nothing at all) on the other half. This, of course, is random 50 percent *partial* reinforcement! In each case, remember, we have continued our restriction that the mean amount of reinforcement per response be 10 pellets, but what we have done is to derive continuous and partial reinforcement as *special cases* of a pattern of reinforcement in which amounts of reinforcement vary over trials. Continuous reinforcement, generally speaking, is the limiting case where there is *no* change in amount, and partial reinforcement is the limiting case where there is *maximum* change in amount.

Of course, to generalize a bit, we do not have to restrict ourselves to the use of just two amounts of reinforcement, as we have done in the examples above. We could pick a certain mean amount and then select half a dozen amounts to give to the rat from trial to trial. We could make each amount occur with a different frequency over a group of trials. In general, there are an infinite number of patterns that could be developed with different amounts of reinforcement, just as there are an infinite number of possible schedules of reinforcement and nonreinforcement.

To what extent do patterns of reinforcement of the type we have discussed have common effects upon behavior? Let us turn to this problem now as we look at some of the things that have been learned about the matter in the laboratory.

THE EFFECTS OF PATTERNS OF REINFORCE-MENT ON LEARNING AND EXTINCTION

PATTERNS OF REINFORCEMENT AND LEARNING

Partial reinforcement If we tried to train a rat to press a lever in a Skinner box by reinforcing it once for every 10 responses, we would have a long wait before the animal would learn to press the lever and begin to perform consistently. This would be true because the strengthening effects of one reinforcement upon behavior would be pitted against the weakening effects of nine nonreinforcements. Of course, once the response was learned, a rat reinforced on FR 10 would respond at a much faster rate than another rat reinforced continuously. But the course of acquisition would be much slower in the former case than in the latter. As a practical matter, rats that are to be placed on schedules of reinforcement in free-responding situations are generally "shaped" toward the final schedule. Thus, we begin by reinforcing quite frequently, gradually decreasing the frequency of reinforcement as the rat's behavior develops.

Much of the same effect holds for discrete-trial learning situations. A running response in a straight alley, for example, tends to develop at a much slower rate when partial as compared with continuous reinforcement is used. In discrete-trial situations, too, the strength of a partially reinforced response at the time learning is complete tends to be no greater—and is often less—than the strength of a response that has been continuously reinforced. This is perhaps even more the case for Pavlovian conditioning. As a matter of fact, one of the primary distinctions—perhaps the major empirical distinction—between Pavlovian and instrumental conditioning is the fact that it is extremely difficult to get successful Pavlovian conditioning with partial reinforcement (Kimble, 1961). This is not to say that it cannot be done, but even where conditioning is successful, its strength fails to match that obtained under comparable conditions with continuous reinforcement. To return to our original point, then, partial reinforcement in discrete-trial learning situations tends to slow the development of learning. There are some exceptions to be noted in the literature (e.g., Weinstock, 1958; Goodrich, 1959; see Robbins, 1971, for a review), but the effect is generally so prepotent that it can be taken as a safe rule of thumb.

Variable amounts of reinforcement If a pattern of appetitive reinforcement like food is used in which amounts of reinforcement vary over trials, organisms often tend to behave during the learning of a response as if they were responding to some sort of *average* of the amounts involved in the pattern. Response strength does not develop in the manner to be expected if the organism were responding alone to either the largest or the smallest amount in the pattern. Instead, the organism behaves as if it were being reinforced by an amount somewhere between these extremes. As a matter of fact, if a specific mean amount is established in advance, a number of patterns of different amounts of reinforcement can be used over training trials, and the rate of development of response strength will be about the same in each case. In many cases an organism behaves as if it were being reinforced by a single amount somewhere near the middle of the range of amounts used (Logan, Beier, & Ellis, 1955; Yamaguchi, 1961; Hulse & Firestone, 1964; Bevan, 1966, 1968).

Yamaguchi's experiment demonstrates this point nicely. He ran hungry rats in a straight runway for 40 acquisition trials and then for 30 extinction trials. During acquisition, one group was rewarded with 9 units of wet mash on a random half of the trials and 1 unit on the other

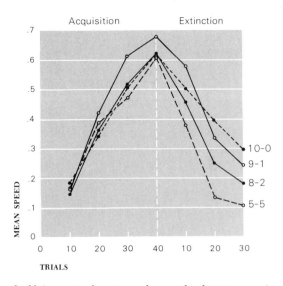

Figure 5.5
Mean running speeds for groups of rats receiving variable amounts of reward. During acquisition all groups run at about the same speed (the 9-1 group is not reliably faster than the others statistically), but during extinction, the greater the range of variability in amount, the greater the running speed. (Yamaguchi, 1961.)

half (1 unit of wet mash weighed 0.05 gram). A second group received 8 and 2 units, a third group received 5 and 5 units (continuous reinforcement), while a fourth received 10 and 0 units (partial reinforcement). Note that the mean amount of reinforcement per response in each case was 5 units—the amount that the continuously reinforced group received.

The results of the experiment are shown in Figure 5.5. If you look at the left half, which shows the acquisition data, you will see that all groups learned at just about the same rate. The group given 9 units and 1 unit ran somewhat faster than the others, but Yamaguchi's statistical analyses show that this difference is due to chance variability in the data. Thus, in Yamaguchi's experiment, as long as the mean amount of reinforcement is constant, the course of learning is essentially independent of the range of amounts that occur over successive responses.

While the effect that Yamaguchi reported is by no means limited to rats and runways, because similar effects can be obtained in free-responding situations (Hulse & Firestone, 1964; Hulse, 1973b), it would be a mistake to think that organisms *always* behave as if they were averaging magnitudes of reinforcement in some fashion. A good example of an exception comes from some work of Boe (1971), who varied the intensity of a *punishing* stimulus (electric shock) and studied how effectively it would suppress some learned behavior. Without going into the details of his experiment, we can note simply that he found that rats exposed to patterns of punishment which varied from 50 volts to 110 volts (with an average intensity of 80 volts) succumbed to the effects of punishment to a greater extent than other rats exposed to a constant 80-volt intensity. In other words, the inclusion of extreme higher intensities made shock a more effective general punishing event—as a matter of fact, the rats in the variable-intensity group eventually behaved much as if they were being shocked continuously at the extreme 110-volt value.

In another context, we have already examined an experiment in Chapter 2 (Hulse, 1973a) in which rats showed *contrast effects* if they had been preexposed to a pattern of reinforcement containing two magnitudes of food. In that case, if you will recall, a negative contrast effect was obtained only if the animals had been exposed to *both* large and small rewards and then trained to respond for the small reward. Here, clearly, the animals learned to distinguish between the large and small amounts in some sense at least and responded to them differentially—rather than averaging them together and responding to them as if they were, psychologically, a single unitary amount. Once again, it is useful to remember that a concept of a pattern of reinforcement stresses the notion that reinforcers are *stimuli* and that stimuli in turn are subject to the many different rules regarding stimuli—rules which range from psychophysical rules of the sort we touched upon in Chapter 3 to principles of discrimination learning that we will examine in detail in Chapter 7. It would be surprising if reinforcers always worked the same way when combined into patterns of one kind or another.

There are a number of other cases where the concept of variable amounts of reinforcement has been applied, ranging from some excellent work of Logan (1965, 1968) on choice behavior to some work of McHose (1970) on differential conditioning. You are encouraged to check these references and the others to which they will lead you if you wish to pursue the matter further.

PATTERNS OF REINFORCEMENT AND EXTINCTION

Extinction produces the most dramatic effect of patterns of reinforcement upon behavior. All patterns affect resistance to extinction somewhat differently, but it is an important general rule that a pattern which involves some change in the nature of reinforcement conditions from response to response will produce greater resistance to extinction than a condition where all responses are reinforced immediately, 100 percent of the time, in just the same way.

Results obtained by many, many investigators show that a pattern of partial reinforcement greatly increases resistance to extinction. Skinner (1938) and Humphreys (1939) demonstrated this in some of the earliest experiments on the problem, and since that time, literally hundreds of experiments have repeated these results with a wide variety of subjects, apparatuses, and experimental procedures (Jenkins & Stanley, 1950; Lewis, 1960; and Robbins, 1971, provide extensive reviews of the literature concerned with this phenomenon).

The large effects of a pattern of intermittent reinforcement on resistance to extinction can be seen in Figures 5.6 and 5.7. Figure 5.6 shows the course of extinction following instrumental conditioning with continuous reinforcement and with aperiodic (variable-interval) reinforcement. The data come from an early classic experiment (Jenkins, McFann, & Clayton, 1950). When a VI schedule is used, 200 reinforcements during training produce about five times as many responses during extinction as when continuous reinforcement is used. The upper

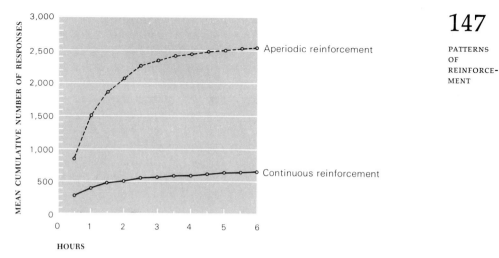

Figure 5.6
Cumulative records of extinction following intermittent and continuous reinforcement. For the intermittent reinforcement condition, the animals in both
groups received 200 reinforcements before extinction began. (Jenkins, Mc-
Fann, & Clayton, 1950.)

curve in Figure 5.7 shows resistance to extinction following 560 reinforcements on different FR schedules, including continuous reinforcement
(Boren, 1961). The number of individual responses emitted in the first
three, out of a total of five, 1-hour extinction sessions increases rapidly as
the size of the fixed ratio increases.

Figure 5.7
Number of extinction responses as a function of the size of
the fixed ratio of reinforcement. The solid curve gives the
total number of individual lever presses made during extinction. The lower dashed curve shows the same data
plotted in terms of response units, one response unit
representing the number of responses that had been required to produce one reinforcement during training. (Bor-
en, 1961.)

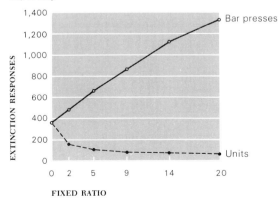

Resistance to extinction following conditioning with a pattern of variable amounts of reinforcement increases as the range, or variability, of the amounts increases. This is shown quite clearly in Yamaguchi's (1961) data, which appear in the right half of Figure 5.5. Greatest resistance to extinction was obtained following training with 10 units on half the trials and 0 units on the other half (partial reinforcement), and resistance to extinction was least if all trials had been reinforced with the mean amount of 5 units (continuous reinforcement). The important point, however, is that intermediate resistance to extinction was obtained when the range in amounts given from trial to trial lay between the extremes of continuous and partial reinforcement: the 9-1 and 8-2 groups arrange themselves neatly between the 5-5 group and the 10-0 group by the end of extinction.

Yamaguchi's data on variable amounts of reinforcement are to be supplemented by data from a growing number of other experiments which show that resistance to extinction increases as variability in the amount of reinforcement increases (e.g., Hulse & Firestone, 1964; Leonard, 1969; Hulse, 1973b). Furthermore, there is now considerable evidence that shows the phenomenon holds even if learning is based on patterns of negative reinforcement and punishment. In the Boe (1971) experiment cited earlier, for example, the effects of punishment were far more durable if punishment had been patterned in intensity during learning than if it had been held constant at some fixed value. Since nonreinforcement and direct punishment of responses appear to share some properties in common (Brown & Wagner, 1964), it is perhaps not surprising that this result should obtain. Indeed, to summarize at this point, it is a safe generalization to conclude that essentially *anything* which makes conditions of reinforcement variable from response to response during acquisition will tend to increase the persistence of a response during extinction. Furthermore, there is apparently no limit to the extent to which a pattern of reinforcement, particularly a pattern based upon a schedule of reinforcement and nonreinforcement, can increase resistance to extinction. Even in the laboratory it is possible to produce habits that will resist the shattering effects of thousands of unreinforced responses. As a matter of fact, Skinner (1950) suggests that if conditions are proper, it is possible to produce an extinction curve with no curvature at all; in other words, the organism goes on responding without reinforcement ad infinitum. Incidentally, Skinner remarks, such a result is a telling blow against a theory of extinction built upon the supposed accumulation of response-produced inhibition.

The effect of patterns of reinforcement upon resistance to extinction is of the greatest theoretical, practical, and adaptive significance. For one thing, we have a key to the understanding of why behavior in natural settings is likely to be so persistent: most behavior is probably not reinforced for all tries, and when reinforcement does come, it tends to come in amounts which vary from try to try. It is fortunate that organisms have evolved to respond the way they appear to do to patterns of reinforcement, since the real world seems to be arranged so that reinforcement is inconsistent, often unpredictable, even capricious.

Indeed, the occasions on which conditions of reward and punishment
fail to change from one time to the next are the occasions which provide
the true anomalies in nature. Perhaps it is equally adaptive that behavior
not be persistent when reinforcement is withdrawn under such conditions.

THEORETICAL INTERPRETATIONS OF THE
EFFECTS OF PATTERNS OF REINFORCEMENT

We have seen that the importance of patterns of reinforcement is
twofold. First of all, at least in the case of schedules of reinforcement
based on reinforcement and nonreinforcement, momentary characteristics of response strength depend upon the particular schedule of reinforcement under which an organism performs. Thus, we have postreinforcement pauses with FR schedules and scalloping with FI schedules.
Second, we saw that patterns of reinforcement have the very prepotent
effect of increasing resistance to extinction. This is perhaps the most
fundamental point; at least, it is the one which has received by far the
most theoretical attention.

Given the fact that patterns of reinforcement based on variables other
than reinforcement and nonreinforcement are relative newcomers to the
experimental study of learning, it is not surprising that the head
scratching of most psychologists has been aimed at the extinction
phenomena associated with partial reinforcement. This is not to say that
other patterns of reinforcement have not received their share of theoretical scrutiny, and eventually it is going to be the case that a theory which
accounts for behavior under one pattern will also account for behavior
under another with only minor modifications. But right now, we must
use the theoretical tools which are at our immediate disposal, and these
are all best designed to pry into the secrets associated with partial
reinforcement. Let us turn our attention, then, to the theoretical analysis
of the *partial reinforcement effect*: the fact that partial reinforcement
produces greater resistance to extinction than continuous 100 percent
reinforcement.

Broadly speaking, there have emerged two general approaches to the
problem (Lawrence, 1958). One says that the partial reinforcement effect
occurs because of things the organism learns about the *sequence* of
reinforcements and nonreinforcements as conditioning trials progress.
This way of looking at things emphasizes the importance of *inter*trial
events—the things that happen from one trial to the second, to the next,
and so on. The second approach places emphasis on how organisms
learn to respond specifically to the reinforced trial as distinct from the
nonreinforced trial. This way of looking at things is concerned not so
much with the effects over a number of trials of the sequence or pattern
of reinforcement and nonreinforcement, but with what organisms learn

to do *within particular trials*, especially those that are not reinforced. That is, the second approach emphasizes *intra*trial events.

INTERTRIAL PHENOMENA AND THE PARTIAL
REINFORCEMENT EFFECT

Expectancy The expectancy approach says that organisms come to expect over a series of trials that reinforcement is associated in a particular fashion with responding. Thus, a rat reinforced 100 percent of the time for pressing a lever comes to expect food after each response. If an animal is reinforced only part of the time during training, however, it will not expect a reinforcement on every occasion, and so when reinforcement stops altogether, the animal is likely to be more persistent. This explanation has great commonsense appeal, and it would almost certainly satisfy your grandmother.

The concept of expectancy does not satisfy many psychologists, however, and it has been roundly and justifiably criticized on several grounds. The most serious criticism of the notion of expectancy is that it is, in its bare form, an ad hoc explanation. It would be acceptable if it were defined in some operational way, such as demanding that an organism be able to respond to a conditional cue before the unconditioned stimulus appears. If this is all that one means by expectancy, there is no quarrel. But nothing much has been explained, either. The basic problem with an expectancy approach to the partial reinforcement effect is not that the notion of expectancy explains too little. Rather, the bare notion of expectancy explains too much too easily.

Discrimination Another simple idea used to account for the partial reinforcement effect says that under partial reinforcement it is less easy for the organism to discriminate between conditions of reinforcement and those of extinction than it is under continuous reinforcement. This implies that the major determiner of resistance to extinction is the extent to which the overall stimulus situation—particularly that prevailing at the time extinction begins—is the same as that during original reinforced training. In partial reinforcement, organisms have a chance over a number of conditioning trials to learn to respond in a stimulus situation which sometimes contains reinforcement and sometimes does not. Consequently, when extinction begins, it is difficult for the organism to tell when original training ends and extinction begins. For a continuously reinforced organism, this is not the case at all, of course. The change from reinforcement conditions of acquisition to those of extinction is marked, abrupt, and therefore easy to discriminate. And so the organism should be able to detect the failure of reinforcement easily and stop responding quickly.

Let us look at a bit of data to see the discrimination hypothesis at work. Tyler, Wortz, and Bitterman (1953) ran rats down a runway. When the rats got to the end, they had to jump a short distance into a goal box, leaping through a window covered with an easily movable card. The purpose of the card was to keep the rats from seeing what was in the goal box until they got there. Two groups of rats were run. One group was reinforced on a random 50 percent of 120 training trials and then extinguished. A second group was also reinforced on 50 percent of 120 training trials and extinguished, but things were set so that *every other* trial was reinforced during acquisition. Thus, in contrast to the rats of the first group, it was possible for the rats of the second group to learn something about the regular serial nature of the pattern of reinforcement. Whether rats could learn to discriminate a pattern of single alternation of reinforcement and nonreinforcement of this sort was, of course, an experimental question, but as things turned out, they could indeed. By the end of training, the rats in the single-alternation group had learned to run quickly on a trial that was to be reinforced and slowly on a trial that was not. The rats in the random group, on the other hand, ran at just about the same speed on all training trials; there was no particular set sequence of reinforcement and nonreinforcement that they could learn to detect.

Perhaps you can already predict the extinction results: the rats in the single-alternation group extinguished faster than the rats in the random group. According to the discrimination hypothesis, the rats in the former group had learned a good deal about the pattern with which reinforcements came during training, and it was relatively easy for them to discriminate the change in the pattern when extinction began. Not so for the rats in the random group; there was no consistent pattern of reinforcement and nonreinforcement during training which could help them discriminate the change from training to extinction, and so they maintained their performance for a longer time.

There are other experiments which support the bare discrimination hypothesis (e.g., Longnecker, Krauskopf, & Bitterman, 1952), but more recent work suggests that it must be modified and complicated a bit if it is to do an adequate job of accounting for the partial reinforcement effect.

Discrimination and blocks of continuous and partial reinforcement Jenkins (1962) and Theios (1962), working independently, asked a very simple question about the effects of partial reinforcement on extinction. What would happen, they wondered, if during the course of training, animals were partially reinforced for a while, but were then continuously reinforced for a number of trials just before extinction began? Would the effects of the early partial reinforcement procedure weather the effects of the subsequent continuously reinforced trials in such a way that the partial reinforcement effect would still appear? Or would the animals behave during extinction as if they had been continuously reinforced throughout training? A bare discrimination theory would predict that they would behave as if they had always been continuously reinforced. This would be true because on the trials prior to extinction, the pattern of continuous reinforcement then in effect ought to make it easy for the animals to discriminate the change to the consistent nonreinforcement characteristic of extinction. But that is not the way things worked out.

Theios, with rats in a runway, and Jenkins, with pigeons in a Skinner box, found that subjects who were first partially reinforced for a block of trials, then continuously reinforced for a block of trials, behaved during extinction very much as if they had not been continuously reinforced at all. In Theios's experiment, for example, all rats first received 30 preliminary training trials in a runway. One group of rats then received 70 trials reinforced at random 40 percent of the time, followed by 70 additional continuously reinforced trials. The group which had the mixture of partial followed by continuous reinforcement was far more resistant to extinction than the group which had continuous reinforcement throughout training. Its resistance to extinction was almost, but not quite, as great as that of another control group which, following preliminary training, had received nothing but partial reinforcement.

By and large, other experiments cast in the same vein as those of Jenkins and Theios have supported the principle that the partial reinforcement effect can be sustained through a block of continuously reinforced training trials (e.g., Sutherland, Mackintosh, & Wolfe, 1965; Theios & McGinnis, 1967; see Sutherland & Mackintosh, 1971, for a review).

Though the data at which we have just looked are quite damaging to the discrimination theory as we have introduced it, there is no reason why the discrimination theory could not be appropriately modified to account for the new information. All we would have to do is to postulate that organisms, once exposed to a pattern of partial reinforcement, can carry with them through a series of continuously reinforced trials some kind of *permanent trace* of their experience with the pattern of partial reinforcement. When extinction begins, the first nonreinforced trial or two reintroduces the conditions characteristic of partial reinforcement, and the organism begins to behave once again as it ought to according to the rules associated with that pattern. What we are saying, basically, is that a rat, a pigeon, or a person ought to be able to "remember" its experience with partial reinforcement and that subsequent experience with continuous reinforcement ought not to interfere very much with that memory. When viewed from the vantage point of common experience, this does not seem to be too rash a working assumption, though like all such assumptions, it must withstand the rigors of experimental test before we can accept it. Let us turn now, then, to a theory of extinction and the partial reinforcement effect which does, in fact, stress the idea that organisms can learn about and remember certain features of patterns of reinforcement.

A sequential theory Capaldi (1966, 1967, 1970) has developed a theory which stresses the things that animals are supposed to learn as they experience *transitions* from nonrewarded to rewarded trials under partial reinforcement. The details of this theory are rich and a bit too complex for full development here (by all means pursue them if you wish), but his basic observation about learning with partial reinforcement is, first, that animals learn to approach goal objects in response to distinctive stimuli associated with nonreinforcement. He labels these stimuli S^N. Capaldi postulates that this will not happen, however, unless S^N is followed by reward; that is, an animal learns nothing about approaching a goal in the presence of cues signaling nonreinforcement (including those the animal remembers from just-preceding nonreinforced trials) unless and until those cues are followed on the very next occasion of the response by positive reinforcement. Note that it is the specific *sequence* of things that is important here. It is not so much that animals are exposed to lots and lots of nonreinforcement in partial reinforcement; rather it is the fact that nonreinforced trials are ultimately followed directly by reinforced trials that conditions the animal to approach when exposed to S^N and so increases resistance to extinction. Beyond this basic postulate, Capaldi adds the notion that the *strength* of the tendency to approach the goal under S^N will depend upon factors such as the *number of transitions* there have been from nonreinforced to reinforced trials over the course of acquisition. This follows from the fact that the greater the number of transitions, the greater the opportunity for responding to nonreinforcement to be strengthened by reward. His theory also says that the strength of S^N will increase as a function of the *number of nonreinforced trials* preceding any given reinforced trial (N-length), and the *number of different N-lengths* that a set of acquisition trials contains.

Given the foregoing principles for establishing S^N in partial reinforcement, then, Capaldi postulates that when entering extinction and exposed to S^N there, the organism remembers the things that were associated with nonreinforcement during training—namely, to approach the goal in the face of cues signaling nonreinforcement—and so continues to perform the learned response for a long time. An animal exposed to continuous reinforcement during acquisition has not, of course, had an opportunity to learn to respond to cues associated with nonreinforcement, has no memory of what to do when faced with nonreinforcement, so to speak, and so extinguishes relatively rapidly.

Capaldi's theory has been subjected to a variety of tests, and by and large it withstands the rigors of experimental scrutiny pretty well. Capaldi (1964) showed, for example, that resistance to extinction increased if a pattern of reinforcement was used during training in which reward was preceded by two nonreinforced trials (an N-length of 2) as compared with one nonreinforced trial (an N-length of 1) or zero nonreinforced trials (that is, continuous reinforcement). Furthermore, he showed that if he used a pattern in which reward was sometimes preceded by one nonreinforced trial, sometimes by two, and so on (that is, if a number of different N-lengths were used), resistance to extinction also increased relative to a condition which contained just one N-length. There are many other deductions that have been made from the theory too, of course, and you may check sources such as Capaldi (1970) if you want to find out more about them. We turn now, however, to another intertrial approach to the partial reinforcement effect, one that is of special interest both because of its intuitive appeal and because of its historical interest—it was perhaps the first formalized theory of the partial reinforcement effect to be developed.

Response units   This approach to the partial reinforcement effect is well suited to free-responding situations. As a matter of fact it is not easily applied to other kinds of experimental situations at all. It is a theoretical account that we owe to Mowrer and Jones (1945).

For most purposes, we define the unit of response as that which will produce reinforcement. Thus in the Skinner box, a response is often defined as a lever press capable of operating the device that delivers the reinforcer. It does not make any difference how the animal presses the lever so long as it is pressed hard enough. By the same token, we might argue that in a partial reinforcement situation in a Skinner box—at least, one where reinforcement is delivered on a ratio of some kind—the unit of response is defined by the *number* of lever presses necessary to activate the reinforcement device. If we did this, we would consider all the nonreinforced lever presses between reinforced ones to be part of the activity necessary for reinforcement, and we would count them as just one response. For example, if we were to use an FR 10 schedule of reinforcement, in which we reinforce every tenth lever press, we would count 10 lever presses as *one response unit*. We might then suppose that organisms can learn to chunk their behavior, perhaps discriminating or learning something about the number of responses that constitute a chunk.

When applied to extinction behavior, the response-unit hypothesis predicts equal resistance to extinction for all ratios of reinforcement—so long as extinction performance is examined in terms of the appropriately sized response unit and each unit has been reinforced the same number of times during training. Thus, an FR 10 schedule might give many more *individual* lever presses than an FR 20 schedule during extinction, but both should give the same number of response units. In order that there be an equal number of response units in this particular example, an animal trained on FR 20 would have to emit twice as many individual lever presses during extinction as an animal trained on FR 10.

Unfortunately, though the response-unit hypothesis has great intuitive appeal, the data do not support the hypothesis very well. Mowrer and Jones themselves found that as the fixed ratio increased, the number of response units emitted during extinction did not remain the same, but decreased. You can see this for yourself in the lower curve of Figure 5.7 where Boren (1961) has plotted his data in terms of response units. Boren reports, too, that when he inspected the individual extinction records of his rats, there was no indication of the chunking of responses that might be expected if the animals had been counting their responses somehow and responding on the basis of some sort of response unit. In spite of its intuitive appeal, in short, the response-unit hypothesis does not withstand experimental test very well, and it has not received very much attention as a consequence.

INTRATRIAL PHENOMENA AND THE PARTIAL
REINFORCEMENT EFFECT

Let us turn now from an approach to the partial reinforcement effect which emphasizes intertrial events, like learning to discriminate something about the overall pattern with which reinforcement and nonreinforcement occur, to an approach which emphasizes the fact that organisms learn how to respond in certain ways *within* a reinforced or nonreinforced trial. The general point to be made here is that training with partial reinforcement provides an opportunity—through the nonreinforced trial—for an organism to learn how to cope with and to maintain its behavior in the absence of reinforcement. Continuous reinforcement does not do this, since by definition continuous reinforcement does not include nonreinforced trials. And so when extinction begins, the partially reinforced organism is better equipped than the continuously reinforced organism to resist the effects of a complete withdrawal of all reward.

While all theories of the intratrial type look within individual trials in search of an explanation for the partial reinforcement effect, they differ in terms of what they find going on there. For example, Weinstock is responsible for the development of a theory which holds that nonreinforced training trials tend to elicit responses which are incompatible with the response that the experimenter wants to condition with partial reinforcement (Weinstock, 1954, 1958, 1970; Robbins, 1969, 1971). But as training proceeds and the organism is exposed to more and more nonreinforced trials, the incompatible responses tend to *habituate*; that is, they tend to extinguish (because they are not reinforced) and to disappear from the organism's repertoire of behavior. When extinction begins, the organism continues to respond for a relatively great many trials because, compared with an organism that has been continuously reinforced, there is less extraneous incompatible behavior to interfere with the response the experimenter has conditioned during training.

Frustration and the partial reinforcement effect   In Chapter 3 we developed the concept of incentive motivation from the fractional anticipatory goal response and the r_g-s_g mechanism, and in Chapter 4 we looked at a parallel concept, the fractional anticipatory frustration response and the r_f-s_f mechanism, to show how this played a role in a theoretical account of the general phenomenon of extinction. If we combine these two mechanisms, we have a tool that we can use to account for the partial reinforcement effect (Amsel, 1958, 1967, 1972).

Once a rat has been run in a runway to food, say, for a few trials, incentive motivation will have developed to some extent; that is, r_g-s_g will have grown in strength, and the cues of the runway will be eliciting for the rat the rather exciting prospect of a morsel of food in the goal box. If we now remove the food for a few trials, we have set the stage for the parallel development of r_f-s_f, since nonreinforcement now will produce a frustrating state of affairs and this, too, can become anticipatory so that it is elicited by cues in the runway. As training continues, and we continue to mix reinforced and nonreinforced trials together, the rat faces a dilemma and is, in fact, in quite a state of conflict. On the one hand, the cues of the runway promise an ultimate payoff of food, but on the other hand, the same cues also promise the upsetting frustration of an empty goal box. Nevertheless, the rat continues to run—unless we provide altogether too few rewards—since reinforcement is available at least some of the time.

The important point, however, is that the animal has been conditioned to make the running response to *one* identical set of runway cues that signals *two* distinct goal events and their associated properties: the "excitement" of reinforcement (mediated by the r_g-s_g mechanism) and the "frustration" of nonreinforcement (mediated by the r_f-s_f mechanism). In effect, while the r_f-s_f mechanism typically mediates and elicits behavior that is incompatible with running, as we have seen earlier, partial reinforcement trains the rat to run in the presence of such frustration-produced cues. While all this is true of a partially reinforced rat, it is not true of a continuously reinforced rat. The latter is conditioned to make the running response to cues that signal just one sort of goal event—reinforcement.

Perhaps you have already anticipated the next step. If we now extinguish the running response, the partially reinforced rat runs for a relatively long time because it has been *conditioned* during training to maintain its behavior in the face of cues that signal the frustration associated with nonreinforcement. The continuously reinforced rat, of course, has not had the benefit of this unpleasant but educating experience. When extinction begins following continuous reinforcement, frustration occurs for the first time, produces incompatible responses, and leads to relatively rapid extinction.

On the face of things, this theoretical system does not sound enormously different from that of, say, Weinstock; we are simply postulating another thing which subjects can learn about on nonreinforced trials that will stand them in good stead during extinction. The frustration approach does add one important element, however, which—as things have turned out—gives it some rather unique advantages among intratrial explanations of the partial reinforcement effect. Frustration is assumed to have the properties of a "motive" that, in a partial reinforcement situation, can add to the vigor with which a response is performed (recall the fact that in the Amsel and Roussel experiment, rats ran relatively faster in the second runway if they had just been frustrated in the first goal box). Let us look at some experiments which show the usefulness of this extra feature.

Amount of reinforcement and the partial reinforcement effect What happens to the size of the partial reinforcement effect when a response is conditioned initially with different amounts of reinforcement? Hulse (1958) and later Wagner (1961) and Hulse and Bacon (1962) sought an answer to this question. Hulse trained rats to run a runway, reinforcing one group on 46 percent of the training trials, and another group on 100 percent of the training trials. Within each group, half the animals were rewarded with a piece of food that weighed 0.08 gram, and half were rewarded with a piece of food that weighed 1.0 gram. At the end of training, the continuously reinforced groups ran faster than the partially reinforced groups, and large rewards produced faster running speeds

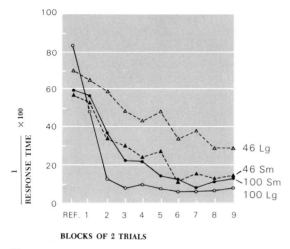

Figure 5.8
Running speeds during extinction as a joint function of
percentage of reinforcement and amount of reinforcement.
The rats had been reinforced 100 or 46 percent of the time
with either a 1.0-gram (L_g) or an 0.08-gram (S_m) food reward. The reference point includes data from the last
training trial and the first extinction trial. (Hulse, 1958.)

than small rewards. But the extinction data are of primary concern; they
are shown in Figure 5.8.

Look first at the extinction performance of the groups that had
received a *large* reward during training. The partially reinforced group
was much more resistant to extinction than the continuously reinforced
group. Now look at the data for the groups that received a *small* reward.
Here, there is still some indication that the partially reinforced group was
more resistant to extinction than the continuously reinforced group, but
as you can see, the difference in running speed is quite small. In other
words, the partial reinforcement effect is much greater when large as
compared with small rewards are used during the conditioning of the
response.

How are these data to be accounted for? The frustration approach,
first of all, can handle the data quite well (Wagner, 1961). When large
rewards are used during training, a much stronger conditioned anticipatory goal response r_g results than if small rewards are used. This, in
the case of partial reinforcement, should produce a relatively strong
conditioned anticipatory frustration response r_f and the drive properties
of r_f should channel into running. All this follows from our previous
discussion and from some work of Bower (1962), among others, which
shows that the size of the frustration effect increases as the amount of
reduction in reinforcement becomes larger. When extinction begins,
partial reinforcement should produce faster running than continuous
reinforcement because partial reinforcement trains the rat to keep

running in the face of cues that signal frustration, but continuous reinforcement does not. This accounts for the bare partial reinforcement effect, as we have seen before.

Now for the following reasons, the *magnitude* of the partial reinforcement effect should increase with increases in amount of reinforcement. First of all, with *partial* reinforcement, large as compared with small rewards should produce greater frustration drive, and hence faster running speeds during extinction. Following *continuous* reinforcement, similarly, large rewards should produce greater frustration during extinction. But what happens as a result of this frustration? It cannot channel directly into running because there has been no opportunity for the rat to learn to cope with frustration in this way during training. Instead—and this is the interesting and critical point—the larger the reward, the greater the frustration that is elicited as extinction begins. This, in turn, assures that large as compared with small rewards will produce more vigorous incompatible responses and lead to a relatively quick collapse of the running response. In other words, our thinking has led us to predict that with continuous reinforcement, large rewards should produce *less* resistance to extinction than small rewards; and if you go back and check Figure 5.8, you will see that this is exactly what happened in Hulse's experiment.

You should not be left with the impression that the frustration approach is the only one that can do an adequate job of accounting for Hulse's data. Capaldi's (1967) theory can do just as adequate a job, and Capaldi, as a matter of fact, has often chosen Hulse's experiment as a vehicle to show his theory at work. As we have seen, Capaldi specifies that resistance to extinction following partial reinforcement is a simple function of the strength of the tendency to approach the goal in the presence of S^N, the cues that are distinctively associated with nonreinforcement. He says further, if you will recall, that the strength of this tendency is a direct function of the frequency with which nonreinforced-to-reinforced–trial transitions have occurred during training, of the N-length that has been involved, and so on. To account for the fact that large rewards under partial reinforcement generate greater resistance to extinction than small rewards, Capaldi simply postulates that the strength of the tendency to approach the goal under S^N is also a direct function of the *magnitude* of reinforcement that is incorporated in the nonreinforced-to-reinforced transition. To account for the fact that small rewards generate greater resistance to extinction than large rewards if continuous reinforcement is used during acquisition, Capaldi invokes a variety of discrimination theory, noting that the shift from a small reward to no reward in extinction involves less of a stimulus change than a shift from large reward to no reward. Since the small-reward animal is responding under conditions which are relatively close to those prevailing during training, it ought to continue running faster during extinction, as indeed it does.

Capaldi's approach to this problem has led to some other important predictions about the effects of patterns of different magnitudes of reward upon resistance to extinction (e.g., Leonard, 1969; Capaldi, 1970). Among them, as you might expect, is the prediction—confirmed by data—that the *order* in which various magnitudes of reinforcement occur during training is an important variable determining resistance to extinction. If an arrangement is worked out, for example, in which three magnitudes of reward occur in the sequence large (*L*), nothing (*O*), small (*S*)—the sequence being repeated over and over again—resistance to extinction is less than it is if the sequence *S-O-L* is used. This happens in spite of the fact that while differing in order, each pattern contains exactly the same magnitudes. Note, however, that in the *L-O-S* pattern, the nonreinforcement-reinforcement transition is from nothing to a small reward, while in the *S-O-L* pattern, it is from nothing to a large reward. The former case ought, therefore, to generate a weaker tendency to approach in the face of S^N in extinction, as indeed it does.

Frustration and blocks of reinforcement and nonreinforcement Let us return very briefly to the fact that the partial reinforcement effect can be sustained through a block of continuously reinforced trials (Theios, 1962) and see how the frustration theory would apply there. If you will recall, we spoke rather loosely of the rat being able to "remember" something about its experience with partial reinforcement, and we said that perhaps this memory could carry through a period of continuous reinforcement and still work to produce a partial reinforcement effect during extinction. The concept of conditioned frustration furnishes a vehicle that is quite a bit more specific and concrete than the notion of a rat being able to remember something.

The key word here is *conditioned*; conditioned frustration has the properties of a permanent habit. During initial training with partial reinforcement, conditioned frustration develops as a result of nonreinforcement. During subsequent training with continuous reinforcement, the motivation associated with conditioned frustration extinguishes to some extent. Thus, while the rat runs in the presence of cues that have acquired the ability to elicit conditioned frustration, the reinforcer for conditioned frustration—primary frustration from nonreinforcement—has been removed. What does not extinguish, however, is the tendency for the rat to make compatible as opposed to incompatible responses to frustration cues when they do appear. This stays with the rat through the period of continuous reinforcement, and when extinction finally does begin, the rat with a history of partial reinforcement has a greater tendency to run to frustration cues than the rat without such a history. And so the partial reinforcement effect is indeed sustained through a block of continuously reinforced trials.

Once again, you should not leave this material with the impression that intratrial theories in general, and the frustration approach in particular, are the only ones that can handle the Theios-Jenkins phenomenon. By this time it should be easy to see just how a theory such as Capaldi's—based as it is upon the reinstatement during extinction of things that are learned about nonreinforcement as a function of nonreinforcement-to-reinforcement transitions—could handle the phenomenon quite easily. Again, the importance of memory for features of patterns of reinforcement experienced in the past becomes self-evident.

SUBORDINATE AND SUPERORDINATE PATTERNS OF REINFORCEMENT

Before we leave the general concept of patterns of reinforcement, there are some things to be developed that are sufficiently new to have not yet found their final niche in any particular theoretical system. They lead to some interesting examples of new phenomena that theories of the future will have to account for successfully. The context we now wish to develop, accordingly, is that based on the concepts of *subordinate* and *superordinate* patterns of reinforcement (Hulse, 1973b). These concepts draw together many of the organizing principles about patterns of reinforcement that we have examined in this chapter and lead, in turn, to some interesting new empirical developments.

Subordinate patterns of reinforcement   Thus far, we have paid almost exclusive attention to patterns of reinforcement which we now want to identify with the new label *subordinate* patterns of reinforcement. A subordinate pattern of reinforcement, in bare form, exists whenever the reinforcement of a response *varies* in some fashion from one response to the next. If that is the case, we can refer to the specific events which change from response to response as the *elements* of the pattern. Elements, in turn, have *attributes* which categorize them, first of all, as rewards or punishers. Beyond that, elements can also have attributes based on other dimensions of reinforcement, such as amount, intensity, delay, and so on.

Patterns are built from elements according to certain *rules*. Thus, in the case of simple FR schedules of reinforcement, the rule is that every *n*th response is reinforced, while the intervening responses go unreinforced. Note that this pattern, just like all the standard schedules of reinforcement, is built from two elements that consist, quite simply, of *reward* and *nonreward* for successive responses. Another example might be drawn from some of the research of Capaldi (e.g., 1970) in which successive responses were followed by *three* elements; recall the experiment in which alley responses were paid off with large, small, or zero magnitudes of reward. In this case, the pattern was composed of elements drawn from a dimension based on *magnitude* of reinforcement, and the rule of the pattern was that elements had to follow one another in some preset orders that were important according to some deductions from Capaldi's theory. As we suggested at the beginning of the chapter, it is easy to go on and think in these terms of other patterns: Yamaguchi's (1961) experiment is a good example of a two-element pattern based on randomly changing magnitudes of reward, while a VI schedule is a good example of a two-element pattern based on reward and nonreward in which a timing rule is also used to define the pattern. Hulse (1973b) discusses some other examples of subordinate patterns, particularly some that are especially good generators of reinforcement contrast effects (Chapter 2), and you can check that work if you wish to pursue the matter further.

Superordinate patterns of reinforcement If you have the concept of a subordinate pattern clearly in mind, let us define a *superordinate* pattern of reinforcement. This pattern is one in which the elements of the pattern are, themselves, *subordinate* patterns of reinforcement. Thus far in this chapter, we have looked in detail at just one example of a superordinate pattern. That was the pattern that Theios and Jenkins used in their studies of the effect of blocks of partial and continuous reinforcement upon resistance to extinction. In the terms we are using now, a *block* of continuous reinforcement and a *block* of partial reinforcement in their experiments would each constitute one *element* of a superordinate pattern. We might call this superordinate pattern an RC or a CR pattern, depending upon the rule we use to order the blocks of random (R) partial reinforcement or continuous (C) reinforcement. If you recall, Jenkins and Theios, together with others after them, found that with an RC pattern, resistance to extinction was just as great as it was if continuous reinforcement alone were used.

Other examples of superordinate patterns can be obtained from some of the schedules of reinforcement that have been developed within the Skinnerian tradition. We mentioned some of them in passing earlier in this chapter: multiple schedules and tandem schedules, for example. A tandem schedule, accordingly, is one in which two schedules, such as FR 15 and VI 3 minutes, are used in alternation, with the subject performing first on one and then on the other. The two component schedules constitute the subordinate patterns, while the two subordinate patterns jointly determine the superordinate pattern, the tandem schedule. It has been typical within the Skinnerian tradition to study the behavior that is correlated with each of the subordinate patterns, perhaps examining what happens when a sudden switch is made from one of the subordinate patterns to the other. A good example of this is the case of *behavioral contrast* (Chapter 2), in which response rates in one component of a multiple schedule are influenced by conditions in the other component of the multiple schedule. It is not typical, however, to watch an organism's reaction to the general experience of being placed on the entire multiple schedule itself, that is, to watch how the organism responds to the multiple schedule regarded *as a whole*. And sometimes organisms can abstract some interesting things from entire superordinate patterns of reinforcement. Let us look at one example now.

Super extinction Hulse (1973b) designed an experiment that was inspired by experiments modeled after those of Theios and Jenkins.

However, he wondered what the effects of stringing *three* patterns of reinforcement together might be, building a superordinate pattern which would contain not two, but three components. In particular, the experiment incorporated continuous reinforcement (C), partial reinforcement on a random 50 percent of the training trials (R), and the pattern that Tyler, Wortz, and Bitterman (1953) used in their experiment: single alternation of reinforcement in which every other trial was reinforced (S). Rats were trained on combinations of these patterns and then extinguished in a Skinner box which incorporated discrete trials—a lever was made available until it was pressed on a trial, then it was removed until it was time for the next trial to begin. For some rats, the subordinate patterns were arranged in the order CSR; the rats began acquisition with a block (lasting through several daily sessions) of continuous reinforcement, switched to single alternation for several days (until their latency data showed fast responding on reinforced trials and slow responding on nonreinforced trials), then concluded training with a final block of random partial reinforcement. For other rats, the superordinate pattern was built from the same subordinate patterns, but they were arranged in *reverse order* so that the rats learned to lever-press on an RSC pattern. Finally, two control groups were run, one which was trained on continuous reinforcement throughout acquisition (CCC), and one which was, similarly, trained on random reinforcement throughout acquisition (RRR). The animals all responded at the same latency at the end of the final period of acquisition—regardless of which terminal subordinate pattern they were on—and so they all entered extinction with the same level of performance. The extinction data are shown in Figure 5.9, which plots the number of responses the animals produced during successive fifths of the first extinction session (later extinction sessions showed the same pattern of results).

It is quite apparent in Hulse's data, first of all, that if training *ended*

Figure 5.9
Resistance to extinction of lever pressing following training with a superordinate pattern of reinforcement. If training ended with random reinforcement (dashed lines), resistance to extinction was greater in general than if training ended with continuous reinforcement (solid lines). A superordinate pattern composed of random, single-alternation, and continuous reinforcement (RSC) produced most rapid extinction, more rapid even than that produced by continuous reinforcement alone (CCC). (Hulse, 1973b.)

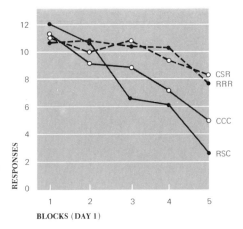

with random reinforcement (even if it had included earlier S or C components), extinction was relatively slow; the animals were still producing substantial numbers of responses at the end of the session. The data are also consistent with other data in showing a conventional partial reinforcement effect: the RRR condition (and the CSR condition, for that matter) both generated greater resistance to extinction than the CCC condition. But notice what happened in the RSC condition. Here, the most rapid extinction of all occurred. By the end of the day, the animals exposed to the RSC sequence in a superordinate pattern *were far less persistent than the animals in any of the other conditions of the experiment.* They had, if you will, demonstrated a "super" loss of response persistence. Note that this is *not* the result that would be expected from an extension of the Theios and Jenkins data, nor is it a result that would be predicted by either Capaldi's intertrial theory or Amsel's intratrial theory. Both of the latter theories would predict that extinction ought to be at least reasonably characteristic of that associated with random partial reinforcement—on the assumption at least that the effects of the random subordinate pattern ought to carry directly through the other subordinate patterns in at least moderately intact form. Instead, persistence was, if anything, at a polar opposite from that characteristic of partial reinforcement.

It is not at all easy at this point to account for the foregoing data in precise theoretical terms. It is much as if, however, the rats "abstracted" some general feature from the entire RSC superordinate pattern, some feature which "emerged" from the pattern experienced as a whole (in the gestalt sense of the term). One possibility is that the animals were able to abstract some rudimentary notion that reinforcement was becoming more *predictable* as the superordinate pattern ran its course. Note that in the RSC pattern, reward is at first both intermittent and unpredictable, then intermittent and predictable (and the long and short latencies on nonreinforced and reinforced trials showed that the rats "understood" the pattern), then continuous and predictable. Perhaps the animals became acutely set to detect whether reward was to be available or not, a set which could lead them to very quickly discriminate the beginning of extinction and to stop responding very rapidly. Clearly, the addition of the single-alternation subordinate pattern must have had something important to do with this, since that was the only feature distinguishing Hulse's experiment from any of the earlier ones.

Now all this is quite ad hoc, and it attributes cognitive capabilities to rats which they may not possess—although these wily creatures have coexisted with man and survived *his* cognitive attempts to do them in in rather remarkable fashion for a great many centuries. Nevertheless, the data seem to appeal to explanation in such terms. In any event, they certainly indicate that there are new things to be discovered from further experimental development of the concept of a superordinate pattern of reinforcement, and it will be interesting to watch future developments in this domain.

We have looked at a rather large number of theories concerning the partial reinforcement effect, perhaps a larger number than the general approach of this book warrants. It is unfortunately true, however, that we have simply mirrored the current state of affairs with respect to what psychologists think about the effects of patterns of reinforcement upon resistance to extinction. Someone has said that in the absence of fact there will be theory, and nowhere does this seem a more appropriate comment than in connection with the partial reinforcement effect. In all likelihood, what will eventually emerge will be a general theory that will combine features of a number of less comprehensive theories, some of which are already available so that we have been able to see what they have to say, and some of which remain to be developed. Already, it seems clear that important things go on both between and within trials which, as we understand things now, help to account for the effects of patterns of reinforcement upon resistance to extinction. Which of these will still be of value to the theoretician in the future remains to be seen.

SIX

LEARNING AND THE CONCEPTS OF EMOTION AND MOTIVATION

Most psychologists make a distinction between the things we learn—our habits—and the things which prompt us to use these habits—our motives. In general terms, we can think of motives and emotions as things which provide the impetus behind behavior; that is, we can think of them as *needs* or *drives*. To constructs of this sort, which emphasize the energy behind behavior, many psychologists would add as a closely related construct the concept of "goals," things which provide *direction* to motivated behavior. Earlier in this book, you were warned that the distinction between reinforcement and motivation would be a difficult one to maintain, particularly when the incentive characteristics of reinforcing stimuli are emphasized. In this chapter you will be able to sense some of the problems that the psychologist might encounter were he to insist on a rigid separation of the two. Nevertheless, we shall find it useful to make at least a loose distinction between operations which energize behavior—whether we call them motives, drives, or emotions —and operations which tend to focus energized behavior in some particular direction, toward some goal or incentive.

At the outset we must, as usual, admit to having culled a few topics for discussion from an enormous number that would appropriately fit into a chapter such as this one. We shall attempt to be rigid in limiting discussion to points where there is a clear relation between motivation, emotion, and *learning*. We shall see how motivation and emotion affect the learning process, and conversely, we shall see how learning processes can play a role in the acquisition of new motives and emotions.

The problem of defining motives   If we limit ourselves to the relatively simple world of animals for a moment, we can think of motivation as having two fundamental components, a need state and a goal—or some appropriate change in external stimulation—which tends to reduce or eliminate that need. Some needs tend to be periodic or cyclic in character, in which case they usually depend upon changes in the internal physiological or neurological balance of the organism. Hunger and thirst are such cyclic needs. Not all needs are governed by internal changes, however, since some exist at a more or less constant level, awaiting only the occurrence of the appropriate external stimulus to set off the appropriate behavior. The avoidance of pain is such a need, and in all animals there are many other such needs—needs we often characterize as instincts.

Obviously, though the animal world is complex enough, we find that things are much more complicated when we look at the realm of human behavior. People are motivated in a rich variety of ways, most of which do not have much of anything to do with basic physiological needs or drives (though there are certainly places in the world where this statement would be justifiably debatable). Instead, most adult human behavior is based upon *learned* motivation; people acquire much of their motivation through experience, with the "need" for money, for fame, for a new car, and so forth, being cases in point. There is an enormous literature which represents the attempts of psychologists to study, describe, and classify human motives of this sort, and there is a corresponding variety of emphasis and of definition of the concepts of motivation and emotion. It would be beyond the scope of this book to go into this material in detail, and we shall not do so. Nor shall we offer a rigorous definition of the concepts of emotion and motivation—beyond definitions that you may be able to abstract for yourself from our selection of the topics and the experiments we shall discuss.

It will be useful, however, to look briefly at some things having to do with the way in which psychologists *use* concepts like that of motivation when they go into the laboratory to perform experiments. Kimble (1961), following Spence (1948), distinguishes two general approaches here. Both take note of the fact that motivation is, after all, a *concept* which depends for its meaning upon operational definitions. Thus, on one hand, we can define a motivational state of affairs by exposing an organism to a particular set of antecedent conditions involving something that we do to the organism or to its environment and then measuring some resulting change in the organism's behavior. In the case of hunger motivation, for example, we might deprive organisms of food for a fixed period of time, prefeed different groups of them with different amounts of food (or at different moments in time prior to test), and then see how efficiently and quickly food would be ingested when it could be earned by performing some simple operant response or when it was made freely available. If we were to define hunger in rats by different amounts of prefeeding and measure it by rate of lever pressing for food, we would find that response rate decreased regularly as the amount of food previously eaten increased in quantity. If we were to define hunger for people by giving them a standard-size preload of Metrecal after a standard period of fasting, but at various times before we allowed them to go ahead and freely ingest more Metrecal, we would get the data shown in Figure 6.1. There, the data indicate the cumulative amounts of Metrecal people ingested from moment to moment as they sucked it from a stainless steel straw (Stellar, 1966; Jordan, Weiland, Zebley, Stellar, & Stunkard, 1966). The data Stellar and Jordan et al. obtained are not perfectly orderly because more Metrecal was ingested just one

167

LEARNING
AND THE
CONCEPTS OF
EMOTION AND
MOTIVATION

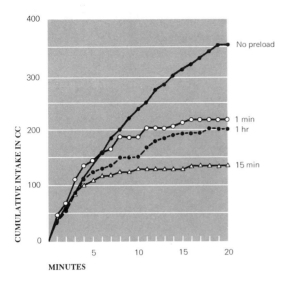

Figure 6.1
Effect of a one-can (235-cubic-centimeter) preload of Metrecal at various times before eating a test meal of Metrecal in humans. With the exception of a one-minute wait, the longer the wait, the greater the amount taken. (Stellar, 1966.)

minute after taking the preload than if 15 minutes had elapsed (possibly due to effects associated with simple stomach distension or absorption), but they certainly show that, in general, the closer the period of prefeeding to the test meal, the smaller the test meal ingested. Incidentally, the curves of Figure 6.1 look just like those that can be obtained under similar conditions when rats ingest fluids (Stellar & Hill, 1952).

The second way to do something with a motivational variable, according to Spence and Kimble, is to measure one aspect of an organism's behavior and see how this aspect co-varies or is *correlated* with a second aspect of the organism's behavior. Thus, if we stick with rats for a moment, we could deprive different groups of rats for various periods of time and then see how fast they would eat a given quantity of food when it was made available to them. Then we could reintroduce the various conditions of food deprivation and see how fast the rats would press a lever for food rewards. Finally, we would see if rate of lever pressing were correlated with speed of eating, guessing that the faster the rats ate the food (i.e., the "hungrier" they were) the faster they would press. Note that this way of looking at things is by no means necessarily independent of the first; in fact, we used deprivation time as the operation to establish differential rates of eating. The important difference lies in the nature of the thing we finally choose to use as an independent variable—in the first case we use some antecedent condition defined apart from the organism, while in the second we use some aspect of the organism's behavior itself.

The data obtained with the correlational approach testify to its general usefulness. With animals (e.g., Bolles, 1967; Miller, 1956), generally good agreement is obtained across measures like amount of food ingested, rate of lever pressing for food, frequency of stomach contractions, and amount of adulteration with bitter quinine that an animal will tolerate. All variables tend to co-vary sensibly with each other as indices of hunger—barring some discrepancies such as the fact that stomach contractions increase for only the first few hours of food deprivation and then taper off.

With people, the correlational approach attains equal success. The data of Figure 6.2 constitute a scattergram for the Jordan et al. (1966) data, showing a subjective rating (on an 11-point scale ranging from not hungry to hungriest ever) of how hungry a person was and the amount of Metrecal then ingested during the next five minutes of test. As you can see, the relationship is quite high; for these data the correlation coefficient was 0.89.

Another common approach with people is to give them a form of pencil-and-paper test which is designed to tap some of their motivational makeup and to use it to predict how well they will then perform at some learning task. For example, a self-report inventory such as the Manifest Anxiety Scale (Taylor, 1956) can be used. The assumption behind this test (which consists of items such as "I am sometimes troubled by what others think of me," to which true or false answers are given), and others like it, is that the items composing the scale tap an emotional responsiveness which is related to drive or motivational level. In this case, those scoring high on the inventory are said to be anxious, and their anxiety state is assumed to act as a generalized motivator of behavior. There appears to be fairly good evidence that Pavlovian conditioning occurs more readily among people scoring high on the test than among those scoring low (Taylor, 1951; Spence, 1958). Similar evidence has been obtained with the California Personality Inventory (Gough, 1964, 1968). The test, which is designed to tap motivation to achieve, among other things, and which is used to predict "superior and/or effective performance," does a good job of forecasting, for example, those who will do well in high school and those who will then go on to college.

Motivation and learning jointly determine performance At this point it would be well to recall something we have mentioned in other places, not

Figure 6.2
A scattergram showing the correlation between a subjective rating of how hungry people felt and how much they then ate on a five-minute test. (Jordan et al., 1966.)

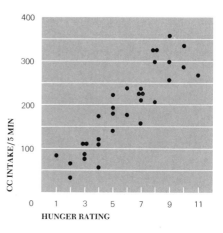

only in connection with the concept of motivation, but also in connection with concepts such as the amount of reinforcement (Chapter 2). The factors which influence behavior are divided by contemporary psychologists into two classes, associative and nonassociative. Both factors are responsible for the overt performance of any instrumental act. If an animal performs a particular act, it is highly probable that this is because (1) it has learned to do so and (2) it is motivated to do so. In short, the response strength of any habit at any given moment will be a function of how well the habit has been learned (determined, say, by how much the habit has been practiced) as well as of the strength of motivation present at the time—on the assumption, of course, that we have held other factors such as amount of reinforcement or delay of reinforcement at some constant value.

169

LEARNING
AND THE
CONCEPTS OF
EMOTION AND
MOTIVATION

It is important to recognize that the foregoing says nothing at all about the way in which motivation might *modify* learning—that is, whether what is learned under high as compared with low motivation is quantitatively or qualitatively different. Is a habit that has been learned under high motivation different from one that has been learned under low motivation, or does level of motivation simply determine the momentary strength with which a given response will be displayed? If high motivation affects the learning process in a way which is different from that of low motivation, what is the nature of the difference? Let us turn now to questions such as these and see what psychologists have learned about them.

THE EFFECT OF MOTIVATION UPON LEARNING

If we are to assess the effects of motivation upon learning, we are faced at the outset with the problem of finding some way of disentangling the effects of motivation upon momentary performance from those it may have upon actual habit strength. As you can see, rats that run down an alley under high hunger drive may run faster than those under low hunger drive, but we do not know from this information alone whether we are dealing with two different amounts of learning or habit strength or with the same amount of learning energized at different levels by our two degrees of hunger. The solution to this problem involves, in general, conditioning animals under one set of motivational levels and then changing something about the task or the motivational conditions under which the animals are run. If the original motivational conditions are creating permanent differences in habit strength—as opposed to momentary differences in the strength with which a given habit is displayed in performance—then we would expect some relatively long-lasting effects of our original conditions to appear when we *transfer* to the new set of conditions. This approach is based, of course, on the reasonable assumption that learned habits are basically stable things, while simple performance of a given habit is a fleeting state of affairs which quickly changes, adjusting almost immediately to the conditions of the moment.

In practice, psychologists have used a number of different kinds of *transfer experiments* in assessing the effects of motivation upon learning. One of the most common procedures is to condition animals under a number of different motivational conditions and then to *extinguish* them under some common level of motivation. Here, the assumption is that if different levels of motivation produce different effects upon amount of learning, resistance to extinction in the various groups should be different (even though all animals are extinguished under the same motivation), because resistance to extinction should reflect the effects of the original conditions of learning. Another similar procedure is to condition under one set of motivational conditions and then to *shift to another set*, watching behavior as practice continues for residual effects of the old set of motivational conditions upon the new. A third, less common, procedure is to condition under one set of motivational conditions, to allow a period of time to pass during which the effects of the original conditioning are presumably "forgotten" in part, and then to *recondition* under another set of motivational conditions. Here, we look for residual effects of the original set of motivational conditions upon the course of reconditioning.

Experiments comparing the effects of level of motivation upon learning Let us now look briefly at some examples of experiments that have been done in connection with the strategies we have just outlined to assess the influence of motivation upon learning. A great many have been done, and they have been surveyed extensively elsewhere (Kimble, 1961; Cofer & Appley, 1964; Deese & Hulse, 1967), and so we will not devote a great deal of time to them. Unfortunately, the picture that emerges from the literature is by no means a clear one. If we look, first of all, at experiments that have used different levels of motivation during conditioning and a common level during extinction, we find negative results most often. Resistance to extinction in the Skinner box, at least, does not vary with the motivational level used during training (Kendler, 1945). Barry (1958), on the other hand, found a significant carry-over of level of motivation during training in a straight runway to performance during extinction.

If we test for the effects of motivation upon learning by shifting drive levels during the conditioning process, we find some experiments indicating that level of motivation affects learning (e.g., Deese & Carpenter, 1951; Theios, 1963) but some indicating that it does not (e.g., Hillman, Hunter, & Kimble, 1953). Equally muddled results appear if a reconditioning procedure is used. Thus, if we take a general look, there seems to be some evidence which, on its face, suggests that level of motivation will affect habit strength or amount learned. There are many experiments, however, which show negative results, and the effect is elusive at best.

There is a very important reason why this may be so, and it is worth some development. Organisms, whether they be rats or people, may *learn to do different things* under high as compared with low motivation.

171

LEARNING
AND THE
CONCEPTS OF
EMOTION AND
MOTIVATION

In other words, the effects of two levels of motivation may *not* be to modify the "strength" of some single habit, but may, instead, be to assure that an organism learns to do one thing under low motivation and something entirely different under high motivation. When, for example, residual effects of low motivation turn up when a shift is made to high motivation, the effects may be due to the fact that the organism is busily going about learning some entirely new and different response. An experiment by Cotton (1953) illustrates this general point very well. He trained a group of rats to run a runway and then tested the group at different times under 0, 6, 16, or 22 hours of food deprivation. In analyzing the behavior of the animals in the runway, however, Cotton went a step farther than the usual procedure of looking at overall running times or speeds. He broke trials into two classes: those in which the animals ran directly to the goal box, and those in which the animals made some sort of competing response, a response (such as stopping to sniff in a corner or retracing) which interfered with direct progress into the goal box. Looking at the data this way produced results which showed that on trials involving no competing responses, running times did not vary with deprivation time at all, while on trials in which there were competing responses, overall running times decreased as deprivation increased. Viewed another way, the data indicate that rats do not *run* more slowly under low as compared with high motivation; instead, they are more apt to engage in *extraneous activity*, the hand on the running-time clock moving all the while. Campbell and Kraeling (1954) have made the same point. They observed that rats run under low as compared with high motivation were less apt to be oriented toward the start-box door as a trial was about to begin.

The upshot of all this is that motivation affects learning in the limited sense that there must be enough of it to get an organism to behave—to expose itself to the problem it must learn and to reinforcing or other events which then ensue. Beyond this, however, it looks as if the associative mechanisms of instrumental learning are largely independent of level of motivation. Where there are apparent effects of motivation upon learning, it is a good idea to see if the situation does not afford the opportunity to learn different things as a function of the prevailing level of motivation.

THE EFFECT OF LEARNING ON MOTIVATION: ACQUIRED DRIVES AND EMOTIONS

In this section, we shall reverse the basic question of the last one and ask how organisms come to acquire new motives through a learning process. For a long time many psychologists took the view that there was but a handful of unlearned motives, most of which, if not all, were tied to biological needs. If one takes this view, of course, it is difficult to describe all the elaborate motives of adult human behavior unless great emphasis is placed upon the development of learned motives. All the complicated motives not directly and obviously connected with biological motives have been considered by some in the past to be derived from biological needs by a process of learning.

Although today most psychologists grant an important role to learned motives, the prevailing opinion seems to be that the view stated above is too simple. We are less sure that all *unlearned* motives are exhausted by a simple catalog of biological needs. Yet, whatever the original source of "pure" motivation, there is little question that learning plays an important part in the elaboration of motives. It will be our task now to see what psychologists have found out about this important matter.

The task immediately returns us to some things we considered in Chapter 1, namely, Pavlovian conditioning, instrumental conditioning, and their interaction. What may now be termed the classical view of acquired motivation depends heavily upon the conditioning of emotions by means of techniques patterned after the Pavlovian model, that is, the pairing of a neutral stimulus with some other stimulus that has the built-in ability to elicit a response—an emotional response in particular. We shall take a brief look at the role of that model in acquired motivation and some of the things that followed from it historically. Then we shall examine another, more recent application of the Pavlovian model, an application which stresses that organisms learn a *predictive relationship* between the two stimuli that enter into Pavlovian conditioning and that this association can have some profound effects upon *instrumental* conditioning. Finally in this regard, we shall apply both these models to the problem of *avoidance learning*, then move on to some other things of interest in connection with motivation and emotion.

CONDITIONING OF EMOTIONS WITH PAVLOVIAN PROCEDURES

A major feature of emotional activity that is of interest to psychologists is that, while it is under the control of many cognitive factors, it is also characterized by elaborate activity in the autonomic nervous system— that part of the peripheral nervous system controlling the actions of the heart, endocrine glands, and smooth muscles, if you will recall. While it is now clear that autonomically controlled response systems are amenable to conditioning with instrumental procedures, it is also the case that they are especially easy to condition with Pavlovian procedures (Chapter 1). For historical as well as practical reasons, therefore, it is not surprising that early attempts to condition emotions took advantage of their reflex-like properties and used Pavlovian techniques. Let us look at a classic example of such an attempt.

The Watson and Raynor study   One of the best known of such studies is by Watson and Raynor (1920). These investigators were interested in the development of fears in infants, and they made a long series of observations of a number of infants. One baby boy, who was about a year old at the time, was the subject of their conditioning study.

173

LEARNING
AND THE
CONCEPTS OF
EMOTION AND
MOTIVATION

Previously, they had discovered that a number of stimuli which one might ordinarily think would arouse fear were not fear-producing for this youngster. White rats, dogs, masks, burning newspapers—none of these produced fear, but one stimulus that did produce a startle reaction followed by crying and other signs of emotional activity was a loud sound. Consequently, they decided to use the loud sound as an unconditioned stimulus for emotional activity.

In the actual conditioning procedure, they paired the sight of a white rat (previously not fear-producing) with the occurrence of the sound. A very few pairings were sufficient to elicit a full-scale emotional response simply by presenting the white rat alone. An interesting development is that this conditioned fear generalized to other animals and to other furry objects, such as a wad of cotton.

This was a rather clear and dramatic demonstration of the possibilities of conditioned emotions, as well as a demonstration of the importance of such principles as stimulus generalization in the extension of the conditioned reaction. Watson and Raynor thought that this experiment could serve as a model for the way in which the complex and irrational fears of daily life might arise. They placed much emphasis upon the importance of emotional reactions in the child's personality development—emphasis which some, but not all, present-day psychologists would find altogether appropriate. Nevertheless, the Watson and Raynor experiment stands as one of the very first examples of the conditioning of an emotion.

FEAR AS A LEARNED DRIVE

Another early and important demonstration of some properties of emotional conditioning comes from some work of May (1948) and Neal Miller (1948, 1951). Their research emphasized the fact that emotions acquired through conditioning could have the properties of *drives* or *motives*, and they hypothesized that if that were true, then *reduction* of such a drive or motive ought to serve as *reinforcement* for instrumental activity—on the assumption, of course, that drive reduction is a tenable reinforcement process. Let us see how this line of reasoning fared in the laboratory.

Miller (1948, 1951) presented us with the classical example of fear as a learned drive. A rat is introduced into an apparatus like that illustrated in Figure 6.3. There are two compartments in the apparatus, a white one with an electrically wired grid as the floor and a black one with a smooth, solid floor. There is a door between the two compartments; the rat can open this door either by pressing a lever at the side of the white compartment or by turning a wheel at the end of the white compartment. First of all, the rat is shocked in the white compartment and allowed to escape through the door into the black compartment. This procedure pairs the cues of the white compartment with the painful shock stimulus and presumably conditions a learned fear reaction. It also teaches the rat that a run to the black compartment leads to safety. In order to see if

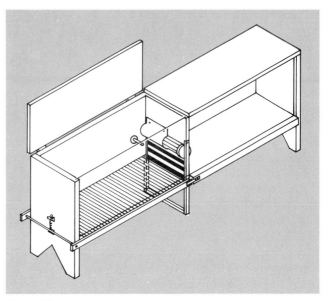

Figure 6.3
Apparatus for demonstration of fear as a learned drive. One compartment is white and one is black. The door between the compartments can be opened either by pressing a lever or by turning a wheel. The rat learns to escape from the white compartment by the association of pain from electric shock with the stimuli from that compartment. (N. E. Miller, 1948.)

conditioned fear of this sort has drive properties, however, it is necessary to find out whether the rat will learn a *new* response to escape from the white compartment *without further electric shocks*. If such a response can be learned, it would have to be learned not on the basis of the pain produced by the shock as a motivator, but on the basis of the conditioned fear as a motivator. Miller showed that rats could learn to turn the wheel when the reinforcement consisted of a reduction in fear correlated with escape into the black compartment. Figure 6.4 shows that each time the rat is placed in the white compartment, it takes less time to get around to turning the wheel.

The conditioned emotional response (*CER*)   Still another application of fear as a learned drive yields a phenomenon known as a *conditioned emotional response* (CER). The phenomenon arises when a neutral stimulus which has acquired the ability to elicit conditioned fear functions to *suppress* ongoing behavior. The conditions which typically produce this (Estes & Skinner, 1941; Brady & Hunt, 1955) involve, first of all, training a rat in a Skinner box to work for food on a variable-interval schedule. After the response is well established, a neutral stimulus is turned on and followed three minutes later with a brief electric shock. The shock is *not* contingent in any fashion upon bar pressing; it occurs independently of anything the animal is doing at the moment. Initially, the neutral stimulus has no effect on lever-pressing behavior, but as successive presentations of neutral stimulus and shock occur, the animal

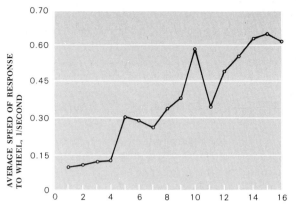

TRIALS WITH WHEEL FUNCTIONING TO OPEN DOOR

Figure 6.4
Learning to turn the wheel, with escape from the conditioned fear of the shock compartment as the motive. The rat is shocked in the white compartment, from which it can escape by an open door. On subsequent nonshock trials, the rat must learn to turn the wheel, which now opens the door, in order to escape from the white compartment. (N. E. Miller, 1948.)

175

LEARNING
AND THE
CONCEPTS OF
EMOTION AND
MOTIVATION

begins to reduce the rate at which it presses the lever during the period of time that the neutral stimulus is on. Eventually, if the strength of the shock is strong enough, for example, the animal may stop its lever-pressing behavior altogether during the "danger" period, resuming rapid lever pressing as soon as the shock occurs. The general technique that is used to develop a CER—which you should note is patterned after the *model* for Pavlovian conditioning—has found numerous applications in many domains of the psychology of learning. It affords an excellent procedure to use in studying how stimuli of one kind and another become associated so as to lead to the eventual suppression of responding reinforced with simple reward training.

Fear as a learned drive, then, can have many effects. Of primary importance, it can lead to *both* the facilitation and suppression of behavior, sometimes demonstrating in the process that it can function as a motivator for the acquisition of new responses. It is well to keep in mind, in other words, Bolles' (1970, 1972) admonition that organisms react to reinforcing events in patterns that are sometimes unique to their species, to the type of reinforcing event, to its mode and site of delivery, and so on. We shall see the continued salience of this point as we turn now to a discussion of avoidance learning and to an examination of some of the facts and theory associated with that paradigm for instrumental testing.

LEARNING THE PREDICTIVE VALUE OF A STIMULUS

In Chapter 1, if you will recall, we analyzed one important interaction between Pavlovian and instrumental conditioning: the fact that autonomic response systems, while conditionable with Pavlovian procedures, could also be easily conditioned with instrumental procedures. Some further interesting things appear if we look at the relationship between these two procedures from another point of view, a point of view which we owe primarily to Rescorla and Solomon (1967) for initial development. The basic idea is that Pavlovian procedures can be used to teach an organism that two stimuli, the CS and the UCS in particular, stand in some consistent relationship to each other such that one reliably *predicts* that the other will occur. While this approach does not deny that a CS can acquire some capacity to produce conditioned emotion or motivation when paired with the appropriate UCS, it chooses to emphasize the cognitive idea that organisms possess the capacity to appreciate that one event reliably forecasts that another will soon occur. Emotion may be part of the situation, but for many reasons, it is not necessarily the most salient part.

The empirical development of the foregoing has taken place in an experimental setting which incorporates the following sequence of events. First, an animal is trained to perform some instrumental response using conventional reinforcement procedures. Then, the animal is subjected to Pavlovian conditioning in which a suitable CS is paired with a suitable UCS. Following the Pavlovian phase, finally, the animal is returned to the instrumental conditioning situation, and the experimenter watches its behavior there when the new Pavlovian CS is introduced into the environment for occasional test periods. The order of these events is important: instrumental conditioning, Pavlovian conditioning, then a return to instrumental conditioning. We shall see later that some remarkably different things occur if the initial period of instrumental training is omitted. Let us look at an experiment of Rescorla and LoLordo (1965) to see an example of the basic procedure at work.

These experimenters placed dogs in a shuttle box and trained them to avoid a strong electric shock using a so-called Sidman avoidance procedure (Sidman, 1953). With this procedure, a schedule of reinforcement was set up such that shock occurred once every 10 seconds unless the dog jumped the hurdle from one side of the box to the other. If the dog did jump, the next shock was postponed for 30 seconds. The dog could continue to avoid shock indefinitely by responding at least once every 30 seconds, but if the dog failed to respond, shocks were reintroduced at their former 10-second intervals until the dog responded again. Notice that this avoidance-training procedure does not involve the use of an external discriminative cue—the dog must depend upon whatever internal timing cues it can develop and respond to in order to avoid shock. Note also that this procedure treats avoidance responding in the shuttle box as a free operant; the dogs are free to jump the hurdle at any point in time.

After three days of avoidance training during which the avoidance response was established initially, the dogs were locked in one compartment of the box and exposed to a series of Pavlovian conditioning trials. In fact, Rescorla and LoLordo studied a variety of Pavlovian paradigms,

but it will be sufficient if we look at that which involved a simple
Pavlovian discrimination. On some trials, a 1,200-hertz tone, which we
can label CS+, came on for five seconds and was followed immediately
by an unavoidable shock through the grid floor of the box. On other
trials, a second tone of 400 hertz, which we can label CS−, came on for
five seconds, but this time no shock followed the end of the tone. With
this procedure, obviously, CS+ could come to signal that shock was
about to arrive, while CS− could come to signal that shock would be
omitted. Days of Pavlovian training of this type were alternated with
days in which the dogs were returned to the basic Sidman avoidance
procedure until the animals had received a total of five Pavlovian
conditioning days and seven avoidance training days. On the next day,
the crucial test trials were run. The dogs began the day on the Sidman
avoidance schedule (although, to keep things uncomplicated, shock was
omitted if the dogs made one of their rare failures to jump the hurdle in
time), and at random times during the one-hour session, CS+ or CS−
was turned on. The experimenters then watched any changes in hurdle-
jumping rate associated with one as compared with the other stimulus.

Before we look at the results of this experiment, note the following.
First, the dogs were not taken from the apparatus, placed in a Pavlovian
harness, and so on, during the Pavlovian phase of the experiment. While
it turns out that precisely the same results are obtained if Pavlovian
training is carried out in some place other than that in which instrumental training is done—such as the traditional Pavlovian harness—use
of this device is not required to satisfy the procedures called for by
Pavlovian conditioning. Those simply demand that a CS be paired in
time with a UCS, and Rescorla and LoLordo's experiment certainly meets
that requirement. Note also that the development of no particular overt
CR was measured, although conditioning of fear undoubtedly occurred
(in the sense that we discussed that concept in the last section), and there
may have been some consistent postural adjustments in the apparatus
conditioned to the CS, too. However, the experimenters in this case were
not interested so much in the conditioning of any particular response
system as they were in the conditioning of an acquired associative
relationship between shock as a UCS and tones as CS+ and CS−. In
particular, they assumed that CS+ would become a reliable predictor of
"shock about to arrive"; that is, it would predict *danger* and so become a
danger signal, while CS− would become a reliable predictor of a period of
time free from shock and so become a *safety signal*.

The results of the experiment are shown in Figure 6.5, which indicates
the jumping rate of the dogs just before the CS+ or CS− was turned on,
the rate during the CS+ and CS−, and the rate for the next 30 seconds
after CS+ and CS− were turned off. It is readily apparent that there were
some marked changes in the instrumental avoidance behavior as a
function of whether CS+ or CS− appeared in the animals' environment.
If CS+ appeared, there was a rapid tripling of jumping rate, while if CS−
appeared, the rate fell to near zero, to recover slowly after CS− had gone
off.

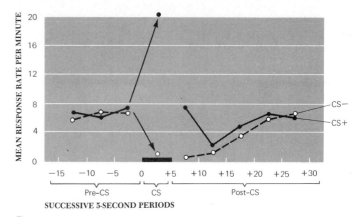

Figure 6.5
The effect on a Sidman avoidance response of turning on a cue that dogs had learned predicted the presence of shock (CS+) or the absence of shock (CS−). Although the shock is now turned off in the hurdle-jumping apparatus, jumping rate goes up markedly when CS+ appears and drops when CS− appears. Responding returns to base line after either of the cues has been turned off. (Maier, Seligman, & Solomon, 1969.)

Experiments of this type show clearly that the results of Pavlovian procedures can have marked effects when they are superimposed on an already established instrumental response. Perhaps you can imagine that the sudden appearance of the CS+ must have been quite a galvanizing experience as the dogs were, so to speak, casually and efficiently avoiding shock with matter-of-fact hurdle jumps. A sensible, perhaps even automatic, reaction to that event would be to speed up the rate of a response the dogs had learned would minimize electric shock, pain, and fear. By the same token, the appearance of CS−, a stimulus which regularly signaled the *absence* of shock in Pavlovian conditioning, may well have inhibited the fear present during avoidance responding and led the dogs to relax their vigorous hurdle-jumping behavior momentarily. In effect, they were being given a signal which had, during Pavlovian training, reliably indicated a safety period and a time-out from shock.

Effects comparable to those obtained by Rescorla and LoLordo are by no means limited to situations involving unpleasant things like electric shock. Trapold and Winokur (1967), for example, were able to show that rats could acquire a discrimination in a lever box much more rapidly if the discriminative cue had been previously used as CS+ in a Pavlovian arrangement in which the cue was paired with the automatic delivery of food. A cue which reliably signaled the absence of food during the Pavlovian phase slowed the development of the discrimination correspondingly. More recently, Hearst and Peterson (1973) were able to show that CS+ and CS− stimuli which had gained their respective properties in an arrangement incorporating one response, generalized their effectiveness to enhance or suppress a second response. This important observation shows that it is unlikely that the effects we have been discussing are effects *mediated* by some characteristic *response*

179

LEARNING
AND THE
CONCEPTS OF
EMOTION AND
MOTIVATION

system the subjects learn fortuitously during the Pavlovian phase of the experiment (recall our discussion of that problem in Chapter 1). It emphasizes, instead, that the effects are due in large measure to the things that organisms can learn about the significance of stimuli as predictors of certain other stimulus events about to follow. In this connection, also recall Hulse's (1973a) experiment on reinforcement contrast effects (p. 52).

There are now an enormous number of experiments amplifying and developing the basic points we have just made (see Bolles & Moot, 1972; Trapold & Overmier, 1972, for important reviews and commentary). The burden of all this information is that, in addition to the motivational and emotional features associated with Pavlovian conditioning, that experimental procedure also endows stimuli with predictive properties which are processed in a highly cognitive fashion even by animals of the capacity of the rat. Furthermore, those properties have potent effects upon whatever ongoing behavior may be under way when they appear in an organism's environment.

Before we leave this topic and move on to apply our thinking to the problem of avoidance learning, there is one final comment to be made. To this point, you may have developed the impression that Pavlovian conditioning refers to some rather fusty old procedures carried out in obscure laboratories in which psychologists or physiologists exhibit a rather strange and curious interest in esoteric, messy responses like salivation, knee jerks, and what have you. By this time, however, you should recognize that modern-day psychologists are interested not so much in the specific product of Pavlovian conditioning—that is, the salivation or knee jerk—as they are in the fact that these overt responses are important evidence that an *association* is being formed between two stimuli through the process of learning. It is the formation of the association, the things that control that process, and the other systems to which its end results can be applied that fascinate psychologists. And that can become a complicated, cognitive process—as well as an emotional and motivational one.

AVOIDANCE LEARNING

In Chapter 1, if you will recall, we described how a dog could learn to *avoid* shock in a shuttle box by leaping over a barrier in response to a cue, and we have just examined a variation on this basic theme, Sidman avoidance. We also noted toward the end of Chapter 1 that while it was a trivial matter to get a rat to press a lever for food, it was very difficult to get the animal to learn to press a lever in order to avoid shock. There are some paradoxes here, and in this section we want to identify them and discuss some of the strategies that psychologists have used in connection with the problem of avoidance learning.

One paradox is the simple fact that avoidance learning occurs at all. It is fairly easy to guess that when an animal *escapes* a noxious stimulus such as shock, this constitutes a rewarding state of affairs, reward arising through straightforward fear reduction after the fashion of the Miller (1948) experiment. But why should *avoidance* of the noxious stimulus be rewarding? How can a stimulus not experienced by the animal be said to be a source of reinforcement?

Common sense would say, of course, that the animal comes to anticipate shock and that this is why it responds to a warning signal such as a buzzer. The learning theorist is not likely to be satisfied with this answer, however, since he will want to know how and why the anticipation develops. A number of theorists have tackled the problem, and a full treatment of all that has been put together both empirically and theoretically on the matter would be far beyond the scope of this book. Consequently, we will restrict ourselves to a discussion based on the roles of fear and fear reduction (a classical theory), on the one hand, and of species-specific defense reactions and safety signals, on the other. Bolles (1972) has written a marvelous review of this material—we have borrowed heavily from his work—and you are referred to his remarks for a fuller development of the matter.

THE CLASSICAL TWO-FACTOR THEORY OF AVOIDANCE LEARNING

We owe to Mowrer (1947) an early explanation of avoidance learning. Mowrer said that an animal in an avoidance-learning situation first learns to give a conditioned emotional response—fear—to the tone or buzzer that precedes shock or other noxious stimulus and that fear is conditioned according to Pavlovian principles. As we saw earlier in this chapter, fear has the properties itself of a drive or motivational state. If the organism performs an instrumental response that reduces the emotional disturbance, this is a reinforcing state of affairs, and on subsequent occasions, the animal will again choose this response. Thus, if leaping a hurdle in a shuttle box to escape shock also serves to reduce the emotional responsiveness to the discriminative cue, it will be a response that comes to be preferred by the animal. In a nutshell, then, Mowrer's theory says that the animal avoids the shock not just in order to avoid it, but to escape from the emotional state now conditioned to the buzzer.

In this form of his theory, Mowrer considered the development of avoidance learning as a two-stage process, and the term *two-factor theory* was applied to his approach. Learning to avoid an unpleasant shock consisted first of all in acquiring a *Pavlovian* emotional response to the buzzer or tone (the first factor) and, secondly, in acquiring some *instrumentally* conditioned response, reinforced by fear-drive reduction, that would get the organism away from the fear-producing buzzer or tone (the second factor).

Extinction of avoidance behavior If the classical two-factor approach runs into some difficulties, as we shall see, it has nevertheless generated some important empirical observations. Some of these have appeared when the extinction of avoidance responding has been studied. This process, viewed from both an empirical and a theoretical vantage point, is an exceptionally interesting one that has many implications for a general theory of learning. At the simplest level, we would expect avoidance learning to be more resistant to extinction than simple escape learning. This would be true because, during conditioning, according to the avoidance-learning paradigm, the organism is exposed to what is essentially a partial reinforcement situation. The animal takes the shock on those occasions where it fails to respond in time to the warning signal, but the shock is omitted on those trials in which successful avoidances occur. With escape learning, on the other hand, the shock occurs no matter what the organism does. Sheffield and Temmer (1950) showed that this thinking is essentially correct; avoidance learning produced greater resistance to extinction than escape learning.

Solomon and his associates (Solomon, Kamin, & Wynne, 1953; Solomon & Wynne, 1954) have looked at the extinction of avoidance behavior from another point of view. In particular, they have asked what happens to conditioned emotion in an avoidance situation under conditions where the intensity of the shock that an animal must avoid is extraordinarily intense. Solomon and Wynne (1953) trained dogs in a shuttle-box apparatus to avoid a shock that was just subtetanizing; had the shock been stronger, the animals would have been thrown into muscular tetany so that they would have been unable to move. An interval of 10 seconds was used between a CS and the onset of the shock, and the dogs could avoid the shock by leaping from one side of the box to the other within this 10-second interval. Figure 6.6 shows the behavior of a typical dog in this situation.

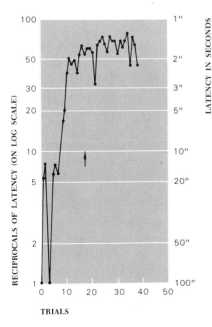

Figure 6.6
Traumatic avoidance learning. Here, a typical dog takes the strong shock for a few trials but then begins to avoid the shock by responding to the warning stimulus within 10 seconds. Once an avoidance response occurred, this dog never again took a shock. Note, too, that response latencies continue to decrease for a few trials after the first successful avoidance. (Solomon & Wynne, 1953.)

Two features of the data are particularly interesting. First of all, the animal goes along for a few trials making simple escapes, but then a single successful avoidance occurs, and *never again does the animal fail to avoid the shock*. Secondly, the latencies with which the animal makes successful avoidances *continue to decrease* even though the animal is no longer being shocked. What is more, Solomon, Kamin, and Wynne found that the avoidance response under these conditions would persist for *hundreds* of trials—it was essentially nonextinguishable unless special "therapeutic" procedures were used, like introducing a glass barrier into which the dogs crashed as they attempted to leap from one side to the other. Furthermore, these results are not restricted to dogs. Turner and Solomon (1962) trained human subjects to avoid a traumatically strong shock by, for example, requiring that they move a lever on a box placed in front of them back and forth from one side to the other (an apparatus designed to be analogous to the shuttle box used with the dogs). Resistance to extinction under this, and a number of other conditions, was extremely great; of those who learned the avoidance response, only 9 of 36 extinguished at all. Most subjects continued to respond for 200 trials or so, at which point the experimenters ended the experiment since there was little indication that extinction was ever going to occur.

How are these things to be explained, particularly the extraordinary persistence of the avoidance behavior after shock had been removed completely from the situation? One explanation, suggest Solomon and Wynne, lies in the fact that the animals perform the avoidance response very rapidly, so rapidly in fact that there is not enough time for the conditioned fear established during the first few escape trials to appear in full-blown form. This would have to happen, of course, for conditioned fear to extinguish. Therefore, they argue, conditioned fear is *conserved* by extremely rapid avoidance responding.

Of course, although this kind of reasoning suggests that extinction of avoidance ought to be a very protracted affair, it does predict that extinction ought to occur *sometime*, a prediction that runs counter to the results Solomon and his associates obtained. To handle this fact, Solomon and Wynne introduce a second concept, that of "partial irreversibility," which says in a nutshell that anxiety conditioned under the traumatic procedures used in these experiments is simply so strong that it will *never* extinguish completely (without the use of therapeutic procedures, at least).

These things provide a grim prospect for those concerned with the role of trauma in human personality development. But the implications of the results are important. They suggest at the very least that many of the mechanisms of neurotic behavior are learned responses used by the individual to reduce in part some learned fear or anxiety. And they suggest, too, that severe human anxiety may be very difficult to deal with when it is brought to the attention of the therapist. But in order to solve problems, one must have a clear picture of the problem that is there to be solved, and Solomon's work—to the extent that it can be generalized to the clinic—is very important in this respect.

The fate of the classical two-process theory of avoidance learning   Earlier, we warned you that the two-factor theory of avoidance learning has some difficulties connected with it—in spite of the fact that it has generated a wealth of important experimental facts over the years. One of its primary problems is that it depends heavily on the validity of conditioned fear as a mediator of the acquisition of the avoidance response itself. That is, the theory specifies that the avoidance response is acquired through the reduction of conditioned fear, and this, in turn, calls for a close correspondence between the waxing and waning of conditioned fear and the performance of the instrumental avoidance response. In fact, the close correspondence between the two processes often fails to appear (Rescorla & Solomon, 1967). The two-factor theory predicts, to be specific, that there ought to be some close relationship between, say, heart rate (as an index of conditioned fear) and the extinction of avoidance responding. If conditioned fear underlies avoidance learning, then heart rate ought to subside in orderly fashion as the avoidance response extinguishes. But this does not happen—conditioned heart rate tends to extinguish *before* the avoidance response extinguishes (Black, 1959), and theoretically, that means the motivational base for the avoidance response is gone long before the avoidance response itself. This is an uncomfortable situation.

The discomfort is not relieved appreciably by some other facts that have come from the laboratory, facts which raise once again the important role of organisms' innate reactions to unpleasant, aversive events. An experiment of Bolles (1969, 1970) sets the stage. Bolles was interested in the possible relation that might exist between the response an animal was trained to make to avoid shock and the response the animal was then required to learn to escape shock if, on a given trial, it failed to avoid. Earlier work (Mowrer & Lamoreaux, 1946) had suggested that escape contingencies might facilitate learning avoidance contingencies, facilitation mediated by fear as called for by two-process theory. But that was not the point that interested Bolles. He trained rats to avoid shock signaled by a noise in a running wheel. For some rats, the avoidance response was running until at least a quarter-turn was achieved. For other rats, the avoidance response was turning about-face in the running wheel (without necessarily turning it), while for a third group, the avoidance response was standing up on the hind legs in the running wheel. If the rat failed to avoid within the 10-second signal–shock interval, the animal was then required to escape shock by performing either the same response involved in the avoidance contingency or, for different rats, one of the other two responses. The experiment thus called for nine groups, each trained with one combination of avoidance and escape response. After 80 training trials, the results appearing in Figure 6.7 were obtained.

The data show, first of all, that for running and turning avoidance responses, at least, the acquisition of avoidance was helped if the escape response was the same as the avoidance response. This is particularly clear for the case where turning was the avoidance response. Note,

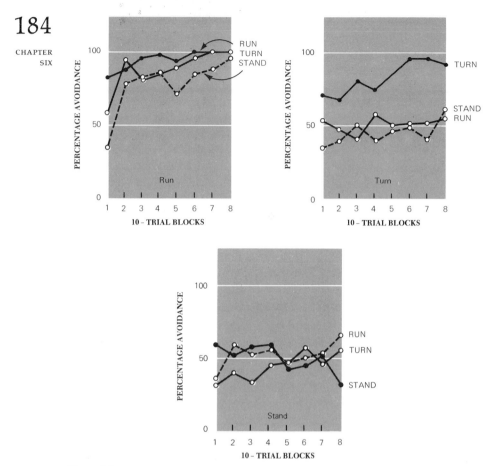

Figure 6.7
Avoidance performance of rats that were required to run, turn, or stand in an activity wheel to avoid shock. Within each avoidance condition, if the rats failed to avoid on a given trial, they could then escape only by running, turning, or standing. Thus, the escape response was either the same as or different from the avoidance response. The labels on the individual curves in each panel of the figure designate the escape requirement, while the labels at the bottom of each panel of the figure designate the avoidance requirement. (Bolles, 1972; adapted from Bolles, 1969.)

however, that the rats showed no improvement whatever in the development of avoidance if standing in the wheel was the avoidance response. Bolles concludes that the single feature that best describes these data is *not* something that can be ascribed to learned fear, or the like. Instead, he insists that the common denominator of the data is the nature of the specific motor response called for in order to escape or avoid shock. Running was best, turning was possible, but the animals were essentially unable to learn to stand up to avoid or escape shock (in the sense, at least, that their performance failed to improve with practice).

SPECIES-SPECIFIC DEFENSE REACTIONS AND SAFETY SIGNALS

Bolles' analysis of the data from his experiment (together with data from a number of others) led him to the development of a new theoretical approach to avoidance learning. His newer theory is a two-factor theory, too, in a sense, but the factors are quite different from anything that has been emphasized in this connection thus far. Specifically, he says that an adequate account of avoidance learning can be developed from two facts: (1) organisms possess innate, characteristic methods of responding to dangerous situations (species-specific defense reactions) and (2) organisms can learn that certain signals *predict* that certain other events will follow. Bolles does not deny that fear can become conditioned to neutral cues in the environment (although he points out that nature often does not allow an opportunity for such conditioning to take place—woe to the creature that does not escape or avoid at once, without practice), but he does insist, first, that it is the animal's natural reaction to danger that is the critical thing. In Bolles' experiment that we examined in the last section, therefore, we would conclude that running was a natural reaction to shock in rats, that turning around was less so, and that standing up was quite unnatural. So far so good.

But how can it be, Bolles now asks, that if animals can only learn to avoid noxious events using responses that are species-typical reactions to noxious events, they *can* learn to use relatively *unnatural* responses like pressing levers and standing up if the experimenter is just a little patient and takes care to arrange things just so? To answer this question, Bolles invokes his second factor, a factor which we covered in some detail earlier in this chapter: animals can learn that certain signals are accurate *predictors* of other events in their environment. Thus, cues which are regularly followed by shock or other aversive stimuli become *danger signals,* while other cues become *safety signals* because they forecast the end of an unpleasant state of affairs and predict a time *free* from aversive stimuli. The organism may also be effectively scared to death as well (or relieved, as the case may be), but fear and fear reduction are not the things that lead to successful escape or avoidance. Instead, to summarize, Bolles postulates that danger signals evoke species-specific defense reactions, reactions that get the animal away from danger. If these work, the animal's problem is solved. If they fail to work, the animal's only recourse is to stumble around, willy-nilly, trying one response that is perhaps close to a response in its natural defense arsenal. Eventually, it may find one—recall the rats that were required to turn around in Bolles' experiment to avoid shock. If it fails to find one, however, it may fail to learn to escape or avoid altogether—recall the rats that had to stand up to escape and avoid shock, and recall the fact that rats have an extremely difficult time learning to press a bar to avoid shock. Under these conditions, in Bolles' (1972) words, the animal's

. . . best chance to solve the problem is to learn about the one positive contingency that exists in the welter of negative contingencies. A particular response, such as pressing the bar, predicts safety (because it removes shock). The animal freezes in front of the bar, and does press it from time to time. If the response produces a cue to safety, this may help the critical contingency be discriminated from the rest. Whether the animal ultimately learns about this contingency and solves the problem will depend upon how far removed the required response is from its species-specific defense reaction repertoire, how much safety the response produces, and, of course, the ability of the animal to learn about such a contingency [p. 139].

Bolles' account of avoidance learning is not the only one that is cast in a similar vein. Seligman and Johnston (1973) have provided another that makes somewhat related assumptions, an account which parallels Bolles' in that it stresses the things that animals learn about the contingent outcomes of one class of responses as opposed to some other. By now you should not be surprised that both stress the role of the cognitive capacities of organisms to solve the fundamental problems of prediction and anticipation that are the very definition of avoidance learning.

LEARNED HELPLESSNESS

In the last few sections we have emphasized the consequences of teaching an organism some instrumental behavior, subjecting it to Pavlovian conditioning, and then retesting it with the Pavlovian CS superimposed upon the ongoing instrumental behavior. We saw, in particular, not only how neutral cues can acquire emotion- and motivation-producing capacities, but also how organisms can come to use them as predictors of danger or safety. In this section, we examine the consequences of an apparently minor adjustment in this sequence of events. Specifically, we shall see what happens when we omit the initial instrumental training, exposing our organism to the Pavlovian contingencies first and then requiring that it learn some new instrumental response for the first time. In this case, an apparently minor modification in procedure produces some rather major and remarkable phenomena. Maier, Seligman, and Solomon (1969), in reporting the results of a number of experiments involving dogs, shuttle boxes, Pavlovian harnesses, and strong electric shocks, summarize things neatly, and we can do little but follow their thoughts closely to properly introduce things.

If a dog is placed in one compartment of a shuttle box (or in the Pavlovian harness) and subjected to a series of brief, very intense, unavoidable and inescapable electric shocks, that dog is rendered *unable* to learn some simple response—like jumping the hurdle into the second compartment—when instrumental contingencies are introduced and hurdle jumping will now lead to escape from or avoidance of electric shock. Furthermore, it does not matter if the experimenter follows the strict Pavlovian procedure and pairs shock with some specific CS, or if shock simply occurs and pairs itself with whatever unspecified "CS" may be provided by the general environment at the moment. Maier et al. (1969) put things this way:

> In dramatic contrast to a naive dog, a dog which has experienced inescapable shocks prior to avoidance training soon stops running and howling and remains silent until shock terminates. The dog does not cross the barrier and escape the shock. Rather it seems to give up and passively accept the shock. On succeeding trials, the dog continues to fail to make escape movements and will take as much shock as the experimenter chooses to give.

187

LEARNING
AND THE
CONCEPTS OF
EMOTION AND
MOTIVATION

. . . such dogs occasionally jump the barrier and escape or avoid, but then revert to taking the shock; they fail to profit from exposure to the barrier-jumping-shock-termination contingency. In naive dogs a successful escape response is a reliable predictor of future, short-latency escape responses [pp. 311–312].

Some sample data showing this extraordinary and remarkable interference with new learning are shown in Figure 6.8. These data were obtained in experiments in which dogs were previously exposed to unavoidable shock (prior-shock condition) or not so exposed (naive condition) and then placed in the shuttle box with a 10-second interval between the beginning of a discriminative cue and the beginning of a strong shock. The shock persisted for 50 seconds unless the dog avoided it or escaped from it. As you can see, the median latency for animals exposed to prior shock was the full 60-second duration of a trial—that is, the typical dog failed to cross the hurdle—while the median latency for the naive dogs declined steadily toward the 10-second mark and the total avoidance of shock. The figure is a trifle misleading in one respect because it suggests that no dog in the prior-shock group learned at all, whereas Maier et al. report that, in fact, only two-thirds of the dogs failed to learn (in contrast to just 6 percent of the naive animals). The key lies in the nature of the statistic—median latency—reported in Figure 6.8, since that statistic reflects just the middlemost latency among the prior-shock group. The data indicate, in other words, that more than half the animals, at least, exhibited the maximum 60-second latency, a figure that corresponds appropriately to the two-thirds figure of Maier et al.

Figure 6.8
If dogs received prior uncontrollable shock in the Pavlovian harness (prior shock), they were unable to learn an escape-avoidance response in the shuttle box. Their latencies match the complete 60-second duration of each trial, indicating they failed to respond during the 10-second interval between the onset of the warning stimulus and the onset of shock and that they also failed to respond during the 50 seconds of shock which followed. Naive dogs learned to escape rapidly, and eventually they began avoiding shock by responding during the initial 10 seconds of each trial. (Seligman, Maier, & Solomon, 1971.)

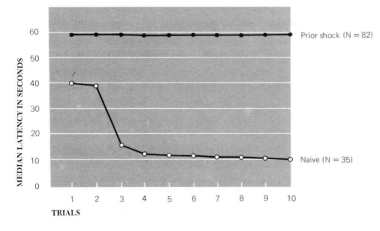

After careful consideration of the available data, Maier et al. reject the notion that adaptation to shock from extensive experience with it could lead to the phenomenon. They also reject the idea that the dogs could have learned some response during the first, Pavlovian, phase of the experiment which would compete or interfere with the acquisition of the new avoidance response in some mechanical way. They conclude that the phenomenon represents a psychological state which they label "learned helplessness."

Learned helplessness, say Maier et al., is an emotional and cognitive condition which arises when an organism is led to conclude from experience that "nothing I do matters," i.e., that the consequence of any given response is just as apt to be the occurrence of a very painful event as the absence of that painful event. And that, of course, is just the state of affairs assured by noncontingent, unavoidable shocks. Thus these investigators stress that the organism learns about the extent to which it can *control* and *predict* the pleasant and unpleasant things in its environment, and by this time, that general idea should be a very familiar one to you.

Learned helplessness is by no means restricted to dogs in Pavlovian harnesses and shuttle boxes. Seligman and Beagley (1974) report that it is obtainable in rats, and Hiroto (1974) reports that it is obtainable in humans, using, in this case, extremely loud sound as the punishing event. Seligman (1974) has summarized this work, together with a good bit of theorizing about the problem and its clinical implications for human behavior.

What can be done about a "helpless" organism? A helpless dog can be rendered competent once again if the experimenter literally pulls the animal with a long leash across the shuttle box and teaches it that shock can be escaped (Seligman, Maier, & Geer, 1968). Also, a dog can be "immunized" against helplessness by exposing it initially to shock in a situation where the dog can acquire control over the shock (Seligman & Maier, 1967). And that, if you will recall, is precisely the set of circumstances we described in an earlier portion of this chapter: dogs first learned an avoidance response and then learned about some relations between a CS and shock during Pavlovian training before, finally, reentering a period of instrumental avoidance training. As we noted before, it is important to keep the sequence of the various phases of Pavlovian and instrumental training in mind. Learned helplessness occurs only under those conditions in which Pavlovian training occurs before the organism is called upon to learn the relevant instrumental behavior.

IS THERE AN APPETITIVE ANALOG TO LEARNED HELPLESSNESS?

Do things analogous to learned helplessness occur when rewards rather than punishments are used? While the available evidence is by no means as extensive as that dealing with learned helplessness, the answer to that question appears to be "yes." We must be cautious here simply because not enough data have yet been obtained to place things on a completely firm footing. Nevertheless, Hulse (1973b), for example, placed one group of hungry rats in a Skinner box and, for each of 14 daily sessions, provided them with 40 free food pellets delivered automatically, one at a time, from a food magazine—all quite independent of anything the animals did. The impending delivery of a food pellet was signaled by a brief tone which ended just as the food pellet arrived; tone–food pellet combinations occurred once every 30 seconds. A second group of rats received food pellets, too, but according to a different pattern. Instead of receiving a food pellet each time the tone sounded, the probability that a food pellet would appear decreased over the 14-day period from 1 to 0 for these animals. That is, the rats experienced a set of events in which the tone was paired with a steadily decreasing supply of food. Following this initial training—which by now you should recognize as a straightforward Pavlovian procedure in which the tone functioned as a CS and food pellets functioned as a UCS—an instrumental procedure was initiated. On day 15 of the experiment, a lever was inserted into the box, and the animals could earn a food pellet if they pressed it. When they pressed it, or if they failed to press it for 30 seconds, it withdrew from the box to reappear for the next trial after a 30-second pause. The facility with which the animals would learn the lever-pressing response was the question of interest, and the data appear in Figure 6.9. The figure shows how long it took the rats on the average to move to the lever and to press it on every other of the 30 trials that were used on day 1.

As you can see, the treatments during the Pavlovian phase of the experiment produced very different rates of learning of the new instrumental response. It is clear that if the tone had signaled the certain arrival of the food pellet on every trial during Pavlovian training, then learning was retarded severely. As a matter of fact, the data show absolutely no indication that the rats improved their performance on day 1, and three of the eight animals in this group failed to learn the simple response after several more days—and 180 trials—of lever-press training.

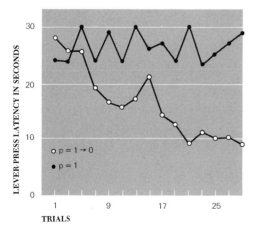

Figure 6.9
Animals learning to press a lever following preliminary training in which free, response-independent food pellets were given every time a signal came on ($p = 1$) and where the probability of a food pellet had decreased steadily from 1 to 0 ($p = 1 \rightarrow 0$). Lever presses for both groups, if they occurred, were always reinforced with one food pellet during learning. The animals in the $p = 1$ group were "indolent," in that they were slow to learn to press the lever. (After Hulse, 1973b.)

If, on the other hand, the tone had signaled a decreasing probability of a food pellet during Pavlovian training, then learning of the response was quite rapid. By the end of the day, the animals were working at a fast level which they were able to improve only slightly over the remaining days of the experiment.

While an abundance of data remains to be collected with regard to this phenomenon, as we indicated earlier, there are some other examples of it. Hulse (1973b) discussed some of them, and Engberg, Hansen, Welker, and Thomas (1972) showed that pigeons were very slow to learn a new key-pecking response if they had had previous experience receiving a supply of free, non-response-contingent reward. If, on the other hand, they had had previous experience performing some other *response* to obtain reward, then they had a relatively easy time switching their behavior to the new key-pecking response and learning that one.

Hulse has applied the term "learned indolence" to the slow learning following steady, consistent, non-response-contingent reward because the phenomenon seems clearly parallel to that of learned helplessness based on free, non-response-contingent punishment. But the parallel may well end there, because Hulse's experiment showed that learned indolence could be turned into something apparently its polar opposite (learned diligence?) by the simple expedient of patterning the delivery of free food pellets during the Pavlovian phase of the experiment. Remember that if the tone was associated with a decreasing probability of food pellets, the rats were very efficient learners when they had to work for reward. This runs counter to the explanation that Maier et al. gave for learned helplessness, i.e., that dogs learned their helpless attitude by concluding there was nothing they could do to *control* the delivery or absence of punishment. Hulse's rats had no control over food pellets either; yet the simple procedure of "fading away" the food pellets was sufficient to turn learned indolence into learned diligence during the subsequent instrumental conditioning phase of the experiment. Clearly, there is much that remains to be learned and developed here, and it is especially important to remember the caution with which we began this section: the concepts of learned indolence and diligence are potentially important, but they require much empirical development before they can be accepted unequivocally into the psychology of learning. But because the psychology of learning stresses the development of learned emotion and motivation, the task is especially important to undertake.

PUNISHMENT

In general, a response is punished when some painful stimulation or the threat of such stimulation is made contingent upon the response. Usually, punishment is administered to ongoing behavior in order to stop it, although as we shall see, things do not always work this way. Indeed, the effects of punishment upon behavior are enormously complex, and it will be our task in this section to unravel some of that tangle.

CLASSICAL WORK ON PUNISHMENT

191

LEARNING
AND THE
CONCEPTS OF
EMOTION AND
MOTIVATION

For many years, experimental and theoretical work on punishment was dominated by the views of the late E. L. Thorndike. For most of his professional life he was an educational psychologist, and consequently, his concern with the problem of punishment was influenced by the formal demands of the classroom. In a word, he was concerned with the influence of verbal praise and reproof upon behavior. Since his views and experiments were very influential, let us look briefly at them.

Thorndike's views and experiments In his earliest writing, Thorndike simply adopted the commonsense view that punishment would reduce the tendency to repeat behavior which it immediately followed (weakened connections, as Thorndike put it). Later, however, Thorndike (1932a) examined the problem more thoroughly and came to another conclusion. He decided that punishment really has no inherently weakening effect upon behavior. Let us see how Thorndike arrived at this rather surprising position.

Thorndike argued that wherever punishment appears to weaken a response, it is an *indirect* effect. Punishment may or may not weaken a response, but it clearly cannot be the mirror image of the action of reward. This is true, at least in the sense that if a response is rewarded, it is apparent to the organism in a typical test that repetition of *this* response will be rewarding; but if a response is punished, it is not clear to the organism which of the other available responses will be rewarded. In effect, punishment does an exemplary job of telling the organism what not to do, but it carries no information by itself which tells an organism what particular alternative course of behavior should be followed.

What happens, however, when the *only* response that is appropriate for a particular motivational state of affairs is punished? The youngster who is punished for taking cookies from the cupboard may know no other way to satisfy a craving for sweets. No matter how many raps on the knuckles (or elsewhere) the youngster may receive, the cookies lose none of their attraction, and the child is not likely to find another way of getting cookies. This leads us to some of the very fundamental questions about punishment, questions which force us into the controlled world of the animal laboratory to find answers to them. Let us look at a couple of the classical experiments on punishment in free-responding situations.

The experiments of Skinner and Estes Skinner (1938) studied the effect of punishment upon the lever-pressing response in the Skinner box. In his experiment, the punishment was a sharp slap on the paws from the lever itself. To measure the effects of punishment, Skinner obtained extinction curves for four rats following training with a fixed-interval schedule of reinforcement. Two rats were slapped at the beginning of the extinction period, and two were not. The result was that the rats slapped at the beginning of extinction showed a much lower rate of responding during extinction. As a matter of fact, the punishment seemed to *suppress* the response entirely for a period of time. The curious thing, however, is that by the time extinction was complete, the slapped rats had caught up, in terms of total number of responses emitted, with the rats which were not slapped.

Skinner interpreted the data to mean that punishment has only a temporary effect upon behavior—an unfortunate interpretation, as later research has shown. Nevertheless, Skinner thought that punishment does not affect the total number of responses which the animal will eventually emit during extinction; it only affects the rate at which some total will be emitted. Early in extinction the punished animals show a lower rate of responding; their response rate is suppressed. But eventually, the suppression disappears and the rates accelerate so that in the end the punished animals give just as many responses altogether as the unpunished animals.

Estes (1944) followed Skinner's work with an intensive investigation of the factors affecting punishment of an isolated instrumental response—again, lever pressing in the rat. In these experiments, he substituted an electric shock for Skinner's slap. The shock was delivered through the lever so that rats used to receiving food as the result of lever pressing sometimes received the shock instead.

Estes' first conclusion was much like Skinner's: the effect of punishment is primarily upon the rate of responding rather than upon the total overall tendency to emit a particular response. Estes did find, however, that if the punishment were intense enough or lasted long enough, there was a slight permanent depression in the total number of responses the animals would emit. Nevertheless, punishment was never able to eliminate the extinction curve completely—rats always came back to respond after punishment, even though they were never again reinforced. It is interesting that when Estes punished his rats only now and then, instead of for every response, the depression of the rate of responding was not nearly so severe, *but it lasted longer.* Thus the results of partial punishment are quite like the results of partial reinforcement, a fact which, incidentally, is now very well established (Azrin, 1956; Azrin, Holz, & Hake, 1963; Boe, 1971).

THE SUPPRESSION OF BEHAVIOR BY PUNISHMENT

The most characteristic feature of a punishment operation, as the experiments of Skinner and Estes clearly suggest, is to reduce at least temporarily the strength of the response that is being punished. There are many exceptions to this rule, however, and we shall look at some of them later. Right now let us see what has been done to pin down the conditions under which behavior is reduced in strength by punishment. As it turns out, this is a particular characteristic of instrumental responses that are established by *positive reinforcement* before punishment begins.

Some parameters of punishment One of the first things that comes to mind is the question of how punishment varies in effectiveness as its intensity changes. A good deal is now known about the subject (Church,

1969, provides a good review). Camp, Raymond, and Church (1967) trained rats to lever-press for food on a VI 1-minute schedule of reinforcement until the response was well established, then divided them into groups that were punished with shocks of intensities that ranged from 0 to 2.0 milliamperes. Each shock lasted 2.0 seconds. Not all lever presses were punished; instead, shocks were distributed throughout a session of lever pressing according to a ratio schedule of reinforcement. The ratio schedule was set for each rat so as to assure that the rat would get one punished response per minute if it maintained its lever-pressing rate at a constant level. Figure 6.10 shows the results.

As you can see, the rats suppressed their behavior more, the greater the intensity of the punishing shock. Camp et al. also report that there was a slight tendency to recover from the suppressive effects of the shock if the intensity was not too great, and you can see that the curves for shocks in the range of 0.1 to 0.5 milliamperes do tend to rise a trifle as punishment sessions run their course. This is not an uncommon finding (Church, 1963) and probably reflects adaptation to the shock stimulus. Sometimes, recovery from suppression can be almost complete providing the intensity of the punishment is not too great (e.g., Azrin, 1960). Under these conditions, an animal may return to its prepunishment level of responding in spite of the fact that punishment continues (remember that responses are also rewarded so that it is worth the animal's while to do so).

What happens when punishment is removed in instrumental situations like those we have just examined? Generally speaking, responding

Figure 6.10
Suppression of food-reinforced lever pressing by punishment. Control animals received no punishment. Suppression ratios are a relative index of lever pressing during punishment and just before punishment. A ratio of 0.5 indicates that the rate during punishment was the same as the rate before punishment, while a ratio of 0.0 reflects complete response suppression. The data show that the greater the punishment-shock intensity the greater the response suppression. (Camp, Raymond, & Church, 1967.)

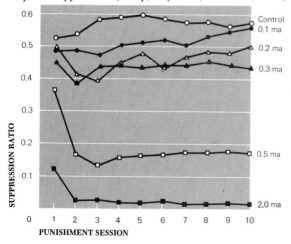

recovers to prepunishment levels, provided that the organism continues to be positively reinforced for its behavior (e.g., Azrin, 1960; Appel, 1963). Similarly, Estes and Skinner, if you will recall, found that if positive reinforcement were removed during punishment, and the test for the effects of punishment carried out during extinction, the rate of extinction was slowed, but the punished animals eventually produced just as many responses as the unpunished animals. Punishment, in other words, seemed to have no permanent effects on the persistence of behavior.

Boe and Church (1967) found something substantially different, however. They trained rats to press a lever for food on a FI 4-minute schedule until the response was well established. Then, following Estes' (1944) general procedure, they turned off food and delivered shocks for the first lever press to occur in successive 30-second intervals of the first 15 minutes of extinction. For the remainder of the first one-hour session, and for the eight sessions which followed, no shocks were delivered and, of course, no food was given either since the tests for the effects of punishment were carried out during extinction. Figure 6.11 gives the results. The data in the figure are cumulative percentages of the number of responses rats made during various portions of extinction as compared with the number made during the last session of reinforced training.

It is quite apparent in Figure 6.11, first of all, that punishment reduced responding to zero during the initial 15-minute period that it was on. Following that, however, it is equally apparent that responding did *not* recover altogether and that the magnitude of this effect depended upon

Figure 6.11
The effect of punishment upon extinction of a food-reinforced response. The data are cumulative percentages of the amount of responding at various stages of extinction as compared with responding during prior reinforced training. Punishment was administered for 15 minutes of the first extinction session (at *P*). Weak or no punishment produced almost no permanent effect, but severe punishment produced very little subsequent responding during later periods of extinction. (Boe & Church, 1967.)

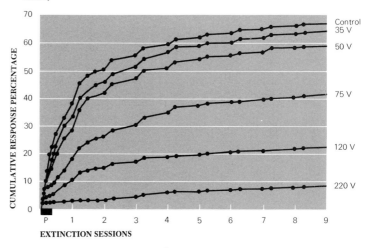

the intensity of the punishing shock with which extinction began. At the extreme 220-volt intensity, there was just a bare trace of recovery, for example, while recovery was almost complete at 35 volts in the sense that the animals extinguished under this condition took just about as long to extinguish as the animals extinguished without any initial punishment at all. Boe and Church, in reconciling their data with those of both Estes and Skinner, note that the intensity of the punishment in the earlier experiments almost certainly was less than the intensity they used, and they suggest that this accounts for the differences in results.

To summarize, then, punishment can have *permanent* effects upon behavior in the sense that it can markedly reduce an animal's persistence during the extinction of a response that has been previously reinforced with some appetitive reinforcer like food. This is to be contrasted with the *temporary* suppressive effects of punishment upon behavior when behavior is also being rewarded at the time that punishment is administered. Under the latter condition, behavior may be suppressed as long as punishment occurs, but it recovers once punishment is removed.

The effects of contingent versus noncontingent punishment In an earlier portion of this chapter, we discussed briefly the concept of the *conditioned emotional response* (CER). If you will recall, we said that a CER was established by a Pavlovian procedure: a neutral stimulus, like a light, is paired with a punishing stimulus, like shock, quite independently of anything the organism happens to be doing at the time. And, if you will also recall, we noted that the appearance of the light eventually tended to suppress ongoing behavior, suppression of behavior being the critical change to which the label CER is attached. The difference between the CER procedure and the conventional punishment procedure is that punishment is contingent upon some particular response in the latter, while it is *not* contingent upon any particular response in the case of the CER. With the CER procedure, instead, punishment is contingent upon the occurrence of some particular *stimulus*, the stimulus which signals that shock will occur at the end of some period of time.

What are the differential effects of response-contingent as compared with non-response-contingent punishment? It is important to recognize that both procedures produce primary effects which are more similar than dissimilar: both suppress behavior in a situation that has been associated with an aversive event like shock. Hunt and Brady (1955), for example, trained two groups of rats to press a lever for food in a Skinner box. After stable performance was reached, a neutral cue was turned on for three minutes. For animals in a punishment group, each response that occurred during the three-minute interval was followed with a brief electric shock. For animals in a CER group, no responses were punished during the three-minute interval, but a brief unavoidable shock occurred just as the neutral stimulus went off. The results showed that both groups of animals reduced their rate of responding during the presence of the neutral cue; both groups, in fact, eventually stopped responding altogether while the cue was on. However, Hunt and Brady also found that it took longer for the effects of the CER procedure to extinguish than it did for the effects of the contingent procedure. When shock was removed from the situation, animals in the CER group showed suppression in the presence of the neutral cue for a longer period of time than did animals in the punishment group. Furthermore, animals in the CER group tended to do things during the presence of the neutral cue that were different from the things that animals in the punishment group did. In the case of the former, a common pattern of behavior was to crouch, freeze, urinate, and defecate, while for the punishment group, the common pattern was to tickle and tease (but not press) the lever until the neutral stimulus went off.

Since Hunt and Brady's initial work, more recent experimentation has shown beyond little doubt that response-contingent punishment does a more direct and effective job of suppressing some particular response than the response-independent CER procedure (e.g., Myer, 1971; Church, Wooten, & Matthews, 1970a; Church, Wooten, & Matthews, 1970b). This is probably so because contingent punishment tends to have its effects upon a much more restricted segment of an organism's behavior—the segment that is being punished in particular. The non-response-contingent procedure, on the other hand, tends eventually to knock out a large part of all the behavior that occurs in the punishment situation. In effect, and speaking a bit loosely, the animal subjected to response-contingent punishment has a relatively easy time figuring out what it is in the situation that must not be done, while for the animal subjected to the CER procedure, it is impossible that this can ever become clear. The latter may continue pressing the lever more than the animal exposed to response-contingent punishment (providing the punishment is not too intense), but in general, a much greater cross section of the animal's behavior will be punished in the long run—in fact, anything the animal happens to be doing at the time the unavoidable shock comes on (but see Church et al., 1970b, for some further thinking on this point). Such an animal is left, traumatized by the consistent contingency between a danger signal and unavoidable shock that does exist in the situation, to "take" the shock and handle its "situational anxiety" as best it can, perhaps in some species-typical fashion (Myer, 1971).

On the basis of the foregoing reasoning, we might make the additional straightforward deduction that because the CER procedure apparently knocks out more of an organism's response repertoire, it ought to take longer for the organism to recover from the effects of the noncontingent punishment once it is removed. That is, of course, exactly what Hunt and Brady discovered. More recent research shows, however, that we do not yet have all the answers here. Church et al. (1970b) showed quite clearly that response-contingent punishment led to *slower* extinction of response suppression than the CER procedure—a result in direct contradiction to that of Hunt and Brady. Church et al. did find, however—in agreement with our thinking—that response-contingent punishment led to suppression of specific components of the organism's behavior—those components that were, in fact, being punished—while the CER procedure tended to suppress behavior in the situation much more generally and uniformly.

197

LEARNING
AND THE
CONCEPTS OF
EMOTION AND
MOTIVATION

The practical use of suppression produced by punishment While it is far beyond the scope of this book to go into the matter in any detail at all, it is useful to recognize that the use of suppression produced by punishment can be an important technique to incorporate in clinical settings, particularly those which adopt the newer methods of behavior modification. Among other techniques, punishment can be combined with reward for alternative responses to produce rather dramatic changes in the behavior of disturbed or retarded people or of people institutionalized for one reason or another. This is an important and rapidly expanding area in clinical and applied psychology, and we have yet to realize its full potential. If you want to pursue the matter, you can read material such as Neuringer & Michael (1970), Wolpe (1974), or any of the current issues of journals such as *Behavior Research and Therapy*. It is interesting to note, incidentally, that practically all the techniques of behavior therapy come from procedures developed initially in the animal laboratory. This is another good example of how fundamental, basic research can lead eventually to important practical usefulness.

SOME NONSUPPRESSIVE FUNCTIONS OF PUNISHMENT

In the last section, we examined some of the ways that punishment works to knock out rewarded behavior, and we saw that the use of a punishing stimulus not only does a pretty good job of doing this—at least temporarily, and sometimes more permanently—in a number of different situations. Now, let us turn things around a bit and look at some situations in which a punishing stimulus not only does not suppress behavior, but can actually be used to facilitate learning, to elicit important innate responses, and to maintain useful behavior. Along the way we shall meet some rather strange paradoxes which, at the very least, suggest that we have a great deal to learn before we shall have much more than a rudimentary understanding of the effects of punishment upon behavior.

The use of punishment as a cue What happens if, instead of following a usually rewarded response with an electric shock, we use the electric shock to signal that if a response is made, a reward can be obtained? In other words, what happens if we *reverse* the usual temporal relation between a "punishing" stimulus and reinforced behavior, using the punishing stimulus as a discriminative cue? Will behavior be suppressed under these conditions? Solomon (1964) thinks not, and there is considerable evidence to support his point of view. The key here is to think of a punishing event not so much in terms of its unpleasantness, but in terms of its properties as a *stimulus*, a cue which ought to function like any other cue.

An experiment of Holz and Azrin (1961) demonstrates that an electric shock can function in exactly the same way as a buzzer or a light in simple discrimination learning. These experimenters trained pigeons to peck at a key on a VI 2-minute schedule of food reinforcement. When the response was running along at a steady rate, they added an electric shock to the situation so that each response on the key produced the shock. The intensity of the shock was adjusted so that the rate of key pecking was reduced by about half. When this condition was well established, extinction periods were introduced in which pecks produced neither food nor shock. This procedure—periods of reinforcement in the presence of a cue (shock) interspersed with periods of no reinforcement in the absence of the cue—is precisely that used to establish the cue as a discriminative stimulus. Under these conditions, we would expect shock to come to signal that food was available, and we would look for the pigeon to reserve most of its responding for the period in which the shock was delivered following each response. This is exactly what happened. The pigeon responded hardly at all during the period of no punishment, but responded quite rapidly *when each response was followed by shock.* Clearly, punishment had been established as a cue which set the occasion for responding for a positive reinforcer.

In a long series of experiments, Muenzinger (1934, etc.; see Church, 1963, for a review) demonstrated another aspect of punishment as a cue for learning. In one of his experiments, he ran rats in a discrimination box, rewarding them with food if they made a correct response, and punishing them with shock if they made an error. Not surprisingly, perhaps, he found that the group run under these conditions made about one-third as many errors as a group that received food alone for a correct response. But here comes a surprise. Muenzinger was also able to demonstrate that shocking an animal after a *correct* response leading to food produced learning that was almost as rapid as shocking the animals for incorrect responses (both conditions, of course, leading to faster learning than if no punishment at all were used).

How are we to account for this rather astonishing result? Muenzinger felt that the function of shock for correct responses was to slow down the animal and, in effect, make the animal do a little more deliberating before making a choice. Wischner (1947) emphasized the fact that Muenzinger used a correction procedure in discrimination training and found a much-reduced effect when a noncorrection procedure was used (that is, when the animal was not allowed to correct an error by retracing and making the proper choice). It is quite possible that such procedural factors may play some minor role in the phenomenon, but on the basis of things we have been developing in this section, another approach suggests itself (Fowler & Wischner, 1969). This is simply that shock in these experiments is paired with food and as such can come to function as a discriminative cue—signaling to the rat just after it has made its choice that it has indeed made the correct one. The key here, once again, may be to look at the *information* that shock gives the rat about its choice behavior.

199

LEARNING
AND THE
CONCEPTS OF
EMOTION AND
MOTIVATION

Recent research suggests that the foregoing analysis is probably correct. In a series of experiments, Fowler and Wischner and their associates have shown that shock for correct responses is especially beneficial in solving difficult as compared with easy discriminations (Fowler, Spelt, & Wischner, 1967). Furthermore, the *feedback* properties of shock as opposed to neutral stimuli for correct choices, that is, the *emphasis* that shock places on a correct choice that it follows, has been shown to be of significance (Fago & Fowler, 1972). Among the varied functions that punishment can play in discrimination learning tasks of this sort (see Taylor, 1974, for some others), in other words, its cue properties play an exceptionally important role, perhaps far more important than its emotion-producing properties. After all, a bit of punishment (and remember that we are talking about fairly mild punishment here) may be a trifle upsetting at the moment, but can this be more than a fleeting state of affairs if it signals at the same time that a positive reward lies just ahead?

Some other paradoxes: the elicitation of behavior by punishment Think, for a moment, of the conventional avoidance-learning experiment. A dog is trained to jump a hurdle in response to a discriminative cue, and if the leap occurs within a prescribed time interval, punishment (electric shock, etc.) is avoided. As we have seen, this behavior is readily established and quickly becomes quite stable. Now let us perform an experimental operation which would lead us to expect suppression of behavior; that is, let us punish the animal for making the avoidance response. A simple way to do this would be to electrify the formerly safe grid floor so that the animal now jumps into shock. We could combine this with an extinction procedure so that if the animal fails to leap and stays in the start compartment, shocks no longer occur there. Under these conditions—on the basis of what we have seen to be the case for responses based on positive rewards—we would expect the dog to quickly suppress its jumping behavior and to stop jumping much sooner than another dog, say, that was not punished. But things simply do not work that way—there is now a great deal of evidence which shows that punishment administered under these conditions *increases* the tendency to respond far beyond what we find if punishment is not used. Solomon et al. (1953) reported in their experiments on traumatic avoidance learning that dogs would jump *faster* and *more vigorously* into shock than they would under conventional extinction procedures, and Church (1963) in his review of the literature cites a host of experiments showing essentially the same thing.

Another example of the elicitation of behavior by punishment in an apparently paradoxical fashion comes from some work demonstrating so-called *vicious-circle* behavior. Brown, Martin, and Morrow (1964) trained rats to run an alley in order to *escape* shock. The rats were dropped onto an electrified grid in the start box and had to run the entire length of the electrified alley before reaching safety in the goal box. After this response was well learned, the animals were extinguished under one of three conditions. For one group, regular extinction was used—after a few trials during which shock intensity was gradually reduced, all shock was turned off in the apparatus. For a second, "short-shock," group, shock was left on in the final 2-foot segment of the alley just before the goal box, but was turned off elsewhere. For a third, "long-shock," group, the entire 6-foot length of the alley was electrified, but shock was absent in the start and goal boxes. You can see the extinction results in Figure 6.12.

In terms of running speed in the last 2 feet of the alley, the group that extinguished *first* was the group which *received no shock at all*. The other two groups, which were both punished for making the former escape response, showed much greater resistance to extinction and were in fact running about 3.5 feet per second after six days of extinction (60 extinction trials). Here was truly "masochistic" behavior on the part of the rats, since all they had to do to avoid shock entirely was to sit still in the start box!

How are we to account for such a paradoxical effect? As you might expect, there are many ways of looking at the problem, but the one favored by Brown et al. (see also Saunders, 1974) holds that vicious-circle

Figure 6.12
Resistance to extinction of an escape response as a function of punishment conditions during extinction. In the long-shock condition, the entire alley was electrified, while in the short-shock condition, the last 2 feet of the alley were electrified. In the no-shock condition, shock was absent throughout the apparatus. Resistance to extinction was least when the alley contained no shock, while it was greatest when the animals ran into shock. (J. S. Brown, Martin, & Morrow, 1964.)

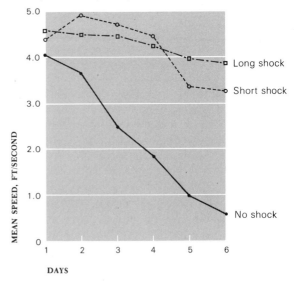

behavior occurs because it is potentiated by the fear that shock evokes in the situation. Shock during extinction operates not so much to suppress specific responses like running as it does to maintain fear in the situation, and when shock appears, animals continue to run because the motivational base for that response is enhanced.

201

LEARNING
AND THE
CONCEPTS OF
EMOTION AND
MOTIVATION

An alternative explanation of vicious-circle behavior rests on yet another class of phenomena associated with behavior evoked by a punishing stimulus. This class has to do with the species-specific behaviors that punishment can produce in animals. There are a host of these, as we have seen throughout this book, ranging from simple running away to some interesting social behavior. Thus, animals ranging from rat to monkey will spontaneously *fight* when punishing shock is turned on if another rat or monkey is in the immediate neighborhood (O'Kelly & Steckle, 1939; Azrin, Hutchinson, & Hake, 1967). In the rat this generally assumes the form of a characteristic "boxing" posture in which two rats stand, face each other, and hit with their front paws. This highly stereotyped behavior can be elicited for hundreds of "trials" with little or no sign of diminishing in probability or intensity. Myer (1971) has provided an elegant review of this and related phenomena, and he has suggested some things which we can use to account for vicious-circle behavior without invoking the concept of fear as Brown et al. did. Myer suggests, fundamentally, that an important effect of punishment in a situation may be the potentiation of any response that an animal may have made there, either because the animal has learned to make the response or—more to the point—the response is some high-probability, species-typical reaction to punishment. The rats in the Brown et al. experiment had obviously learned a highly specific response— running—to a punishing shock, a response which is also a natural, high-probability unconditioned response to shock, as we have stressed on a number of occasions before. Consequently, when they stumbled into shock during extinction, a highly potentiated response was immediately available, and they did what they had always done in the situation when that stimulus appeared: they ran—fast.

One final comment about punishment seems in order. It should be clear from all we have said in this section that punishment can have rather dramatic effects in quashing behavior. At the same time, however, we have seen that punishment can be equally useful in helping along the learning process—particularly when it is used as an information-carrying cue and when it is combined with reward for some other kinds of behavior. Some of the earlier classical work on punishment (that of Skinner, for example) placed primary emphasis on only one side of a coin that has two sides—and an edge as well. From this literature, one can gain the strong impression that punishment is a maladaptive, ineffective, and wasteful technique to use in the establishment and guidance of behavior. Such is patently not the case, and we should welcome further research aimed at an area of the psychology of learning that has not received all the attention it deserves.

This has been a long chapter, and it could have been a good deal longer. Following our opening warning, however, we have not included many things that could have been quite legitimately included in a chapter on motivation and emotion—topics such as conflict, experimental neurosis, the effect of stress upon learned behavior, and more generally, a study of the facts and broad theories of motivation and their application to psychology. These things, while they are unquestionably important to behavior theory, are best treated in other places, and there are now a number of excellent sources which deal specifically with the topic of motivation. To name a few, we can mention Cofer and Appley (1964), Hinde (1970), and Bolles (1974). To this list, we can add any of the annual editions of the *Nebraska Symposium on Motivation*. All this will lead you to still more excellent material.

What we *have* attempted to do in this chapter is to develop a place for motivation and emotion within the psychology of learning, looking specifically at how these things enter into the learning process itself, on the one hand, and how learning produces new emotions and motives, on the other.

SEVEN

GENERALIZATION AND DISCRIMINATION

One of the most fundamental requirements of adaptive behavior in both lower animals and man is that the right behavior occur at the right time. This generally means that *on signal* an organism performs a response which is already part of its basic behavior. Sometimes the relevant behavior seems to be built in biologically, and learning assumes a less salient role. When we looked at the concept of species-specific defense reactions in Chapter 1, for example, we pointed out that nature sometimes does not permit leisurely opportunities to acquire complicated responses to particular stimuli through practice—particularly so if the behavior pattern is one upon which the animal must depend in sudden, unexpected, life-and-death situations involving hunter and prey. Even at less dramatic moments, nature may downplay the role of learning in attaching response to stimulus. For example, in the case of the three-spined stickleback fish, a very crude model of a female will elicit the *innate* pattern of mating behavior in the male, providing the model is painted red on its underneath surface (Tinbergen, 1951). Here, the critical feature of the stimulus seems to be its red color.

If nature is rigid, demanding fixed patterns of action to stimuli on some occasions, it is plastic, permitting wide variation in the attachment of cue to response on many other occasions. Indeed, man likes to think that a hallmark of his behavior is that it is adjustable, that it can be arranged to accommodate the pitfalls and pratfalls of the moment. And it is certainly true that animals lower than man can learn to respond to a single given stimulus in many different ways—depending upon environmental requirements of the moment. Under all conditions, then, it is important to study how organisms learn to distinguish one pattern of cues from another and how these cues are to be attached to the many complicated things that living organisms can do. Some psychologists maintain that in this simple sense at least, all learning is little more than a process of discrimination (Logan, 1971).

In this chapter and especially the next, perhaps more than in any other thus far, we shall be incorporating data from experimentation based upon both animal and human subjects. In contrast to the development of some areas within the psychology of learning, the study of discriminative abilities uses data from species ranging from rat to bird to monkey to man. There is probably good reason for this. While it may be true that many facets of behavior are species-specific or more or less prepared for learning as a function of phylogenetic niche, there is especially good reason to believe that animal and man share at least some of the fundamental methods and capacities for searching and gathering information from their environments, information which then guides their behavior. For example, there is good evidence that many animals share with man the capacity to attend selectively to the stimulus dimensions of the outside world and to process information that such attention fosters. We shall be looking at some of that data and the interpretations that psychologists have placed upon it in due course. But in many respects this chapter and the next can be viewed as a bridge between the psychology of learning that has emerged primarily from a study of lower animals and the psychology of learning that has developed primarily from an analysis of human behavior, and the verbal skills that are uniquely characteristic of man.

GENERALIZATION

While it is patently clear that telling the difference between one pattern of cues and another is of tremendous importance for the proper behavior of organisms, it is equally clear that there are occasions where it is best to respond to two cue patterns as if they were more or less the same. Thus, a given cue pattern—considered purely as an array of light intensities or sound waves striking a receptor—never reaches the organism in *exactly* the same form on any two given occasions. This can be true for the simple reason that an organism is almost certain to orient its body toward some object in its environment in different ways at different times. In the limit, the cues to which a response is to be attached through learning are never truly identical, though of course, they are apt to be quite highly similar. Here, then, is another important problem: What happens when an organism is asked to respond to two or more cues that, while different, are nevertheless *similar* in some particular way? How similar must the cues be before the organism responds to them as if they were identical? What happens to behavior as we progressively reduce the similarity among the cues? Before we turn to a discussion of the process of discrimination *per se* and the factors which help determine how organisms tell when things are *different*, let us look at the phenomenon of *stimulus generalization* and the factors which can lead an organism to conclude that things are *the same*.

There are two fundamental points about stimulus generalization: (1) the effectiveness of a conditioning operation is not limited to the stimulus originally used in conditioning, and (2) the ability of a stimulus to elicit a conditioned response decreases as the stimulus becomes less similar to the one used during original conditioning. There is little argument about the first point: as an empirical fact, two different stimuli can—under the proper conditions—elicit the same response, albeit at different strengths, perhaps. There is more controversy about the second point, however, particularly when it comes to deciding how concepts like "related" or "similar" should be defined. Here, as we shall see, psychologists have talked in terms of some simple physically defined dimension, such as distance along the skin or the wavelength or intensity of a light, and they have also talked in terms of some psychophysically determined *scale* of similarity. Let us elaborate both points by turning to some things that have emerged from the laboratory.

205

GENERALIZA-
TION
AND
DISCRIMINA-
TION

Generalization with Pavlovian conditioned responses   Hovland (1937a) was among the first to look for generalization gradients in human subjects using Pavlovian procedures. His classic work studied generalization based upon different pitches and intensities of sound. It is particularly interesting because, instead of using tones arrayed along a dimension of raw physical frequencies, he did some preliminary psychophysical work to select the stimuli to be used. In his experiment with tonal frequencies, he picked four frequencies of sound—153, 468, 1,000, and 1,967 hertz—such that neighboring pairs of tones were separated from each other by 25 j.n.d.'s (*just noticeable differences*). Thus, when the tones were equated for loudness, the 153-hertz tone was as different from the 468-hertz tone as the 468-hertz tone was different from the 1,000-hertz tone in terms of the number of discriminably different steps in pitch between them. What Hovland did with this procedure, in effect, was to translate a physical scale based on simple frequencies of sound into a psychological scale where his stimuli were about equally spaced in terms of their apparent pitch.

After selecting his stimuli in this manner, Hovland conditioned the galvanic skin response (GSR) to the 153-hertz tone for half his subjects and to the 1,967-hertz tone for the other half.[1] Shock was used as the unconditional stimulus. Then he tested for generalization by presenting the tones during extinction. Testing was carried out in such a way that the data from the two groups could be pooled, and the results of the experiment are shown in Figure 7.1. As you can see, Hovland obtained a progressively greater decrease in the amplitude of the GSR the farther test tones were removed in similarity from the original CS. In another experiment (Hovland, 1937b), a very similar set of results was obtained for tones arranged along a dimension of loudness.

While Hovland's work is indeed classic, and deserves recognition for that fact, there is recent reason to believe that for some unknown reason it may have been empirically flawed. Attempts to replicate Hovland's experiment (Epstein & Burstein, 1966; Burstein, Epstein, & Smith, 1967) have been unsuccessful. The "gradients" that these investigators have obtained range from U-shaped (with a maximal GSR not only to the

---

[1]The galvanic skin response is associated with the electrical activity of the sweat gland cells when they are excited. These glands are largely innervated by the sympathetic branch of the autonomic nervous system; hence this response is often termed an "emotional" one.

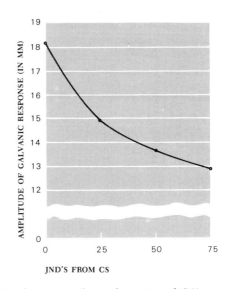

Figure 7.1
Generalization of the galvanic skin response (GSR) for tones differing in frequency. In preliminary work, four tones were determined that differed from each other by 25 j.n.d.'s in pitch, and conditioning was carried out for different subjects using the highest or the lowest tone as the conditional stimulus. The data show that, on test trials, the amplitude of the GSR decreased as the test tones became progressively less similar to the original CS. (Data from Hovland, 1937a.)

original CS but also to the stimulus *farthest away* from the original CS) to completely flat. In the latter case, the gradient consists of GSR levels which are the same for *all* test stimuli, a result which raises serious question that there was any significant control of behavior acquired by the original CS at all. Burstein et al. (1967) suggest that the problem may have to do with the characteristics of the GSR itself, for it can be formidably difficult to bring under good laboratory control—quite apart from its use as an index of the development of stimulus generalization. In spite of these difficulties, Hovland's early classic work is especially important in theoretical terms because it introduced psychophysical techniques into the definition of the dimension along which stimulus generalization takes place.

If responses other than the GSR are used, good stimulus generalization can be obtained with Pavlovian procedures. Moore (1972) conditioned the nictitating membrane response in rabbits (the nictitating membrane is one of the rabbit's three eyelids) using one of two conditioning procedures. Under one, the *C* condition, the closure of the membrane was conditioned to a single 1,200-hertz tone. Under the second, the *T-T* condition, differential conditioning was established with a 1,200-hertz tone as a CS+ and a 2,400-hertz tone as a CS− (the tones were equated for loudness). An electric shock delivered to the skin near the eye served as a UCS; this produces a reliable unconditioned closure of the nictitating membrane. Following conditioning, the rabbits were tested in extinction for conditioning to the original CS+ and for generalization of conditioning to tonal frequencies different from that stimulus, and the results appear in Figure 7.2. The data are plotted in terms of the *relative* number of conditioned responses that the rabbits produced at each of the test frequencies. In the *C* group, for example, about 30 percent of the *total* CRs produced throughout all testing were given to the 1,200-hertz tone, about 12 percent to the 400-hertz tone, and so on.

207

GENERALIZA-
TION
AND
DISCRIMINA-
TION

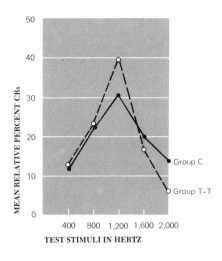

Figure 7.2
Stimulus generalization associated with Pavlovian conditioning of the rabbit's nictitating membrane. Under the *C* condition, the response was conditioned originally to a single 1,200-hertz tone as CS, while under the *T-T* condition, the response was differentially conditioned with a 1,200-hertz tone as CS+ and a 2,400-hertz tone as CS−. Note that the generalization gradient for the *T-T* condition is relatively more peaked at 1,200 hertz and that it falls off steeply toward the high frequencies. (Moore, 1972.)

There are several things to note about Figure 7.2. First of all, maximum responding occurred to CS+, with smaller and smaller tendencies to respond associated with stimuli either above or below CS+. The result, of course, is a stimulus generalization gradient, with response strength falling off on either side of the original CS+. In the case of group *C*, the gradient is more or less symmetrical about CS+. Second, the effect of differential conditioning was to *sharpen responding* to CS+ relative to the other frequencies; group *T-T* reserves a much greater percentage of its total responding for CS+. Finally, and this point is related to the last, the gradient for group *T-T* is *asymmetrical* about CS+. The gradient falls off steeply in the high frequencies, that is, those frequencies approaching the 2,400-hertz tone that was used as CS− and never reinforced. Evidently, differential conditioning generated decreased responding to stimuli nearest CS−, "pushing" the rabbits' maximal tendency to respond down toward the lower frequencies.

Generalization with instrumentally conditioned responses Generalization in Pavlovian conditioning is a relatively straightforward matter, since some stimulus is always used to elicit the conditioned response, and we have very precise control over the properties of that stimulus and what we do with it in the conditioning situation. In simple instrumental conditioning, however, we do not ordinarily attach a response by direct experimental means to some specific stimulus. In fact, as we saw in Chapter 1, we are hard pressed (perhaps impossibly so) to identify the precise stimulus which comes to control the behavior we study. We can, of course, arrange things so that we are more sure of stimulus control by using the technique of simple discrimination training that we also discussed in Chapter 1, and we shall look at experimental work in which this was done in a moment (meeting, incidentally, a few surprises). Right now, however, let us look at some experiments in which no *direct* attempt was made to assure that the stimulus dimension along which generalization was tested had control over behavior.

In one experiment, Guttman and Kalish (1956) tested pigeons for generalization along a continuum of wavelengths of light—that is, along a dimension of hue or color. They did this by training pigeons in a Skinner box to peck at a key upon which was projected a CS light of a particular wavelength. Different pigeons were trained initially to peck under CS wavelengths ranging from 530 to 600 nanometers. After some preliminary training, pecks were reinforced on a VI 1-minute schedule during 60-second periods in which the light was on the key. Successive light-on periods were separated by 10-second "time-out" periods in which the key and the entire environment of the pigeon were completely dark (pigeons will not respond under such conditions). Tests for generalization were made under extinction conditions where the pigeon was permitted to peck for 30-second periods on each of 11 test wavelengths spread about the original CS. The data from the experiment are shown in the upper part of Figure 7.3.

Once again, well-defined generalization gradients were obtained. A regular gradient appears about both sides of each of the CS wavelengths used during initial training, and while there is a considerable difference in the total number of responses emitted during the generation of the several gradients, there is no marked difference in their overall shape.

In developing their experiment, Guttman and Kalish reasoned that the

Figure 7.3
The upper panel shows the generalization gradients that were obtained for each of several training stimuli that differed in wavelength of light. There is a progressive decrease in response strength as test stimuli become farther removed in wavelength from the original training stimulus. The lower panel shows, for humans and for pigeons, how much change in wavelength (Δλ) is required to produce a discriminable change in hue at different points along the spectrum. (Guttman & Kalish, 1956.)

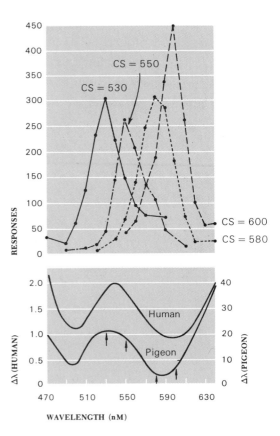

209

GENERALIZA-
TION
AND
DISCRIMINA-
TION

shape of the generalization gradient might be a function not so much of the physical dimension of wavelength per se as of a psychological dimension associated with wavelength (reasoning analogous to Hovland's). In particular, they thought that the shape of their generalization gradients might be related to *discriminability functions* for color, two of which are plotted in the lower part of Figure 7.3 (one for human vision and one for pigeon vision). If their reasoning was correct, the generalization gradient should be quite broad and flat for a CS picked at a high point on the discriminability function—that is, a point say in the middle of the greens, where a relatively large change in wavelength must be made before an observer can tell that a change has occurred. Correspondingly, of course, the gradient should be steep at a low point on the discriminability function—a point like that around 590 nanometers, where there is a *transition* from one broad range of hues to another and a relatively small change in wavelength can be detected. Of course, as we have already seen, the shapes of the generalization gradients did not change in this experiment as a function of the CS wavelength, and so Guttman and Kalish concluded that hue generalization in the pigeon at least was not related in any systematic way to the ability of the bird to detect simple differences in hue, per se.

The failure of Guttman and Kalish to obtain a relationship between hue discriminability and stimulus generalization may be due to any of a number of possible factors. Marsh (1965), cited in Riley (1968), showed that one *could* find such a relationship in pigeons, providing that a relatively small number of points—two versus four—were tested for generalization during extinction. Riley suggests that testing during extinction over an extensive array of stimulus values may generate inhibitory effects which tend to wipe out the relation between discriminability and stimulus generalization. On the other hand, the effect may be associated with fundamental features of the process of association itself, such as the amount of training an organism receives on the original CS. Hearst has shown (Hearst & Koresko, 1968; Hearst, 1969) that stimulus generalization gradients of a type directly analogous to those of Guttman and Kalish became much more peaked and sharply "tuned" at the original CS value the greater the *amount* of training prior to the test for generalization. These data do not speak directly to the issue, since Hearst did not explore gradient shapes across the full range of a stimulus dimension such as hue, but they imply that there are many factors at work in the determination of the shape of generalization gradients which could mask some real relation between generalization and discriminability in an experiment of the Guttman and Kalish variety.

WHAT UNDERLIES THE GENERALIZATION GRADIENT?

The empirical phenomenon of the generalization gradient is a fact with which no one argues. As we noted before, however, there is considerable argument over what lies behind that fact. Pavlov (1927) and Hull (1943, 1952) thought of generalization of the type demonstrated in the Hovland experiment as a more or less primary process closely associated with fundamental physiological events in the cerebral cortex or in afferent sensory systems like touch, sight, and sound. They emphasized the *physical* as opposed to the *functional* nature of stimuli, in other words (Chapter 1). The function of the association of a given stimulus with reinforced responding was to develop the strength of a habit to that stimulus, habit strength which would then appear to other stimuli to the extent that the other stimuli were similar along some simple physical scale like the frequency of a sound or the wavelength of a light. Explicit here was the assumption that stimulus generalization ought to be closely tied to the things that were known about the psychophysics of stimuli: their similarity, how far apart they were on some psychological scale, and so on. Implicit in this approach, in turn, was the notion that stimulus generalization ought, therefore, to be related directly to the degree with which one stimulus could be discriminated from another. But the process of discrimination itself, the experience of comparing one stimulus with another, was not of fundamental theoretical importance to the *development* of a stimulus generalization gradient.

Lashley and Wade (1946), on the other hand, maintained that generalization gradients depend crucially upon the opportunity afforded an organism to *learn* about the various properties of a stimulus dimension along which generalization is to take place. In this sense, in other words, they postulate a *functional* stimulus. If an organism has no experience at all telling the difference between one stimulus and another along some dimension like sound intensity, for example, why should the organism respond differently to one stimulus as opposed to the other on a generalization test? Why shouldn't the two stimuli be reacted to as if they were the same? Thus, most simply, organisms would have to be taught about stimulus dimensions by being trained to make *discriminations* among stimuli located along them. If this were done, not only would the stimulus dimension as a whole become relevant to the behavior of the organism, but also the organism ought to be set to respond differentially to one stimulus from that dimension as opposed to another, and the generalization gradient ought to appear. In the absence of such experience, however—in the absence of familiarity with a sensory dimension as a dimension *relevant* for behavior—the organism ought to respond to one stimulus in just the same way that it responds to any other. Under these conditions, a generalization gradient ought to be completely *flat*, with equivalent response strength at all test stimuli. Clearly, discrimination is crucial to the process of *developing* a generalization gradient in the first place for Lashley and Wade—in contrast to the secondary role afforded discrimination in this regard by Pavlov and by Hull.

There is some evidence to support, in a limited sense, the point of view taken by Lashley and Wade with respect to stimulus generalization. First of all, simple discrimination training (Chapter 1) can have marked effects upon generalization gradients. Jenkins and Harrison (1960), for example, ran an experiment in which they tested for generalization of pitch in the pigeon. Pigeons were run in a Skinner box under one of two conditions. In one, training to a CS of a 1,000-hertz tone was carried out in a manner essentially identical to that of Guttman and Kalish: periods of reinforced responding in the presence of the CS, separated by short "blackouts." In a second condition, the birds were reinforced for pecks in the presence of the CS, but they were also exposed to a number of other intervening periods in which the CS was absent. During these periods, the pigeons were free to peck, but *pecking was not reinforced*. This, if you will recall our discussion in Chapter 1, is simple discrimination training, and it normally leads—as it did for Jenkins and Harrison—to a state of affairs where the pigeon reserves most of its pecks for the periods of time that the discriminative cue of the tone is on. When the pigeons in both groups were tested subsequently under extinction for the strength of their responding to tones arranged about the 1,000-hertz CS, they produced the generalization gradients shown in Figures 7.4 and 7.5.

The nature of the "gradients" shown in Figures 7.4 and 7.5 is interesting indeed. Following training in which the 1,000-hertz tone was *not* used as a discriminative cue (Figure 7.4), there is essentially no gradient at all—the pigeons demonstrated about the same response strength to each of the test stimuli and—curiously enough—to no tone at all. However, when the 1,000-hertz tone was used as a discriminative cue (Figure 7.5), marked differences in response strength to the test stimuli appeared, and gradients much like those of Guttman and Kalish were obtained. These results provide important confirmation for a point of view which stresses the role of discrimination as a contributing factor in stimulus generalization. When discrimination training was not used, the birds showed *complete* generalization—they responded to one tone in just about the same way that they responded to any other (including silence)! In effect, sound was not a relevant stimulus dimension at all from the pigeons' point of view. Discrimination training, however,

211

GENERALIZA-
TION
AND
DISCRIMINA-
TION

Figure 7.4
Generalization gradients for three pigeons following training in which the training tone of 1,000 hertz (S^D) was not used as a discriminative cue. The gradients are flat, indicating that all pigeons generalized completely to all test tones— including no tone at all. (H. M. Jenkins & Harrison, 1960.)

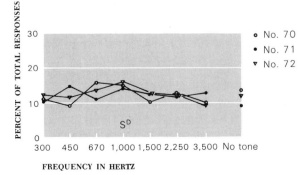

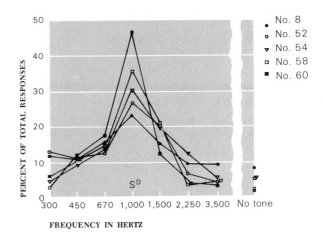

FREQUENCY IN HERTZ

Figure 7.5
Generalization gradients for five pigeons following training in which the training tone of 1,000 hertz (S^D) was used as a discriminative cue. Here, typical generalization gradients were obtained that show that familiar falloff in response strength as test tones become progressively less similar to the training tone. Responding to no tone at all (S^Δ) was quite low. (H. M. Jenkins & Harrison, 1960.)

seems to have brought the pigeons' behavior under control of auditory stimuli. In common terms, this procedure singled out sound as an important stimulus dimension, one that was attention-getting and relevant to the pigeons' task in the experiment. Thus, when faced with a series of different tones in the test for generalization, the pigeons demonstrated that they could, in effect, tell the difference between the original training tone and the new, different ones.

It is important to recognize that the Jenkins and Harrison experiment supports only a limited and restricted interpretation of the Lashley and Wade approach to generalization. Strictly speaking, that approach would require that discrimination training take place between at least two *real stimuli* along the dimension that was to be made relevant; e.g., Jenkins and Harrison would have had to make their birds learn a discrimination between a 1,000-hertz and, say, a 2,250-hertz tone instead of a discrimination between a 1,000-hertz tone and silence. What the Jenkins and Harrison experiment *does* show is that simple discrimination training brings the birds' behavior under general control of auditory stimuli and that this procedure is necessary, apparently, for stimulus generalization gradients to appear to auditory stimuli in this species. The effects upon generalization gradients of forming a discrimination between two stimuli drawn from a given stimulus dimension—the procedure called for by a strict interpretation of Lashley and Wade—do no violence to the Lashley and Wade approach, but they are best treated later because they introduce some additional phenomena which are of special interest in a slightly different context.

If you have read carefully, you will have noted that Guttman and

Kalish were able to obtain gradients under experimental conditions where Jenkins and Harrison could not. That is, the Guttman and Kalish procedure did not involve any deliberate discrimination training involving color, yet stimulus generalization gradients appeared. There are many possible answers to this question, but one is that pigeons are basically more of a "visual" animal than they are "auditory"—in the sense that they probably depend more on the sense of sight than the sense of hearing to get around in the world. In other words, we may have another example of species-specific behavior at hand.

213

GENERALIZA-
TION
AND
DISCRIMINA-
TION

General laws for generalization gradients   Much of the original impetus for the study of generalization was provided by the hope that experimental work would reveal some kind of general mathematical law that could be used to describe the "shape" of generalization gradients for a wide variety of response and stimulus dimensions. Psychologists have worried, often for theoretical reasons, whether gradients should be "concave upward" or "concave downward," and whether the ultimate gradient would be relatively "flat" or "steep" along some stimulus dimension. An enormous amount of work has been done in the laboratory on this and on related problems (Mednick & Freedman, 1960; Kimble, 1961; Mostofsky, 1965; Hearst, 1969), and while we may be progressing toward some general rules about stimulus generalization and the shape of the generalization gradient, there is still considerable ground to cover before we reach any kind of final answer—if, indeed, one is there to be obtained.

There are many good reasons why an exact mathematical law of stimulus generalization has not been determined. Some of these are purely mechanical. For example, even for the case of the galvanic skin response, there are many ways in which a response can be measured—as electrical resistance, as current flow, as electrical potential, and if ac circuits are used, as other quantities. Unfortunately, there is no rational choice for the basic measure that should be used. This precludes a fundamental mathematical law of stimulus generalization for even so restricted a case as the Pavlovian GSR, and of course, things do not become simpler for instrumentally conditioned responses. If you check, you will find that experiments of the Guttman and Kalish type have used the rate, relative frequency, or perhaps the probability with which responses occur during extinction as indices of generalization. Yet again, there is no rational consideration which suggests that any of these indices is to be preferred to any other.

Just as there are problems in choosing the proper response index to use in tests for generalization, so are there problems when it comes to choosing the proper way to define a rational stimulus dimension along which generalization presumably occurs (Blough, 1965). In Hovland's (1937a) experiment, we saw one attempt to do this—the use of a psychophysical scale of just noticeable differences between adjacent test frequencies of sound. But in the Guttman and Kalish experiment, we saw that there was little correspondence between generalization and a very similar psychophysical function, a discriminability function for light wavelength. On the other hand, good correspondence between a psychophysical function and generalization is sometimes obtained (Kalish, 1958; Moore, 1972).

Part of the problem associated with this seeming mass of inconsistency also has to do with factors which are themselves, in part at least, apparently independent of the process of generalization per se. We have already noted that the amount of training given prior to the test for generalization can have the effect of "tuning" behavior toward more precise control by the original training stimulus (Hearst, 1969), and we could generalize this point concerning amount of training to a number of other factors which appear in generalization as well (Terrace, 1966; Selekman, 1973). Then, too, there are things associated with the *way in which we go about testing* for generalization which modify the shape of the gradient. Perhaps you have noticed that in all of the work discussed thus far, testing for generalization has been carried out in extinction. Perhaps, too, you have deduced the reason for this—testing must be carried out in extinction to avoid building response strength to one of the generalized test stimuli, response strength which would certainly accrue if responses were reinforced during the test itself. Yet the *nonreinforcement* of behavior, particularly if it occurs in the general context in which reinforcement has been forthcoming, can have some marked inhibitory effects on generalized behavior, even though the inhibition may not be tied specifically to anything more precise than the general environment in which generalization testing is carried out.

A path out of the problem of the shape of generalization gradients may be provided by work which stresses new methods for conceptualizing the stimulus and response dimensions along which generalization is presumed to take place. Shepard (1957, 1958, 1965) has argued that if we are willing to accept a measure such as probability of response as an index of generalization (recognizing the problems inherent in this assumption), then it ought to be possible to develop stimulus dimensions for generalization by means of scaling techniques rather more sophisticated than those used to generate the simple scales described above. To this end, Shepard has used *multidimensional scaling* to define points that are equally distant from each other in "psychological space" and has shown how generalization gradients can be deduced from mathematical models based on such scales. Thus in physical terms, stimuli like pure tones may be specified in one dimension, frequency. But in psychological space, two or more dimensions may be required to specify relations among pure tones. For example, as Shepard (1965) reminds us, Blackwell and Schlosberg (1943) found that there was greater generalization between two tones if they were an octave apart than if they were just less than an octave apart. Thus, psychologically, the similarity between two tones may be determined by two things: their frequency and whether or not they stand together as an octave.

Any further discussion of Shepard's work would carry us quickly beyond the scope of this book, but he and others, like Torgerson (1965) and Hearst (1969), are attempting to find new ways of describing how stimuli are *similar* to each other, or how techniques can be developed which *transform* one response index into another so as to make better sense out of theoretical and empirical generalization gradients.

215

GENERALIZA-
TION
AND
DISCRIMINA-
TION

Extinction also generalizes   We have seen that the effects of reinforcement generalize to stimuli other than those specifically used in training. As might be expected, the inhibitory processes associated with extinction also generalize in this way. Suppose we use Pavlovian conditioning to condition a galvanic skin response in human subjects by pairing a tone of a certain frequency with electric shock (Hovland, 1937a). After conditioning, we shall, of course, find that another frequency will elicit the response. Suppose, however, we *extinguish* the conditioned response to the *second* tone, then go back and test with the first tone. If we do this, we shall find that extinction of the response to the second tone will reduce the tendency to respond to the first. Thus, the inhibitory effects of extinction generalize, as do the effects of reinforcement. Furthermore, the phenomenon is not limited to Pavlovian conditioning, since the same thing can be shown for instrumentally conditioned responses. Kling (1952) and Honig (1961) were among the first to demonstrate this in instrumental conditioning, while Dubin and Levis (1973) provide a more recent example.

The generalization of the excitatory and inhibitory effects associated with reinforcement and extinction are extremely important in the theory of discriminative learning, and a large portion of the remainder of this chapter will be devoted to an application of these principles to an understanding of discriminative learning.

DISCRIMINATIVE LEARNING

Organisms come to *discriminate* among stimuli when they are trained to respond differentially to them. In an empirical, operational sense, then, discrimination is the opposite of generalization, and we can look upon discriminative learning in a general way as the process of breaking down generalizations.

There are many ways to set up laboratory studies of the process by which organisms come to discriminate among stimuli. You are already familiar with one: simple discrimination training in a Skinner box, where the organism is reinforced for making some response in the presence of one stimulus (S^D) and not reinforced when the response occurs in the absence of that stimulus (S^Δ). Under these conditions, as we noted in Chapter 1, the organism comes to reserve most of its responding for the S^D period and responds very little during the S^Δ period. The process by which this occurs is gradual. Initially, as S^D and S^Δ are alternated, an animal continues to respond through both periods, but gradually, the opposing effects of reinforcement and extinction that are associated with the two take hold, and the animal tends to respond only when it is appropriate to do so—during S^D, when reinforcement is available. Sometimes a discrimination of this sort is called a "go, no-go" discrimination in the sense that the organism's task is to learn under what conditions it is appropriate to respond (go) and under what conditions it is appropriate to withhold responding (no-go).

Another procedure for the study of discriminative learning involves the use of the Lashley jumping stand (Figure 7.6), or a device which incorporates the functional features of that apparatus. The problem illustrated in Figure 7.6 requires the rat to make a discrimination between vertical and horizontal stripes, jumping to one or the other of the two stimuli. If the correct choice is not made, the door does not open and the rat falls to the net below. Thus, typically, the Lashley jumping stand makes use of punishment. The essential feature of the discrimination problem posed in the Lashley jumping stand—or in other apparatuses like it—is that the organism must *choose* between some stimulus (S+), which is "correct" and associated with positive reinforcement, and another stimulus (S−), which is "incorrect" and associated with no reinforcement or with punishment. This is to be contrasted with the go, no-go type of discrimination in which the organism "chooses" by either responding or failing to respond.

Despite the outward simplicity of the procedures associated with discriminative learning, the events that go on in the organism must be complicated indeed. Let us look at some of the attempts that have been made to deal with the problem both theoretically and experimentally.

Figure 7.6
The Lashley jumping stand. The rat jumps from the stand to one door or the other. If the choice is correct, the stimulus card gives way; if the choice is wrong, the rat falls to the net below. (Lashley, 1930.)

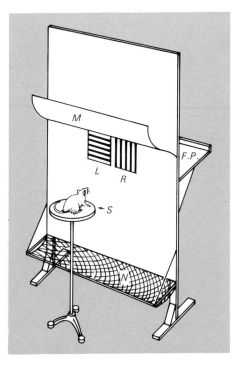

Theories of discriminative learning fall into two broad classes. One of these places great emphasis upon the development and interaction of gradients of excitation and inhibition to correct and incorrect stimuli. The other stresses the importance of the active problem-solving character of discrimination and the all-or-nothing properties of hypotheses that organisms might use in learning to discriminate. The latter theory also places special emphasis on the principles of attention and information processing. As you might expect, neither of these theories by itself can account for all the data—a familiar state of affairs in the psychology of learning—but together they do a good job of accounting for the information available to us at the moment about the discriminative process.

THE ALGEBRAIC SUMMATION AND CONTINUITY THEORY

The theory of discrimination learning that makes use of the concepts of generalized excitation and inhibition comes initially from the work of Spence (1936, 1937, 1952, 1960), though most of the fundamental notions are close to those of Hull (1943, 1952).

First of all, Spence and Hull insisted that gradients of stimulus generalization interact algebraically. Suppose that an animal is trained on a discrimination problem by the reinforcement of a response to one stimulus (S+) and the extinction of the response to a second stimulus (S−). As we have just seen in this chapter, the excitatory effects associated with S+ will generalize to other stimuli, and so will the inhibitory effects associated with S−. Now according to this view, the strength of the tendency to respond to any given stimulus is obtained by *subtracting* the strength of the generalized *inhibition* associated with that stimulus from the strength of the generalized *excitation* associated with that stimulus. The ultimate tendency to respond, in other words, is a *net* tendency to respond.

The hypothesis at hand is illustrated in Figure 7.7. Here, the curve labeled *E* represents the generalization of excitation associated with the stimulus S+, to which responses are reinforced, while the curve labeled *I* shows the generalization of inhibition associated with the stimulus S−, to which responses go unreinforced. The dashed curve labeled *R* shows the net response strength that is obtained after *I* is subtracted from *E* at every point along the stimulus continuum. The exact form of all these generalization curves is unknown, of course—as we have indicated in the earlier portions of this chapter—and to the extent that deductions from the theory depend upon the shape of the curves, they may or may not be supported by data. Nevertheless, the theory does make some testable predictions which have been supported by experimentation; let us turn to some of these now.

Peak shift If you will take another look at Figure 7.7, you will note that reinforcing responses to S+ and extinguishing them to S− generates a

Figure 7.7
The algebraic summation theory of discrimination learning. Net response strength (R) is the result of the subtraction of the effects of generalized inhibition (I) from the effects of generalized excitation (E). Note that in this example, the net response strength is *shifted* away from the original S+ stimulus in a direction opposite that of the original S− stimulus. Net response strength is at a maximum at S_P. The numbers along the stimulus dimension refer to stimulus sizes in an experiment discussed in the text. (After Spence, 1937a.)

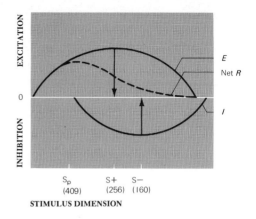

net gradient of stimulus generalization which is *not* symmetrical but which has the bulk of response strength *displaced* along the stimulus dimension in the direction of S+ and away from S−. That is, as you go to the left along the stimulus dimension in the figure, the curve for net response strength rises, reaching a peak not at the original S+, but at a point to the left of S+ which is labeled S_P in the figure. Experimental data are available which show that, in fact, such displacements of generalization gradients are obtained following discrimination training incorporating differential reinforcement to S+ and S− stimuli (Hanson, 1959; Terrace, 1968, 1972; see Purtle, 1973, for a review). Hanson, for example, trained pigeons to respond to a 550-nanometer wavelength of light as S+ and, for different groups, to S− stimuli that ranged from 555 to 590 nanometers. Responses to S+ were reinforced, while those to S− were not.[2] When the pigeons were then tested for generalization, they produced the generalization gradients shown in Figure 7.8.

Figure 7.8 shows several things quite clearly. First, there is a readily apparent shift of the bulk of responding during generalization testing to the left, that is, along the wavelength dimension away from the S− stimulus. This corresponds exactly to what the Spence-Hull theory predicts. Second, the *peaks* of the generalization gradients, that is, the points of maximum response, are *shifted* in the same direction—so much so that they lie to the left of the original S+ stimulus of 550 nanometers. The amount of the shift is greater, the closer the S− stimulus was to the S+ stimulus. The Spence-Hull theory does not necessarily predict this *peak shift* per se (although Figure 7.7 was drawn to indicate it), and it

---

[2]Note that this is a *different* sort of discrimination training from that used by Jenkins and Harrison (1960), who taught their pigeons to respond in the presence of a tone and to stop responding in the *total absence* of the tone. Hanson taught his pigeons to respond to one of two stimuli that were both picked from the same stimulus dimension—wavelength of light. In other words, Hanson's procedure used an *intradimensional* discrimination.

219

GENERALIZA-
TION
AND
DISCRIMINA-
TION

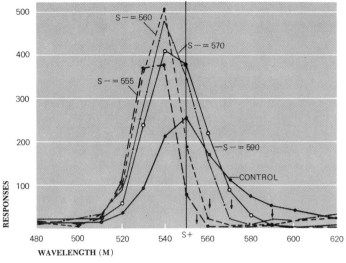

Figure 7.8
Examples of the "peak shift" phenomenon. The peaks of the generalization
gradients are shifted away from S+ in a direction opposite that of the stimulus
wavelengths used as S− stimuli in original training. The amount of the shift in
the peak is greater the closer the S− stimulus to the S+ stimulus. The control
data are taken from the Guttman & Kalish (1956) experiment. (Hanson, 1959.)

undoubtedly depends upon a great number of factors such as the shape of
the underlying gradients of excitation and inhibition; but the theory does
predict the overall shift in the area of maximum net response strength,
and the thrust of Hanson's data represents a striking confirmation of the
Spence-Hull position. Incidentally, the fact that Hanson's postdis-
crimination generalization gradients are higher than the *control* gradient
taken from the Guttman and Kalish experiment, discussed earlier in this
chapter, probably represents an example of behavioral contrast at work
(p. 53). Intradimensional discrimination training, you will note, provides the necessary conditions—alternating periods of reinforcement and
nonreinforcement each paired with its own cue—to generate exaggeratedly increased rates to the S+ stimulus and exaggeratedly decreased
rates to the S− stimulus (Terrace, 1972).

If you go back and check Moore's data in Figure 7.2, by the way, you
will see a shift of the bulk of responding away from S− and an
exaggerated amount of responding to S+ there, too, and so these
phenomena appear in Pavlovian conditioning as well as in instrumental
conditioning. The data of Figure 7.2 do not show a peak shift, but Moore
(1972) reports that he could obtain it in some other analogous experiments that he did.[3]

---

[3]For some research which stresses an additional approach to an understanding of the peak
shift, see Blough (1973).

Errorless discrimination training   Terrace (1964, 1966, 1972) was able to devise a technique which enabled pigeons to learn a visual discrimination without ever making errors, that is, without ever responding to S− and experiencing the nonreinforcement associated with that stimulus. He did this by "fading in" the negative stimulus, using a variety of procedures which assured that it first appeared in the bird's environment gradually and, if you will, unobtrusively, becoming "stronger" and more salient by stages as the experiment progressed. Under these conditions, his pigeons learned the discrimination in the sense that they responded to S+, but never responded to S−, even when S− was presented at full strength late in the experiment. Now note that Terrace's procedure should produce an interesting thing from the point of view of the Spence-Hull theory. It should produce a discrimination in which there should be no gradient of inhibition built up to S− for the very simple reason that inhibition is based on the extinction of responding through nonreinforcement, and such extinction can't occur unless responses to S− occur. Consequently, the Spence-Hull theory would predict that a peak shift, or a shift in the bulk of responding toward S+ in a direction away from S−, would fail to occur in the case of a generalization test following errorless discrimination learning. And that is precisely what Terrace observed.

Transposition   One of the most interesting capabilities of the Spence-Hull theory is the way in which it can be used to account for a phenomenon in discriminative learning known as *transposition*. Transposition is the apparent ability of organisms to make *relational* discriminations. We can best illustrate what these are by an example.

Kohler (1915) trained chickens to respond (with food as reinforcement) to the darker of two gray surfaces. The chickens were never reinforced when they responded to the lighter surface. When this discrimination was well established, the animals were presented with a new choice between the original reinforced gray and one *darker still*. When faced with this new problem, the chickens chose the darker of the two grays, even though they had always been reinforced for choosing the other one. In other words, argued Kohler, the animals had learned the *relationship* "darker than" rather than the specific association of a particular stimulus with reinforcement.

This result poses a problem for the Spence-Hull theory, which says that organisms learn by attaching responses to specific absolute stimuli, for here is a case in which reinforcement apparently has no effect (or even a negative effect) on choice of the particular gray surface that was paired with reinforcement initially. It turns out, however, that this example of transposition can be explained by the principle of stimulus generalization. Let us see how Spence went about the matter.

Spence (1937a, 1937b) used an illustration based on a study of the discrimination of visual size in chimpanzees. He trained animals to discriminate between two squares, 256 and 160 square centimeters in size. The response to 256 was reinforced, and the response to 160 was extinguished. Then, after the discrimination between stimuli 256 and 160 was well established, the values of the stimuli were shifted to 256 and 409. The animals then chose 409—a stimulus which had never been reinforced.

221

GENERALIZA-
TION
AND
DISCRIMINA-
TION

The theoretical analysis of this problem is contained in Figure 7.7, to which we have already referred. If you look at that figure again, and check the generalization of inhibition gradient around S− (160 square centimeters in this case), you will see that inhibition generalized to S+ (256 square centimeters) to some extent. By the same token, excitation to 256 square centimeters generalized to a stimulus value at S_p (409 square centimeters). To arrive at the comparative value of response strength after discrimination of 256 and 409, we subtract the amount of generalized excitation at each point. And if we do this, as the figure shows, the *net* response strength is greater for 409 than it is for 256. Thus we would predict that on the average, animals would choose to respond to 409 instead of 256. This, of course, is a prediction of the transpositional effect. Obviously, however, the success of Spence's analysis depends upon the relative shape, relative location, and slope of the generalization curves, and we have already seen the difficulties inherent in that problem. The Spence-Hull theory suggests that the occurrence of transposition depends upon factors which stem from the characteristics of generalization gradients, characteristics which can be determined by extent of training, amount of reinforcement, and so on.

The obvious way to *prevent* transposition is to make the positive and negative stimuli very different from each other. A demonstration of what this would do can be seen by moving the curves in Figure 7.7 apart. In general, experimenters have found that when they move the stimuli far apart along some stimulus dimension, there tends to be a failure of transposition. Thus Kendler (1950) and Ehrenfreund (1952) found that as they systematically increased the difference between stimuli, the percentage of responses showing transposition decreased—results that would be expected from generalization gradients.

THE NONCONTINUITY THEORY

The theory of discriminative learning we have just examined places great emphasis upon the gradual accumulation of habit strength and upon the algebraic summation of gradients of generalization based on reinforcement and extinction. In general, this theory has been contrasted with one which emphasizes the problem-solving behavior of organisms in discriminative learning. This is generally called a *noncontinuity* theory, because it implies that learning a discrimination is not a continuous accumulation of positive and negative habit strength, or the like. The essential idea is that organisms try out hypotheses about the discrimination problem they have to solve, now paying attention to one aspect of the problem, now to another, trying out this hunch, then that one, and so on. Eventually the problem is solved—perhaps all at once—as the result of a more or less strategic attack upon it. Obviously the strategies that are available will depend to a very large extent upon the inherent capabilities of the learning organism: people are going to be much better than rats in their problem-solving ability. But rats can behave in ways which suggest a noncontinuous process at work; let us look now at an example of how this might happen.

A rat is trained to jump to one or another window in the Lashley jumping stand. The problem for the rat is to learn to jump to the white window and to avoid the black one. When the rat is faced initially with a choice between black and white, the white window might by chance be on the right side. If the rat jumps successfully to the white window, it might learn either that the white is correct or that the right side is correct. Let us suppose that it learns right to be correct. The rat will then work on this hypothesis until it is either punished or extinguished. The rat might then adopt some other hypothesis, based upon a chance contingency of reinforcement and some aspect of the environment. This would continue until the rat happened on the correct hypothesis and kept at it long enough to convince the experimenter that the rat had solved the problem.[4]

In other words, instead of gradually learning a single habit through the accumulation of the effects of reinforcement and nonreinforcement, the rat would have adopted a number of different strategies, learning (and unlearning) a whole series of habits analogous to those that human beings would call hypotheses.

This notion, that animals adopt a succession of strategies or hypotheses in solving problems, has been advanced by many investigators, most notably Krechevsky (1932) and Lashley (1938, 1942; Lashley & Wade, 1946). The noncontinuity theory has never been entirely expressed by one author, and many more points than the simple one about hypotheses have been made. Lashley, for example, in nearly all his publications emphasizes the momentary attentional set the animal may have in perceiving a portion of the stimulus field set in front of it by the experimenter.

The theorists who have supported the noncontinuity viewpoint have tended to look at experimental problems that arise out of intuition. The continuity theorists, on the other hand, have tended to develop experimental hypotheses in more rigorous fashion, choosing them from formal (and sometimes mathematical) principles. In the light of this difference in approach, it is not always possible to compare the continuity and noncontinuity theories line for line, as it were; but let us look at some of the experimental problems designed for this purpose and see what the outcome has been.

COMPARISON OF THE CONTINUITY AND NONCONTINUITY THEORIES

The effects of changing the problem   Some of the best evidence on the comparative adequacy of the continuity and noncontinuity theories has

---

[4]Olton (1972, 1974) has provided an elegant new analysis of this process in rat discrimination learning.

come from experiments in which a problem is altered partway through the training program. One way to do this is to *reverse the discriminative cues* early in training while an animal is still responding at a chance level. Here is how this could be done. Suppose that we start to train a rat to discriminate between white and black cards. We reinforce choices of the black card and extinguish choices of the white one. Then after a few trials, we reverse the cues so that the white card is now associated with reinforcement and the black card with nonreinforcement. What effect will this have on the speed with which the animal learns the problem? If the animal has been following a wrong hypothesis (a position hypothesis, say) during the initial phase of training, we should expect no effect if we reverse the cues, since the animal has not yet begun to associate black and white cues with the presence or absence of reinforcement. If, however, each trial adds a small increment both of habit strength to the positive stimulus and of inhibition to the negative stimulus, as the continuity theory would suggest, then reversing the cues ought to lead to negative transfer or interference—and thus to relatively slow learning. Note that this reasoning holds only for early trials where the animal is responding at a chance level, that is, during the *presolution period*, where, presumably, noncontinuity rats have not had a chance to stumble upon and to identify a hypothesis as correct.

There are a number of experiments which have used the technique of reversing cues during the presolution period, and the overwhelming majority show that reversing cues *does* retard learning (Ehrenfreund, 1948; Mackintosh, 1965; Sutherland & Mackintosh, 1971). It is clear, then, that the results of discrimination experiments in which cues are reversed early in learning favor the continuity view.

The continuity theory does not fare so well, however, if we reverse cues during a later stage in the learning process. Suppose we train animals on a discrimination problem until they have learned the problem well. Then suppose we give them a large number of additional training trials on the problem; that is, we *overtrain* or permit the animals to *overlearn* the problem. While noncontinuity theory might not have any specific prediction to make about behavior if we now reverse cues, continuity theory would have a very specific prediction to make—namely, that it ought to be progressively more difficult for the animals to reverse their behavior as the number of overtraining trials increases. This would be true because overtraining should add additional habit strength to the correct solution to the original problem (though perhaps not an overwhelming amount, given what we know about the relation between number of reinforcements and habit strength). Consequently, it ought to be more difficult for the animals to drop (extinguish) their original behavior and to respond appropriately to reversed cues.

But in a number of experiments, this does not seem to be the case at all. The data indicate that overtraining *speeds up* the process of learning the reversal (Reid, 1953; D'Amato & Jagoda, 1961; Sperling, 1965a, 1965b; Lovejoy, 1966; J. Mandler, 1968; Suter, 1970). The reasons for this are, at best, complicated, but the phenomenon—termed the *over-*

223

GENERALIZA-
TION
AND
DISCRIMINA-
TION

learning reversal effect—is worrisome to a continuity theorist. This is especially so since it now seems fairly certain that a major factor in the overlearning reversal effect is the relative attention that the animal pays to the rewarded S+ cue in the discrimination as opposed to the unrewarded S− cue (Mandler, 1968; Suter, 1970).

Suter (1970), for example, showed that rats are under close control of S− during the course of early discrimination training; that is, they learn to make correct responses by learning to *avoid* the negative S− cue. Overtraining tends to modify this tendency, however, so that the animals shift their attention to the S+ cue and respond on the basis of it. When discrimination reversal occurs, the old S+ cue now becomes the new S− cue. Overtrained animals should have a relatively easy time with the new discrimination because they have already learned to pay attention to the new S− cue, the cue that rats first use to solve discrimination problems. Rats without overtraining are less well off, however, because they have not had an opportunity to learn to pay attention to the cue that will be S− following the reversal. They must, in effect, begin all over again.

There are a number of theories which are akin to Suter's (e.g., Lovejoy, 1966; Biederman, 1968), and as Suter points out, most could account for his data with some relatively minor modifications in their assumptions. All share in common, however, the notion that the overlearning reversal effect depends upon attentionlike processes which are quite acutely and differentially tuned to the stimuli that are involved in a discrimination—attention processes that do not arise from a gradual buildup of excitation and inhibition and may totally ignore one or the other of an S+ and S− stimulus at various stages of the discrimination process. This is hardly the type of data or theoretical analysis which would sit well with the continuity theorist.

Discrimination among stimuli implying relationships   Since the noncontinuity view stresses the notion that animals actively attend to and compare stimuli in the process of learning a discrimination, what would happen if an experiment were done in which the discriminative stimuli actually consisted of *relations* among stimuli? Let us look at a classic experiment on this problem, that of Lawrence and DeRivera (1954), which was arranged to test predictions that the continuity and noncontinuity theories would make about transposition.

Lawrence and DeRivera used a Lashley jumping stand for their experiment, and an array of stimuli were chosen and used as follows. Stimulus cards were prepared that consisted of two brightnesses. The bottom half of each card was always a middle gray, a brightness of 4 on a scale ranging from 1 (bright) to 7 (dark). The top half of each card consisted of a gray selected from one of the other scale values. Thus, card $^1/_4$ had the top half brighter than the bottom half, while card $^7/_4$ had the top half darker than the bottom half. During initial training, identical cards were placed over *both* windows of the apparatus. If the top half of the cards was lighter than the bottom half, the rats had to jump to the right to obtain a food reward; if the top half was darker, a jump to the left produced a reward. In effect, the rats could approach the discrimination problem in one of two ways. They could respond to a *relationship*: top lighter than bottom—jump right; top darker than bottom—jump left; or they could respond to the *absolute brightness* of the top half of the cards (since the bottom was always the same brightness): top bright (value 1, 2, or 3)—jump right; top dark (values 5, 6, or 7)—jump left. After initial training, the experimenters tried to find out which strategy the rats were, in fact, using by subjecting them to a series of transposition tests. In general, this was done by changing the brightness of the *bottom* half of the cards to values other than the single one used during training.

Think, for a moment, of the stimulus card $3/1$, one of the cards used during the transposition tests. If the rats had learned to respond during training to the absolute brightness of the top part of the card, a rat faced with a $3/1$ card during transposition should jump to the right, since both the 3 stimulus and the 1 stimulus were rewarded during initial training for this response. If, however, the rats had learned to respond on the basis of the *relation* between the top and bottom brightness, a rat faced with a $3/1$ card should jump to the left, since initial training set things so that jumps to the left were rewarded when the top of the card was darker than the bottom.

Lawrence and DeRivera used a great many combinations of this sort and found that about 80 percent of the responses during transposition fitted a relational interpretation of what the rats had learned during initial training, and only 20 percent fitted an absolute interpretation. Once again it appears that rats will learn to respond in a relational way—providing we set things so that the task which the animal faces is one that clearly implies a relationship.

An evaluation of the continuity and noncontinuity theories It should be evident by now that there is much to be said for both these points of view. Certainly the continuity theory is correct in asserting that animals can be trained to have positive responses to certain stimuli without comparing these stimuli with others on the same sensory continuum. On the other hand, there are abundant data to show that animals do not react simply to stimuli, any stimuli, that come within range; they are selective in what they attend to. Furthermore, there is good evidence that animals test "hypotheses" about the nature of a problem and that they can behave in a relational manner if we present them with a problem which, in a more or less obvious way, leads them to respond relationally. As we turn in the next chapter to an examination of how organisms acquire the capacities and skills that ultimately make up their ability to discriminate, we shall have yet other examples of how data can be interpreted through a combination of the continuity and noncontinuity approaches.

225

GENERALIZA-
TION
AND
DISCRIMINA-
TION

EIGHT

THE ACQUISITION OF DISCRIMINATIVE CAPACITY

William James has described the perceptual experience of an infant as a "blooming, buzzing confusion." The study of how both animals and man come to create an orderly, sensible world out of such a chaotic beginning is the study of perceptual learning. In this chapter, we shall consider the part of this domain that leads most naturally from our discussion of the fundamental rules of generalization and discrimination. Specifically, we shall consider how an organism *develops the capacity for making more and more accurate discriminations as a result of practice.* In a sense, we have already looked at some aspects of this problem when we examined, for example, some of the things that had to be done to bring a pigeon's behavior under the control of some simple sensory dimension like the frequency of a tone (remember the Jenkins and Harrison experiment). Now, however, we want to look at things when the situation becomes more complicated in terms of the variety of information that the organism must learn to handle in a meaningful, sensible way. As you can imagine, it becomes especially appropriate at this point to pay increasing attention to the abilities of primates—particularly the human variety—and by the time we reach the end of this chapter, we shall be dealing with data and theory devoted primarily to the behavior of human beings. We begin with a discussion of the phenomenon of *learning sets,* then go on to present the theories and facts that psychologists have produced as they study how organisms develop the capacity to discriminate among the many events in the world around them.

DISCRIMINATION LEARNING SETS

One of the major characteristics of the discriminative process, as it is viewed by the continuity theorist, is that learning is a fairly gradual process taking place over a number of trials. Another class of experiments shows, however, that it is possible to produce a kind of behavior on a discrimination problem in which there does not appear to be much learning at all because the organism solves the problem immediately. In such an experiment, for example, two stimuli are presented to a monkey;

one of the stimuli, say, is a red cylinder and the other is a blue pyramid.
Under one of these objects is a hidden peanut. When the two stimuli are
exposed to a monkey, it carefully examines each and chooses to look
under one. If, by chance, it looks under the wrong one, on the very next
trial it looks under the other one and will continue to do so with almost
no errors on subsequent trials. The discrimination is perfect, and it is
only a matter of chance whether the monkey discovers the reward on the
first or on the second trial.

Immediate and perfect discrimination of this sort does not, of course,
happen automatically. It comes from a history of learning to make such
discriminations. As animals solve a *number* of successive discrimination
problems of the same type, they show an orderly and gradual improvement in their ability to solve any given problem until finally they can
produce an essentially immediate solution. An improvement in ability of
this sort has been called by Harlow, who was the first to study the
phenomenon in detail, the formation of a *learning set*.

Let us look at one of Harlow's experiments (Harlow, 1949) to see in a
bit of detail how a learning set develops. Eight monkeys were trained in a
special apparatus to pick one of two stimulus objects that were exposed
on a tray side by side; a reward was found under one object that the
experimenter designated correct, while nothing was found under the
other. After the monkeys spent some time on one problem, they were
shifted to another, then a third, and so on, until they had worked on 344
successive problems. The stimuli varied from problem to problem in
terms of their shape, color, height, etc., but in all cases, the monkeys'
basic task was simply to learn which of the two different objects of the
moment hid the reward. On each of the first 32 problems, the monkeys
were given 50 practice trials. On each of the remainder of the problems,
the monkeys received 6 to 11 practice trials. The results of the experiment
are shown in Figure 8.1, which indicates the percent of correct responses
that the monkeys made on the *first* 6 practice trials for successive blocks
of the total number of discrimination problems.

The figure shows that on early (preliminary) problems, there was
gradual improvement over the first six trials. The improvement continued over the remaining 44 practice trials that were used on each of
these problems, though this is not shown in the figure. By the time the
monkeys were working on problems 101 to 200, however, they were
correct about 85 percent of the time after just one trial (remember that
the nature of each problem set things so that they could perform no
better than chance on the first trial). And on the last block of 56
problems, they were correct on the second trial 95 percent of the time,
maintaining their accurate performance from this point on. In other
words, the monkeys eventually "learned how to learn" discrimination
problems so efficiently that their performance on any given discrimination problem was essentially perfect from the outset.

On the basis of these results, we might imagine—with Harlow
(1959)—that there ought to be some particular number of practice trials to
use with each successive problem that would produce maximally efficient

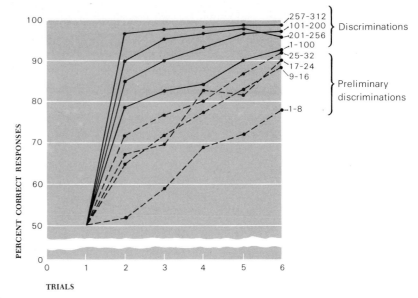

Figure 8.1
The development of a discrimination learning set. Early discriminations require a large number of trials to master, but later ones are learned in essentially one trial. (Harlow, 1949.)

development of a learning set. We might not have to use so many trials on each problem that animals would learn to discriminate perfectly, but offhand we might guess that the number required might have to be large enough to produce a good deal of learning on one discrimination before moving to the next. Over quite a broad range of practice trials per problem, this does not seem to be the case at all (Miles, 1965; Levine, Levinson, & Harlow, 1959). Rather, as long as there is some minimal amount of practice given on each successive problem, say 3 or 4 trials, the development of a learning set is correlated with the number of *problems* to which the learner is exposed. The greater the number of problems the better the learning-set formation.

TYPES OF LEARNING SETS

The type of learning set we have examined so far is one which involves a simple discrimination between two stimulus objects, one of which is "correct" and the other "incorrect." Learning-set formation is by no means limited to rather simple *object-quality* discriminations of this sort. For example, monkeys can easily learn a *discrimination-reversal* learning set. Harlow (1950) trained his animals on a series of 112 problems, each problem consisting of 7, 9, or 11 trials of simple discrimination training between two objects followed by 8 trials in which the stimulus that was formerly incorrect was now correct. The monkeys gradually learned over a series of problems to reverse their choice at the appropriate time in each problem; by the time they had been exposed to the full set of problems, the sudden discovery of no reward for picking an object produced an immediate shift to the other object on almost all occasions. This observation should remind you of our earlier discussion of reversal learning; but keep in mind that here the animals had experience with a great many reversals, while in the work we looked at earlier, our main interest was in the things that happened the first time an animal met a discrimination reversal.

229

THE
ACQUISITION
OF
DISCRIMINA-
TIVE
CAPACITY

Another kind of learning set is called a *response-shift* learning set. Here, the monkey is faced with the usual object-quality discrimination on trial 1 of a problem, selects one of the stimulus objects, and finds a reward no matter which object gets picked. On the *second* trial within a problem, however, the monkey must shift its choice to the other object of the pair in order to obtain a reward. An experiment by Brown and McDowell (1963) showed that monkeys could learn this kind of problem very well. Note that a response-shift learning set is quite similar to a discrimination-reversal learning set, except that with the former the animal must use its first choice, per se, as a cue to what to do, while with the latter, the monkey uses the *outcome* of a response (sudden nonreward of a choice) as a cue to shift its behavior.

There are many other kinds of learning sets that have been developed and studied. Furthermore, the phenomenon is not limited to monkeys, since it can be shown in species ranging from rats and raccoons to dolphins and humans (Herman, Beach, Pepper, & Stalling, 1969; Kintz, Foster, Hart, O'Malley, Palmer, & Sullivan, 1969). It has also led to the development of a number of models describing how learning sets can be expressed in mathematical terms (Levine, 1959, 1965; Restle, 1957, 1958). These are beyond the scope of this book, but they are well worth pursuing should you choose to do so.

THE THEORETICAL SIGNIFICANCE OF LEARNING SETS

How are we to place the phenomenon of learning sets within a theoretical framework designed to describe how organisms develop the capacity to discriminate? In a purely descriptive sense, it would seem that learning sets provide an elegant example of a *combination* of the continuity and noncontinuity approaches to discriminative learning—insofar as these theories are differentiated on the basis of a gradual incremental learning process as opposed to a sudden insightful one. Thus, the initial development of a learning set is a gradual affair in that early problems are solved only after a number of practice trials, skill developing slowly and incrementally as more and more problems are tackled by the learner. But the ultimate outcome of this process—instant, one-trial solution of a problem—bears all the hallmarks of a noncontinuity process at work. Perhaps this bears on a point we made earlier in Chapter 1 (p. 28): a learning "curve" can be gradual and continuous or "jumpwise," depending upon the amount of already acquired information the learner brings to the new task. However, while learning sets may *look* like a noncontinuity process arising from a continuity process at the empirical level, further scrutiny of this suggestion shows it to be inadequate. To begin with, Riopelle (1953) has shown that transfer from problem to problem based upon stimulus generalization of cues associated with successful solution becomes less and less as additional problems are solved. On the assumption that there are some stimulus similarities among the cues used from one problem to the next in learning-set formation, animals in fact learn that they cannot rely on such similarities to lead them to rapid solution of successive problems. This means that stimulus generalization of the type we discussed in the last chapter becomes either completely suppressed or radically altered in character.

Warren (1954) points out that testwise monkeys approach each recombination of stimuli as a *new* problem, however many times the specific stimuli required in the discrimination have been differentially rewarded. Thus, even if one of the stimuli had been much more frequently rewarded than the other in the past, the animals would not tend to choose this stimulus more often. Warren suggests that this means that the analysis of discriminative learning according to the excitatory and inhibitory strengths built up to particular stimuli as the result of reinforcement and extinction does not apply to animals which have learned many problems. Furthermore, the *non*reward of a stimulus choice can function just as well as the reward of a stimulus choice in establishing a learning set. If we add to this the fact that monkeys, at least, can acquire a learning set by simply *watching* other monkeys perform in a discrimination situation (Darby & Riopelle, 1959), we would be properly hesitant to fit the phenomenon of learning sets into any kind of standard theoretical account of discriminative learning.

Error factors Harlow (1950, 1959) has approached the theoretical analysis of learning sets in terms of *error factors*. His basic assumption is that the formation of a learning set stems essentially from the elimination or suppression of response tendencies that lead to mistakes or errors. He lists four such error factors: *position preference, stimulus perseveration, differential cue,* and *response shift*. An animal may have a built-in tendency to respond consistently to the left, say, of two stimulus objects (position preference), and it may also tend to continue picking an object that it has just picked (stimulus perseveration). By the same token, an animal may spontaneously shift on occasion from one object to another even though it has been picking the first, and correct, one consistently for a great many trials (response shift)—a factor which Harlow attributes to the monkey's tendency to explore. Also, an animal can be fooled early in learning a two-object discrimination by the fact that the things which determine a correct choice are ambiguous at the outset of a problem (differential cue). From the animal's point of view, picking a particular object *could* be correct because the object is on the left, say, or because the object is red. The animal might begin responding initially on the basis of the position cue rather than the color cue, a factor that could produce errors if this happened to be the incorrect approach.

According to Harlow, then, learning is *not* basically a process of building response strength for a correct choice; it is basically a process of reducing the strength of incorrect ones. This is an interesting idea—an idea that would, for example, not unfairly describe some of the things that go on in the classrooms of many elementary schools. Often the teacher's problem is not one of getting across to the pupil the idea that something is correct. To the contrary, it is often the problem of getting the pupil to understand what is incorrect.

231

THE
ACQUISITION
OF
DISCRIMINA-
TIVE
CAPACITY

Regardless of theory, the phenomenon of learning sets is a very good example of one elementary way in which organisms develop their discriminative capacity. Given extensive experience with discrimination problems as a *class* of events that occur in the world, creatures are no longer limited to the simple notion that red objects or square objects are associated with reinforcement; they learn that one of two objects will lead to reward, that the object reinforced last time will not be reinforced this time, and so on. Learning sets, then, provide one means by which organisms reduce James' "blooming, buzzing confusion." Let us now look at some other mechanisms which enter into the process and see if we can make further sense out of things.

ATTENTION TO CUES

We have to this point mainly considered situations in which subjects have to choose between stimuli that vary in a single dimension such as form, color, pitch, and so on. Suppose we complicate matters—slightly at first—by looking at a classic experiment which defines one approach to the concept of relative attention to cues when stimuli vary in *more* than one dimension. We can then go on to a more general discussion of the problem.

The experiment was simple (Reynolds, 1961). Two pigeons were trained to peck for food at a key in a Skinner box. Sometimes, a white triangle on a red background was projected on the key, and under this S+ condition, responses were reinforced. At other times, a white circle on a green background appeared on the key, and under this S− condition, responses were not reinforced. Once the birds had learned this simple discrimination, Reynolds asked an interesting question: What would happen when the stimuli were broken down and their components were presented singly to the birds; that is, what would happen when the forms circle and triangle and the colors red and white were each projected by themselves on the key? When this was done, it turned out that one bird responded to the white triangle and not to the other three stimuli, while the second bird responded to the red key and not to the other three stimuli. In other words, one bird was responding to one feature (form) of the S+ stimulus, while the other bird was responding to the other feature (color) of the S+ stimulus. Put still another way, one bird was paying attention to one dimension of the positive stimulus, while the other bird was paying attention to the second dimension of the positive stimulus. And this was purely an idiosyncratic affair— there was nothing in the experiment to lead the birds to pick one dimension over the other since both were equally efficient predictors of reward.

In Reynolds' experiment, there was nothing done to make it more likely that a bird would pick the form dimension over the color dimension. But suppose we set out to bias an organism in some way so that it would be more likely to pay attention to one dimension of a multidimensional set of stimuli than to some other dimension. The possibility that we could do this is obviously consistent with *noncontinuity theory* as we discussed it in the last chapter, and it is also one approach we might choose in training an organism to acquire a special capacity to discriminate among the features of a complicated stimulus display.

LAWRENCE'S EXPERIMENTS

Some evidence about the manipulability of attention comes from two studies by Lawrence (1949, 1950), which established that when rats learn to discriminate among cues, they can transfer this discrimination to new situations in which entirely different instrumental responses are required. Thus the distinction between cues is not correlated exclusively with the responses used in discrimination learning, and therefore discrimination learning cannot simply be a matter of stimulus-response bonds. Instead, during discrimination learning, subjects learn something about the stimuli that can be transferred to new situations.

Lawrence (1949) trained rats in stage 1 of an experiment to make a simultaneous discrimination. One group of animals was trained to step across a short gap to one compartment of a two-compartment box on the basis of, e.g., the brightness (black or white) of the two compartments—with black, say, being the correct choice rewarded with food and white being the incorrect choice punished by dropping the floor of the apparatus and letting the rats fall a short distance to a platform. A second group had to choose between compartments with rough or smooth floors, while a third had to discriminate between a large or a small compartment.

After they had learned to do this, the animals were shifted in stage 2 to another problem involving a different response, a *successive* discrimination in which they had to learn to go right or left in a T maze. In the T maze, the animals were exposed to two sets of cues. One set, say black versus white, was *relevant*—the rats had to turn to the right if the maze was black on a given trial, to the left if the maze was white. Correct responses were rewarded with food. Another set, say rough floor versus smooth floor, was *irrelevant*—besides the difference in brightness, the T maze had a rough floor on some trials, a smooth floor on others—but these cues were not correlated in any consistent fashion with the brightness cues the rats had to use to learn the new discrimination. The critical variable in the experiment was the relation between the relevant and irrelevant cues in the second (T-maze) problem and the set of cues that had been used in the first (simultaneous-discrimination) problem. Lawrence's experimental design was considerably more complete than this; but we shall simplify things a bit by talking about only part of it.

Now think for a moment of rats who, for example, learn the stage 2

233

THE
ACQUISITION
OF
DISCRIMINA-
TIVE
CAPACITY

T-maze problem with black versus white as the relevant cue and rough versus smooth as the irrelevant cue. Some of these animals had learned the simultaneous discrimination on the basis of black versus white. Lawrence ventured the guess that these animals would learn the T-maze problem relatively rapidly—on the assumption that black versus white had acquired some special distinctiveness, by virtue of being used in the simultaneous discrimination, that would transfer to the successive discrimination and help learning there. Other animals, however, had learned the stage 1 simultaneous discrimination on the basis of rough versus smooth cues. If these cues had acquired some special distinctiveness, and if the rats used them in the T-maze problem, they would be responding not to the relevant cues but, in fact, to the irrelevant ones. Consequently, interference ought to occur, and the rate at which the rats learned the successive discrimination would be relatively slow. The third group of animals, trained initially on wide versus narrow alleys, should be neither helped nor hurt on the successive discrimination, since that particular stimulus dimension was not varied in the T maze. Thus the rate at which they ought to learn should lie somewhere between the rates of the other two groups. In general, the data supported Lawrence's reasoning, particularly for those conditions where the stimulus dimension used on the first problem was the relevant one on the second. These animals learned the T-maze discrimination relatively quickly—more quickly, say, than the animals who had had no prior experience with the relevant stimulus dimension. Clearly then, animals seem to learn something about a stimulus dimension when acquiring one response in one experimental situation that will transfer to another experimental situation and facilitate learning of another response there. Again, the animal cannot be transferring on the basis of some simple stimulus-response bond because, while the stimulus dimension is the same in the two learning situations, the responses are different.[1] Instead there must be some kind of central coding process (Lawrence, 1963), a kind of general abstraction having to do with the distinctiveness of "brightness as a cue" that, once learned in one situation, can function to mediate and speed up learning in a new situation.

An important outcome of this work has been to point toward the solution of some of the issues in the continuity-noncontinuity controversy. Lawrence and his associates (Lawrence & Mason, 1955; Goodwin & Lawrence, 1955) have suggested that in complicated discrimination problems, organisms learn several habits simultaneously. First of all, they can learn to attend to a particular kind of stimulus dimension (brightness, for example), and secondly, they can learn an actual discrimination (a *particular* brightness is reinforced). Suppose, however, that there are other cues present, such as the height of a hurdle over

---

[1]It has been argued that there is more similarity between the stage 1 and stage 2 responses used by Lawrence than meets the eye and that the strength of Lawrence's argument is thereby weakened. Readers interested in pursuing this point are referred to the discussions by Riley (1968, pp. 131–140), Siegel (1967), and Sutherland and Mackintosh (1971, pp. 167–181).

which an animal must jump. If the experimenter changes the problem so that the height of the hurdle becomes the relevant cue, the animal need not necessarily unlearn the brightness discrimination. All that is necessary is that attention toward brightness be extinguished. If this is so, the animal can learn the new discrimination without disturbing much of what it has learned about the old one.

INTRADIMENSIONAL AND EXTRADIMENSIONAL SHIFTS

The basic prediction of an attentional theory of discrimination learning is that the relative salience of different dimensions can be manipulated by prior training. The feature of Lawrence's experiments that permits this prediction to be tested is the radical change in response from stage 1 to stage 2 which, presumably, prevents direct transfer between the two tasks. There is still another way of testing this basic prediction in the absence of direct task-to-task transfer. We can do this by arranging things so that the discriminations to be learned in stage 1 and stage 2 share the same dimensions yet use different specific stimuli drawn from those dimensions. We can then compare performance on an *intradimensional shift* (IDS) of this sort with performance on an *extradimensional shift* (EDS) in which an entirely new dimension becomes relevant for the solution of the discrimination problem as we go from stage 1 to stage 2. A comparison of the two schemes appears in Figure 8.2. In stage 1, form is relevant (square +, circle −), while orientation of inscribed lines is irrelevant (neither vertical nor 45-degree right is consistently reinforced). For the IDS, in stage 2, form remains relevant (triangle +, cross −), and orientation remains irrelevant (neither 45-degree left nor horizontal is consistently reinforced). For the EDS, in stage 2, orientation becomes relevant (45-degree left +, horizontal −), and form becomes irrelevant

Figure 8.2
Intradimensional and extradimensional shifts. In each case, subjects first learn discrimination on the left, where form is the relevant dimension and orientation of interior lines is the irrelevant dimension. In the case of an intradimensional shift, subjects then learn a second discrimination in which form is still relevant. In the case of an extradimensional shift, the previously irrelevant dimension becomes relevant so that now subjects must respond on the basis of orientation. Stimuli are usually presented in pairs, the elements of which differ simultaneously in both form and orientation.

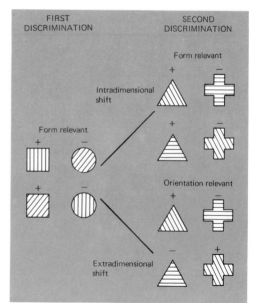

(neither triangle nor cross is consistently reinforced). If the relative salience of a dimension per se can indeed be modified by learning, then you can see that it ought to be easier to learn in stage 2 if stage 2 incorporates an intradimensional shift than if it incorporates an extradimensional shift.

235

THE
ACQUISITION
OF
DISCRIMINA-
TIVE
CAPACITY

Many factors appear to affect relative performance in IDS and EDS problems, factors as diverse as age, number of values along each dimension, and degree of stage 1 learning (see Sutherland & Mackintosh, 1971, and Wolff, 1967, for reviews of this literature). However, for our purpose we may ignore these complicating factors and simply point out the fact that intradimensional shifts are usually easier to learn than extradimensional shifts by animals (e.g., Mackintosh & Little, 1969; Shepp & Eimas, 1964) as well as by humans (e.g., Campione, Hyman, & Zeaman, 1965; Isaacs & Duncan, 1962; Uhl, 1966). Thus, organisms find a discrimination easier to master if they have had to master a previous discrimination in which the same dimension was relevant. It is interesting to note that during stage 1, subjects seem to learn both to attend to the relevant dimension and to ignore the irrelevant dimension (Kemler & Shepp, 1971).

REVERSAL AND NONREVERSAL SHIFTS

Another closely related problem has to do with the effects of *reversal* and *nonreversal shifts* upon discriminative learning (Kendler & Kendler, 1962). The two are diagramed in Figure 8.3. Subjects first learn a discrimination in which two stimulus dimensions are used, only one of which is relevant. In Figure 8.3, the stimuli vary in both size and brightness, but size is the relevant cue; large objects are positive (correct) and small objects are negative (incorrect). Now the subjects are shifted to another discrimination involving the same stimulus dimensions. In the case of a *reversal* shift, the *same* stimulus dimension is still relevant, but the subject must reverse his choice behavior; small objects are now positive and large objects negative. In the case of a *nonreversal* shift, the previously *irrelevant* stimulus dimension becomes *relevant*. Thus brightness becomes the relevant stimulus dimension; black is positive and white negative. By this time you have probably noticed that a reversal shift is an example of an intradimensional shift, while a nonreversal shift is an example of an extradimensional shift. The major methodological difference between intra- and extradimensional versus reversal and nonreversal shifts is that in the latter pair of paradigms the same stimuli are used in stages 1 and 2.

Now here is the critical question: Which should be learned faster, a reversal shift or a nonreversal shift? Following some of our thinking in connection with the overlearning reversal effect (p. 223), we might expect that a nonreversal shift would be learned faster than a reversal shift, since at the time the shift occurs, there is a relatively strong habit for reversal-shift subjects to continue responding to the stimulus that was correct but is now incorrect. If we think in terms of attention to dimensions, however, we might predict just the opposite. If subjects had

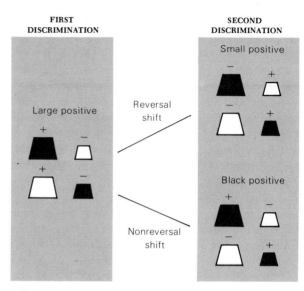

Figure 8.3
Reversal and nonreversal shifts. In each case, subjects first
learn the discrimination on the left, where size is the relevant dimension and brightness is the irrelevant dimension.
In the case of a reversal shift, subjects then learn a second
discrimination in which size is still relevant, but *small* is
now the positive cue. In the case of a nonreversal shift, the
previously irrelevant dimension becomes relevant so that
now subjects must respond on the basis of brightness.
Stimuli are usually presented in pairs, the elements of
which differ simultaneously in both form and brightness.
(After Kendler & Kendler, 1962.)

coded something about size in general as a relevant cue in the first
problem, they would still be attending to the relevant dimension when
the reversal shift occurred, and all they would have to do is reverse their
overt choice responses. With the nonreversal shift, however, they would
have to learn not only to make the appropriate choice behavior, but also
to make it on the basis of a *newly* relevant stimulus dimension.

The experimental data on this problem are interesting. It turns out
that for college students reversal shifts are easier to learn than nonreversal shifts (Buss, 1956; Harrow & Friedman, 1958; Kendler & D'Amato,
1955). However, a wide variety of animal species find nonreversal shifts
easier to learn than reversal shifts (Brookshire, Warren, & Ball, 1961;
Kelleher, 1956; Mackintosh, 1962; Tighe, 1964). Preschool children learn
a nonreversal shift faster than a reversal shift; their behavior is more like
that of a rat than of a college student (Kendler, Kendler, & Wells, 1960).
However, by kindergarten age children learn reversal and nonreversal
shifts at about the same rate (Kendler & Kendler, 1959).

Systematic investigation of the developmental change in the ability to
learn reversal shifts requires a task applicable to a variety of ages that
yields a quantitative index of performance. The best technique for such
investigation is known as the *optional shift paradigm* and is shown in
Figure 8.4. This task yields meaningful data in subjects ranging from rats
to human adults.

237

THE
ACQUISITION
OF
DISCRIMINA-
TIVE
CAPACITY

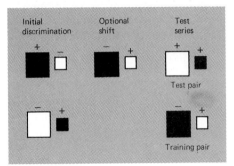

Figure 8.4
The optional shift paradigm, described in text. (After Kendler & Kendler, 1968.)

In the first stage, the initial discrimination shown in the figure requires that subjects learn that color is relevant (black +, white −) and size irrelevant. The second stage is presented immediately after criterion is reached in the initial discrimination. Only two of the four stimuli are presented, and the reward pattern is reversed from the initial discrimination. This shift is called optional because both dimensions are relevant and they vary redundantly (i.e., + is small, white and − is large, black). The subject may learn to respond on the basis of either or both dimensions. The question of interest is: What is the basis of the optional shift? Does the subject respond on the basis of size (nonreversal shift) or color (reversal shift)? In the third stage the test pair, on which any choice is rewarded, is alternated with the training pair used during the second stage. The subject will continue to respond as before on the training pair (i.e., small, white is +, large, black is −). To determine the basis of the optional shift, the responses to the test pair are examined. If the subject consistently selects the large white square, then his response throughout the third stage is primarily to white regardless of size. Since the initial discrimination required the selection of black, the subject has made an optional reversal shift. Conversely, if he consistently selects the small black square, then his responses are primarily to small regardless of color in the test series, and we infer that he has made an optional nonreversal (i.e., extradimensional) shift. If he fails to select either test figure consistently, he is considered to have made a nonselective shift.

The data in Figure 8.5 show that the propensity to make optional reversal shifts is greater for children than for rats and that it increases in children as a function of age (Kendler, Kendler, & Silfen, 1964; Tighe & Tighe, 1966).

How are these data to be explained? Clearly, there is little to be gained, once again, by sticking to an approach couched in terms of simple stimulus-response bonds, since this does not do a very adequate job of accounting for all the data (though it might explain the behavior of rats and preschool children). Kendler and Kendler (1968) favor a *mediating response* notion—an external cue sets off an *implicit* response which, in turn, has its own cue properties that become attached to the final set of overt choice responses. The mediating response acts as a sort of generalized go-between, linking a number of different (though related) stimulus inputs and response outputs. The precise nature of the

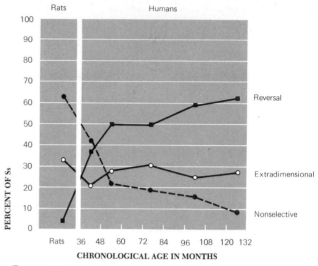

Figure 8.5
The percentage of subjects demonstrating reversal, extradimensional, and nonselective shifts in the optional shift paradigm for rats and for children of varying ages. (Kendler & Kendler, 1968.)

mediating response is not yet known; however, one likely candidate is implicit verbal behavior. In effect, children learn to *label* a relevant dimension on a reversal shift, for example, with a general implicit verbal tag (e.g., "*size* is relevant"), and they learn to use such mediating labels to help make the switch from one discrimination problem to its reverse. Moreover, children's facility with verbal labels ought to increase with age, and they ought to respond increasingly often on the basis of these mediating responses. That they clearly appear to do so is shown by the data in Figure 8.5. Nonverbal organisms do not have this helping hand available, of course, and so they tend to respond on reversal and nonreversal shifts much as if they *were* making simple direct associations between stimuli and responses.

It is worth pointing out that children undergo a rather massive intellectual revolution between the ages of 5 and 7 and that an increased use of verbal mediators is only one aspect of this revolution (White, 1965). Further research will be necessary to pin down precisely the cause of the change with age in the relative ease of reversal and nonreversal learning (see Wolff, 1967, for a review of evidence pertaining to several alternative hypotheses).

Reversal-shift effects with verbal stimuli   The emphasis in the preceding section was on stimuli that varied along obvious perceptual dimensions such as color, form, and size. It is interesting to note that the superiority of reversal shifts over nonreversal shifts (for adults) has also been shown with verbal stimuli. Kendler and Kendler (1968, pp. 225–232) used as stimuli eight words that could be easily put into two categories such as clothing and vegetables. Their design is shown schematically in Table 8.1. The letters *A* and *B* simply refer to two different responses. During stage 1 all the words related to clothing were assigned response A; all the vegetables were assigned response B. During stage 2, the subjects were split into two groups, half learning a reversal shift and half learning a nonreversal shift. As in the usual case where stimuli vary along perceptual dimensions, in the reversal shift, responses are reversed for all stimuli, while in the nonreversal shift, responses are reversed for only half the stimuli. The results closely parallel the findings we have reported previously for adults: The reversal shift was learned more quickly than the nonreversal shift.

An even more striking experiment was reported by Bogartz (1965). He used eight nonsense words (e.g., LEV) that had no relevant attribute in common. Four stimuli (let's call them group 1) were associated with one response, saying "dot," and the other four (group 2) with another response, saying "cross." After initial acquisition, the subjects were split into two groups. The reversal group had to learn now to respond "dot" to group 2 stimuli and "cross" to group 1 stimuli. For the nonreversal group, two A-dot associations and two B-cross associations were kept intact, while the two remaining A and B associations were reversed. Despite the fact that the reversal group had more associations to relearn, they learned faster in stage 2 than the nonreversal group, thus reproducing the basic reversal-shift phenomenon. Since the stimulus set did not contain any obvious dimension, we can conclude that the reversal-shift effect does not require mediating responses to dimensions of stimuli. Of course, this is not to say that mediation or attention to cues may not still be appropriate in cases where there are obvious dimensions of stimulus variation.

OBSERVING RESPONSES

Some psychologists have attempted to explain attention to cues in terms of *observing* or *orienting* responses (Wyckoff, 1952; Reid, 1953; Spence, 1960). An observing response can be defined as any response that results

Table 8.1
Design of Kendler and Kendler (1968) study of reversal and nonreversal shifts with verbal stimuli

STIMULUS	RESPONSE		
	STAGE 1	STAGE 2	
		REVERSAL	NONREVERSAL
Shirt	A	B	A
Hat	A	B	A
Dress	A	B	B
Pants	A	B	B
Pea	B	A	A
Potato	B	A	A
Carrot	B	A	B
Bean	B	A	B

in exposure to a discriminative stimulus (Stollnitz, 1965). What is meant by this is that an organism must make the "response" of orienting its receptors to the relevant stimulus in any kind of discrimination problem before it can go on to produce the specific choice behavior that will lead, say, to reinforcement. If it does not "observe" the stimulus, it obviously does not have the information it needs to solve the problem. The property of observing responses that makes them of interest to us in connection with things like reversal and nonreversal shifts is that they are presumed to vary in the *probability* with which they occur initially, and in the facility with which they are learned and with which they extinguish.

For example, Stollnitz (1965) tells us that monkeys tend to look where they put their fingers. If we pick a discrimination problem in which a monkey must actually touch the relevant cue—a pattern in the center of a card, for example—and push it in order to move the card aside and obtain a reward, the probability that the monkey will observe the cue ought to be very high. If, however, we require the monkey to touch a point some distance away from the cue, the probability ought to be correspondingly lower—at first, at least—that the monkey will observe the cue. In fact, this seems to be the case; monkeys have a relatively difficult time solving certain kinds of discrimination problems if there is any appreciable separation between the locus of a cue that must be used to solve the problem and the locus of the spot where the monkey must put its finger to indicate its choice. The distance does not have to be large—on the order of $1/2$ to $3/4$ inch.

The application of the concept of the observing response to the problems associated with discrimination learning is not hard to imagine. Consider, for example, a fairly subtle case where rats are given training on a discrimination between a black horizontal and white vertical rectangle. One might think that there is no way for the rats to orient themselves so as to perceive the orientation differences without seeing the color differences, and vice versa. However, Kendler and Kendler (1966) suggest that in this case the rats may conceivably discriminate brightness differences by fixating on the centers of the stimuli and may discriminate orientation by fixating on the edges of the figures.

As reasonable and useful as the notion of observing responses may be, it turns out that it is simply inadequate as a *general* explanation of mediational and attentional phenomena. One example will do.

Superior performance on intradimensional over extradimensional shifts has been demonstrated even when the choice of stimuli prevents the possibility of differential orienting responses. Shepp and Howard (1973) had children learn discriminations based on the dimensions of hue and "tint" (i.e., saturation). While many stimuli used in discrimination experiments could involve different overt orienting responses—one might move the eyes or fixate in a different way looking at a triangle as opposed to a blank card, for example—hue and tint are necessarily properties of precisely the same location on a physical stimulus. Consequently, no *overt* differences seem possible (or necessary) for learning the two discriminations. The fact that an intradimensional shift was learned more easily than an extradimensional shift under these conditions suggests that such concepts as attention and mediation are better understood as central and implicit rather than as peripheral and overt.

241

THE
ACQUISITION
OF
DISCRIMINA-
TIVE
CAPACITY

IS ATTENTION SELECTIVE?

Most research and theory on attention is based on the assumption that it is limited in amount. Thus, if a subject learns to pay more attention to one cue, less must be available for other cues. This assumption seems to accord well both with common sense and with a great deal of evidence from the study of human perceptual capacities (e.g., Egeth, 1967; Kahneman, 1973). It also accords well with a substantial body of evidence from the learning laboratory. However, some recent learning research has seemingly contradicted the notion that attention is selective. We shall first consider a study consistent with the classical conception of attention before turning to some of the newer, contradictory evidence.

Mackintosh (1965) used a three-stage paradigm to explore the effects of dimensional learning on attention. His experimental design is diagramed in Figure 8.6. Three groups of rats were used, two experimental groups and one control group. In stage 1, the two experimental groups learned a successive discrimination task based on brightness (turn left when two white stimuli are shown, turn right when two black stimuli are shown). For group BW, the stimuli were simply black or white squares. For group BW$_{hv}$, the stimuli were long thin rectangles, again black or

Figure 8.6
Three-stage experiment by Mackintosh (1965) to determine if attention can be manipulated by prior training. Stage 1 required a successive discrimination; the letter beneath each pair of stimuli indicates the direction the subject had to turn to be reinforced when that pair was displayed. Stage 2 required a simultaneous discrimination; the subject was reinforced only for selecting (i.e., jumping to) the + stimulus. Stage 3 also required a simultaneous discrimination. The three pairs of stimuli were presented in a random order, and the subject made a selection of one or the other member of a pair on each trial. (Note: Cross-hatching indicates a gray stimulus.)

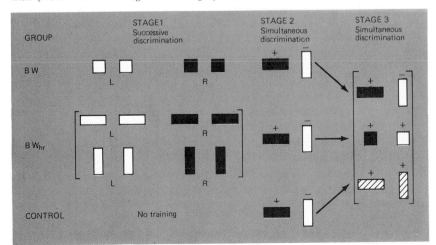

white. When a pair was shown, the two rectangles were either both horizontal or both vertical, but orientation was irrelevant in that it was uncorrelated with reward. The control group received no training during this stage.

In stage 2, all subjects learned a single simultaneous discrimination: approach a horizontal black rectangle and avoid a vertical white rectangle. The question of interest is what subjects learned in this second stage. Did they learn to approach horizontal forms and avoid vertical forms, or to approach black forms and avoid white forms; or did they learn both of these habits about equally? Most importantly, were the things subjects learned in stage 2 dependent on their training during stage 1? To answer these questions, two kinds of test trials were used in stage 3. On one, a black and a white square were shown together. On the other, a horizontal and a vertical gray rectangle were shown together. In addition to the test trials, all of which were reinforced, subjects also continued receiving training trials as in stage 2. As expected, stage 1 training *did* affect stage 2 learning as shown by stage 3 test performance. Consider the orientation test (vertical versus horizontal gray rectangles). Group BW subjects selected the horizontal rectangle (that had been correct in stage 2) less often than the control subjects. Presumably, this is because they were initially trained on a brightness discrimination and continued discriminating on this basis when they were switched to stage 2. The BW_{hv} subjects selected the horizontal rectangle even less often than the BW subjects, presumably because they had learned to ignore orientation during stage 1. Mackintosh (1965) pointed out that these data refute both an extreme continuity position and an extreme noncontinuity position because the animals neither learned about just one cue at a time nor learned about all cues equally. Instead, the degree of attention paid to each of the two dimensions of variation in stage 2 was dependent upon past experience. In other words, prior experience discriminating values on dimension A decreased the attention subsequently paid to dimension B. Similar findings have been reported with octopuses (Sutherland, Mackintosh, & Mackintosh, 1965) and humans (Eckstrand & Wickens, 1954).

By contrast, several studies seem to indicate that prior experience with one dimension *increases* the amount of attention paid to another dimension (e.g., Honig, 1969; Switalski, Lyons, & Thomas, 1966; Thomas, 1969). In Honig's study (1969), pigeons in the experimental condition were first trained to peck at a key that could be illuminated with colored light. Blue was positive (S+) and green was negative (S−). Birds in the control condition did not have to discriminate between the colors because pecking was reinforced equally when the key was blue or green. After the birds had had substantial training in this task, they were presented with a new task in which the positive stimulus displayed on the key consisted of three vertical black bars on a white background. The negative stimulus was simply the white background without any bars. After some training on this task, the birds were then given a generalization test in which the orientation of the bars was varied systematically and the number of responses emitted to each orientation was tabulated. **243**

THE
ACQUISITION
OF
DISCRIMINA-
TIVE
CAPACITY
The data appear in Figure 8.7. The chief assumption underlying the
interpretation of this study is that the steepness of a generalization
gradient for a dimension is an index of the amount of attention that is
paid to the dimension. That is, if a subject is paying attention to a
dimension, he ought to be readily able to detect differences in test stimuli
drawn from that dimension, and this in turn ought to reflect itself in a
relatively quick drop in responding to stimuli different from the original
training stimulus. Thus the data in Figure 8.7 are taken to mean that the
experimental subjects paid more attention to orientation than did the
control subjects. This is rather surprising since the only difference
between the groups is that the experimental subjects had earlier received
training on the *unrelated* dimension of color.

Thomas, Burr, and Svinicki (1969) attempted a more direct test of the
proposition that attention is selective. They reasoned that if attention is
limited in amount, then there should be an *inverse* relationship between
the amount of attention given to one aspect of a complex stimulus and
the amount given to another. They trained pigeons to respond to a white
vertical line on a green background. Subsequently the pigeons were
given separate generalization tests along the dimensions of wavelength
and line angle. In contrast to the prediction made on the assumption of
attentional selectivity, they found a *direct* relationship between generalization slopes along the two test dimensions. Thus birds that attended
more to wavelength also attended more to line orientation.

Is attention selective? Despite the provocative results of the generalization studies, it seems most reasonable to conclude that attention is
limited in amount, that it is selective rather than generalized. The basic
problem with the "general attention" position is that supporting data
come from transfer tasks that do not pit one dimension against another.
Under such circumstances steepened generalization gradients may simply be due to prior discrimination training giving animals a "set to

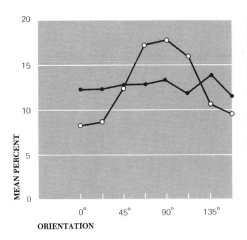

Figure 8.7
Stimulus generalization as a function of
test-stimulus orientation for experimental and control subjects. The functions represent percentage generalization gradients—the total number of
responses to each of the orientations
was divided by the total number of responses to all the orientation values.
This procedure takes into account the
possibility of different levels of overall
response output in different groups.
(Honig, 1969.)

discriminate" that carries over to any new generalization task (Reinhold & Perkins, 1955). Further, the direct relationship between the amounts of attention paid to two dimensions found by Thomas, Burr, and Svinicki may be attributed to individual differences among pigeons in their tendency to be discriminative. Thus a pigeon who discriminates sharply among colors may also be expected to discriminate sharply among the values of any other dimension (see also Hansen, Miller, & Thomas, 1971). The crucial question is how subjects allocate their attentional capacity when stimuli vary along both test dimensions simultaneously, and both dimensions are capable of controlling the response. This was the approach used in Mackintosh's (1965) study that demonstrated attentional selectivity.

ACQUIRED-COMPOUND THEORY

It is obvious that the capacity to make fine discriminations is, at least in part, the result of learning. Professional judges such as wine tasters, wool graders, and color mixers are capable of making discriminations that far exceed the capacity of the inexperienced layman. How do they come to such a refined state? Indeed, how do any of us manage to learn to make a discrimination that we find initially difficult or even impossible? Certainly the processes we discussed in the preceding section are important in the development of fine discriminations, but other processes may also be involved, especially where humans are concerned. In addition to attention to cues, two other principles have been proposed to account for the acquisition of discriminative capacity. One of these is known as *acquired compounding* of stimuli, and the other is known as *stimulus differentiation*. We shall consider these principles in this and the following section.

Perhaps the first psychologist to concern himself with questions of discrimination learning was someone to whom we have already referred, William James. To account for the ability to discriminate between stimuli that are very similar, James proposed that other highly discriminable stimuli may be attached to the to-be-discriminated stimuli, thus forming *compound stimuli* that are easier for the subject to learn to distinguish. An example of this mechanism was given by James (1890) when he explained how one might learn to distinguish burgundy wine from claret.

> Probably they have been drunk on different occasions. When we first drank claret we heard it called by that name, we were eating such and such a dinner, etc. Next time we drink it, a dim reminder of all these things chimes through us as we get the taste of the wine. When we try burgundy our first impression is that it is a kind of claret; but something falls short of full identification and presently we hear it called burgundy. During the next few experiences, the discrimination may still be uncertain—"which," we ask ourselves, "of the two wines is this present specimen?" But at last the claret-flavor recalls pretty distinctly its own name, "claret," "that wine I drank at So-and-so's table," etc; and the burgundy-flavor recalls the name burgundy and someone else's table. And only when this different SETTING has come to each is our discrimination between the two flavors solid and stable. After a while the

245

THE
ACQUISITION
OF
DISCRIMINA-
TIVE
CAPACITY

tables and other parts of the setting, besides the name, grow so multifarious as not to come up distinctly into consciousness; but *pari passu* with this, the adhesion of each wine with its own name becomes more and more inveterate, and at last each flavor suggests instantly and certainly its own name and nothing else. The names differ far more than the flavors, and help to stretch these latter further apart. Some such process as this must go on in all our experience [p. 511].

In this example the verbal labels and the settings at which claret and burgundy were drunk are presumably more distinctive than the wines themselves, and thus the acquired-compound stimuli, consisting of wines plus names plus settings, are more distinctive than the "simple" stimuli consisting of just the wines.

You may have noticed that according to James' plan the compound stimuli are the product of a form of S-S learning. More recently, there has been an effort to recast the account into S-R terms (Miller & Dollard, 1941; Dollard & Miller, 1950; Goss, 1955). These theorists assume that an organism experiences sensory feedback (s) from any response (R) that it makes, even if that response is implicit—even, that is, if the response is a simple *thought* instead of some overt muscle movement or act. If this response is learned to an external stimulus (S), then the external stimulus and the feedback stimulus (called a response-produced cue) form a compound stimulus that is mediated by the response (R). The notation for the compound stimulus is S-R·s (after Saltz, 1971), although a lowercase r may be used if the response is implicit. The compound stimulus is conditionable to overt responses by the ordinary mechanism of reinforcement. As you may have concluded already, incidentally, this is nothing but an additional example of mediation at work (p. 90).

Suppose, now, that we have two stimuli, S_1 and S_2, to be discriminated and that through mediating responses R_1 and R_2 the response-produced cues s_1 and s_2 are attached to S_1 and S_2. If the implicit stimuli s_1 and s_2 differ from each other to a greater extent than S_1 and S_2, then it should be easier to learn to discriminate the two compound stimuli than to discriminate S_1 from S_2. This is known as *acquired distinctiveness of cues*. It is interesting to consider what happens if the stimuli s_1 and s_2 are more similar to one another than are S_1 and S_2. According to the theory, the compounds should now be *more* difficult to discriminate than S_1 and S_2. This is known as *acquired equivalence of cues*. One common way to produce equivalence is to attach several different stimuli to the same response during stage 1. We shall next consider a few of the numerous empirical tests of the acquired-compound theory that have been performed to date. These experiments will help to clarify the somewhat abstract approach we have used so far.

ACQUIRED DISTINCTIVENESS OF CUES—STIMULUS PREDIFFERENTIATION

Experiments on this topic generally involve a two-stage design. In stage 1, the experimental subjects learn to attach a distinctive response, commonly a verbal label like a word, to each of several stimuli. These verbal responses (R's) presumably give rise to distinctive implicit stimuli (s's) which in turn result in distinctive compound stimuli. In stage 2, subjects are tested to determine whether stage 1 *predifferentiation training* was effective. Three kinds of test have been used in stage 2 (Ellis, 1973). *Transfer tests* measure the ease with which new responses can be associated with the pretraining stimuli following labeling practice. *Recognition and discrimination tests* are used to determine if stimuli are more accurately recognized, or if discrimination between training and test stimuli is facilitated, after labeling practice. *Mediated generalization tests* measure changes in the probability of generalization among a set of stimuli following predifferentiation training.

The basic question of the transfer paradigm is whether stage 1 predifferentiation training facilitates learning in stage 2. If it does, we would like to conclude that the initial training made the stimuli less confusable with one another, that it differentiated them, in other words. However, for this conclusion to be valid, at least two other conditions must be met. First, the responses used in the two stages must be unrelated to one another so that stimulus-response relationships learned in one stage will not transfer directly from one stage to the other simply because the responses required are the same. Second, the measure of facilitation should be made against an appropriate control group. The simplest control condition would be to run a group of subjects in stage 2 without any stage 1 pretraining. Unfortunately, subjects in such a condition would suffer the disadvantage of not being "warmed up" or as practiced for the task at hand as subjects who also had learning trials during stage 1 (see p. 341). A more appropriate control, therefore, would be to give subjects discrimination training during phase 1 on stimuli as difficult as, but very different from, those used by subjects in the experimental condition. This should ensure that these subjects do not have the opportunity to acquire specific information about the stimuli that are to be used during the later test. Regrettably, many studies have lacked this kind of control condition.

An early study by Gagné and Baker (1950) provides an example of the results of predifferentiation research. The four stimuli were lights that differed in color and position (top or bottom, red or green) on a display board. The predifferentiation training required subjects to learn to associate the letters *J, V, S,* and *M* with the stimuli (one letter per stimulus). Subjects received either 0, 8, 16, or 32 trials in the letter-light association task. They were then switched to a task in which they were required to learn to flip a specified switch to each of the lights. The main result was that the larger the number of predifferentiation trials, the better the subjects performed during stage 2.

The stimuli used by Gagné and Baker may not seem to be difficult to discriminate initially, and yet predifferentiation training rendered them functionally still more distinctive. It is important to note that predifferentiation training is also effective when the stimuli are selected so as to be genuinely difficult to discriminate. For example, Goss and Greenfeld

247

THE
ACQUISITION
OF
DISCRIMINA-
TIVE
CAPACITY

(1958) used four lights that differed only slightly in intensity. Here, too, attachment of distinctive verbal labels resulted in improved performance on a subsequent motor learning task as compared with a control group that received no predifferentiation training.

Neither of the preceding studies used the ideal control condition described earlier. However, on the basis of other studies, it is now clear that predifferentiation training with verbal labels has facilitative effects above and beyond the effects of general transfer factors such as warm-up. For example, Cantor (1955) used colored lights as stimuli. For all subjects, stage 2 involved learning a motor response to each of six colored lights in the red-yellow range. The experimental subjects received verbal predifferentiation training on the same six colors, while control subjects received pretraining on six lights in the blue-green range. Training on the specific colors used in stage 2 resulted in substantially better performance than training on a set of different colors. Another finding from this study is that there was no difference between the subjects who saw the "irrelevant" blue-green stimuli and a control who received no pretraining at all. Thus, in this particular study there was no warm-up or other general transfer in evidence—a fortunate thing, but not to be counted on as a very general finding.

ACQUIRED EQUIVALENCE OF CUES

Saltz (1971) has pointed out the importance of distinguishing between a "strong" and a "weak" form of acquired equivalence. The theory of acquired compounds (see Goss, 1955) leads to the prediction that differences should become less discriminable for subjects for whom these stimuli have acquired equivalence than for subjects who have had no explicit practice with the stimuli. This is the strong form of equivalence, and evidence of it may be considered to support the general S-R position from which the theory is derived.

A weak form of equivalence is one in which there is a *relative* equivalence effect but not an absolute decrement in stage 2 learning. For example, consider an experiment in which there are three conditions of stage 1 training: (1) a distinctiveness condition in which each stimulus is assigned a different label, (2) an equivalence condition in which all stimuli are assigned the same label, and (3) a control condition in which subjects do not see the test stimuli at all (recall, however, that some kind of learning task is required here to control properly for *general transfer*). Suppose that the subjects in the equivalence condition learn the stage 2 task more slowly than the subjects in the distinctiveness condition but more quickly than those in the control condition. The fact that in this hypothetical experiment the equivalence condition resulted in poorer stage 2 learning than the distinctiveness condition is interesting and deserving of explanation. However, such a pattern of results would only indicate a weak equivalence effect, since there is no evidence that equivalence training actually impaired stage 2 learning relative to the control treatment. For the strong form of acquired equivalence to be supported would require that the equivalence group learn more slowly in stage 2 than the control group.

Robinson (1955) performed an experiment that compared various kinds of pretraining with a control condition of no pretraining at all. The stimuli were 10 fingerprints. In the distinctiveness condition, subjects learned to associate a different nickname with each fingerprint (e.g., Moll, Duke, Slim, Nick). In the equivalence condition, five of the fingerprints were associated with the label "cops" and five with the label "robbers." This should tend to reduce the distinctiveness of stimuli attached to the same responses. In the same-different condition, subjects simply compared pairs of fingerprints, indicating whether they were the same or different; these subjects did not attach labels to stimuli.

In stage 2, the subjects had to indicate on each trial which of a set of comparison fingerprints was the *same* as or *different* from a standard (the standard changed from trial to trial). The data revealed that all three of the experimental groups were better than the control group in stage 2; but the experimental groups did not differ reliably from one another. The data indicate the presence of a predifferentiation effect of *some* sort, but they fail to support the Miller-Dollard-Goss acquired-compound theory because there was not even a weak equivalence effect, much less a strong effect. However, the fact that the distinctiveness group did not discriminate stimuli more accurately than the same-different group is *not* embarrassing to an acquired-compound theory, because the same-different group (and only that group) had direct practice on the test task during stage 1. It is worth observing that this is the first experiment we have come across that used a perceptual discrimination task in stage 2, rather than a transfer learning task. While such a change in method may seem slight, we shall see later that it may have important consequences.

DeRivera (1959) also used fingerprints as stimuli in a study that compared several conditions of pretraining with a control condition of no pretraining at all. With respect to phase 2 learning of fingerprint-digit associations, the control group was distinctly the poorest. Thus, there was no evidence in this study of a strong form of acquired equivalence. However, there is some evidence for a kind of weak equivalence that is worth going into in some detail. One group of subjects served in a standard distinctiveness condition, learning to associate a unique letter with each of the 10 fingerprints. The interesting variation in this study is that there were two kinds of equivalence conditions. In both, subjects were pretrained to attach five randomly selected fingerprints to the letter *C*, the other five to the letter *G*. The difference between the conditions is that in one, subjects were told that the stimuli attached to a common response had nothing in common but the response and that they should try to form separate associations between each fingerprint and the label assigned to it. In the other condition, they were told that the task of learning print-letter associations would be facilitated if they would look for common characteristics among the prints assigned to each letter. Note that even though the assignments of prints to the labels *C* and *G* were actually random, with such complex stimuli, subjects instructed to

look for common features were often successful. The data, errors during
stage 2 learning, indicated that the distinctiveness condition and the
"nothing in common" equivalence condition were the most effective
forms of pretraining. The "common characteristics" equivalence pretraining condition resulted in significantly more errors than the two other
pretraining conditions, but significantly fewer errors than the control
that received no prior training at all. Thus the data indicate, at best, a
weak equivalence effect. Note, however, that the chief determinant of
the pretraining effect is not the number of distinct external labels used in
predifferentiation training, since the distinctiveness (10 labels) and
"nothing in common" equivalence condition (2 labels) resulted in equal
performance, while the two 2-label groups differed substantially in
performance. Such data indicate the importance of implicit mediational
responses, since this is all that could have differed between the two
equivalence conditions.

There have been several other experiments that have failed to
demonstrate even a weak equivalence effect (e.g., Hake & Eriksen,
1955). Rather than consider these studies in any detail, let us turn instead
to two studies that have been interpreted as supporting the acquired-
compound theory (Malloy & Ellis, 1970; Katz, 1963).

Katz (1963; see also Katz & Zigler, 1969) used the four stimuli shown
in Figure 8.8 along with the verbal labels BUZ, RIC, JAN, and SOL. The
subjects, seven- and nine-year-old children, were divided into three
pretraining conditions. The distinctive label group was taught to associate a different one of the labels with each of the four figures; the
common label group used two labels and was taught to associate two
figures with each; and the no label group was shown the figures without
labels.

In stage 2, subjects were shown pairs of stimuli and were required to
decide whether the stimuli were the same or different. Once again, this
operation represents an effort to determine if perceptual accuracy is
enhanced by practice in labeling.

The measure most relevant to the acquired-equivalence hypothesis is
the number of "same" judgments made to pairs of stimuli that were

249

THE
ACQUISITION
OF
DISCRIMINA-
TIVE
CAPACITY

Figure 8.8
Stimulus figures used in a study of children's
discrimination learning. (Katz, 1963.)

actually "different." If labeling affects the distinctiveness of stimuli, we would expect that pairs assigned a common label ought to be falsely called "same" more often than pairs assigned either no labels or distinctive labels. The mean numbers of same responses for such pairs were 4.31, 3.06, and 1.94, respectively. Thus the distinctive label condition resulted in fewer false same judgments than the no label control, while the common label condition resulted in more false sames. Although this experiment appears to support acquired-compound theory, it suffers from several weaknesses. First, the control group was inappropriate since they saw the stimuli prior to the stage 2 test. We shall present evidence later that mere exposure to stimuli can result in some degree of differentiation. Second, it is difficult to know what basis Katz' subjects used in judging sameness and difference. The children may not have clearly understood that the experimenter's criterion was physical identity since no training was given to drive this point home. Suppose, for example, they had been shown the two triangles below. Would they

have decided that they were the same because they share the label "triangle," or would they have decided that they were different because they lack physical identity? We do not know. Third, Kendler and Kendler (1968) have pointed out that Katz' data may be interpreted in terms of differential attention to cues rather than acquired compounds. A common label could encourage the subject to attend to the similar portions of two shapes, while distinctive labels could encourage him to attend to the portions of the shapes that are obviously different.

Malloy and Ellis (1970) attempted to design a test of acquired-compound theory that would be free of the problems that had plagued earlier investigators. They used a mediated generalization paradigm in a three-stage experiment. The first stage was designed to establish acquired distinctiveness and equivalence effects by means of verbal pretraining. In the second stage a new verbal response was attached to some of the pretrained stimuli. The third stage was a test designed to determine the extent to which the responses conditioned in stage 2 would generalize to other, similar, stimuli not shown in stage 2.

The theory predicts that generalization from one stimulus to another, similar, stimulus should be increased, relative to a no-pretraining control, when the two stimuli have been attached to the same label in stage 1. Further, generalization should be decreased when the two stimuli have been attached to distinctive responses in stage 1. Both of these predictions were supported by the data.

This study very nearly avoided all three of the problems mentioned in connection with the Katz study. First, a control condition was included in which stimuli were not exposed at all during stage 1 training. Second, the

subjects were adults who understood that the basis for responding in
stage 3 was physical identity. Third, some additional conditions were
added to control for the possibility that attention to cues may have
determined the results. Comparison of the equivalence and distinctiveness conditions with these extra control conditions indicated that the
acquired-equivalence effect observed in the experiment could not be
explained in terms of attention to cues. However, the acquired-
distinctiveness effect could *not* be unambiguously attributed to the
mediational mechanisms of acquired-compound theory; attention to
cues could not be ruled out.

251

THE
ACQUISITION
OF
DISCRIMINA-
TIVE
CAPACITY

Further comments on predifferentiation training We have to this point
not considered the nature of the stimuli that have been used in
predifferentiation experiments. However, some recent work indicates
that stimulus characteristics are crucial in determining the outcome of the
experiment. We have also failed to consider the nature of the transfer
task used to assess the effects of various kinds of pretraining. This is also
an important determinant of the experimental outcome.

Ellis and Muller (1964) observed that the outcomes of previous
predifferentiation experiments seemed to depend upon the nature of the
stage 2 transfer task. When stage 2 required learning to attach a
discriminative response to each stimulus, performance was usually better
following stage 1 verbal labeling practice (e.g., Gagné & Baker, 1950).
However, when stage 2 involved a perceptual task such as making
same-different judgments, prior verbal labeling practice usually did not
enhance performance (e.g., Robinson, 1955). Ellis and Muller performed
two experiments to determine the significance of this observation.

In the first experiment, two sets of stimuli were used that differed in
complexity (simple 6-point forms and complex 24-point forms). There
were three different types of predifferentiation training: distinctiveness,
observation, and equivalence. The distinctiveness group learned a different label for each of eight stimuli, the equivalence group learned two labels
(four stimuli per label), and the observation group was simply instructed
to examine the stimuli when they were shown. As a test of transfer, a
recognition task was used in stage 2. On each recognition trial the subject
had to indicate if one of the original stimuli was present on a card
containing a set of five similar stimuli. For the simple shapes, the
observation group performed better in stage 2 than either the equivalence
or the distinctiveness groups, but for the complex shapes, the distinctiveness group was superior to the other two groups. Thus, the nature of the
stimuli affects the relative performance of various pretraining conditions.
This finding set the stage for the second experiment. Ellis and Muller had
found stimuli (simple shapes) for which labeling pretraining did *not* lead
to superior recognition when compared with simple observation. What
would happen if these same stimuli were now used in an experiment in
which a discriminative response had to be attached to each stimulus
during stage 2?

Two groups of subjects were used: distinctive labels and observation.

The stimuli were six-point forms. In stage 2, subjects learned to push a different button for each of the forms. With this new task, the transfer data were different; now the distinctiveness group performed better than the observation group.

In sum, these findings raise some questions about the implications of research on predifferentiation. If pretraining with distinctive labels really makes stimuli more discriminable, then why doesn't this show up routinely in experiments that use perceptual transfer tasks such as sameness and difference detection or recognition? Ellis and Muller suggest that enhanced positive transfer to a discriminative-response task may occur not only as a result of increased distinctiveness, but also as a result of increased availability of differential responses. Learning to attach verbal responses to stimuli may have the specific effect of facilitating the attachment of other responses to the same stimuli. To put the matter differently, distinctiveness pretraining may make stimuli more *associable* rather than more *distinctive*.

GIBSON'S DIFFERENTIATION THEORY

In 1940, Gibson, a student of Hull's, proposed that the critical change occurring during discrimination learning is a sharpening or steepening of the generalization gradients surrounding each stimulus as a result of the reinforcement of correct responses and extinction of incorrect responses. Gibson gave the name *differentiation* to this process. Differentiation shows up as a reduced tendency for a stimulus to evoke incorrect responses, which means, considering a set of stimuli as a whole, that there will be less interstimulus competition and confusion after differentiation training. Furthermore, once training has conferred differentiation upon a set of stimuli for a subject, differentiation becomes a property of that set that will influence subsequent learning involving those stimuli.

Saltz (1971) has pointed out just how radical Gibson's theory was for its time. According to conventional theory, learning was supposed to involve S-R bonds, and thus the facilitation of one task by another required some degree of similarity or relevance between the S-R associations involved in each of the tasks. However, Gibson's theory suggested that transfer could also be effected by manipulation of a stimulus factor alone (differentiation) without involving the between-tasks similarity of S-R associations.

Over a period of years, Gibson's theory evolved into a form that was even more radically different from a standard S-R theory in that differentiation was thought to be possible even in the absence of differential reinforcement (e.g., Gibson & Gibson, 1955; Gibson, 1967). In the revised theory, differentiation results from an increase in sensitivity to stimulus variables that may be difficult or impossible to detect at first. The increase is apparently the direct result of experience with stimuli and need not be mediated by reinforcement.

Empirical support for Gibson's theory comes from a variety of sources. First of all, studies that demonstrate acquired distinctiveness of cues

(e.g., Gagné & Baker, 1950) are consistent with Gibson's theory since
the conditions of stage 1 learning in those studies should have permitted
differentiation to occur. (Recall that these studies were designed to
prevent the direct transfer of stage 1 S-R associations to stage 2
learning.) Moreover, the failure to find strong equivalence of cues is also
consistent with Gibson's theory since her theory does not specifically
suggest that any form of pretraining ought to *reduce* differentiation. The
series of studies that investigated the effects of response specificity
during predifferentiation training also support the Gibsonian view.
Recall, for example, the DeRivera (1959) study in which 10 fingerprints
were used, labeled in various ways during pretraining. Subjects who
were encouraged to search for distinctive features of the stimuli performed better than subjects who were encouraged to search for common
features, even when the degree of response specificity was controlled.
Such a finding suggests that any behavior that encourages the subject to
attend to the distinguishing features of stimuli should produce positive
transfer (Tighe & Tighe, 1966).

Perhaps the most striking part of Gibson's theory is the assertion that
differentiation can occur in the absence of reinforcement. This has been
demonstrated in some of the studies previously mentioned. For example,
in Robinson's study, the same-different judgments were not corrected
and thus were not reinforced. Also the aesthetic judgments in Rasmussen and Archer's study were not reinforced. Most importantly, these are
not isolated examples. It seems to be the rule rather than the exception
that simply allowing subjects to experience a set of stimuli is sufficient to
produce some degree of differentiation. This is not to say, of course, that
simple observation would produce *as much* differentiation as an appropriately designed pretraining task.

This conclusion is consistent also with Robinson's (1955) finding that
simply having subjects tell whether pairs of fingerprints were the same or
different was as effective as any condition in which explicit labels were
attached to them. Even making aesthetic judgments of forms is as
effective a form of pretraining as labeling (Rasmussen & Archer, 1961).

Some demonstrations of the non-necessity of differential reinforcement for differentiation come from studies on environmental enrichment
during early life. For example, Gibson and Walk (1956) raised rats from
birth to 90 days of age in one of two different environments. Each home
cage in this study was surrounded by a white cardboard wall several
inches from the cage. For the experimental group, four metal forms (two
circles and two triangles) were hung on the cardboard walls and thus out
of reach of the animals. The positions of the forms were changed from
time to time to make sure that no association was formed between a form
and, say, a favorite place for eating. No forms were displayed to the
control animals. At about 90 days of age the rats were trained to
discriminate between a circle and a triangle like those on the wall. The
rats in the experimental condition far surpassed those in the control
condition, even though the forms were simply shown for 90 days without
any kind of differential reinforcement. The rats were not fed or in any
other way explicitly reinforced for responding to either stimulus during

the 90-day pretraining period, and thus the study demonstrates that *differential* reinforcement is not necessary for differentiation to occur. However, some subsequent studies (Kerpelman, 1965; Bennett & Ellis, 1968) have shown that reinforcement of a *nondifferential* sort *is* important in differentiation learning. In both of these experiments, rats were raised for 90 days in cages like those used by Gibson and Walk. However, for some rats the circular and triangular training forms were removed during the daily feeding periods, while for other rats the forms were present throughout the feeding period. The rats that had the forms present during meals learned the subsequent discrimination task more quickly than the rats that did not.

WHEN DIFFERENTIATION WORKS

Suppose differentiation effects are compared for two sets of stimuli. One set, let's call it A, is composed of four stimuli that differ widely from one another, while the other set, B, is composed of stimuli that are quite similar to one another. Ellis (1973) has pointed out that according to Gibson's theory, stimulus differentiation training should be more beneficial for set B than for set A. This conclusion is based on the assumption that a relatively large part of the total effort involved in first-task learning must be devoted to discrimination when stimuli are similar to one another. When stimuli are dissimilar, discrimination is a relatively smaller part of the total effort. Thus, in transfer studies, when subjects must learn to attach new responses to the stimuli, the beneficial effect of prior differentiation training should be greater under conditions of high stimulus similarity than under conditions of low stimulus similarity.

As plausible as this prediction may seem, it has not been verified in several studies. For example, Del Castillo and Ellis (1968) used sets of lights that differed from one another in intensity. In one condition the intensity differences were small; in another condition they were large. Nevertheless, transfer was not reliably different in the two cases.

More recently, however, Ellis (1973) has reported that there are circumstances in which the prediction from Gibson's theory is verified. In particular, the transfer of differentiation depends on the nature of the stimulus elements. Relatively simple stimuli such as lights or nonsense words (e.g., XAJ) do not show transfer of differentiation, but complex stimuli such as 24-point random shapes or 3 by 3 letter matrices do show such transfer. Apparently the prediction holds as long as selection of cues must be made from a large variety of alternative features. This interpretation would seem to bring Gibson's theory and the theory of attention to cues close together.

EVALUATION OF THEORIES

The acquired-compound theory has fared rather badly. Its prediction of acquired equivalence has been verified only in the study by Malloy and Ellis (1970), and its prediction of acquired distinctiveness is not unique since other theories also predict the phenomenon. In sum, it seems likely that labels per se do not render stimuli more discriminable; any effect they have seems to be the result of encouraging the detection of relevant distinctive features.

Attention to cues (or acquired salience of dimensions) seems to be an important factor in discrimination learning. Attention theory has been severely criticized for being too vague and for generating predictions on an intuitive level rather than through explicit, formal rules (Kendler & Kendler, 1966, 1968; Saltz, 1971). While this has been true in the past, recent versions of attention models have been explicitly mathematical and are less subject to such criticisms (e.g., Lovejoy, 1966, 1968; Sutherland & Mackintosh, 1971; Trabasso & Bower, 1968; Zeaman & House, 1963).

The great advantage of Gibson's theory is that it is not based on reinforcement principles and can thus account for all the studies in which differentiation is obtained without differential reinforcement. The theory may, however, have dispensed too completely with reinforcement because it cannot explain why nondifferential reinforcement facilitates differentiation learning (Kerpelman, 1965; Bennett & Ellis, 1968). It seems reasonable to conclude that the principles of both differentiation and attention to cues are operative in discrimination learning.

From the preceding discussion it is obvious that psychologists have not yet reached agreement on the theoretical interpretation of discrimination learning and the acquisition of discriminative capacity. However, we should not let this obscure the fact that a great deal of reliable evidence has been accumulated about both of these topics.

NINE

CONCEPT IDENTIFICATION AND THE LEARNING OF RULES

The dictionary tells us that a concept is a thought or an idea, and so, according to the dictionary, this chapter must be about how we acquire ideas. That is a reasonable description of the chapter for informal purposes, but it leaves too many loose ends to be entirely satisfactory. For one thing, it is not very explicit, and for another, it implies a distinction between perception and thinking that does not apply to the learning of concepts. Our perceptions are the meaningful impressions that the world makes upon our senses, while our thoughts are activities that can go on independently of the external impressions of the moment. However, that difference is not necessary to an understanding of how we learn concepts. The learning of both perceptual and cognitive concepts depends upon the way in which we organize the components to make unitary concepts, and that dependence is the most significant aspect of concept learning. In most laboratory experiments, as a matter of fact, the object of study is the development of concepts based upon perceptual events, but the results are meant to apply to purely cognitive concepts as well. Thus, the distinction between perception and thinking is not relevant to the major conditions that determine how we come to learn concepts, and experiments on concept identification have implications both for how we perceive the world and for how we think about it. What we need, however, is an account of the idea of *concept* itself, independent of the distinction between perception and thinking. We can, then, examine how we go about investigating concept learning.

CONCEPTS AND CONCEPT-IDENTIFICATION EXPERIMENTS

A *concept* is a set of features connected by some rule. In order to make sense out of that definition, we must know what is meant by "feature" and what is meant by "rule." The notion of feature is widely used in contemporary psychology. It originally arose in connection with theories about the nature of speech and studies of the perception of speech. But the idea of feature has very general utility, and it has long been used in psychology under a variety of other names, such as attribute, property, characteristic, or even, somewhat inaccurately, dimension. A *feature* is any aspect of an object or event that can be abstracted from that object or event and be said to be identical to the same feature abstracted from any other object or event. Grass is green in the summer. Greenness, then, is a feature of grass. It is also a feature of other objects, automobiles for example (though it is not necessarily a defining feature for either—it may be as irrelevant to the *concept* of grass as to that of automobile). We can define features as precisely or loosely as we choose. We could define green by reference to a precise pair of wavelengths, or we could simply allow it to be defined by loose judgments of agreement, such as "Yes, I'd say your car is about the color of grass." Features cannot exist in themselves. They are always abstractions of objects or events. Green cannot exist without something to be green.

Features always exist in more than one state. They must always contrast with something. If everything in the world were the same shade of green, green would not be a feature because there would be nothing to contrast it with. We need to contrast green with red or some other color before we can say that it is a feature. In the description of concepts and concept attainment, we emphasize this contrastive property of features by pointing out that features must always exist in different states. Therefore, it is more accurate to say that green is a feature-state of the general feature of color rather than to say that green itself is a feature. However, the term feature is often used to mean the state of some feature as well as the contrasting property itself.

Another important characteristic of features is that they are practically endless in number. We can always invent new features simply by describing some contrast that has never been made before. We might invent a new concept, "Center-Wash," for example, by identifying an area in Washington, D.C., bounded by Fourteenth Street, Eighteenth Street, and G and N Streets. This area, Center-Wash, would contrast with the rest of Washington (or the rest of the world, if we chose). Such a simple geographical concept may not be very useful, but consider the equally arbitrary notion of "Greenwich Villlage." Need for new concepts develops all the time, and we often invent them by making new distinctions which give rise to new features. Therefore, we cannot possibly learn to identify all possible features or all possible concepts. In learning about new concepts, we must identify what features are being contrasted, even though they may be totally strange to us, and find out how those features are connected to form concepts.

Not all features in the real world are independent. In fact, features usually contain other features. There is an important feature that divides all things in the world into living and nonliving objects. The category of living contains other distinctions. These features are plainly organized in a hierarchy, and many sets of features that we use in everyday life are so organized. Just how these are related to one another depends upon the semantic structure of the particular language we speak. Different semantic structures influence the way in which we learn and think, and the ease with which we can acquire new ideas depends in part upon the feature-structure of the particular language or languages we know. The important point for the moment, however, is simply that features are not fixed but are the result of the active operation of human minds.

The other part of the definition of concept concerns the nature of rules. A *rule* is an instruction for doing something. Thus, it is a rule of sorts that if you try to start an automobile engine when it is hot by pressing on the accelerator too hard, you are likely to flood the engine and make it impossible to start. It is also a rule that if you add two or more numbers together and the sum is greater than nine, you must carry the first digit of the sum over to the next column of figures. These two examples illustrate an important difference between kinds of rules. Some rules are heuristic and some are algorithmic. The rule about flooding the carburetor is a heuristic one, and the rule about carrying forward digits is an algorithmic one. Heuristic rules are general principles that apply with discretion. Algorithmic rules are precise, and they apply automatically and blindly. Both heuristic and algorithmic processes occur in human thinking, and later in the chapter we shall be concerned with this distinction.

But, what does it mean to say that a concept is a set of features connected by some rule? It means that any concept we can think of—the game of football, George Washington's false teeth, or the theory of biological determinism—can be defined by the relation among certain features. These relations are spelled out by the rules. A golf ball, for example, is a circular object of a certain composition, size, and weight used for the purpose of playing a particular game. Here the rule combining the features is one of conjunction. The features are added together to form the concept. A golf ball is something that is this *and* that *and* something else. The concept of being a citizen of the United States can also be described by a set of features, but the rule for combining the features in this case is different. An American citizen is one who is born in the United States, *or* born abroad of American parents, *or* someone who has lived in the United States for a period of time *and* has gone through the process of naturalization. The rule is clearly a more complicated one. It includes disjunctive relations, revealed by the connective *or*, as well as conjunctive relations, revealed by the connective *and*.

Thus, it is clear that there are at least two components in learning new concepts. We must come to identify the features, and we must learn how those features are connected by rules. These two components usually go together in the same process of learning. We have already examined some of the problems of how we learn to identify features in the chapters concerned with stimulus control and with perceptual learning. Therefore, in this chapter we shall concentrate largely on the problem of learning to cope with rules of different sorts.

Concepts in the Laboratory

Earlier investigators of concept identification believed that the principles of conditioning and simple associative learning would suffice to explain how people learned concepts. These theories generally stated that people came to identify concepts by associating features together through contiguity (see Restle, 1955, for one version of such a theory). The trouble is, of course, that such a theory, in its simplest form, would account only for learning of conjunctive concepts. While it is certainly the case that conditioning and other simple principles of learning can describe how some simple concepts are learned by human beings as well as by animals, the extension of these notions to the most interesting and complicated forms of concept identification is forced and clumsy. Therefore, contemporary theorists of concept learning have abandoned simple learning theory as the fundamental basis for concept learning. These theorists, of course, recognize that the performance in a concept-identification task is under the control of reinforcement and other conditions identified in simple learning. Current theories emphasize logical analyses of concept-learning tasks, as we shall see. Whatever the theory, however, an analysis of the logical structure of concepts is important to the study of concept learning.

THE VARIETY OF RULES

There are a number of logically possible ways in which features can be combined in concepts. For 2 features, there are 16 possibilities for feature combination, of which only 10 are unique (Bourne, 1970). These 10 can be reduced to 5 pairs which are really mirror images of one another. In the interests of simplicity only 1 of each pair is presented in Table 9.1. Table 9.1 also gives an example of a concept taken from ordinary experience that illustrates each rule. These examples should help you to understand the principle, but don't press the examples too far, for one of the things about concepts in ordinary life is that they are not always precisely and explicitly defined.

One important thing to remember is that the rules in Table 9.1 are logical rules. They are derived from the propositional calculus. In ordinary experience we do not cast things in the form of the propositional calculus. We learn to construct grammatical sentences, to do arithmetic, to judge people, and to make moral decisions—all with rules that, on the surface at least, take very different forms and certainly not very often the forms of the rules in Table 9.1. However, such rules may be reducible to the rules of the propositional calculus. The point is that the logical structure of rules is simply a way of characterizing them for logical purposes—a way of determining their implications. There is no necessary implication that people implicitly or explicitly think in terms that are stated in the rules themselves. However, it is important that concepts and the rules behind them be characterized in unambiguous ways, and the logical rules of Table 9.1 provide just such a characterization. One of the things that the exposition of logical rules, such as those in Table 9.1, does is to show us that logical relations are sufficiently complex so that no simple psychological theory about how people deal with concepts and learn to identify them will be adequate.

Occasionally, investigators of concept identification in laboratory experiments will have subjects learn to identify concepts from ordinary experience. More often, however, investigators invent artificial concepts. These have special properties that enable us to tease apart and control various aspects of the processes in concept learning. Figure 9.1 shows some materials that might be used in a laboratory experiment on concept identification. Each panel in Figure 9.1 contains an example of a possible concept. These exemplars have been constructed by making all possible combinations of three binary features. Binary features are ones that can exist in only two possible states. One feature in Figure 9.1 is shape; all the objects pictured in it are either square or round. Another is size; the squares and circles are either large or small. Finally, all exemplars are one of two colors, gray or white. There are eight possible objects or exemplars in this conceptual universe. A given concept from this universe will consist of some subset of all possible combinations. One subset, for example, is defined by the affirmative rule; the concept consists of all square things. Exactly half of the objects in this universe will be examples of this concept since half of the objects are square. Another concept might be defined by the conjunction of size and shape. One such concept consists of all square things that are small. The subset of objects defined by this particular concept is smaller than the affirmative concept. It consists of only two exemplars. Still another concept might be defined by the inclusive disjunction of objects that are either gray or round or both. Here, six out of the eight possible objects are exemplars of the concept. Incidentally, the simple universe of possible objects in Figure 9.1 illustrates one very important point: All objects can be members of more than one concept. In fact the number of possible concepts in such a universe is greater than the number of objects. Finally,

Table 9.1
Some of the ways in which features may be combined by rule to form concepts

NAME	DESCRIPTION OF THE RULE	DESCRIPTION OF THE CONCEPT
Affirmative	R	All red objects are examples of the concept.
Conjunctive	$R \cap S$	All objects that are both red and square are examples of the concept.
Inclusive disjunctive	$R \cup S$	All objects that are red or square or both are examples of the concept.
Conditional	$R \longrightarrow S$ $[\overline{R} \cup S]$	If an object is red, then it must be square to be an example of the concept.
Biconditional	$R \longleftrightarrow S$ $[(R \cap S) \cup (\overline{R} \cap \overline{S})]$	Red objects are examples if and only if they are square.

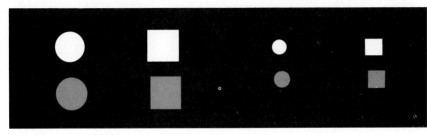
261

CONCEPT
IDENTIFICATION
AND THE
LEARNING
OF RULES

Figure 9.1
Stimuli that could be used in a concept-learning experiment. There are three features: size, color, and shape. There are two states for each feature, resulting in eight stimuli. These could define a large number of concepts, depending upon the rules governing the relations among stimuli.

note that for some concepts, some features will be relevant and others will be irrelevant. Relevant attributes are those mentioned in the rule defining the concept, while irrelevant attributes are all the remaining ones in the universe. For example, if size and shape are relevant, color would be irrelevant. Members of the concept-set might be small and square, irrespective of whether they are white or black.

PROCEDURES IN CONCEPT-ATTAINMENT EXPERIMENTS

Nearly every experiment in concept learning differs from the next one in some small procedural detail. However, there are certain variations in method that are important, and you will need to understand these in order to follow the ideas presented in this chapter.

There are two general classes of experiments in concept learning. One of these uses a *method of reception* and the other a *method of selection* (Bourne, Ekstrand, & Dominowski, 1971). In both kinds of experiments, subjects are exposed to objects or pictures of objects like those in Figure 9.1. The subjects guess which objects are examples of the concept, and from this information they try to form an idea of the objects that form the concept as well as of the rule that defines the concept. The way in which this is done, however, differs between the receptive and the selectional paradigms.

In the method of reception, the subject is presented with each successive object, and he makes some decision as to whether it is an example of the concept or not. He then is told whether his decision is correct or not. The important feature of the receptive paradigm is that the selection of each example presented to the subjects is in the hands of the experimenter. Thus, if the subject has a particular hypothesis about what the concept is which he is to learn, he may not be able to test that hypothesis until a relevant object comes along. The experimenter may simply not present him with an object containing what the subject believes to be the relevant or crucial feature-states.

There are several ways of doing a receptive experiment. In the simplest form, the subject learns just one concept, and he may indicate that concept by saying "yes" or "plus" for objects that he thinks are exemplars of the concept and saying "no" or "minus" for those object which he thinks are not examples of the concept. In more complicated versions of the receptive experiment, subjects may have to associate nonsense names with each object. The set of objects will be divided up into a number of mutually exclusive subsets, each defined by some concept rule. This is a more difficult task because the subject has to learn several concepts instead of just one. Learning multiple concepts and associating each concept with a nonsense name is more characteristic of older experiments than of more recent ones (e.g., Heidbreder, 1947). Other variations of the receptive paradigm ask subjects to sort objects or otherwise indicate how objects are to be distributed among concepts. These are minor variations; the important property of the receptive method is that the subject has no control over the order in which he receives exemplars.

The method of selection allows the subject to choose which object he will test as an example of the concept on each trial. The best-known experiment using the selective paradigm made use of the objects illustrated in Figure 9.2 (Bruner, Goodnow, & Austin, 1956). In this set of objects there are four features: shape, color, number of objects, and number of borders. Since each feature exists in three states, there are $3 \times 3 \times 3 \times 3$ or 81 objects in all. The subjects in this experiment were told that various combinations of objects would define concepts, and it was the task of the subjects to find out what the concepts were by choosing various objects as examples of the concepts. The subjects would thus point to or name the exemplars which they thought defined the concept, and the experimenter would tell them whether they were right or not. Of course, a subject's initial choice is presumably a random one, and in that respect is not very different from being presented with an initial object by the experimenter. Thereafter, however, the subject can choose his own examples in order to test various hypotheses. That is precisely the advantage of the selective paradigm. It enables us to make inferences about what hypotheses the subjects have in mind by following the choices they make.

Other variations in methods and materials are possible, though the difference between the receptive and selective method defines the most important procedural difference. Perhaps the next most important difference lies in the kinds of objects used. The kinds of objects illustrated in Figures 9.1 and 9.2 are typical of most experiments in concept identification. They are arbitrarily constructed nonsense figures or objects. There is no concept in our ordinary experience that is exemplified by a row of three green crosses or by a small white square (as opposed, say, to a large black circle). Some experimenters have argued that even if the objects define arbitrary concepts, the features of which they are composed ought to cohere in some natural way. These experimenters argue that subjects should be presented with schematized or stylized objects which could conceivably be real objects or distortions of real objects.

Some materials used in concept-attainment experiments look like fanci-
ful bugs (Gottwald, 1971), while others suggest human faces (see
Bourne, Ekstrand, & Dominowski, 1971, p. 178). Circles with appropriately placed pairs of dots, a vertical line, and a horizontal line will
irresistibly suggest a human face. The human face can be made to seem
to be smiling by curving the horizontal line upward and made to seem
sad by curving the line downward. Thus, the feature associated with the
mouth can be in two states. Similar variations can be imposed on the
other features. There is no logical difference between concepts defined
by such figures and the kinds of concepts exemplified in Figures 9.1 and
9.2, but some experimenters have argued that it is more natural and
easier for subjects to deal with concepts in which the various combinations of features form coherent patterns.

263

CONCEPT
IDENTIFICATION
AND THE
LEARNING
OF RULES

EXPERIMENTAL STUDIES OF CONCEPT LEARNING

CONCEPT ATTAINMENT AS A FUNCTION OF KIND OF RULE

The most important cognitive characteristic of concepts is the structure of
the rules that define them, and it is not surprising, therefore, that such
rules are responsible for wide variations in the difficulty of learning

Figure 9.2
Stimuli from a concept-learning task used to investigate strategies in concept attainment.
The forms varied in: shape, color, and number of borders. There were three values for each
attribute (color was either red, black, or green). (Bruner, Goodnow, & Austin, 1956, p. 42.)

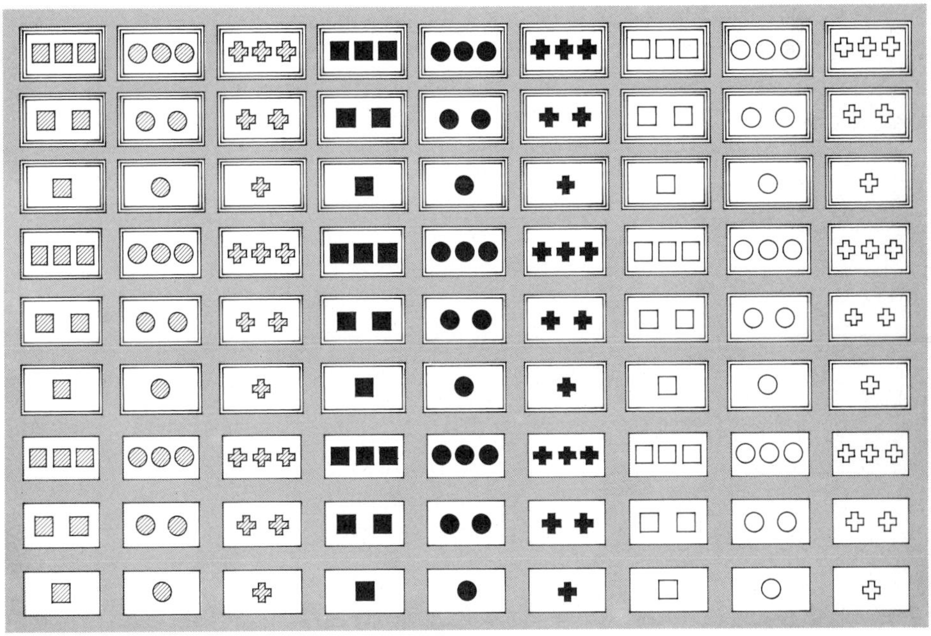

concepts. An experiment by Neisser and Weene (1962) illustrates that point.

Neisser and Weene asked subjects to look at some filing cards on which were printed four letters composed of various combinations of the consonants J, Q, V, X, and Z. There are 625 possible combinations of these letters (JJJJ, JJJQ, JJQQ, JQQQ, etc.). Certain combinations defined concepts. For example, any card containing the letter Q might define an affirmative concept. All cards with at least one Q on them would be instances of the concept, and those cards without Q's would not be instances of the concept. A conjunctive concept might be defined by all those cards containing at least one J and one Z. The subjects in this experiment looked at each card and guessed whether it was a member of the concept they were to discover. The experimenter informed the subjects after each guess whether or not they were correct. The object of the experiment was to see how many examples or trials it took subjects to reach a criterion of 25 consecutive correct guesses when the concepts were defined by different kinds of rules.

Some of the data from this experiment are presented in Table 9.2, which lists the logical rule defining each kind of concept studied in the experiment and the median number of trials it took the subjects in the experiment to attain each kind of concept. The rules defining the concepts in this experiment are defined in slightly different ways from those in Table 9.1, but they are reducible to the rules of Table 9.1. Notice that the experimenters divided the kinds of concepts into three levels. These levels are natural outcomes of the ways in which rules define concepts. Level I concepts, for example, include only those defined by a single feature. Level II concepts define combinations of features, and level III concepts are produced by joining combinations of disjunctive pairs from level II. Some concepts were so difficult that subjects could not

Table 9.2
Trials to criterion for different types of problems
(Neisser & Weene, 1962, p. 643)

TYPE OF CONCEPT	CYCLE 1 MEDIANS	CYCLE 2 MEDIANS
LEVEL I		
Affirmation (present)	11.0	4.0
Absence	7.0	1.5
LEVEL II		
Conjunction	13.0	18.0
Inclusive disjunctive	21.0	24.0
Conditional	28.0	17.0
Disjunctive absence $(\overline{A} \cup B)$	50.0	23.0
Conjunctive absence $(A \quad B)$	29.0	8.0
Implication	∞	19.5
LEVEL III		
Either/or $(A \cap \overline{B}) \cup (\overline{A} \cap B)$	68.0	41.5
Both/neither $(A \cap B) \cup (\overline{A} \cap \overline{B})$	∞	53.5

reach the criterion in the time allotted for the experiment. Also, notice that conjunctive concepts are just about as easy as concepts defined by the presence of a single feature. The relative degree of ease in learning conjunctive and affirmative concepts will depend somewhat upon the particular conditions of the experiment. If there are a great many features defining the universe of possible examples, then chance might make it very difficult for subjects to discover which feature defines a simple affirmative concept. A conjunction of several features might make it easier for subjects to detect, simply by guessing, correct examples. However, the differences between various kinds of conjunction and disjunction do not depend upon such more or less mechanical matters but are a reflection of the logical structure of the concepts themselves.

265

CONCEPT
IDENTIFICATION
AND THE
LEARNING
OF RULES

Neisser and Weene remind us that a computer programmed to discover the concepts with maximum efficiency would find it just as easy to learn those concepts that are difficult for human beings as it would the concepts that are easy for human beings. These authors argue that subjects must have available the components of concepts that are defined by combinations of rules in order to learn. Thus subjects must learn three things in level III concepts: the features, the conjunction of features, and the combination of conjunctive-disjunctive rules. Such an argument does not, however, account for the large differences among level II concepts. Disjunctive absence, for example, is very difficult. The subjects in this experiment had difficulty in seeing that a concept could be defined by the absence of J *or* the absence of Z. The difficulty lies in the fact that examples containing *both* J and Z would be positive examples of the concept. Thus, positive instances would be QQVQ, VXQX, *and* JZQQ, but not JQQV or VXZZ. Here, the logical rule is not tied to a simple pattern among the features but to a complicated one. Garner (1962), in a series of investigations in the learning of perceptual patterns, shows us that people find it very difficult to perceive the organization among features when the features are tied together by complicated contingent rules. Thus, it is more than just the number of things the subjects must learn; it is the degree of congruence between rules and the simplicity of patterns among features that determines the ease of learning concepts. The learning of concepts is partly a matter of perceiving the patterns that result from combinations of features. The simple presence or absence of a given feature is much easier to detect than some contingent rule which allows features to be absent under some conditions defining the concept and present under still others.

The essential results of the experiment by Neisser and Weene have been duplicated many times. A series of experiments summarized by Bourne (1970) shows that it is much easier for subjects to solve concepts in which the logical rules consist of simple affirmation, negation, or conjunction than concepts that consist of disjunctive or biconditional rules. However, more than this, the experiments by Bourne and his colleagues show that subjects, through proper training, can come to be very much better in dealing with difficult logical rules than they were initially. In fact, instruction in formal logic, particularly instruction that gives subjects experience in the use of truth tables, shows a strong positive transfer to the ability to perform concept-attainment tasks (Dodd, Kinsman, Klipp, & Bourne, 1971). In order to develop a strategy based upon logical truth tables, subjects must systematically notice the association of the presence or absence of a given feature with some rule. In fact, truth tables are just that. They are tables for showing whether a given feature is true (T) or false (F). True in the context of experiments on concept learning means that the feature is present in a particular exemplar, and false means that it is absent.

Observing how pairs of relevant attributes in all possible combinations are classified as being correct or not will enable any subject to induce the logical rules underlying the concept by applying the rules connecting T and F, or presence and absence, to the logical rules. For example, consider the pairs of features, color and shape, in Figure 9.1. The subjects would have to see examples containing each combination: black present, square present; black present, square absent; black absent, square present; black absent, square absent. Just by knowing whether examples containing each of the above combinations were examples of a particular concept or not would tell the subjects what the rule was defining the concept and enable them to pick future examples that would always be correct. Given the selectional paradigm, the subjects could attain any such concept in a maximum of just four trials.

Bourne and his associates have been able to show that subjects behave as if they were using truth tables after they have had long experience at learning concepts in the laboratory. Figure 9.3 shows the number of trials to solution for subjects learning nine successive concepts embodying two different logical rules (Bourne, 1967). On the first trial, there is a large difference in mean trials to solution between a simple disjunctive concept and a biconditional concept. By the sixth problem, however, all differences in trials to solution had disappeared. That was because subjects

Figure 9.3
The difference in trials to solution for successive problems in learning concepts defined by biconditional and disjunctive rules. (From Bourne, 1967, p. 17.)

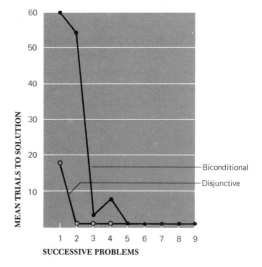

were applying truth-table-like rules, and when they did so, difficulty with different kinds of problems disappeared.

267

CONCEPT
IDENTIFICATION
AND THE
LEARNING
OF RULES

Subjects can learn truth-table strategies on their own as the result of long experience at learning concepts in the laboratory, and they can be taught to use truth-table strategies by deliberate instruction. This does not mean that in their ordinary experience people make use of a truth-table strategy in learning concepts, but it does illustrate that they are capable of learning how to use highly efficient logical strategies as the result of experience. People can, under some circumstances, behave like efficiently programmed computers. Research investigators, trouble-shooters, and other people who have to solve problems that have well-defined structures make use of strategies like the truth-table strategy in solving problems. The number of relevant attributes must be very small, however, or these people must have access to some way of writing down their successes and failures, for the limitations of human memory would preclude the application of the truth-table strategy to a large number of relevant attributes unless notes and records aid memory.

Bourne (1970), in discussing this phenomenon, suggests that there is a kind of hierarchy in concept learning. Subjects must first learn what the attributes are. These attributes then must be coded into the objects that are the stimuli in a concept-learning experiment, though in ordinary experience it is probable that it is the other way around—subjects know the objects and must tease out the attributes. At the next level, subjects learn to group objects into various kinds of concepts. With increased experience in dealing with the way in which the world is divided into classes by concepts, people can learn to use the various logical rules in a systematic way. People then acquire an implicit knowledge of the propositional calculus. Not all human beings, of course, completely master the ability to form concepts in this most abstract of ways, but it is apparent that such potential is there even though it may not be properly exhibited. Many people seem to get by without ever using the distinction between conditional and biconditional concepts.

INFORMATION PROCESSING IN CONCEPT LEARNING

The amount of information present in any array of objects which must be classified in a concept-attainment experiment determines the ease with which concepts may be learned. The amount of information, if all states of all attributes are to be represented in the universe of possible objects, increases directly with the number of features. Obviously, it is harder to learn that a concept is defined by the simple presence of some single feature (an affirmative concept) when the number of features from which to choose is 12 than when it is 2. For any kind of rule, increasing the number of irrelevant features (features that do not define the concept in question) increases the time it takes to learn concepts (Archer, Bourne, & Brown, 1955). The more irrelevant features there are, the harder it is to discover those features correlated with the concept and the rule connecting them. This result holds even when the irrelevant features are correlated with one another so that they are redundant (Bourne &

Haygood, 1959). However, the influence of correlated irrelevant features will depend upon the particular pattern of possible objects that are deleted as the result of the correlation. A correlation among features requires that some objects conceivable in the total universe will be missing in a particular set. If, for example, size and shape were correlated in Figure 9.1 (so that, say, all large objects are also black), some of the objects (those that are small and black) would be missing.

However, a more puzzling result is the fact that human beings seem to be able to use the information in positive instances (examples of the concept) better than they can in negative instances (objects not examples of the concept), even when the information transmitted is the same for objects that are instances and objects that are not. An early experiment (Smoke, 1933) showed that subjects seemed to learn very little from negative instances. The experimenter reported that his subjects appeared to profit little from being told what were not instances of the concept. For a time this result was accepted as a general conclusion. A more careful analysis revealed, however, that the result was possibly an artifact, for the conditions of the experiment were such that negative instances contained much less information than positive instances. Therefore, it was not surprising that subjects learned more from the positive instances. However, a later experiment (Hovland & Weiss, 1953) showed the same result when the conditions of the experiment were controlled so that exactly the same amount of information was contained in positive and negative instances. In order to have the same amount of information in negative and positive instances, it means that just as many objects in the universe must be members of the concept as there are objects that are not members of the concept. This means that on any given occasion, a subject must have an equal probability of receiving either an instance of the concept or one that is not.

Freibergs and Tulving (1961) thought people might learn more from positive instances simply because, in ordinary experience—in contrast to laboratory experience—negative instances are very seldom informative. Because there are an infinite number of concepts in the real world (remember that we can invent features), being told what a concept is not provides no information whatever. Being told that I am not thinking of the paving blocks in the Piazza San Marco does not tell you anything about what is on my mind at the moment. In the artificial universes of laboratory experiments, being told what is not an example of the concept in question eliminates some possibilities, and if conditions are right, a negative instance could be as informative as a positive instance. Therefore, even though people transfer their experience in the world at large to the laboratory, it ought to be possible to undo that experience through laboratory training. Freibergs and Tulving compared the gains subjects made from positive instances with those made from negative instances after the subjects had experience in the laboratory, learning concepts either entirely through positive instances or through negative instances. These investigators used geometric forms as objects, and these forms varied in three features. There were 4 possibilities for each feature, and so there were 12 instances in all for each problem. The problems were **269**

CONCEPT
IDENTIFICATION
AND THE
LEARNING
OF RULES
such that they could always be solved either through four positive
instances or through four negative instances. Half of the subjects were
asked to identify each concept after being exposed to the four positive
instances, and half were asked to identify the concept after four negative
instances.

On the initial problem, the subjects who inspected positive instances
did much better than those who inspected only negative instances. After
20 problems, however, the median performance in time to solution was
almost precisely the same for those having positive and negative
instances. Practice with solving problems with negative instances results
in subjects being able to use negative information about as efficiently as
they use positive information. This result is not so unimportant for the
real world as it sounds. Many people, including medical diagnosticians,
must learn to pay attention to negative information, and it often seems to
be the case that they do not do so as much as they should. They carry
over the experience of ordinary life to the demands of their professions.
It is often necessary, through deliberate programmed instruction, to
cause people to attend to negative information.

OTHER CONDITIONS DETERMINING CONCEPT ATTAINMENT

How the objects are displayed influences the way in which people learn
concepts. First of all, the stimuli used as objects make a difference
(Archer, 1962). If stimuli are distinct from one another on some
particular feature but not terribly distinct on another feature, subjects will
not treat the features equally but will pay attention to the one that is clear
and distinct. For example, if size is used as a feature and the large objects
are very large compared with the small objects, then size will be one of
the features seized upon by subjects early in practice. If, on the other
hand, differences in size appear to be trivial, then subjects will pick some
other dimension.

The *dominance* of a feature for a particular concept will be an
important determiner of how easy it is for subjects to learn that concept
(Bourne, 1966). Dominance refers to the saliency of a feature for a
particular concept, not just the saliency of some feature in general, as in
the size example just discussed. In ordinary experience some objects are
more salient exemplars of some features than others. Underwood and
Richardson (1956) were able to demonstrate this fact by collecting some
normative data. They asked a large group of subjects to give descriptive
qualities to a list of various concepts. Some qualities are much more often
associated with some concepts than with others, even though those
qualities would apply equally well to all the concepts in question. "Milk,"
"chalk," "snow," and "teeth" are all strong exemplars, according to the
data collected by Underwood and Richardson, for the feature "white."
More than 70 percent of the subjects in this study listed white as a quality
for these concepts. On the other hand, "baseball," "fang," "paste," and

"sugar" are all unpopular exemplars for "white," though the feature of whiteness applies equally well or poorly to all of these concepts. "Sugar," of course, is preeminently "sweet," and "paste" is "sticky." Coleman (1964) was able to demonstrate that the learning of simple affirmative concepts was influenced by the dominance level of the features used to define them. There are no data on the matter, but it is very likely the case that learning more complicated concepts would likewise be influenced by the dominance level of the underlying features for the concepts in question.

As you might expect, patterns of reinforcement and varieties of information in feedback after performance influence the rate of concept attainment (see Bourne, 1966; Bourne, Ekstrand, & Dominowski, 1971). Simply exposing someone to exemplars without providing informational feedback has a relatively minor effect upon performance (Bourne, Guy, & Wadsworth, 1967). It may help subjects to identify the underlying features, but they cannot learn anything about the conceptual structure of the array of objects they inspect.

One important situation is that in which features are tied to a concept by rules that function in a probabilistic way rather than in a completely deterministic way. A concept might be defined by the conjunction of two attributes, but every now and then, simply by chance error, an experimenter may fail to indicate a conjunction of those two features as correct and may, on other occasions, indicate an object as correct even though it does not exhibit a conjunction of the two features in question. The same condition will hold in our ordinary experience in even a richer and more varied form. Not all those who teach us about the world will define a given concept in the same way. We learn to adjust to the fact that nothing is certain. Rules change and features are misidentified. The information supplied by our senses is often of dubious reliability and validity. Through all these variations, however, we must suppose that there is an underlying deterministic structure to the universe, and our task is to find it. People can learn to make appropriate inferences under conditions of probabilistic variations in concepts, but the process is a slow and difficult one (Deane, Hammond, & Summers, 1972), particularly when the features to be detected are not sharply distinct from one another but vary in some graded way.

STRATEGIES IN CONCEPT LEARNING

The most important aspect of how people learn concepts is the way in which they go about it. The problem of strategies in concept attainment has been the object of investigation since publication of the now-famous study by Bruner, Goodnow, and Austin (1956). These authors discovered the power of the selective method for finding out what kinds of strategies people employ in learning concepts. The selectional method provides data on what particular choices subjects make, and from this information it is possible to infer the hypotheses the subjects use. The relations

among the various hypotheses tell us something about the overall
strategies subjects employ. Bruner, Goodnow, and Austin used the
materials illustrated in Figure 9.2, and the concepts they asked their
subjects to learn were all conjunctive ones. Thus, their actual empirical
work is limited to conjunctive concepts. However, people in the ordinary
course of things prefer to use conjunctive concepts if at all possible, and
furthermore, there is every reason to believe that the main conclusions
reached by these investigators would have only been strengthened by an
examination of other kinds of problems. It is the case, however, that the
particular strategies employed by their subjects were constrained by the
fact that the concepts were all conjunctive.

Consider a conjunction of all green circles with two borders (imagine
that the shaded objects in Figure 9.2 are green as they were in the experiment itself). For such a concept there are 255 possible arrangements.
A first positive example eliminates 240 of the possibilities, and there is
a similar value for all positive and negative instances thereafter. A computer could keep track of all the possibilities eliminated by any given
choice and thus solve the problem in the minimum number of choices.
In short, for this problem as for others, there is a logically best strategy,
and such a strategy would, in the long run, produce the most efficient
learning. In order to solve the problem logically, however, the subjects
must remember each card and the combination of feature-states that it
contains. Furthermore, they must remember whether each object they
have tested is an example of the concept or not. These requirements produce an impossibly difficult task for human memory. A few people, mainly those with some logical training or training in computer programming, try to keep to such a strategy, but without an external record of
what has happened, they do not do very well. The logically best strategy is an efficient one for human beings only when the number of objects
is comparatively small and the concepts are limited to pairs of features.

FOCUSING

A more reasonable strategy for people is what Bruner, Goodnow, and
Austin call focusing. There are two varieties of focusing, conservative
focusing and focus gambling. In conservative focusing, the subject uses
his first success in identifying an instance of the concept as a point of
departure. He begins with a hypothesis based upon all the feature-states
contained in that object. For example, suppose that the first correct card
a subject picks is one containing three green circles and two borders. He
would then systematically test one feature at a time. He might, for
example, test the border feature and thus select a card with three green
circles and three borders. This, of course, would be a wrong choice, and
so he would know that the two-border state is critical to the concept, for
that is the only difference between his successful choice and the
subsequent unsuccessful one. The subject might then test color as the
next choice and choose a card with three circles and two borders but of a
different color. Again, he would find that he was wrong. This time he
would know that both color and borders are relevant features and that

271

CONCEPT
IDENTIFICATION
AND THE
LEARNING
OF RULES

green and two borders are critical to the concept. Next, he might choose to vary the number of circles, moving from a choice of three to a choice of one. This time he would find that his choice was still correct; consequently, he would know that the number of objects was irrelevant. After testing for shape by choosing, say, crosses instead of circles, he would know that shape was critical. With, perhaps, a few more choices to make sure, the subject would be reasonably certain that he could identify the concept.

The important property of conservative focusing is that only one feature is changed at a time. The subject, therefore, only has to remember back one choice. All his previous choices are irrelevant.

Another possible strategy is focus gambling. In focus gambling, the subject takes a chance and varies two or more attributes at a time. Given, for example, a positive choice of two green circles with two borders, the subject might guess two red circles with three borders. He would, in so doing, be changing two features, color and number of borders. If that turned out to be positive, the subject would have learned a great amount at one stroke, for he would know that number of shapes and color are both irrelevant to the concept in question. However, he would be taking a chance, and in this particular example, he would have lost. He would not have known whether it was changing the color or changing the number of borders that produced the error.

On the average, ordinary subjects do better with conservative focusing than with anything else, though nearly all subjects change their strategies from time to time. Given an initial negative choice, subjects may try focus gambling, but when they hit upon a correct choice, they settle down to conservative focusing. Any strategy, however, is under the control of the cumulation of experience that subjects have had, for such general patterns of action as strategies are subject to control by reinforcement much as are individual responses. However, those subjects who have had much good luck in early problems tend to shift from conservative focusing to focus gambling, and so it is not entirely a matter of the pattern of reinforcement of the successful strategies. Subjects assess the situation and make predictions for the future.

The superiority of focusing strategies over purely logical strategies (or no strategy at all) is greater the greater the burden upon memory and the assimilation of information. If subjects try to treat the concept-attainment experiment purely as a paired associate experiment in which they must learn, by rote, whether each stimulus is correct or not, the burden on memory would be intolerable for universes of the size used by Bruner, Goodnow, and Austin. This burden, Bruner, Goodnow, and Austin call "cognitive strain." To demonstrate the importance of cognitive strain, these investigators asked some subjects who had been working at a variety of problems using the display of objects in Figure 9.2 to solve some problems in their heads. That is to say, the subjects were exposed to the objects and then asked to solve problems without actually seeing the objects. Those subjects who were used to doing conservative focusing had an easy time of it. In general they took no more time to solve problems than when they had the display before them. Subjects who used other strategies, however, had an extremely difficult time. They had to remember not only the objects, but how they had done on all previous choices.

273

CONCEPT
IDENTIFICATION
AND THE
LEARNING
OF RULES

STRATEGIES IN RECEPTION EXPERIMENTS

Subjects do employ strategies in receptive experiments, though it is harder to determine what these strategies are. Some investigators, however, have invented a variety of techniques for inferring what strategies the subjects have in reception experiments, and to the extent that such can be managed by the subjects, they tend to be focusing strategies (Levine, 1966). The problem is that the subject must remember a great deal. One experiment (Coltheart, 1971) shows that subjects have poor recognition and recall memory for the particular objects they have seen, but they can remember reasonably well the hypotheses they have tested. This is a reflection of a sensible strategy on the part of subjects faced with the receptive paradigm. It would not be important to remember whether or not you have seen a particular exemplar before (unless you are learning by rote), but it is very sensible to remember if you have tested some particular hypothesis before. Memory for hypotheses is not perfect, but it is much better than memory for objects tested. Even in the receptive paradigm, however, subjects do seem to remember their initial object, and so there is something like a primacy effect in remembering items in a concept-learning experiment (Trabasso & Bower, 1964).

Ordinary experience is probably a mixture of the situations encountered in receptive and selectional experiments, but in the main it is probably more like the selectional case than the receptive case. Certainly, in scientific investigation, in medical diagnosis, in troubleshooting, and other such applications of problem solving, we generally can choose the things with which we test our hypotheses. However, even when we cannot, as in the pure receptive paradigm of the laboratory, we still operate with hypotheses, and we store these hypotheses in memory.

As we have already noted, it is possible to teach subjects to use a strategy based upon truth tables, and indeed, they learn to use such a strategy out of their own experience when relevant. Such a strategy is relevant when subjects must learn concepts formed by using a variety of rules. It would not be terribly profitable for situations in which subjects know beforehand the nature of the rule connecting features, but it does occur, even in the receptive paradigm if it is necessary and success at problem solving has shaped such a strategy.

One final note: Strategies do not characterize the totality of the approach subjects take to the problem of learning concepts. Sometimes, people deliberately change strategies as a strategy in itself. As Heidbreder (1947) noted, subjects sometimes adopt a passive attitude and simply watch the instances go by, giving responses more or less randomly while they take in the situation. In terms of a distinction made earlier in the chapter, strategies are heuristic rather than algorithmic in practice, although it is quite possible to state a given strategy as an algo-rithmic rule. People try them out, and if they work they stick with them.

The problem of discovering what strategies people use is complicated by the fact that people do not always know what they are doing, or at least they find it difficult to put into words a description of the procedures by which they solved some problem. Research on the psychology of thinking has been plagued with this problem. In studies of concept learning, we usually infer strategies from the choices subjects make, just as we infer their knowledge of the concept from their performance. For most subjects we use performance rather than explanations as a criterion of solution. Highly practiced subjects and subjects deliberately trained for the purpose, of course, can give detailed accounts of the hypotheses and concepts they use as well as provide logically clear and correct descrip-tions of the concepts they indicate through their choice of exemplars. Even here, however, there are problems. One of them is that subjects must use language to describe or explain their concepts. Descriptions reflect not only the linguistic skills of the subjects but the peculiar features of a given language and languages in general. In short, we may use the information subjects supply us from their introspections during problem solving, but when that information appears to be in conflict with other information, we are more likely to accept the other information.

THEORIES OF CONCEPT LEARNING

Associative Theories

The early theories invented to account for the performance of individuals in concept-learning experiments were all based upon the idea that learning occurred through association. These theories described concept learning as a process of association of responses emitted during learning and the instances which defined the concepts. In short, concept learning was no different from any other elementary process of learning. It was merely that concept learning was built upon a background of experience.

Theories which describe concept learning this way are now regarded as being too limited to describe the rich range of facts available to us; but aspects of these theories apply to certain situations, and other aspects of them appear in more recent theories. Furthermore, the particular failures of these theories tell us something about the important aspects of learning concepts. Therefore, there is ample justification for reviewing them.

OLDER THEORIES

Associative theories of concept learning are of two kinds (Bourne, Ekstrand, & Dominowski, 1971). The older variety of theories were based upon the principle that the entire complex of the stimulus provided by each object was associated with the response emitted to that stimulus. This principle had its experimental roots in the fact that all components of compound conditioned stimuli seem to be associated with the condi-

tioned response (Chapter 8). It creates a complication, however, for all
positive instances of a concept will differ from one another in some
details. For each instance of the concept some feature will be irrelevant,
and the irrelevant features will vary from instance to instance. In short,
the stimulus changes in an irregular and essentially unpredictable way.
This, in fact, defines the principal difference in actual practice between
concept learning and learning of a simpler sort.

275

CONCEPT
IDENTIFICATION
AND THE
LEARNING
OF RULES

The problem of the variation in stimuli associated with the correct
response is readily solved by invoking the principle of stimulus generalization. However much the positive instances differ among themselves,
they will, in the long run, be more like one another than they will be like
the negative instances. Furthermore, the more irrelevant features there
are, the slower one would expect learning to be. This is because stimulus
generalization would be less from one example to another than when
there are fewer irrelevant features. That is the case in actual experiments
(Archer, Bourne, & Brown, 1955). The result of applying the notion of
stimulus generalization is to reduce concept learning to a kind of
discrimination learning in which generalization associated with reinforcement gradually increases the probability of the correct responses
being associated with positive instances. Theories of discrimination
learning were reviewed in Chapter 8, and we shall not repeat them here.
Suffice it to say that such theories apply in certain situations, particularly
those situations in which "concepts" are heavily influenced by good
perceptual organization. Well-organized stimuli do function as un-
analyzed wholes, and to the extent that the principle of association is
appropriate, association to all aspects of the stimulus will occur. There is,
then, a genuine continuity between discrimination learning and concept
learning.

NEWER THEORIES

The newer associative theories of concept learning differ from the older
ones in that the association between stimulus and response does not
occur to all components of the stimulus. It is rather the features provided
by successive instances that are associated with responses. Responses to
the relevant features are reinforced and those to the irrelevant features
are extinguished during learning. The major difference in shifting the
process of association from the entire stimulus to features is that it allows
systematic variation from trial to trial in the particular feature that is the
focus of attention. In fact, such theories of concept learning are regarded
as theories about attentional processes in learning.

The earliest version of such a theory is by Restle (1962), and
successive versions by Restle and others have appeared regularly.
Perhaps the most definitive form of such a theory is that provided by
Trabasso and Bower (1968). In this version of the theory, as well as in
others, features are associated with appropriate response categories.
Irrelevant features are associated with whatever response is appropriate
to negative instances, and relevant features are associated with the
responses to positive instances. The association of features with respon-

ses is independent and additive, though provision is made in the version of the theory by Trabasso and Bower for the possibility that some features will be more salient than others.

The essential characteristic of the theory is that learning is by an all-or-none process (p. 25). Conditioning of a given attribute is all or none and is accomplished on a single trial. Learning can occur only on those trials in which subjects make errors, for the correct response provides no opportunity for the elimination of irrelevant features. Generally, the details of the theory are designed to explain the distribution of choices and the rate of learning in the learning of a particular kind of concept. It is what Trabasso and Bower call the "redundant relevant cue problem." In this terminology, features are cues. In all the problems Trabasso and Bower investigated, the relevant features were correlated with one another, and the concepts were defined by conjunctive rules. The correlation of features makes the problems identical to the compound stimulus problems in discrimination learning, and this fact emphasizes the continuity between discrimination learning and concept learning. Discrimination learning can be regarded as the special case of concept learning in which features are correlated and in which conjunctive rules are always applied. Correlated features always reduce the total population of objects. If, for example, a concept is defined by black circles and the features of color and shape are correlated, there will be no black squares and no white circles in the universe of instances.

Given this somewhat restricted situation, Trabasso and Bower were able to make some accurate predictions of the results of certain experiments in which adult subjects learned concepts formed from stimuli like those in Figure 9.1 or Figure 9.2. They were able, for example, to predict the effects of testing with only one component of the stimuli associated with the concept. However striking their predictions, the situation is a limited if not unusual one, and the theory makes a number of assumptions which are highly suspect. Some of the assumptions, in fact, are in outright contradiction to empirical data. For example, Trabasso and Bower assume that subjects remember instances for only one trial back (in Restle's original version of the theory, the subject was allowed no memory for previous trials at all). We know that subjects do remember more than this, at least on occasion. Furthermore, the assumption that no learning occurs on correct trials appears to be incorrect (Levine, 1966).

It is not surprising, therefore, that these theories have limited utility. They do serve to show that it is at least feasible to suppose that simple associative processes apply to the learning of conjunctive concepts, but they ignore the more difficult kinds of concepts which human subjects can learn. These theories may well apply to the kind of learning that lies on the borderline between discrimination learning and concept learning, but since these theories ignore the rule structure of concepts, they cannot apply to the full range of concept-learning experiments without considerable modification.

The study of artificial intelligence is another source of theories about concept learning. Artificial intelligence means the study of the intellectual capabilities of computers. Computers can be programmed to mimic the intellectual functions of human beings, and so the study of human functions is one aspect of artificial intelligence. It is not that computers "think like people," but it is possible to program digital computers to do some of the things people do. The significance of so doing lies in the fact that we must at least know what is required of human intelligence when we program a machine to duplicate it. This helps us make explicit our knowledge of the abilities which are the basis of human thinking and perception.

Almost every intellectual function that human beings can perform has been the subject of one or more computer programs. Human visual perception, in the form of pattern recognition, has been one of the most frequently studied problems (Selfridge & Neisser, 1960). There are programs that mimic the human use and understanding of language (Winograd, 1972), and there is even something called the "general problem solver" (Newell & Simon, 1972). All these programs for simulating aspects of human intelligence require some of the aspects of concept learning that we have discussed thus far. Pattern-recognition devices, for example, require feature analysis. A program for the understanding of human learning must make use of something like a truth table, in much the way truth tables are used in concept-learning experiments. However, rather than examine these more specialized problems, we shall look at programs specifically aimed at producing concept learning in machines.

INFORMATION PROCESSING

The earliest efforts to produce programs that will allow machines to learn concepts are those of Hovland (1952), Hovland and Hunt (1960), and Hunt (1962). The Hovland and Hunt models have generally been called information processing models of concept learning.

Information processing models require three phases: perception, definition of positive instances, and development of a decision tree. Perception means simply the identification of features. In concept-learning models this stage can be made quite simple, though any attempt to simulate the way human beings do it would require much more sophisticated treatment than is generally found in concept-learning models. The critical matter in concept-learning programs is the development of a method for discovering concepts. Hunt characterizes this activity as the selection of positive instances. Hunt built into one version of his computer program for learning concepts a strategy for the selection of positive instances that is essentially a focusing strategy. Selecting positive instances, however, does not define the concept based upon them. Therefore, some procedure must be included which serves to define concepts. This procedure Hunt called developing a decision tree. A decision tree can be characterized as a plan for or description of a sequence of decisions. For example, a subject may first ask, "Is the concept a triangle or a square?" He may then ask, "Is it red or green?" He will move through all possible choices of features until a decision is reached which uniquely sorts all objects in the universe. A real subject may not go all the way through such a tree but may jump to some conclusions.

MACHINE INDUCTION

Concept learning describes a process of induction. The learner acquires some information about the structure of the world through experience. Hunt, Marin, and Stone (1966) made explicit this parallel between induction and concept learning by developing a program which duplicates a concept-learning experiment. Here are the steps for an experiment using a reception paradigm:

1. A sample of objects is selected from the universe by some random procedure. The sample is arbitrarily ordered for presentation to the subject (which in this instance is a computer).
2. The first object is perceived and remembered by the learner.
3. The learner uses the information in its memory (including memory based on step 2) to compute a possible concept.
4. The next object is presented to the learner.
5. The possible concept generated in step 3 is used to classify the new object.
6. If the classification is correct, the system returns to step 4 for presentation of a new object. If the classification is incorrect, the learner returns to step 3.
7. The experiment stops when there are no more objects to be classified.

A program developed in this way will be able to learn concepts. If the experimental paradigm is selective rather than receptive, a slightly more complicated sequence is required in order to provide the opportunity for the learner to choose successive objects based upon some hypothesis being operated upon at the moment.

Such a program learns complex concepts much more rapidly than human subjects do under comparable conditions. Therefore, it is probable that the program does not operate precisely in the way a human being does. One reason why it may not is because the program has too good a memory. It remembers all possible objects and all the hypotheses evaluated up to any given point. Human beings usually do not remember this much. Consequently, Hunt, Marin, and Stone considered programs with less than perfect memories. In one of their programs, for example, each time a new object is presented, the memory for an old one, chosen at random, is erased. This, of course, is not the way human memory operates, but it is closer to human memory than the perfect memory of the program outlined above. Consequently, it is not surprising that it produces data more like those found with human learners. A more complex system explored by Hunt, Marin, and Stone stores positive and negative instances separately. The same rule of erasing memory for an old object at random applies when a new one appears. Because, for many concepts, positive instances will be far less common than negative instances, there will be less turnover in the memory for positive instances, a condition which is probably more like that in human memory. We are more likely to remember those things that exemplify a concept we are trying to learn than those things that do not.

The rules introduced into the program generally are algorithmic. They are designed to produce specific outcomes. The program, because it is entirely algorithmic, is awkward. What the computer needs is some criterion for selecting objects to be tested and for varying hypotheses to be considered. One possibility would be to give the computer some heuristic rule to tell it to test items similar to those which previously produced errors. However, in general, these programs do miss the flexibility of human thinking, largely because it is extremely difficult to be explicit about these kinds of rules.

279

CONCEPT
IDENTIFICATION
AND THE
LEARNING
OF RULES

An Eclectic View

Human beings are capable of operating as purely associative devices or as truth-table testing devices, as the occasion and conditions demand. In short, no single process describes the superficial characteristics of the way in which human beings learn concepts. It is possible that some very general process may be able to encompass all the information we have about the ways in which people *can* acquire concepts, but at present we have no single view which does justice to all the facts of concept learning. Bourne's (1970) hierarchical description of the development of skill at concept learning reflects the fact that some processes depend upon others. People must be able to extract features from objects before they can learn class concepts. The formation of class concepts leads to the explicit development of rules. And rules, when organized in some very efficient and abstract way, become a logical system. Within the confines of the laboratory and with laboratory materials, as Bourne demonstrates, it is possible to illustrate this progression.

There are, furthermore, problems associated with the variety of forms real concepts take. Real concepts have more variable structures than most of the concepts studied in the laboratory. Approximations to socially defined concepts will often do as well at a certain stage as the entirely correct conceptual structure. For example, the morphological rules of language (those governing past-tense verbs in English, for example) are learned in a hierarchical fashion. Children learn the lower-order (conditional) rules first, and they generalize these rules to exceptions (strong or irregular verbs). Later they learn rules governing the exceptions, rules which will take complex conditional and disjunctive forms. Initially, before children learn any rules at all, they may do very well with strong verbs in English, because these occur very frequently. They will, however, lose their facility with these verbs (perhaps originally learned by association) when they begin to acquire the rules governing the regular forms. An experiment by Palermo and Eberhart (1968) shows that this is not simply an outcome of the developmental sequence children must go through. Adults learning a laboratory concept of the same structure show the same overgeneralization of the regular rule, a result that retards the learning of the irregular forms or the exceptions.

Perhaps one of the most persistent problems in understanding human concept learning is the rule of human memory as a limiting factor. The strategies people adopt and other aspects of their approaches to the learning of conceptual structures appear to be determined by human limitations of memory. These are both limitations in short-term memory and limitations due to long-term forgetting. These conditions, more than anything else we know about, appear to make the correspondence between machine-based problem solving and human problem solving less than perfect. As we have seen, some computer models of human concept learning attempt to mimic human limitations of memory, but the fact is that we do not know well enough how human memory operates to make these simulations very convincing. Concept learning is complicated. It depends upon memory and limitations of memory, associations, associative structures, the knowledge of and ability to use particular strategies, and both implicit and explicit knowledge of logical structures.

TEN

LANGUAGE AND LANGUAGE LEARNING

There are few things more important that people learn than language. The whole of human culture depends upon learning to speak and understand language. There are no cultures, no matter how primitive, that do not possess a highly developed and sophisticated means of communicating. Those persons who, for one reason or another, are handicapped in the use of language always require special care and extraordinary treatment in order to survive in any human society. For these reasons alone, then, no account of the psychology of learning applied to the human species is complete without a detailed account of how human beings acquire their languages. The next two chapters are devoted to this question. This chapter examines the nature of language itself and presents those features of learning peculiar to language, while the following chapter gives an account of some of the special techniques for investigating the learning of verbal materials in the laboratory. This chapter contains an introduction to linguistic theory and some psychological data on the learning of language, while the next chapter concentrates on the methods and results of the verbal learning laboratory.

Human languages have some special properties, and these are responsible for some problems unique to the learning of language. Some contemporary theorists have argued that almost none of the basic principles of elementary learning apply to the learning of language (see McNeill, 1970). This is not the case, as we shall see, but it certainly is the case that learning a language raises some questions not generally discussed as part of the general principles of learning. When we talk about learning in general, we are seldom concerned with the peculiar features of particular skills or particular responses under consideration. There are surely important differences in the way in which pigeons learn to peck at keys and rats learn to press levers, but these differences are almost entirely irrelevant to the general *principles* of learning. The same laws of reinforcement scheduling apply to both, for example. However, everywhere in the learning of language, the special properties of human languages intrude themselves. The nature of speech, for instance, creates a fundamental problem which tells us right away that we are dealing with a peculiar set of stimuli for which special rules of learning must apply. We hear speech as a succession of separate sounds, sounds that we can transcribe into the discrete symbols of the alphabet. Yet speech itself is a continuous stream of noise, and what is more, those features that identify a particular sound and thus enable us to write it as a particular letter are often part of the physical stimulus associated with the preceding or following sound. This makes the identification of speech sounds almost hopelessly complex. It means that the "same" speech sounds are never really the same on two successive occasions—they depend upon what particular sounds precede and follow them, and they vary, depending upon the idiosyncratic characteristics of speakers and occasions. Thus, the simple principles of discrimination learning can supply only a very small part of the answer to the question of how children come to identify the sounds of the language they speak. Such principles are more easily applied to the learning of the more or less arbitrary code for those speech sounds, the alphabet.

In fact, the question of the complexity of speech identification as well as the peculiar features of the grammars of human language have led some students of language to the view that the most essential aspects of what we know about language are given to us by characteristics innate in the human species (see Chomsky, 1968). The metaphor that has sometimes been used to describe the child learning a language is to portray him as a linguist or cryptographer deducing a code—the language his parents and other adults speak—from some principles he has available simply from the maturation of his brain. The notion that language is innate in the human species is an old one, but recent theories in linguistics and psycholinguistics have revived interest in it. Consequently, our discussion of the acquisition of language will be intertwined with various ideas about what it is about the human capacity for language that is prior to and necessary for the learning of human languages.

Although it is tangential to our main interest, the fact that language seems to have such unique properties leads us to say a word about the physical structures associated with the competence for language. There is very strong evidence, extending all the way back to the middle of the nineteenth century, to show that much of the competence in the use of language centers in structures located in the left cerebral hemispheres of most human beings. We say most human beings because a minority of people may well have their competence for language primarily centered in the right cerebral hemisphere. These are individuals who are genetically left-handed. The fact that not all human beings are bilaterally asymmetrical in linguistic function in precisely the same way suggests that there is a period in our lives during which the brain is plastic in linguistic function. The asymmetry that results from this plastic period is part of the acquisition process of language itself. Lenneberg (1967) has presented a thorough account of the evidence for such a view of the nature of the biology of language.

Finally, we must remind ourselves that language and thought in the human being are almost inextricably intertwined. This fact has given rise to the ancient question of whether or not the special properties of human thought are the result of or are dependent in some way upon language.

Again, this is a question beyond the scope of this book, but certain facts relating to the question are of significance to the learning of language. The evidence on how we learn rules and attain concepts, which we reviewed in the last chapter, shows us that the understanding of concepts is not totally dependent upon language, for we can sometimes demonstrate conceptual knowledge that we cannot make explicit in language. However, to the extent that thought is expressed in language, it is at the mercy of the special features of language. Most of our thinking does end up either being expressed in language or being performed in some particular language, and it must surely be the case that the peculiar features of particular languages have deep and ineradicable influences upon thinking. All these concerns mean that we must, in any account of the basic principles of learning intended to apply to human beings, give an account of the nature of language.

THE NATURE OF LANGUAGE

Language serves two functions for people. It allows us to communicate with one another, and it provides some machinery for thinking. Not only does it supply us with the tools for thought, but it provides us with a method of ordering our ideas in such a way as to enable us to test their truth value. We can compare our ideas with the state of the world and determine whether the world and our ideas agree. We can also compare our ideas among themselves and determine whether or not they contradict one another. These activities are expressed in language.

The communicative function of language is not unique to the human species. Throughout the animal world, noises provide the most widely used means by which one member of a species communicates with others of the same species. However, animal communication, so far as we know, is radically different in principle from human communication in a most important respect. There is no animal language, so far as anyone really knows, that permits the expression of an infinite number of propositions with but a small collection of finite elements (the speech sounds mentioned earlier). This principle—that we can express an infinity of ideas with finite means—has been the foundation of nearly all serious thought about human language, and it is one that we must keep in mind if we are not to fall into a too-facile comparison of human communication with animal communication.

Human languages are capable of expressing ideas. By that statement we mean to point out that they can express logical relations and implications, and provide the vehicle for the expression of judgments about logical relations and the world. The languages of animals do not permit the expression of logical implications in the most general sense. It is very possible that animals with highly developed central nervous systems, such as the great apes, may be able to draw logical inferences of a sort, but they cannot express those inferences by the communicative acts characteristic of their species. In short, animal languages consist of signals, not symbols. The signals serve to arouse particular reactions in other organisms. Human communications are sometimes intended to create particular reactions, but more generally they are intended to communicate ideas. Human language, as Chomsky has so often pointed out, is creative. We can, in the next breath, express an idea that has never been said before. The creation of new signals in the animal world must be rare indeed.

Human beings, of course, use signals as well as symbols. Particular tones of voice, facial expressions, crying, laughing—all have communicative functions. These signals are partly learned and partly determined by species-specific characteristics. Purely arbitrary human signals are possible, and we can teach animals such signals through instrumental conditioning. But such signals are not part of that essential component of human language that permits the expression of an indefinite number of propositions by the use of a finite set of elements.

It is possible that animals may be capable of using the basic principles of human language. There have been, over the years, a number of experiments aimed at teaching chimpanzees to use human language. Most of these have completely failed, but several more recent attempts may be closer to success (Gardner & Gardner, 1969; Premack, 1971). These more recent studies have not attempted to teach chimpanzees human speech but, rather, have attempted to teach them some other system of symbols which embodies the same abstract rules as does human speech. We shall have occasion to comment on these studies later in this chapter.

It is possible that we do not need the special properties of speech in order to communicate with one another, as the experiments with chimpanzees suggest. But we do need some sort of abstract system that embodies a set of rules or principles. In this sense, the fundamental characteristic of human language is not that it is composed of speech sounds, but that it is a system of communication regulated by rules. Rules are expressed in the grammars of various languages. Therefore, if we want to get to the heart of the nature of language, we must turn to a study of grammar.

Grammar

In the most general sense the grammar of a language is a set of rules for combining elements in such a way as to make intelligible sentences. For the grammars of human languages, the elements are, at various levels, speech sounds, words, and phrases. The learning of the grammar of a language is the learning of how speech sounds, words, and phrases are combined in that language to form sentences. The rules of human languages are special in many ways, or else we would have treated the problem of learning grammatical rules in the last chapter, where we considered general questions about the learning of rules.

The basic elements of human languages are speech sounds. As babies, we have the problem of learning to differentiate one sound of the language spoken by the adults around us from another. We also must learn to combine these sounds to make and understand sensible sentences. It cannot be just a matter of some simple discrimination learning and the chaining together of some responses, though some behavioristic analyses of language learning have assumed that is all there is to the learning of language (Staats, 1971). One of the difficulties with such a view is that learning a language is not a matter of learning to put stimuli and responses together. For one thing, the elements of human languages that we ordinarily think about when we think about language—the speech sounds and the words—are not the only ones. There are other elements of language that are not themselves responses in the ordinary use of language, elements such as phrases, sentences, and such relational notions as subject, predicate, and proposition. These abstract notions, as linguists remind us (see Bever, Fodor, & Garrett, 1968) are not responses, nor do they appear in theories of conditioning and simple learning, yet they are absolutely essential to an understanding of how we learn to use language. It will not do to say that a child learning a language is only learning to combine words into such chains, typical of the language of small children (see McNeill, 1970), as "bye-bye Daddy," "more milk," "big dog," "no bed." The child must also be learning, while he is exhibiting his use of such combinations, abstract notions and relations such as subject, predicate, verbs, nouns, parts of sentences that express the agentival role, parts that are recipients of action, and a host of other subtle principles. In short, the child learns not only what linguists call a "terminal vocabulary" (the words of the language he speaks), but he also learns a set of grammatical principles. He cannot, of course, make these principles explicit. In fact, since linguistic theory itself is incomplete, no one at present can make all of these principles completely explicit in a satisfactory way. But the very fact that children learn to form sentences shows that they know these principles implicitly.

There are many ways to express the fundamental principles of the grammars of human languages, and linguists are by no means agreed upon the best way (see Steinberg & Jakobovits, 1971). The best we can do at present is point to those kinds of rules which express the competence people have to use language and to eliminate those kinds of rules which are of limited utility in understanding human languages. People learn in a variety of ways. We saw in the last chapter that some very respectable theories about some kinds of learning will not describe the competence people have for learning to use logical rules in general. Much the same is true of the competence people have for language, and one of the major purposes of this section is to point out those kinds of rules that best express what people know, implicitly or explicitly, about the rules of the language they speak.

One word about the most fundamental concept in language, that of "sentence." So far as linguistic theory is concerned, the basic element in human languages is the sentence or, more accurately, the proposition or structure underlying simple sentences. The rules of grammar of a particular language are the rules for composing all the sentences that could conceivably be said in that language. Since the number of sentences that can be said in any language is infinite, the rules of grammar must describe an infinite set of objects. The rules themselves should be finite, however. The automatic application of the rules of a completely adequate grammar for a given language should generate nothing but sentences which would make sense in that language. Sentences that do not make sense or sentences that are just jumbles of words should never be produced by the application of linguistic rules if they are the correct ones. Such a grammar of sentences must have three components. It must have a phonological component. This is the part that expresses the rules for producing and combining sounds. It must have a component that arranges the grammatical elements in the correct way and allows for proper modification of these. This is the grammatical part. The grammar, in turn, consists of syntax, which is concerned with the arrangement of words, and morphology, which is concerned with how words are modified. The final part consists of rules for assigning correct semantic interpretations. There is some question about how much such rules for assigning correct semantic interpretations are linguistic in nature. Semantic interpretation depends in part upon linguistic knowledge, but it also depends upon knowledge of the world and knowledge of logic. In fact, we could regard much of the material in the preceding chapter on how people learn concepts as the study of the learning of a kind of semantic component of language. In any event, most of what we will have to say about grammar will be about how people come to acquire an implicit knowledge of grammar—that is to say, of syntactic and morphological rules. We shall comment on seman-tic aspects of language later.

Syntax has received more attention in modern linguistics than mor-phology. While more recent accounts of grammatical theory have made syntax less important, the effect of the early prominence of syntactic studies remains. As a result, much of the experimental work on the learning of grammar centers on rules of syntax: how to arrange elements so as to have them make sense. The sentence "Jack and Jill went up the hill" is easily distinguished from the nonsense string "and went Jack hill Jill the up." One string obeys the rules of English syntax, the other does not, and all speakers of English, even very young ones, recognize that. In the section that follows we shall examine some approaches to the study of syntax and how it is learned.

FINITE-STATE RULES

The simplest kind of grammar that can form strings of words by the application of some rules is a finite-state grammar. A finite-state grammar is one in which the state of the system at the moment limits the possible options for the next state of the system. Translated into the problem of determining how strings of words go together, it means that the choice of one word invokes a rule that determines the choice of the next. In order to generate a sentence by finite-state rules, we start with some initial state. It tells us which word to select first. That word, in turn, tells us what options are open to us, having made this selection. For example, if the first word chosen is the English article *the*, we would have the option of following it with all English nouns (except some proper ones), adjectives, quantifiers, and some others. However, verbs and conjunctions would not be allowed. Thus, by finite-state rules, sentences unfold from left to right, from beginning to end, just as we say them. Hence there is a certain kind of appeal to the application of a finite-state grammar to language. Finite-state grammars generate Markov chains. We have already seen that some elementary theories of learning conceive of human learning as being produced by all-or-none processes (Chapter 1). These are varieties of Markov processes.

Figure 10.1 illustrates the application of a finite-state grammar to a miniature artificial language (Miller, 1958). This language contains only the words S, N, X, and G. All sentences must start with S or N, for they are the only paths (as the choices allowed in a finite-state grammar are sometimes called) that lead from the initial state 0. If N is chosen, it leads to state 1; if S is chosen, it leads to state 3. The options from state 1 permit us to go to state 0' or to state 3. If we go to state 0', we must select G and end the sentence, since the only transition allowed from state 0' is "finish." The choice of state 3 leads either to S (which leads to state 2) or to X (which loops back to state 3).

There are some obvious features of all the strings (sentences) that can be generated by this miniature grammar. All sentences must begin with N or S and end with G. Sentences can be infinitely long because of the recursive loop at state 3 and because it is possible to loop indefinitely through 1, 3, 2. Some of the possible sentences generated by this grammar are listed in Table 10.1 together with some purely random strings composed of the same four letters. The random strings appear to the naked eye to be much like the strings generated by the grammar (labeled as redundant strings in Table 10.1). They are not, however. They were constructed by choosing the letters, one at a time, with the help of a table of random numbers. The only rule imposed on the random strings is that each one had to be the same length as one of the finite-state–generated strings.

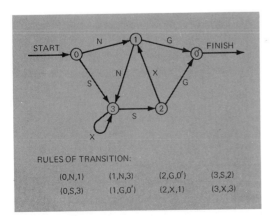

Figure 10.1
Diagram of a finite-state generator. A string is any sequence of letters generated by starting at state 0 and finishing at 0'. A letter is added to the string by taking the path labeled by that letter from one state to another. (Miller, 1958, p. 486.)

The reason for presenting this example at such length is because the strings in Table 10.1 were used in an experiment which compared the ability of adult subjects to learn the redundant and the random strings. The strings were arranged in lists. That is why the first column of redundant strings is labeled L_1 and the second L_2. The subjects in this experiment learned to recall nine strings in each list by first looking at each string separately and then trying to write down all the strings. One glance through the list and an attempt to recall it constituted one trial. The subjects studied the lists for 10 trials or until they could correctly reproduce all nine strings of either random or redundant strings. The results are shown in Figure 10.2 (Miller, 1958).

The results are clear. There is a large difference in the rate at which the redundant and random strings were learned. In short, the subjects in this experiment told us that they could, in their performance, detect the difference between random strings and the rule-generated strings. It is too bad, in a way, that this experiment did not require the subjects who studied the redundant strings to generate additional ones like the ones they had learned. If this had been done, the experiment would have been a kind of concept-learning experiment. Undoubtedly it would have taken much more practice with, in all probability, more strings, to make it possible for the subjects to correctly generate other possible sentences in the language underlying the redundant strings. In any event, the simple results achieved do tell us that subjects are able to detect structures generated by finite-state grammars.

However, for a variety of reasons, most linguists and psychologists find it difficult to believe that real languages are built on the principle of finite-state generators. There was a time, in the early 1950s, when people thought this might be the case. This was largely the result of the introduction of information theory to psychologists and the application of Markov processes to the analysis of learning generally. However, it is

Table 10.1
Lists of redundant and random strings used in an experiment on the learning of structure
(From Miller, 1958, p. 487)

STRUCTURED (REDUNDANT)		RANDOM	
L_1	L_2	R_1	R_2
SSXG	NNSG	GNSX	NXGS
NNXSG	NNSXG	NSGXN	GNXSG
SXSXG	SXXSG	XGSSN	SXNGG
SSXNSG	NNXSXG	SXNNGN	GGSNXG
SXXXSG	NNXXSG	XGSXXS	NSGNGX
NNSXNSG	NNXXSXG	GSXXGNS	NGSXXNS
SXSXNSG	NNXXXSG	NSXXGSG	NGXXGGN
SXXXSXG	SSXNSXG	SGXGGNN	SXGXGNS
SXXXXSG	SSXNXSG	XXGNSGG	XGSNGXG

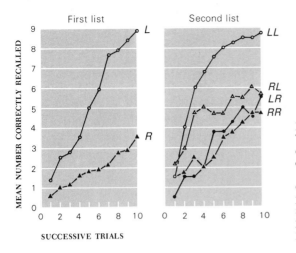

Figure 10.2
The mean number of letters correctly recalled in free recall of random (R) and redundant (L) lists of letters. Notice that on the second list, those exposed to L lists at first performed better than those exposed to R lists. (Miller, 1958, p. 487.)

very implausible that natural human languages really are based upon finite-state rules. For one thing, certain kinds of grammatical constructions that occur in many languages could not be generated by finite-state rules. These are, in general, constructions which allow an unlimited number of embedded phrases to occur within other phrases. Chomsky (1957) used this fact as the principal formal reason why finite-state grammars would not work for real languages. However, such structures are rare in practice, and it is even possible that a theory of grammar could be constructed that would account for sentences in real languages without assuming infinite embedding.

A more commonsense objection to finite-state grammars is that they do not accord with any sensible view of human knowledge and how we construct sentences to communicate that knowledge. Some of the time at least, we must know what we are going to say before we begin a sentence. Finite-state grammars imply that we choose one word and then let that choice determine where we go next. We may well do that when we are merely letting our voices run on while we stall for time, but when we are trying to communicate ideas, it is hard to see how the logical propositions behind sentences we speak could be imposed upon a finite-state generating device. Most of the time, when we are speaking in order to communicate something to someone else or even when we are thinking to ourselves, we must have some general idea where our sentences are going. The end of a sentence may be just as important in the formation of the total structure of the sentence as the beginning.

Therefore, despite the fact that people are able to appreciate the structure of finite-state strings and may even occasionally themselves act as finite-state generators, finite-state rules are not the rules by which we construct and understand sentences in natural languages. No student of the way in which children learn their first language has thought to do experiments based on finite-state rules for the good reason that no one thinks that is the way in which children learn languages.

A radically different kind of grammar is one which Chomsky (1957) called phrase-structure grammar. It is a grammar of a completely different sort. The device that generates sentences in a phrase-structure grammar can be described by a tree. Such a tree is generated by a series of rules that moves from the most general set of elements to the most specific. A tree diagram for a simple phrase-structure grammar is presented in Figure 10.3. This time, because phrase-structure grammars naturally appear to be appropriate as the grammars for real languages, we can allow the rules to generate a possible sentence in English. The rules implied by the tree in Figure 10.3 will generate only a tiny number of correct English sentences (and, unfortunately, some incorrect ones), but it does illustrate the point of phrase-structure grammars.

In phrase-structure grammars, instead of states we have nodes. Nodes have branches coming from them, and these lead to other nodes. Thus the node in Figure 10.3 labeled S (for sentence) leads to a node labeled SU (for subject) and to a node labeled P (for predicate). In a realistic grammar we would probably have a separate node for the verb, but here we have put the verb as a node under P along with another node labeled O (for object). SU and P are alike in that they both lead to nodes labeled A (for article) and N (for noun). We could then add a vocabulary to this structure to make it possible to produce sentences in English. For example, we might designate the articles as *a* and *the*, while *boy, cat, dog,* and *ball* would serve as nouns. We might well allow only one verb, say, *chases*. The grammar would then generate such sensible sentences as "The boy chases the ball" and "The dog chases a cat." Unfortunately, this syntactic grammar coupled with the vocabulary in the simple way outlined above would also produce such curious sentences as "A ball chased the cat."

A tree, such as that in Figure 10.3, generates a phrase marker. For more complicated sentences, one would need a different tree, and hence a different phrase marker. The sentence "The boy throws the ball to the

Figure 10.3
A tree diagram generating a simple English sentence according to phrase-structure rules.

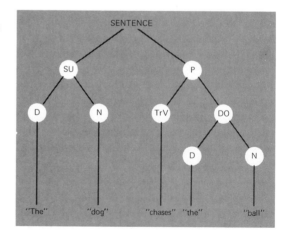

dog" would require a more elaborate phrase marker in order to accommodate the prepositional phrase "to the dog." That reveals one of the problems with a pure phrase-structure grammar. Every different sentence type would require a new tree or a new phrase marker. There are too many different kinds of sentences in any language to permit a phrase-structure grammar to be an efficient way of describing the syntax of a language. However, it is possible to supplement phrase-structure rules in various ways, and Chomsky (1965) has argued that there is a small set of phrase markers at the base of all languages. The more complicated forms of sentences actually spoken are derived, in this theory, from what Chomsky calls transformational rules.

There are, however, good reasons for believing that something like the rules of a phrase-structure grammar are implicitly understood by human users of a language and that they are reflected in the way in which people think about languages. We shall point to many pieces of evidence on that score in the pages to come. However, since we have just considered an experiment describing the fact that people can use the informational structure produced by a finite-state grammar, we would do well to examine the results of an experiment that investigates the differences between learning based upon phrase-structure rules and learning based upon finite-state rules for the same set of materials.

This is not difficult to do, for the fact is that, for the generation and description of sentences, phrase-structure rules or finite-state rules will do indifferently well. As long as the set of sentences is limited in number, it can be produced by applying either phrase-structure rules or finite-state rules. In short, these kinds of grammars can produce identical strings. There are, however, whole classes of sentences which phrase-structure grammars can produce but finite-state grammars cannot. For many cases, including most sentences in ordinary language, either will do. How is it possible, then, to determine whether subjects are using phrase-structure rules or finite-state rules to learn or to understand patterns that could be generated by either? Strictly speaking, there is no way to produce direct evidence regarding which kind of rule might be employed by human subjects, but an experiment by Saporta, Blumenthal, and Reiff (1963) provides some indirect evidence that phrase-structure rules produce more rapid learning.

The phrase-structure rules for the strings in Table 10.1 would divide each string into two or more phrases, and each phrase would have to obey the same rule. For example, we could say that the initial phrase can be N, GN, or NN, but never G alone, and never NS. Such rules would result in the patterns found in the second column of Table 10.2. The difference between the first column and the second column of Table 10.2 is only in the introduction of spaces to mark the phrases that could generate the strings. Otherwise, the finite-state column and the phrase-structure column are identical. Subjects in this experiment practiced the nine sentences without the phrase-marking spaces or the nine sentences with the phrase-marking spaces. Figure 10.4 shows the results. Initially, there is not a big difference between the condition which shows the phrase divisions to the subjects and the condition which does not, but after a few trials there is a sudden increase in the number of correct responses given by the subjects shown the correct phrase divisions. Notice that the learning is slow compared with the data presented in Figure 10.2, and there is little difference between the random and the finite-state conditions. That is because (1) a different method of practice was used and (2) "random" means something different in this experiment than it did in the previous one. Random in this experiment refers to random placement of the spaces rather than to the random selection of letters in the string. The strings are actually identical to those in the finite-state and phrase-structure conditions.

ADDITIONAL LINGUISTIC RULES

Linguists generally view it as an impossibility to write a grammar of a language solely by expanding phrase-structure rules. Various alternatives are possible. One is to supplement phrase-structure rules by transformational rules. That is what Chomsky (1957, 1965) proposes. Transformational rules, like phrase-structure rules, are instructions to rewrite a particular symbol as some other symbol or symbols.

Transformational rules cannot be represented in simple trees as phrase-structure rules can because they depend upon the context in which they occur. They are contingent rules. A transformational rule asserts that some symbol may be rewritten as one or more other symbols *only* under conditions imposed by the presence of certain other symbols. In general, transformational rules rearrange elements derived from phrase-structure trees and provide formal means for introducing the actual words used in sentences. They vastly expand the possibilities of producing sentences and enable linguists to simplify the grammars they write for particular languages.

Other linguists, however, regard the syntactically based grammar advocated by Chomsky as artificial and perhaps even unworkable. A number of linguists have favored grammars which generate or explain the syntax and morphology of a language entirely by semantic rules.

Table 10.2
Finite-state strings divided by phrase marking and randomly

FINITE STATE	PHRASE STRUCTURE	RANDOM
N X S	N X S	N X S
N S X N	N S XN	N S XN
N X N S	N XN S	N XN S
G N S X	GN S X	G N SX
N X N X N	N XN XN	N X NXN
G N X N G N	GN XN GN	GNX N GN
N X N X G N	N XN XGN	N XN XGN
N X G N X	N XGN X	NX GN X
G N X G N X	GN XGN X	G NX GNS
G N X G N X G N	GN XGN XGN	GNXGN XG N

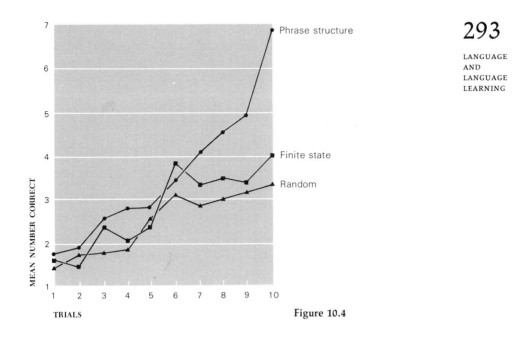

Figure 10.4

Such grammars seem to be more in accord with the assumption that we know what we are going to say before we say it. Syntactically based grammar appears to imply (though not necessarily so) that meaning is secondary to the syntactic form itself. Semantically based grammars, on the other hand, make the assumption that the meaning of the sentence is primary and that all syntactic and other rules serve only to communicate basic meaning. Semantically based grammars vary from being case grammars (Fillmore, 1968) to being any one of a variety of generative semantic grammars (see Steinberg & Jakobovits, 1971). Generative semantic theories have been particularly important to students of memory, who make the altogether reasonable assumption that we usually do not remember the grammatical structure of sentences we hear but that we do remember the essential idea behind the sentence (Sachs, 1967). Consequently, we shall have more to say about generative semantic theories in an account of the basis of semantic memory.

DEEP AND SURFACE STRUCTURES

One of the important contributions of Chomsky (see Chomsky, 1965) is the distinction between deep and surface structure. The distinction is a subtle one and has not always been used by Chomsky (or by others, for that matter) in consistent ways. In general, however, it refers to the fact that the actual spoken or written sentences we produce and understand are based upon an elaborate structure which is never apparent in the spoken language as such. Base phrase markers, like the one illustrated in Figure 10.3, provide the deep structure for one theory of language. A series of transformations is required that relates deep structure to the surface sentence. Deep structures, as the generative semantic theorists have been particularly fond of pointing out, provide the basic meaning of what is in the surface sentence, but they do not include the particular words by which that meaning may be expressed. In fact, it is entirely possible to think of deep structure simply as a set of features related by rules of the sort described in the last chapter. Such a view tends to make the surface structure appear to be ephemeral and unimportant. What is important is what we mean—the deep structure. Be that as it may, if we are to produce sentences in the languages we speak, and if others are to understand those sentences, we must learn the rules that relate the surface sentences to the deep structures and the rules that connect various parts of the surface structures to one another.

Coming to understand concepts in the world, applying logical operations, and testing the truth value of assertions are all part of the deep structure behind what we say. And we must learn how to do these as well as how to apply them to particular concatenations of features in the world before we can use language in all its power. But we must also learn the surface structure of sentences, and we must learn the ways in which ideas can come from the deep structure to the surface of sentences.

LEARNING GRAMMAR

Grammar, in a general sense, refers to all the rules of language, and only in a special sense does it refer to the rules of syntax and morphology. Because the communication of ideas requires the use of rules at all levels of language, we should use the word grammar in its general sense. However, because grammar has conventionally meant the study of the rules of syntax and morphology and because studies of how language is learned have made a distinction among learning phonological rules, semantic rules, and grammatical rules, we shall observe the distinction. This section, then, will mainly concern the acquisition of grammar in the sense of syntax and morphology. Later in this chapter and in Chapter 14 we shall deal with semantics.

Learning Surface Structure

SENTENCES AS FRAMES

One way to learn something about the surface structure of sentences is to use what linguists call the slot-in-frame technique. It provides a way of finding out what words or parts of words can substitute for the original in sentences without changing the grammatical structure of those sentences or making them ungrammatical. Fries (1952) used the method to arrive at a new classification of English parts of speech. Fries' reclassification of English has some uses, though generative theorists point out that such purely empirical methods as those used by Fries can never lead to a complete grammatical description of any language. Nevertheless, teachers use the method as a way of showing students how words can be grammatically equivalent to one another. By using a very general frame, such as, "The (book) was good," it is possible to show that only nouns of a certain type will fit into the place left vacant by the word book.

At one time there was a belief that children learned the grammatical structure of their native language by using something like a slot-in-frame approach. Ervin (1961) even argued that the process was consistent with contiguity theories of learning, and she tried to bolster her argument by pointing to the changes in the kinds of associations children give to words as they get older. Young children give response words in free association that could easily follow the stimulus word in some sentence. For example, they are likely to give BALL as an association to BIG. Older children—and adults—tend more often to give the same part of speech. Older individuals give SMALL as an association to BIG. They do so, Ervin argued, because older children have learned grammatical equivalences by learning what words can substitute for one another in sentences. The equivalence among responses in association, by this view, is mediated through the stimuli. Equivalence among words of the same grammatical class, in the more general situation, is mediated by the sentence frames in which they occur.

Generative theorists (McNeill, 1970) argue that children must have some hypotheses to test before they can go about learning grammatical equivalences (or equivalences of any sort) in language. Language learning occurs too rapidly for the development of mediational activity by the simple principles of ordinary associative learning. By the time most children are five years old, they understand thousands of words, and they have grasped the essentials of the structure of their native language no matter how complicated that structure may be (Brown, 1973). Even more of a problem is the fact that some of the equivalences to be learned have no consistent physical representation (Garrett & Fodor, 1968). That means children must learn disjunctive concepts of various sorts in order to understand linguistic equivalences.

Nevertheless, it is possible to appreciate the surface structure of some sentence without knowing what the sentence means. That is accomplished by cues provided in the sentence (the frame of the slot-in-frame method). There is no question about the grammatical structure of the sentences in Lewis Carroll's poem, "The Jabberwocky." "Twas brillig and the slithy toves did gyre and gimble in the wabe. . . ." Words like *and, the,* and even, in most of their uses, words like *did* and *was* serve to tell us what parts of speech *gyre* and *toves* must be. *And* and *the* are words that have no meaning aside from the grammatical function they serve. Even words like *did* and *have* have a purely grammatical meaning in most of their uses.

EXPERIMENTS ON SURFACE STRUCTURE AND MEMORIZATION

Many experiments show that the occurrence of such grammatical signals makes sentences easy to learn and remember, even when the learning is by rote. One such experiment is that of Epstein (1961), from which the data in Table 10.3 are taken. If you look at the two sentences under category I in Table 10.3, you will see that the essential grammatical features of ordinary English are retained, even though nonsense material is substituted for nouns, verbs, etc. Category II presents the same nonsense material without the suffixes which identify grammatical position. Category III has no grammatical structure, and category IV includes grammatical elements, but these are arranged contrary to the structure of English.

Subjects looked at these sentences (or strings) one at a time. The numbers in Table 10.3 are the number of exposures or trials required, on the average, for the subjects to recall the sentences without error. Notice that of all the nonsense sentences, the one containing the grammatical structure of English was the easiest to learn. The only sentence easier to learn was the sentence employing normal English syntax together with common English words. Despite the fact that the same nonsense sequences occurred in all the nonsense sentences, those sequences containing English syntactical elements in the correct position were easier to learn. The sentence taking the greatest number of repetitions was the nonsense sentence containing cues contrary to ordinary English.

There have been many similar studies. Anglin and Miller (1968) showed that sentences with words grouped according to their phrase structures were easier to recall than sentences grouped contrary to phrase structure. In reviewing studies of this sort, O'Connell (1970) points out that there is no question but that they show grammatical structure to help the recall of strings of words, even when the strings and the words in them make no sense. Undoubtedly, this in part is because such superficial matters as locations of the function words (*and*, *the*, etc.) and affixes to words help us to locate potential deep structures. While it is true that the deep structure of language really requires some meaningful proposition and, in any event, could never be grasped by anything like learning what substitutes for what by a slot-in-frame method, such learning must play some role in how children come to sort out the complexities of the surface structure of language. Every teacher of what

Table 10.3
Types of nonsense sentences used in experiments on grammatical structure and learning. The number of trials to learn is the average for each pair of sentences of a different type.
(After W. Epstein, 1961)

CATEGORY	SENTENCE	TRIALS
I	A VAPY KOUBS DESAKED THE CITAR MOLENTLY UM GLOX NERFS.	
	THE YIGS WUR VIRMLY RIXING HUM IN JEGEST MIV.	5.77
II	A VAP KOUB DESAK THE CITAR MOLENT UM GLOX NERF.	
	THE YIG WUR VUM RIX HUM IN JEG MIV.	7.56
III	KOUBS VAPY THE UM GLOX CITAR NERFS A MOLENTLY.	
	YIGS RIXING WUR MIV HUM VUMLY THE IN JEGEST.	8.15
IV	A VAPY KOUBED DESAKS THE CITAR MOLENTS UM GLOX NERFLY.	
	THE YIGLY WUR VUMS RIXEST HUM IN JEGING MIV.	6.90
V	CRUEL TABLES SANG FALLING CIRCLES TO EMPTY PENCILS LAZY	
	PAPER STUMBLED TO SHALLOW TREES LOUDLY FROM DAYS.	3.50

are now called language arts knows the value of these techniques in the practical matter of getting children to correctly identify grammatical concepts.

First Language Acquisition

The really important questions about the learning of grammar concern how children learn their native tongues. This, however, is a complicated matter, and the psychology of learning, as we ordinarily think of it, is relevant only to aspects of the problem. Many students of the language of children are convinced that children know a great deal about language natively. Even if we are skeptical about how much innate knowledge of language there is, there are all those questions about what happens when children create new sentences and how they relate what they know about the world to sentences. Some of these questions are questions about learning, but others are matters of maturation and problems in the study of human thinking. Nevertheless, the psychology of learning does have something to say about how children acquire language.

CONTEXTUAL GENERALIZATION

The simplest point of view about how children acquire language is based upon the principle we have just discussed, the slot-in-frame technique. Applied to the problem of how babies learn to talk their native language and acquire its grammar, it is called "contextual generalization" (Braine, 1963a, 1963b). The label, contextual generalization, brings the principle into the mainstream of learning theory, for it suggests that we apply the principles of stimulus and response generalization to the problem of first language learning. Braine's investigations consisted of two parts: The first shows that children talk in two-word sentences when they first learn to talk. They seem to use one word as a pivot or frame, and the other word is the position in which a variety of concepts can be substituted. Braine also performed some experiments to show that older children could learn the grammar of a miniature language by contextual general- ization. In these experiments he told his subjects that they were going to learn a bit of a strange language, one in which they would not know what any of the words meant. In the simplest of the experiments, the words were but two sentences long, and they consisted of two classes of words, "pivot" words which seemed as the frames and "open" words. The open words were KIV, JUF, and FOJ, while the pivot words were BEW, MUB, and YAG. The words were presented in pairs with the open words on the right and the pivot words on the left. After presenting two of the open words with two of the pivot words in all possible combinations, Braine tested for contextual generalization by asking his subjects whether the third word from each class belonged in the right-hand position or in the left-hand position. Children do quite well at this task. In more complicated experiments, Braine showed that children can easily learn to generalize within more complicated syntactic structures, even when those struc- tures are exemplified in strings of nonsense words.

Braine's two classes of words are labeled open and pivot because it expresses the point of view about how language is learned that Braine developed from his experiments on artificial languages and his observations on two-word sentences in very young children. The idea is that there is a small class of words which serves a grammatical function only. This class comprises pivot words. A larger, unlimited class of words can be used in various combinations with the grammatical or pivot words to express syntactic relations. If the child learns sentences from the fixed or pivot words, he can fill in words from the unlimited class by using their semantic characteristics. As the language of the child becomes more complicated, the class of pivot words subdivides into several classes of grammatical words, and the open class becomes the nouns, verbs, adjectives, and adverbs of adult language.

LEARNING LINGUISTIC ABSTRACTIONS

Braine's distinction between pivot and open words, while influential in early studies of language development, has not fared well recently (Brown, 1973). Furthermore, some linguists have argued that Braine's experiments are irrelevant to language learning (Bever, Fodor, & Weksel, 1965; Garrett & Fodor, 1968). These linguists point out that children must have some abstract principle that will generate surface structures. Simply learning what can substitute for what is not enough to produce the variety of sentences children can use and understand. The surface structures of language are too numerous and, in any event, must be referred to some deep representation for interpretation. Furthermore, if children learned by applying a simple principle of contextual generalization, they would make errors in their speech that they do not make. Of course, children's speech is, from the standpoint of the adult dialect, full of errors, but these are not the kinds of errors that a notion of contextual generalization would lead one to expect. Rather they are the kinds of errors that would happen if children had incompletely mastered transformational rules. Bever, Fodor, and Weksel (1965) point out that children never make the mistake of converting to the passive form sentences that do not make sense in the passive voice. Very young children know that "The window was broken by Bobby" is the equivalent of "Bobby broke the window." But they also know that "The bike costs 10 dollars" cannot be converted into "Ten dollars was cost by the bike."

The kinds of mistakes children make often reflect deep regularities in language that are, for some reason, lost in the usually accepted surface form. Children regularize strong verbs at a certain stage of development. Brown (1973) points out that most American children use the form *hisself* for *himself* at about age four. That usage is clearly on a model established by the other reflexive pronouns such as *myself*, *yourself*, and *herself*. The masculine possessive pronoun is *his*, not *him*. Four-year-olds apparently know this and apply it to the formation of reflexives.

Language is relational, and children are early aware of the importance of word order in English for conveying relations of meaning. Very young children understand the distinction between the two sentences "Make the truck hit the car" and "Make the car hit the truck" as instructions about what to do with toy vehicles (Brown, 1973). Yet their own sentences are filled with mistakes in word order. These mistakes are often as not ignored by adult hearers, though such adult hearers will go to great trouble to correct children's mistakes in pronunciation or in word usage. Once again, such mistakes cannot be based upon contextual generalization. Rather they reflect the child's incomplete grasp of the rules for getting from a deep conceptual level to the surface level necessary to express meaning to adults and others. Thus, a child will say "Why he is mad?" instead of "Why is he mad?" He understands that the *wh* element in *who, why,* and *when* questions comes at the beginning in English, but he doesn't understand that the verbal auxiliary must be moved forward in the sentence (and added to the sentence if none is present in the declarative form).

Children search for simple and orderly rules in the production and understanding of language. They take it for granted that the linguistic information they receive (and produce) is not entirely accurate and must be, in some way, a degeneration of something which has a much more regular conceptual structure than what they actually hear does. Without such an assumption, children would probably find it impossible to learn human languages. Furthermore, at the same time they must learn all the problems of applying logical systems to the world they perceive. Modern developmental psychologists argue that there is a more or less invariant sequence in which children's conceptual abilities emerge, both because experience dictates such a sequence and because biological maturation requires it. Children learn to appreciate the fundamental aspects of the grammars of their native languages very early, but it is a long time before they approach adult usage. In fact, it isn't until children reach what Piaget calls the "operational stage" that they begin to use the full range of sentence structures.

SEMANTICS AND THE USE OF LANGUAGE

We have maintained a rather arbitrary distinction between the grammatical and semantic aspects of language because that is the way the linguistic and psychological literature on language and the learning of language is organized. Rules apply, however, not just to the grammar, but to the semantic component of language, for without some systematic structure to semantics, we would not be able to communicate our meaning to one another and relate it to the world outside. Furthermore, some theories of language acquisition would insist that we learn about syntactic rules only through semantic representation (Slobin, 1971). In this section we shall examine some ideas about how semantic rules are organized, consider how they might be learned, and then turn to the question of how the conditions of learning affect the way in which we learn language.

Representing the World in Language

How do people represent the world to themselves, and how do they learn to code that representation into language? There can be no single answer to a question as complicated as that one, but in recent years we have begun to put together some ideas that at least have the virtue of showing us what asking that question means in detail. These ideas come from linguistics, from computer sciences, and from experimental psychology.

WHAT REPRESENTING THE WORLD REQUIRES

An old tradition in psychology and philosophy says that when we think, we think in images. We generate pictures of the things we think about—"faint copies," to use Hume's term, of what were originally perceptions. In this tradition the problem of translating thinking into language and language into thinking is the problem of how to relate images to language. This is a problem that has received treatment at the hands of several contemporary experimental psychologists (Bugelski, 1970; Bower, 1972). However, other recent theorists have argued that the way in which we represent things to ourselves is, like the deep structures of language, inaccessible to awareness. Pylyshyn (1973) presents some very persuasive evidence that this must be so, and he further argues that the way in which thinking is translated into language is not available to conscious experience. Though we may have an image when we link the two words *boy* and *plays* to form a sentence, the essential relation is the abstract one of predication. Or, put in a way familiar to the readers of Chapter 10, the words in syntactic arrangement serve to bring together a set of features unique to the proposition, *the boy plays*. If we store our impressions of the world, they must be stored, according to this analysis, in some way that reflects the relations of the predicate calculus. We must retain in memory propositions statable in the predicate calculus together with whatever axioms are necessary to do the computing for retrieval from memory. We do not store impressions as such but generate impressions in memory, just as we generate sentences when we speak. The consequences of the generation of an impression from memory may be the awareness of an image, or it may be simply the ability to make a statement in language.

Computer scientists have imagined various ways in which a predicate calculus might be coupled with the real world and with ordinary language in such a way as to mimic the human ability to talk about the world in a sensible way. One of the most convincing analogies to human understanding is provided by a computer program invented by Winograd (1972). It both understands and uses ordinary English. The program enables a computer to perceive a miniature world displayed to it, to understand English sentences about that world, and to talk about it to a person. The miniature world is much like the miniature universes used in concept-attainment experiments, a fact that is not without significance. It consists of small objects of various shapes, sizes, and colors. These can be moved about in various ways, and the computer can describe the relations among the objects. For example, it can answer, in ordinary English, a question such as; "Is there a red pyramid on top of any of the green cubes?"

The essential aspect of Winograd's program is a feature representation of both the world and language coupled with a deductive system. The features of the world include such things as color, location, and size, as well as such purely relational features as *on* or *beside*. The deductive system is designed so that it is capable of deducing certain facts from direct knowledge of other facts.

The language used in the program is a reduced version of ordinary English that is also analyzed by features. Linguistic features include syntactic entities, such as *noun phrase* and *verb phrase*. The program for the computer includes routines which enable it to identify these, often by the use of methods like those of the slot-in-frame technique. There is also a semantic analyzer in the program. It associates the features of the world with the features of language. This semantic analyzer knows more than just how to relate the world of reality to the vocabulary; it has the deductive system at its command. It can arrive at new facts by deduction. From the features associated with pyramids, for example, the system may be able to deduce the fact that pyramids cannot support other structures. From this deduction it would be able to answer "no" to the question, "Is there a sphere on the large red pyramid?" without ever bothering to examine the state of its miniature world at the moment. In short, the entire program can be described as the operation of deductive inference upon a set of feature structures. In this respect, the computer operates upon its miniature world in much the same way that a highly practiced subject will operate upon the miniature world of the concept-attainment experiment.

While we cannot conclude from this parallel between human thinking and the understanding Winograd's program allows a computer that the program is a description of how human beings go about making judgments and statements about the world, it does tell us what kinds of things human beings must be able to do, for the computer does only those things that a human being can easily do. Human beings must have feature analyzers (and some way of inventing new features) together with a means of coding those features onto a lexicon. Human beings must also have ways of analyzing or decoding the syntax of sentences, and this cannot be done simply by having a list of all possible sentences stored in one's head. We must be prepared to deal with total novel sentences, just as Winograd's computer can, within the limits of its vocabulary and grammar. Finally, human beings must have some way of deducing new facts from those that we have available.

Another way of finding out what being able to use a language entails is to know what is needed in order to teach a human language to a member of another species. There have been several attempts to teach chimpanzees to talk, on the assumption that they would be better candidates for the job than any other species because of both their temperament and their intelligence. These attempts have not been very successful. Recently, however, two experiments have made more progress, not in teaching chimpanzees to speak but in teaching them to use human language through other means. One of these experiments is worth describing in some detail because it makes use of an approach that uses a feature analysis and the rudiments of a deductive system. It is by Premack (1971).

Rather than trying to teach his experimental subject, a chimpanzee named Sarah, to talk, Premack instructed her in the use of a special language which made use of small plastic objects of various colors, sizes, and shapes. Some of these served as words and others as important linguistic relations. These plastic symbols were backed with thin metal strips so that they would adhere to a magnetic writing board. Communication between ape and man consisted of sentences written by placing the plastic counters on the magnetic board. Sentences were written from top to bottom rather than from left to right as in ordinary English writing.

Each plastic counter served as a concept. One denoted Sarah herself, and others named her fellow chimpanzees and the human beings who worked with her. Objects were also given plastic names. A small set of verbs included *is, give, take, insert,* and *wash.* Certain important linguistic and logical relations were also named. For example, a blue triangle denoted the logical relation "if-then." Other relative concepts, such as that of conjunction, or the idea of "name of" were also assigned plastic counters. The latter enabled Sarah to learn new concepts easily. Finally, a series of adjectives described features of things that Sarah could communicate.

The initial training used instrumental conditioning. First of all, Sarah was trained to pick up a banana placed near a pink plastic chip. Then the banana was moved out of her reach. Now, in order to obtain the banana, Sarah had to transfer the pink chip to the magnetic board. After Sarah had mastered this task, she was given another plastic chip, this time a blue one, in order to get an apple. The next step was to introduce the plastic chip denoting *give* and require Sarah to write sentences such as "give banana" or "give apple" to get what she wanted. In order to know the meaning of *give,* however, it had to be contrasted with something else, and so other verbs, such as *wash,* were introduced. Sarah could now instruct her human experimenter to wash an apple or give her a banana. Then, Sarah was introduced to three-word sentences. Now, in order to be reinforced, she had to give the experimenter's name, the verb, and her own name, all in the correct order. She learned that if she used someone else's name, either nothing happened or that person (or chimpanzee) got

what was requested.

She was taught the meaning of *same* and *different* by being given three objects, two of which were alike, such as a spoon and a pair of cups. This, of course, is just a version of the oddity problem, which has long been used in research with primates. Learning the concepts "name of" and "not name of" enabled the experimenter to teach Sarah new nouns directly without the laborious approximation through reinforcement. She was taught conditional relations by being given an apple and a banana, with a piece of chocolate in plain view. If she chose the apple, she got the chocolate, but she did not get the chocolate if she chose the banana. The symbol for if-then was introduced. This was an exceedingly difficult problem for Sarah, and it took her a long time to learn it well enough to apply it consistently over the range of her vocabulary. Finally, Sarah was taught to obey written commands as a way of testing her comprehension.

Sarah's performance provides a fascinating demonstration, though there are still problems in interpreting what it is she is doing. Her productive vocabulary is so limited that it is impossible to tell whether she is really learning the concept of "syntax" or whether she is learning a large number of specific responses to particular cues. This problem always plagues investigators who use the receptive paradigm in studying concept attainment (p. 261). Unless subjects are required to identify a very large number of negative and positive instances, the experimenter never really knows whether they have simply learned a large number of specific associations or have mastered an abstract concept. This problem in interpreting Sarah's performance will remain as long as her vocabulary remains small and the variety of types of sentences she can use is small.

There is also the possibility that she is receiving covert cues from her trainer, a possibility that Premack knows about and for which he has provided specific tests. These tests reveal that at least some of what Sarah does can only be accurately demonstrated with trainers who know the code Sarah is supposed to be using. Finally, Sarah does not use her vocabulary with complete reliability. For some words, despite extended practice, reliability is only about 60 percent. Small children are seldom this unreliable in their use of words. They misuse words until corrected, but they do so with a fair degree of consistency.

Granting all these problems, Sarah's performance is remarkable. She does not do as well as Winograd's computer, but she illustrates many of the same characteristics (assuming that no artifact accounts for her performance). Neither the computer nor the chimpanzee has access to the full range of human language, and until one or the other of them does, we cannot say that the methods used to program the one and train the other really reveal processes in the learning of language. They have the virtue, however, of showing us the minimal kind of competence the use of language requires. These demonstrations are impressive enough to make us believe that the feature-plus-deduction analysis of language is a useful way to look at the way in which people learn to use language.

The Use of Language

Thus far we have had relatively little to say about those conditions of practice which influence the rate at which we acquire information about language. Common belief has it that children learn language by imitating adults. There is, however, a surprising degree of skepticism about this view among students of the development of language (see Slobin, 1968). Children seldom spontaneously copy adult utterances with any exactitude. Furthermore, most of the utterances spoken by children could not have been previously spoken by adults. Language is creative, and individual sentences are composed to meet the needs of the moment, even by children, and not what has been learned in the past.

Adults sometimes try to correct children's speech by what students of language call "expansion." The child may say, "Have cookie," to which the parent replies, "Say, 'please may I have a cookie?'" The parent may then require the child to repeat his expanded version. Slobin (1968) estimates that about 15 percent of all children's imitative utterances is accounted for by responses to expansions. In addition, some students of behavioral modification have been able to provide evidence that tuition requiring some form of imitation does facilitate language development. Such demonstrations have centered around the concept of "modeling" (Bandura, 1971).

MODELING

Modeling encompasses imitation and more, as we saw in Chapter 3 (p. 99). It describes any kind of situation in which one individual provides a model for another. Thus, if a child can learn from the parent just by observing the parent, even though he does not imitate the parent, the learning is through modeling. If modeling is to be used to teach the abstract relations of language, Zimmerman and Rosenthal (1973) argue, it is necessary to use the method of a concept-attainment experiment. The feature to be taught is held constant across instances while all other features are varied. Modeling of this sort makes it possible to teach children both new linguistic usages and the ability to state explicit grammatical principles (Zimmerman & Rosenthal, 1973). With children who are not severely retarded, explicit reinforcement of correct usage or correct statements of a principle adds but little to the training. Apparently, the reinforcement provided intrinsically by the task is sufficient. Explicit reinforcement is necessary, however, when children are severely deficient in linguistic performance (Wheeler & Sulzer, 1970), perhaps because linguistic performance for such children is intrinsically punishing, and this effect needs to be counteracted by some overt reinforcement.

Modeling depends for its effectiveness in part upon social interaction, or so, at least, the proponents of modeling argue. However, there is little information to tell us whether or not the same information displayed by, say, a teaching machine might have the same effect. The main thing that this rather extensive literature tells us is that it is possible to teach linguistic rules by deliberate tuition and that the use of the newly learned rules generalizes to other situations. In short, it tells us that the principles of rule learning discovered in the concept-attainment experiments apply to how children learn language.

OTHER CONDITIONS OF PRACTICE

The brief discussion of modeling should serve to remind us that all the conditions that determine the course of practice in other skills also determine the course of the acquisition of language, for viewed in one way, language is but another skill. Carroll (1971) has brought together all the literature relevant to learning from ordinary discourse. Much of the material in that book could apply to a general book on the learning of skills. A book edited by Reed (1971) brings together the ideas of a number of individuals on the learning of language. The book ranges over the kinds of problems we have discussed in this chapter in addition to such applied topics as language instruction in secondary schools. It has, however, little to say about any special conditions of practice, for there are very few that are specific to language. The exceptions are mainly concerned with learning phonology, and here the emphasis is upon the existence of technological aids such as tape recorders and sound spectrographs.

One point does deserve mention, however, and it arises out of a particular school of linguistic theory, contrastive linguistics. Contrastive linguistics emphasizes the fact that language is built upon the contrast of features or feature-states. We know that the two words *bin* and *pin* are different even when they are spoken by an artificial voice. They are exactly alike except that the initial sounds /b/ and /p/ differ in but a single feature that is distinctive for the difference in meaning. That single feature is "voicing." The initial consonant in *bin* is voiced (the vocal cords vibrate during the sound), and the initial consonant in *pin* is not voiced (the vocal cords are silent). The principle of minimal contrast, as it is called, can be applied to meaning and grammar as well as to phonology.

Contrastive linguists (see Stockwell & Bowen, 1965) emphasize the importance of contrast both in the analysis of language and in learning language, particularly the learning of second languages. They provide evidence and persuasive argument that the learning of a second language is facilitated by pointing out to the student just how the student's native language and the new language differ. It is more than just a matter of reducing interference or increasing positive transfer (see p. 340), it is a matter of getting the student to be aware of the basic structure of the two languages. Once again, it is a matter of concept learning. Contrastive analysis helps point out the features distinctive to a language and the rules that govern the arrangement of those features. Perhaps this simply emphasizes once more the continuity from discrimination learning to concept learning.

ELEVEN

VERBAL LEARNING

The last chapter was about the nature of language and how people learn to use and understand language. It had relatively little to say about how people acquire information that happens to be in verbal form. That topic has been a major concern of students of human learning, and this chapter is given over both to a discussion of the methods psychologists have used to investigate this problem and to some of the results they have achieved. The methods themselves are important because they are used in the study of memory as well as in applied studies of human learning.

EXPERIMENTAL TECHNIQUES IN VERBAL LEARNING

Most of the methods experimental psychologists have used to study verbal learning are associative in nature. Associations are relations, and so this means that the basic technique of the learning laboratory is to teach subjects the relations among elements of various sorts. The elements may be words, nonsense syllables, letters, numbers, and sometimes whole sentences and connected discourse. The methods of the verbal learning laboratory are associative in another, narrower, meaning as well. They originated in a theory of learning which asserted that the basic principle in all learning is association by contiguity. That means that one element comes to be related to another—or the one comes to be able to elicit the other—simply because they have been perceived together. Therefore, the oldest techniques of the learning laboratory are simply ways of presenting verbal items to subjects in temporal contiguity. There are special methods for ensuring that subjects do not skip around, but rather, practice the items in precisely the order dictated by the experimenter. For example, many laboratories still make use of memory drums, which are devices for exposing verbal material one item at a time in orders prearranged by the experimenter.

In order to study the processes in verbal learning, investigators have used two principal kinds of variations: the nature of the materials given to subjects to learn and the methods of presentation and practice. We shall examine both of these.

Materials in the Study of Verbal Learning

The reader of the last two chapters might suppose that the most commonly used materials in the verbal learning laboratory would be designed to produce variations in logical, semantic, and linguistic relations. In recent years such has been the case, but the investigation of memory and the study of the cumulative effects of practice antedate the current interest in logical and semantic relations. Consequently, many of the materials used in earlier studies of verbal learning reflect other interests. The earliest materials of the verbal learning laboratory are nonsense syllables.

NONSENSE SYLLABLES

Nonsense syllables were first used by the German experimental psychologist Hermann v. Ebbinghaus, who, in 1885, published the first experimental study of human memory. In company with most experimental psychologists of his day, Ebbinghaus had a particular theory about the nature of verbal learning. He believed that it consisted of association, by temporal contiguity, of ideas. These ideas could later be remembered if one of them could elicit all the others. Associations were made in the first place by rote practice, and so the earliest methods of the experimental learning laboratory, strongly influenced by the work of Ebbinghaus, were techniques of rote memorization (Postman, 1968).

Ebbinghaus knew that ordinary words, which carried the meaning of ideas, would be, for adult subjects in the laboratory, associated with countless other words simply as the result of ordinary experience. He wanted to study how new ideas were acquired, and so, he argued, he could not use ordinary German words because there would already be too many associations among these words. Learning and retention of material learned in the laboratory would be contaminated by relations learned outside the laboratory. Therefore, Ebbinghaus formed words that he thought would be totally meaningless and devoid of associations by combining all the possible consonant-vowel-consonant combinations that did not make real German words. These are the celebrated CVC nonsense syllables, familiar to generations of students in the learning laboratory.

Nonsense syllables, because they were devoid of associations, were supposed to be uniformly difficult or easy to learn. They could be learned in any order or combination, and each would be about as difficult as the next. That made it possible for Ebbinghaus to perform the experiments he did, for he used himself alone as an experimental subject, and he compared the learning of various combinations of CVC syllables under different conditions of practice and after different retention intervals. Since the materials were all nearly alike, differences in performance could be ascribed to the differences in conditions of practice and retention intervals. While Ebbinghaus's syllables were not all exactly alike (something about which he was aware), it is a testimony to his methods that his results hold up today.

Nonsense syllables are not devoid of meaning, and they are most certainly not uniform in the ease with which they may be associated with one another in rote practice. There has been nearly a century of work devoted to finding out just how different Ebbinghaus's syllables are and how they differ from ordinary words in meaning and in ease of association. The work with these syllables has led to systematic efforts to measure the important characteristics of all kinds of verbal materials.

With nonsense syllables, as with other kinds of verbal materials, there are two characteristics that make them vary in the ease with which they may be learned and associated with one another. One of these is their internal structure, and the other is their, presumably previously learned, relations with other items. All kinds of materials used in verbal learning experiments, even individual letters and numbers, have internal structures. The internal structure of individual letters is determined by the way in which features combine to form them, and there is evidence to show that the ease of learning and remembering combinations of letters depends upon the feature-structure of individual letters and how they relate to one another (Wickelgren, 1966). Nonsense syllables certainly have different kinds of internal structures. The relations among the letters BEK form a good syllable in English. There is no English word like it, but it is easy to pronounce and has the feel of an English word. XYF, on the other hand, does not. It is a rare combination of letters, and most people would have difficulty pronouncing it. Both these syllables, incidentally, may be found in Table 11.1. What is more, we have the feeling that it would be easier to associate BEK rather than XYF with other words. I, for example, think of *Bic pens*.

These two aspects of verbal materials are not always easy to separate, and since they both have the effect of producing variation in rates of learning and retention, they have often been lumped together. Indeed, most of the methods used to assess the structural and associative values of verbal materials do not differentiate between them. However, some important facts will hinge on the difference, and it is a good idea to keep the distinction in mind as you read the balance of this chapter.

Table 11.1

Association value or meaningfulness for selected CVC trigrams

The numbers are the percent of subjects indicating that a given syllable is meaningful to them. (Data from Archer, 1960)

TRIGRAM	% S_s	TRIGRAM	% S_s	TRIGRAM	% S_s
XYF	3	DUJ	13	BUP	34
YEQ	4	BIW	15	LOZ	40
MYV	5	RUV	16	VOX	46
QEJ	6	TIW	18	QIN	50
NIJ	7	QED	20	MYR	58
WUQ	8	HOJ	22	BEK	66
GEX	9	BIQ	24	VIK	74
PYB	10	SIW	26	NEV	80
ZOF	11	DYT	28	DAT	90
NYV	12	TAZ	32	TEX	100

The earliest attempt to assess the learnability of nonsense syllables is the measurement of *association value* by Glaze (1928). Glaze showed a large number of nonsense syllables one at a time to subjects and asked these subjects to indicate whether or not each syllable produced an association or not. Glaze's procedure was casual, and he used only 15 subjects. As with Ebbinghaus's original research, it is a testimony to the robustness of the phenomenon that Glaze investigated to say that his measurements proved to be reliable and valid predictors of all kinds of measures of the comparative speed of learning and retentive qualities of nonsense syllables. The percentage of subjects reporting an association to a given syllable will predict, for example, how many repetitions are required to combine that syllable with other syllables in serial learning.

Since association value proved to be useful to students of verbal learning, there have been several repetitions, under better conditions, of Glaze's observations. The most extensive one is that of Archer (1960). Archer examined the association value of all possible three-letter combinations in the Roman alphabet. Archer's subjects were told to ask themselves the following questions: Is it a word? Does it sound like a word? Does it remind me of a word? Can I use it in a sentence? If the answer was "yes" to these questions, the subjects were supposed to indicate an association with that syllable. Table 11.2 shows the association value, according to Archer's norms, for some selected syllables.

Another closely related technique is generally described as the measurement of *meaningfulness*. This term comes from the idea that the more associations a given verbal item arouses, the more meaningful that item. In most measurements of meaningfulness, people are asked to list all the associations they can think of with a word in a given period of time, say, one minute. Two examples are the number of associations given to some two-syllable nonsense (and real) words by Noble (1952) and to three-letter nonsense syllables by Mandler (1955). Table 11.2 shows the number of associations Noble's subjects gave in one minute to some of his items.

Table 11.2
Disyllables and their meaningfulness values
The meaningfulness value is defined as the average number of associations given to each disyllable in one minute. (Data from Noble, 1952)

DISYLLABLE	M VALUE	DISYLLABLE	M VALUE
GOJEY	0.99	BODICE	2.80
NEGLAN	1.04	JITNEY	3.51
BELAP	1.22	PALLET	3.62
XYLEM	1.24	ORDEAL	3.91
QUIPSON	1.26	YEOMAN	4.60
BODKIN	1.39	KENNEL	5.52
ATTAR	1.71	INCOME	6.24
MAELSTROM	1.84	ZEBRA	7.12
ROMPIN	1.90	JELLY	7.70
JETSAM	2.54	ARMY	9.43

These measures predict rate of learning. For example, Figure 11.1 shows the number of items correctly recalled in an experiment in which students were asked to study, for either one or two minutes, some CVC syllables which differed in association value. You can see from this figure that there is a large variation in the number of syllables correctly remembered (McGeoch, 1930).

Both association value and meaningfulness require, by some judgment or rating, one group of subjects to predict how well another group of subjects will learn or remember a group of verbal items. As you can imagine, there are many features on which verbal items can be judged, and many of these will predict the learnability of those items. Among these is familiarity (Noble, 1953), which assesses how familiar subjects are with verbal items by asking them to rate how often in the past they might have seen certain letters, combinations of letters, or words. Another predictor is imagery, and it is important enough to warrant more extended discussion.

Imagery refers to the degree to which some particular verbal item (usually a word) is able to produce a definite image in a subject. It is typically evaluated by asking subjects to rate verbal items for their ability to produce images (Paivio, 1965, 1971). It is closely related to the concreteness of the concept behind the word in question. Concrete nouns, for example, nearly always produce higher ratings of imagery than do abstract nouns. All these measures—association value, meaningfulness, familiarity, and imagery—are highly correlated with one another. That is to say, if a given item is judged to be high in one of these, it will likely be judged high in the others as well. Paivio, however, presents convincing evidence that imagery is the most potent predictor of performance in verbal learning (Paivio, 1967, 1968). He also points out (Paivio, 1971) that such features as emotionality and evaluation (how good or bad an item is judged to be) are either negatively correlated or

Figure 11.1
The mean number of correct responses during learning as a function of meaningfulness (Glaze association value) of the items learned. (Underwood & Schulz, 1960, p. 29; data from McGeoch, 1930.)

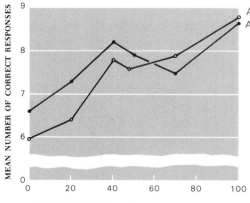

MEANINGFULNESS (GLAZE ASSOCIATION VALUE)

uncorrelated with association value, meaningfulness, and imagery. Because of the power of imagery as a predictor of performance in verbal learning and because asking subjects to image deliberately increases the level of their performance in verbal learning (Bugelski, 1970), many theorists have regarded imagery as having a causative role in facilitating performance in verbal learning. The data, however, are correlational in nature, and it can be argued with equal persuasiveness that the relation between imagery and facilitation of performance exists because both are produced by some more fundamental process (Pylyshyn, 1973).

From the names associated with these judged features, we might suppose that they mainly predict how well an item will be associated with other items. That certainly seemed to be the intent of Glaze's measure of association value, and furthermore, some of the studies of imagery have concerned imaging *relations* between pairs of verbal items. However, for the most part, these measures have been used to predict the degree of difficulty subjects have with the item *per se* rather than with its ability to relate to other items. An elaborate series of experiments by Underwood and Schulz (1960) establishes that point. For example, they show that association value and meaningfulness of nonsense syllables and letter combinations are much more important on the *response* side of paired-associate learning (Chapter 10) than on the stimulus side. That means that subjects have trouble integrating or putting together strings of letters which are low in association value in order to recall them correctly. They have less trouble recognizing them, and in fact, the association values or meaningfulness of letter strings seems not to affect at all how well they can be associated with one another. The effects of association value upon response integration Underwood and Schulz attribute to varying degrees of pronounceability associated with different degrees of association value. Certainly, at the low end of the scale, at least, these measures seem to reflect the internal structure of items rather than the extent to which they can easily be associated with other items. For real words, however, something more must be involved. Imagery and meaningfulness may well reflect the extent to which particular words are semantically encoded.

One other measure that seems to be related to how well people learn specific items is of a different character, and it deserves independent comment. It is frequency of usage. For many languages, particularly highly developed languages, normative information exists which tells us how often, relatively speaking, the average person is likely to have seen or heard any particular verbal item. This comes in the form of word counts. Two well-known counts of American English are those of Kučera and Francis (1967) and Thorndike and Lorge (1944). The latter work expressed the count of 30,000 words in terms of frequency per million. It has often been used to predict rate of verbal learning. One example is seen in Figure 11.2. It shows the number of words correctly recalled after the subjects had heard 20 words. Each group of 20 words that the subjects heard came from a different frequency range of English.

Effects like those in Figure 11.2 occur in many situations, and there are

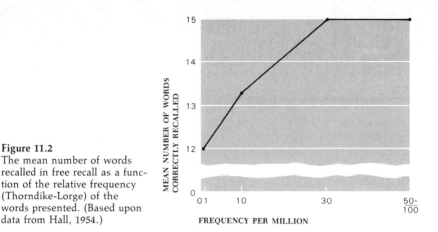

Figure 11.2
The mean number of words recalled in free recall as a function of the relative frequency (Thorndike-Lorge) of the words presented. (Based upon data from Hall, 1954.)

probably a number of reasons for them. For one, the more common the word, the greater the probability that everyone tested in the experiment has seen the word before and knows what it means (Deese, 1961). Underwood (1969) argues that frequency is one of the fundamental features associated with each item we remember, and frequency, along with some other features such as modality, enables us to discriminate one memory from another and thus retrieve the one we want.

RELATIONS AMONG ITEMS

Most of the measures we have discussed thus far predict the extent to which subjects have previously encoded or integrated the items we wish them to learn. They have relatively little to do with the specific relations those items have with other items. Whether one is an associationist or not, it is necessary to agree that one must learn the relationship among items as well as the items themselves in order to remember most material correctly. Consequently, it is not surprising that students of verbal learning have looked for measures that will predict the ease with which particular items will be related to one another in practice.

One of the most commonly used techniques to establish the preexisting relations people may have among words that will help them in learning a new task is testing for free associations. In a free-association test, a person is given a stimulus word and asked to reproduce the responses to it. The relative frequency with which particular responses are given is taken as a measure of the strength of the association (Cramer, 1968; Cofer, 1971). For example, "chair" is a relatively common response to "table," while "dish" is a relatively rare one. The association of "chair" to "table" is stronger, by this measure, than is "dish" to "table." One of the largest collections of norms of free association is that published by Postman and Keppel (1970).

Free associations predict a number of things about learning and recall. In one experiment (Deese, 1959), students were asked to recall lists of words after hearing each list but once. Each list was 15 words long, but they differed in the degree to which the words composing them were free associates of one another. One list, for example, contained words that, on the average, elicited other words on the list in free association around 30 percent of the time, while other lists contained words that never elicited one another in free association. The results clearly show that the average free-association strength among words in a list predicts the number of words in that list which will be recalled (see Figure 11.3). This is because the same processes seem to take place in free recall as in free association. If "table" makes most people think of "chair," it is easy to remember that "chair" occurred in the list of words you just heard if you remember that "table" occurred.

A closely related measure of relation is provided by *sequential dependencies*. Sequential dependencies are complicated, and they occur at several levels of language. They occur at the level of words and at the level of phonemes or letters. Everyone who has read Poe's story "The Gold Bug" knows that letters in English do not occur with equal frequency. The letter *e*, in the long run, appears more often than any other letter. Consequently, if we were to guess at a missing letter in a passage of ordinary English, our best guess, all other things being equal, would be *e*. However, the accuracy of our prediction would be greatly increased by knowing what letters went before and after the missing letter. If we saw the letter *q* we would know that the next letter must be *u*.

The analysis of the statistical structure of language is part of what is known as "information theory" or "uncertainty analysis" (see Garner, 1962). Information theory has some important methodological and theoretical consequences for the study of learning; however, here we shall draw upon it mainly as a way of summarizing the statistical

Figure 11.3
The mean number of words recalled in free recall as a function of the interitem associative frequency of the lists presented. These lists were all either high-, low-, or zero-frequency associates to particular stimulus words. (Based upon data from Deese, 1959.)

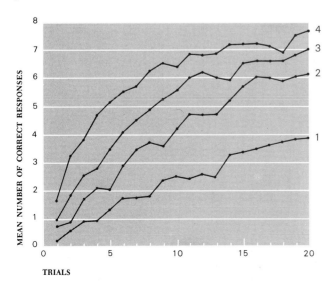

structure of language. The statistical structure of language is revealed in sequential dependencies, and it is the result of many relations operating together and at cross purposes. Some of these relations are grammatical, some are semantic, and some are even phonological. Thus it is a genuine statistical effect in the sense that it is the result of many things acting together.

There have been many studies of sequential relations in language and their effects in learning. One of the most familiar to students of verbal learning is the count by Underwood and Schulz (1960) of the relative frequency of occurrence of various three-letter combinations in English. They counted the frequency with which every possible combination of three letters occurs per 15,000 words of printed English. Table 11.3 presents some trigrams, as these three-letter combinations are called, taken from this count. A common trigram, such as THE, will occur as often as 1,200 times in 15,000 words, while a rare trigram, such as TFI, will occur only once per 15,000 words.

These trigram frequencies predict the rate of verbal learning. Figure 11.4 shows the number of correct responses in 20 trials of paired-associate learning. In a paired-associate task (p. 320), subjects learn to give particular responses to particular stimuli. In this case, subjects had to learn to give trigram combinations to random numbers. As you can see from Figure 11.4, the number of correct responses increases with the increase in frequency of the trigram. Underwood and Schulz attributed this result to the fact that the common trigrams are better integrated. They are easier to pronounce, for example. Therefore, strictly speaking, this result is one more of integration of the items to be learned than of making more available relations among items.

Not only do words consist of sequentially predictable combinations of letters; they are also arranged in predictable sequences. If you see the word *the*, you might expect *people* or *reasons* or *car* to follow, but not the words *for* or *communicate* or *electrify*. In short, there are varying sequential probabilities among words. Furthermore, as with letters, the

Table 11.3
The frequency with which certain trigrams occurred in 15,000 words of running English text
(Data from Underwood & Schulz, 1960)

TRIGRAM	FREQUENCY	TRIGRAM	FREQUENCY
ABB	5	GST	1
ACK	31	IBB	1
ALE	14	IVE	114
BAG	3	LLY	47
BBE	5	MPO	10
BLE	70	NAL	33
DAP	1	NCE	77
DUC	21	ONE	126
EDS	7	SCL	1
ERS	115	THE	1,201
GHT	104	ZZL	3

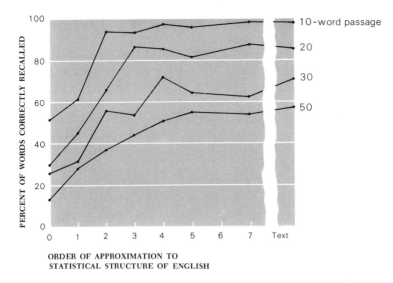

ORDER OF APPROXIMATION TO
STATISTICAL STRUCTURE OF ENGLISH

Figure 11.4
The mean number of correct responses in paired-associate learning as a function
of meaningfulness of the response terms, from low (1) to high (4). (Underwood & Schulz, 1960, p. 133.)

more items you have available in a sequence, the more accurately you
can predict. At one time there was a great interest in *statistical approximations to English*. The idea was that if you had enough predictive
information at hand, you could predict with nearly perfect accuracy some
missing letter or word. While it is certainly true that the more information you have, the more accurately you can predict, statistical predictions
fall short of complete accuracy. The reason is, of course, that language is
not generated statistically. It is generated by placing meaningful propositions in acceptable surface grammatical forms. Furthermore, the notion
that such predictions were strictly sequential from left to right is not
correct, as we saw in the last chapter. The interest in sequential
prediction from left to right grew out of stimulus-response psychology—
the idea that language consists of chains of stimuli and responses. In
fact, however, the prediction of missing letters in words or missing
words in texts is statistically nearly symmetrical (see Garner, 1962). You
can predict backwards with almost as much accuracy as you can predict
forward. We now know that finite-state rules, which might generate
left-to-right statistical sequences, are not adequate to describe the
structure of real language.

   With the realization that a strict stimulus-response approach was of
limited utility in studying the nature of language, and with a loss of
interest in finite-state theories as models of language, interest in
sequential dependencies and statistical approximations in language declined. We can and do detect the statistical structure of things, and such
detection undoubtedly helps the learning and retention of verbal material. But the statistical structure of language is not the central means by
which we encode and retrieve verbal information from memory.

A different kind of measure of the relations among verbal items is of much current interest, largely because it is compatible with the way in which the semantic structure of language is organized (see Chapter 14). This measure is category clustering, an effect first discovered by Bousfield (1953). The phenomenon is based upon the fact that conceptual names readily fall into categories. *Lion, dog,* and *baboon* are all members of the conceptual category *animal,* while *oxygen, sodium,* and *iron* can all be classified as chemical elements. Cohen, Bousfield, and Whitmarsh (1957) developed norms showing the relative frequency with which people think of particular instances, given a general category name. Battig and Montague (1969) have extended these norms, and both sets are used in the experiments on clustering in recall mentioned later. At this point we need only describe the general effect: If a list of 64 words made up of equal numbers of names of animals, chemical elements, vegetables, and occupations is presented to subjects in random order, subjects will tend to recall the words in conceptual groups. In a word, they will *cluster* them. Bousfield's results on category clustering were among the first experiments demonstrating that verbal memory is primarily semantic in nature.

There are many other such predictors of the extent to which verbal items will be learned or recalled, but these are the chief ones. Much research in verbal learning over the past 20 years has been directed toward finding out exactly why these various characteristics of verbal material predict ease of learning. Before turning to these experiments, however, we shall look at some of the principal methods that have been used in research on verbal learning.

Methods in Research on Verbal Learning

There is a bewildering array of conditions under which subjects have been taught verbal materials in the laboratory. Some of these variations in conditions are traditional and some are the results of special theories. The most frequently used methods fall into broad categories, and in order to understand the experimental literature on verbal learning it is necessary to know what these are.

FREE RECALL

The simplest way of testing the effects of subjects studying some set of verbal materials is to ask for free recall. Free recall is a way of saying that subjects can recall the items presented to them in any order they wish. The way in which they actually do recall the material depends upon the material. Figure 11.5 presents data from a study of one of the most important characteristics of *immediate* free recall: the probability of recall of individual items as a function of their position in the list. The material in this experiment (Murdock, 1962) consisted of common unrelated English words. They were presented one at a time, and after the presentation of the complete list, the subjects were told to recall as many words as they could in any order.

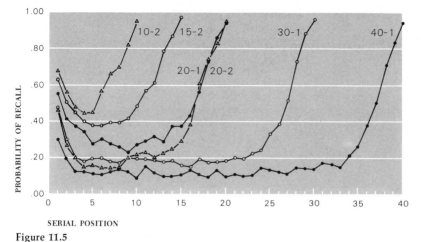

SERIAL POSITION

Figure 11.5
The probability of recall in free recall as a function of serial position of items in the original list. (Murdock, 1962, p. 484.)

The lists were alike except that they varied in number of items from 10 to 40. The results given in Figure 11.5 show a characteristic bowed shape for all the curves. The items most likely to be recalled were those at the ends of the lists, and the probability of recall of the last three items did not vary much for lists of different length. The middle items of all lists were least likely to be recalled, so that the probability of recall is greatest at the end, next greatest at the beginning, and least in the middle, irrespective of the length of the lists.

These serial position curves, as they are called, will vary with the nature of the material and the nature of practice. In Figure 11.5, the most frequently recalled items are those that are *last* in presentation. This recency effect, as it is usually called, is almost certainly a result of the ability of subjects to "read out" items from primary memory before the information is stored in the quasi-permanent form of long-term memory. If recall is delayed, and particularly if some other task is interpolated between presentation and recall, this recency effect will disappear (Glanzer and Cunitz, 1966). It is possible, however, to eliminate the recency effect, as well as alter other characteristics of recall, by introducing structure into the list of words to be recalled. You will recall that the lists from which the curves in Figure 11.5 were taken consisted of unrelated words. If we ask people to recall lists in which there are sequential dependencies, they (1) tend to recall the list in the order of presentation, and (2) do not recall the last few items more frequently (Deese & Kaufman, 1957).

It is also possible to change the relation between the order of recall and probability of recall by instructions. The curves in Figure 11.6 tell the story. In this experiment, subjects were presented with lists consisting of 20 common but unrelated English words. After some practice lists, some experimental lists appeared. For the experimental lists, however, some subjects received different instructions. For the first experimental lists,

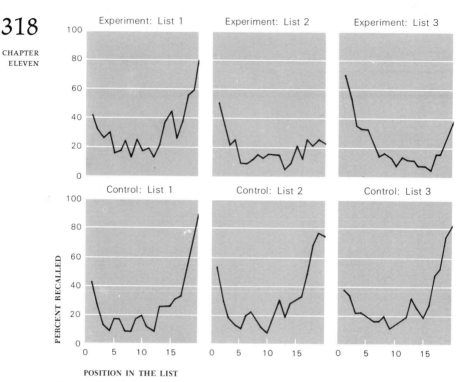

Figure 11.6
Serial position curves in recall as a function of instructions. Exp. list 1 is for instructions for free recall; exp. list 2 for instructions for serial recall after presentation; exp. list 3 for instructions for serial recall before presentation. The control lists are all for instructions for free recall. (Deese, 1957.)

subjects received no instructions before presentation, and so they supposed that they were to recall the items as they occurred to them. The results are that, as is to be expected, the serial position curve did not differ from that for the subjects who heard the "control" lists. However, for the second experimental list, subjects were told after *presentation* that they had to recall the words in order of presentation. The result is to eliminate the recency effect, but notice that the recall of items near the beginning of the list remains unchanged. In the third experimental list, subjects *knew beforehand* that they must recall in the order of presentation. The result is that the tendency to recall more words from the beginning of the list, often called the "primacy effect," is enhanced.

What is not apparent in the curves is that there is a net difference in the number of words the subjects could recall. When the lists could be recalled in any order, subjects recalled about 6.7 words on the average. When the words had to be recalled in serial order, subjects could recall only about 4 items, even when serial order was not scored. The difference is almost certainly a difference between the information that subjects could store in primary memory and that which they had managed, in the course of hearing the complete list, to transfer to secondary memory (p. 385).

The earliest experiments on verbal learning were experiments on serial learning. Ebbinghaus (1885) used what has come to be known as the method of complete presentation. That is to say, he spread the complete set of materials out before himself (he always used only himself as subject) before he began to learn. He read each word only once at the stroke of a metronome and tried to associate it with the next item so that, when given any single item, he could *anticipate* the next one. Thus, despite the method of complete presentation, he learned by serial anticipation.

Serial anticipation produces some interesting and complicated effects in learning, effects which reveal something of the nature of the processes people go through when they try to associate verbal items together. In contemporary experiments, however, the method of complete presentation is seldom used. Instead, subjects see one word at a time in what must surely be the original mechanical teaching machine, the memory drum. When the subject sees a particular word exposed, he is to try to guess or anticipate what the next one will be. Thus, each item serves as a stimulus for the recall of the next. For example, the first item in a list might be the nonsense syllable SYJ. When the list begins, the stimulus for this syllable is provided by some starting signal, such as an asterisk. When, on subsequent trials, the subject sees the starting signal, he is supposed to try to say, "S-Y-J." The next syllable might be LOZ. LOZ will serve as a stimulus for its next item, say, NEP, and so on through the list. If nonsense syllables are used, subjects spell the items, but if ordinary English words are used, the subjects need only pronounce them.

Figure 11.7 shows the typical results from an experiment in serial anticipation. It shows the number of correct responses during practice of

Figure 11.7

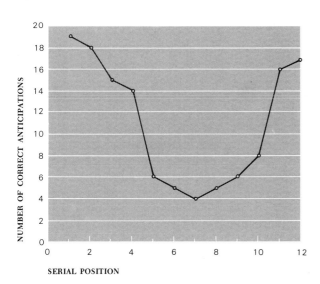

SERIAL POSITION

the list to mastery as a function of position of items in the list. The largest number of correct responses are made at the beginning of the list, the least just slightly past the middle, and the end of the list produces almost as many correct responses as the beginning.

No effect in simple verbal learning has received as much attention as this, the serial position effect in rote serial anticipatory learning. It seems so simple that a simple explanation appears to be in order. Various theories about the cumulation of "inhibitory tendencies" and "reactive inhibition" have been pitted against theories which emphasize perceptual saliency and anchoring effects provided by the beginning and end items in the list. Harcum (1970) presents some persuasive evidence that perceptual saliency of the beginning and end are very important, but immediate memory, proactive and retroactive inhibition (see Chapter 14), must also play a role. In any event, the primacy-recency effects are powerful ones both in the repetitive practice of verbal material and in the scanning of perceptual material (Harcum, 1970).

PAIRED-ASSOCIATE LEARNING

Probably the most common method of presentation used in the learning laboratory is that of paired associates. The paired-associate experiment is used for several reasons. For one, it is commonly viewed as being representative of a wide variety of problems people face in mastering verbal materials. Consider, for example, the learning of a vocabulary of foreign words by traditional methods. The essential feature is a pairing between English words and the words in the foreign language so that when a foreign word is presented, its English equivalent readily comes to mind. However, the greatest impetus behind the use of the paired-associates method is theoretical. It is the model example of the traditional view of association. One member of each pair of items serves as the stimulus for the response, which is the other member. There is a long tradition in psychology of viewing all learning as a matter of acquiring stimulus-response relationships. As a matter of experimental procedure, the paired-associate method does allow us some control over the effects of overt responding upon learning, for while subjects must learn both items in a pair, they need only learn to recognize the stimulus item, while they must actually be able to retrieve the response item.

In a laboratory experiment, subjects will usually be required to learn a set of stimulus-response pairs. Anywhere from 8 to 20 such pairs may constitute a list. The subjects are exposed to the list in something like the familiar flash-card technique. They first see the stimulus item, and then they see the stimulus and response items together. The next time that particular stimulus item appears, the subject is supposed to produce the correct response before the stimulus and the response appear together. Each complete presentation of the list constitutes a trial, and of course, the items are presented in a different order on each trial.

An alternative method is to present the entire set of pairs together and then ask for recall of the responses by presenting the stimuli one at a time. Surprisingly enough, so far as rate of learning is concerned, it doesn't seem to make much difference which way practice is accomplished (Battig, 1961; Lockhead, 1962). This result is surprising because the method of complete presentation does not provide for knowledge of results until the entire series of items has been studied. Many developers of teaching programs have assumed that immediate knowledge of results is beneficial to learning, yet for paired-associate learning that does not seem to be the case.

OTHER METHODS

There are, of course, an endless number of methods of presentation that might be employed in the laboratory. Those we have discussed thus far are the traditional ones. New methods are developed all the time; then there are the whole battery of methods that have been invented primarily for the study of retention. Among these are the various tests for short-term memory and tests for recognition memory. These will be presented in the chapters on memory. Other methods are usually peculiar to some individual problem or experiment, and these can be discussed as they come up.

PROBLEMS AND RESULTS IN VERBAL LEARNING

What do people learn when they practice the various methods we have just described? They learn the relationships we require them to learn, for one thing. But most psychologists would not be satisfied with so superficial an answer. We want to know what, say, learning a list of paired associates entails, or how it is accomplished. Many of the methods described in the preceding section were developed on the assumption that all learning happened by contiguous association. Such a view now appears to be overly simple, and so we are left with the necessity of describing verbal learning in some detail. There are two aspects to the learning of the kinds of relationships that exist in the various tasks we have described. One is the problem of describing what the basis is for relationships formed during the experiment, and the other is the problem of describing the contribution of preexisting information to the learning of those relationships. We shall examine the latter problem first.

The Effect of Existing Information upon Verbal Learning

Subjects who come into the verbal learning laboratory know a great deal at the outset about what they are to learn. They know how to pronounce the letters and words presented to them. They know what some of or all of the words mean, and they know how to put words together to form sentences. All this information bears on verbal learning, and the effects of various kinds of information can be illustrated in many ways. One of the most interesting is provided by category clustering because it depends upon some subtle relations of meaning.

SEMANTIC RELATIONS IN CATEGORY CLUSTERING

Clustering, you will recall, occurs in free recall when words belonging to the same conceptual category follow one another in the order of recall more often than they should by chance. Bousfield (1953), who discovered the effect, argued that clustering was the result of a word's making subjects think of the category name and the category name, in turn, making the subjects think of another word from the list they had just heard which belonged to the same category. This process has sometimes been described as mediation through superordination. To take a particular example: A subject may remember that *cat* is on the list; the word *cat* leads to the mediating concept, *animal*, and that, in turn, helps the subject to remember that *dog* was also on the list. Therefore, in recall, *dog* will be remembered right after *cat*, even though they were widely separated in the list presented to the subject.

This example, it may occur to some readers, might be accounted for without mediation. *Dog* is a common association to *cat* in free association norms. Therefore, the order *cat-dog* in recall might be a direct result of preceding habits rather than the result of the mediation of something else. Deese (1959) so argued on the basis of the fact that the presence of strong associations in a list increases the number of words recalled. This is direct evidence of the influence of associations in recall. Marshall and Cofer (see Cofer, 1965) showed that different pairs of associates, when equal in association frequency according to norms, clustered more frequently when they were also categorically related than when they were not. This fact, as well as other evidence on clustering (see Bousfield, Steward, & Cowan, 1964), suggests that clustering can be both on the basis of direct associations and by categorical mediation. Furthermore, an experiment by Bousfield and Puff (1964) shows that *any* semantic feature connecting words, not just a superordinate feature, will produce clustering. Thus, semantic information is used, without deliberate intention, to organize output in recall. Furthermore, it is by no means certain that associative connections of the sort found in free-association norms are not themselves the result of semantic factors at work (see Deese, 1965). The relation between association and meaning is complicated. Most linguists would be likely to argue that free associations, in part at least, are the result of relations among semantic features that make up the meaning of words. On the other hand, a number of psychologists have recently argued that relations in meaning can be described by more sophisticated versions of association theory. These range from notions that enrich association theory by describing whole networks of connections rather than single associations (Kiss, 1973) to theories that are associational only in the sense that they describe semantic memory as relational and assume that the relations described within it are learned (Kintsch, 1972; Rumelhart, Lindsay, & Norman, 1972).

One of the most interesting of the neoassociation theories is that of Anderson and Bower (1973), and a portion of it bears directly on clustering and free recall. The theory is called HAM, which is, after the fashion of computer-based theories, an acronym, in this case for human associative memory. HAM explicitly denies that words are directly associated together, as earlier theories of verbal learning assumed. Words can be connected to one another only through the mediation of propositions embedded in a complicated grammar. Even the learning of nonsense syllables depends upon propositions. In the theory proposed in HAM, the individual letters of a nonsense syllable like xyj are individually represented by "idea nodes," and in order to encode or integrate this syllable, HAM, which is intended to mimic the mental processes of a human being, would have to develop the proposition "within xyj, an x precedes a y, which precedes a j."

However, Anderson and Bower point out, for many purposes the only important fact is that two words are connected together. It doesn't really matter whether the connection is direct or via a propositional structure. Therefore, it is possible to analyze the results of many experiments as if the words learned by the subjects were connected together directly rather than being linked through some propositional structure. This makes it possible to relate another computer program, FRAN (for free recall in an associative network) to HAM.

Finally, to cap matters, there is some direct evidence that free associations themselves are really truncated propositions or parts of propositions (Hamilton & Deese, 1973). Thus, it doesn't really matter whether free-association norms or category norms better predict the results of clustering experiments. The bringing together of words in recall happens because words are related conceptually. All sorts of conceptual relations can be embedded in propositions, of which a category name is but one example. *Dogs* and *cats* are both animals, but *dogs* also fight *cats*, and *dogs* chase *cats*. People can cluster the same words for different reasons. The essential fact is that clustering is the result of the influence of something previously learned upon the performance of a new task, and that previous learning can be described by propositional relations.

SUBJECTIVE ORGANIZATION

What we have previously learned is not simply a collection of unrelated propositions, but an organized system of information about the world. People impose organization on new material as they learn it, even if there is no inherent (previously learned) organization to that material. Tulving (1962) demonstrated that on successive free-recall trials of the same set of words, people settle down to a fixed sequence in recall, even when the list itself is presented in a different order on each trial. Each individual's sequence is different and reflects principles of organization unique to that individual. Tulving (1966) also argued that the increase in the number of words recalled on successive trials was the *result* of the development of organization and not merely a correlate of it. Simply repeating words does not produce much learning. Tulving asked two groups of subjects to learn, by free recall, the same set of 22 words. One group of subjects saw the words beforehand. They read aloud each word as it was exposed on a memory drum, and each word was exposed six times. This group of subjects and another group then learned to recall the list by ordinary free-recall procedures. After hearing the list, the subjects tried to recall as many words as they could. On the first trial there was a very small difference in favor of the group of subjects that had seen the words ahead of time, but that difference disappeared by the second trial, and both groups learned the list at the same rate. Learning the list entailed forming some sort of organization, and the repetition at the beginning had not helped that organization.

Mandler (1967; 1970; 1972) has argued that the most general form of organization in memory is hierarchical. He reminds us that if there are only five words per category, five categories per level, and five levels, the resulting number of concepts stored would be the enormous number 10^{17} items. However, he also points out that subjects accede to the demands of the world and will form whatever relations are necessary. People will organize things serially, if that is the way things are made easy for them. Mandler argues and shows by data that the reason Tulving's subjects had to fall back upon their own subjective organization is that the lists were always presented to them in different orders on different trials. If the list is always presented in the same order, subjects will adopt that particular order as the mode of organization. In fact, Mandler (1970) argues, serial order is so frequently used a technique in organizing information that it is committed to memory. We often use the highly overlearned alphabetic sequence to encode new information, and city planners used to name streets by numbers and letters in order to make it easy for people to find locations.

An experiment by Mandler and Pearlstone (1966) points out a difference between subjective organization and organization imposed by some general conceptual structure. Subjects were given a list of words to sort into anywhere from two to seven categories. These subjects repeatedly sorted the words until they achieved a stable structure. Another group of subjects learned to sort the same words into a conceptual scheme devised by the experimenters. The subjects who developed their own organization achieved stable structures in many fewer sorts than did those who had to learn the experimenter-defined sorts. Nevertheless, the subjects in the two groups recalled about the same number of words. Once again, it wasn't the amount of exposure that was important, it was the nature of the organization.

However, Mandler (1970) points out that subjective organizations are largely consensual. Different people agree upon similar organizations for a given collection of words. Completely idiosyncratic organizations or reliance on some mnemonic device such as the alphabet only appear in those cases in which a particular collection of words or a list consists of items which come from categories unrelated to one another.

Chunking is the name given by Miller (1956) to the development of subjective organizations of various sorts. Miller points out that people have severely limited capacities for processing information in short-term memory (see Chapter 13). About all we can handle without repetition or help from previous experience is from five to seven separate items. For example, after a single exposure, an adult can recall correctly a string of numbers from five to seven items long. Beyond that, in order to recall more, a person must reorganize the material. Miller gives as an example someone who overlearned the decimal equivalents of binary numbers. He could then remember strings of up to 20 zeros and ones simply by breaking them up into units of three and translating each group of three into its decimal equivalent. In the chapters on retention, we shall examine processes of reorganization in memory in greater detail.

The Nature of the Relations Learned

What are the relations learned in any particular experiment, or in any task outside the laboratory for that matter? From the account of the various methods in verbal learning given earlier in this chapter, we would know that the relations learned in a given task depend in part upon the arrangement of items in the task. Or, more generally, they depend upon the *structure* of the task, which can be defined as the arrangement of items plus the instructions about what is to be learned.

In paired-associate learning, subjects learn to give particular items in response to other items. For example, a subject might be asked to pair 12 adjectives with 12 nonsense syllables. When he sees BEJ, he is supposed to give *limp*; when he sees XYJ, he is supposed to produce *total*, and so on. Even if he learns the task perfectly, he might not be able to write down all the adjectives in the absence of the syllables. In order to retrieve the adjectives without error he would probably need the syllables as mediators. All that paired-associate learning requires is that a subject be able to discriminate among the stimuli and give the correct responses to those stimuli (Ellis, 1973). It does not require the subject to commit the stimuli to memory. If asked, most subjects would be able to recall only a portion of the stimuli used in a paired-associate experiment.

To be able to recall a list in serial order requires something more complicated. The subjects must know at least what item follows every item in the list, but experiments from Ebbinghaus's day on show that subjects learn many more associations than those between successive items. In free recall, or in other tasks, other relations are learned. Some of these are peculiar to the task in question, but others reveal general processes at work. In the section that follows, we shall extract some general principles about structural relations by examining the experimental literature concerned with the relations learned in particular tasks.

Paired-associate learning came to be a favorite laboratory task because it seemed so clearly to exemplify stimulus-response psychology. Given a stimulus, subjects learned to associate a response, and that was it. Thousands of experiments now tell us, however, that a bare stimulus-response conception of paired-associate learning is too simple. In fact, things have gone rather far in the other direction. Anderson and Bower (1973), in their computer program designed (among other things) to simulate paired-associate learning, make the assumption that paired-associate learning always entails an underlying proposition. If, for example, we require a subject to give the response *lawyer* to the stimulus *cow*, Anderson and Bower, or at least their program, would assume that the subject must generate some propositions such as *the cow kicked the lawyer* in order to do so. Even if the pair consisted of a nonsense syllable and a number, the subject, according to Anderson and Bower, would have to generate a proposition such as, BEJ *precedes 12*, or BEJ *is paired with 12*.

For learning meaningful relations, images certainly help. In fact, given the six or seven seconds between pairs of items necessary to allow an image of the relation between a stimulus item and its response to be formed, there is evidence that an indefinitely large number of associates can be committed to memory *on a single trial* (Bugelski, 1970). Evidently, imaging is evidence of a kind of mental reorganization going on that Miller had in mind with his idea of chunking. Bugelski argues that images always occur in learning, and consequently, that the reason it is so hard to learn some kinds of relations is because those relations do not readily lend themselves to images. Paivio (1971) and Anderson and Bower (1973) take a less extreme position. They argue that images help learning relations between pairs of items but that they are not necessary. Pylyshyn (1973), however, argues that some relations are easier to image *and* easier to learn because they exemplify some more basic underlying structure. In short, images and ease of learning are not related by cause and effect but are related because ease of imaging and ease of learning both reflect some more fundamental process that is wholly inaccessible to direct conscious experience and not directly reflected in behavior.

In another sense, though not the sense of stimulus-response psychology, paired-associate learning represents about the simplest kind of relation that can be learned. It is in the sense that the conditions of a paired-associate experiment discourage the subject from learning anything other than *paired* relations. Many-one, one-many, and many-many relations cannot easily be learned because the only thing constant in a paired-associate experiment is the relation between a particular stimulus item and its response. Given this simple situation, there are many alternatives to the idea that the stimulus simply evokes the response. One of the oldest of these alternative ideas is the notion of *redintegration*. Horowitz and his associates have recently revived that idea (Horowitz, Chilian, & Dunnigan, 1969; Horowitz & Prytulak, 1969;

Horowitz, White, & Atwood, 1968). Redintegration occurs when a part makes you think of a whole. Thus, Horowitz and his associates would argue, the stimulus A, in paired-associate learning, does not elicit the response B, but rather, part A elicits the whole A-B, or for that matter, part B could elicit the whole A-B. This is much more compatible with the notions of modern linguistics than the traditional stimulus-response view. In fact, it is closely related to the ideas of many contemporary linguists who hold that complete sentences are often responses to a probe, conceived of as a topic or theme, prompted by preceding sentences or by the need of someone else for information (Hockett, 1966; Chafe, 1970). The complete sentence consists of the topic or theme of the sentence together with the comment upon that topic. Thus, if someone asks us about our mutual friend John, we are not forced to think of weddings, as classical association theory might have it, but we are prompted to remember the whole proposition that John is married and thus might say to someone: "Didn't you know, John got married last month?"

Horowitz and his collaborators are not content to argue from linguistics, but they show from a series of experiments, some of which are experiments in paired-associate learning and all of which arise out of the paired-associate paradigm, that the probability of recall of B, given that the subject knows A or recalls A, is vastly greater than it should be. Most of the experiments performed by these investigators are experiments in free recall, but all the analyses are between pairs of words, and the results are meant to apply to paired-associate learning.

All these ideas—the notion of redintegration, the idea that paired-associate learning requires the development of a proposition relating the stimulus and response items, the idea that paired-associate learning is mediated through images—express in a particular form the general view that the whole is greater than the sum of its parts. When we put this notion together with some of the characteristics unique to paired-associate learning in the laboratory, such as that one member of the pair is better as a cue for recall than the other simply because the subject is not required to practice it overtly, we can account for all the interesting effects in paired-associate learning. The subject is required to retrieve, in all its detail, the stimulus item and then to make the overt response part of a whole, perhaps an abstract proposition or perhaps an event pictured by an image, in order to show that he has learned the paired relation.

SERIAL LEARNING

Serial learning is much more complicated, both experimentally and in theory, than paired-associate learning, though on superficial glance it might appear to be simpler. Computer programs which simulate paired-associate learning are easier to devise than those which will imitate the known phenomena of rote serial learning, and this fact is a reflection of the more complicated series of relations required by rote serial learning as compared with those required by paired-associate learning. The fact that pairs, in paired-associate learning, are in random order from trial to trial makes interpair connections difficult to make and temporary in nature. However, the fixed order of the items from one trial to the next in serial learning makes relations develop not only between adjacent items, but between items at different parts of the list. This phenomenon was observed by Ebbinghaus (1885), and he called it the development of remote associations, though that name does not square very well with modern versions of theories to account for serial processes in learning.

Be that as it may, the name is commonly used, and we shall use it here. Remote associations can be detected in various ways. Ebbinghaus used an indirect technique, but one of considerable power. He would first learn a list in serial order and then rearrange the list and learn it in the new order. In every instance, the rearranged list was learned more rapidly than the list that was completely new. This result could not be accounted for by warm-up or by any of the features of general transfer (see Chapter 14) because Ebbinghaus, by the time he reached this experiment, had acquired vast experience with all the syllables and with the serial learning of them by rote. Rather, it had to do with something internal to the lists. Ebbinghaus believed that associations were made from a given item across other items to items remote in the list by the same process that governed associations between adjacent items. However, these remote associations were weaker, either because the intervening items interfered with the establishment of remote associations or because the elapsed time made the associative connections weaker. Remarkable confirmation of that view comes from Ebbinghaus's observations that there is greater transfer when the distance between adjacent items from the original list is close on the derived list than when the distance is large. If BIJ is separated from GEX by only one item in the original list, the connection between them will be more easily learned on the derived list than if they were separated by, say, six items on the original list.

There is direct evidence for remote associations as well. For example, if you make a subject, who has learned a list by serial anticipation, give free associations to items on the list, he will show a greater probability of giving responses that are close to the stimulus item on the list than to items that are more remote (McGeoch, 1936). However, despite this and other facts, it is pretty certain now that the interpretation of serial learning as a matter of forming a complex of adjacent and remote associations is wrong.

For one thing, the idea of remote associations makes puzzling the similarity between serial position curves obtained in serial anticipation experiments (see Figure 11.7) and similar curves obtained from experiments in perceptual scanning (see Harcum, 1970). Ebenholtz (1972) brought together a large amount of empirical evidence to show that the serial position curve and other effects in rote serial learning result from what he describes as the dimensional properties of the task. Initially, the beginning and end items provide anchors that are easy to identify for the subject. Jensen (1962) points out that subjects really learn the items of a

12-item list in this order: 1, 2, 12, 3, 11, etc. They learn the middle items late, and last of all they learn the item just past the middle, in this case item 7. Ebenholtz argues that this order arises out of the efforts of the subjects to tag each item by some category determined by position in the list. Subjects first learn the first two and the last positions. They then attempt to assign general region tags to the remaining items, and to the extent that they are successful in this, they will be able to anticipate the items in serial order. This cannot be the whole story, for the anticipatory method of presentation guarantees that each item will not only be categorized by its position tag, but by what item precedes it (and, perhaps, by what follows it) as well.

Such a view is consonant with contemporary theories of what Mandler (1970) calls seriation. These theories accord with Lashley's (1951) notion that serial acts are hierarchical. Even though one response must follow another in serial order, the whole is planned in advance. It wasn't until psychologists became aware of the fact that such serial acts as uttering sentences must be planned, at least in part, in advance, that they began to take seriously the notion of hierarchical structures in serial learning. Restle (Restle, 1970; Restle & Brown, 1970) has developed an explicit theory of how serial patterns are learned, a theory based upon structural trees very much like those used in the derivation of sentences in linguistics (see p. 290). He has applied his notions to such diverse phenomena as serial learning and the analysis of musical structures.

Though subjects do make use of hierarchical structures in serial learning, they also make use of the cues provided by individual items. Therefore, the learning of a list by serial anticipation is probably very complicated. As with so many laboratory tasks that were originally designed to make things simple and to provide strong controls, serial anticipation has the effect of making things more complicated. Patterns are easier to discern when subjects can scan all items in any order they wish, and learning a list to some criterion is very much faster by such a method of complete exposure than by the traditional serial method of one item at a time.

Strategies in Learning

Previous information, the structure of the task, and similar conditions can be varied experimentally more or less directly. However, an equally important condition for learning is the strategy a person uses to master some particular task. Strategies in learning cannot be studied quite so directly. The techniques for the study of strategy depend upon (1) giving subjects different kinds of instructions regarding how to go about learning and (2) inducing subjects to adopt some particular strategy by varying the conditions of the experiment. Both of these are uncertain ways of studying exactly what subjects do in learning, but they are both far better than asking subjects how they learn. If there is one message that is common to all these chapters on learning and retention in human beings, it is that people cannot correctly identify the processes that go on in themselves as they learn.

Why is it that practice seems to be effective at some times and not at others? We have already seen that the structural relations among materials account for much of the variation in difficulty associated with different tasks and conditions of learning. Some things require more practice per unit material because the material is unstructured or because the conditions of practice prevent us from perceiving its structure. Even more important, however, is the strategy individuals are induced to adopt in practice or in exposure to some material.

INCIDENTAL LEARNING

We learn some things without trying. Unless we are politicians we seldom make a deliberate effort to learn the names of the large number of people we meet in the course of a year, but most of us manage to learn at least some of these. There is, then, learning without deliberate intent. Most practice is on a continuum between intensive practice and casual, incidental practice. Experimental studies of incidental learning are aimed at finding out what makes the difference between deliberate practice and incidental learning.

Is intent to learn itself the critical feature? Probably not. Postman (1964) and Montague (1972) independently come to the conclusion, after reviewing rather different kinds of experimental studies, that intent per se has no relevance. What really matters is the kind of activities, or in Montague's terms, processing of information results from different levels of intention.

There are two main experimental techniques for comparing incidental and intentional learning. One of these compares exposure of materials without specific instructions to learn with exposure and instructions to learn. The comparison is based upon a test for retention at some time later. Another technique is to give people something to learn, but while they are learning that material, expose them to other materials which they are not specifically instructed to learn. A test of retention compares performance with that of people instructed to learn *all* materials.

In the first instance, performance on recall without specific instructions to learn is compared with performance after instructions to learn. In the second instance, performance after instructions to learn just one aspect of the material exposed is compared with performance after instructions to learn all aspects of the materials. The second kind of approach has the advantage of not needing the cooperation of subjects, but it suffers from the disadvantage arising from interference from the cover task—the task that subjects are instructed to perform.

It is hardly a surprise to learn that nearly every comparison of incidental and intentional learning shows superiority of intentional learning. However, it is greater for some conditions than for others. When, under incidental conditions, subjects are forced by the nature of the cover task assigned to them to respond differentially to each item, the differences between incidental and intentional conditions are drastically reduced (Mechanic, 1962). The task in this experiment was something

like paired-associate learning. The subjects were exposed to pairs of
three-letter nonsense syllables. They had to learn the second member of
each pair, but not the first. However, as a cover task the subjects rated
both members of the pair for phonetic similarity. The task required the
subjects to pronounce both syllables as best they could. They had to
compare the syllables with one another—to respond to *all* syllables
differentially, not just to those to be learned. In another condition, the
rating of pronunciation was replaced by another cover task, one that did
not require the subjects to pronounce items.

The subjects remembered more of the items they had been instructed
to learn, a fact which shows that the instructions to learn had been
followed. The difference between the items learned intentionally and
those learned incidentally markedly declined, however, when the subjects were required to pronounce the items and not just cancel letters in
them. The act of pronunciation itself required subjects to learn something about the syllables. One of the things that happens when people
learn intentionally is that they respond differentially to the items to be
learned. Any task that requires differential responding will result in
something being learned about that task. In summary, intentional
learning accomplishes its results by imposing different activities during
practice than would be the case with no intent to learn. Intent aids
learning only to the extent that it causes people to respond to the
materials to be learned in ways that they would not ordinarily. It is not a
matter of trying harder, it is a matter of what is done during practice.

MEDIATION

Sometimes two things are associated together by sharing something else
in common. When such association occurs, mediation is said to have
taken place. The principle of mediation asserts that associations between
element A and element B occur because they are both associated with C.
The third term bridges the gap between two terms that otherwise would
be unrelated. The principle of mediation was more important when
association theory dominated the study of verbal learning. However,
there is no denying that mediation takes place and is important in
learning. As we shall see, however, current interpretations of mediation
go beyond traditional association theory.

The ways in which a single term can mediate between two others
reduces to three main types (Jenkins, 1963). These types are illustrated
schematically in Table 11.4. You can think of each of the letters as
standing for either a stimulus term or a response term in paired-associate
learning. We can use the column headed stimulus equivalence to
illustrate a typical experiment. The subjects in such an experiment would
first learn to give the responses B to their appropriate stimuli A. On a
second task, the subjects learn to give the same responses B, but now to
new stimuli C. Then on a final task, in which mediation is evaluated, the
new stimuli for the second task C become response terms, which the
subjects must learn to give to the original stimuli A. The rate of learning

the third pairs is compared with the rate for some control pairs, unrelated to the items in the first two phases.

These three types are incomplete, for there is a fourth type possible, reverse chaining. It, however, makes no sense in a stimulus-response analysis, and so it is not shown in the table. It was included, however, in a large experiment by Horton and Kjeldergaard (1961). All the subjects in this experiment learned three lists of paired associates, and each list corresponded to one of the stages in Table 11.4. The lists consisted of eight items, which were short but relatively rare words such as BANAL, KRONE, or UMBER. Practice was by the method of anticipation. In the third stage, half of the items to be learned consisted of related pairs and half consisted of control items. For example, for the chaining paradigm, the subjects might be required to learn the association BANAL-KRONE, then the association KRONE-UMBER. They would tested by the pair BANAL-UMBER.

The net result of this large and carefully controlled experiment was to show that all paradigms produced evidence of mediation in the third stage. In fact, even the impossible paradigm—the reversed chain—produced some evidence of mediation, though not as much as the others. The surprising result, however, was that the paradigms did not differ among themselves. One produced about as much evidence for mediation as another. This was a surprising result because association theory would lead us to expect differences.

Jenkins (1963) reviewed this and other experiments like it and came to the conclusion that the tendency to mediate is something that must be aroused in subjects. It just doesn't occur automatically, although reinforcement and similar conditions control its arousal. Mandler (1963) argued that if reinforcement and other such conditions control the tendency to mediate during verbal learning, then the problem becomes one of knowing whether or not subjects can learn the theory of mediation as a concept. He asserted that subjects can and, furthermore, that the relations in mediation are understood by subjects as logical propositions. If that is the case, the chaining paradigm would read as follows:

If A, then B.
If B, then C. Therefore:
If A, then C.

Mandler points out that of the eight possible arrangements of three items taken two at a time, all but two make logically possible propositions.

Table 11.4
Principal types of mediation paradigms

STAGE	CHAINING	STIMULUS EQUIVALENCE	RESPONSE EQUIVALENCE
Learn:	A–B	A–B	B–A
Then learn:	B–C	C–B	B–C
Test for:	A–C	A–C	A–C

Some, however, are logically stronger than others. The stimulus-equivalence paradigm, for example, leads, in the third stage, to a logically possible conclusion, but not one that is logically necessary. The only unlogical propositions are the reverse chains, and these apparently produce the least mediation.

The relations in experiments designed to teach subjects to use mediators, such as those in the Horton and Kjeldergaard experiments, are complex and not well understood. Undoubtedly, Mandler is correct in principle, however. That is to say, subjects try to form schematic relations to help them in rote learning. One possible schematic relation is that of propositional logic. There are others, however.

We have already examined (p. 325) aspects of a different approach to the problem of mediation. It is the study of what has generally been called natural language mediators. In these investigations, experimenters do not try to teach subjects specific mediating relations but, instead, try to find out what kinds of mediating devices subjects use without instruction. Paivio (1971) shows us that the imagery value of words and their degree of concreteness in meaning are the best predictors of how well those words will be learned in free recall or recognized in experiments on recognition memory. They are better predictors than association value, meaningfulness, or frequency of usage. Paivio argues, therefore, that images serve to mediate during learning and tests for retention. Some words are so low in their capacity to arouse images, however, that any mediation involving them must be verbal, or in any event, conceptual in such a way as not to depend upon the production of images. Purely verbal mediation does occur (Montague, 1972) and is responsible for the comparative ease with which some items can be associated with others in verbal learning experiments. However, verbal mediation will differ from occasion to occasion and from item to item. It is under the control of the person doing the learning and not the experimenter.

However, Prytulak (1971) provides us with an analysis of the kinds of mediators that subjects do, on occasion, use in memorizing CVC nonsense syllables. They do not treat the CVCs as immutable. In fact they alter and transform them in various ways in an effort to relate them to something that is easier to remember. A very few nonsense syllables are identical to a phonetic representation of a real word. An obvious example is TAC. However, for other syllables, subjects must substitute, add to, delete, or build some meaningful phrase upon the syllable given. For example, SAQ might be remembered by a given subject as the word *sag*. Notice, however, that mediating the syllable this way requires the subject to remember the transformation, too. Not surprisingly, Prytulak found that some transformations are more useful than others. The transformations that are the easiest and require the least alteration of the original item are the most useful. However, any deliberate mediation, because it runs the risk of requiring an extensive operation, takes time, and mediation cannot occur with very rapid rates of presentation of items. Learning is very slow with very rapid rates of presentation.

Furthermore, if sufficient time is given between items in paired associate learning and subjects are instructed and practiced in making use of natural language mediators, they can learn long lists on a single presentation.

Almost all the material in this chapter, including the material on mediation, serves to tell us that the most important determiner of the pace at which some new verbal material is learned depends upon how easily subjects can bring their past experience to bear on the new material. That is partly a matter of the material itself. Some things are easily learned because they draw so heavily upon information learned earlier. It is also partly a matter of the strategy subjects use in learning. Knowing the most useful strategy depends not only upon having the store of background information, but upon being able to use it in an effective way.

TWELVE

MEMORY

In the preceding chapters we have been concerned with learning, the relatively permanent change in behavior that results from practice. We turn now to consider retention, a related problem of equal importance. The concepts of learning and memory are closely related to one another since the results of a particular learning experience must be retained in order for experience to be cumulative. Thus, understanding learning necessitates understanding memory. In this chapter we shall use the words *memory*, *retention*, *forgetting*, and *remembering* pretty much in accord with their everyday meanings. Note that a theory of retention (or memory) is at the same time a theory of forgetting since the terms are complementary: Amount forgotten = amount learned − amount retained.

This chapter is organized around the question, Why do we forget? In answering this question we shall examine several theories of forgetting. However, before we plunge into these theories, it will be useful to describe some operations common to all memory systems, be they embodied in computers, rats, or human beings. These operations are *encoding, storage,* and *retrieval.*

It will help us to be objective if we consider a distinctly nonliving memory system. An office filing system will suffice. Suppose a letter comes to the office and a secretary files it. Let us say that it is a letter of complaint from an important customer. This information is needed to properly categorize the letter. If the information is of a new kind, the categorization problem leads to some difficult decisions. If the office has never received complaints before, the secretary must decide whether to put the letter under the customer's name or under a new category "complaints." Categorization must be consistent to work. It won't do for the secretary to file this letter under complaints and the next such letter under a customer's name. In human memory this process of deciding how to classify information is called *encoding.* Encoding includes the perception of information and the abstraction of one or more of the essential characteristics of the information. An important difference between a filing system and human memory is that the input can be retained in the filing system, whereas in human memory only the information that is encoded is retained. Thus, in a paired-associates task, it is possible that the subject will encode the pair XJZ−14 as X−14, and thus in retention be quite unable to supply any information about the other two letters. This important problem of coding and coding variability is discussed in a book edited by Melton and Martin (1972).

The second necessary operation in the memory system is *storage*. In most nonliving systems there is little that needs to be said about this stage. We assume that the letter is not accidentally thrown out and that neither the ink on our letter nor the paper itself will disappear with time. Therefore the information will stay put. Whether this is the case in a living system is a question that we shall consider later in this chapter.

The third stage, *retrieval*, is the converse of encoding. A new secretary frantically looks for a letter of complaint. "Where is this filed? Under complaints? Customer's name? By its date of arrival? Under the name of the executive to whom it was addressed?" All these and more are potential locations for the information, and the secretary will have to search within each of the categories until she either finds the letter or gives up. While we are not conscious of searching in different locations when we try to remember something, we are aware of trying to remember how we *encoded* the information.

We introduced a new secretary to exemplify the retrieval process because it makes it clear that we are not concerned here with the memory system of the secretary, but that of the filing cabinet itself. Nevertheless, it is necessary to suppose that an active agent organizes the process of retrieval. However, there need be nothing mysterious or unscientific about such an agent. For example, in a computer system a similar function is served by the executive program.

This analysis of memory shows that forgetting may be due to a failure of any of the three operations of a memory system. Encoding may be inadequate or incorrect. Information may be degraded during storage, or storage capacity might be too small to hold all the desired information. Finally, retrieval may fail because the search takes place in the wrong part of the file.

DISUSE THEORY

The simplest theory of forgetting is that of disuse or decay. The idea is that learning is the result of practice or use, while during retention intervals, when the information in question is not used, forgetting occurs; therefore, disuse causes forgetting. Such a theory has an implicit physiological basis. It is assumed that learning modifies the central nervous system and that forgetting is produced by deterioration over time of the "trace" in the central nervous system. Thus, forgetting is conceived of as similar to the progressive fading of a photograph over time or the gradual obliteration of the inscription on a tombstone.

Forgetting, by this view, is due to a failure of storage; neither encoding nor retrieval is implicated.

Such a theory is inadequate on several grounds (see, e.g., McGeoch, 1932, 1942). The single biggest objection is that it is possible to demonstrate that forgetting is affected by the activities that a subject engages in during the retention interval (the interval between initial learning and the test of retention). An early study that showed such an effect is that of Jenkins and Dallenbach (1924). There were only two subjects in this rather heroic experiment, and they were both tested several times in each of the experimental conditions. Jenkins and Dallenbach compared the rate of forgetting between intervals of sleep and of waking. Learning took place either late at night or early in the morning. After learning a 10-item list of nonsense syllables to a criterion of one perfect recitation in the morning, subjects went about their daily affairs until the time scheduled for a return to the laboratory one, two, four, or eight hours after original learning. At night, subjects went to sleep for one, two, four, or eight hours immediately after learning. They were awakened by the experimenter for the retention test. The two subjects and the experimenter lived in a room in the laboratory near the experimental cubicle for the duration of the experiment. The retention test consisted of a simple free recall of the learned list, a different list being used each time a subject was tested. The results are shown in Figure 12.1, where number of syllables recalled is plotted as a function of retention interval.

Note that both curves show that forgetting is *negatively accelerated*. Forgetting is rapid at first (e.g., in the first hour after learning) and slower later (e.g., between four and eight hours). This is a general result, first demonstrated by Ebbinghaus in 1885. The important finding is that

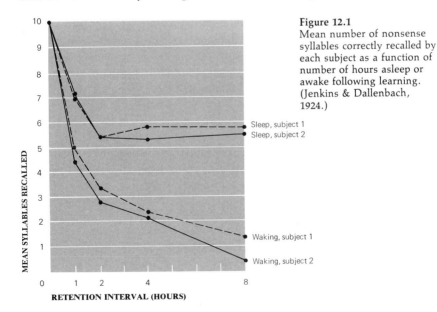

Figure 12.1
Mean number of nonsense syllables correctly recalled by each subject as a function of number of hours asleep or awake following learning. (Jenkins & Dallenbach, 1924.)

there is a substantial difference in retention between the sleep condition and the waking condition. Thus, disuse itself cannot be held to be solely responsible for forgetting. Could the results be due to "cheating" on the part of the subjects? It is possible that they disobeyed their instructions not to think about the lists after leaving the experimental room. However, this should have tended to improve retention during *waking* intervals, and thus cheating cannot explain the difference between the sleep and waking conditions. A more recent investigation has confirmed the differential forgetting rates of sleep and waking conditions (Ekstrand, 1967). Interestingly, most of the forgetting that takes place during sleep occurs during the stage of sleep associated with dreaming (Fowler, Sullivan, & Ekstrand, 1973).

The Jenkins and Dallenbach study is but a single example of the now widely known fact that forgetting is a function of the nature of the activity that fills a retention interval. There are also other kinds of experimental evidence against disuse theory, such as the observation that the nature of the activity that *precedes* original learning also affects forgetting over a fixed retention interval.

We conclude that disuse theory is inadequate as a complete explanation of forgetting. Note, however, that while the negative evidence we have cited shows that disuse does not account for all forgetting, it does not prove that disuse accounts for no forgetting at all.

PERSEVERATION-CONSOLIDATION THEORY

It is not necessary to go so far as to compare sleeping with waking activity to show that forgetting is a function of the nature of the activity interpolated between learning and testing. For example, suppose a subject learns a list of nonsense syllables, then rests (with instructions not to rehearse) for 20 minutes and is then tested for retention of the list. In another condition subjects learn the same list of nonsense syllables, but spend the next 20 minutes learning a new, unrelated list. At the end of that time retention of the initial list is tested. Subjects who "rest" retain more of the original list than the subjects who learn a new list. One of the earliest attempts to account for the difference between the effects of rest and activity during a retention interval is perseveration theory (Müller & Pilzecker, 1900). This is a physiological theory, the idea being that the neural activity produced by learning tends to perseverate (i.e., continue) after the end of explicit practice itself. Perseveration has the function of consolidating learning. There is, of course, ample evidence for the existence of perseverative processes at both the physiological and the psychological levels, e.g., visual afterimages and pathological repetition compulsions. However, whether perseveration is a part of ordinary memorial processes is a question open to investigation.

The theory of Müller and Pilzecker was made more specific by Hebb (1949), who postulated that the memory trace was held in the form of reverberating electrical circuits while a more permanent structural trace is laid down. Some evidence to support this hypothesis was presented by Duncan (1949), who tested the effects of *electroconvulsive shock* (ECS) on avoidance learning in rats. ECS is an electrical current passed through the brain, producing a comatose state during which there is little neuronal activity. If ECS is administered after a trial in a learning experiment, then the trace of the learning experience should be disrupted if it is still in the form of reverberating electrical activity, but not if the structural change has consolidated. The rats in Duncan's experiment were given one trial per day in a simple active-avoidance task. They could avoid punishment by running out of one chamber into another within 10 seconds. In the various conditions of the experment, an ECS followed the avoidance response by 20 seconds, 40 seconds, 1 minute, 4 minutes, 15 minutes, 1 hour, 4 hours, or 14 hours. One group of control animals was given no ECS. The data shown in Figure 12.2 indicate that learning steadily improves as ECS is delayed from 20 seconds to 1 hour. However, ECS delays of 1, 4, and 14 hours all produced learning as rapid as that for the control animals. These data suggest that the process of consolidation, at least in the rat, is essentially completed in one hour. Although there are grounds for criticizing Duncan's conclusions (e.g., Coons & Miller, 1960), at least some of the effect he observed is due to the disruption of consolidation (Spevack & Suboski, 1969).

Perseveration theory has trouble accounting for some of the results of varying the time at which interpolated learning occurs. For example, even allowing for reasonable differences between rat and man, it would seem plausible that consolidation in man ought to be completed within several hours. Nevertheless, a condition of interpolated learning results in substantially worse retention than a "rest" condition, even when the interpolated learning task is given midway in a retention interval of six *weeks* (Bunch & McTeer, 1932). Another finding that poses a problem

Figure 12.2
Mean number of trials on which rats successfully avoided shock (out of 18 trials) as a function of the time between each trial and administration of ECS. Different points on the curve represent different groups. (Duncan, 1949.)

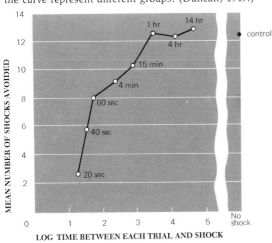

for perseveration theory is that earlier learning can affect the retention of material learned later. Finally, there are effects due to the *similarity* between original and interpolated learning that are not accounted for easily by perseveration theory. If original learning requires memorizing a poem, there would probably be better recall if the interpolated task were memorizing chemical formulae than memorizing another poem. As we shall see in the following section, the systematic exploration of similarity effects in learning serves as the cornerstone for the most important of the theories of retention and forgetting. All this makes it clear that perseveration theory is an inadequate general theory of forgetting. However, the evidence from the studies of ECS suggests that there may be some effects of perseveration on short-term memory (see Chapter 13).

INTERFERENCE THEORY

The most important of the theories of forgetting is interference theory. This theory, as an explanation of the phenomena of forgetting, comes from a specific aspect of a broader view of behavior known as associationism. In interference theory the elemental unit of analysis is the bond between a specific stimulus and a specific response. Once such an S-R connection is established, it is not weakened by the passage of time; however, S-R associations interact with one another, producing behavioral changes that may be either facilitatory or inhibitory. Forgetting is one manifestation of an inhibitory interaction.

If any and all associations may interact with one another, then in understanding the retention of a specific association, *all* experience prior to and subsequent to the acquisition of the association must be taken into consideration. This is impossible for all except perhaps the most rudimentary organisms. What we try to accomplish in laboratory investigations of forgetting is to manipulate the subject's learning history during a limited period of time, in the hope that the laws so discovered are applicable to uncontrolled, real-life situations as well.

TRANSFER

We can study the interaction of S-R associations in either of two contexts. *Transfer* concerns how previous experience affects the *acquisition* of some specific material. *Proaction* and *retroaction* refer respectively to how the *retention* of material learned at some time may be affected by prior learning or subsequent learning. Since performance on one task can be either helped or hindered by the existence of other things learned, we have the following possible effects: in retention we can have proactive or retroactive facilitation and proactive or retroactive inhibition. In acquisition we can have positive or negative transfer.

Although our concern in this chapter is with retention, and thus with proaction and retroaction, it will be useful to consider briefly the nature of transfer experiments. The basic question that a transfer study answers is how prior experience affects later learning. The design of an experiment in transfer requires two groups of subjects, one of which practices a preliminary task either for some specified period of time or to some specified criterion and is then tested on acquisition of a second task. The other group of subjects learns only the second task. Transfer is positive if the experimental group learns more rapidly than the control group and negative if its performance is worse. This experiment requires that the two groups not differ in ability. Equation of the groups is accomplished by random assignment of subjects to the two groups. The basic conditions are summarized in Table 12.1.

In studies of transfer, a distinction is made between *general* and *specific* sources of transfer. Transfer is specific to the extent that it can be attributed to specifiable relations of similarity between the stimuli and/or responses used in successive tasks. General transfer is a catch-all category for any transfer effects that are not demonstrably specific in origin. For example, suppose one wanted to determine if learning Spanish helped in the subsequent learning of another Romance language such as French. A standard transfer design could be used. The experimental group takes a year of Spanish while the control group does not. During the second year both take French. Suppose that testing throughout the second year indicates that the experimental group learns more quickly. What would this indicate? Certainly the data would not speak to the issue of whether learning one Romance language specifically facilitates learning another one. It might be that students in the experimental group picked up some general study skills while learning the first language and not anything pertaining to the features shared by the two languages. It would help to have an additional control group in which students learn a non-Romance language such as Russian during phase one and then French during phase two. If the students who learn Russian do as well as those who learn Spanish in the later acquisition of French, then the transfer due to learning Spanish would probably be general, while if the group that had Russian performed as poorly as those who learned no language, then the transfer due to learning Spanish would be specific to the features shared by French and Spanish.

General transfer is fairly loosely defined. However, it has been possible to distinguish between two categories of general transfer: warm-up and learning how to learn. Warm-up is like limbering-up to perform a motor skill. Warm-up includes such things as adjusting to the rhythm of the memory drum and finding the posture most conducive to attending to the material to be learned. Such adjustments occur in early trials and then disappear fairly rapidly (in a matter of an hour or two) after the end of practice (Hamilton, 1950; Thune, 1950). Even an unrelated task such as color guessing can warm subjects up for subse-

Table 12.1
Experimental design for the study of transfer

GROUP	STEP 1	STEP 2
Experimental	Learns A	Learns B
Control	Rests	Learns B

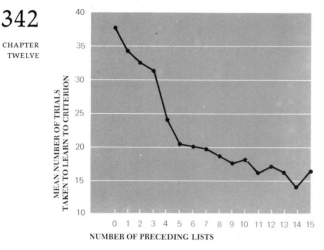

Figure 12.3
Average number of trials required to learn a list as a function of the number of preceding lists learned. (Ward, 1937.)

quent learning if its trials are presented at the same pace as those used in learning the nonsense syllables (Thune, 1950).

Learning to learn results in a more permanent change. As we saw in Chapter 8, it is the acquisition of learning skills with practice. In a study by Ward (1937), subjects learned 16 different lists of paired associates successively. The data in Figure 12.3 show a great reduction in the number of trials needed to learn a list as a result of practice. Since the lists were all different, the improvement in learning was not due to retention of specific items, but of skills useful for learning any list of nonsense syllables. Learning to learn is a general phenomenon. Even animals show it.

Within the category of specific transfer, the most widely investigated topic concerns similarity. The paired-associate task is the method usually used in such investigations since it permits independent manipulation of stimulus and response similarity. The five varieties of paired-associate learning most frequently used in studies of transfer (and proaction and retroaction for that matter) are exemplified in Table 12.2.

In a study of specific transfer effects, the control group would not rest, but would learn a list with stimuli and responses unrelated to the ones

Table 12.2
Some sample lists exemplifying the original and transfer lists for five paradigms of transfer

INITIAL LIST		TRANSFER LIST			
A–B	C–D	A–B$'$	A–D	C–B	A–B$_r$
MAB-pill	FET-dog	MAB-pills	MAB-dog	FET-pill	MAB-sky
DAX-home	JIB-book	DAX-homes	DAX-book	JIB-home	DAX-home
BEM-sky	WUF-car	BEM-skies	BEM-car	WUF-sky	BEM-bug
DIV-bug	PAB-lamp	DIV-bugs	DIV-lamp	PAB-bug	DIV-pill

used in the transfer phase. Thus, the A-B, C-D condition serves as a control for the effects of general transfer.

If the responses in the two tasks are similar, the experimental condition is symbolized A-B, A-B'. In the sample in Table 12.2, the responses are very similar. Lesser degress of similarity might also be used; for example, the B' words might have been *capsule, house, clouds, insect.* The greater the similarity of the responses in the two lists, the greater the degree of positive transfer. At one extreme, transfer is identical to further practice, since A-B, A-B represents continued learning of the initial list. At the other extreme, the response-transfer paradigm becomes A-B, A-D; new responses must be attached to old stimuli. In these circumstances, while learning the second list, stimuli tend to elicit the original B responses rather than the newly correct D responses. Thus this design usually produces negative transfer.

The A-B, C-B condition permits the use of old responses but requires that they be attached to new stimuli. Imagine having to learn to stop at blue traffic lights and go at yellow lights—or having to stop at pink lights and go at turquoise lights. These examples suggest that the degree of facilitation of or interference with subsequent learning will depend on the similarity of the original and transfer stimuli.

The A-B, A-B$_r$ paradigm represents the situation in which the original stimuli and responses are paired randomly during transfer. Imagine having to learn to stop at green lights, slow down at red lights, and go at amber lights. This paradigm produces massive negative transfer.

There have been many attempts to characterize in a simple fashion the various similarity relations observed in transfer studies. By far the best known is the *transfer surface* constructed by Osgood (1949).

In Figure 12.4, positive and negative transfer are represented by vertical distances above and below the horizontal plane of zero transfer. The long dimension represents degrees of response similarity, the steps being: R_I, identical response; R_S, similar response; R_N, neutral (i.e., unrelated) response; R_O, opposite response (e.g., black-white); R_A, antagonistic response (e.g., open fist-clench fist). The short dimension represents various levels of stimulus similarity between two tasks: S_I, identical stimulus; S_S, similar stimulus; S_N, neutral stimulus.

Note that maximum positive transfer occurs when both stimuli and responses are the same, i.e., A-B, A-B or continued practice on a single list. Maximum negative transfer occurs when stimuli are identical and responses are antagonistic. It is difficult to think of antagonistic verbal responses, but the extension versus flexion of a specific muscle provides a good nonverbal example. Note that if stimuli are unrelated (S_N), transfer is zero, regardless of the degree of response similarity. An experiment by Dallett (1962) has verified several of the relations in this surface; however, it is clear that the figure is an incomplete and in part incorrect schematization of the data. It has no way of predicting the massive interference that results from the repairing in the A-B, A-B$_r$ paradigm. Martin (1965) points out that "opposed responses" (e.g., black-white) may be located incorrectly in the diagram. Because they have features in common (they are both color names) they are conceptually close. Opposed responses have some positive degree of similarity and should

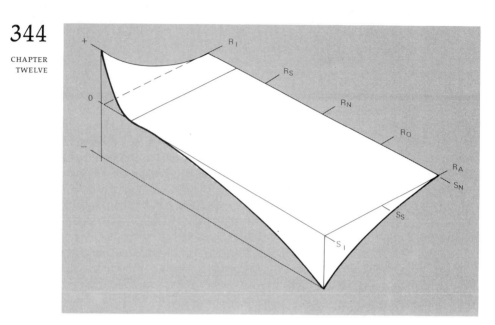

Figure 12.4
The hypothetical stimulus-response transfer surface. (After Osgood, 1949.)

thus be to the left of R_N rather than to the right in the diagram. Postman (1971) has discussed some of the problems of trying to account for transfer with only the two dimensions of stimulus and response similarity. The transfer surface ignores the fact that there are other components of transfer in paired-associate learning (such as response availability, forward associations, backward associations), each of which is subject to similarity effects. Martin (1965) has provided a more detailed analysis of transfer that takes such components into account.

In the next section we turn from transfer to proaction and retroaction. However, remember that the surface proposed by Osgood was designed to account for proaction and retroaction as well as for transfer.

RETROACTION AND PROACTION DESIGNS

The basic design of the transfer study can be adapted to permit the investigation of the effects of other learning experiences upon the *retention* of some specific material. Consider first the proaction design shown in Table 12.3. The time between steps 1 and 2 and between steps 2 and 3 can be varied by the experimenter.

Table 12.3
Experimental design for the study of proaction

GROUP	STEP 1	STEP 2	STEP 3
Experimental	Learns A	Learns B	Retention test on B
Control	Rest	Learns B	Retention test on B

The difference between groups in the amount of task B retained reflects the influence of the learning of task A by the experimental group. If proaction influences retention of task B, it must operate somewhere between the learning of task B and the test for retention of task B. That means the major influence of the prior task is through *its* retention after task B has been learned, for it is the retained aspects of task A that must interfere with the retention of task B.

The retroaction design, shown in Table 12.4, is the easier one to understand because the interfering condition is actually produced during the retention interval for the task tested.

The difference in the amount of retention of task A reflects the influence of the learning of task B by the experimental group. Once again, the duration of the intervals between steps can be varied by the experimenter.

The meaning of rest for the control condition deserves some comment. In an ideal experiment the subjects in the control condition would be held in suspended animation. The experiment by Jenkins and Dallenbach (1924) in which subjects slept during certain retention intervals comes about as close as possible to the ideal, but in ordinary practice it is difficult to impose even this degree of inactivity upon control subjects. The problem is most serious in a retroaction design, for while the experimental subjects are learning an interpolated task, the control subjects may rehearse the original task. We suppose this not to be a matter for serious concern in studies of animal behavior, since animal subjects will not be doing something appropriate to the test task under rest conditions. However, human subjects can rehearse. Consequently, control subjects are not usually allowed to be passive. Rather, they are given some task to perform in the "rest" condition which keeps them occupied but which is unrelated to the eventual test task. This is why the A-B, C-D paradigm often provides the control condition for retroaction and proaction experiments.

In both retroaction and proaction, experimentally produced forgetting takes place when the control group retains more than the experimental group. The classical term for this forgetting is proactive or retroactive *inhibition* (depending on the design). A newer term is *interference*, which is probably better because it avoids the physiological connotations of the term *inhibition*. Of course, it is also possible to select materials and tasks that make the experimental group show better retention than the control group. In that case we say that proactive or retroactive *facilitation* has taken place.

Table 12.4
Experimental design for the study of retroaction

GROUP	STEP 1	STEP 2	STEP 3
Experimental	Learns A	Learns B	Retention test on A
Control	Learns A	Rest	Retention test on A

Before we can turn to a detailed analysis of the experiments that have been done in the tradition of interference theory, it is important that we appreciate some of the complexities involved in measuring retention and evaluating transfer, proaction, and retroaction.

There are both direct and indirect methods of testing retention. The direct methods include *recall* and *recognition* as well as their variations, while the major indirect method is known as *savings*. Each of these methods taps a different aspect of learning and retention, and thus a method cannot be haphazardly selected.

In a typical *free-recall* test, a subject may be presented with a list of items, e.g., words, and after the list has been presented one or more times the subject is asked to simply recall as many of the words as possible, without regard to order, in some specified period of time, say three minutes. This technique places greatest emphasis upon the simple availability of the material. By contrast, *serial anticipation*, which is a form of cued recall, also requires the subject to learn the position within the list of each item. In this procedure, a list of words is presented one word at a time, and the entire list is repeated in the same order until the subject learns it. The task requires the subject to guess the next word in the list on each trial.

Various kinds of materials demand different varieties of recall. For example, in the study of *perceptual memory*, we may ask people to draw or otherwise give their reconstruction of the material which had been exposed to them.

The preceding methods all required the subject to reproduce the learning materials. There is also the important method of *recognition*. There are two forms of recognition tests in common use today. In the *forced-choice* procedure, the subject must select the correct alternative from among two or more alternatives. For example: Which of the following is the name of the third book of the Bible: (1) Exodus, (2) Leviticus, (3) Deuteronomy? In the *Yes-No* procedure, the subject decides whether or not a single item passes a threshold of "acceptability." For example: Is Leviticus the third book of the Bible (Yes or No)? Recognition measures have some interesting properties and are frequently used in sophisticated attempts to construct models of memory processes (see, e.g., Kintsch, 1970, chapter 5).

Recognition is usually considered to be the most sensitive of the direct measures of retention, since it often shows retention when production methods do not. Unlike recall, alternatives are presented to the subject for evaluation; they need not be generated by the subject himself. Thus recognition depends only minimally on availability of responses, knowledge of serial position, or complex retrieved processes. Recognition is usually regarded as a pure measure of storage or of the extent to which people differentiate among items presented to them (Postman & Rau, 1957). Recently, these traditional views of recognition have been called into question by some new findings described later in this chapter.

Indirect methods of measuring retention all rely on the fact that the rate at which some material is relearned depends upon how well it was learned in the first place. Most indirect measures simply compare the amount of time or number of trials it takes to relearn something with the original learning. Thus, if it takes 12 trials to learn a set of nonsense syllables, and then 24 hours later it takes only 2 trials to relearn the same set, we have indirect evidence for retention over the intervening time, even though there may be no direct evidence in recall—that is, on the *first* trial of relearning the subject may obtain a retention score of zero.

The major difficulty with accepting such data as evidence of retention is that people learn how to learn. Even if a person learned two *different* but equivalent lists, one after the other, the second one would be learned in less time than the first. Only when relearning an original list is faster than learning a new second list do we have evidence of retention.

One way to express the improvement in relearning is by a savings score. The savings score reflects the amount of time or number of repetitions saved in relearning compared with the amount in original learning. It is given by the formula

$$\text{Percent savings} = \frac{N \text{ trials to learn} - N \text{ trials to relearn}}{N \text{ trials to learn}} \times 100$$

Critics have rightly condemned the indiscriminate use of the percent-savings measure as a comparative measure of retention when materials differ in difficulty. But this measure of retention does provide an acceptable means to compare materials which require the same number of trials or same amount of time to learn in the first place. In other words, it may be used to determine how retention changes with time in the absence of practice.

THE DEVELOPMENT OF INTERFERENCE THEORY: RETROACTION

McGeoch (1932) stated the original version of interference theory. He assumed that original associations remain intact, while new associations were acquired during interpolated learning. This has been called the *independence hypothesis*, since it suggests that two sets of related associations may exist in storage without mutual interference (Barnes & Underwood, 1959). According to this theory, the cause of forgetting is not a failure of storage, but is competition between alternative responses at recall. Such competition is, unfortunately, all too common an experience. You have probably found yourself trying to recall some name or fact while you perseverated on some obviously incorrect response. Folk wisdom suggests (probably correctly) that when you find yourself so blocked, it is best to stop trying to remember and just wait for the competing response to disappear, thus freeing the sought-after response. In psychoanalytic theory, memory is also permanent; unconscious repression acts as the agent of inhibition at recall. Techniques such as free association and dream interpretation, in the view of psychoanalytic theory, serve as tools to peel back repression.

Two-factor theory The independence hypothesis was undermined in a famous study by Melton and Irwin (1940). These experimenters determined the influence of amount of practice at the interpolated task upon the retention of the first task in a retroaction experiment. The material the subjects learned consisted of nonsense syllables learned by the method of serial anticipation. All subjects practiced the original list for five trials. They then either rested or were given 5, 10, 20, or 40 trials of interpolated learning. Thirty minutes after original practice, all subjects were required to relearn the original list to a criterion of two perfect recitations. The amount of retroactive interference (RI) on the first relearning trial for each of the experimental conditions was computed by subtracting from the recall score for each test condition the recall of the rest condition.

The results are shown by the curve in Figure 12.5 labeled "total obtained RI." Total RI increased rapidly as the amount of practice on the interpolated task increased from zero to a very few trials. However, total RI reached a maximum after about 20 interpolated trials, and it is even possible that there was a decline in total inhibition as practice on the second task continued. When Melton and Irwin came to present reasons for this result, they drew upon some additional data. They tabulated the number of overt errors which occurred during the recall of the first list. They were particularly interested in those errors that were actually *correct* syllables from the second list. These *interlist intrusions* are failures of recall of the first list that can definitely be traced to competition from items learned during practice on the second list. The frequency of these errors is plotted as a function of the number of repetitions of the

Figure 12.5
Retroactive inhibition as a function of the number of trials of interpolated learning. The lower curve shows the inhibition attributable to overt intrusion at recall. The upper dashed curve shows inhibition attributable to factor *X*. (Melton & Irwin, 1940.)

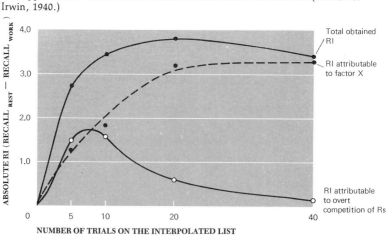

interpolated list in Figure 12.5 as the curve labeled "RI attributable to

overt competition of responses." These errors are common during early
trials of practice on the interpolated list but decline thereafter. Melton
and Irwin argued that this was so because, as the interpolated list became
better learned, it was more easily differentiated from the original list and
therefore less likely to produce intrusions during recall of the original list.

The problem, however, is to account for the fact that retroactive
inhibition continues to be high after overt competitive intrusions have
declined. How do we account for the sustained high retroaction? As
shown in Figure 12.5, Melton and Irwin labeled the difference between
retroactive inhibition attributable to overt competition and total retroaction "factor X." Notice that factor X continues to increase as the result of
additional practice on the interpolated task.

What is factor X? Melton and Irwin argued that it might be *unlearning*
of the material from the first list. They pointed out the analogy to the
experimental extinction of instrumental responses. As subjects learn the
second list, items from the first list occasionally intrude. That is, people
think of, or even overtly give, items from the original material during
practice with the interpolated list. Such responses are incorrect during
the learning of the second list, and so they go unreinforced or may even
be punished. Therefore, the tendency to give items from the first list is
weakened during the learning of the second list. The more the practice
on the second list, the greater the cumulative unlearning of the first.

If unlearning is analogous to extinction, one would expect *spontaneous
recovery* (see. p. 113) to occur. Therefore, some of the inhibiting effects of
the second list would disappear if a time interval were allowed for the
material from the first list to spontaneously recover. Underwood (1948)
used such an analogy to account for the finding that the amount of
retroactive inhibition tends to decline as the time interval is lengthened
between the learning of the second list and the test of retention of the
first.

However, all such evidence is indirect. In the standard techniques of
rote learning, it is very difficult to observe what actually happens to other
responses as the subject learns the material assigned to him. Several
experiments (Briggs, 1954, 1957) have analyzed paired-associate learning
with a *modified free-recall* (MFR) technique that makes it easier to follow
what happens to responses from the first task during the learning of the
second task. The A-B, A-D paradigm is used, and specially designed
recall tasks are inserted during the learning of list 2. The stimuli (i.e., A
terms) are presented, and the subjects make a single response to each
one. These tests show that as the items from the second list are learned,
the responses from the first list become less likely to occur. Furthermore,
the material from the first list "spontaneously" recovers if a time interval
occurs between practice on the second list and recall test. Therefore, the
analogy to extinction seems to be more than circumstantial.

Such experiments suggest two factors at work in the retroactive
inhibition experiment and one in the proactive inhibition experiment. In
the retroaction design, learned responses appropriate to the first task
become unavailable during the learning of the second. In addition, the

second task produces learned responses which compete, at the time of the retention test for the first task, with those of the first task. This is particularly the case if the cues differentiating the occurrence of responses from one or another of the tasks are very much alike. There is confusion at the time of recall between the materials from the two tasks.

In the proaction experiment, only competition is at work. Since the interfering task is learned first, there is no additional learning task interposed before the test for retention that would permit unlearning of the correct responses of the second list. Note however, that the A-B associations of the *first* task are partly unlearned as a result of learning A-D associations in the second task. The mechanism that permits A-B associations to serve as potent competitors with A-D associations in proaction is spontaneous recovery. From the analogy with experimental extinction and from direct experimental evidence, we know that the responses weakened through unlearning recover. One consequence of such recovery is that when equivalent tasks are learned to equivalent degrees, there is very little difference between retroactive and proactive inhibition after a time interval has elapsed prior to the final retention test (Melton & von Lackum, 1941).

The problem with the MFR technique is that it permits only one response to each stimulus. Therefore, it can only show whether the list 1 or list 2 response to a stimulus is the stronger at a particular time. To determine whether list 1 responses become absolutely weaker rather than just weaker relative to list 2 responses, it is necessary to provide an opportunity for both responses to occur in a situation that minimizes the opportunity for response competition. Barnes and Underwood (1959) designed just such an experiment to determine the "fate" of first-list associations. Subjects learned lists of paired associates in which nonsense syllables were the stimuli and unrelated two-syllable adjectives were the responses. There were eight pairs in the lists, and each subject learned two lists. In the critical condition of the experiment, the nonsense syllables (stimuli) were identical for the two lists, but the responses were different. Therefore, the subjects had to learn two different responses to the same stimuli in rapid succession.

At various points during the learning of the second list, subjects were asked to give, in special recall tests, the items appropriate to *both* the first and the second lists. Subjects were allowed a full two minutes for this recall. This technique is a modification of the modified free-recall method and thus is usually referred to as MMFR. The essential results of these recall tests can be seen in Figure 12.6, which shows that the responses appropriate to the first list decline in number during the learning of the second list. This result is demonstrated again by an experiment much like Barnes and Underwood's (Goggin, 1963). Goggin did not, however, do what Barnes and Underwood did in the recall tests; she asked subjects to write down all the items they could possibly remember, even though some of them might be wrong or identified with the wrong stimulus. Her results were almost identical with those of Barnes and Underwood. The only conclusion seems to be that during the learning of the second list,

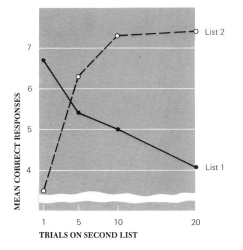

7

6

5

4

MEAN CORRECT RESPONSES

List 2

List 1

1   5   10   20

TRIALS ON SECOND LIST

Figure 12.6
The number of responses correctly recalled from list 1 and list 2 as a function of degree of practice on the second list. The more practice on the second list, the fewer responses subjects
could recall from the first list. (Barnes
& Underwood, 1959.)

the material from the first list becomes unavailable. Therefore, it isn't
just that people learn new responses to old stimuli which are more likely
to occur than the original responses. The original stimulus-response
associations seem to be weakened so that they become difficult to recall.

Response-set interference   At this point in our discussion it appears that
McGeoch's independence hypothesis is wrong, since first-list associations do seem to become weaker as second-list associations are learned.[1]
However, the evidence is not totally convincing. Suppose, for example,
that unlearning does not affect associations *per se*, but instead, that it
represents a generalized tendency, acquired during second-list learning,
to avoid or suppress first-list responses, as a set. Suppose further that the
"selector mechanism" responsible for this suppression is subject to
"inertia" so that it continues to select second-list responses for a while
after the end of second-list training, thus reducing recall of first-list
responses on MMFR tests as well as on conventional recall tests. Such a
hypothesis was first proposed by Newton and Wickens (1956) and was
elaborated by Postman, Stark, and Fraser (1968).

The hypothesis of response-set competition has received support from
studies by McGovern (1964) and Postman and Stark (1969), among
others. In both of these studies of paired-associate learning there were
two kinds of retention tests. One was an ordinary recall test. The other
was designed to eliminate the necessity for response recall; it was a
matching or multiple-choice test. Comparisons between the recall and
matching tasks were made in a variety of experimental conditions, and in
most, the matching test showed much less retroactive inhibition than the
recall test. Indeed, in some conditions there was no significant amount of

---

[1]We are concerned here with the A-B, A-D design because it is one of the standard
paradigms used in the analysis of negative transfer and retroactive and proactive interference. First-list associations do not become weaker during second-list learning in *all*
paradigms, however. A notable exception is A-B, A-B' (Barnes & Underwood, 1959).

retroactive inhibition. Note that the matching task cannot be performed if the stimulus-response association has been unlearned. Therefore, the obtained pattern of results suggests that the relations between stimuli and responses were not unlearned, but that first-list responses were for some reason unabailable in the standard recall situation.

The phenomenon of response-set competition or suppression, although important, cannot account for all retroaction. The best evidence of this is that in the A-B, A-B$_r$ paradigm there is strong retroaction even though the response sets are identical in the first and second lists. Thus, response-set competition should be thought of as an elaboration of two-factor theory rather than an alternative to it (Postman & Underwood, 1973). Our best current guess is that response-set suppression *and* unlearning of specific stimulus-response associations are both implicated in forgetting (Anderson & Bower, 1973, chapter 15).

List differentiation   Suppose a subject learns two lists in succession and is later tested on list 1. The extent to which the subject will be able to recall the responses appropriate to the first list is a function of the degree to which he can tell which responses go with which list (even if all the required responses happen to be highly available). This point was made by Underwood (1945) to explain why interpolated learning did not result in an ever-increasing number of overt intrusions in the study by Melton and Irwin (1940, see Figure 12.5). He reasoned that increasing practice on list 2 makes that list more distinctive from list 1. During the subsequent list 1 retention test, a subject might have a tendency to give a list 2 response rather than the correct list 1 response, but if the lists were well differentiated he would know that the response he wanted to give was inappropriate and he would suppress it. The result would be an error of omission rather than an overt intrusion.

Underwood assumed that the degree of differentiation of two lists would depend on the absolute and relative strengths of the competing associations and the length of time between the end of list 2 learning and the subsequent retention test. The last of these factors was investigated by Deese and Marder (1957). Subjects learned in succession two serial lists of 12 adjectives each. They were then given recall tests after delays varying from 4 minutes to 48 hours. The data showed more between-list confusions (i.e., intrusions) as the delay interval increased. Tests of the absolute and relative strength hypothesis were carried out by Winograd (1968). After learning two lists of 25 words each, subjects were shown all 50 words from both lists in a mixed order, and the subjects assigned each word to list 1 or list 2. When list 1 and list 2 were practiced equally often, and thus had roughly equal relative strengths, list discrimination improved as the amountof practice increased. When lists were unequally practiced (e.g., one repetition for list 1, three repetitions for list 2), list discrimination improved as the imbalance in frequency between the lists increased.

These experiments confirm the importance of list differentiation as a factor contributing to forgetting. As with response-set suppression, it represents an elaboration of classic two-factor interference theory.

Spontaneous recovery The assumption that spontaneous recovery of unlearned associations occurs is a crucial aspect of interference theory, and consequently, several investigators have attempted to find direct evidence of such recovery.

One investigation of this issue is that of Koppenaal (1963). Subjects learned two lists of paired associates of the form A-B, A-D. The key question is, What happens to A-B recall during the retention interval following the end of second-list learning? Presumably, A-B associations should be unlearned as a result of learning A-D. Therefore, if spontaneous recovery occurs, A-B recall should increase with the length of retention interval. To test this notion, subjects were tested for recall of both the B and D responses at seven retention intervals after original learning, varying from one minute to one week, using the MMFR technique of Barnes and Underwood.

There is reason to fear that even if the recovery hypothesis is correct, spontaneous recovery may be masked by other factors that impair performance, such as things learned outside the experiment during the retention interval. As a control for this possibility, another group was tested that learned only A-B, but was tested at the same retention intervals. The data appear in Figure 12.7. Notice that there is no evidence of *absolute* recovery of A-B associations, because recall of first-list items does not rise with time. Moreover, when that function is compared with that of the single-list control group, there is no statistically reliable evidence of *relative* recovery. By contrast, note the relative recovery of the first and second lists in that those two curves have clearly different slopes and even cross-over. However, this relative recovery is not of great theoretical importance. Other investigators have also failed to obtain reliable amounts of absolute recovery (Ceraso & Henderson, 1966; Slamecka, 1966). However, using retention intervals of 2, 8, and 20 minutes, Postman, Stark, and Fraser (1968) showed absolute recovery. Also, Elkstrand (1967), in his study of retention during periods of sleep

Figure 12.7
The number of responses correctly recalled as a function of the delay between the end of learning and the retention test. The lack of a systematic increase in list 1 responses with time indicates spontaneous recovery is not occurring. (Koppenaal, 1963.)

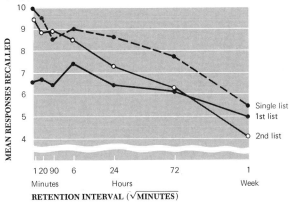

RETENTION INTERVAL (√MINUTES)

and waking, found evidence for absolute recovery of A-B responses during sleep. Thus, although the evidence for spontaneous recovery is not clear-cut, there do appear to be conditions in which it may be observed.

PROACTION IN INTERFERENCE THEORY

Because of the emphasis on retroaction, it was thought for a long time that if a subject learned, say, a list of nonsense syllables in the laboratory and was tested a week later, any forgetting that took place could be attributed to interference from habits learned during that week. To a person not committed to interference theory, this argument may not seem very plausible since the subject was unlikely to have come into contact with nonsense syllables during his everyday life. Interference theory would lead us to suppose that there should not be much retroaction when the interpolated and original materials are very different. However, it is not uncommon to find as much as a 75 percent decrement in recall after a 24-hour retention interval. How, then, might such massive amounts of forgetting be explained without violating the spirit of interference theory? A resolution to the problem was given in an article by Underwood (1957).

An experiment by Greenberg and Underwood (1950) examined whether subjects learn how to recall in the same sense that they learn how to learn. Naive subjects learned a list of 10 paired adjectives to a criterion of 8 out of 10 correct. Recall was after 48 hours. On the day following recall, a new list was learned to the same criterion and recalled after 48 hours. This was repeated for two additional lists. Recall accuracy was studied as a function of number of previous lists learned (this varied from 0 to 3, of course). Recall did not improve, but instead, fell from about 69 percent on the first list learned to about 25 percent on the fourth list. The existence of intrusions from previous lists suggested that proactive interference was the source of the decrement in recall. Thus, the forgetting of material learned in the laboratory may be in large part the result of previous lists learned in the same laboratory.

In the Greenberg and Underwood study, recall after a 48-hour retention interval following the learning of three previous lists was 25 percent, which is approximately the amount of recall found after 24 hours in many studies extending all the way back to Ebbinghaus in 1885. This suggested to Underwood the possibility that in those previous studies, subjects must have learned numerous lists. This proved to be the case. It was standard procedure at one time to have every subject serve in every condition to control experimental variability. Underwood reviewed over a dozen previous experiments in which recall was measured after 24 hours, and he determined for each of these experiments the average number of lists the subjects were required to learn before learning the list on which recall after 24 hours was measured. He then plotted recall as a function of the number of previous lists and produced the graph shown in Figure 12.8. This figure provides clear evidence of the importance of proactive interference in retention.

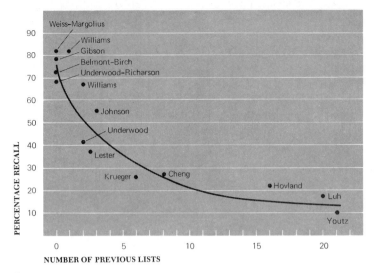

Figure 12.8
Percentage recall as a function of the number of previous lists learned as
determined from a number of studies. (Underwood, 1957.)

It is important to keep clear two very different effects of learning
several lists successively. We have just seen that *recall* gets worse with
successive practice. However, the phenomenon of learning to learn still
asserts itself in that subjects *learn* successive lists to criterion more
quickly with more practice, as demonstrated in Figure 12.3. These two
phenomena illustrate the distinction between proaction and transfer.

Extraexperimental sources of interference in forgetting The proaction
experiment is important because it suggests that the things we have
previously learned can interfere with our retention of something just
learned. Furthermore, it is the proaction effect that allows us to account
for uncontrolled forgetting that occurs in experiments on experimentally
produced forgetting. In most studies the control group shows a loss as
well as the experimental group; it is only that the loss for the experimental group is greater. Uncontrolled forgetting could be the result of
interference from previously learned habits—habits acquired outside the
experimental laboratory.

With such an idea in mind, Underwood and Postman (1960) investigated extraexperimental sources of interference in the retention of simple
verbal tasks in the laboratory. They asked subjects to learn three-letter
syllables by the method of serial anticipation in lists of 12 syllables.
During learning, the subjects tried to anticipate, by spelling, each
syllable before it was shown to them. Retention was tested in exactly the
same way. One group of subjects was tested for retention 30 seconds
after learning and the other group was tested for retention after one
week. The immediate retention test provided a base line against which
the amount of forgetting that took place in a week's time could be
measured. Underwood and Postman took the view that such forgetting

would be the result of previous habits interfering with retention of the experimental lists.

The critical variable was the nature of the lists the subjects learned. The lists were constructed so that some of them would be more subject to interference from previously acquired habits than others. Two possible sources of interference are ordinary sequential relations among letters in spelling and linguistic relations among words. Consider the question of letter sequences. Suppose one of the items is JQB. This sequence is unlikely in ordinary English. If the subjects were required to remember JQB, the more usual sequences of English (A or E following J, etc.) might interfere with the retention of the experimental syllable during the time interval. Underwood and Postman argued that the amount of such interference would be less when the letters in the syllables to be remembered were already like those of ordinary English. Therefore, Underwood and Postman compared the retention of two types of nonsense syllables: those consisting of very probable sequences in English, such as EST and UND, and those which are relatively improbable in English, such as HOK and RHA.

The same argument can be applied to words. Rare words have relatively few associations, argued Underwood and Postman, and these are weaker than those of common words. Consequently, we would expect lists of rare three-letter words such as ADO and RUT to be retained *better* despite their rarity than lists of very common words, such as AGE and USE. There would be more interference from previous associations during the retention interval for the common words.

The results of the experiment were disappointing. There was forgetting during the one-week period for all lists, but there was no statistically reliable differential forgetting among the lists. What differences did appear were contrary to the original hypothesis. There was more forgetting for the uncommon words than for the common words. Virtually the only reliable evidence the investigators found for the notion which led to the experiment was that the high-probability syllables were relearned more rapidly than everything else. While the authors performed a variety of analyses which convinced them that their original hypothesis was still tenable, the whole experiment was a very weak demonstration of the importance of extraexperimental sources of forgetting. It casts doubt on the importance of interference as an explanation of forgetting—for, if anything, one would expect the extensive previous experience with linguistic usage to have produced much bigger effects than it would be possible to achieve with experimentally produced forgetting.

Still another embarrassment for Underwood and Postman's (1960) analysis of the role of extraexperimental language habits was provided by Slamecka (1966). He pointed out that the plausibility of their theory hinges upon the adequacy of the unlearning hypothesis, i.e., that during the learning of a list, extraexperimental associations are actually weakened. He attempted a direct test of this hypothesis in the following way. Ten nouns differing in frequency of usage were selected to be stimulus (i.e., A) items in some lists of paired associates. Before any learning took

place, however, all subjects gave free associations to the 10 words. These free associations were presumably the readiest associations to the stimuli. The subjects were then divided into three groups. Two groups learned either an A-B list or an A-B list and then an A-D list. A control group rested while the other groups learned their assigned paired-associates lists. It is important to note that the B and D response items were selected so that none had occurred as free associations in the first part of the experiment. Next, all subjects were asked to recall their free associations. Subjects did quite well; more importantly, there were no differences among the three groups. Thus learning one or two interpolated lists did not seem to cause any unlearning of preexperimental associations. However, there was evidence of unlearning of *experimentally* learned associations in that recall of the A-B list was significantly worse for the A-B, A-D group than for the A-B, Rest group. Slamecka interpreted his data in terms of differentiation of associations, as did Postman and Stark (1969) in an experiment mentioned earlier.

It is easy to produce differential interference in the laboratory by varying the similarity relations among sets of lists. The question arises then as to *why* extraexperimental sources of interference fail to produce the expected results. Underwood and Ekstrand (1966) proposed two possible answers to this question when they pointed out that extraexperimental linguistic habits are very strong and developed as a result of widely distributed practice. In the usual laboratory experiment, potentially interfering associations are not learned to a very high level, and they are usually learned in a single session. Underwood and Ekstrand attempted to study the effect of proactive inhibition with associations learned under conditions that were meant to simulate the conditions under which linguistic habits are learned. Two lists of 12 paired associates each were learned in succession. The stimulus terms were three-letter words, and the response terms were two-syllable adjectives. The lists formed an A-B, A-D paradigm, and they were learned in the same order by all subjects. Subjects practiced the original lists for 12, 32, 48, or 80 trials, and there were two conditions of learning, massed and distributed. In the massed practice conditions the trials were all given in a single session; in the distributed practice conditions the trials for each degree of learning were spread over four days. Different subjects were assigned to each of the conditions. It should be noted that the original task was not very difficult; it is the kind of task that a typical college student can master in less than 12 trials. Immediately after the last trial of A-B learning, the subjects were required to learn the second, A-D, list to a criterion of one perfect trial. Recall of A-D followed 24 hours later.

The most important result of this experiment was that distributed practice led to little, if any, proactive inhibition, while massed practice led to large amounts of proactive inhibition. The effect of degree of learning was not large and was noticeable only in the massed learning conditions. This result has serious implications for interference theory. If we assume that linguistic habits are learned by distributed practice, then, like the

A-B list, they should not be a major source of interference for habits learned in the laboratory. Why do they not interfere? Mandler (1962) argued that overlearning may result in associations becoming part of a structure which prevents them from interfering with other associations. Whether Mandler's argument is cogent or not, the failure of associations learned under distributed practice to interfere with associations learned in the laboratory is a major embarrassment for interference theory. The fact is that if a list is learned to a fixed criterion in the laboratory by a naive subject, the rate of forgetting is essentially independent of the nature of the list (e.g., whether it is made up of words or nonsense), which should not be the case according to theory.

CURRENT STATUS OF INTERFERENCE THEORY

Interference theory has had a long history. As research accumulates, anomalies and inconsistencies in theories are noted. Some of the problems with interference theory have resulted in changes in the theory, but the resulting confusion cannot be ignored. For example, there is the finding that retroaction in a paired-associates learning task is in part due to the entire set of first-list responses declining in availability (e.g., Postman and Stark, 1969). To incorporate this into the theory, one need only assume that the responses of the first list are associated with contextual stimuli such as the experimental setting, the experimenter, etc. (McGovern, 1964). During interpolated learning, the contextual stimuli remain the same while the responses are changed. In the A-B, A-D paradigm the list stimuli (the As) also remain the same. The explanation for the depression of first-list responses is that it is the context-B associations that have been unlearned. While this may be an ingenious way to account for the data, it is not obvious why the A-B associations are not weakened also.

There are other problems that have not yet been resolved. An example is the failure of the "extraexperimental interference" hypothesis. But what about the theory on its original grounds, intraexperimental forgetting? An experiment by Shiffrin (1970) on the list-length effect bears on this question. The probability of recalling a particular item decreases as the length of the list in which the item is embedded increases (e.g., Deese, 1960; Murdock, 1962). This phenomenon is consistent with interference theory since an item in a long list is preceded (proactive inhibition) and followed (retroactive inhibition) by more items, on the average, than an item from a short list. There are other possible explanations, however. Shiffrin proposed that the probability of a subject recalling a specific item is an inverse function of the size of the set of items through which he searches to retrieve stored information. If the subject can restrict his retrieval to words presented in the list, this model also accounts for the effect of list length on learning and recall. To distinguish between the retrieval and interference explanations, Shiffrin presented his subjects with a number of lists of words of varying lengths and asked for recall of the list *before* the one just presented, not the one just presented as in the usual list-learning experiment. This procedure permits the separation of the effect of the size of the list being recalled from the effect of the total number of words intervening between presentation and recall. Suppose a long list (20 words) is followed by a short list (5 words). The retrieval hypothesis predicts that probability of recall should depend only upon the length of the list being recalled, i.e., good recall for a short list, poor recall for a long list. By contrast, the interference hypothesis would say that probability of recall should depend upon the length of the list intervening between the presentation and the recall of a given list as well as upon the size of the to-be-recalled list. One hypothesis predicts that recall should be independent of the length of the intervening list, while the other predicts the existence of a relationship.

The results of Shiffrin's study were quite striking. Recall of the 5-word lists averaged about 15 percent higher than the 20-word lists. Moreover, there was virtually no difference between the effects of interpolating a 5- or a 20-word list. This finding provides yet another argument against interference theory.

CUE-DEPENDENT FORGETTING

At the beginning of this chapter the notions of encoding and retrieval were introduced as logically necessary parts of the overall process of remembering, but we have not yet described their significance in detail. In this section we shall consider a body of recent research which will show that, "What is stored is determined by what is perceived and how it is encoded, and what is stored determines what retrieval cues are effective in providing access to what is stored" (Tulving & Thomson, 1973, p. 353). To put the matter differently, when we forget something, it does not necessarily mean that the memory trace is lost; it may merely be inaccessible because the current context does not permit retrieval schemes that are congruent with the encoding schemes employed at the time of original learning. This is a thumbnail sketch of the theory of "cue-dependent forgetting" (e.g., Tulving, 1974).

There are several lines of evidence showing that forgetting may be understood as being due to a lack of appropriate retrieval cues at the time of attempted retention. We shall report on: (1) effects of retrieval cues on retroactive interference, (2) effects of contextual biasing, and (3) when recall exceeds recognition.

EFFECTS OF RETRIEVAL CUES ON RETROACTIVE INTERFERENCE

Tulving and Psotka (1971) presented subjects with lists of 24 words, each list consisting of 4 words in each of 6 categories. For example, one list was made up of the following words, with the words grouped as shown to make the categories obvious: *hut, cottage, tent, hotel; cliff, river, hill, volcano; captain, corporal, sergeant, colonel; ant, wasp, beetle, mosquito; zinc, copper, aluminum, bronze; drill, saw, chisel, nail.* Each list was presented three times, and then a free-recall test was given for that list.

Different groups of subjects learned one, two, three, four, five, or six of these lists, with new words and new categories appearing on each list. In each group, after subjects had learned and been tested on each list separately, they were given a test in which they were to recall all the words from all the lists they had seen. After some intervening activity, subjects were given a final test on all the lists they had seen, but now they were presented with the names of all the categories that had been used (e.g., types of building, earth formations, military titles, etc.). This is called a *cued-recall* test. The results of the three tests are shown in Figure 12.9. The curve labeled "noncued recall" shows free-recall performance as a function of the number of lists interpolated between original learning and the eventual *overall* free-recall test. It drops markedly, indicating strong retroactive interference as a result of learning subsequent lists. The crucial finding, however, is that cued recall is nearly as high as original immediate recall. Thus the forgetting observed in this experiment (and indexed by the decline of noncued recall) is reversible.

Tulving (1974) suggests that the reversal of forgetting by the introduction of retrieval cues is not easily accounted for by the chief explanatory mechanisms of modern interference theory, viz., unlearning and general response competition. However, according to Tulving, the data are compatible with the idea of cue-dependent forgetting. During the tests of original learning, the retrieval environment is, presumably, similar to that prevailing during the initial presentation of the items. However, by the time of the overall free-recall test, the retrieval environment has changed as a result of learning and recalling the interpolated lists.

Figure 12.9
Mean number of words recalled from a list of 24 words in three successive tests—(T_1) immediate free recall, (T_2) noncued recall, and (T_3) cued recall—as a function of the number of other lists learned between the list and the second test. T_2 and T_3 are tests for all items presented on all lists; T_1 tests recall of a particular list immediately after that list is learned. (Data from Tulving & Psotka, 1971; figure from Tulving, 1974.)

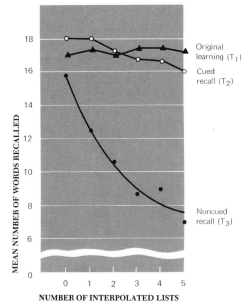

Presentation of the category names for the final overall tests restores the 361
missing information to the subject's retrieval environment and makes
possible nearly full recovery of the stored items. It is worth noting that MEMORY
the slight amount of retroactive inhibition evident in the cued-recall data
could be due to loss from storage (e.g., through decay) since the
cue-dependent-forgetting hypothesis does not rule out the contribution
of other factors.

EFFECTS OF CONTEXTUAL BIASING

The idea that what is stored is determined by what is perceived and how
it is encoded implies that a stimulus is not a rigidly fixed thing, but may
be represented in many different ways depending on the strategy
adopted by the subject at any given time.

A demonstration of this general principle was provided in a series of
experiments on recognition memory for nouns (Light & Carter-Sobell,
1970). During initial learning, nouns were presented (in sentences) in
the biasing context of a specific adjective (e.g., The boy earned a GOOD
GRADE on the test). During a later recognition test, subjects were
shown a long list of adjective-noun pairs and were asked to indicate
whether or not each *noun* had been shown before. In different conditions, the recognition test included pairs that biased either the same
semantic interpretation as before (e.g., *good grade*) or a different
semantic interpretation (e.g., *steep grade*). The crucial finding is that
recognition accuracy was higher when the same semantic bias existed at
the time of retrieval as at the time of initial encoding. A further important
finding was that this was true even when the same general semantic
interpretation was induced with a different specific adjective (e.g., *bad
grade*). Thus the word *grade* does not have a unitary representation in
memory, a representation that may be consulted to determine if the word
grade itself has been experienced in a recently presented list. Instead, it
has at least two representations, and one cannot determine if *grade* in the
sense of *score* has been seen recently if the retrieval cue leads to the
representation of *grade* in the sense of *slope*.

This important result is not due to the specific details of the Light and
Carter-Sobell experiment, since similar conclusions have been reached in
a variety of experimental settings (e.g., Cofer, Segal, Stein, & Walker,
1969; Tulving & Thompson, 1971, 1973). Contrary to popular opinion,
these studies suggest that a rose is not a rose is not a rose.

WHEN IS RECALL HIGHER THAN RECOGNITION?

Tulving and his colleagues have performed several studies on contextual
biasing which have yielded a most striking phenomenon: Under appropriate test conditions, recall performance may be substantially better
than recognition performance (e.g., Tulving, 1968; Tulving & Thomson,
1971; Watkins, 1974). This finding is surprising because many theorists
have assumed that retrieval processes, while necessary for recall, are
bypassed in a recognition memory test (see, e.g., Kintsch, 1970;

McCormack, 1972, for discussions of this point). Thus, in a recall test, a subject implicitly generates "candidate items" and decides for each whether or not it was on the test list. In a recognition test there is no need to generate items since they are provided directly by the experimenter. Thus, according to this analysis a subject should never recall items that he cannot recognize. Despite the apparent reasonableness of the traditional view of memory, it turns out that it is possible for subjects to recall items that they cannot recognize. A demonstration of this effect has recently been reported by Watkins (1974).

Watkins had subjects learn paired-associate lists in which the A and B items were nonsense words of five and two letters, respectively. However, when taken together, the two elements of a pair formed a common word (e.g., AMNES-TY, LIQUE-FY, SPANI-SH). The list was presented just once, at the rate of four seconds per pair.

To test for recognition of the B terms, subjects were presented with the B terms of the list they had just seen, mixed randomly with B terms from a matched list (e.g., IC, UR, EL from a list containing AMNES-IC, LIQUE-UR, SPANI-EL). To test for recall (in this case cued recall) of the B terms, the subjects were shown a list of the A terms they had seen previously and were asked to recall the B term that went with each. The data from this study were quite dramatic. Recognition accuracy was about 9 percent while cued-recall accuracy was 67 percent.

There is some dispute over the meaning of these data. Tulving argues that (1) such data may be explained by the principle of cue-dependent forgetting *and* that (2) the data show that retrieval is more than a trivial part of a recognition task. The argument for point (1) seems quite reasonable. If the term TY was not encoded as such, but only as part of the larger unit AMNESTY, then TY will not be an effective retrieval cue for "itself" during recognition. Apparently, however, the beginning of a word (AMNES-) *is* an effective retrieval cue for the whole word and, consequently, for the last few letters as well. (Note that the theory does not yet have any mechanism to explain this asymmetry between A and B terms, although the difference does seem intuitively reasonable.)

The argument for point (2) is less straightforward. It goes like this: Traditional theory holds that retrieval is not an important component of recognition, but is an important part of recall. Thus recall should never be higher than recognition. Since several studies have shown that recall can exceed recognition, traditional theory is wrong; recognition must also involve retrieval processes to a substantial degree. However, as McCormack (1972) has pointed out, differences in coding schemes used at the time of learning and the time of test may be sufficient explanation of the data. In other words, cue-dependent forgetting is sufficient to explain recall being higher than recognition; the data do not demand the additional statement that recognition involves extensive retrieval. And, indeed, the bulk of the experimental evidence reviewed by McCormack suggests that the traditional distinction between recall and recognition is amply justified.

The theory of cue-dependent forgetting appears to offer several advantages over modern versions of interference theory. Consider, for example, the demonstration that forgetting due to "retroactive inhibition" may be reversible under some conditions (Tulving & Psotka, 1971). According to one version of interference theory, loss of list members at the time of the first *overall* free-recall test is the result of unlearning of associations in the list. Note that both specific (item-to-item) and general (item-to-context) associations are unlearned. The question is, If unlearning refers to an actual weakening or degradation of a trace or association, how can it possibly be reversed? To answer by saying "spontaneous recovery" is not really to answer at all so much as simply to give a name to the phenomenon.

Another version of interference theory would claim that retroactive interference is due to response-set suppression, with earlier lists in the Tulving and Psotka experiment suffering from competing responses from later-learned lists. The problem here is that it is not clear why presenting retrieval cues (e.g., category names) should reduce response competition.

In contrast to the difficulty interference theory has in accounting for the reversibility of forgetting, the theory of cue-dependent forgetting seems to provide an entirely plausible explanation. Other advantages of the theory include its straightforward explanations of recognition failure and semantic biasing.

Among the objections that have been raised against the hypothesis, perhaps the most serious is that, as presently constituted, it is virtually incapable of being disproven since it is always possible to claim that any specific instance of forgetting is due to the lack of an appropriate retrieval cue. To disprove such an assertion requires the acceptance of the null hypothesis—i.e., a rejection of all possible alternative explanations. Although invulnerability to disproof is a serious flaw, the hypothesis is still useful and interesting as a source of experimental questions and hypotheses. Moreover, we may hope that in coming years specific variants of the general theory will be formulated in sufficient detail to make meaningful tests of the theory possible. Progress in this direction is already evident under the general theme of coding and coding variability (see Melton & Martin, 1972). Bower (1972) has even developed a mathematical model of coding that seems to incorporate many of the essential ideas of cue-dependent forgetting. Cue-dependent forgetting will not long suffer from the luxury of being invulnerably vague.

ALTERNATIVES TO INTERFERENCE THEORY

During the past dozen or so years a growing number of psychologists have become dissatisfied with interference theory, but no single, coherent, widely accepted alternative to that theory has yet been proposed.

The idea of cue-dependent forgetting represents one attempt at theoretical reformulation. Another major effort to organize the field of memory has been made by Anderson and Bower (1973), who have proposed what they call a neoassociationistic model of memory. A full discussion of this model presupposes some knowledge of computer programming, symbolic logic, and linguistics and thus is beyond the scope of this book. Still other theorists have adopted what we shall refer to as a *cognitive* viewpoint. This view stresses two general ideas: that the human learner is active rather than passive in his interaction with the informational aspects of the environment, and that what is learned forms a schema or organized mental structure.

Cognitive theories are not entirely new. Indeed, Plato had a nativistic and cognitive theory of memory. However, due to the influence of associationism and behaviorism, especially in America, cognitive theories were neglected in experimental psychology for many years.

Cognitive psychologists have not yet produced a theory powerful enough to make specific predictions about a wide range of phenomena; however, they have demonstrated some very interesting empirical effects that are embarrassing to any straightforward interpretation of interference theory. Some of these important demonstrations are discussed in Chapter 14.

THIRTEEN

SHORT-TERM MEMORY

The term *memory* does not refer to a simple concept. Rather, there are several different aspects to memory. Indeed, recent work suggests that there may even be several kinds of memory.

The possibility of more than one kind of memory is not entirely a new idea. William James distinguished between what he called *primary* and *secondary memory.* An object in secondary memory, according to James, is "recalled, fished up, so to speak, from a reservoir in which, with countless other objects, it lay buried and lost from view. But an object of primary memory is not thus brought back; it never was lost . . . never cut off in consciousness from that of the immediately present moment" (1890, pp. 646–647).

In James' distinction the kind of memory described in the previous chapter is secondary memory, measured in minutes, hours, days, or even longer periods. In this chapter we shall be concerned mostly with primary memory, measured in seconds. There seems to be still another form of memory even briefer in its duration than primary memory which we shall refer to as *sensory memory.* This system retains a fairly complete and accurate representation of the information presented to the senses, but only for a few seconds at the most.

Cutting across the distinction among memories in terms of duration is another distinction based upon modality. Visual and auditory memory are to some extent distinct from one another as well as from a higher level, verbal memory. There is also evidence for the existence of separate tactile, kinesthetic, and olfactory memory systems, but we shall not have space to cover them in this chapter.

Before we begin our discussion we need to define some terms. *Short-term memory* is a theoretically neutral term used to describe experimental situations or tasks requiring retention for up to a minute or so. Its complement is *long-term memory.* Some theorists, James for example, believe there are real differences between the memory required for short-term retention and that for long-term retention. For them the system subserving short-term retention is usually called either *short-term store* or *primary memory*, while the long-term system is usually called either *long-term store* or *secondary memory.* Finally, extremely brief *sensory memory* is also known as *sensory information store*. In discussing particular modalities, we shall use terms such as *visual memory* or *auditory information store* as well as other terms proposed by various theorists to describe modality-specific memories.

SENSORY MEMORY

THE VISUAL INFORMATION STORE

The registration of a complex visual scene on the retina is virtually instantaneous, but the perceptual analysis of that scene takes an appreciable amount of time—in some instances more time than the duration of the physical signal. Some mechanism is needed to maintain the image while the perceptual system accomplishes its task. This is the role of the visual information store.

Some of the properties of the visual information store, which Neisser (1967) has referred to as *iconic memory*, were demonstrated in an important experiment by Sperling (1960). Subjects were given brief presentations (50 milliseconds) of arrays of letters that looked something like this:

```
X   M   R   J
P   N   K   D
L   Q   B   G
```

A subject who tries to report as many of the presented letters as possible will be able to get only four or five correct, on the average. This finding is simply a reaffirmation of the well-known limitation on the *span of apprehension*. The question raised by Sperling was, Why is the span so limited? Can the observer see only four or five elements from such a brief display? Or is it the case that he actually sees them all, but can report only four or five because he forgets some? In Sperling's experiment, subjects were asked to give only a *partial report*. They were to recall, immediately after presentation, only one of the rows of the array. However, they did not know which row to report until an auditory signal was given *after* the presentation. The signal was one of three tones, high, medium, or low in pitch, corresponding to the top, middle, or bottom row. When the cue for partial report was given immediately after the letter array, subjects could report nearly all the letters in the specified row. Since the subjects could not concentrate on any one row ahead of time, they must briefly have had available to them nearly all the 12 letters of the array. As the cue is delayed to one second, performance declines to the level of the whole report, as shown in Figure 13.1. These data suggest that subjects are able to hold a brief memory image of the array for enough time to be able to "read out" any one row from the memory image. Subjects cannot recite the whole array correctly, perhaps because the image fades while they are reciting the first few letters, or perhaps because the recitation of the first few letters interferes with memory for the remaining letters.

Iconic memory is entirely visual in nature, as indicated by the fact that its duration is strongly dependent on viewing conditions. The data of Figure 13.1 indicate that iconic information was available for no longer than one second. In that study the visual field present before and after the exposure of the letter array was dim. When a bright pre- and postexposure field is used, iconic persistence is reduced to about one-half second, and when a dark pre- and postexposure field is used, iconic persistence is extended to about five seconds (Averbach and Coriell, 1961; Averbach & Sperling, 1960; Sperling, 1960). There is also evidence that iconic memory can be destroyed by subsequent visual stimuli. Averbach and Coriell (1961) presented an array of letters in much the same way as Sperling did. After a very short delay, the subjects were told which one of the letters to report by the presentation of a circle around the place where one of the letters had been. The intent of the investigators had been to use the circle as a partial report cue. To their surprise, however, performance was extremely poor. The circle had erased the memory image of the letter.

The duration of the icon is that time during which the partial report score is higher than the whole report score. There are different ways to estimate its duration as well. For example, Haber and Standing (1969) had subjects adjust the temporal spacing of repeated pulses of light so that the image was just barely continuous (i.e., so one pulse did not totally disappear before the next appeared). The average spacing was 250 milliseconds, the time of the memory image. Why should the icon be limited to 250 milliseconds? One plausible explanation notes the identity of this duration and the typical duration of an eye fixation in a free-viewing situation. If iconic persistence exceeded fixation times, we would tend to see a collage of impressions as we moved our eyes about a scene. As interesting as this speculation is, it is teleological and not conclusive. Furthermore, there appear to be conditions that produce substantially longer visual traces.

Posner and Keele (1967) studied trace duration indirectly by using

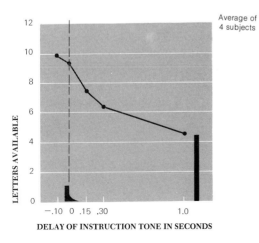

Average of 4 subjects

Figure 13.1
Number of letters available from a 50-millisecond display of 12 letters as a function of delay of instruction tone. Height of bar at right indicates immediate memory for this material when measured by the method of whole report. Width of bar at left indicates exposure duration. As explained in text, number of letters available is estimated from number correctly reported in the partial report technique. (Sperling, 1960.)

LETTERS AVAILABLE

−.10 0 .15 .30   1.0

DELAY OF INSTRUCTION TONE IN SECONDS

reaction time. On each trial a pair of letters was displayed, one after the other, and subjects were to indicate as quickly as possible if the letters had the same *name* or not (e.g., AA = yes; Aa = yes; Ab = no). When such a task is performed with both letters simultaneously present in the center of the visual field, name matching is faster by at least 70 milliseconds when the items are physically identical (e.g., AA) than when they are not (e.g., Aa). To the extent that an advantage for physically identical pairs exists when the subjects have to match the second letter to the memory trace of the first letter, the trace must be preserving the visual aspect of the letter. What Posner and Keele discovered is that the physical-identity advantage decreases as the delay interval between the first and second letter increases, but it does not reach zero until the delay is 1.5 seconds. In other words, the visual information from a single letter decays in about 1.5 seconds.

Subsequent research suggests that the kind of visual memory measured by Posner and Keele is not the same as the memory studied by Sperling, Averbach, and Coriell and Haber and Standing. For example, presenting *visual noise* (a dense jumble of bits and pieces of letters) after a letter array reduces the advantage of partial report (Sperling, 1963). However, in the letter-matching paradigm, visual noise presented after the first stimulus does *not* affect the advantage of physically identical pairs over pairs with just name identity (Posner, Boies, Eichelman, and Taylor, 1969).

THE AUDITORY INFORMATION STORE

The existence of a visual memory permits perceptual analysis even if the physical signal ceases before the analysis is completed. The existence of such a store is even more important in audition, since sound is intrinsically extended in time. Having a faithful reproduction available after the offset of an auditory signal aids in interpreting that signal. Neisser (1967) gives several lines of evidence supporting the necessity for supposing this kind of store, which he calls *echoic memory*, to exist. For example, you can correct a foreigner by saying, "No, not zeal, seal!" If he did not retain a faithful, unencoded representation of both the "z" and the "s" sounds, he could not benefit from the advice offered. The appreciation of music also requires an echoic memory of substantial duration. Neisser points out that perceptual analysis is often guided by context, but in speech the context necessary for the interpretation of a given sound often *follows* the sound. Thus, some echoic persistence would help the retrospective analysis of speech.

There have been several attempts to demonstrate the existence of an echoic memory and to measure its properties. Massaro (1970) used an auditory backward masking paradigm to determine the duration of echoic memory for a pure tone. On each trial one of two test tones was presented for 20 milliseconds, followed at varying intervals by a masking tone. The subjects had to indicate which one of the two possible test tones had been presented. The independent variable was the delay between the presentation of the test tone and the presentation of the masking tone. As the masking tone was delayed from 20 milliseconds to about 250 milliseconds, there was a steady increase in the accuracy of recognition of the test tone. Beyond 250 milliseconds there was little increase in accuracy. Since the test tone lasted only 20 milliseconds, some echoic memory must have been available for perceptual processing to account for the increase in accuracy up to 250 milliseconds. Massaro (1972) has summarized several other studies that point to a limit of about 250 milliseconds for the persistence of echoic memory.

The duration of echoic storage appears to depend on the requirements of the task used to measure it, since estimates longer than 250 milliseconds have been given. Guttman and Julesz (1963) used a method akin to that used by Haber and Standing (1969) to measure the duration of iconic storage. Guttman and Julesz played repetitive segments of white noise and attempted to determine the longest segment that would permit subjects to notice the repetition. The resulting duration was about one second.

There is some evidence that the sound of the human voice reading digits may be retained for at least two seconds (Crowder, 1969, but see also Crowder, 1971). A similar value for human speech was obtained in an experiment by Treisman (1964). She had subjects listen to and "shadow" (i.e., repeat, keeping as close as possible to the original) a message directed to their right ears. At the same time a message was presented to their left ears. Unbeknownst to the subjects, the two messages were identical, although the messages were not in phase. The message on the shadowed ear either preceded or lagged behind the message on the nonshadowed ear. The identity of two supposedly different messages is somewhat startling, and subjects will spontaneously comment on the identity as soon as it is noticed. Therefore, the dependent variable in this experiment was the average lag at which subjects noted the identity of the two messages. The lag was about 4.5 seconds when the shadowed message was leading, but only about 1.4 seconds when the unattended message was leading. In all likelihood this discrepancy reflects the existence of two kinds of memory. The memory that lasts for 4.5 seconds is for speech that has been attended, fully analyzed, and encoded. The memory that lasts for 1.4 seconds is for relatively unencoded speech, i.e., for speech persisting in echoic memory.

Still other experiments have suggested that echoic memory for a simple tone might persist for as long as 10 seconds (e.g., Eriksen & Johnson, 1964). Thus, as was the case with iconic memory, different experimental operations yield different estimated durations for sensory information storage. Considering the complexity and flexibility of the human organism, this result is hardly surprising. Future research will have to consider systematically differences among stimulus materials and task demands that contribute to the wide discrepancies among the available estimates. It is possible that estimates in excess of 250 milliseconds represent the retention of *encoded* auditory information. If subjects are able to encode an auditory signal verbally, extended retention is not surprising.

In the preceding pages we have been discussing memory of very brief duration. Clearly, some more permanent form of storage is necessary for much of our interaction with the world. In this section we shall consider how information from visual sensory memory gets transferred to a more permanent form of storage.

Suppose an array of letters is presented briefly, as in Sperling's experiment (1960), and the subject is to report as many of the letters as he can. Suppose further, that a field of visual noise is presented at some time after the letter array. The purpose of the visual noise is to control the amount of time the display is available for visual processing by terminating the extraction of new visual information from the original display. Sperling (1963) found that subjects could report an additional letter for each 10 milliseconds of exposure. However, this rate of increase was limited to the first three or four letters. An additional one or two letters was added more slowly, and there was no further increase beyond 100 milliseconds, as shown in Figure 13.2. It is worth noting that the 100-letters-per-second processing rate found by Sperling is too high to be implicit speech. Landauer (1962) had subjects count to themselves or repeat well-learned materials such as the alphabet. Covert speech was not much faster than overt speech, both averaging about 150 milliseconds per letter or per digit.

Sperling (1963) attempted to describe the subjects' performance in terms of three components: visual information storage, internal scanning of the array, and rehearsal. We have already noted the characteristics of the visual information store: it maintains the perceptual properties of the initial input, it has a large capacity, and it decays rapidly. The next step, scanning, involves the selective conversion of perceptual information into a form suitable for rehearsal. The rate of scanning or "readout" is an important parameter of this model since it determines how many

Figure 13.2
Number of letters correctly reported as a function of delay of postexposure visual noise for two subjects. The time axis here has also been interpreted as "effective exposure duration," on the assumption that visual noise prevents extraction of new visual information from the icon. (Sperling, 1963.)

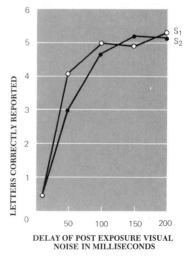

letters can be processed before the clarity of the display decays below a useful level.

The end product of readout is some representation of the input suitable for rehearsal and more durable than an iconic representation. What is the nature of this representation?

One clue comes from the kinds of errors subjects make when they attempt recall. Sperling (1963) reported that subjects often confuse letters that sound alike, for example writing "D" for "T" or "F" for "X". This kind of confusion was first observed by Smith (1896). The auditory nature of these errors was established clearly by Conrad (1964). In the first part of Conrad's experiment, subjects identified letters spoken in a noisy background. In the second part of this experiment, subjects recalled visually presented letters. The result was that the same letters were confused with one another in the two experiments. Recall errors were much like listening errors, even though recall was of visual items. This finding accords with the subjective experience that rehearsal of letters or digits seems to take the form of subvocal repetition. According to Sperling, once scanning has operated on the visual trace to extract the name of the letter for subsequent rehearsal, the information is in short-term memory.

A FURTHER COMMENT ON VISUAL MEMORY

Visual information is often transformed into an auditory or phonological form for short-term storage, as Sperling and Conrad thought. However, it is important to recognize that this transformation does not always occur and that visual information can be stored as such for the short term or even the long term. An example is provided by our ability to recognize scenes and faces that we have not seen for several years.

Consider, for example, an experiment by Kroll, Parks, Parkinson, Bieber, and Johnson (1970). Subjects had to remember a single letter on each trial, and this letter was presented either visually or aurally. The 1-second, 10-second, or 25-second retention interval was filled with an aural shadowing task in which subjects were asked to repeat letters as they were spoken. At one second, the visual and aural letters were recalled equally well, which tells us that they were equally well perceived. However, at 10 and 25 seconds, the aural memory letters were recalled less well than the visual memory letters because the shadowing task interfered more with retention of the aural letters than with the visual letters. The implication of this result is that visual letters were retained in a visual form for at least 25 seconds. Had they been coded phonologically, as suggested by Sperling and Conrad, they would have suffered the same degree of interference as the letters presented aurally in the first place.

The authors speculate that they found visual rather than phonological coding because they presented just one letter on each trial, rather than many, as Sperling and others have done. Phonological coding and rehearsal may be the optimal strategy in certain circumstances, while visual coding and rehearsal may be optimal in others.

It is likely that there are actually several different ways in which visually presented information may be retained in memory. If we accept William James' definition of primary memory as being whatever is in immediate consciousness, then primary memory holds whatever attention is focused on. Primary memory may be verbal, visual, auditory, olfactory, or whatever, depending on the kind of information being held in consciousness. This line of reasoning suggests that there are three kinds of memory: a sensory representation, a long-term memory, and a primary memory. In vision, the sensory representation lasts for about one-half second under ordinary viewing conditions. Primary memory lasts for as long as the subject can maintain the necessary degree of attention. Long-term memory is permanent. Visual information may be retained as such, or it may be recoded for retention in primary or long-term memory. Further work will be required to describe the nature of the information retained by each of the three proposed storage systems.

SHORT-TERM RETENTION

EARLY RESEARCH ON THE MEMORY SPAN

One of the oldest measures of mental ability is the digit span task. A string of unrelated digits is read to a subject, who must then repeat them back in the same order. The span for the normal adult is approximately seven; performance in excess of seven does not necessarily indicate high intelligence, but a score below five may be evidence of feeblemindedness (Horrocks, 1964).

An important fact about the memory span is that it is about the same size for a variety of materials. Thus, a subject can retain approximately the same number of random digits, random letters, or unconnected words (Woodworth & Schlosberg, 1954). Those readers familiar with computer terminology will notice that presentation of a random digit transmits fewer *bits* (less information) than a random letter, which is in turn much less informative than a randomly selected word. Thus, the apparent constancy of memory span is not due to capacity being limited to a fixed amount of information.

Another measure was described by Miller (1956) in an article entitled "The magical number seven, plus or minus two: Some limits on our capacity for processing information." He proposed that immediate memory was limited to 7 ± 2 *chunks*, where a chunk is a unit reflecting the organization imposed on the stimulus material by the subject himself. For example, the nominally independent digits 1, 4, 9, 2, might be reorganized (recoded) by the subject into a single unit (1492), as "Discovery of America by Columbus," or perhaps just "Columbus" (see pp. 323–325). Unfortunately, there is no mathematical formula available for calculating the number of chunks in a message; indeed, since chunking is subjective, the number might well differ from person to person. Thus, although there is no disputing the importance of Miller's insight that amount retained is a function of how material is organized, perhaps we should not take too seriously any excessive emphasis on exact quantification of memory in terms of number of chunks.

SUB-SPAN MEMORY

Consider the following question: Should a subject be able to remember a consonant trigram (e.g., X J D) for, say, 18 seconds? Since the memory span is 7 ± 2, the answer must be "yes." Fortunately, the obviousness of this answer did not deter Peterson and Peterson (1959) from testing the question experimentally. There isn't much doubt that if subjects were free to rehearse X J D during an 18-second retention interval, they would show perfect retention; however, Peterson and Peterson included a *distractor task* to eliminate or at least reduce the subject's opportunity to rehearse. The distractor task they introduced was counting backwards by three's or four's from a three-digit number (e.g., 487, 484, 481, etc.). On each trial a consonant trigram was presented, followed by a three-digit number. The subjects repeated the number (a new one was used on each trial) and then counted backwards in time, with a metronome beating once per second until they were asked for recall. The relation between percentage of correct recall and retention interval is shown in Figure 13.3. When rehearsal is not permitted, recall of a sub-span number of letters decreases drastically within 18 seconds. Subsequent work has established the generality of this finding. Figure 13.3 also presents results from a study by Murdock (1961). Using the Peterson and Peterson technique, he gave his subjects either a single

Figure 13.3
Percentage of correct recall of three-consonant trigrams (Peterson & Peterson, 1959; Murdock, 1961) and one-word and three-word units (Murdock, 1961). The similarity of the functions for stimuli consisting of three unrelated letters and three unrelated words gives strong support to the idea that the "chunk" is the unit of short-term memory. (Melton, 1963).

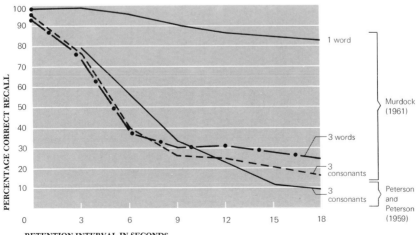

word, a consonant trigram, or three simple words on each trial. His data show that retention for a single word is quite good over the entire retention interval and that retention is equal for three unrelated consonants and three unrelated words. Thus each letter in the nonsense syllable acts like a word. This finding corroborates the importance of chunking in short-term memory. Peterson and Peterson suspected that their data indicated that verbal information was subject to rapid decay when rehearsal was prevented. In the next section, we shall consider this possibility along with several alternatives.

SINGLE-PROCESS AND DUAL-PROCESS THEORIES OF SHORT-TERM RETENTION

It is important to find out if loss of information is governed by the same principles for short-term as for long-term memory. The difference in rate of forgetting seems so drastic as to suggest that different principles must operate in the two domains.

There are two views on this issue. One view holds that there are several different storage systems in human memory, including what we have called primary memory and secondary memory. Hebb (1949) argued that the physiological basis of memory is dual in nature. According to his theory there are two phases in the establishment of the physiological substrate for memory. The first of these phases is dynamic. It consists of a network of activity in a group of nerve cells which recurrently excite one another. This phase, Hebb asserts, is responsible for a memory trace of very short duration. Long-term or permanent memory Hebb attributes to structural changes in these nerve networks which are the result of repeated elicitation of the active phase. The most straightforward interpretation of Hebb's theory is that forgetting in primary memory is due to passive decay. Since structural changes are permanent, it would be plausible to conclude that forgetting in secondary memory is due to a principle like competition at recall (McGeoch, 1932). In other words, decay and interference would both be required to explain forgetting. Many theorists have modeled their theories after Hebb's analysis.

The idea that there are two stages in memory is not necessarily linked to the idea that decay and interference are the mechanisms of forgetting. In primary memory at least two principles of forgetting have been proposed in addition to decay. One is *displacement* (e.g., Waugh & Norman, 1965). An item is retained in primary memory until it is displaced or bumped out by a subsequent item. Another is *acid-bath interference* (Posner & Konick, 1966). Forgetting in primary memory is an interaction of both decay and interference. The interaction may be conceived of as analogous to an acid bath. Suppose a metal plate with a message cut into its surface is plunged into a bath of acid. The degree to which the message is obliterated is a function of the time that the plate is exposed to the acid (decay) and also of the strength of the acid (i.e., the level of interference).

There are theorists who argue that scientific parsimony may be
violated by a proliferation of storage systems. They try to show that the
same principles apply to both short-term and long-term memory. For
Melton (1963) and others, this has amounted to trying to show that the
principles of interference theory, long used in the analysis of long-term
memory, are also applicable to short-term memory. Sensory memory
may be outside this explanatory scheme. Most theorists are willing to
concede that decay operates in this domain.

To account for primary and secondary memory with a single set of
principles does not require one to be an interference theorist. For
example, we shall see that Craik and Lockhart (1972) have tried to show
that it is more fruitful to consider apparently different kinds of memory
stores to be the result of differential depth of processing of perceptual
inputs.

In the following pages we shall consider some of the data pertaining to
the single-store versus multiple-store positions. We shall first consider
the adequacy of the various principles that have been proposed to
account for forgetting from primary memory. If different principles of
forgetting are operative in primary and secondary memory, we can
conclude that those two stores are functionally different. Then we
consider some other evidence that has been advanced to support the
dual-store hypothesis, and finally, we present some arguments for a
single-store hypothesis that is based on grounds other than classical
interference theory.

Decay Some early evidence in support of decay theory comes from a
series of experiments by Brown (1958). He compared retention of
consonants with and without rehearsal over a 4.7-second retention
interval. In one condition, rehearsal was limited following the presentation of the consonants by asking subjects to name digits that were
presented during the retention interval. Digit naming served the same
purpose as counting backward in the Peterson and Peterson (1959)
experiment. In the other condition, no task was required during the
retention interval. Subjects were free to rehearse if they wished. Brown
assumed that digit naming blocks rehearsal but that it is not a source of
retroactive interference in the classical sense (because of the categorical
difference between digits and letters). The data showed that performance
was much better when rehearsal was allowed. Thus a delay of several
seconds before recall produced forgetting.

In a second experiment, Brown attempted to show that the interpolated task was not influencing the results by means of retroactive interference. He reasoned that if decay were the cause of forgetting, then the
similarity of the interpolated and to-be-remembered material should not
affect retention. Thus with consonants to be remembered, performance
should be the same regardless of whether the interpolated material
consists of digits or of other consonants. His data supported that
argument.

Finally, in a third experiment, Brown added a blank interval between the presentation of the to-be-remembered items and the additional, rehearsal-preventing items. As the length of this interval was increased from 0.78 seconds to 4.68 seconds, recall improved from 41 to 59 percent. This improvement in recall is consistent with a perseveration-con-solidation notion in which loss of information from primary memory is due to decay. Subsequent research has not born out all of Brown's con-clusions. In particular, the similarity of interpolated and to-be-remem-bered material *does* seem to affect retention (e.g., Wickelgren, 1965).

Another kind of evidence for decay comes from studies in which rate of presentation of a single string of elements is varied. If subjects are instructed to begin their recall as soon as the list of elements is completed, then increasing the rate of presentation of elements ought to decrease the amount of time that material must remain in store. Thus, if recall is higher when presentation rate is higher, this would be evidence that time in store, and hence decay, is an important factor in retention. Several studies have demonstrated improved recall for faster rates of presentations. For example, Conrad and Hille (1958) used eight-digit sequences presented once at a rate of either 90 digits per minute or 30 digits per minute. For the condition in which both presentations and recall were fast, mean recall was 41 percent versus 31 percent where both were slow. Fraser (1958) and Posner (1964) also reported that fast presentations can lead to better recall than slow presentation rates. The issue is complicated by the fact that numerous studies have shown the opposite result. As Aaronson (1967) points out, there are several good reasons why performance should be better with slower presentations. For example, there is more time for accurate perception of the elements of the series when the presentation is slow. Also, there is more time for rehearsal, coding, and organization at slow rates. It is because all these factors oppose finding good recall with fast presentation that the occasional finding of this effect must be accorded considerable weight.

Interference   The early work on primary memory was interpreted to mean that decay was operative (e.g., Brown, 1958; Conrad & Hille, 1958; Peterson & Peterson, 1959). This viewpoint was criticized in an experi-ment by Keppel and Underwood (1962). This study was addressed to the interpretation of the Peterson and Peterson experiment. They pointed out that if the Petersons' experiment is to be explained in terms of interference theory, then proactive inhibition (PI) will have to bear most of the explanatory burden since the digits used in the interpolated task should not cause much retroactive interference.

Remember that PI increases with the number of interfering associa-tions (e.g., Underwood, 1945, 1957). Therefore, PI should increase over trials, Keppel and Underwood pointed out.

Also, the logic of the PI paradigm requires an increase in interference as a function of the length of the retention interval due to the recovery of extinguished associations (Briggs, 1954; Underwood, 1948). Note that this principle is capable of explaining decay-like losses of retention over time.

Peterson and Peterson showed that the degree of forgetting was the same throughout the course of their experiment. In other words, they found no evidence that PI increased over trials. This might seem to be persuasive evidence that interference theory is not applicable to short-term memory experiments. However, Keppel and Underwood pointed out that subjects received two practice trials before the experiment proper. It is possible that PI builds up very rapidly; two practice trials may create considerable interference.

To test these ideas they performed some experiments using a method similar to that of Peterson and Peterson. However, each subject was tested for only three trials. Figure 13.4 shows data for single CCC items in which the letters were read aloud to the subject. Figure 13.4 also shows data from a modification of the Peterson and Peterson experiment in which each trigram was shown visually for two seconds to increase the degree of learning. The most important finding is that for both experiments there is less forgetting on the first test than on the second or third tests. Thus, the PI created by even a single prior trial is substantial.

In a follow-up study, Loess (1964) tried to show that PI continues to increase in magnitude with successive trials beyond the third. It did not. PI again reached its maximum after the second or third trial. The build-up of PI in short-term memory depends upon the similarity of the items presented on successive trials. If subjects are given three digits to remember on each of four successive trials, recall accuracy will decline from the first to the fourth trial. However, if on the fourth trial they are given three consonants to remember, retention improves dramatically (Wickens, Born, & Allen, 1963). Improved recall upon changing the category of to-be-remembered items is called "release from PI," and it occurs over a wide variety of materials (Wickens, 1972).

Although PI has been the focus of much research on primary memory, some attention has been paid to retroactive inhibition (RI) as

Figure 13.4
Proportion of correctly recalled consonant trigrams as a function of retention interval for the first, second, and third trials of a three-trial experiment. The figure on the left shows results of an experiment in which stimuli were read aloud to subjects. The figure on the right shows results of an experiment in which stimuli were displayed visually for two seconds. (Keppel & Underwood, 1962.)

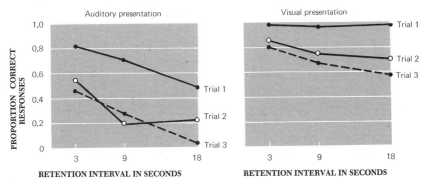

well. Wickelgren (1965) had subjects read off a series of 12 letters. The first four had to be recalled later; the last eight served simply as interpolated material. The chief independent variable was the degree of acoustic similarity between the interpolated and to-be-remembered material. When acoustic similarity was high there was much more forgetting than when it was low.

Results such as the preceding have lent support to the single-store hypothesis since they tend to indicate that the principles of interference theory are operative in both short-term and long-term memory.

Acid-bath interference A simple decay theory cannot account for the effects of similarity relations on forgetting without making additional assumptions. Posner and Konick (1966) discussed two alternative possibilities. One is like that of classical interference theory (McGeoch, 1932), holding that similarity does not affect the rate at which information decays, but only the difficulty of discriminating the correct from the interfering items at the time of the retention test. This is the response competition notion. The second model was based on the "acid-bath" analogy: rate of retention loss should be a function of the similarity of the correct and interfering items (i.e., to strength of acid) and also of the number of interfering items present (amount of acid). These two models differ in that the acid-bath idea proposes that forgetting is caused by events occurring during the retention interval, while the competition model proposes that forgetting is caused by events occurring at the time of attempted retrieval.

A comparison of these two ideas has been provided by Hawkins, Pardo, and Cox (1972). These investigators examined factors affecting PI in short-term recognition memory. A series of lists was presented, each list composed of four phonetically similar words. At some points within the series, the subject was given two successive lists, 1 and 2, that contained items drawn from a set of items either phonetically similar or phonetically dissimilar; for example:

	LIST 1	LIST 2
Similar	lob, fox, top, boy	dog, rot, cop, sod
Dissimilar	weak, team, reap, bead	dog, rot, cop, sod

Interest was focused on retention of list 2 under the two conditions of similarity. Retention was tested either immediately after the presentation of list 2 or after a 20-second interval of counting backward by three's. The subject was provided with an array containing the four correct items plus two distractor items. The task was to choose the four correct items from this array and arrange them in the order of their appearance in the original list. In the "competition" condition, the two distractors used following a similar list 2 had appeared in the preceding list 1. In the "noncompetition" condition, the two distractors used following a similar list 2 had not appeared in the preceding list 1. Distractors appearing in the recognition array following a dissimilar list 2 also had not appeared in list 1. (There was no "competition" condition for the dissimilar lists.)

According to the acid-bath model, PI arises as a function of the
similarity of list 1 and list 2 items. Therefore, there should be more
forgetting for the similar than the dissimilar list 2. This should be equally
true for the competition and noncompetition conditions, since forgetting
reflects processes occurring during storage, not at the time of the
retrieval test.

According to the response competition model, the competition that
produces PI comes from the subject's inability to distinguish between list
2 and similar list 1 items at the time list 2 retention is tested. Such
competition should not occur in the noncompetition condition of this
experiment, because list 1 items were not present in the recognition
array. Consequently, the crucial prediction from this model is that if
competition is eliminated, the rate of forgetting should not differ for a
similar list 2 and a dissimilar list 2. The data supported this prediction,
not the one based on acid-bath interference.

Displacement All the preceding ideas are consistent with the fact that
there is a loss of information over time (assuming no rehearsal, of
course). For decay, the reason is obvious. For acid-bath interference,
there is more erosion of the plate the longer it is in the acid. For
interference theory, there is spontaneous recovery of unlearned associations in time. Thus, if retention declines with time, all the preceding
models are supported equally. There is another view of memory,
however, which leads to the prediction that retention should be independent of time even when no rehearsal is permitted. This model
holds that primary memory is limited in capacity and that information is
lost only when an item is displaced by a subsequent item.

Evidence in support of this notion comes from a study by Waugh and
Norman (1965). This experiment was designed to study recall of an item
as a joint function of amount of time and number of other items
following its presentation. Lists of 16 single digits were prepared on tape
by a speaker at a constant rate of either one or four digits per second.
Subjects were instructed to rehearse by thinking of only the current digit,
not any of the earlier ones. The last digit in the series was one that had
appeared exactly once before in the list; it was accompanied by a
high-frequency tone. This digit was considered a *probe digit*, and its
presentation was a cue for the subject to attempt to recall the digit that
had originally followed it in the list.

The responses were scored to yield a serial position curve for each rate
of presentation. The curve related the proportion of correct recall to the
distance from the end of the list. Consider the recall of an item i digits
from the end of the list. At the one-per-second presentation rate this
digit would be followed by i items and i seconds before recall. At the
four-per-second presentation rate the digit would still be followed by i
items, but by only $1/4$ seconds. Therefore, if recall of an item i digits from
the end of the slow list is equal to recall of an item $4i$ digits from the end
of the fast list, then it is reasonable to conclude that time in store is the
crucial factor. However, if recall of an item i digits from the end of the

slow list is equal to recall of an item *i* digits from the end of the fast list, then time in store is not a crucial factor, but number of subsequent items is. The results are plotted in Figure 13.5, which shows probability of recall as a function of number of interfering items, i.e., distance from end of list. This figure shows that the effect of rate is small relative to the effect of serial position, and in fact the differences between the two sets of points representing the two presentation rates were not statistically significant.

This experiment suggested that time in store was not an important determinant of retention. It is crucial to know if this finding can be verified in other than the rather special circumstances of the probe-digit task. Ideally, to decide this issue would require that the subject try to retain something over a short retention interval, during which time no additional inputs enter his short-term memory and he does not rehearse. Reitman (1971) tried to meet these conditions. The material to be remembered consisted of triads of common words, and the retention interval was 15 seconds. The crucial variation concerned the nature of the distracting task, whose purpose was to control rehearsal. In one condition the task required the subject to indicate, by pressing a key, whenever a very soft tone occurred in a background of white noise. It was hoped that this condition would block rehearsal and yet not cause any new material to be entered into short-term memory. In another condition the task consisted of detecting when the spoken syllable "toh" occurred in a background series of "doh's." This condition should also block rehearsal; however, the verbal nature of the detection stimuli might lead to some interference with to-be-remembered material. As control conditions, subjects also detected the tones and syllables without having to memorize the word triplets.

The data indicated that detection performance was equally good in the experimental and control conditions. On the assumption that rehearsal

Figure 13.5
Proportion of correct recall of a digit as a function of the number of subsequent digits in the list, using the probe-digit technique. (Waugh & Norman, 1965.)

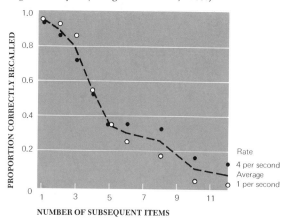

of the words would have disrupted detection, this result suggests that subjects successfully avoided rehearsal. How good was memory under these conditions? In the tonal detection task, 13 of 18 subjects had recall scores of 100 percent. Thus for most subjects, retention of three words was perfect for 15 seconds. This performance may be compared with that shown in Figure 13.3. In the syllabic detection task, median recall was 74 percent. These findings indicated to Reitman that verbal material is not subject to spontaneous decay, but that interpolated word-like stimuli could interfere with material being held in short-term memory. This finding was replicated and extended to 40 seconds by Shiffrin (1973).

Since these findings have wide implications, Reitman (1974) has tried to replicate them in a more carefully designed experiment. This study differed from the original one in two ways. First, the material to be remembered consisted of five words rather than three. She argued that 100 percent recall in the previous experiment showed that the task was too easy to detect memory loss in many subjects. Second, a better assessment was made of whether subjects were rehearsing or not. The analysis showed that most subjects did rehearse even when instructed not to. However, a few did not. The important finding was that for these nonrehearsing subjects, in the tonal detection task, retention declined substantially over 15 seconds. In the syllabic detection task, retention declined even more than in the tonal detection task. Reitman concluded that both decay *and* interference (or displacement) affect forgetting.

Evaluation of mechanisms of short-term forgetting Since the prediction of the acid-bath interference notion was not confirmed in the study by Hawkins et al. (1972), we shall not consider that idea further.

The idea of decay received support in Reitman's (1974) experiment. Subjects who successfully avoided rehearsal showed retention losses while engaged in a task that should not have caused new material to be entered into short-term memory. However, decay cannot be considered the sole mechanism of short-term forgetting because Keppel and Underwood (1962) and Loess (1964) showed that forgetting rate depends on the number of prior trials, as interference theory would predict. We may tentatively conclude that decay and either interference or displacement operate in short-term memory.

It is, at the present time, difficult to choose between the notions of displacement and interference. The major problem with the displacement hypothesis is that it suggests that items are displaced randomly. However, it is known that similarity effects operate in short-term memory. For example, Wickelgren (1965) showed greater retroactive interference for phonologically similar interpolated items than for phonologically dissimilar items. Thus, displacement of items from short-term memory is not random, but is dependent on similarity. The problem this poses for displacement theory is that once a theorist starts taking similarity relations seriously, he is liable to end up reinventing interference theory. This may not be inevitable, however. Perhaps there is some way to construct an adequate displacement theory that is different from interference theory. We do not yet know.

Interference theory is consistent with many of the data from short-term-memory experiments (Melton, 1963). However, there are a few inconsistencies as well. For one, in long-term memory, proactive inhibition increases with the length of an intertrial interval. In short-term memory, Peterson and Gentile (1965) found the opposite to be true. Another problem is that some interference phenomena that operate in long-term memory do not operate in short-term memory. Baddeley and Dale (1966) examined retroactive interference with paired-associate learning in both short-term and long-term memory. They used an A-B, A'-D paradigm, with an A-B, C-D control. As expected, in long-term memory, retroactive interference was observed. However in short-term memory no interference was found. Pairs of adjectives were no more likely to be forgotten when followed by a pair with a similar stimulus than when followed by an unrelated pair. Wickelgren (1967) has obtained similar results.

In summary, none of the mechanisms of forgetting that we have considered can, alone, explain all of short-term forgetting. If we accept Reitman's conclusion that decay does occur, it is still necessary to postulate that an additional factor is implicated. What is this factor? We do not yet know. Interference is not entirely satisfactory, and displacement is uncomfortably vague. This inconclusive state of affairs should not obscure one important result of our survey. We have found evidence that not all the classical interference phenomena operate in short-term memory (Baddeley & Dale, 1966; Peterson and Gentile, 1965; Wickelgren, 1967). This evidence supports the dual-process point of view.

Further evidence for multistore models We have to this point focused on the question of whether primary and secondary memory are governed by the same laws of retention. However, even if we were to assume that they were, it might still be possible to maintain that they are separate systems, if appropriate evidence could be found. Two kinds of evidence for the separation of primary and secondary memory have been presented: the existence of experimental factors that influence one kind of memory but not the other and physiological dissociation.

Serial position curves. Some evidence for two-process theory comes from studies of the serial position curve in free-recall experiments. A list of unrelated words is read to a subject who is asked to recall the list in any order he chooses. One of the most important characteristics of free recall is the variation in probability of recall of individual items as a function of their position in the list presented to the subject. Figure 11.5 (p. 317), taken from an extensive experiment by Murdock (1962), shows probability of recall as a function of serial position for six experimental conditions. The first number in the description of a condition is the number of words in the list (10, 15, 20, 30, 40). The second number (1 or 2) represents the number of seconds for which each word was presented.

Actually the words were spoken to the 1-per-second beat of a metro-nome; for the 2-second lists, the experimenter simply skipped every other beat. This figure demonstrates that for relatively long lists, say, 20 items or longer, the curve seems to have three distinct segments in that the last few items are the best recalled, the first few are next best recalled, and the middle items are the least well recalled. Accuracy is correlated with order of recall; subjects report the last items first, the first items next, and then items from the middle. The enhanced accuracy of the first few serial positions is said to represent a *primacy* effect and of the last seven or so a *recency* effect. The low middle part of such curves is often referred to as the *asymptote*. Theorists who believe in the existence of two separate memory stores argue that the recency section of the serial position curve is the result of retrieval from primary memory. If this is the case, it should be possible to eliminate the contribution of primary memory to total recall with an interpolated task and thus eliminate the recency effect. Glanzer and Cunitz (1966) performed such an experiment, interpolating either 0, 10, or 30 seconds of counting out loud after list presentation. The data, shown in Figure 13.6, indicate that the recency effect is indeed eliminated by 30 seconds of counting. Similar data were obtained by Postman and Phillips (1965).

Dual-process theorists consider recall from the middle, asymptotic, segment of the serial position curve to reflect recall from secondary memory. If this is the case, then variables that affect secondary memory should affect recall of the middle of the list but not of the last items. Sumby (1963) used lists that were constructed of either high-frequency

Figure 13.6
Proportion of words correctly recalled from a 15-word list as a function of serial position in the list, for 0-, 10-, and 30-second delays of recall. (Glanzer & Cunitz, 1966.)

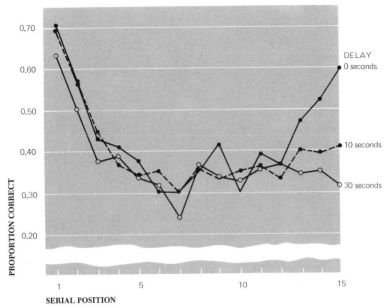

or low-frequency words from the Thorndike-Lorge (1944) count of the frequency of occurrence of words in English. For words at the end of the list, recall was independent of frequency, but for words at the middle, recall was better for the high-frequency words. Another variable that influences secondary memory is presentation rate. As may be seen in Figure 11.5, for the 20-word lists the recency portion of the curve is the same for one- and two-second rates, but the middle serial positions are markedly different for the two rates.

What of the primacy effect? It, too, is seen as representing recall from secondary memory. The enhancement over the asymptote may be due to the fact that primary memory is relatively "empty" at the beginning of a list, and so the material encountered early may stay in storage longer than later items and may benefit from the opportunity for a few extra rehearsals. Support for this analysis comes from an experiment done by Rundus (1971) in which subjects were asked to rehearse out loud rather than covertly. Rehearsals of the subjects were tape-recorded and were later analyzed to explore the relationships between probability of recall of specific items and amount of rehearsal these items had received. Throughout the primacy and middle sections of the list there was a close correspondence between the mean number of rehearsals and the prob-ability of recall. The correspondence broke down within the recency segment. Probability of recall was high there, even though rehearsal frequency was low. This fact is yet another demonstration that the recency effect is independent of factors that influence other segments of the serial position curve in free recall.

It is interesting to note that primacy sometimes fails to occur. In such circumstances it is likely that the explanation lies in the nature of the rehearsal allowed or required by the experimental task. Recall the probe-digit experiment of Waugh and Norman (1965). In that study, retention improved regularly with recency; the first few items were *not* well remembered. According to Waugh and Norman, this occurred not because their task used the probe technique rather than free recall, but because subjects were instructed to rehearse only the current item. Thus the first few items did not get more than their share of rehearsals and they were not recalled disproportionately well.

Semantic and phonological similarity. Another line of evidence has frequently been interpreted to mean that there are two separate memory stores. Similarity effects are based chiefly upon phonological features in primary memory but chiefly upon semantic features in secondary memory. By similarity effects we mean the kinds of proactive and retroactive phenomena discussed in the section on transfer in Chapter 12.

The importance of semantic similarity in accounting for variations in secondary memory is well established. To cite just one example, McGe-och and McDonald (1931) found that the amount of interference in serial learning increased as a function of the similarity in meaning of the words making up the two successive lists. The importance of phonological similarity in primary memory is also well established. The point is made by Conrad's (1964) demonstration that the errors made in short-term retention of visually presented letters are very similar to the listening errors that occur when the letters are presented aurally. These memory errors were once considered to be *acoustic* confusions. However, there is now some evidence that the important features may be *articulatory* rather than acoustic (Hintzman, 1967). We shall try to avoid prejudging this issue by using the neutral term *phonological similarity*.

Kintsch and Buschke (1969) used the probe paradigm introduced by Waugh and Norman (1965) to compare phonological and semantic similarity. Their lists were 16 words long. In one experiment, two different kinds of lists were constructed; one consisted of 16 unrelated words and the other consisted of 8 pairs of synonyms. In each case the 16 words were presented in a random order. In the other experiment the two kinds of lists were unrelated words and homophone pairs (e.g., bare, bear). The authors made the assumption that the items in the last few serial positions are stored in secondary memory. Given this assumption, the data shown in Figure 13.7 show that the semantic factor (synonymity) has a negative effect on secondary memory, and the phonological factor (homonymity) has a negative effect on primary memory.

Baddeley (1966) assessed the influence of phonological and semantic similarity on *secondary* memory. He chose as a task learning of lists by rote, with a few modifications to ensure that primary memory had no influence on retention. Each presentation of a list was followed immediately by a task requiring short-term retention of a sequence of digits. This task destroyed any residue of the word list in primary memory. It was followed by recall. There were four lists, each list learned by a separate group. The lists are shown in Table 13.1. List B was matched with list A, and list D with list C in terms of Thorndike-Lorge (1944) frequency. After four learning trials, subjects performed for 15 minutes in a digit-copying task and were then given a final recall test.

The results showed little effect of phonological similarity on either learning or the delayed retention test. However, it proved to be substantially harder for subjects to learn and recall the semantically similar list than its control.

Figure 13.7
Probability of correct recall as a function of serial position. The figure on the left shows that intralist synonymity had its (negative) effect only *before* the recency portion of the serial position curve, while the figure on the right shows that intralist homonymity had its (negative) effect only *within* the recency portion of the curve. (After Kintsch & Buschke, 1969.)

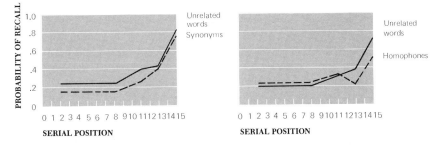

The data we have surveyed suggest that phonological similarity is important only in primary memory and not in secondary memory, while the reverse is true of semantic similarity. Anyone interested in this topic should see Shulman's (1971) review paper in which the preceding generalization is disputed, and Baddeley's (1972) rejoinder in which Shulman's analysis is in turn criticized.

Neurophysiological evidence. Some important evidence in support of two-process theory comes from a series of papers by Milner (1966; Milner, Corkin, & Teuber, 1968) on the side effects of a neurosurgical treatment for epilepsy. Bilateral surgical lesions in the hippocampal region produce a severe and persistent memory disorder in human patients. Patients with such lesions show no loss of skills learned prior to the operation, and their performance on IQ tests is also unaffected. What is aberrant about these patients is that they are unable to add new material to secondary memory, with the possible exception of new perceptual-motor skills. Primary memory is unaffected. The digit span is normal, and as long as rehearsal is permitted, material can be retained. However, disruption of rehearsal leads to rapid loss. This pattern of evidence has suggested to many psychologists (e.g., Atkinson & Shiffrin, 1968) that the lesions have destroyed the ability either to enter new information into secondary memory or to retrieve new information from it.

In contrast to Milner's subject, Warrington and Shallice (1969; Shallice & Warrington, 1970) have reported observation on a patient with another neurological problem and with the opposite memory defect: his primary memory is drastically reduced while his secondary memory is quite normal. The adequacy of his secondary memory was established by the use of a variety of standard tasks in which his performance fell well within the normal range. However, when short-term retention was tested, performance was poor.

Table 13.1

Lists used in Baddeley's (1966) study of phonological and semantic similarity

LIST A	LIST B	LIST C	LIST D
PHONOLOGICALLY SIMILAR	CONTROL	SEMANTICALLY SIMILAR	CONTROL
man	pit	great	good
cab	few	large	huge
can	cow	big	hot
cad	per	huge	safe
cap	sup	broad	thin
mad	bar	long	deep
max	day	tall	strong
mat	hat	fat	foul
cat	rig	wide	old
map	bun	high	late

For example, in free recall of 10-item lists, the serial position curve was flat over the middle 8 positions. Although primacy was reduced here, what is of greater interest in this context is that the recency effect, indicating primary memory, existed for only the last item. The patient was also tested with a task in which the to-be-remembered items were three common words, and the distracting task consisted of simple counting rather than counting backward by three's, which he could not do efficiently. His retention curve started out low at immediate recall, but it showed no further decline over 15 seconds. This suggests the absence of a rapid-loss primary memory; recall may have been from a more permanent secondary store.

Shallice and Warrington (1970) draw two conclusions from their observations. First, they believe they have shown yet another dissociation of primary and secondary memory. Second, and this is the more novel of their conclusions, they feel their data disallow any theory in which information must enter primary memory before entering secondary memory. Since their subject had a normal secondary memory even though his primary memory was grossly defective, there must be a way for information to get into secondary memory without having to "pass through" primary memory. Taking into account their own data as well as data on semantic and phonological confusions, they propose a model with parallel inputs into primary and secondary memory, as shown in Figure 13.8. This kind of flowchart model is not really explicit enough to lead to many testable predictions, but it can serve as a useful explanatory aid. According to this model, the patient may have sustained damage to the phonemic short-term store or to the pathway linking the phonemic analysis unit with the short-term store.

We have finished our brief summary of the evidence showing the

Figure 13.8
Model suggested by Shallice and Warrington (1970) to account for retention in auditory verbal memory experiments. Auditory input is subjected to both phonemic analysis and semantic analysis. The results of phonemic analysis are placed in short-term store at the same time that the results of semantic analysis are placed in long-term store. Ordinary rehearsal may be represented by the loop A-B-C. The output connections from the long-term store are unspecified because the experiments performed by Shallice and Warrington (1970) provided no relevant evidence.

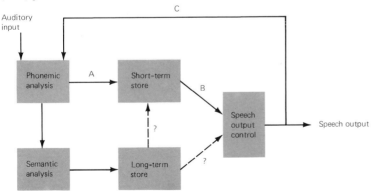

separate existence of a short-term primary memory and a more durable secondary memory. This evidence is impressive because it comes in so many different forms. No one piece of it would be enough to lead to the conclusion that there are two separate memory stores, but in concert they make an impressive case. Nevertheless, there are those who would like to maintain that all memory (except perhaps for sensory storage) operates according to a single set of principles. We turn now to consider their case.

THE ARGUMENT FOR A ONE-PROCESS THEORY

In an influential article, Melton (1963) argued that what we have called primary and secondary memory are points on a continuum rather than a dichotomy. For Melton the unitary explanation was classical two-factor interference theory, which he concluded was as appropriate for primary as for secondary memory. The dual-process theory he argued against was clearly Hebb's: labile activity traces for primary memory, permanent structural changes for secondary memory (Hebb, 1949). On the basis of the literature we have reviewed in this chapter, it seems that Melton's confidence in classical interference theory may not have been vindicated. Indeed, it seems that none of the principles we have described so far is going to be able to explain all the data on forgetting. However, it is important to note that Melton's more general point that primary and secondary memory are essentially the same is by no means a dead issue. Several theorists, in a desire for parsimony, have proposed ways in which a single set of principles could predict the results of a wide variety of learning and memory studies. We shall briefly consider an example of such an effort here.

The levels-of-processing view of memory   Craik and Lockhart (1972) have argued that the data offered as evidence for the existence of multiple storage systems can be explained just as well in terms of *levels of processing*. Their idea is based on the widely accepted notion that perception involves the rapid analysis of stimuli at a number of levels or stages (Selfridge & Neisser, 1960). Preliminary stages analyze stimuli into sensory features such as lines, angles, frequencies, and amplitudes. Later stages use the results of preliminary analyses to match stimuli against stored representations (pattern recognition) and to extract meanings from messages. After a stimulus has been recognized, it may undergo still further processing, e.g., by triggering associations or images based on the subject's past experience. The idea that processing involves a series or hierarchy of stages means that stimuli may be processed to different "levels" or "depths," depending on factors such as the nature of the stimuli and the amount of time available for processing.

   Craik and Lockhart go on to say that one of the results of perceptual analysis is the memory trace, and that trace persistence is a function of depth of analysis, with deeper levels resulting in more durable traces. The basic determinant of how long information will be retained is the depth to which it has been processed. However, stimuli can also be retained, at a given level of processing, by rehearsal. This mechanism is called primary memory.

For unknown reasons, there is great variability in the ease with which information at different levels can be maintained in primary memory. The phonemic features of words are easy to maintain by rehearsal, while the iconic representation of a large array of letters appears to be impossible to maintain. When attention is diverted from an item in primary memory, information will be lost at a rate that depends on its level of processing. How can such a model account for the kinds of data we have presented as evidence for the dual-store position? We shall consider the argument below.

Phonological and semantic coding. Short-term retention of words appears to be based on a phonological code, while secondary memory is based on a semantic code. Several theorists have pointed out that this does not necessarily mean that there are two memory systems with fundamentally different properties (Wickelgren, 1973). It might mean, instead, that subjects process items differently, depending on the demands of an expected retention test. If the subject's task is to reproduce some words a few seconds after hearing them, it may not be necessary to code those words at a level deeper than phonological analysis. If the words form a sentence, or if retention will be tested after a long retention interval, it may be more appropriate to process at the semantic level.

The fact that, in the absence of rehearsal, phonologically coded information is lost more rapidly than semantically coded information is also not indicative of the existence of two distinct memory systems. There are far fewer phonemes (sound units) in the language than there are morphemes (meaning units). Thus, a phonologically coded message will be more similar, on the average, to interfering material than will a semantically coded message. Since rate of information loss is dependent on the similarity of material to be remembered and interfering material, we would expect phonologically encoded items to be lost more rapidly even if there were only a single storage system.

Serial position effects. Following presentation of a list for free recall, if subjects are required to engage in interpolated interfering activity, the terminal section of the serial position curve is depressed, but the rest of the curve is relatively unaffected (see Figure 13.6). This fact has usually been interpreted as support for the dual-process notion. However, it need not be so interpreted. Gruneberg (1970) and Wickelgren (1973) have pointed out that items before the terminal section have already been subjected to interfering interpolated activity in that they have been followed by other items to be remembered. On this view the last few items have an advantage that can be overcome with extra interpolated activity.

The level-of-processing view is that the recency effect is due to the last few items being available in a phonological code (as well as in whatever other code is responsible for long-term retention in free recall). However, the phonological code is transient, and if recall is delayed by interpolated activity, the superiority of the last few serial positions vanishes.

Neurophysiological evidence. Milner's studies (1966; Milner, Corkin, & Teuber, 1968) have shown that surgery can produce subjects with intact short-term and long-term retention but no ability to transfer *new* information into long-term memory. The levels-of-processing approach suggests that such patients have lost the ability to process new information at deep levels. This analysis has been applied to patients suffering from another neurological problem (Korsakoff's syndrome) that also results in an inability to store new information in long-term memory (Cermak, 1974).

Evaluation of levels of processing In addition to accounting for the short-term memory effects discussed in the preceding section, the levels-of-processing view is consistent with effects of different orienting tasks on *incidental memory* (pp. 330–331). For example, Schulman (1971) had subjects scan a list of words for targets defined graphologically (words containing the letter A) or semantically (words naming living things). After the scanning task, subjects were given an unexpected recognition test to see how many words from each type of list were retained. Incidental memory for words from the semantically defined target condition was superior to that for words from the graphological condition. Since words must be analyzed more deeply in the semantic task than the graphological task, the data are consistent with the theory.

We see that the idea of processing levels is consistent with data from a variety of experimental situations. However, as a general theory of memory, it suffers from several defects as it is now stated. For one, it is not a complete theory in that it explains differences in rates of forgetting, but does not explain the cause of forgetting for material processed to any given depth. For another, no rules have been given for ascertaining the processing level required by any given task. We can all agree that searching for a word containing an A is a lower-level task than searching for a word meaning *living thing*. This is intuitively obvious. However, intuition may not be adequate for more subtle cases. Finally, it is not yet clear whether this theory will be able to handle the observation that some of the interference effects that operate in long-term memory seem not to operate in short-term memory (Baddeley & Dale, 1966; Peterson & Gentile, 1965; Wickelgren, 1967).

RELATIONS BETWEEN SHORT-TERM AND LONG-TERM RETENTION

Chapters on learning and memory are usually kept quite separate. In part, this is due to the necessity for imposing some kind of order on a large field of endeavor. In addition, it is the case that different people have worked in these two fields. Recently, however, there has been a change in that many workers who have proposed models and theories in one field have recognized an obligation to attempt an explanation broad enough to encompass the other field.

Melton (1963) stresses the common principles of memory and learning. Learning can be defined as the modification of behavior as a function of experience. There has been learning if there has been a change in behavior from trial n to trial $n + 1$. Trials n and $n + 1$ may be the presentation and test trials in a test of short-term memory, or they may be two successive trials in any repetitive learning situation. Melton pointed out that the change in behavior from trial n to $n + 1$ is referred to, according to psychological convention, in three different ways, depending upon the conditions of experimentation. If the variable of interest is the ordinal number of trial n, and not the temporal interval between n and $n + 1$, the behavior change is referred to as a *learning* change. When the variable of interest is the interval between n and $n + 1$, and the events occurring therein, the behavior change is referred to as a *retention* change. When learning and retention are studied, the experimental situation is usually the same on trials n and $n + 1$. When any task or situation variables are systematically varied between n and $n + 1$, the investigation is of *transfer*, i.e., the utilization of the products of trial n in the different situation of $n + 1$.

The foregoing analysis is purely formal, and one might wonder whether there is any substantive relationship between learning and memory and, in particular, short-term memory. The answer appears to be "yes," according to an analysis by Tulving (1964). Tulving was concerned with the trial-to-trial improvement in performance found in free-recall tasks. The same long list (22 words in Tulving's experiment) was presented in a new scrambled order on each trial. After each trial the subject tried to recall as many of the words as he could.

Tulving's analysis begins with the observation that the items are presented slowly enough to be perceived clearly, and that immediately after each item is presented the subject is able to repeat it back correctly. Therefore, one could claim that even on the first trial, subjects have learned the entire list, even though they might not be able to recall more than about five items from it after presentation of the entire list. The fact that recall is so poor does not mean that learning was incomplete, but rather that retention was incomplete. Many of the causes of short-term retention loss in this kind of situation have been examined earlier in this chapter. The recall score on the first trial reflects the joint effects of one-trial learning and intratrial forgetting. The net effect of these Tulving referred to as *intratrial retention*.

Performance on the second trial and all subsequent trials can also be considered to be the result of retention. However, on these trials *two* retention components must be considered. Some items could be remembered during the recall phase of the second trial, even without being re-exposed during the input phase of the second trial; the subject remembers these items from the previous trial. The number of these responses indicates the level of *intertrial retention*. In addition, the subject may recall during the output phase of the second trial some items that were not recalled from the first trial but were recalled from the input phase of the second trial. These responses indicate the level of *intratrial retention* for trials beyond the first.

The preceding analysis suggests the possibility of examining inter- and intratrial retention over successive pairs of trials. On successive trials $n - 1$ and n, there are four possible subsets of events defined by the conjunction of recalling (C) or not recalling (N) an item on each trial.

1. *CC* represents items that one recalled on both $n - 1$ and n. This is a measure of intertrial retention.
2. *NC* consists of items recalled on n but not on $n - 1$. This is a measure of intratrial retention.
3. *CN* consists of items that are recalled on $n - 1$ but not recalled on n. This is a measure of intertrial forgetting.
4. *NN* consists of items that are not recalled on either $n - 1$ or n. This is a measure of intratrial forgetting.

If the size of each of the four subsets is computed from the data for all pairs of consecutive trials (0 and 1, 1 and 2, . . . , $n - 1$ and n), four curves are obtained. Since forgetting and retention bear a complementary relation to one another, any two of the curves may be derived from the other two. This means that the traditional learning curve, in which performance (P) is plotted as a function of trials, can be described in terms of just two of its four logical components. Tulving was concerned mainly with intertrial retention and intratrial retention, which are related to performance according to the following formula:

$$P = CC + NC$$

To determine what merit, if any, this analysis has, Tulving collected

Figure 13.9
Mean sizes of subsets corresponding to four different components of performance derived from a trial-by-trial analysis of recall data. (Tulving, 1964.)

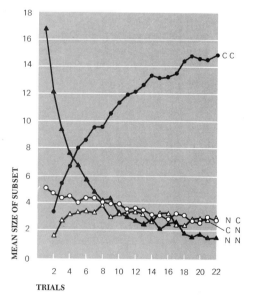

data from subjects attempting free recall of a 22-word list. Subjects were
allowed 22 trials. The data from the componential analysis appear in
Figure 13.9. The intertrial retention (CC) curve is the only one that rises
systematically over trials, while the intratrial retention curve (NC) is
nearly linear with a negative slope. When the overall learning curve was
"predicted" from the CC and NC components the fit was impressive.
The learning curve had the form $P = a \log n - bn + c$ (where n
represents trials). The component $a \log n$ represents the contribution of
the CC function, and the component $c - bn$ represents the NC
contribution.

The negative slope of the intertrial retention function (NC) may be
the result of a relatively short list. Tulving presents a persuasive
argument that the function is generally flat, i.e., independent of n. If
intratrial retention is independent of n it is also independent of intertrial
retention. Thus, regardless of the number of items remembered from a
previous trial, the subject will recall the same number of "new" items on
each trial. (A "new" item is one that was not recalled on the previous
trial).

The important remaining problem is how subjects increase intertrial
retention over trials. Subjects do not simply recall more and more items
from the input list, but they impose an increasing degree of organization
on the list as practice continues. Since the list is made up of unrelated
words that are presented in a different random order on each trial, one
might wonder what kind of structure the subjects could possibly impose
on the words. Subjects recall certain items close to one another even
though they are separated in the input list. Since the sequences that
develop are often idiosyncratic and since it may not be obvious to the
experimenter what the basis for a sequence or cluster is, Tulving (1962)
has referred to this phenomenon as *subjective organization* (SO). He
devised a measure of the extent to which recall on successive trials is
structured sequentially. Of course, to the extent that recall is structured
in, say, clusters and not sequentially, Tulving's measure of SO will yield
an underestimate of structure, but it has in fact proved to be a useful tool
nevertheless. It should be noted that Tulving's measure is especially
useful when unrelated words are used. If the experimenter has designed
a list to contain several clusters there are other methods of analysis that
may be more appropriate (see p. 316).

Tulving (1964) showed that there was a very close relationship over
trials between his measure of SO and intertrial retention (CC). Moreover, the data from individual subjects show that there is a nearly zero
correlation between SO and intratrial retention (at least early in practice)
but a strong correlation ($+.58$) between SO and intertrial retention.
Thus, intratrial retention does not seem to depend on organization
whereas intertrial retention does.

If we can assume that SO indicates the extent to which seemingly
unrelated items are organized into what are called "higher-order subjective units," then the increase in intertrial retention may be interpreted as
a sign of an increase in the size of subjective units rather than an increase

in their number. "Repetition does not change the basic storage capacity of memory. Rather, organizing processes accompanying repetition lead to an apparent increase in capacity by increasing the information load of individual units" (Tulving, 1962, pp. 344 ff.).

Higher-order subjective units may be considered an analog in secondary memory to the chunks proposed by Miller (1956) as a unit for short-term retention. Tulving suggests that it is possible that the same limitations that apply to primary memory may thus apply to the handling of information in a repetitive verbal learning experiment.

FOURTEEN

MEMORY FOR MEANING

Why is it necessary to have a separate chapter on memory for meaning? It is because human language and human cognitive processes continuously act upon and change what we know. What we know is the product of our memory, and while we have considered how conditions of learning and retention influence memory and how memory is structured, we have not yet considered how what we remember is altered and cast into new forms by our ongoing linguistic and intellectual processes. Most of what we know about how such continuous reorganization takes place is the result of two sorts of studies: investigations into the semantic structure of memory, and research on cognitive reorganization during the process of remembering. This chapter is mainly given over to these two topics.

First, however, a word on the relation of these topics to the studies of memory we have examined thus far. While we have, in the course of considering verbal learning, examined some of the effects of semantic structures on organizational processes (see, for example, clustering in free recall, p. 322), our main emphasis has been upon how the conditions and materials we learn induce patterns of forgetting. We have, in studying memory, chiefly been concerned with how much we forget of certain kinds of things under particular kinds of conditions. In short, our major interest has been in the quantitative aspects of memory, an interest that has a long history back to the work of Ebbinghaus (1885).

However, the very fact that quantitative studies of forgetting have been in the tradition of Ebbinghaus has meant that these studies have largely overlooked reorganizational processes. Ebbinghaus initiated the view in the study of memory that it is necessary to control or eliminate meaning from the materials learned in order to reduce so complex a problem to the limitations of the laboratory. To this end, for example, Ebbinghaus made use of nonsense syllables. As we have seen, subsequent investigators have moved beyond the nonsense syllable, but the view that one must eliminate or at least severely restrict meaning in order to study memory still persists. Cofer (1973, p. 537) characterizes the contemporary concern with memory as "determining the conditions for the acquisition and retention of specific verbal associations and the factors that make acquisition easy or difficult and that facilitate or inhibit retention of associations and their transfer to other lists." Cofer goes on to point out that one of the distinguishing methodological characteristics of the research carried out in this tradition is reliance upon accuracy of recall or recognition of the items presented to the subjects. Errors are supposed to provide clues to the processes, such as proactive inhibition, that produce deficits in memory.

There is, however, another tradition in the study of memory, though it has occupied far less attention than the Ebbinghaus tradition, at least until recent years. It is a tradition that takes natural materials as the source of study. Subjects are asked to remember sentences, stories, and other kinds of material that have coherent structures. This tradition is less distinguished from the Ebbinghaus tradition by its materials and methods, however, than it is by its emphasis upon what the subject is to remember. Ebbinghaus studied rote learning, and the overwhelming majority of experiments upon forgetting have used rote learning. However, in the tradition for which Sir Frederic Bartlett (1886–1969) is largely responsible, the emphasis is on the meaning the subject is trying to remember and how that meaning is transformed by the act of recollection itself. Before turning to the work of Bartlett and those who have followed in his tradition, however, we shall examine contemporary views concerning how semantic information is stored in memory, for such stored semantic information provides the elements of meaning from which reconstruction in recall can take place.

SEMANTIC STORAGE IN MEMORY

How do we store the huge number of words whose meanings we must remember in order to produce and understand language? Do we have something like a dictionary in our heads, from which we can look up or retrieve the general meanings of words which we can then use in particular sentences? Some investigators have thought so, though their conception of the nature of the subjective dictionary is very different from the plan on which most ordinary dictionaries are made. While many of these theories are interesting to linguists rather than to psychologists, a few of them have psychological implications, and indeed, some of them were designed specifically to account for problems in semantic memory. These have led to experimental investigations of memory. Our account of semantic structures will concentrate on these theories.

TYPES OF SEMANTIC STRUCTURES

Network structures   One of the most common ideas about the subjective dictionary is that it is organized as a network of interconnected pathways of relations. One type of network that has received close attention in this regard is the *hierarchy*. Schemes for showing how our vocabularies are hierarchically organized go back a considerable time, but some of the more recent theories have specifically addressed themselves to the psychological implications of a hierarchical organization. One such theory is by Quillian (1968). In Quillian's theory, each word in a vocabulary has a set of features associated with it. Thus, the meaning of the word *canary* stems from the fact that, among other things, we know canaries to be yellow and to be able to sing. The features of yellowness and ability to sing are stored with the entry, *canary*. Canaries also have wings and feathers, and they can fly. These features, however, are not stored with *canary*. These features are general characteristics of birds, and hence they are stored with the entry, *bird*. In this way, only the information appropriate to a given level in a hierarchy is stored at that level. If someone asks us, "Do canaries sing?" we can answer that question by going directly to the word *canary*. If, however, someone asks us "Do canaries fly?" we must answer that question by going to the entry *canary*, discovering that the information is not stored with that entry, and then going to the next highest entry, *bird*, and discovering the information there. This general arrangement is illustrated in Figure 14.1.

This theory leads to the hypothesis that it should take longer to answer the question "Do canaries fly?" than to answer the question "Do canaries sing?" To examine this kind of hypothesis, Collins and Quillian (1969) performed an experiment in which subjects answered "true" or "false" (by pressing the appropriate button) to various propositions. Some of the propositions used by Collins and Quillian include "An oak

Figure 14.1
A hierarchical model for semantic storage. Features are stored at the appropriate nodes. (Collins & Quillian, 1969.)

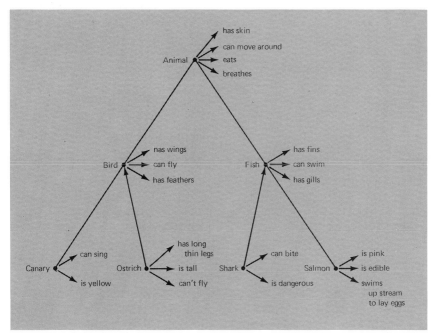

has acorns" (true, with the features stored with the word *oak*), "A spruce has branches" (true, with the features stored at one level up the hierarchy), "A birch has seeds" (true, with the feature stored two levels up the hierarchy), and "A juniper is a grain" (false). Collins and Quillian measured the reaction time for correct answers to these propositions. They also measured the reaction times to propositions indicating relations in the hierarchy ("An oak is a tree," "An oak is a plant"). The data from their experiment can be seen in Figure 14.2.

Collins and Quillian argued that the further away, in the hierarchy, the information is stored, the longer it should take to answer the question. They also argued that reaction times to questions about relations in the hierarchy should also be longer the greater the distance between the terms in question. Both results appear to hold.

Several experiments, as you might imagine, have followed this investigation. Some of these experiments appear to confirm the results found by Collins and Quillian, while others do not or lead to alternative interpretations. Anderson (1972) asked subjects to recall the nouns that served as direct objects in some simple sentences. The subject of the sentence served as a cue for recall of the object noun. Recall was better when the word serving as a cue was a close superordinate rather than a remote superordinate for the word to be recalled. These results are in accord with the notions of Collins and Quillian.

Landauer and Meyer (1972) were able to confirm the basic experimental results achieved by Collins and Quillian, but they argued that the results are not due to semantic distance but to category size. If you

Figure 14.2
Reaction times for responding "true" or "false" to statements based upon semantic features stored at different levels. (Collins & Quillian, 1969.)

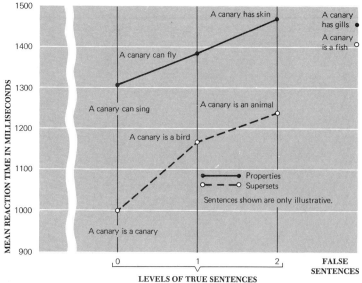

examine the tree, it becomes clear that there are more things that are

members of the categories near the top of the tree than categories near
the bottom. All the varieties of birds are also varieties of animals.
Landauer and Meyer argue that it takes longer to retrieve information
from large categories than from small ones, and that the semantic
distance effect in Figure 14.2 is really a result of the nesting of semantic
categories in Figure 14.1. One might suppose that it would be easy to
settle this question by comparing the reaction times to sentences of the
form "X is a Y" for two categories which are not nested but which differ
in size. For example, it would be possible to compare reaction times to
sentences like "A perch is a fish" with reaction times to sentences like
"A collie is a dog." Presumably, there are more fishes than dogs.
However, it isn't that simple, for the average subject in an experiment
may actually know more varieties of dogs than of fishes. Consequently,
the issue has remained unsettled at this level.

Given this state of affairs, one group of experimenters attempted to
determine whether or not the category effect is due to semantic distance
or to category size by using artificial features (Smith, Haviland, Buckley,
& Sack, 1972). Subjects would learn such relations as "A Hawk is a 4"
and "A bird is a 2." They were instructed in the hierarchical organization
so that they knew that any property true of birds was also true of hawks,
but that properties specifically attributed to hawks would not necessarily
be true of all birds. When the subjects were trained on a two-leveled
hierarchy, the results were very much in accord with the proposal made
by Collins and Quillian. However, the results for a three-leveled hierarchy were more complicated and did not fit the notion of semantic
distance. In fact, the data from this portion of the experiment agreed
with the notion that information in memory is always stored with the
lexical item in question and is not arrived at by deduction combined with
a knowledge of hierarchical relations. While people can employ deduction in memory, they are not likely to do so if the inference is difficult to
make. Hence the features or semantic information appropriate to a given
word appears to be stored both with the word and, if appropriate, with its
superordinate. Thus, there is no particular efficiency in Quillian's proposal, and that was its principal claim. However, the experiments by
Collins and Quillian and by others do show us that deductive inference
can be used in retrieval from memory and apparently is automatically
and directly so used if the inference is simple, as from a word to its
immediate superordinate.

Hierarchical relations are but one of the types of network relations
that can hold among words of similar meaning. Other models of
semantic storage in memory have described how different patterns of
relations can account for facts of memory and performance.

One formal model of how information is represented in memory that
has attracted much attention is by Rumelhart, Lindsay, and Norman
(1972). These authors represent knowledge stored in memory by means
of a network in which the nodes stand for concepts or events, and the

directed, labeled lines that connect the nodes stand for the meaningful relations. An example of such a representation is given in Figure 14.3. This rather abstract picture of what is stored in memory is supplemented in this account by a set of sensory-motor plans. One of the features of this model of memory is that, as in Quillian's model, semantic information is stored in an efficient manner. Whenever a new example of a general class is encountered, only the properties unique to that example will be stored with it; everything else is stored at the more general level. Moreover, a concept may belong to any number of classes, and thus information about it can be retrieved through any of the classes.

Information in this model is represented as a set of propositions that consist of actions, actors, and objects. Since the action taking place is generally described by a verb, it is the verb that becomes the central relation to which the actors and objects are attached. For example, the proposition "A cat chases mice" is focused on the action "chases." The cat is the actor, and mice are the objects of the action. This analysis suggested to Yates and Caramazza (1974) a possible test of the model. Subjects were given sentences to remember. Recall of the sentences was cued by the presentation of a single word from the original sentence, either the verb or a noun serving another grammatical function in the sentence. The idea was that recall should be better when it was cued by the verb than by any other sentence element, because the verb is central to the representation of the sentence and is thus associatively linked with all the other elements. The data indicated that recall was the same for the various kinds of recall cues and thus failed to support this aspect of the Rumelhart, Lindsay, and Norman model.

Aspects of a more recent model, one by Anderson and Bower (1973) were described earlier (p. 323). It was described in an earlier chapter,

Figure 14.3
Representation of the semantic information required to be stored for an understanding of the sentence, "John murders Mary at Luigi's." (Rumelhart, Lindsay, & Norman, 1972.)

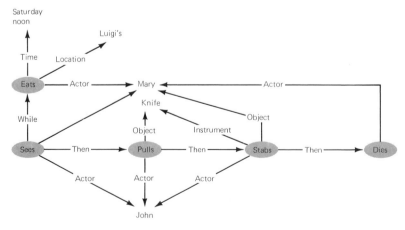

even though it is basically a model of semantic retrieval, because it was used by its authors to account for the results of some traditional experiments in paired-associate learning and interference.

Set structures In network models, words are represented by interconnected pathways of relations. To verify a proposition such as "A robin is a bird," the stored relation between robin and bird is retrieved and compared with the proposition. Although verification includes both retrieval and comparison, the retrieval process is considered the more important. These models represent just one tradition in semantic memory research. In contrast, *set-theoretic models* represent words as sets of features. To verify the proposition that "A robin is a bird" requires retrieving the attributes of bird and robin and comparing them. However, retrieval is treated as fairly "automatic"; comparison is the process of chief interest.

The idea that propositions are verified by a comparison of the attributes of the words constituting the proposition was proposed by Schaeffer and Wallace (1969, 1970) to account for some findings that are not easily handled by Collins and Quillian's hierarchical model. Propositions containing semantically similar items are verified more quickly than propositions containing dissimilar items. You will recall that "An oak is a tree" is verified more quickly than "An oak is a plant." This finding is consistent with the hierarchical model because there are fewer "steps" between oak and tree than between oak and plant. However, the opposite is true for negative judgments. For example, Rips, Shoben, and Smith (1973) found that False reaction time increased with the semantic relatedness of the items in a proposition. Statements like "A robin is a mammal" take longer to disconfirm than statements like "A robin is a car." Similar findings have been obtained by Schaeffer and Wallace (1969, 1970) and Wilkins (1971).

The fact that semantic similarity interferes with judging that two items are *not* related, suggests that attributes that are logically irrelevant to the decision are included in the decision process. This has suggested to several theorists that the verification of propositions, and other semantic memory tasks, includes a stage in which an *overall* comparison is made of all the attributes of the key words. Smith, Shoben, and Rips (1974) have proposed a two-stage theory that includes such an overall comparison as its first stage. If the results of the initial comparison indicate either very high or very low overlap between the sets of attributes constituting the terms being compared, a judgment can be made immediately. However, if the degree of overlap is neither very high nor very low, a second stage of comparison is required in which just the features that are considered *defining* are considered (see also Meyer, 1970).

In the model proposed by Smith and his colleagues, the notion of *defining* features is distinguished from the notion of *characteristic* features. To illustrate the distinction, consider the word *robin*. Among the facts that an individual may know about this category are that robins are bipeds, have wings, have distinctive colors, perch in trees, are undomesticated, and have a certain average size. Smith, Shoben, and Rips (1974) argue that the first three of these features are more defining of the concept of robin than the latter three, which, for most individuals, would be merely characteristic features of robins. One would probably *not* specify average size if one were trying to define the concept of robin for a foreign friend. Higher level concepts (such as bird or animal) also have characteristic and defining features.

The distinction between defining and characteristic features helps to explain some otherwise puzzling phenomena. For example, Rips, Shoben, and Smith (1973) showed that, for any given category, it takes longer to judge that some items belong to that category than other items. Thus sparrow and pigeon are judged to be birds more quickly than are chicken and goose. Technically speaking, chickens and geese are birds; any differences in reaction time among birds thus cannot be due to differences among items in terms of defining features. More plausibly, chickens and geese share fewer characteristic features with the category labeled birds than do sparrows and pigeons. Chickens and geese are less *typical* of the category birds than are sparrows and pigeons (Rosch, 1973).

The set-theoretic model is not limited to problems of class membership. In fact Smith, Rips, and Shoben (1974) have extended their model to a wide variety of tasks, including the solution of analogy problems and the understanding of metaphor.

Evaluation of models of semantic structure   The term "semantic memory" was first used by Quillian in 1968, and so the field is still very young. Although some interesting and important work has been done since that time, right now we must admit that we do not know how semantic information is stored. It is possible that it is retained in memory in some as yet not understood way and is retrieved only in some particular way depending upon the person's needs of the moment. Sometimes we need to remember that a *dog* is an *animal*, while at other times we may need to remember only that *dogs* and *cats* are to be found around the house. In one case we call upon a superordinate-subordinate relation, while in the other we call upon a coordinate or, perhaps, a completely unlabeled associative relation. In short, the relations, labeled or otherwise, that tie two pieces of semantic information together may be a process that occurs only at the time of retrieval. What we may remember may be something quite different. One possibility is that we store undifferentiated features and that when a critical set of features is brought together, it trips off the name of a concept. Thus, the collection of features, *furry, mammalian, domestic, barks* readily arouses the word *dog*. While this view comes closer to that expressed by Anderson and Bower (1973) than any other, these authors do not explicitly address themselves to how features are related to arousal of particular words. An interesting set of experiments do relate to this problem, however, and we shall consider these experiments in the following section.

SOME FURTHER EXPERIMENTS IN SEMANTIC MEMORY

At this point it is useful to introduce a distinction Tulving (1972) makes between episodic memory and semantic memory. Episodic memory deals with information about episodes and events that have particular beginnings and endings. Tulving points out that the act of retrieving information from episodic memory also serves as a special kind of input to episodic memory and thus changes the content of episodic memory. Partly because of its susceptibility to change as the result of retrieval and partly for other reasons, episodic memory is more subject to transformations of various sorts and to loss than is semantic memory. Semantic memory is the memory necessary for the use of language. It is generally the kind of thing we refer to as "knowing something" rather than "remembering something," though, of course, we know that knowledge depends upon memory. Semantic memory is a relatively stable system that permits the retrieval of information without significant alteration in content. As with episodic memory, however, our success in retrieving information in semantic memory depends in part upon the nature of the cues with which we are presented and upon the conditions of the moment. Thus failures and partial successes in semantic memory are possible, and these provide us with additional experimental information about the nature of semantic memory.

The tip of the tongue effect Everyone has had some experience with the tip of the tongue phenomenon. It occurs when we cannot think of something, usually a proper name, but we feel that we are on the verge of being able to remember it. We say to ourselves, "Wa . . . , Watson—no, Wilber—no, Willia . . . that's it—Wilkins." The inability to recall something that we know we know leaves us feeling distinctly uncomfortable, and we may ruminate about it for hours and even days before we satisfy ourselves that we have finally remembered the correct name or word.

Brown and McNeill (1966) realized that this phenomenon might help us to understand how semantic information is stored in memory. As in the example given above, it often happens that our incorrect guesses contain many of the same sounds and other characteristics of the correct word or name. Therefore, Brown and McNeill argued, it might be possible to demonstrate via the tip of the tongue phenomenon that semantic storage is actually by distinctive features, and that partial assemblage of features might lead to erroneous recall of items similar to the target word.

Therefore, these investigators invented an ingenious way of studying the phenomenon in the laboratory. They read definitions to subjects. These definitions were of rare words taken from the *American College Dictionary*. Examples include *apse, nepotism, cloaca, ambergris,* and *sampan*. If the subjects could immediately identify the word from its definition, they were to do nothing further. If, however, they could not think of the word but felt sure that they knew what it was, they supplied the investigators with information about their guesses as to the number of syllables in the correct word, its initial letter, words of similar sound and meaning, and also the word they had in mind in case it turned out that the real word was not the one they were thinking of.

Brown and McNeill found a total of 360 instances in which subjects thought they were in a tip of the tongue state. Of these, 233 were actually tip of the tongue states. The words that came to mind were classified by the subjects into 224 words that sounded like the target word and 95 words that were similar in meaning. In short, while the larger portion of the tip of the tongue phenomenon was phonetic in nature, there were also semantic effects. For example, words similar in meaning to *sampan* and thought of by the subjects when they heard the definition included *barge, houseboat*, and *junk*. These are clearly semantically related.

Brown and McNeill came to the conclusion that what people store in semantic memory is features. When enough features are retrieved, the correct word can be remembered. The features necessary to word memory are both phonetic—how to pronounce the word in question— and semantic—what it means. Brown and McNeill likened semantic memory to a keysort system. Keysort cards have holes punched in them, and each hole corresponds to some particular piece of information. It is possible to retrieve all the cards that relate to that particular piece of information by locating all the cards that have a hole punched in that particular position. What happens in memory according to this analogy is that the subject thinks of one or more features, and these allow him to retrieve a number of words (or batch of cards). By remembering more and more features, the subject can narrow the words down to the single one that is correct, or the one word that is uniquely defined by a particular set of features. Brown and McNeill called this process retrieval from generic memory.

A subsequent investigation (Yarmey, 1973) confirms this general interpretation but shows us that search for the correct set of features is clearly helped by imagery and by verbal mediators. In trying to identify well-known people from photographs, subjects used episodic information: "I remember seeing his picture in the paper this morning while I was reading at breakfast—yes, it's Pablo Picasso." Thus, while semantic information may be stored in the form of generic features, its retrieval will also depend upon the use of episodic mediators.

Ease of recall of semantic information   The tip of the tongue experiments provide convincing evidence that we use the semantic features associated with a given word to retrieve that word in memory. Granted that such is the case, it is still puzzling why we can easily retrieve some words but others only with difficulty. The tip of the tongue phenomenon does not seem to help us solve the puzzle. In the laboratory we must deal with strange and unusual words, and in our daily experience with the effect there are too many things unique to a given situation to let us find a general answer. An experiment closely related to the tip of the tongue experiments, however, suggests that frequency of usage and dominance level (p. 269) are correlates of the ease of retrieval (Freedman and Loftus, 1971).

In this experiment, subjects responded to some superordinate concepts by giving an example of that concept. In addition to giving an example of the superordinate, however, they had to restrict themselves to a case that began with a certain letter or which was characterized by a particular feature. For example, the subjects saw *animal-z*. They were then to give an example of an animal that began with the letter *z* (*zebra*, of course, readily comes to mind). In another example, the subjects saw the pair *flower-yellow*. They had to respond with the name of a flower that was yellow (*daffodil*). The dependent measure was the speed of response.

The results showed that the time it took subjects to retrieve a correct example was unrelated to estimates of the size of the category. For example, the speed of response to *month-winter* was almost identical to the item, *vegetable-green*, though there are many more green vegetables than there are winter months. However, frequency of usage of the responses given by the subjects and the dominance level of potential responses to the categories did make a difference. Figure 14.4 shows the results. The responses given by the subjects were classified in one of five levels of frequency of usage, according to a count of how often words occur in ordinary English. Notice that the reaction time decreases as the frequency of usage of the responses increases. There is also a correlation between dominance level and reaction time. Dominance refers to the readiness with which a given category instance is aroused, given the category name. For example, *trout* readily comes to mind as an example

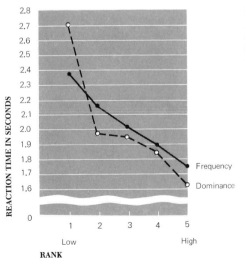

Figure 14.4
Reaction time in naming examples of concepts as a function of the frequency and dominance levels of the concept names (Freedman & Loftus, 1971.)

of a *fish*, while *sea robin* would scarcely occur to anyone asked to simply name a fish. Freedman and Loftus used category norms to determine the dominance level for the concepts they gave their subjects. They found, in the norms, the most commonly given example that would fit each concept. The higher the dominance level the shorter the reaction time. Notice that these results do not imply that frequency and dominance *cause* an easier retrieval, merely that they are related to it.

We can apply these results to the tip of the tongue effect. They suggest that certain features are *salient* for certain concepts. Even though the color yellow would apply to roses or violets (both of which can be yellow) as logically as to daffodils (which are sometimes white), when we are asked to think of a yellow flower we more easily think of daffodils than of roses or violets. Thus, in searching our memory for the name of the concept we are trying to retrieve, if we are lucky we will get ahold of a feature that is salient for the concept in question. We may well, however, think of a feature that is logically appropriate but low in saliency for that concept. In that case, it may take us a very long time to retrieve the concept name from memory.

Thus, while there is no logical reason why some features are more closely associated with the concepts they characterize than other features, there are psychological reasons for believing that some features are better associated than others. Differences in association between feature and concept make for some of the variability in the ease of retrieving concepts from semantic memory. If we find it difficult to remember something, it may be because we are working with the wrong feature as cue. Given this fact, however, it is difficult to see why some features are more salient than others for concepts. Word frequency is merely a correlate, and dominance level is simply another way of showing that there is differential association between feature and concept. These measures do not account for differential association; they simply make it more plausible that it exists. We do not yet have any well-supported theory that would account for differences in association between concepts and the features that compose them.

RECONSTRUCTION IN MEMORY

Memory for meaning must consist in part of the storage of semantic information, information about our world and our experience in it. However, the actual process of remembering something consists of more than retrieving it from memory. It also consists of reconstruction of missing parts—and hence dynamic change in memory—as well as of the assimilation of past memories to ongoing experience. Reconstruction draws upon other memories, but it also draws upon the making of inferences—in short, upon reasoning. The importance of reconstruction in memory was first pointed out by Bartlett (1932), and it is to his work that we turn.

Bartlett's studies Bartlett's book, *Remembering* (1932), contains a wealth of original and incisive investigation into perceiving, imaging, and remembering, from the point of view of both individual psychology and social psychology. Our main concern is with his observations on memory and his use of the method of repeated reproduction. In these experiments, Bartlett gave subjects a story, an argumentative prose passage, or sometimes simply a drawing to study. Subjects would examine these materials under a particular set of instructions for a period of time. They would then be asked to reproduce what they had studied after an interval of about 15 minutes. From many of his subjects, Bartlett would obtain subsequent reproductions at irregular intervals of increasing length—up to 10 years in a few cases.

Here is one of the stories he used. It was read twice at the initial study period by each subject.

The War of the Ghosts

One night two young men from Egulac went down to the river to hunt seals, and while they were there it became foggy and calm. Then they heard war-cries, and they thought: "Maybe this is a war-party." They escaped to the shore, and hid behind a log. Now canoes came up, and they heard the noise of paddles, and saw one canoe coming up to them. There were five men in the canoe, and they said:

"What do you think? We wish to take you along. We are going up the river to make war on the people."

One of the young men said: "I have no arrows."

"Arrows are in the canoe," they said.

"I will not go along. I might be killed. My relatives do not know where I have gone. But you," he said, turning to the other, "may go with them."

So one of the young men went, but the other returned home.

And the warriors went on up the river to a town on the other side of Kalama. The people came down to the water, and they began to fight, and many were killed. But presently the young man heard one of the warriors say: "Quick, let us go home: that Indian has been hit." Now he thought:

"Oh, they are ghosts." He did not feel sick, but they said he had been shot and made a fire. And he told everybody and said: "Behold I accompanied the ghosts and we went to fight. Many of our fellows were killed and many of those who attacked us were killed. They said I was hit, and I did not feel sick."

He told it all, and then he became quiet. When the sun rose he fell down. Something black came out of his mouth. His face became contorted. The people jumped up and cried.

He was dead. (Bartlett, 1932, p. 65)

Here is a reproduction given by one of Bartlett's subjects twenty hours after he had read the story.

The War of the Ghosts

Two men from Edulac went fishing. While thus occupied by the river they heard a noise in the distance.

"It sounds like a cry," said one, and presently there appeared some men in canoes who invited them to join the party on their adventure. One of the young men refused to go, on the ground of family ties, but the other offered to go.

"But there are no arrows," he said.

"The arrows are in the boat," was the reply.

He thereupon took his place, while his friend returned home. The party paddled up the river to Kaloma, and began to land on the banks of the river. The enemy came rushing upon them and some sharp fighting ensued. Presently someone was injured and the cry was raised that the enemy were ghosts.

The party returned down the stream, and the young man arrived home feeling none the worse for his experience. The next morning at dawn he endeavored to recount his adventures. While he was talking something black issued from his mouth. Suddenly, he uttered a cry and fell down. His friends gathered around him.

But he was dead. (Bartlett, 1932, p. 66).

Notice, first of all, that the reproduction suffers from gross inaccuracies. Such is the rule rather than the exception, unless, of course, the material is studied exhaustively. In addition, however, Bartlett made the following comments about this particular reproduction.

1. The story has been considerably shortened, largely by omissions.

2. The language of the story has been assimilated to the habitual usage of the subject. The story, as you might have guessed, is a transcription of a North American Indian folk tale, and something of the exotic character of the original story teller is retained in the version used by Bartlett. His subjects, however, reproduced the story in something closer to standard British usage.

3. The story has become, again from the standpoint of our culture, more coherent than the original.

4. There are many omissions and some transformations. For example, "boat" replaced the less familiar (to Cambridge undergraduates) "canoe." "Hunting seals" becomes "fishing." This, incidentally, is a transformation present in the overwhelming majority of reproductions of this story by American students. The inference seems to be, if the two young Indians were going to the river they must have been going to fish, not to hunt. Proper names are misremembered. On a more thematic level, the main point about the ghosts is entirely misunderstood. The two excuses made by the reluctant men change places.

Eight days later the same subject made another reproduction, and all the trends noted in the original reproduction were simply accentuated.

Here is another reproduction made by a subject $6^{1/2}$ years after the original reading. This subject had made only one previous reproduction. His later version is:

1. Brothers.
2. Canoe.
3. Something black from mouth.

4. Totem.

5. One of the brothers died.

6. Cannot remember whether one slew the other or was helping the other.

7. Were going on a journey, but why I cannot remember.

8. Party in war canoe.

9. Was the journey a pilgrimage for filial or religious reasons?

10. Am now sure it was a pilgrimage.

11. Purpose had something to do with totem.

12. Was it on a pilgrimage that they met a hostile party and one brother was slain?

13. I think there was a reference to a dark forest.

14. Two brothers were on a pilgrimage, having something to do with a totem in a canoe, up a river flowing through a dark forest. While on their pilgrimage they met a hostile party of Indians in a war canoe. In the fight one brother was slain, and something black came from his mouth.

15. Am not confident about the way the brother died. May have been something sacrificial in the manner of his death.

16. The cause of the journey had both something to do with a totem, and with filial piety.

17. The totem was the patron god of the family and so was connected with filial piety. (Bartlett, 1932, p. 77).

What is so striking about this reproduction is that it is constructive in nature. The subject gradually reconstructs the main outline of the story, but in so doing he makes changes and introduces alien elements. Bartlett points out that this subject was most pleased with those elements that were purely his invention—the totem, the filial piety, the pilgrimage, the dark forest. He was also most certain about these points.

Still another subject was asked for a reproduction 10 years after the original presentation. She wrote "Egulac" and "Calama" but could go no farther. She then said she had a visual image of a sandy bank and of two men going down a river in a boat. That was all.

These reports exemplify the major features observed by Bartlett in hundreds of reproductions. There are deletions and simplification, extrapolation and invention, as well as systematic distortion. In order to do justice to the rich and varied nature of the reproductions, Bartlett proposes that what is remembered is not only determined by the stimulus materials themselves but by preexistent, active, organized settings that he called schemas (or schemata, in the Latin spelling). A schema is a plan or general point of view with all of the details left out. Bartlett argues that preexisting schemas influence a person's perception of complex events and memories for that event.

Although nearly everyone accepts Bartlett's main points now, his work leaves us unsatisfied. His theories are general rather than specific, and his experiments are such that we do not know whether the qualitative changes he observed are the result of changes taking place during storage or are the result of processes activated at retrieval. Most commentators have assumed that the reproductions reported by Bartlett reflect changes taking place all during the retention interval or changes induced by the reproduction process itself (as Bartlett himself seemed to think), but the fact is that we really do not know what the subjects learned in the first place in these experiments. Some investigators have argued that it is not important whether the changes occur during learning or retention (see Paul, 1959). But if we are to make use of these experiments in understanding the nature of learning and forgetting, the distinction is an important one. Another problem in Bartlett's observations is that he must infer the nature of the preexistent schemas from the occurrence of systematic distortion in the reproductions, but he had no way to control or produce such schemas and hence to control the systematic distortions. There are some experiments in which memory has been studied after schemas of various sorts have been experimentally induced. These are discussed in the next section.

Experimental induction of schemas A famous experiment is one by Carmichael, Hogan, and Walter (1932) in which verbal labels were shown to influence memory for simple pictures. The pictures are shown in the center column of Figure 14.5. These pictures were shown one at a time. Before each picture was shown, the experimenter said, "The next figure resembles . . ." (giving one of the two names assigned to the next figure to appear). The names were divided into two lists, as shown in Figure 14.5. One group of subjects heard list I, another heard list II, and a third or control group heard no list at all. The series was repeated until the subjects could produce a recognizable representation of all 12 figures. The investigators then examined the productions and found that they were strongly influenced by the names assigned the figures. Some selected examples of the effect of the names can be seen in Figure 14.5.

A study by Hanawalt and Demorest (1939) used materials like those in the experiment just described, but it differed from the earlier one in an important respect; verbal labels were not presented during the learning phase of the experiment. They were presented only at the time of recall. The labels served as suggestions or cues to the subject; e.g., "Draw the figure which resembled curtains in a window." This study also showed distortion under the influence of the verbal label. Thus, there is evidence that memory traces and current schemas interact at the time of reproduction. There may also be changes during the period of retention, though at present we can only guess at what these would be.

These studies differed from those of Bartlett in that there was no overall schema to determine the nature of the reproduction. Each label provided a simple schema for each separate figure. However, there have been some more recent studies aimed at determining the influence of generalized schemas in retention. To appreciate the problem to which these studies have been addressed, read the following paragraph.

> The procedure is actually quite simple. First you arrange things into different groups depending on their makeup. Of course, one pile may be sufficient depending on how much there is to do. If you have to go somewhere else due to lack of facilities that is the next step, otherwise you are pretty well set. It is important not to overdo any particular endeavor. That is, it is better to do too few things at once than too many. In the short run this may not seem

important, but complications from doing too many can easily arise. A mistake can be expensive as well. The manipulation of the appropriate mechanisms should be self-explanatory, and we need not dwell on it here. At first the whole procedure will seem complicated. Soon, however, it will become just another facet of life. It is difficult to foresee any end to the necessity for this task in the immediate future, but then one never can tell. (Bransford & Johnson, 1972, p. 722).

If your only instructions were to try to understand this passage and remember it for later reproduction, how well do you think you would do? If you were like the subjects in an experiment by Bransford and Johnson (1972), you would be able to remember very little of the paragraph.

Figure 14.5
A study of the effects of verbal labels on the retention of visually presented forms. The stimulus figures are shown in the center column. Flanking this column are the alternative verbal labels given to two groups of subjects. In the extreme left and right columns are shown some examples of reproductions that illustrate the effects of the verbal labels. (Carmichael, Hogan, & Walter, 1932.)

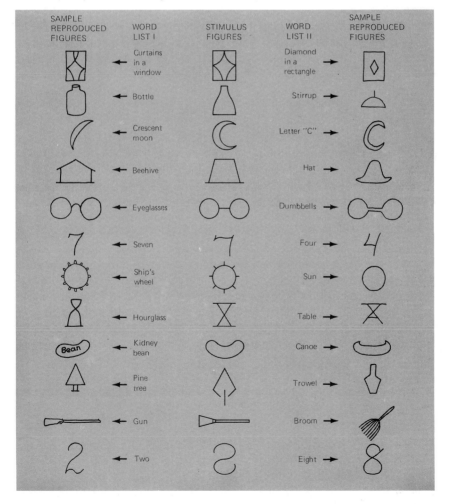

However, if before reading the passage you had been told that the paragraph was about washing clothes, you would have done much better. For this paragraph, when Bransford and Johnson's subjects knew the topic, they recalled nearly twice as many "idea units" as when they did not. The context provided by the topic provides a kernel around which the otherwise nearly nonsensical passage coalesces. However, knowledge of the topic is not, in itself, sufficient to permit an enhancement of recall and comprehension. Subjects who were told the topic *after* they had heard the paragraph did relatively poorly. Thus, it is crucial for the proper context to be present when the material is being studied (see also Dooling and Lachman, 1971).

Facilitation from an appropriate set is a very general characteristic of cognition (Egeth, 1967). We do not accept information passively, but we always must structure information as it is received if we are to understand and retain it. There is no raw experience, impartially analyzed, for all our experience is analyzed within the limits provided by the set of the moment. That set will yield particular schemas within which understanding will take place.

Experiments on serial order   Even in situations which superficially appear as though the simple principles of association would suffice for their explanation, schematic relations appear to determine what subjects learn and retain. In an experiment by DeSoto and Bosley (1962), subjects learned which of the labels "freshman," "sophomore," "junior," or "senior" was to be paired with each of 16 persons' names. The task was one in paired-associate learning (p. 320), and the experimenters recorded the nature of the errors the subjects made while learning to pair the labels with the names by rote practice. These errors were not randomly distributed, but rather reflected the "distance" between the correct label and the label mistakenly given. Suppose, for example, that *Dave* is a "freshman." If a subject made an error with the name *Dave*, it would most likely be "sophomore" and least likely be "senior." Thus, the name-label relations, even in this rote, paired-associate task, were not learned simply as isolated associations, but as part of a larger schema in which names were attached to four different locations along some conceptual dimension of "years in college."

Another experiment (Potts, 1972) reveals the strength and ubiquity of the serial ordering schema. In this experiment, subjects learned about four elements, which can abstractly be referred to as A, B, C, and D. Information was presented about the order of the elements in a paragraph, and after the subjects had studied the paragraph, they were tested for their knowledge of the ordering. The design of the experiment was complicated by requiring that the subjects learn information about two different orderings in each paragraph. Here is a paragraph the subjects studied.

In a small forest just south of nowhere, a deer, a bear, a wolf, and a hawk were battling for dominion over the land. It boiled down to a battle of wits, so intelligence was the crucial factor. The bear was smarter than the hawk, the hawk was smarter than the wolf, and the wolf was smarter than the deer. On a small pond in the middle of the same forest, another contest for dominion was being waged. The contenders were a frog, a clam, a duck, and a fish. In this case, however, the battle was to be decided by an election, and friendliness was the crucial factor. The fish was friendlier than the frog, the frog was friendlier than the clam, and the clam was friendlier than the duck. In addition, the fish was friendlier than the clam, the frog was friendlier than the duck, and the fish was friendlier than the duck. In the end each of the battles was decided in its own way and tranquility returned to the area (Potts, 1972, p. 730).

Note that information about all six possible pairs of elements is provided for the dimension of friendliness (A>B, B>C, C>D, A>C, A>D, B>D) but about only the three "adjacent" pairs for the dimension of intelligence (A>B, B>C, C>D). We shall refer to these as the explicit and implicit conditions, respectively, since information about the three "remote" pairs (i.e., that A>C, A>D, B>D) is only given implicitly in the second case. Subjects indicated their knowledge of the orderings by answering true-false questions as quickly as possible.

If we attempt to analyze this situation in terms of classical associationism, we would assume that subjects remember best exactly what is presented. Therefore, when the remote pairs are not presented, performance on these pairs should be poorer than performance on the adjacent pairs. Moreover we would predict that performance on the remote pairs should be better when these pairs were actually presented than when they were not. Neither of these predictions was confirmed. Subjects were faster and more accurate on questions dealing with the remote than with the adjacent pairs, and this was true whether or not the relations between remote pairs were explicit or had to be deduced. These results are consistent with the notion that subjects may use a serial-order schema in learning and remembering relations among elements.

DEEP AND SURFACE STRUCTURE IN MEMORY

In the experiment we have just described, it seems likely that the subjects extracted the underlying meaning or structure of the relations described in the paragraph. Their responses to the true-false questions were more dependent upon the inferred structure than on the forms of the actual sentences presented. However, we might want to know if some representation of those sentences had been stored in memory. There is no evidence from that experiment on the question, but other experiments do address themselves to this problem. They are, in general, experiments concerned with the relation between the surface form of the information we receive and the deep structural relations from that information that we actually retain.

Sachs' experiment One of the most frequently cited recent experiments on memory is one by Sachs (1967) aimed at finding out what features people retain from the reading of ordinary prose. The subjects in this experiment listened to and tried to understand some prose passages. Unknown to the subjects, each passage contained what Sachs called a base sentence. It was the object of the experiment, and it occurred either 0, 80, or 160 syllables from the end of the passage. At the end of the passage, subjects were presented with a sentence that was either identical to the base sentence or a changed version of it. They were asked to indicate whether the test sentence was the same as the base sentence or whether it had been changed. There were four kinds of relations between test sentences and base sentences in the experiment. The test sentence could be identical to the base, or it might differ from it in one of three ways: semantically (a change in meaning), formally (a change in detail that does not change meaning), or in voice (a change from active to passive or vice versa). For example, one passage concerned the Dutch optician who discovered the principle of the telescope and communicated the information to Galileo. The base sentence in the passage was: "He sent a letter about it to Galileo, the great Italian scientist." The semantically altered test sentence was: "Galileo, the great Italian scientist, sent him a letter about it." The alteration in voice was: "A letter about it was sent to Galileo, the great Italian scientist." The formal change was: "He sent Galileo, the great Italian scientist, a letter about it."

The principal data from the experiment are the percentages of correct responses to each of the four kinds of test sentences as a function of the amount of material interpolated between the base sentences and the test sentences. These data can be seen in Figure 14.6. Subjects can detect a semantic change reasonably well, even after 160 syllables have been interpolated. However, after 160 syllables the accuracy of identifying changes in voice or the form of the sentence declines to nearly chance levels. Notice that all sentence types were correctly categorized with no interpolated material. This fact has been taken as evidence that the grammatical form (and other nonsemantic features) of the sentence is

Figure 14.6
Percentage of correct judgments for each of four kinds of test sentence as a function of distance from end of passage of the base sentence. To be counted as correct, Identical test sentences must be judged *same,* while the Semantic, Passive/Active, and Formal test sentences must be judged *different.* (Sachs, 1967.)

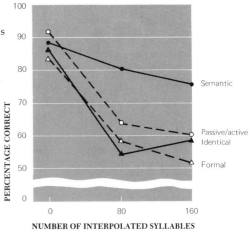

preserved in primary or short-term memory, while only the meaning is preserved in secondary or long-term memory. This corresponds to a difference between surface structure and deep structure. Only the deep structure of linguistic information is retained for future use, unless there is some premium placed upon remembering something else (which sentence is printed in red, for example). Even then, memory for the nonsemantic aspect, because it is not part of a schematic whole, will likely be poorer than for the semantic aspect of the material in question.

The abstraction of linguistic ideas   Some experiments on the abstraction of linguistic ideas serve to show how the schematic information in deep structures may be combined during retention and/or retrieval to form new structures only implicit in the original material learned by subjects. These experiments are reported in a study by Bransford and Franks (1971).

These experiments take advantage of the relatively high accuracy of recognition memory. An experiment by Shepard (1967), for example, shows that we can easily recognize a simple sentence that we have seen before, even if we have seen hundreds of other sentences in the meantime. Thus, subjects who had seen the sentence before would have no difficult recognizing "The rock rolled down the mountain," when that sentence is embedded in a long list of unrelated sentences. However, Bransford and Franks provide some conditions in which subjects will *not* recognize having seen such a sentence before. These conditions are part of an experiment which studies the way in which ideas, contained in separate sentences, are integrated.

Bransford and Franks made use of what they called idea sets. Each idea set could be expressed as a complex sentence. For example, one idea set could be expressed by the sentence, "The ants in the kitchen ate the sweet jelly which was on the table." Another is, "The rock which rolled down the mountain crushed the tiny hut at the edge of the woods." Each of these complex sentences can be broken down into four simple declarative sentences. These simple sentences Bransford and Franks called *ones* because they contained one simple idea each. These *ones* can be combined into *twos* and *threes*, consisting of two or three of the four ideas underlying the complex sentences. For example, a *two* such as "the sweet jelly was on the table" consists of an underlying idea "the jelly was sweet" plus the idea "the jelly was on the table."

During the acquisition phase of the experiment, subjects heard a long list containing, in random order, some of the *ones*, *twos*, and *threes* (but no *fours*) that could be generated from each of the four idea sets used in the experiment. Shortly after hearing these sentences, the subjects were given a recognition test. That test consisted of some sentences the subjects had heard before (called "old" sentences), some sentences not heard before but consistent with the ideas presented before ("new" sentences), and some sentences inconsistent with those ideas (called "noncases"). An example of a noncase would be, "The rock crushed the ants in the kitchen of the tiny hut." The task of the subjects was to indicate which sentences they had actually heard before and which they had not. In addition, they were asked to say how confident they were of their answer on a five-point rating scale ranging from "very low" to "very high" confidence. This resulted in a 10-point scale ranging from $+5$ (very high confidence that the item had been heard before) to -5 (very high confidence that the item had not been heard before). Remember that no *fours* were presented originally. They were always new sentences presented in the recognition test.

Many new sentences received positive ratings, indicating that the subjects thought they had heard the sentences before. In fact, there was no evidence that subjects could discriminate between old and new sentences. Secondly, confidence increased as the number of ideas in a sentence increased (see Figure 14.7). Thirdly, noncases were accurately judged to have not been heard before. Since the noncases were always *fours*, this result shows that positive ratings are not due solely to the length of the sentences in the recognition test. This is important because the greatest confidence was expressed for *fours*, but no *fours* had been presented during acquisition.

This experiment and others like it that have been carried out since show that people store something more general or abstract than just the particular set of sentences heard during acquisition. Bransford and Franks' subjects integrated information from related sentences to construct an idea of the meaning behind those sentences. These ideas are what they retained, not the particular sentences. The recognition ratings depended upon the degree to which a test sentence exhausted the set of four ideas contained in the original complex idea. Integration is particu-

Figure 14.7
Mean confidence ratings for the recognition of test sentences as a function of the number of "idea units" contained in the sentences. The similarity of the ratings for *old* and *new* sentences indicates that subjects had trouble discriminating sentences they had heard before from sentences they had not heard before. (Bransford & Franks, 1971.)

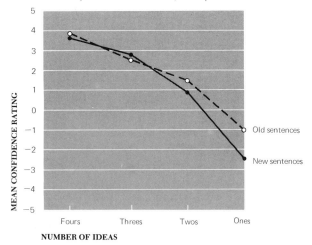

larly impressive here since, during acquisition, the sentences from each
of the four idea sets were intermixed in such a way that sentences from
the same idea set were never adjacent.

Other interpretations of this experiment are possible (see, for example, Reitman & Bower, 1973). However, when we put these results
together with the results of Sachs' experiment and when we consider the
kinds of transformations evident in the protocols from Bartlett's subjects,
the evidence seems strong that ideas rather than chains of linguistic
elements are retained in memory. These ideas can be combined and
altered by other information learned simultaneously or at other times.

A word of caution   From what we have reported in the preceding pages,
it might seem that human beings are incapable of exact, literal recall.
That, of course, is incorrect, as the countless experiments on rote
learning demonstrate. It is true that memory for gist is probably more
important than memory for detail, but this should not obscure the fact
that human beings are capable of literal recall. Although mastery of a
12-word list by the method of serial anticipation may be tedious and
slow, it *is* possible. However, when we come to meaningful material, the
evidence of this chapter suggests that it is the meaning that is retained in
secondary memory, not necessarily the linguistic form. However, that all
depends upon the context.

One excellent example of the importance of context comes from a
study by Anderson and Bower (1973) on the retention of voice. They
found that the active-passive distinction would be retained for a short
period of time when subjects were asked to recognize sets of unrelated
sentences. When the sentences formed meaningful passages, rapid loss
of information about voice was observed, as in Sachs' original study.
More important, however, is the observation by Anisfeld and Klenbart
(1973) to the effect that different grammatical paraphrases of the same
idea sometimes convey different meanings. For example, it is notorious
that the passive voice is weaker than the active voice (see Johnson, 1967).
If the listener or reader perceives the particular grammatical form of a
sentence as conveying a meaning of some importance, he may well
integrate that meaning into the secondary memory for the idea and thus
be able to recognize or reproduce the exact grammatical form.

Furthermore, Cofer (1973) points out that attention to form and
attention to meaning may be, to some extent, incompatible. Thus it may
be possible to achieve verbatim recall only by ignoring semantic content.
Some evidence of this sort is suggested by Osborne (1902), who reported
a case study of an actor who was able to "wing" a part, i.e., learn the
lines for the next scene while waiting in the wings. What is especially
interesting about the case is that he claimed that after so learning a part
he had no idea what the play was about and would have to reread it
afterwards to find out.

BIBLIOGRAPHY

AARONSON, D. Temporal factors in perception and short-term memory. *Psychol. Bull.*, 1967, **67**, 130–144.

ADELMAN, H. M., & MAATSCH, J. L. Resistance to extinction as a function of the type of response elicited by frustration. *J. exp. Psychol.*, 1955, **50**, 61–65.

AMSEL, A. The role of frustrative nonreward in noncontinuous reward situations. *Psychol. Bull.*, 1958, **55**, 102–119.

AMSEL, A. Frustrative nonreward in partial reinforcement and discrimination learning: Some recent history and a theoretical extension. *Psychol. Rev.*, 1962, **69**, 306–328.

AMSEL, A. Partial reinforcement effects on vigor and persistence: Advances in frustration theory derived from a variety of within-subjects experiments. In K. W. Spence & J. T. Spence (Eds.), *The psychology of learning and motivation: Advances in research and theory.* Vol. 1. New York: Academic, 1967.

AMSEL, A. Positive induction, behavioral contrast, and generalization of inhibition in discrimination learning. In H. H. Kendler & J. T. Spence (Eds.), *Essays in neobehaviorism: A memorial volume to Kenneth W. Spence.* New York: Appleton Century Crofts, 1971.

AMSEL, A. Behavioral habituation, counterconditioning, and a general theory of persistence. In A. Black & W. Prokasy (Eds.), *Classical conditioning II: Current theory and research.* New York: Appleton Century Crofts, 1972.

AMSEL, A., & ROUSSEL, J. Motivational properties of frustration: I. Effect on a running response of the addition of frustration to the motivational complex. *J. exp. Psychol.*, 1952, **43**, 363–368.

ANDERSON, J. R. & BOWER, G. H. *Human associative memory.* Washington, D.C.: Winston & Sons, 1973.

ANDERSON, R. C. Semantic organization and retrieval of information from sentences. *J. verb. Lng. verb. Behav.*, 1972, **11**, 794–800.

ANGLIN, J. M., & MILLER, G. A. The role of phrase structure in the recall of meaningful material. *Psychon. Sci.*, 1968, **10**, 343–344.

ANISFELD, M., & KLENBART, I. On the functions of structural paraphrase: The view from the passive voice. *Psychol. Bull.*, 1973, **79**, 117–126.

APPEL, J. B. Punishment and shock intensity. *Science*, 1963, **141**, 528–529.

ARCHER, E. J. Re-evaluation of the meaningfulness of all possible CVC trigrams. *Psychol. Monogr.*, 1960, **74**, No. 497.

ARCHER, E. J. Concept identification as a function of obviousness of relevant and irrelevant information. *J. exp. Psychol.*, 1962, **63**, 616–620.

ARCHER, E. J., BOURNE, L. E., JR., & BROWN, F. G. Concept identification as a function of irrelevant information and instructions. *J. exp. Psychol.*, 1955, **49**, 153–164.

ATKINSON, R. C., & SHIFFRIN, R. M. Human memory: A proposed system and its control processes. In K. W. Spence & J. T. Spence (Eds.), *The psychology of learning and motivation.* Vol. 2. New York: Academic, 1968.

AVERBACH, E., & CORIELL, A. S. Short-term memory in vision. *Bell System Technical Journal*, 1961, **40**, 309–328.

AVERBACH, E., & SPERLING, G. Short-term storage of information in vision. In C. Cherry (Ed.), *Information theory.* London: Butterworth, 1961.

AYLLON, T., & AZRIN, N. H. *A motivating environment for therapy and rehabilitation.* New York: Appleton Century Crofts, 1968.

AZRIN, N. H. Some effects of two intermittent schedules of immediate and non-immediate punishment. *J. Psychol.*, 1956, **42**, 3–121.

AZRIN, N. H. Effects of punishment intensity during variable-interval reinforcement. *J. exp. Anal. Behav.*, 1960, **3**, 123–142.

AZRIN, N. H., HOLZ, W. C., & HAKE, D. F. Fixed-ratio punishment. *J. exp. Anal. Behav.*, 1963, **6**, 141–148.

AZRIN, N. H., HUTCHINSON, R. R., & HAKE, D. F. Attack, avoidance, and escape reactions to aversive shock. *J. exp. Anal. Behav.*, 1967, **10**, 131–148.

BACON, W. E. Partial-reinforcement extinction effect following different amounts of training. *J. comp. physiol. Psychol.*, 1962, **55**, 998–1003.

BADDELEY, A. D. The influence of acoustic and semantic similarity on long-term memory for word sequences. *Quart. J. exp. Psychol.*, 1966, **18**, 302–309.

BADDELEY, A. D. Retrieval rules and semantic coding in short-term memory. *Psychol. Bull.*, 1972, **78**, 379–385.

BADDELEY, A. D., & DALE, H. C. A. The effect of semantic similarity on retroactive interference in long- and short-term memory. *J. verb. Lng. verb. Behav.*, 1966, **5**, 417–420.

BANDURA, A. Influence of models' reinforcement contingencies on the acquisition of imitative responses. *J. Pers. Soc. Psychol.*, 1965, **1**, 589–595.

BANDURA, A. Vicarious and self-reinforcement processes. In R. Glaser (Ed.), *The nature of reinforcement.* New York: Academic, 1971.

BARNES, J. B., & UNDERWOOD, B. J. "Fate" of first-list associations·in transfer theory. *J. exp. Psychol.*, 1959, **58**, 97–105.

BARRY, H., III. Effects of strength of drive on learning and extinction. *J. exp. Psychol.*, 1958, **55**, 473–481.

BARTLETT, F. C. *Remembering: A study in experimental and social psychology.* Cambridge: Cambridge University Press, 1932.

BATTIG, W. P. Comparison of anticipation and recall methods of paired-associate learning. *Psychol. Rep.*, 1961, **9**, 59–65.

BATTIG, W. F., & MONTAGUE, W. E. Category norms for verbal items in 56 categories: A replication and extension of the Connecticut norms: *J. exp. Psychol.*, 1969, **80**, 1–46.

BEACH, F. A. The snark was a boojum. *Amer. Psychol.*, 1950, **5**, 115–124.

BENNETT, T. L., & ELLIS, H. C. Tactual-kinesthetic feedback from manipulation of visual forms and nondifferential reinforcement in transfer of perceptual learning. *J. exp. Psychol.*, 1968, **77**, 495–500.

BEVAN, W. An adaptation-level interpretation of reinforcement. *Percept. Mot. Skills*, 1966, **23**, 511–531.

BEVAN, W. The contextual basis of behavior. *Amer. Psychol.*, 1968, **23**, 701–714.

BEVER, T. G., FODOR, J. A., & GARRETT, M. A formal limitation of associationism. In T. R. Dixon & D. L. Horton, *Verbal behavior and general behavior theory.* Englewood Cliffs, N.J.: Prentice-Hall, 1968.

BEVER, T. G., FODOR, J. A., & WEKSEL, W. Theoretical notes on the acquisition of syntax: A critique of "contextual generalization." *Psychol. Rev.*, 1965, **72**, 467–482.

BLACK, A. H. The extinction of avoidance responses under curare. *J. comp. physiol. Psychol.*, 1958, **51**, 519–524.

BLACK, R. W. Shifts in magnitude of reward and contrast effects in instrumental and selective learning. *Psychol. Rev.*, 1968, **75**, 114–126.

BLACKWELL, H. R., & SCHLOSBERG, H. Octave generalization, pitch discrimination, and loudness thresholds in the white rat. *J. exp. Psychol.*, 1943, **33**, 407–419.

BLANCHARD, E. B., & YOUNG, L. B. Self-control of cardiac functioning: a promise as yet unfulfilled. *Psychol. Bull.*, 1973, **79**, 145–163.

BLOUGH, D. S. Two-way generalization peak shift after two-key training in the pigeon. *Anim. Lng. Behav.*, 1973, **1**, 171–174.

BOAKES, R. A., & HALLIDAY, M. S. (Eds.). *Inhibition and learning.* New York: Academic, 1972.

BOE, E. E. Variable punishment. *J. comp. physiol. Psychol.*, 1971, **75**, 73–76.

BOE, E. E., & CHURCH, R. M. Permanent effects of punishment during extinction. *J. comp. physiol. Psychol.*, 1967, **63**, 486–492.

BOGARTZ, W. Effects of reversal and nonreversal shifts with CVC stimuli. *J. verb. Lng. verb. Behav.*, 1965, **4**, 484–488.

BOLLES, R. C. *Theory of motivation.* New York: Harper, 1967.

BOLLES, R. C. Avoidance and escape learning: simultaneous acquisition of different responses. *J. comp. physiol. Psychol.*, 1969, **68**, 355–358.

BOLLES, R. C. Species-specific defense reactions and avoidance learning. *Psychol. Rev.*, 1970, **77**, 32–48.

BOLLES, R. C. The avoidance learning problem. In G. H. Bower (Ed.), *The psychology of learning and motivation.* Vol. 6. New York: Academic, 1972.

BOLLES, R. C. *Theory of motivation.* (2d ed.) New York: Harper, 1975.

BOLLES, R. C., & MOOT, S. A. Derived motives. *Ann. Rev. Psychol.*, 1972, **23**, 51–72.

BOREN, J. J. Resistance to extinction as a function of the fixed ratio. *J. exp Psychol.*, 1961, **61**, 304–308.

BOURNE, L. E., JR. *Human conceptual behavior.* Boston: Allyn and Bacon, 1966.

BOURNE, L. E., JR. Learning and the utilization of conceptual rules. In B. Kleinmuntz (Ed.), *Memory and the structure of concepts.* New York: Wiley, 1967.

BOURNE, L. E., JR. Knowing and using concepts. *Psychol. Rev.*, 1970, **77**, 546–556.

BOURNE, L. E., JR., EKSTRAND, B. R., & DOMINOWSKI, R. L. *The psychology of thinking.* Englewood Cliffs, N.J.: Prentice-Hall, 1971.

BOURNE, L. E., JR., GUY, D. E., & WADSWORTH, N. Verbal-reinforcement combinations and the relative frequency of informative-feedback in a card-sorting task. *J. exp. Psychol.*, 1967, **73**, 220–226.

BOURNE, L. E., JR., & HAYGOOD, R. C. The role of stimulus redundancy in concept identification. *J. exp. Psychol.*, 1959, **58**, 232–238.

BOUSFIELD, W. A. The occurrence of clustering in the recall of randomly arranged associates. *J. gen. Psychol.*, 1953, **49**, 229–240.

BOUSFIELD, W. A., & PUFF, C. R. Clustering as a function of response dominance. *J. exp. Psychol.*, 1964, **67**, 76–79.

BOUSFIELD, W. A., STEWARD, J. R., & COWAN, T. M. The use of free associational norms for the prediction of clustering. *J. gen. Psychol.*, 1964, **70**, 205–214.

BOVET, D., BOVET-NITTI, F., & OLIVERIO, A. Genetic aspects of learning and memory in mice. *Science*, 1969, **163**, 139–150.

Bower, G. H. Application of a model to paired-associate learning. *Psychometrika*, 1961, **26**, 255–280. (a)

Bower, G. H. A contrast effect in differential conditioning. *J. exp. Psychol.*, 1961, **62**, 196–199. (b)

Bower, G. H. The influence of graded reductions in reward and prior frustrating events upon the magnitude of the frustration effect. *J. comp. physiol. Psychol.*, 1962, **55**, 582–587.

Bower, G. H. Mental imagery and associative learning. In L. Gregg (Ed.), *Cognition in learning and memory*. New York: Wiley, 1972.

Bower, G. H. Stimulus-sampling theory of encoding variability. In A. W. Melton & E. Martin (Eds.), *Coding processes in human memory*. Washington, D.C.: Winston & Sons, 1972.

Bower, G. H., & Grusec, T. Effect of prior Pavlovian discrimination training upon learning an operant discrimination. *J. exp. Anal. Behav.*, 1964, **7**, 401–404.

Bower, G. H., & Miller, N. E. Rewarding and punishing effects from stimulating the same place in the rat's brain. *J. comp. physiol. Psychol.*, 1958, **51**, 669–674.

Bower, G. H., & Trabasso, T. Concept identification. In R. C. Atkinson (Ed.), *Studies in mathematical psychology*. Stanford, Calif.: Stanford University Press, 1964.

Bowlby, J. Critical phases in the development of social responses in man and other animals. In J. M. Tanner (Ed.), *Prospects in psychiatric research*. London: Oxford, 1952.

Braine, M. D. S. The ontogeny of English phrase structure: The first phase. *Language*, 1963, **39**, 1–14. (a)

Braine, M. D. S. On learning the grammatical order of words. *Psychol. Rev.*, 1963, **70**, 322–348. (b)

Bransford, J. D., & Franks, J. J. The abstraction of linguistic ideas. *Cognitive Psychology*, 1971, **2**, 331–350.

Bransford, J. D., & Johnson, M. K. Contextual prerequisites for understanding: Some investigations of comprehension and recall. *J. verb. Lng. verb. Behav.*, 1972, **11**, 717–726.

Breland, K., & Breland, M. The misbehavior of organisms. *Amer. Psychol.*, 1961, **16**, 681–684.

Briggs, G. E. Acquisition, extinction and recovery functions in retroactive inhibition. *J. exp. Psychol.*, 1954, **47**, 285–293.

Briggs, G. E. Retroactive inhibition as a function of degree of original and interpolated learning. *J. exp. Psychol.*, 1957, **53**, 60–67.

Brookshire, K. H., Warren, J. M., & Ball, G. G. Reversal and transfer learning following overtraining in rat and chicken. *J. comp. physiol. Psychol.*, 1961, **54**, 98–102.

Brown, J. Some tests of the decay theory of immediate memory. *Quart. J. exp. Psychol.*, 1958, **10**, 12–21.

Brown, J. S., Martin, R. C., & Morrow, M. W. Self-punitive behavior in the rat: Facilitative effects of punishment on resistance to extinction. *J. comp. physiol. Psychol.*, 1964, **57**, 127–133.

Brown, P. L., & Jenkins, H. M. Auto-shaping of the pigeon's key-peck. *J. exp. Anal. Behav.*, 1968, **11**, 1–8.

Brown, R. Development of the first language in the human species. *Amer. Psychol.*, 1973, **28**, 97–106.

Brown, R. T., & Wagner, A. R. Resistance to punishment and extinction following training with shock or nonreinforcement. *J. exp. Psychol.*, 1964, **68**, 503–507.

Brown, R. W., & McNeil, D. The "tip-of-the-tongue" phenomenon. *J. verb. Lng. verb. Behav.*, 1966, **5**, 325–337.

Brown, W. L., & McDowell, A. A. Response shift learning set in rhesus monkeys. *J. comp. physiol. Psychol.*, 1963, **56**, 335–336.

Bruner, J. S., Goodnow, J. J., & Austin, G. A. *A study of thinking*. New York: Wiley, 1956.

Bugelski, B. R. Words and things and images. *Amer. Psychol.*, 1970, **25**, 1002–1012.

Bunch, M. E., & McTeer, F. D. The influence of punishment during learning upon retroactive inhibition. *J. exp. Psychol.*, 1932, **15**, 473–495.

Burstein, K. R., Epstein, S., & Smith, B. Primary stimulus generalization of the GSR as a function of objective and subjective definition of the stimulus dimension. *J. exp. Psychol.*, 1967, **74**, 124–131.

Buss, A. H. Reversal and nonreversal shifts in concept formation with partial reinforcement eliminated. *J. exp. Psychol.*, 1956, **52**, 162–166.

Butter, C. M., & Thomas, D. R. Secondary reinforcement as a function of the amount of primary reinforcement. *J. comp. physiol. Psychol.*, 1958, **51**, 346–348.

Camp, D. S., Raymond, G. A., & Church, R. M. Temporal relationship between response and punishment. *J. exp. Psychol.*, 1967, **74**, 114–123.

Campbell, B. A. The fractional reduction in noxious stimulation required to produce "just noticeable" learning. *J. comp. physiol. Psychol.*, 1955, **48**, 141–148.

Campbell, B. A. The reinforcement difference limen (RDL) function for shock reduction. *J. exp. Psychol.*, 1956, **52**, 258–262.

Campbell, B. A. Absolute and relative sucrose preference thresholds for hungry and satiated rats. *J. comp. physiol. Psychol.*, 1958, **51**, 795–800.

Campbell, B. A. Interaction of aversive stimuli: summation or inhibition? *J. exp. Psychol.*, 1968, **78**, 181–190.

Campbell, B. A., & Kraeling, D. Response strength as a function of drive level and amount of drive reduction. *J. exp. Psychol.*, 1954, **47**, 101–103.

Campione, J., Hyman, L., & Zeaman, D. Dimensional shifts and reversals in retardate discrimination learning. *J. exp. Child Psychol.*, 1965, **2**, 255–263.

Cantor, J. H. Amount of pretraining as a factor in stimulus predifferentiation and performance set. *J. exp. Psychol.*, 1955, **50**, 180–184.

Cantor, M. B. Signaled reinforcing brain stimulation facilitates operant behavior under schedules of intermittent reinforcement. *Science*, 1971, **174**, 610–613.

CAPALDI, E. J. Effect of N-length, number of different N-lengths, and number of reinforcements on resistance to extinction. *J. exp. Psychol.*, 1964, **68**, 230–239.

CAPALDI, E. J. Partial reinforcement: A hypothesis of sequential effects. *Psychol. Rev.*, 1966, **73**, 459–477.

CAPALDI, E. J. A sequential hypothesis of instrumental learning. In K. W. Spence & J. T. Spence (Eds.), *The psychology of learning and motivation.* Vol. 1. New York: Academic, 1967.

CAPALDI, E. J. An analysis of the role of reward and reward magnitude in instrumental learning. In J. H. Reynierse (Ed.), *Current issues in animal learning.* Lincoln, Neb.: University of Nebraska Press, 1970.

CAPEHART, J., VINEY, W., & HULICKA, I. M. The effect of effort upon extinction. *J. comp. physiol. Psychol.*, 1958, **51**, 505–507.

CARMICHAEL, L. L., HOGAN, H. P., & WALTER, A. A. An experimental study of the effect of language on the reproduction of visually perceived form. *J. exp. Psychol.*, 1932, **15**, 73–86.

CARROLL, J. B. *Learning from verbal discourse in educational media: A review of the literature.* Princeton, N.J.: Educational Test Services, 1971.

CERASO, J., & HENDERSON, A. Unavailability and associative loss in RI and PI: Second try. *J. exp. Psychol.*, 1966, **72**, 314–316.

CERMAK, L. S., & BUTTERS, N. Information processing deficits of alcoholic Korsakoff patients. *Quart. J. Studies Alcohol*, 1973, **34**, 1110–1132.

CHOMSKY, N. *Syntactic structures.* The Hague: Mouton, 1957.

CHOMSKY, N. *Language and mind.* New York: Harcourt, Brace & World, 1968.

CHURCH, R. M. Emotional reactions of rats to the pain of others. *J. comp. physiol. Psychol.*, 1959, **52**, 132–134.

CHURCH, R. M. The varied effects of punishment on behavior. *Psychol. Rev.*, 1963, **70**, 369–402.

CHURCH, R. M. Response suppression. In B. A. Campbell & R. M. Church (Eds.), *Punishment and aversive behavior.* New York: Appleton Century Crofts, 1969.

CHURCH, R. M., WOOTEN, C. L., & MATTHEWS, T. J. Contingency between a response and an aversive event in the rat. *J. comp. physiol. Psychol.*, 1970, **72**, 476–485. (a)

CHURCH, R. M., WOOTEN, C. L., & MATTHEWS, T. J. Discriminative punishment and the conditioned emotional response. *Lng. Motiv.*, 1970, **1**, 1–17. (b)

CLIFFORD, T. Extinction following continuous reward and latent extinction. *J. exp. Psychol.*, 1964, **68**, 456–465.

COFER, C. N. Properties of verbal materials and verbal learning. In J. W. Kling & L. A. Riggs (Eds.), *Woodworth & Schlosberg's experimental psychology.* New York: Holt, 1971.

COFER, C. N. Constructive processes in memory. *Amer. Scient.*, 1973, **61**, 537–543.

COFER, C. N., & APPLEY, M. H. *Motivation: Theory and research.* New York: Wiley, 1964.

COFER, C. N., SEGAL, E., STEIN, J., & WALKER, H. Studies in free recall of nouns following presentation under adjectival modification. *J. exp. Psychol.*, 1969, **79**, 254–264.

COHEN, B. H., BOUSFIELD, W. A., & WHITMARSH, G. A. *Cultural norms for verbal items in 43 categories.* Storrs, Conn.: University of Connecticut Press, 1957.

COLE, M., & ABRAHAM, F. Extinction and spontaneous recovery as a function of amount of training and extinction intertrial interval. *J. comp. physiol. Psychol.*, 1962, **55**, 978–982.

COLEMAN, E. B. Verbal concept learning as a function of instructions and dominance level. *J. exp. Psychol.*, 1964, **68**, 213–214.

COLLIER, G., & MARX, M. H. Changes in performance as a function of shifts in the magnitude of reinforcement. *J. exp. Psychol.*, 1959, **57**, 305–309.

COLLINS, A. M., & QUILLIAN, M. R. Retrieval time from semantic memory. *J. verb. Lng. verb. Behav.*, 1969, **8**, 240–247.

COLTHEART, V. Memory for stimuli and memory for hypotheses in concept identification. *J. exp. Psychol.*, 1971, **89**, 102–108.

CONRAD, R. Acoustic confusions in immediate memory. *Brit. J. Psychol.*, 1964, **55**, 75–83.

CONRAD, R., & HILLE, B. A. The decay theory of immediate memory and paced recall. *Canad. J. Psychol.*, 1958, **12**, 1–6.

COONS, E. E., & MILLER, N. E. Conflict versus consolidation of memory traces to explain "retrograde amnesia" produced by ECS. *J. comp. physiol. Psychol.*, 1966, **61**, 34–42.

COTTON, J. W. Running time as a function of amount of food deprivation. *J. exp. Psychol.*, 1953, **46**, 188–198.

CRAIK, F. I. M., & LOCKHART, R. S. Levels of processing: A framework for memory research. *J. verb. Lng. verb. Behav.*, 1972, **11**, 671–684.

CRAMER, P. *Word association.* New York: Academic, 1968.

CRESPI, L. Quantitative variation of incentive and performance in the white rat. *Amer. J. Psychol.*, 1942, **15**, 467–517.

CROWDER, R. G. Improved recall for digits with delayed recall cues. *J. exp. Psychol.*, 1969, **82**, 258–262.

CROWDER, R. G. Waiting for the stimulus suffix: Decay, delay, rhythm, and readout in immediate memory. *Quart. J. exp. Psychol.*, 1971, **23**, 324–340.

DALLETT, K. M. The transfer surface re-examined. *J. verb. Lng. verb. Behav.*, 1962, **1**, 91–94.

DALY, H. B. Excitatory and inhibitory effects of complete and incomplete reward reduction in the double runway. *J. exp. Psychol.*, 1968, **76**, 430–438.

D'AMATO, M. R. Secondary reinforcement and magnitude of primary reinforcement. *J. comp. physiol. Psychol.*, 1955, **48**, 378–380.

D'AMATO, M. R., & FAZZARO, J. Discriminated lever-press avoidance learning as a function of type and intensity of shock. *J. comp. physiol. Psychol.*, 1966, **61**, 313–315.

D'AMATO, M. R., FAZZARO, J., & ETKIN, M. Discriminated bar-press avoidance maintenance and extinction in rats as a function of shock intensity. *J. comp. physiol. Psychol.*, 1967, **63**, 351–354.

D'AMATO, M. R., & JAGODA, H. Analysis of the role of overlearning in discrimination reversal. *J. exp. Psychol.*, 1961, **61**, 45–50.

DARBY, C. L., & RIOPELLE, A. J. Observational learning in the rhesus monkey. *J. comp. physiol. Psychol.*, 1959, **52**, 94–98.

DEANE, D. H., HAMMOND, K. R., & SOMMERS, D. A. Acquisition and application of knowledge in complex inference tasks. *J. exp. Psychol.*, 1972, **92**, 20–26.

DEAUX, E. B., & PATTEN, R. L. Measurement of the anticipatory goal response in instrumental runway conditioning. *Psychon. Sci.*, 1964, **1**, 357–358.

DEESE, J. Extinction of a discrimination without performance of the choice response. *J. comp. physiol. Psychol.*, 1951, **44**, 362–366.

DEESE, J. Influence of inter-item associative strength upon immediate free recall. *Psychol. Rep.*, 1959, **5**, 305–312.

DEESE, J. Frequency of usage and number of words in free recall: The role of association. *Psychol. Rep.*, 1960, **7**, 337–394.

DEESE, J. From the isolated unit to connected discourse. In C. N. Cofer (Ed.), *Verbal learning and verbal behavior*. New York: McGraw-Hill, 1961.

DEESE, J., & CARPENTER, J. A. Drive level and reinforcement. *J. exp. Psychol.*, 1951, **42**, 236–238.

DEESE, J., & HULSE, S. H. *The psychology of learning*. (3rd ed.) New York: McGraw-Hill, 1967.

DEESE, J., & KAUFMAN, R. A. Serial effects in recall of unorganized and sequentially organized verbal material. *J. exp. Psychol.*, 1957, **54**, 180–187.

DEESE, J., & MARDER, V. J. The pattern of errors in delayed recall of serial learning after interpolation. *Amer. J. Psychol.*, 1957, **70**, 594–599.

DEL CASTILLO, D. M., & ELLIS, H. C. The role of response-produced cues in paired-associate transfer as a function of stimulus similarity. *Psychon. Sci.*, 1968, **10**, 197–198.

DELGADO, J. M. R., ROBERTS, W. W., & MILLER, N. E. Learning motivated by electrical stimulation of the brain. *Amer. J. Physiol.*, 1954, **179**, 587–593.

DENNY, M. R. A theory of experimental extinction and its relation to a general theory. In H. Kendler & J. Spence (Eds.), *Essays in neobehaviorism: A memorial volume to Kenneth W. Spence*. New York: Appleton Century Crofts, 1971.

DE RIVERA, J. Some conditions governing the use of the cue-producing response as an explanatory device. *J. exp. Psychol.*, 1959, **57**, 299–304.

DE SOTO, C. B., & BOSLEY, J. J. The cognitive structure of a social structure. *J. abnorm. soc. Psychol.*, 1962, **64**, 303–307.

DEUTSCH, J. A. Learning and electrical self-stimulation of the brain. *J. theoret. Biol.*, 1963, **4**, 193–214.

DEUTSCH, J. A. Prolonged rewarding brain stimulation. In G. Bower (Ed.), *The psychology of learning and motivation*. Vol. 7. New York: Academic, 1973.

DEUTSCH, J. A., & HOWARTH, C. I. Some tests of a theory of intracranial self-stimulation. *Psychol. Rev.*, 1963, **70**, 444–460.

DI VESTA, F. J., & RICKARDS, J. P. Effects of labeling and articulation on the attainment of concrete, abstract, and number concepts. *J. exp. Psychol.*, 1971, **88**, 41–49.

DODD, D. H., KINSMAN, R. A., KLIPP, R. D., & BOURNE, L. E., JR. Effect of logic pretraining on conceptual rule learning. *J. exp. Psychol.*, 1971, **88**, 119–122.

DOLLARD, J., & MILLER, N. E. *Personality and psychotherapy*. New York: McGraw-Hill, 1950.

DOOLING, J. L., & LACHMAN, R. Effects of comprehension on retention of prose. *J. exp. Psychol.*, 1971, **88**, 216–222.

DUBIN, W. J., & LEVIS, D. J. Generalization of extinction gradients: A systematic analysis. *J. exp. Psychol.*, 1973, **100**, 403–412.

DUNCAN, C. P. The retroactive effect of electroshock on learning. *J. comp. physiol. Psychol.*, 1949, **42**, 32–44.

DUNHAM, P. J. Contrasted conditions of reinforcement: A selective critique. *Psychol. Bull.*, 1968, **69**, 295–315.

EBBINGHAUS, H. *Über das Gedächtnis*, Leipzig: Duncker und Humbolt, 1885. (H. A. Ruger and C. E. Bussenius, Tr.) New York: Teachers College, Columbia, 1913. Revised, New York: Dover, 1964.

EBENHOLTZ, S. M. Serial learning and dimensional organization. In G. H. Bower (Ed.), *The psychology of learning and motivation*. Vol. 6. New York: Academic, 1972.

ECKSTRAND, G. A., & WICKENS, D. D. Transfer of perceptual set. *J. exp. Psychol.*, 1954, **47**, 274–278.

EGETH, H. Selective attention. *Psychol. Bull.*, 1967, **67**, 41–57.

EGGER, M. D., & MILLER, N. E. Secondary reinforcement in rats as a function of information value and reliability of the stimulus. *J. exp. Psychol.*, 1962, **64**, 97–104.

EGGER, M. D., & MILLER, N. E. When is a reward reinforcing? An experimental study of the information hypothesis. *J. comp. physiol. Psychol.*, 1963, **56**, 132–137.

EHRENFREUND, D. An experimental test of the continuity theory of discrimination learning with pattern vision. *J. comp. physiol. Psychol.*, 1948, **41**, 408–422.

EHRENFREUND, D. A study of the transposition gradient. *J. exp. Psychol.*, 1952, **43**, 83–87.

EKSTRAND, B. R. Effect of sleep on memory. *J. exp. Psychol.*, 1967, **75**, 64–72.

ELLIS, H. C. Stimulus encoding processes in human learning and memory. In G. H. Bower (Ed.), *The psychology of learning and motivation*. Vol. 7. New York: Academic, 1973.

ELLIS, H. C., & MULLER, D. G. Transfer of perceptual learning following stimulus predifferentiation. *J. exp. Psychol.*, 1964, **68**, 388–395.

ENGBERG, L. A., HANSEN, G., WELKER, R. L., & THOMAS, D. R. Acquisition of key pecking via autoshaping as a function of prior experience: "learned laziness"? *Science*, 1972, **178**, 1002–1004.

423

ENGEL, B. T. Comment on self control of cardiac functioning: a promise as yet unfulfilled. *Psychol. Bull.*, 1974, **81**, 43.

EPSTEIN, S., & BURSTEIN, K. R. A replication of Hovland's study of stimulus generalization to frequencies of tone. *J. exp. Psychol.*, 1966, **72**, 782–784.

EPSTEIN, W. The influence of syntactical structure on learning. *Amer. J. Psychol.*, 1961, **74**, 80–85.

ERIKSEN, C. W., & JOHNSON, H. J. Storage and decay characteristics of nonattended auditory stimuli. *J. exp. Psychol.*, 1964, **68**, 28–36.

ERVIN, S. M. Changes with age on the verbal determinants of word association. *Amer. J. Psychol.*, 1961, **74**, 361–372.

ESTES, W. K. An experimental study of punishment. *Psychol. Monogr.*, 1944, **57**, No. 263.

ESTES, W. K. Toward a statistical theory of learning. *Psychol. Rev.*, 1950, **57**, 94–107.

ESTES, W. K. Statistical theory of spontaneous recovery. *Psychol. Rev.*, 1955, **62**, 145–154.

ESTES, W. K. The statistical approach to learning theory. In S. Koch (Ed.), *Psychology: A study of a science.* Vol. 2. New York: McGraw-Hill, 1959.

ESTES, W. K. Learning theory and the new "mental chemistry." *Psychol. Rev.*, 1960, **67**, 207–233.

ESTES, W. K. All-or-none processes in learning and retention. *Amer. Psychol.*, 1964, **19**, 16–25. (a)

ESTES, W. K. Probability learning. In A. W. Melton (Ed.), *Categories of human learning.* New York: Academic, 1964. (b)

ESTES, W. K. New perspectives on some old issues in association theory. In N. J. Mackintosh & W. K. Honig (Eds.), *Fundamental issues in associative learning.* Halifax, N.S.: Dalhousie University Press, 1969.

ESTES, W. K. *Learning theory and mental development.* New York: Academic, 1970.

ESTES, W. K. Reward in human learning: Theoretical issues and strategic choice points. In R. Glaser (Ed.), *The nature of reinforcement.* New York: Academic, 1971.

ESTES, W. K. Memory and conditioning. In F. J. McGuigan & D. B. Lumsden (Eds.), *Contemporary approaches to conditioning and learning.* Washington, D.C.: Winston & Sons, 1973.

ESTES, W. K., & BURKE, C. J. A theory of stimulus variability in learning. *Psychol. Rev.*, 1953, **60**, 276–286.

ESTES, W. K., HOPKINS, B. L., & CROTHERS, E. J. All-or-none and conservation effects in the learning and retention of paired associates. *J. exp. Psychol.*, 1960, **60**, 329–339.

ESTES, W. K., & SKINNER, B. F. Some quantitative properties of anxiety. *J. exp. Psychol.*, 1941, **29**, 390–400.

FAGO, G., & FOWLER, H. Facilitated discrimination learning as affected by response-contingent neutral and aversive stimuli. *Lng. Motiv.*, 1972, **3**, 20–30.

FEARING, F. *Reflex action: A study in the history of physiological psychology.* Baltimore: Williams & Wilkins, 1930.

FERSTER, C. B., & SKINNER, B. F. *Schedules of reinforcement.* New York: Appleton Century Crofts, 1957.

FILLMORE, C. The case for case. In E. Bach & R. T. Harms (Eds.), *Universals in linguistic theory.* New York: Holt, 1968.

FLAHERTY, C. F., RILEY, E. P., & SPEAR, N. E. Effects of sucrose concentration and goal units on runway behavior in the rat. *Lng. Motiv.*, 1973, **4**, 163–175.

FOWLER, H., SPELT, P. F., & WISCHNER, G. J. Discrimination performance as affected by training procedure, problem difficulty and shock for the correct response. *J. exp. Psychol.*, 1967, **75**, 432–436.

FOWLER, H., & WISCHNER, G. J. The varied functions of punishment in discrimination learning. In B. A. Campbell & R. M. Church (Eds.), *Punishment and aversive behavior.* New York: Appleton Century Crofts, 1969.

FOWLER, M. J., SULLIVAN, M. J., & EKSTRAND, B. R. Sleep and memory. *Science,* 1973, **179**, 302–304.

FOWLER, R. L., & KIMMEL, H. D. Operant conditioning of the GSR. *J. exp. Psychol.*, 1962, **63**, 563–567.

FRASER, D. C. Decay of immediate memory with age. *Nature,* 1958, **182**, 1163.

FREEDMAN, J. L., & LOFTUS, E. Retrieval of words from long term memory. *J. verb. Lng. verb. Behav.*, 1971, **10**, 107–115.

FRIEBERGS, V., & TULVING, E. The effect of practice on utilization of information from positive and negative instances in concept identification. *Canad. J. Psychol.*, 1961, **15**, 101–106.

FRIES, C. C. *The structure of English.* New York: Harcourt, Brace, 1952.

GAGNÉ, R. M. The effect of spacing trials on the acquisition and extinction of a conditioned operant response. *J. exp. Psychol.*, 1941, **29**, 201–216.

GAGNÉ, R. M., & BAKER, K. E. Stimulus predifferentiation as a factor in transfer of training. *J. exp. Psychol.*, 1950, **40**, 439–451.

GALLISTEL, C. R. Self-stimulation: The neurophysiology of reward and motivation. In J. A. Deutsch (Ed.), *Physiological basis of memory.* New York: Academic, 1973.

GALLUP, G. G., & ALTOMARI, T. S. Activity as a postsituation measure of frustrative nonreward. *J. comp. physiol. Psychol.*, 1969, **68**, 382–384.

GARCIA, J., ERVIN, F. R., & KOELLING, R. A. Learning with prolonged delay of reinforcement. *Psychon. Sci.*, 1966, **5**, 121–122.

GARCIA, J., KIMMELDORF, D. J., & KOELLING, R. A. Conditioned aversion to saccharin resulting from exposure to gamma radiation. *Science,* 1955, **122**, 157–158.

GARCIA, J., & KOELLING, R. A. Relation of cue to consequence in avoidance learning. *Psychon. Sci.*, 1966, **4**, 123–124.

GARDNER, R. A., & GARDNER, B. T. Teaching sign language to a chimpanzee. *Science,* 1969, **165**, 664–672.

GARNER, W. R. *Uncertainty and structure as psychological concepts.* New York: Wiley, 1962.

GARRETT, M., & FODOR, J. Psychological theories and linguistic constructs. In T. R. Dixon & D. L. Horton (Eds.), *Verbal behavior and general behavior theory*. Englewood Cliffs, N.J.: Prentice-Hall, 1968.

GIBSON, E. J. A systematic application of the concepts of generalization and differentiation to verbal learning. *Psychol. Rev.*, 1940, **47**, 196–229.

GIBSON, E. J. *Principles of perceptual learning and development*. New York: Appleton Century Crofts, 1967.

GIBSON, E. J., & WALK, R. D. The effect of prolonged exposure to visually presented patterns on learning to discriminate them. *J. comp. physiol. Psychol.*, 1956, **49**, 239–242.

GIBSON, J. J. The concept of the stimulus in psychology. *Amer. Psychol.*, 1960, **15**, 694–703.

GIBSON, J. J. *The senses considered as perceptual systems*. Boston: Houghton Mifflin, 1966.

GIBSON, J. J., & GIBSON, E. J. Perceptual learning—differentiation or enrichment? *Psychol. Rev.*, 1955, **62**, 32–41.

GLANZER, M., & CUNITZ, A. R. Two storage mechanisms in free recall. *J. verb. Lng. verb. Behav.*, 1966, **5**, 351–360.

GLAZE, J. A. The association value of non-sense syllables. *J. genet. Psychol.*, 1928, **35**, 255–269.

GLICKMAN, S. E., & SCHIFF, B. B. A biological theory of reinforcement. *Psychol. Rev.*, 1967, **74**, 81–109.

GOGGIN, J. Influence of the written recall measure on first-list associations. *J. exp. Psychol.*, 1963, **65**, 619–620.

GOODRICH, K. P. Performance in different segments of an instrumental response chain as a function of reinforcement schedule. *J. exp. Psychol.*, 1959, **57**, 57–63.

GOODWIN, W. R., & LAWRENCE, D. H. The functional independence of two discrimination habits associated with a constant stimulus situation. *J. comp. physiol. Psychol.*, 1955, **48**, 437–443.

GOSS, A. E. A stimulus-response analysis of the interaction of cue producing and instrumental responses. *Psychol. Rev.*, 1955, **62**, 20–31.

GOSS, A. E., & GREENFELD, N. Transfer to a motor task as influenced by conditions and degree of prior discrimination training. *J. exp. Psychol.*, 1958, **55**, 258–269.

GOTTWALD, R. L. Attribute-response correlations in concept attainment. *Amer. J. Psychol.*, 1971, **84**, 425–436.

GOUGH, H. G. Academic achievement in high school as predicted from the California Psychological Inventory. *J. educat. Psychol.*, 1964, **55**, 174–180.

GOUGH, H. G. College attendance among high-aptitude students as predicted from the California Psychological Inventory. *J. counsel. Psychol.*, 1968, **15**, 269–278.

GRANT, D. A. Classical and operant conditioning. In A. W. Melton (Ed.), *Categories of human learning*. New York: Academic, 1964.

GREENBERG, R., & UNDERWOOD, B. J. Retention as a function of stage of practice. *J. exp. Psychol.*, 1950, **40**, 452–457.

GRICE, G. R. The relation of secondary reinforcement to delayed reward in visual discrimination learning. *J. exp. Psychol.*, 1948, **38**, 1–16.

GRICE, G. R. Stimulus intensity and response evocation. *Psychol. Rev.*, 1968, **75**, 359–373.

GRICE, G. R. Conditioning and a decision theory of response evocation. In G. Bower (Ed.), *The psychology of learning and motivation*. Vol. 5. New York: Academic, 1972.

GRICE, G. R., & HUNTER, J. J. Stimulus intensity effects depend upon the type of experimental design. *Psychol. Rev.*, 1964, **71**, 247–256.

GRUNEBERG, M. M. A dichotomous theory of memory—Unproved and unprovable? *Acta Psychologica*, 1970, **34**, 489–496.

GUTHRIE, E. R. *The psychology of learning*. New York: Harper, 1935.

GUTHRIE, E. R. *The psychology of learning*. (Rev. ed.) New York: Harper, 1952.

GUTHRIE, E. R. Association by contiguity. In S. Koch (Ed.), *Psychology: A study of a science*. Vol. 2. New York: McGraw-Hill, 1959.

GUTHRIE, E. R., & HORTON, G. P. *Cats in a puzzle box*. New York: Holt, 1946.

GUTTMAN, N. Operant conditioning, extinction, and periodic reinforcement in relation to concentration of sucrose used as a reinforcing agent. *J. exp. Psychol.*, 1953, **46**, 213–224.

GUTTMAN, N., & JULESZ, B. Lower limits of auditory periodicity analysis. *J. acoust. Soc. Amer.*, 1963, **35**, 610.

GUTTMAN, N., & KALISH, H. I. Discriminability and stimulus generalization. *J. exp. Psychol.*, 1956, **51**, 79–88.

HAKE, H. W., & ERIKSEN, C. W. Effect of number of permissible response categories on learning of a constant number of visual stimuli. *J. exp. Psychol.*, 1955, **50**, 161–167.

HAMILTON, C. E. The relationship between length of interval separating two learning tasks and performance on the second task. *J. exp. Psychol.*, 1950, **40**, 613–621.

HAMILTON, H. W., & DEESE, J. Marking and propositional effects in associations to compounds. *Amer. J. Psychol.*, 1974, **87**, in press.

HANAWALT, N. G., & DEMAREST, I. H. The effect of verbal suggestion in the recall period upon the reproduction of visually perceived forms. *J. exp. Psychol.*, 1939, **25**, 159–174.

HANSEN, G., MILLER, J. T., & THOMAS, D. R. Individual differences as a factor influencing generalization slope and discrimination learning. *J. comp. physiol. Psychol.*, 1971, **77**, 456–462.

HANSON, H. M. Effects of discrimination training on stimulus generalization. *J. exp. Psychol.*, 1959, **58**, 321–334.

HARCUM, E. R. Defining shape for perceptual element-position curves. *Psychol. Bull.*, 1970, **74**, 362–372.

HARLOW, H. F. The formation of learning sets. *Psychol. Rev.*, 1949, **56**, 51–65.

HARLOW, H. F. Performance of catarrhine monkeys on a series of discrimination reversal problems. *J. comp. physiol. Psychol.*, 1950, **43**, 231–239.

HARLOW, H. F. Learning set and error factor theory. In S. Koch (Ed.), *Psychology: A study of a science.* Vol. 2. New York: McGraw-Hill, 1959.

HARRIS, A. H., GILLIAM, W. J., FINDLEY, J. D., & BRADY, J. V. Instrumental conditioning of large-magnitude, daily, 12-hour blood pressure elevations in the baboon. *Science,* 1973, **182,** 175–177.

HARROW, M., & FRIEDMAN, G. B. Comparing reversal and nonreversal shifts in concept formation with partial reinforcement controlled. *J. exp. Psychol.,* 1958, **55,** 592–598.

HAWKINS, H. L., PARDO, V. J., & COX, R. D. Proactive interference in short-term recognition: Trace interaction or competition? *J. exp. Psychol.,* 1972, **92,** 43–48.

HEARST, E. Excitation, inhibition, and discrimination learning. In N. J. Mackintosh & W. K. Honig (Eds.), *Fundamental issues in associative learning.* Halifax, N.S.: Dalhousie University Press, 1969.

HEARST, E., & KORESKO, M. B. Stimulus generalization and the amount of prior training on variable-interval reinforcement. *J. comp. physiol. Psychol.,* 1968, **66,** 133–138.

HEARST, E., & PETERSON, G. B. Transfer of conditioned excitation and inhibition from one operant response to another. *J. exp. Psychol.,* 1973, **99,** 360–368.

HEBB, D. O. *The organization of behavior.* New York: Wiley, 1949.

HEIDBREDER, E. The attainment of concepts: III. The process. *J. gen. Psychol.,* 1947, **24,** 93–138.

HELSON, H. *Adaptation-level theory: An experimental and systematic approach to behavior.* New York: Harper, 1964.

HERMAN, L. M., BEACH, F. A., PEPPER, R. L., & STALLING, R. B. Learning set formation in the bottlenose dolphin. *Psychon. Sci.,* 1969, **14,** 98–99.

HILGARD, E. R., & BOWER, G. H. *Theories of learning.* (4th ed.) New York: Appleton Century Crofts, 1974.

HILGARD, E. R., & MARQUIS, D. M. *Conditioning and learning.* New York: Appleton Century Crofts, 1940.

HILL, W. F. *Learning.* (Rev. ed.) Scranton, Pa.: Chandler, 1971.

HILL, W. F., & SPEAR, N. E. Resistance to extinction as a joint function of reward magnitude and the spacing of extinction trials. *J. exp. Psychol.,* 1962, **64,** 636–639.

HILLMAN, B., HUNTER, W. S., & KIMBLE, G. A. The effect of drive level on the maze performance of the white rat. *J. comp. physiol. Psychol.,* 1953, **46,** 87–89.

HINDE, R. A. *Animal behavior.* (2nd ed.) New York: McGraw-Hill, 1970.

HINDE, R. A., & STEVENSON-HINDE, J. (Eds.). *Constraints on learning.* London: Academic, 1973.

HINTZMAN, D. L. Articulatory coding in short-term memory, *J. verb. Lng. verb. Behav.,* 1967, **6,** 312–316.

HIROTO, D. S. Locus of control and learned helplessness. *J. exp. Psychol.,* 1974, **102,** 187–193.

HIRSCH, J. (Ed.). *Behavior genetic analysis.* New York: McGraw-Hill, 1967.

HABER, R. N., & STANDING, L. Direct measures of short-term visual storage. *Quart. J. exp. Psychol.,* 1969, **21,** 43–54.

HOLZ, W. C., & AZRIN, N. H. Discriminative properties of punishment. *J. exp. Anal. Behav.,* 1961, **4,** 225–232.

HOMME, L. E. Spontaneous recovery and statistical learning. *J. exp. Psychol.,* 1956, **51,** 205–212.

HONIG, W. K. Generalization of extinction on the spectral continuum. *Psychol. Rec.,* 1961, **11,** 269–278.

HONIG, W. K. Attentional factors governing the slope of the generalization gradient. In R. M. Gilbert & N. S. Sutherland (Eds.), *Animal discrimination learning.* New York: Academic, 1969.

HOROWITZ, L. M., CHILIAN, P. C., & DUNNIGAN, K. P. Word fragments and their redintegrative powers. *J. exp. Psychol.,* 1969, **80,** 392–394.

HOROWITZ, L. M., & PRYTULAK, L. S. Redintegrative memory. *Psychol. Rev.,* 1969, **76,** 519–531.

HOROWITZ, L. M., WHITE, M. A., & ATWOOD, D. W. Word fragments as aids to recall: The organization of a word. *J. exp. Psychol.,* 1968, **76,** 219–226.

HORROCKS, J. E. *Assessment of behavior.* Columbus, Ohio: Merrill, 1964.

HORTON, D. L., & KJELDERGAARD, P. M. An experimental analysis of associative factors in mediated generalizations. *Psychol. Monogr.,* 1961, **75,** No. 11.

HOVLAND, C. I. "Inhibition of reinforcement" and phenomena of experimental extinction. *Proc. Nat. Acad. Sci. Wash.,* 1936, **22,** 430–433.

HOVLAND, C. I. The generalization of conditioned responses: I. The sensory generalization of conditioned responses with varying frequencies of tone. *J. gen. Psychol.,* 1937, **17,** 125–148. (a)

HOVLAND, C. I. The generalization of conditioned responses: II. The sensory generalization of conditioned responses with varying intensities of tone. *J. genet. Psychol.,* 1937, **51,** 279–291. (b)

HOVLAND, C. I. The generalization of conditioned responses: IV. The effects of varying amounts of reinforcement upon the degree of generalization of conditioned responses. *J. exp. Psychol.,* 1937, **21,** 261–276. (c)

HOVLAND, C. I. A "communication analysis" of concept learning. *Psychol. Rev.,* 1952, **59,** 461–472.

HOVLAND, C. I., & HUNT, E. B. Computer simulation of concept attainment. *Behavioral Science,* 1960, **5,** 265–267.

HOVLAND, C. I., & WEISS, W. Transmission of information concerning concepts through positive and negative instances. *J. exp. Psychol.,* 1953, **45,** 175–182.

HULL, C. L. Knowledge and purpose as habit mechanisms. *Psychol. Rev.,* 1930, **37,** 511–525.

HULL, C. L. Goal attraction and directing ideas conceived as habit phenomena. *Psychol. Rev.,* 1931, **38,** 487–506.

HULL, C. L. *Principles of behavior.* New York: Appleton Century Crofts, 1943.

HULL, C. L. *A behavior system.* New Haven, Conn.: Yale Univ. Press, 1952.

HULSE, S. H. Amount and percentage of reinforcement and duration of goal confinement in conditioning and extinction. *J. exp. Psychol.*, 1958, **56**, 48–57.

HULSE, S. H. Partial reinforcement, continuous reinforcement, and reinforcement shift effects. *J. exp. Psychol.*, 1962, **64**, 451–459. (a)

HULSE, S. H. Discrimination of the reward in learning with partial and continuous reinforcement. *J. exp. Psychol.*, 1962, **64**, 227–233. (b)

HULSE, S. H. Reinforcement contrast effects in rats following experimental definition of a dimension of reinforcement magnitude. *J. comp. physiol. Psychol.*, 1973, **85**, 160–170. (a)

HULSE, S. H. Patterned reinforcement. In G. H. Bower. (Ed.), *The psychology of learning and motivation,* Vol. 7. New York: Academic, 1973. (b)

HULSE, S. H., & BACON, W. E. Supplementary report: Partial reinforcement and amount of reinforcement as determinants of instrumental licking rates. *J. exp. Psychol.*, 1962, **63**, 214–215.

HULSE, S. H., & FIRESTONE, R. J. Mean amount of reinforcement and instrumental response strength. *J. exp. Psychol.*, 1964, **67**, 417–422.

HUMPHREYS, L. G. Acquisition and extinction of verbal expectations in a situation analogous to conditioning. *J. exp. Psychol.*, 1939, **25**, 294–301.

HUNT, E. B. *Concept learning.* New York: Wiley, 1962.

HUNT, E. B., MARIN, J., & STONE, P. J. *Experiments in induction.* New York: Academic, 1966.

HUNT, H. F., & BRADY, J. V. Some effects of punishment and intercurrent "anxiety" on a simple operant. *J. comp. physiol. Psychol.*, 1955, **48**, 305–310.

HUTT, P. J. Rate of bar pressing as a function of quality and quantity of food reward. *J. comp. physiol. Psychol.*, 1954, **47**, 235–239.

IRWIN, F. D. *Intentional behavior and motivation: A cognitive theory.* Philadelphia: Lippincott, 1971.

ISAACS, I. D., & DUNCAN, C. P. Reversal and nonreversal shifts within and between dimensions in concept formation. *J. exp. Psychol.*, 1962, **64**, 580–585.

ISON, J. R. Experimental extinction as a function of number of reinforcements. *J. exp. Psychol.*, 1962, **64**, 314–317.

JAMES, W. *Principles of psychology.* New York: Holt, 1890.

JENKINS, H. M. Resistance to extinction when partial reinforcement is followed by regular reinforcement. *J. exp. Psychol.*, 1962, **64**, 441–450.

JENKINS, H. M. Effects of the stimulus-reinforcer relation on selected and unselected responses. In R. A. Hinde & J. Stevenson-Hinde (Eds.), *Constraints on learning.* London: Academic, 1973.

JENKINS, H. M., & HARRISON, R. H. Effect of discrimination training on auditory generalization. *J. exp. Psychol.*, 1960, **59**, 246–253.

JENKINS, J. G., & DALLENBACH, K. M. Oblivescence during sleep and waking. *Amer. J. Psychol.*, 1924, **35**, 605–612.

JENKINS, J. J. Mediated associations. In C. N. Cofer & B. S. Musgrave (Eds.), *Verbal behavior and learning.* New York: McGraw-Hill, 1963.

JENKINS, W. O., McFANN, H., & CLAYTON, F. L. A methodological study of extinction following aperiodic and continuous reinforcement. *J. comp. physiol. Psychol.*, 1950, **43**, 155–167.

JENKINS, W. O., & STANLEY, J. C., JR. Partial reinforcement: A review and critique. *Psychol. Bull.*, 1950, **47**, 193–234.

JENSEN, A. R. An empirical theory of the serial-position effect. *J. Psychol.*, 1962, **53**, 127–142.

JOHNSON, M. G. Syntactic position and rated meaning. *J. verb. Lng. verb. Behav.*, 1967, **6**, 240–246.

JORDAN, H. A., WEILAND, W. F., ZEBLEY, S. P., STELLAR, E., & STUNKARD, A. J. The direct measurement of food intake in man: A method for the objective study of eating behavior. *Psychosomatic Medicine*, 1966, **28**, 836–842.

KAHNEMAN, D. *Attention and effort.* Englewood Cliffs, N.J.: Prentice-Hall, 1973.

KALAT, J. W., & ROZIN, P. "Learned safety" as a mechanism in long-delay taste-aversion learning in rats. *J. comp. physiol. Psychol.*, 1973, **83**, 198–207.

KALISH, H. I. The relationship between discriminability and generalization: a re-evaluation. *J. exp. Psychol.*, 1958, **55**, 637–644.

KATKIN, E. S., & MURRAY, E. N. Instrumental conditioning of autonomically mediated behavior: Theoretical and methodological issues. *Psychol. Bull.*, 1968, **70**, 52–68.

KATZ, P. A. Effects of labels on children's perception and discrimination learning. *J. exp. Psychol.*, 1963, **66**, 423–428.

KATZ, P. A., & ZIGLER, E. F. Effects of labels on perceptual transfer: Stimulus and developmental factors. *J. exp. Psychol.*, 1969, **80**, 73–77.

KEESEY, R. Duration of stimulation and the reward properties of hypothalamic stimulation. *J. comp. physiol. Psychol.*, 1964, **58**, 201–207.

KELLEHER, R. T. Discrimination learning as a function of reversal and nonreversal shifts. *J. exp. Psychol.*, 1956, **51**, 379–384.

KELLEHER, R. T. Conditioned reinforcement in chimpanzees. *J. comp. physiol. Psychol.*, 1957, **50**, 571–575.

KELLEHER, R. T., & GOLLUB, L. R. A review of positive conditioned reinforcement. *J. exp. Anal. Behav.*, 1962, **5**, 543–597.

KELLER, F. S., & SCHOENFELD, W. N. *Principles of psychology.* New York: Appleton Century Crofts, 1950.

KEMLER, D. G., & SHEPP, B. E. Learning and transfer of dimensional relevance and irrelevance in children. *J. exp. Psychol.*, 1971, **90**, 120–127.

KENDLER, H. H. Drive interaction: II. Experimental analysis of the role of drive in learning theory. *J. exp. Psychol.*, 1945, **35**, 188–198.

KENDLER, H. H., & D'AMATO, M. F. A comparison of reversal shifts and nonreversal shifts in human concept formation. *J. exp. Psychol.*, 1955, **49**, 165–174.

KENDLER, H. H., & KENDLER, T. S. Vertical and horizontal processes in problem solving. *Psychol. Rev.*, 1962, **69**, 1–16.

KENDLER, H. H., & KENDLER, T. S. Selective attention versus mediation: Some comments on Mackintosh's analysis of two-stage models of discrimination learning. *Psychol. Bull.*, 1966, **66**, 282–288.

KENDLER, H. H., & KENDLER, T. S. Mediation and conceptual behavior. In K. W. Spence & J. T. Spence (Eds.), *Psychology of learning and motivation*. Vol. 2. New York: Academic, 1968.

KENDLER, T. S. An experimental investigation of transposition as a function of the difference between training and test stimuli. *J. exp. Psychol.*, 1950, **40**, 552–562.

KENDLER, T. S., & KENDLER, H. H. Reversal and nonreversal shifts in kindergarten children. *J. exp. Psychol.*, 1959, **58**, 56–60.

KENDLER, T. S., KENDLER, H. H., & SILFEN, C. K. Optional shift behavior of albino rats. *Psychon. Sci.*, 1964, **1**, 5–6.

KENDLER, T. S., KENDLER, H. H., & WELLS, D. Reversal and nonreversal shifts in nursery school children. *J. comp. physiol. Psychol.*, 1960, **53**, 83–88.

KEPPEL, G., & UNDERWOOD, B. J. Proactive inhibition in short-term retention of single items. *J. verb. Lng. verb. Behav.*, 1962, **1**, 153–161.

KERPELMAN, L. C. Preexposure to visually presented forms and nondifferential reinforcement in perceptual learning. *J. exp. Psychol.*, 1965, **69**, 257–262.

KIMBLE, G. A. *Hilgard and Marquis' conditioning and learning.* (2nd ed.) New York: Appleton Century Crofts, 1961.

KIMBLE, G. A., MANN, L. I., & DUFORT, R. H. Classical and instrumental eyelid conditioning. *J. exp. Psychol.*, 1955, **49**, 407–417.

KIMBLE, G. A., & SHATTEL, R. B. The relationship between two kinds of inhibition and the amount of practice. *J. exp. Psychol.*, 1952, **44**, 355–359.

KIMMEL, H. D. Instrumental conditioning of autonomically mediated responses in human beings. *Amer. Psychol.*, 1974, **29**, 325–335.

KINTSCH, W. *Learning, memory, and conceptual processes.* New York: Wiley, 1970.

KINTSCH, W. The structure of semantic memory. In E. Tulving & W. Donaldson (Eds.), *The organization of memory*. New York: Academic, 1972.

KINTSCH, W., & BUSCHKE, H. Homophones and synonyms in short-term memory. *J. exp. Psychol.*, 1969, **80**, 403–407.

KINTZ, B. L., FOSTER, M. S., HART, J. O., O'MALLEY, J. J., PALMER, E. L., & SULLIVAN, S. L. A comparison of learning sets in humans, primates, and subprimates. *J. gen. Psychol.*, 1969, **80**, 189–204.

KISS, G. R. The acquisition of word classes: A theory and its computer simulation. In G. H. Bower (Ed.), *The psychology of learning and motivation*. Vol. 7. New York: Academic, 1973.

KLING, J. W. Generalization of extinction of an instrumental response to stimuli varying in the size dimension. *J. exp. Psychol.*, 1952, **44**, 339–346.

KLING, J. W. Speed of running as a function of goal-box behavior. *J. comp. physiol. Psychol.*, 1956, **49**, 474–476.

KLING, J. W., & RIGGS, L. A. (Eds.). *Woodworth and Schlosberg's Experimental Psychology.* (3rd ed.) New York: Holt, 1971.

KOPPENAAL, R. J. Time changes in the strengths of A-B, A-C lists; spontaneous recovery? *J. verb. Lng. verb. Behav.*, 1963, **2**, 310–319.

KRECHEVSKY, I. "Hypotheses" in rats. *Psychol. Rev.*, 1932, **38**, 516–532.

KROLL, N. E. A., PARKS, T., PARKINSON, S. R., BIEBER, S. L., & JOHNSON, A. L. Short-term memory while shadowing: Recall of visually and aurally presented letters. *J. exp. Psychol.*, 1970, **85**, 220–224.

KUČERA, H., & FRANCIS, W. N. *Computational analysis of present-day American English.* Providence, R.I.: Brown University Press, 1967.

LAMBERT, W. W., & SOLOMON, R. L. Extinction of a running response as a function of distance of block point from the goal. *J. comp. physiol. Psychol.*, 1952, **45**, 269–279.

LANDAUER, T. K. Rate of implicit speech. *Percept. mot. Skills*, 1962, **15**, 646.

LANDAUER, T. K., & MEYER, D. E. Category size and semantic-memory retrieval. *J. verb. Lng. verb. Behav.*, 1972, **11**, 539–549.

LASHLEY, K. S. The mechanism of vision: I. A method of rapid analysis of pattern-vision in the rat. *J. genet. Psychol.*, 1930, **37**, 453–460.

LASHLEY, K. S. An examination of the "continuity theory" as applied to discriminative learning. *J. gen. Psychol.*, 1942, **26**, 241–265.

LASHLEY, K. S. The problem of serial order in behavior. In L. A. Jeffress (Ed.), *Cerebral mechanisms in behavior*. New York: Wiley, 1951.

LASHLEY, K. S., & WADE, M. The Pavlovian theory of generalization. *Psychol. Rev.*, 1946, **53**, 72–87.

LAWRENCE, D. H. Acquired distinctiveness of cues: I. Transfer between discriminations on the basis of familiarity with the stimulus. *J. exp. Psychol.*, 1949, **39**, 770–784.

LAWRENCE, D. H. Acquired distinctiveness of cues: II. Selective association in a constant stimulus situation. *J. exp. Psychol.*, 1950, **40**, 175–188.

LAWRENCE, D. H. Learning. *Annu. Rev. Psychol.*, 1958, **9**, 157–188.

LAWRENCE, D. H. The nature of a stimulus: Some relationships between learning and perception. In S. Koch (Ed.), *Psychology: A study of a science.* Vol. 5. New York: McGraw-Hill, 1963.

LAWRENCE, D. H., & DE RIVERA, J. Evidence for relational discrimination. *J. comp. physiol. Psychol.*, 1954, **47**, 465–471.

LAWRENCE, D. H., & HOMMEL, L. The influence of differential goal boxes on discrimination learning involving delay of reinforcement. *J. comp. physiol. Psychol.*, 1961, **54**, 552–555.

LAWRENCE, D. H., & MASON, W. A. Systematic behavior during discrimination reversal and change of dimension. *J. comp. physiol. Psychol.*, 1955, **48**, 267–271.

LENNEBERG, E. H. *The biological foundations of language.* New York: Wiley, 1967.

Leonard, D. W. Amount and sequence of reward in partial and continuous reinforcement. *J. comp. physiol. Psychol.*, 1969, **67**, 204–211.

Levine, M. A model of hypothesis behavior in discrimination learning set. *Psychol. Rev.*, 1959, **66**, 353–366.

Levine, M. Hypothesis behavior. In A. M. Schrier, H. F. Harlow, & F. Stollnitz (Eds.), *Behavior of nonhuman primates.* Vol. 1. New York: Academic, 1965.

Levine, M. Hypothesis behavior by humans during discrimination learning. *J. exp. Psychol.*, 1966, **71**, 331–336.

Levine, M., Levinson, B., & Harlow, H. F. Trials per problem as a variable in the acquisition of discrimination learning set. *J. comp. physiol. Psychol.*, 1959, **52**, 396–398.

Lewis, D. J. Partial reinforcement: A selective review of the literature since 1950. *Psychol. Bull.*, 1960, **57**, 1–28.

Lewis, D. J., & Cotton, J. W. The effect of intertrial interval and number of acquisition trials with partial reinforcement on performance. *J. comp. physiol. Psychol.*, 1959, **52**, 598–601.

Light, L., & Carter-Sobell, L. Effects of changed semantic context on recognition memory. *J. verb. Lng. verb. Behav.*, 1970, **9**, 1–11.

Lockhead, G. R. Methods of presenting paired associates. *J. verb. Lng. verb. Behav.*, 1962, **1**, 62–65.

Loess, H. Proactive inhibition in short-term memory. *J. verb. Lng. verb. Behav.*, 1964, **3**, 362–368.

Logan, F. A. *Incentive.* New Haven, Conn.: Yale Univ. Press, 1960.

Logan, F. A. Decision making by rats: Delay versus amount of reward. *J. comp. physiol. Psychol.*, 1965, **59**, 1–12.

Logan, F. A. Incentive theory and changes in reward. In G. H. Bower (Ed.), *The psychology of learning and motivation.* Vol. 2. New York: Academic, 1968.

Logan, F. A. *Fundamentals of learning and motivation.* Dubuque, Iowa: Wm. C. Brown, 1969.

Logan, F. A. Essentials of a theory of discrimination learning. In H. H. Kendler & J. T. Spence (Eds.), *Essays in neobehaviorism: A memorial volume to Kenneth W. Spence.* New York: Appleton Century Crofts, 1971.

Logan, F. A., Beier, E. M., & Ellis, R. A. Effect of varied reinforcement on speed of locomotion. *J. exp. Psychol.*, 1955, **49**, 260–266.

Longnecker, E. G., Krauskopf, J., & Bitterman, M. E. Extinction following alternating and random reinforcement. *Amer. J. Psychol.*, 1952, **65**, 580–587.

Lovejoy, E. Analysis of the overlearning reversal effect. *Psychol. Rev.*, 1966, **73**, 87–103.

Lovejoy, E. *Attention in discrimination learning.* San Francisco: Holden-Day, 1968.

MacKinnon, J. R. Interactive effects of the two rewards in a differential magnitude of reward discrimination. *J. exp. Psychol.*, 1967, **75**, 329–338.

MacKinnon, J. R. Competing responses in a differential magnitude of reward discrimination. *Psychon. Sci.*, 1968, **12**, 333–334.

Mackintosh, N. J. The effect of overtraining on a reversal and a nonreversal shift. *J. comp. physiol. Psychol.*, 1962, **55**, 555–559.

Mackintosh, N. J. Incidental cue learning in rats. *Quart. J. exp. Psychol.*, 1965, **17**, 292–300.

Mackintosh, N. J., & Little, L. Intradimensional and extradimensional shift learning by pigeons. *Psychon. Sci.*, 1969, **14**, 5–6.

Maier, S. F., Seligman, M. E. P., & Solomon, R. L. Pavlovian fear conditioning and learned helplessness: effects on escape and avoidance behavior of (a) the CS-US contingency and (b) the independence of the US and voluntary responding. In B. A. Campbell & R. M. Church (Eds.), *Punishment and aversive behavior.* New York: Appleton Century Crofts, 1969.

Malloy, T. E., & Ellis, H. C. Attention and cue-producing responses in response-mediated stimulus generalization. *J. exp. Psychol.*, 1970, **83**, 191–200.

Malloy, T. E., & Proctor, S. Electrodermal responses as affected by subject- versus experimenter-controlled noxious stimulation. *J. exp. Psychol.*, 1973, **97**, 370–377.

Mandler, G. Associative frequency and associative prepotency as response measures of nonsense syllables. *Amer. J. Psychol.*, 1955, **68**, 662–665.

Mandler, G. From association to structure. *Psychol. Rev.*, 1962, **69**, 415–427.

Mandler, G. Comments on Professor Jenkins' paper. In C. N. Cofer & B. S. Musgrave (Eds.), *Verbal behavior and learning.* New York: McGraw-Hill, 1963.

Mandler, G. Words, lists and categories. In J. L. Cowan (Ed.), *Thought and language.* Tucson, Ariz.: University of Arizona Press, 1972. (a)

Mandler, G. Organization and recognition. In E. Tulving & W. Donaldson (Eds.), *Organization and memory.* New York: Academic, 1972. (b)

Mandler, G., & Pearlstone, Z. Free and constrained concept learning and subsequent recall. *J. verb. Lng. verb. Behav.*, 1966, **5**, 126–131.

Mandler, J. M. The effect of overtraining on the use of positive and negative stimuli in reversal and transfer. *J. comp. physiol. Psychol.*, 1968, **66**, 110–115.

Marsh, G. The inverse relationship between discriminability and stimulus generalization as a function of the number of test stimuli. Unpublished doctoral dissertation, University of California, Berkeley, 1965.

Martin, E. Transfer of verbal paired-associates. *Psychol. Rev.*, 1965, **72**, 327–343.

Massaro, D. W. Preperceptual auditory images. *J. exp. Psychol.*, 1970, **85**, 411–417.

Massaro, D. W. Preperceptual images, processing time, and perceptual units in auditory perception. *Psychol. Rev.*, 1972, **79**, 124–145.

May, M. A. Experimentally acquired drives. *J. exp. Psychol.*, 1948, **38**, 66–77.

McCormack, P. D. Recognition memory: How complex a retrieval system? *Canad. J. Psychol.*, 1972, **26**, 19–41.

McGeoch, J. A. The influence of associative value upon the difficulty of non-sense syllable lists. *J. genet. Psychol.*, 1930, **37**, 421–426.

McGeoch, J. A. Forgetting and the law of disuse. *Psychol. Rev.*, 1932, **39**, 352–370.

McGeoch, J. A. The direction and extent of intra-serial associations at recall. *Amer. J. Psychol.*, 1936, **48**, 221–245.

McGeoch, J. A. *The psychology of human learning.* New York: Longmans, 1942.

McGeoch, J. A., & McDonald, W. T. Meaningful relation and retroactive inhibition. *Amer. J. Psychol.*, 1931, **43**, 579–588.

McGovern, J. B. Extinction of associations in four transfer paradigms. *Psychol. Monogr.*, 1964, **78** (Whole No. 593).

McHose, J. H. Relative reinforcement effects: S_1/S_2 and S_1/S_1 paradigms in instrumental conditioning. *Psychol. Rev.*, 1970, **77**, 135–146.

McLaughlin, B. *Learning and social behavior.* New York: Free Press, 1971.

McNeill, D. *The acquisition of language.* New York: Harper, 1970.

Mechanic, A. Effects of orienting task, practice, and incentive on simultaneous incidental and intentional learning. *J. exp. Psychol.*, 1962, **64**, 393–399.

Mednick, S. A., & Freedman, J. L. Stimulus generalization. *Psychol. Bull.*, 1960, **57**, 169–200.

Meehl, P. E. On the circularity of the law of effect. *Psychol. Bull.*, 1950, **47**, 52–75.

Melton, A. W. Implications of short-term memory for a general theory of memory. *J. verb. Lng. verb. Behav.*, 1963, **2**, 1–21.

Melton, A. W., & Irwin, J. M. The influence of degree of interpolated learning on retroactive inhibition and the overt transfer of specific responses. *Amer. J. Psychol.*, 1940, **53**, 173–203.

Melton, A. W., & von Lackum, W. J. Retroactive and proactive inhibition in retention: Evidence for a two factor theory of retroactive inhibition. *Amer. J. Psychol.*, 1941, **54**, 157–173.

Melton, A. W., & Martin, E. *Coding processes in human memory.* Washington, D. C.: Winston & Sons, 1972.

Menzel, E. W. Chimpanzee spatial memory organization. *Science*, 1973, **182**, 943–945.

Messing, R. B., & Campbell, B. A. Summation of pain produced in different anatomical regions. *Percept. Psychophys.*, 1971, **10**, 225–228.

Meyer, D. E. On the representation and retrieval of stored semantic information. *Cog. Psychol.*, 1970, **1**, 242–300.

Miles, R. C. The relative effectiveness of secondary reinforcers throughout deprivation and habit-strength parameters. *J. comp. physiol. Psychol.*, 1956, **49**, 126–130.

Miles, R. C. Discrimination-learning sets. In A. M. Schrier, H. F. Harlow, & F. Stollnitz (Eds.), *Behavior of nonhuman primates.* Vol. 1. New York: Academic, 1965.

Miller, G. A. Free recall of redundant strings of letters. *J. exp. Psychol.*, 1958, **56**, 485–491.

Miller, G. A. The magical number seven, plus or minus two: Some limits on our capacity for processing information. *Psychol. Rev.*, 1956, **63**, 81–97.

Miller, G. A., Galanter, E., & Pribram, K. H. *Plans and the structure of behavior.* New York: Holt, 1960.

Miller, N. E. Studies of fear as an acquirable drive: I. Fear as motivation and fear-reduction as reinforcement in the learning of new responses. *J. exp. Psychol.*, 1948, **38**, 89–101.

Miller, N. E. Learnable drives and rewards. In S. S. Stevens (Ed.), *Handbook of experimental psychology.* New York: Wiley, 1951.

Miller, N. E. Effects of drugs on motivation: The value of using a variety of measures. *Ann. N. Y. Acad. Sci.*, 1956, **65**, 318–333.

Miller, N. E. Liberalization of basic S-R concepts: Extensions to conflict behavior, motivation and social learning. In S. Koch (Ed.), *Psychology: A study of a science.* Vol. 2. New York: McGraw-Hill, 1959.

Miller, N. E. Some reflections on the law of effect produce a new alternative to drive reduction. In M. R. Jones (Ed.), *Nebraska symposium on motivation.* Lincoln, Neb.: University of Nebraska Press, 1963.

Miller, N. E. Learning of visceral and glandular responses. *Science*, 1969, **163**, 434–445.

Miller, N. E., & DiCara, L. Instrumental learning of heart rate changes in curarized rats: Shaping, and specificity to discriminative stimulus. *J. comp. physiol. Psychol.*, 1967, **63**, 12–19.

Miller, N. E., & Dollard, J. *Social learning and imitation.* New Haven, Conn.: Yale Univ. Press, 1941.

Miller, N. E., & Kessen, M. L. Reward effects of food via stomach fistula compared with those of food via mouth. *J. comp. physiol. Psychol.*, 1952, **45**, 555–564.

Milner, B. Amnesia following operation on the temporal lobes. In C. W. M. Whitty & O. L. Zangwill (Eds.), *Amnesia.* London: Butterworth, 1966.

Milner, B., Corkin, S., & Teuber, H.-L. Further analysis of the hippocampal amnesic syndrome: 14-year follow-up study of H. M. *Neuropsychologia*, 1968, **6**, 215–234.

Moeller, G. The CS-UCS interval in GSR conditioning. *J. exp. Psychol.*, 1954, **48**, 162–166.

Moltz, H. Latent extinction and the reduction of secondary reward value. *J. exp. Psychol.*, 1955, **49**, 395–400.

Moltz, H. Latent extinction and the fractional anticipatory response mechanism. *Psychol. Rev.*, 1957, **64**, 229–241.

Montague, W. E. Elaborative strategies in verbal learning and memory. In G. H. Bower (Ed.), *Psychology of learning and motivation.* Vol. 6. New York: Academic, 1972.

Moore, B. R. The role of directed Pavlovian reactions in simple instrumental learning in the pigeon. In R. A. Hinde & J. Stevenson-Hinde (Eds.), *Constraints on learning.* London: Academic, 1973.

MOORE, J. W. Stimulus control: Studies of auditory generalization in rabbits. In A. H. Black & W. F. Prokasy (Eds.), *Classical conditioning II: Current theory and research.* New York: Appleton Century Crofts, 1973.

MOSTOFSKY, D. E. (Ed.). *Stimulus generalization.* Stanford, Calif.: Stanford University Press, 1965.

MOWRER, O. H. On the dual nature of learning—a reinterpretation of "conditioning" and "problem-solving." *Harvard educ. Rev.,* 1947, **17**, 102–148.

MOWRER, O. H., & JONES, H. Extinction and behavior variability as functions of effortfulness of task. *J. exp. Psychol.,* 1943, **33**, 369–386.

MOWRER, O. H., & JONES, H. Habit strength as a function of the pattern of reinforcement. *J. exp. Psychol.,* 1945, **35**, 293–311.

MOWRER, O. H., & LAMOREAUX, R. R. Avoidance conditioning and signal duration—a study of secondary motivation and reward. *Psychol. Monogr.,* 1942, **54**, No. 247.

MUENZINGER, K. F. Motivation in learning. I. Electric shock for correct response in the visual discrimination habit. *J. comp. Psychol.,* 1934, **17**, 267–277.

MÜLLER, G. E., & PILZECKER, A. *Experimentelle Beiträge zur Lehre vom Gedächtnis. Zeitschrift für Psychologie,* 1900, **1**, 1–300.

MURDOCK, B. B., JR. The retention of individual items. *J. exp. Psychol.,* 1961, **62**, 618–625.

MURDOCK, B. B., JR. The serial position effect of free recall. *J. exp. Psychol.,* 1962, **64**, 482–488.

MYER, J. S. Some effects of noncontingent aversive stimulation. In F. R. Brush (Ed.), *Aversive conditioning and learning.* New York: Academic, 1971.

NEISSER, U. *Cognitive psychology.* New York: Appleton Century Crofts, 1967.

NEISSER, U., & WEENE, P. Hierarchies in concept attainment. *J. exp. Psychol.,* 1962, **64**, 640–645.

NEURINGER, C., & MICHAEL, J. L. (Eds.). *Behavior modification in clinical psychology.* New York: Appleton Century Crofts, 1970.

NEWELL, A., & SIMON, H. A. *Human problem solving.* Englewood Cliffs, N.J.: Prentice-Hall, 1972.

NEWTON, J. M., & WICKENS, D. D. Retroactive inhibition as a function of the temporal position of interpolated learning. *J. exp. Psychol.,* 1956, **51**, 149–154.

NILSSON, N. J. *Learning machines.* New York: McGraw-Hill, 1965.

NOBLE, C. E. An analysis of meaning. *Psychol. Rev.,* 1952, **59**, 421–430.

NOBLE, C. E. The meaning-familiarity relationship. *Psychol. Rev.,* 1953, **60**, 89–98.

NORTH, A. J., & STIMMEL, D. T. Extinction of an instrumental response following a large number of reinforcements. *Psychol. Rep.,* 1960, **6**, 227–234.

NOTTERMAN, J. M., & MINTZ, D. E. *Dynamics of response.* New York: Wiley, 1965.

O'CONNELL, D. C. Facilitation of recall by linguistic structure in nonsense strings. *Psychol. Bull.,* 1970, **74**, 441–452.

OLDS, J. Satiation effects in self-stimulation of the brain. *J. comp. physiol. Psychol.,* 1958, **51**, 675–678.

OLDS, J., & MILNER, P. Positive reinforcement produced by electrical stimulation of septal area and other regions of the rat brain. *J. comp. physiol. Psychol.,* 1954, **47**, 419–427.

O'KELLY, L. I., & STECKLE, L. C. A note on long enduring emotional responses in the rat. *J. Psychol.,* 1939, **8**, 125–131.

O'LEARY, K. D., & DRABMAN, R. Token reinforcement programs in the classroom: A review. *Psychol. Bull.,* 1971, **75**, 379–398.

OLTON, D. S. Discrimination behavior in the rat: Differential effects of reinforcement and nonreinforcement. *J. comp. physiol. Psychol.,* 1972, **79**, 284–290.

OLTON, D. S., & SAMUELSON, R. Decision making in the rat: Response-choice and response-time measures of discrimination reversal learning. *J. comp. physiol. Psychol.,* 1974, in press.

OSBORNE, H. F. Rapid memorizing, "winging a part," as a lost faculty. *Psychol. Rev.,* 1902, **9**, 182–183.

OSGOOD, C. E. The similarity paradox in human learning: A resolution. *Psychol. Rev.,* 1949, **56**, 132–143.

PAIVO, A. Abstractness, imagery, and meaningfulness in paired-associate learning. *J. verb. Lng. verb Behav.,* 1965, **4**, 32–38.

PAIVO, A. Paired associate learning and free recall of nouns as a function of concreteness, specificity, imagery and meaningfulness. *Psychol. Repts.,* 1967, **20**, 239–245.

PAIVO, A. A factor-analytic study of word attributes in verbal learning. *J. verb. Lng. verb Behav.,* 1968, **7**, 41–49.

PAIVO, A. *Imagery and verbal processes.* New York: Holt, 1971.

PALERMO, D. S., & EBERHART, V. L. On the learning of morphological rules: An experimental analogy. *J. verb. Lng. verb. Behav.,* 1968, **7**, 337–344.

PASSEY, G. E. The influence of intensity of unconditioned stimulus upon acquisition of a conditioned response. *J. exp. Psychol.,* 1948, **38**, 420–428.

PASSEY, G. E., & WOOD, D. L. Effects of patterns of reinforcement on the conditioned eyelid response. *J. exp. Psychol.,* 1963, **66**, 241–244.

PATTEN, R. L., & DEAUX, E. B. Classical conditioning and extinction of the licking response in rats. *Psychon. Sci.,* 1966, **4**, 21–22.

PAUL, I. H. Studies in remembering: The reproduction of connected and extended verbal material. *Psychol. Issues,* 1959, **1**, 152.

PAVLOV, I. P. *Conditioned reflexes.* (Translated by G. V. Anrep). London: Oxford, 1927.

PERIN, C. T. Behavior potentiality as a joint function of the amount of training and degree of hunger at the time of extinction. *J. exp. Psychol.,* 1942, **30**, 93–113.

PERIN, C. T. A quantitative investigation of the delay-of-reinforcement gradient. *J. exp. Psychol.,* 1943, **32**, 37–51.

PETERSON, L. R., & GENTILE, A. Proactive interference as a function of time between tests. *J. exp. Psychol.,* 1965, **70**, 473–478.

PETERSON, L. R., & PETERSON, M. J. Short-term

retention of individual verbal items. *J. exp. Psychol.*, 1959, **58**, 193–198.

PFAFFMANN, C. The pleasures of sensation. *Psychol. Rev.*, 1960, **67**, 253–268.

PFAFFMANN, C. Taste preference and reinforcement. In J. Tapp (Ed.), *Reinforcement and behavior.* New York: Academic, 1969.

POSNER, M. I. Rate of presentation and order of recall in immediate memory. *Brit. J. Psychol.*, 1964, **55**, 303–306.

POSNER, M. I., BOIES, S. J., EICHELMAN, W. H., & TAYLOR, R. L. Retention of visual and name codes of single letters. *J. exp. Psychol. Monogr.*, 1969, **79**, No. 1.

POSNER, M. I., & KEELE, S. W. Decay of visual information from a single letter. *Science*, 1967, **158**, 137–139.

POSNER, M. I., & KONICK, A. E. On the role of interference in short-term retention. *J. exp. Psychol.*, 1966, **72**, 221–231.

POSTMAN, L. Short-term memory and incidental learning. In A. W. Melton (Ed.), *Categories of human learning.* New York: Academic, 1964.

POSTMAN, L. Herman Ebbinghaus. *Amer. Psychol.*, 1968, **23**, 149–157.

POSTMAN, L. Transfer, interference and forgetting. In J. W. Kling & L. A. Riggs (Eds.), *Woodworth & Schlosberg's Experimental Psychology.* (3rd ed.) New York: Holt, 1971.

POSTMAN, L., & KEPPEL, G. (Eds.). *Norms of word association.* New York: Academic, 1970.

POSTMAN, L., & PHILLIPS, L. W. Short-term temporal changes in free recall. *Quart. J. exp. Psychol.*, 1965, **17**, 132–138.

POSTMAN, L., & RAU, L. Retention as a function of the method of measurement. *Univ. Calif. Publ. Psychol.*, 1957, **8**, 217–270.

POSTMAN, L., & STARK, K. The role of response availability in transfer and interference. *J. exp. Psychol.*, 1969, **79**, 168–177.

POSTMAN, L., STARK, K., & FRASER, J. Temporal changes in interference. *J. verb. Lng. verb. Behav.*, 1968, **7**, 672–694.

POSTMAN, L., & UNDERWOOD, B. J. Critical issues in interference theory. *Mem. Cognit.*, 1973, **1**, 19–40.

POTTS, G. R. Information processing strategies used in the encoding of linear orderings. *J. verb. Lng. verb. Behav.*, 1972, **11**, 727–740.

PREMACK, D. Toward empirical behavioral laws: I. Positive reinforcement. *Psychol. Rev.*, 1959, **66**, 219–233.

PREMACK, D. Reinforcement theory. In D. Levine (Ed.), *Nebraska symposium on motivation.* Lincoln, Neb.: University of Nebraska Press, 1965.

PREMACK, D. Catching up with common sense or two sides of a generalization: Reinforcement and punishment. In R. Glaser (Ed.), *The nature of reinforcement.* New York: Academic, 1971.

PREMACK, D. Language in chimpanzee? *Science*, 1971, **172**, 808–822.

PROKASY, W. F., JR., GRANT, D. A., & MEYERS, N. A. Eyelid conditioning as a function of unconditioned stimulus intensity and intertrial interval. *J. exp. Psychol.*, 1958, **55**, 242–246.

PRYTULAK, L. S. Natural language mediation. *Cog. Psychol.*, 1971, **2**, 1–56.

PUBOLS, B. H., JR. Incentive magnitude, learning, and performance in animals. *Psychol. Bull.*, 1960, **57**, 89–115.

PURTLE, R. B. Peak shift: A review. *Psychol. Bull.*, 1973, **80**, 408–421.

PYLYSHYN, Z. W. What the mind's eye tells the mind's brain. *Psychol. Bull.*, 1973, **80**, 1–24.

QUILLIAN, M. R. Semantic memory. In M. Minsky (Ed.), *Semantic information processing.* Cambridge, Mass.: MIT, 1960.

RASMUSSEN, E. A., & ARCHER, E. J. Concept identification as a function of language pretraining and task complexity. *J. exp. Psychol.*, 1961, **61**, 437–441.

REED, C. B. (Ed.). *The learning of language.* New York: Appleton Century Crofts, 1971.

REID, L. S. The development of noncontinuity behavior through continuity learning. *J. exp. Psychol.*, 1953, **46**, 107–112.

REINHOLD, D. B., & PERKINS, C. C., JR. Stimulus generalization following different methods of training. *J. exp. Psychol.*, 1955, **49**, 423–427.

REITMAN, J. S. Mechanisms of forgetting in short-term memory. *Cog. Psychol.*, 1971, **2**, 185–195.

REITMAN, J. S. Without surreptitious rehearsal, information in short-term memory decays. *J. verb. Lng. verb. Behav.*, 1974, **13**, 365–377.

REITMAN, J. S., & BOWER, G. H. Storage and later recognition of exemplars and concepts. *Cog. Psychol.*, 1973, **4**, 194–206.

RESCORLA, R. A. Pavlovian conditioning and its proper control procedures. *Psychol. Rev.*, 1967, **74**, 71–80.

RESCORLA, R. A. Pavlovian conditioned inhibition. *Psychol. Bull.*, 1969, **72**, 77–94.

RESCORLA, R. A. Informational variables in Pavlovian conditioning. In G. Bower (Ed.), *The psychology of learning and motivation.* Vol. 6. New York: Academic, 1972.

RESCORLA, R. A. Second-order conditioning: Implications for theories of learning. In F. J. McGuigan & D. B. Lumsden (Eds.), *Contemporary approaches to conditioning and learning.* New York: Wiley, 1973.

RESCORLA, R. A., & LoLORDO, V. M. Inhibition of avoidance behavior. *J. comp. physiol. Psychol.*, 1965, **59**, 406–412.

RESCORLA, R. A., & SOLOMON, R. L. Two-process learning theory: Relationships between Pavlovian conditioning and instrumental learning. *Psychol. Rev.*, 1967, **74**, 151–182.

RESCORLA, R. A., & WAGNER, A. R. A theory of Pavlovian conditioning: Variations in the effectiveness of reinforcement and nonreinforcement. In A. Black & W. F. Prokasy, Jr. (Eds.), *Classical conditioning II.* New York: Appleton Century Crofts, 1972.

RESTLE, F. A theory of discrimination learning. *Psychol. Rev.*, 1955, **62**, 11–19.

RESTLE, F. Theory of selective learning with probable reinforcements. *Psychol. Rev.*, 1957, **64**, 182–191.

RESTLE, F. Toward a quantitative description of learning set data. *Psychol. Rev.*, 1958, **65**, 77–91.

RESTLE, F. The selection of strategies in cue learning. *Psychol. Rev.*., 1962, **69**, 320–343.

RESTLE, F. Theory of serial pattern learning: Structural trees. *Psychol. Rev.*, 1970, **77**, 481–495.

RESTLE, F., & BROWN, E. Organization of serial pattern learning. In G. H. Bower (Ed.), *Psychology of learning and motivation*. Vol. 6. New York: Academic, 1972.

REUS, J., LYNCH, J., & GANTT, W. H. Motor response device. *Cond. Refl.*, 1966, **1**, 135–136.

REVUSKY, S., & GARCIA, J. Learned associations over long delays. In J. T. Spence & G. Bower (Eds.), *The psychology of learning and motivation*. Vol. 4. New York: Academic, 1970.

REYNOLDS, G. S. Behavioral contrast. *J. exp. Anal. Behav.*, 1961, **4**, 57–71. (a)

REYNOLDS, G. S. Attention in the pigeon. *J. exp. Anal. Behav.*, 1961, **4**, 203–208. (b)

REYNOLDS, R. W. The relationship between stimulation voltage and rate of hypothalamic self-stimulation in the rat. *J. comp. physiol. Psychol.*, 1958, **51**, 193–198.

RILEY, D. A. *Discrimination learning*. Boston: Allyn and Bacon, 1968.

RIOPELLE, A. Transfer suppression and learning sets. *J. comp. physiol. Psychol.*, 1953, **46**, 108–114.

RIPS, L. J., SHOBEN, E. J., & SMITH, E. E. Semantic distance and the verification of semantic relations. *J. verb. Lng. verb. Behav.*, 1973, **12**, 1–20.

ROBBINS, D. Effect of duration of water reinforcement on running behavior and consummatory activity. *J. comp. physiol. Psychol.*, 1969, **69**, 311–316.

ROBBINS, D. Partial reinforcement: A selective review of the alleyway literature since 1960. *Psychol. Bull.*, 1971, **76**, 415–431.

ROBINSON, J. S. The effect of learning verbal labels for stimuli on their later discriminations. *J. exp. Psychol.*, 1955, **49**, 112–115.

ROBERTS, C. L., MARX, M. H., & COLLIER, G. Light onset and light offset as reinforcers for the albino rat. *J. comp. physiol. Psychol.*, 1958, **51**, 575–579.

ROSCH, E. On the internal structure of perceptual and semantic categories. In T. E. Moore (Ed.), *Cognitive development and acquisition of language*. New York: Academic, 1973.

ROSS, S. M., & ROSS, L. E. Comparison of trace and delay classical eyelid conditioning as a function of interstimulus interval. *J. exp. Psychol.*, 1971, **91**, 165–167.

ROZIN, P., & KALAT, J. W. Specific hungers and poison avoidance as adaptive specializations of learning. *Psychol. Rev.*, 1971, **78**, 459–486.

RUMELHART, D. E., LINDSAY, P. H., & NORMAN, D. A. A process model for long term memory. In E. Tulving & W. Donaldson (Eds.), *Organization of memory*. New York: Academic, 1973.

RUNDUS, D. Analysis of rehearsal processes in free recall. *J. exp. Psychol.*, 1971, **89**, 63–77.

SACHS, J. S. Recognition memory for syntactic and semantic aspects of connected discourse. *Perception and Psychophysics*, 1967, **2**, 437–442.

SALTZ, E. *The cognitive bases of human learning.* Homewood, Ill.: Dorsey, 1971.

SALTZMAN, I. J. Maze learning in the absence of primary reinforcement: A study of secondary reinforcement. *J. comp. physiol. Psychol.*, 1949, **42**, 161–173.

SAPORTA, S., BLUMENTAL, A., & REIFF, D. G. Grammatical models and language learning. *Monograph Series on Language and Linguistics*, 1963, **16**, 133–142.

SAUNDERS, T. R., JR. Effects of US intensity and number of CS-US pairings on maintenance of vicious-circle behavior in rats by secondary punishment. *J. comp. physiol. Psychol.*, 1974, **86**, 535–542.

SCHAEFFER, B., & WALLACE, R. Semantic similarity and the comparison of word meanings. *J. exp. Psychol.*, 1969, **82**, 343–346.

SCHAEFFER, B., & WALLACE, R. The comparison of word meanings. *J. exp. Psychol.*, 1970, **86**, 144–152.

SCHLOSBERG, H. The relationship between success and the laws of conditioning. *Psychol. Rev.*, 1937, **44**, 379–394.

SCHNEIDERMAN, N. Interstimulus interval function of the nictitating membrane response of the rabbit under delay versus trace conditioning. *J. comp. physiol. Psychol.*, 1966, **62**, 397–402.

SCHRIER, A. M. Comparison of two methods of investigating the effect of amount of reward on performance. *J. comp. physiol. Psychol.*, 1958, **51**, 725–731.

SCHULMAN, A. I. Recognition memory for targets from a scanned word list. *Brit. J. Psychol.*, 1971, **62**, 335–346.

SCULL, J. W. The Amsel frustration effect: Interpretations and research. *Psychol. Bull.*, 1973, **79**, 352–361.

SELEKMAN, W. Behavioral contrast and inhibitory stimulus control as related to extended training. *J. exp. Anal. Behav.*, 1973, **20**, 245–252.

SELFRIDGE, O. G., & NEISSER, U. Pattern recognition by machine. *Scientific American*, 1960, **203**, 60–68.

SELIGMAN, M. E. P. On the generality of the laws of learning. *Psychol. Rev.*, 1970, **77**, 406–418.

SELIGMAN, M. E. P. *Helplessness*. San Francisco: Freeman, 1974.

SELIGMAN, M. E. P., & BEAGLEY, G. Learned helplessness in the rat. *J. comp. physiol. Psychol.*, 1974, **67**, in press.

SELIGMAN, M. E. P., & HAGER, J. L. *Biological boundaries of learning*. New York: Appleton Century Crofts, 1972.

SELIGMAN, M. E. P., & JOHNSTON, J. C. A cognitive theory of avoidance learning. In F. J. McGuigan & D. B. Lumsden (Eds.), *Contemporary approaches to conditioning and learning*. Washington, D.C.: Winston & Sons, 1973.

SELIGMAN, M. E. P., & MAIER, S. F. Failure to escape traumatic shock. *J. exp. Psychol.*, 1967, **74**, 1–9.

SELIGMAN, M. E. P., MAIER, S. F., & GEER, J. H. Alleviation of learned helplessness in the dog. *J. abnorm. Psychol.*, 1968, **73**, 256–262.

SELIGMAN, M. E. P., MAIER, S. F., & SOLOMON, R. L. Unpredictable and uncontrollable aversive events.

In R. F. Brush (Ed.), *Aversive conditioning and learning.* New York: Academic, 1971.

SEWARD, J. P., & LEVY, N. Sign learning as a factor in extinction. *J. exp. Psychol.*, 1949, **39**, 660–668.

SHALLICE, T., & WARRINGTON, E. K. Independent functioning of verbal memory stores: A neuropsychological study. *Quart J. exp. Psychol.*, 1970, **22**, 261–273.

SHAPIRO, D., SCHWARTZ, G. E., & TURSKY, B. Control of diastolic blood pressure in man by feedback and reinforcement. *Psychophysiology*, 1972, **9**, 296–304.

SHEFFIELD, F. D. A drive induction theory of reinforcement. In R. N. Haber (Ed.), *Current research in motivation.* New York: Holt, 1966.

SHEFFIELD, F. D., ROBY, T. B., & CAMPBELL, B. A. Drive reduction versus consummatory behavior as determinants of reinforcement. *J. comp. physiol. Psychol.*, 1954, **47**, 349–354.

SHEFFIELD, F. D., & TEMMER, H. W. Relative resistance to extinction of escape training and avoidance training. *J. exp. Psychol.*, 1950, **40**, 287–298.

SHEFFIELD, F. D., WOLFF, J. J., & BACKER, R. Reward value of copulation without sex drive reduction. *J. comp. physiol. Psychol.*, 1951, **44**, 3–8.

SHEPARD, R. N. Stimulus and response generalization: A stochastic model relating generalization to distance in psychological space. *Psychometrika*, 1957, **22**, 325–345.

SHEPARD, R. N. Stimulus and response generalization: Tests of a model relating generalization to distance in psychological space. *J. exp. Psychol.*, 1958, **55**, 509–523.

SHEPARD, R. N. Approximation to uniform gradients of generalization by monotone transformations of scale. In D. I. Mostofsky (Ed.), *Stimulus generalization.* Stanford, Calif.: Stanford University Press, 1965.

SHEPARD, R. N. Recognition memory for words, sentences, and pictures. *J. verb. Lng. verb. Behav.*, 1967, **6**, 156–163.

SHEPP, B. E., & EIMAS, P. D. Intradimensional and extradimensional shifts in the rat. *J. comp. physiol. Psychol.*, 1964, **57**, 357–361.

SHEPP, B. E., & HOWARD, D. V. Are differential orienting responses necessary for dimensional learning and transfer? *J. exp. Psychol.*, 1973, **100**, 122–134.

SHIFFRIN, R. M. Forgetting: Trace erosion or retrieval failure? *Science*, 1970, **168**, 1601–1603.

SHIFFRIN, R. M. Information persistence in short-term memory. *J. exp. Psychol.*, 1973, **100**, 39–49.

SHULMAN, H. G. Similarity effects in short-term memory. *Psychol. Bull.*, 1971, **75**, 399–415.

SIDMAN, M. Two temporal parameters of the maintenance of avoidance behavior by the white rat. *J. comp. physiol. Psychol.*, 1953, **46**, 253–261.

SIEGEL, S. Overtraining and transfer processes. *J. comp. physiol. Psychol.*, 1967, **64**, 471–477.

SIEGEL, S., & DOMJAN, M. Backward conditioning as an inhibitory procedure. *Lng. Motiv.*, 1971, **2**, 1–11.

SIEGEL, S., & WAGNER, A. R. Extended acquisition training and resistance to extinction. *J. exp. Psychol.*, 1963, **66**, 308–310.

SKINNER, B. F. Two types of conditioned reflex and a pseudo type. *J. gen. Psychol.*, 1935, **12**, 66–77.

SKINNER, B. F. The generic nature of the concepts of stimulus and response. *J. gen. Psychol.*, 1935, **12**, 40–65.

SKINNER, B. F. *The behavior of organisms.* New York: Appleton Century Crofts, 1938.

SKINNER, B. F. Superstition in the pigeon. *J. exp. Psychol.*, 1948, **38**, 168–172.

SKINNER, B. F. Are theories of learning necessary? *Psychol. Bull.*, 1950, **57**, 193–216.

SLAMECKA, N. J. Differentiation versus unlearning of verbal associations. *J. exp. Psychol.*, 1966, **71**, 822–828.

SLOBIN, D. I. Imitation and grammatical development in children. In N. S. Endler, L. R. Boulter, & H. Osser (Eds.), *Contemporary issues in developmental psychology.* New York: Holt, 1968.

SLOBIN, D. I. Developmental psycholinguistics. In W. O. Dingwall (Ed.), *A survey of linguistic science.* College Park, Maryland: Linguistics Program, University of Maryland, 1971.

SMITH, E. E., HAVILAND, S. E., BUCKLEY, P. B., & SACK, M. Retrieval of artificial facts from long-term memory. *J. verb. Lng. verb. Behav.*, 1972, **11**, 582–592.

SMITH, E. E., RIPS, L. J., & SHOBEN, E. J. Semantic memory and psychological semantics. In G. H. Bower (Ed.), *The psychology of learning and motivation.* Vol. 8. New York: Academic, 1974.

SMITH, E. E., SHOBEN, E. J., & RIPS, L. J. Structure and process in semantic memory: A featural model for semantic decisions. *Psychol. Rev.*, 1974, **81**, 214–241.

SMITH, T. L. On muscular memory. *Amer. J. Psychol.*, 1896, **7**, 453–490.

SMOKE, K. L. Negative instances in concept learning. *J. exp. Psychol.*, 1933, **16**, 583–588.

SNYDER, H. L., & HULSE, S. H. Effect of volume of reinforcement and number of consummatory responses on licking and running behavior. *J. exp. Psychol.*, 1961, **61**, 474–479.

SOLOMON, R. L. Punishment. *Amer. Psychol.*, 1964, **19**, 239–253.

SOLOMON, R. L., KAMIN, L. J., & WYNNE, L. C. Traumatic avoidance learning: The outcomes of several extinction procedures with dogs. *J. abnorm. soc. Psychol.*, 1953, **48**, 291–302.

SOLOMON, R. L., & WYNNE, L. C. Traumatic avoidance learning: Acquisition in normal dogs. *Psychol. Monogr.*, 1953, **67**, No. 354.

SOLOMON, R. L., & WYNNE, L. C. Traumatic avoidance learning: The principles of anxiety conservation and partial irreversability. *Psychol. Rev.*, 1954, **61**, 353–385.

SPENCE, K. W. The nature of discrimination learning in animals. *Psychol. Rev.*, 1936, **43**, 427–449.

SPENCE, K. W. The differential response in animals to stimuli varying within a single dimension. *Psychol. Rev.*, 1937, **44**, 430–444. (a)

SPENCE, K. W. Analysis of formation of visual

discrimination habits in the chimpanzee. *J. comp. Psychol.*, 1937, **23**, 77–100. (b)

SPENCE, K. W. Continuous versus non-continuous interpretations of discrimination learning. *Psychol. Rev.*, 1940, **47**, 271–288.

SPENCE, K. W. The role of secondary reinforcement in delayed reward learning. *Psychol. Rev.*, 1947, **54**, 1–8.

SPENCE, K. W. The postulates and methods of behaviorism. *Psychol. Rev.*, 1948, **55**, 67–68.

SPENCE, K. W. Theoretical interpretations of learning. In S. S. Stevens (Ed.), *Handbook of experimental psychology.* New York: Wiley, 1951.

SPENCE, K. W. The nature of the response in discrimination learning. *Psychol. Rev.*, 1952, **59**, 89–93.

SPENCE, K. W. *Behavior theory and conditioning.* New Haven, Conn.: Yale Univ. Press, 1956.

SPENCE, K. W. A theory of emotionally based drive (D) and its relation to performance in simple learning situations. *Amer. Psychol.*, 1958, **13**, 131–141.

SPENCE, K. W. *Behavior theory and learning.* Englewood Cliffs, N.J.: Prentice-Hall, 1960.

SPERLING, G. The information available in brief visual presentations. *Psychol. Monogr.*, 1960, **74**, (Whole No. 498).

SPERLING, G. A model for visual memory tasks. *Human Factors*, 1963, **5**, 19–31.

SPERLING, S. E. Reversal learning and resistance to extinction: A review of the rat literature. *Psychol. Bull.*, 1965, **63**, 281–297.

SPEVACK, A. A., & SUBOSKI, M. D. Retrograde effects of electroconvulsive shock on learned responses. *Psychol. Bull.*, 1969, **72**, 66–76.

SPOONER, A., & KELLOGG, W. N. The backward conditioning curve. *Amer. J. Psychol.*, 1947, **60**, 321–334.

STAATS, A. W. *Child learning, intelligence and personality.* New York: Harper, 1971.

STAATS, A., FINLEY, J., MINKE, K. A., WOLF, M., & BROOKS, C. A reinforcer system and experimental procedure for the laboratory study of reading acquisition. *Child Development,* 1964, **35**, 209–231.

STADDON, J. E. R., & SIMMELHAG, V. L. The "superstition" experiment: A reexamination of its implications for the principles of adaptive behavior. *Psychol. Rev.*, 1971, **78**, 3–43.

STANLEY, W. C., & AAMODT, M. S. Force of responding during extinction as a function of force requirement during conditioning. *J. comp. physiol. Psychol.*, 1954, **47**, 462–464.

STEINBERG, D. D., & JAKOBOVITS, L. A. (Eds.). *Semantics.* London: Cambridge, 1971.

STELLAR, E. Hunger in man: Comparative and physiological studies. *Amer. Psychol.*, 1966, **21**, 105–117.

STELLAR, E., & HILL, J. H. The rat's rate of drinking as a function of water deprivation. *J. comp. physiol. Psychol.*, 1952, **45**, 96–102.

STOCKWELL, R. P., & BOWEN, J. D. The sounds of English and Spanish. In C. A. Ferguson (Ed.),

Contrastive structure series. Chicago: The University of Chicago Press, 1965.

STOLLNITZ, F. Spatial variables, observing responses, and discrimination learning sets. *Psychol. Rev.*, 1965, **72**, 247–261.

SUMBY, W. H. Word frequency and the serial position effect. *J. verb. Lng. verb. Behav.*, 1963, **1**, 443–450.

SUTER, S. Position preferences and selective attention in animal discrimination learning. Unpublished doctoral dissertation. Johns Hopkins University, 1970.

SUTHERLAND, N. S., & MACKINTOSH, N. J. *Mechanisms of animal discrimination learning.* New York: Academic, 1971.

SUTHERLAND, N. S., MACKINTOSH, N. J., & MACKINTOSH, J. Shape and size discrimination in octopus: The effects of pretraining along different dimensions. *J. genet. Psychol.*, 1965, **106**, 1–10.

SUTHERLAND, N. S., MACKINTOSH, N. J., & WOLFE, J. B. Extinction as a function of the order of partial and consistent reinforcement. *J. exp. Psychol.*, 1965, **69**, 56–59.

SWITALSKI, R. W., LYONS, J., & THOMAS, D. R. Effects of interdimensional training on stimulus discrimination. *J. exp. Psychol.*, 1966, **72**, 661–666.

TAYLOR, G. T. Varied function of punishment in differential instrumental conditioning. *J. exp. Psychol.*, 1974, **102**, 298–307.

TAYLOR, J. A. The relationship of anxiety to the conditioned eyelid response. *J. exp. Psychol.*, 1951, **41**, 81–92.

TAYLOR, J. A. Drive theory and manifest anxiety. *Psychol. Bull.*, 1956, **53**, 303–320.

TEICHNER, W. H. Experimental extinction as a function of the intertrial intervals during conditioning and extinction. *J. exp. Psychol.*, 1952, **44**, 170–178.

TERHUNE, J. G., & PREMACK, D. On the proportionality between the probability of not-running and the punishment effect of being forced to run. *Lng. Motiv.*, 1970, **1**, 141–149.

TERRACE, H. S. Wavelength generalization after discrimination learning with and without errors. *Science*, 1964, **144**, 78–80.

TERRACE, H. S. Stimulus control. In W. K. Honig (Ed.), *Operant behavior: Areas of research and application.* New York: Appleton Century Crofts, 1966.

TERRACE, H. S. Discrimination learning, the peak shift, and behavioral contrast. *J. exp. Anal. Behav.*, 1968, **11**, 727–741.

TERRACE, H. S. By-products of discrimination learning. In G. H. Bower (Ed.), *The psychology of learning and motivation.* Vol. 5. New York: Academic, 1972.

THEIOS, J. The partial reinforcement effect sustained through blocks of continuous reinforcement. *J. exp. Psychol.*, 1962, **64**, 1–6.

THEIOS, J. Drive stimulus generalization increments. *J. comp. physiol. Psychol.*, 1963, **56**, 691–695.

THEIOS, J., & McGINNIS, R. W. Partial reinforcement before and after continuous reinforcement. *J. exp. Psychol.*, 1967, **73**, 479–481.

THOMAS, D. R. The use of operant conditioning techniques to investigate perceptual processes in animals. In R. M. Gilbert & N. S. Sutherland (Eds.), *Animal discrimination learning.* New York: Academic, 1969.

THOMAS, D. R., BURR, D. E. S., & SVINICKI, M. D. Evidence for a positive relationship between degree of control acquired by two dimensions of a complex stimulus. *Nature*, 1969, **223**, 420–421.

THORNDIKE, E. L. Animal intelligence. *Psychol. Monogr.*, 1898, **2**, No. 8.

THORNDIKE, E. L. *Animal intelligence.* New York: Macmillan, 1911.

THORNDIKE, E. L. Reward and punishment in animal learning. *Comp. Psychol. Monogr.*, 1932, **8**, No. 39.

THORNDIKE, E. L., & LORGE, I. *The teacher's word book of 30,000 words.* New York: Columbia University Press, 1944.

THUNE, E. L. The effects of different types of preliminary activities on subsequent learning of paired-associate material. *J. exp. Psychol.*, 1950, **40**, 423–438.

TIGHE, T. J. Reversal and nonreversal shifts in monkeys. *J. comp. physiol. Psychol.*, 1964, **58**, 324–326.

TIGHE, L. S., & TIGHE, T. J. Discrimination learning: Two views in historical perspective. *Psychol. Bull.*, 1966, **66**, 353–370.

TINBERGEN, N. *The study of instinct.* Oxford: Clarendon Press, 1951.

TINBERGEN, N. *The herring gull's world.* London: Collins, 1953.

TOLMAN, E. C. *Purposive behavior in animals and men.* New York: Appleton Century Crofts, 1932.

TOLMAN, E. C. Cognitive maps in rats and men. *Psychol. Rev.*, 1948, **55**, 189–208.

TOLMAN, E. C. *Collected papers in psychology.* Berkeley, Calif.: University of California Press, 1951.

TOLMAN, E. C. Principles of purposive behavior. In S. Koch (Ed.), *Psychology: A study of a science.* Vol. 2. New York: McGraw-Hill, 1959.

TORGERSON, W. S. Multidimensional scaling of similarity. *Psychometrika*, 1965, **30**, 379–393.

TRABASSO, T., & BOWER, G. H. Memory in concept identification. *Psychon. Sci.*, 1964, **1**, 133–134.

TRABASSO, T. R., & BOWER, G. H. *Attention in learning: Theory and research.* New York: Wiley, 1968.

TRAPOLD, M. A., & OVERMIER, J. B. The second learning process in instrumental learning. In A. H. Black & W. F. Prokasy (Eds.), *Classical conditioning II: Current research and theory.* New York: Appleton Century Crofts, 1972.

TREISMAN, A. M. Monitoring and storage of irrelevant messages in selective attention. *J. verb. Lng. verb. Behav.*, 1964, **3**, 449–459.

TROLAND, L. T. *The fundamentals of human motivation.* Princeton, N.J.: Van Nostrand, 1928.

TROWILL, J. A., PANKSEPP, J., & GANDELMAN, R. An incentive model of rewarding brain stimulation. *Psychol. Rev.*, 1969, **76**, 264–281.

TULVING, E. Subjective organization in free recall of "unrelated words." *Psychol. Rev.*, 1962, **69**, 344–354.

TULVING, E. Intratrial and intertrial retention: Notes toward a theory of free recall verbal learning. *Psychol. Rev.*, 1964, **71**, 219–237.

TULVING, E. Subjective organization and effects of repetition in multitrial free-recall learning. *J. verb. Lng. verb. Behav.*, 1966, **5**, 193–197.

TULVING, E. When is recall higher than recognition? *Psychon. Sci.*, 1968, **10**, 53–54.

TULVING, E. Episodic and semantic memory. In E. Tulving & W. Donaldson (Eds.), *Organization and memory.* New York: Academic, 1972.

TULVING, E. Cue-dependent forgetting. *Amer. Scientist*, 1974, **62**, 74–82.

TULVING, E., & PSOTKA, J. Retroactive inhibition in free recall: Inaccessibility of information available in the memory store. *J. exp. Psychol.*, 1971, **87**, 1–8.

TULVING, E., & THOMSON, D. M. Retrieval processes in recognition memory: Effects of associative context. *J. exp. Psychol.*, 1971, **87**, 116–124.

TULVING, E., & THOMSON, D. M. Encoding specificity and retrieval processes in episodic memory. *Psychol. Rev.*, 1973, **80**, 352–373.

TURNER, L. H., & SOLOMON, R. L. Human traumatic avoidance learning: Theory and experiments on the operant-respondent distinction. *Psychol. Monogr.*, 1962, **76**, No. 40.

TYLER, D. W., WORTZ, E. C., & BITTERMAN, M. E. The effect of random and alternating partial reinforcement on resistance to extinction in the rat. *Amer. J. Psychol.*, 1953, **66**, 57–65.

UHL, C. N. Eliminating behavior with omission and extinction after varying amounts of training. *Anim. Lng. Behav.*, 1973, **1**, 237–240.

UHL, C. N., & GARCIA, E. E. Comparison of omission with extinction in response elimination in rats. *J. comp. physiol. Psychol.*, 1969, **69**, 554–562.

UHL, C. N., & SHERMAN, W. O. Comparison of combinations of omission, punishment, and extinction methods in response elimination in rats. *J. comp. physiol. Psychol.*, 1971, **74**, 59–65.

UHL, N. P. Intradimensional and extradimensional shifts as a function of amount of training and similarity between training and shift stimuli. *J. exp. Psychol.*, 1966, **72**, 429–433.

UNDERWOOD, B. J. The effect of successive interpolations on retroactive and proactive inhibition. *Psychol. Monogr.*, 1945, **59**, No. 3.

UNDERWOOD, B. J. Retroactive and proactive inhibition after five and forty-eight hours. *J. exp. Psychol.*, 1948, **38**, 29–38.

UNDERWOOD, B. J. Interference and forgetting. *Psychol. Rev.*, 1957, **64**, 49–60.

UNDERWOOD, B. J. Attributes of memory. *Psychol. Rev.*, 1969, **76**, 559–573.

UNDERWOOD, B. J., & EKSTRAND, B. R. An analysis of some shortcomings in the interference theory of forgetting. *Psychol. Rev.*, 1966, **73**, 540–549.

UNDERWOOD, B. J., & POSTMAN, L. Extraexperimental sources of interference in forgetting. *Psychol. Rev.*, 1960, **67**, 73–95.

UNDERWOOD, B. J., & RICHARDSON, J. Some verbal

materials for the study of concept formation. *Psychol. Bull.*, 1956, **53**, 84–95.

UNDERWOOD, B. J., & SCHULZ, R. W. *Meaningfulness and verbal learning.* Philadelphia: Lippincott, 1960.

VALENSTEIN, E. S., & WEBER, M. L. Potentiation of insulin coma by saccharin. *J. comp. physiol. Psychol.*, 1965, **60**, 443–446.

WAGNER, A. R. Effects of amount and percentage of reinforcement and number of acquisition trials on conditioning and extinction. *J. exp. Psychol.*, 1961, **62**, 234–242.

WAGNER, A. R. Conditioned frustration as a learned drive. *J. exp. Psychol.*, 1963, **66**, 142–148.

WAGNER, A. R. Stimulus validity and stimulus selection in associative learning. In N. J. Mackintosh & W. K. Honig (Eds.), *Fundamental issues in associative learning.* Halifax, N.S.: Dalhousie University Press, 1969.

WARD, L. B. Reminiscence and rote learning. *Psychol. Monogr.*, 1937, **49** (Whole No. 220).

WARREN, J. M. An analysis of the formation of visual discriminative habits of rhesus monkeys. *Amer. J. Psychol.*, 1954, **67**, 517–520.

WARRINGTON, E. K., & SHALLICE, T. The selective impairment of auditory verbal short-term memory. *Brain*, 1969, **92**, 885–896.

WATKINS, M. J. When is recall spectacularly higher than recognition? *J. exp. Psychol.*, 1974, **102**, 161–163.

WATSON, J. B., & RAYNOR, R. Conditioned emotional reactions. *J. exp. Psychol.*, 1920, **3**, 1–4.

WAUGH, N. C., & NORMAN, D. A. Primary memory. *Psychol. Rev.*, 1965, **72**, 89–104.

WEIMER, W. B. Psycholinguistics and Plato's paradoxes of the *Meno. Amer. Psychol.*, 1973, **28**, 15–33.

WEINSTOCK, S. Resistance to extinction of a running response following partial reinforcement under widely spaced trials. *J. comp. physiol. Psychol.*, 1954, **47**, 318–322.

WEINSTOCK, S. Acquisition and extinction of a partially reinforced running response at a 24-hour intertrial interval. *J. exp. Psychol.*, 1958, **56**, 151–158.

WEINSTOCK, S. A contiguity analysis of learning in the runway. In M. H. Marx (Ed.), *Learning: Theories.* New York: Macmillan, 1970.

WHEELER, A. J., & SULZER, B. Operant training and generalization of a verbal response form in a speech deficient child. *J. appl. Behav. Anal.*, 1970, **3**, 139–147.

WHITE, S. H. Evidence for a hierarchical arrangement of learning processes. In L. P. Lipsitt & C. C. Spiker (Eds.), *Advances in child development and behavior.* Vol. 2. New York: Academic, 1965.

WICKELGREN, W. A. Acoustic similarity and intrusion errors in short-term memory. *J. exp. Psychol.*, 1965, **70**, 102–108.

WICKELGREN, W. A. Phonemic similarity and interference in short-term memory for single letters. *J. exp. Psychol.*, 1966, **71**, 396–404.

WICKELGREN, W. A. Exponential decay and independence from irrelevant associations in short-term recognition memory for serial order. *J. exp. Psychol.*, 1967, **73**, 165–171.

WICKELGREN, W. A. The long and the short of memory. *Psychol. Bull.*, 1973, **80**, 425–438.

WICKENS, D. D. Characteristics of word encoding. In A. W. Melton & E. Martin (Eds.), *Coding processes in human memory.* Washington, D.C.: Winston & Sons, 1972.

WICKENS, D. D., BORN, D. G., & ALLEN, C. K. Proactive inhibition and item similarity in short-term memory. *J. verb. Lng. verb. Behav.*, 1963, **2**, 440–445.

WIKE, E. L. *Secondary reinforcement: Selected experiments.* New York: Harper, 1966.

WILKINS, A. T. Conjoint frequency, category size, and categorization time. *J. verb. Lng. verb. Behav.*, 1971, **10**, 382–385.

WILLIAMS, D. R., & WILLIAMS, H. Auto-maintenance in the pigeon: Sustained pecking despite contingent nonreinforcement. *J. exp. Anal. Behav.*, 1969, **12**, 511–520.

WILLIAMS, S. B. Resistance to extinction as a function of the number of reinforcements. *J. exp. Psychol.*, 1938, **23**, 506–522.

WILSON, W., WEISS, E. J., & AMSEL, A. Two tests of the Sheffield hypothesis concerning resistance to extinction, partial reinforcement, and distribution of practice. *J. exp. Psychol.*, 1955, **50**, 51–60.

WINOGRAD, E. List differentiation as a function of frequency and retention interval, *J. exp. Psychol. Mongr. Suppl.*, 1968, **76**, No. 2, Part 2.

WINOGRAD, T. Understanding natural language. *Cog. Psychol.*, 1972, **3**, 1–191.

WISCHNER, G. J. The effect of punishment on discrimination learning in a noncorrection situation. *J. exp. Psychol.*, 1947, **37**, 271–284.

WOLFE, J. B. Effectiveness of token-rewards for chimpanzees. *Comp. Psychol. Monogr.*, 1936, **12**, No. 60.

WOLFF, J. L. Concept-shift and discrimination-reversal learning in humans. *Psychol. Bull.*, 1967, **68**, 369–408.

WOLPE, J. *The practice of behavior therapy.* (2nd ed.) Elmsford, N.Y.: Pergamon, 1974.

WOODWORTH, R. W., & SCHLOSBERG, H. *Experimental psychology.* (Rev. ed.) New York: Holt, 1954.

WYCKOFF, L. B., JR. The role of observing responses in discrimination learning. Part I. *Psychol. Rev.*, 1952, **59**, 431–442.

YAMAGUCHI, H. The effect of continuous, partial, and varied magnitude reinforcement on acquisition and extinction. *J. exp. Psychol.*, 1961, **61**, 319–321.

YARMEY, A. D. I recognize your face but I can't remember your name: Further evidence on the tip-of-the-tongue phenomenon. *Mem. Cognit.*, 1973, **1**, 287–290.

YATES, J., & CARAMAZZA, A. Prompted recall of grammatical cases. Paper read at Eastern Psychological Association, Philadelphia, April 1974.

YERKES, R. M., & MORGULIS, S. The method of Pavlov in animal psychology. *Psychol. Bull.*, 1909, **6**, 257–273.

YOUNG, P. T. *Motivation of behavior.* New York: Wiley, 1936.

Young, P. T. *Motivation and emotion: A survey of the determinants of human and animal activity.* New York: Wiley, 1961.

Young, P. T. *Emotion in man and animal.* Huntington, N. Y.: R. E. Krieger, 1973.

Zeaman, D. Response latency as a function of the amount of reinforcement. *J. exp. Psychol.*, 1949, **39**, 466–483.

Zeaman, D., & House, B. J. The role of attention in retardate discrimination learning. In N. R. Ellis (Ed.), *Handbook of mental deficiency: Psychological theory and research.* New York: McGraw-Hill, 1963.

Zeiler, M. D. Eliminating behavior with reinforcement. *J. exp. Anal. Behav.*, 1971, **16**, 401–405.

Zimmerman, B. J., & Rosenthal, T. L. Observational learning of rule governed behavior by children. *Psychol. Bull.*, 1974, **81**, 29–42.

NAME INDEX

Page numbers in *italic* indicate References.

SUBJECT INDEX